The London Guildhall

An archaeological history of
a neighbourhood from early
medieval to modern times

PART II

David Bowsher, Tony Dyson, Nick Holder
and Isca Howell

MoLAS Monograph 36

MUSEUM OF LONDON ARCHAEOLOGY SERVICE

Front cover (parts I and II): foundation stones for the new Guildhall chapel, rebuilt in the 1440s and 1450s

These two stones, discovered face-up and side by side at the base of the foundation trench for the new north aisle of the chapel, suggest a formal foundation ceremony took place to mark the start of construction. This ceremony would have been attended by aldermen and Common councillors, including the current mayor, the warden of the Guildhall College and perhaps John Croxtone, the chapel's architect. They presumably remained safely at ground level while one of Croxtone's workmen went down a ladder into the foundation trench and laid the stones nearly 4m below their feet.

The inscriptions, painted in a formal manuscript style known as 'blackletter Gothic', name (in Latinised versions) Henry (Henricus) Frowyk and Thomas Knolles (Knollys). Frowyk, a former and future mayor, was one of three aldermen appointed in 1440 to supervise the construction of the chapel; in 1442, Thomas Knolles, perhaps the son of a former mayor, joined this committee. From this we can conclude that Frowyk and Knolles were present at the formal foundation ceremony in 1440 or 1441; not only were they involved in the project but may have been two of the main financial contributors. Quickly hidden under foundation rubble, their names were intended to be 'known to God'.

CONTENTS

6

Early medieval settlement, churches and the Guildhall: discussion of the evidence

6.1 The expanding Late Saxon town and the topographic influence of the Roman amphitheatre

The street pattern

Following King Alfred's reoccupation of the walled city, the area between the Thames and Cheapside was subdivided by streets, north of Queenhithe–Garlickhithe in the late 9th century AD and elsewhere from the mid 10th. Not until the 11th century is there evidence at Milk Street of comparable development north of Cheapside, and by the 12th century this north–south street was joined by another, Ironmonger Lane (Horsman et al 1988, 115).

Further north still, beyond the line of Cat Street (modern Gresham Street), the original Guildhall of the early 12th century was sited between two more streets of this type, Aldermanbury to the west and Basinghall Street to the east. These extended as far as the city wall and formed part of a series of similar streets, including Noble Street and Wood Street to the west and Coleman Street to the east. Further east, much of this northern area of the city, within the wall as well as outside it, was marshland, known as *la Mora* and undrained before the 15th century (Dyson 1977, 15–16). Up to that time, the Guildhall/Cripplegate area, bounded to the north and west by the Roman and medieval walls, would thus have been more compact and secluded in character than it subsequently became. Within this fairly regular pattern, the outlines of Aldermanbury and Basinghall Street contrast sharply with that of their fellows. Where the latter follow straight, purposeful courses, these two are markedly sinuous in form, curving away from each other around the Guildhall area and then swerving back towards each other as if to avoid some sizeable obstacle that only now can be understood as the still substantial surviving remnants of the Roman amphitheatre (Fig 281). The two must certainly have been in place by the early 12th century, while the former amphitheatre bank was still visible, and perhaps by *c* 1050, before it became too eroded to have any real influence on the local topography (Fig 282).

The two streets have another feature in common beyond mere shape. Both preserve the name of ancient districts through which they ran. 'Aldermanbury' originally denoted a prominent early medieval tenement on the north side of the parish church of St Mary (below, 6.7). It also gave its name to a soke (ie an area of early 'private' legal jurisdiction) which was probably coterminous with the parish itself, at whose centre the tenement and church lay. Similarly, Basinghall Street preserves the name of *Basinghaga*, meaning 'enclosure of the men of Basing' (Ekwall 1954, 94), later known as Bassishaw and first recorded in 1160–80 (HMC 1883, 206). The original Bassishaw was very probably coterminous with the medieval parish of St Michael, all the more so because the parish was (and still is) a City ward – the only instance in London where a parish and ward were co-extensive, and of significance on that account. Several London wards, especially those based on City gates like Aldgate and Cripplegate,

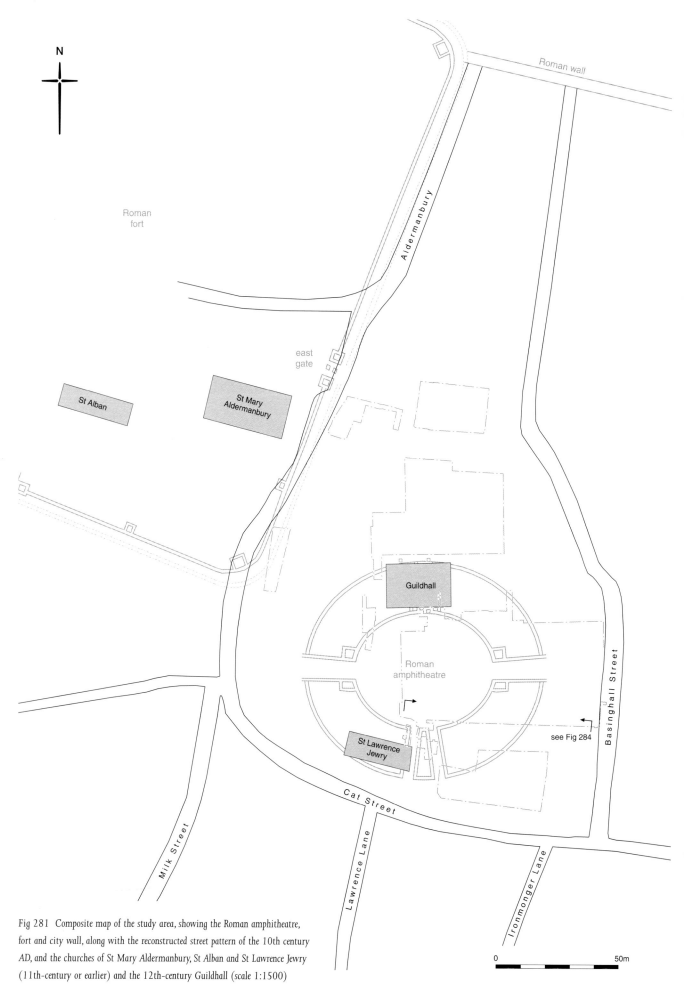

N

Roman
fort

St Alban

St Mary
Aldermanbury

east
gate

Aldermanbury

Roman wall

Guildhall

Roman
amphitheatre

St Lawrence
Jewry

see Fig 284

Basinghall Street

Cat Street

Milk Street

Lawrence Lane

Ironmonger Lane

Fig 281 Composite map of the study area, showing the Roman amphitheatre,
fort and city wall, along with the reconstructed street pattern of the 10th century
AD, and the churches of St Mary Aldermanbury, St Alban and St Lawrence Jewry
(11th-century or earlier) and the 12th-century Guildhall (scale 1:1500)

0   50m

Fig 282 Artist's reconstruction of the study area in the 1060s (Judith Dobie)

appear to have evolved from private sokes, and it is as a soke that Aldermanbury first appears. Aldermanbury and Bassishaw should therefore be seen as closely similar territories, evidently representing significant early units of occupation and lordship. Only a little further afield to the west, around the parish and lane of St Mary Staining, was *Staeninghaga*, the 'enclosure of the men of Staines' (Ekwall 1954, 123–4), first recorded in 1053–66 (Sawyer 1968, no. 1142). *Staeninghaga* lay to the south of the old Roman Cripplegate fort (Fig 281), with Aldermanbury and Bassishaw lying east of it, and like Bassishaw was named after a place outside London. In fact, both places, Staines and Basing(stoke), have something else in common: locations on the Roman road that led through Newgate to Winchester and beyond. This seems to hint at some West Saxon presence and influence in the City that can hardly date from before the late 9th century AD.

Although their origin and nature remain obscure, these distinctive forms of pre-Conquest occupation in the vicinity of the former Roman fort and amphitheatre seem to mark it out from the rest of the City. Early date and atypical character apart, they have no obvious bearing on its selection as the seat of civic government. If anything, the choice is remarkable for its eccentricity, remote from the waterfront which was the source of the refounded city's prosperity, and even from Cheapside, its central axis and main trading centre. Moreover, the overall configuration of streets in the area has a haphazard quality at odds with the more or less regular street pattern in evidence further to the south, but matched by the improvisatory character of the east–west 'Gresham Street' route (formerly Cat Street/Lad Lane). Early maps show this to have resembled a major thoroughfare only where it passed through the Jewry and near Guildhall, between Wood Street to the west and Lothbury to the east.

The ultimate function of the 'Gresham Street' route was to link Aldersgate and Aldgate while skirting the *Mora* that occupied much of the north-central part of the walled city. There seems to have been little integration across it, between the Guildhall district and the rest of the City to the south. If anything, it may have acted as a boundary between them, an impression reinforced by the lack of any direct route connecting Guildhall with Cheapside. Until the devastation of the Great Fire of 1666 presented the opportunity of constructing King Street to serve just that purpose, the approach was by way of the comparatively minor Lawrence Lane, which led primarily to the parish church after which it is named. The Guildhall, it would seem, arrived on the scene later than the church and the street, as is confirmed by the dating of the relatively crude street gridding between Gresham Street and Cheapside to the 11th century, on the evidence of Milk Street (Schofield et al 1990, 153–9), whereas the Guildhall appears only to have existed from the third decade of the 12th century. Some other explanation is thus required for the choice of its out-of-the-way location.

Archaeological evidence adjacent to the study area

Excavations to the south of the study area and north of Cheapside (between Milk Street and Ironmonger Lane) show that this area was resettled by the 10th century AD. At Milk Street excavations in 1976 revealed two sunken-featured buildings and associated pits dating from the late 9th to 11th centuries AD (Horsman et al 1988, 23). Recent archaeological work at 30 Gresham Street (GHT00) found numerous Late Saxon cesspits and rubbish pits across the site. The earliest of these pits date from c 1000, but the majority of them from c 1050–c 1150. The surviving Saxo-Norman buildings on the site consisted of several sunken-floored timber structures, the most complete example being of rectangular plan and showing evidence of stave-built walls (Blair and Watson 2004). The ceramic evidence from recent excavations further to the west at 10 Gresham Street (GSM97) indicates reoccupation of this area of the city during the 10th century AD, probably in the first half, with an increase in activity from c 1050 onwards (Casson et al in prep). At a similar distance north of Cheapside, excavations at Ironmonger Lane (Horsman et al 1988, 30–2) revealed two sunken-floored buildings dating to the late 9th to 10th centuries AD behind the Ironmonger Lane street frontage, which is thought to have developed in the post-Conquest period. A Late Saxon sunken-floored building was also found at 36–37 King Street (KNG95). Immediately south of the study area at 15–17 King Street and 44–46 Gresham Street (KIG95) archaeological investigations found the remains of two north–south aligned sunken-floored buildings of 10th- to 11th-century AD date (Blair 2000, 24).

There is little evidence from nearby archaeological sites for any occupation in this part of the City, north of Gresham Street, in the 10th or early 11th century AD. Residual pottery from recent excavations within the former Roman fort at Cripplegate, to the west of the study area, suggests that there was limited local activity, perhaps of an agricultural nature, in the late 10th or early 11th century AD, while the earliest post-Roman reoccupation is dated from the late 11th century (Howe and Lakin 2004, 61; Lyon 2004).

Archaeological evidence in the study area

There is little evidence for reoccupation of the Roman amphitheatre site prior to the 10th century AD. The presence of a Merovingian copper-alloy buckle <S1> (Fig 283) of the 6th or early 7th century AD (but found in a later 12th-century deposit) is intriguing. Finds of this date are extremely rare within the walls of the former Roman town, although a similar buckle was found in a burial in Lundenwic (Chapter 8.8). Given the lack of any other finds or pottery of this date from the site to suggest any occupation, it probably came to be there as a chance loss by an individual; other explanations might be that it was an exotic curiosity finally discarded by someone in the late 12th century, or even that it came from a nearby disturbed burial.

The sunken-floored timber building (B134) constructed in the 10th century AD (Chapter 2.1) appears to stand in isolation. As has been shown to the south of Gresham Street, between Milk Street and Ironmonger Lane, there is evidence of dispersed pre-1050 Late Saxon settlement but no corresponding evidence to the north of the street. It may be that the unique topography

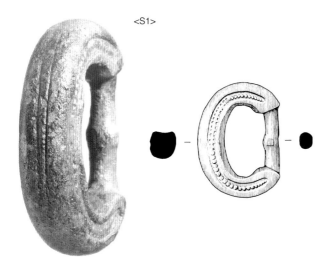

<S1>

Fig 283 Merovingian copper-alloy buckle <S1> of the 6th or early 7th century AD (scale: line drawing 1:1, photograph c 2:1)

of the study area made it more attractive to settlement than other areas north of Gresham Street at this time. The microstratigraphic and pollen studies from period 9 imply the presence of a freely-draining grassland soil, not one suffering from boggy or waterlogged conditions to create an inhospitable environment. A general lack of woodland cover is indicated by the pollen analysis, with some evidence for hedgerows and scrubby copses.

Building 134 was cut into the rear of the former bank flanking the eastern 'hollow way' leading to the enclosed depression of the former arena. It may have controlled and used this 'natural' feature for keeping livestock or growing crops. Within the enclosed area there was a near absence of pits and only ephemeral evidence for flimsy structures or fences. It seems likely that livestock was herded on this 'greenfield' site, and the evidence of plant remains and micromorphological study indicates rotting organic matter such as dungheaps. The pits in the 10th to early 11th century AD (Chapter 2.1) appear to have been concentrated around the former eastern entrance to the amphitheatre, both on the bank and within the entranceway around Building 134. There was also a further

concentration of pits to the south outside the former amphitheatre bank, perhaps suggesting the presence of early buildings along the north side of Cat Street.

The limited evidence for Late Saxon metalworking is discussed in Chapter 6.6.

The topographic influence of the Roman amphitheatre

The physical appearance of the site of the former amphitheatre to any Late Saxon settlers would have been as a fairly prominent feature in the landscape: a large oval depression surrounded by a low bank bisected by 'hollow ways' marking the former entrances into the arena. The settlers of this area in the 10th century AD would have seen a bank standing up to c 1.1m high from within the former arena and 1.6m outside the amphitheatre, at the eastern edge of the site (Fig 284). By the middle of the 11th century, dumping or soil accumulation had reduced the height of the bank to c 0.8m and 1.2m respectively. Continued dumping or soil accumulation within the former amphitheatre arena indicated that by c 1080 (the end of period 10 phase 2) the former amphitheatre bank now stood as a low mound c 0.6m high. By the time of the construction of the Guildhall in the 1120s (period 10 phase 5), the contemporary ground surface lay at c 0.2m *above* the top of the former amphitheatre bank, and the relict earthwork was no longer visible. It is unlikely that the low mound had exerted any significant topographic influence after c 1080. The site of the early Guildhall may lie centrally over the northern bank of the former Roman amphitheatre (Fig 281) but this apparent relationship can now be seen as mere coincidence. The land to the south had already been enclosed and developed, and so the Guildhall may simply have been sited on available open land at the edge of the developing town. The Guildhall was set back from Aldermanbury, and its location may well have been influenced by the former royal and/or civic *burh* of Aldermanbury just to the north-west (below, 6.7).

There is tentative evidence for a connection between the alignment of the former amphitheatre and the church of St Lawrence Jewry. The alignment of the east wall of the later

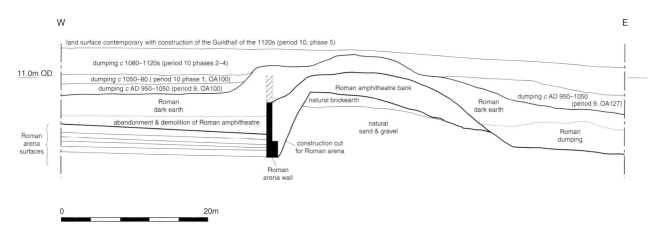

Fig 284 Reconstructed cross-section across the former Roman amphitheatre bank and arena to show the topographic effect on subsequent medieval occupation of the area (vertical scale 1:100; horizontal scale 1:500)

church of St Lawrence Jewry appears to coincide with the alignment of the walls of the southern entrance to the Roman amphitheatre and may hint at a very early date for the foundation of the church (Fig 281; Bateman and Miles 1999, fig 14). Why this should have occurred is uncertain. It may have been due to pragmatic considerations of siting the church on the bank of the former amphitheatre and aligning it 'parallel' to the curving relict earthwork. Some walls of the southern entranceway could have been visible and might have constrained the position of the church. The east end of the church may even have reused the amphitheatre entrance wall. Whatever the modalities, the alignment of the east end of the church was then transferred to the churchyard boundaries and adjacent lane, and subsequently on through the later timber buildings. This model for the transference of alignment from the former Roman amphitheatre to the medieval layout shows that the church was built first and thus became the primary topographic influence on this part of the study area.

The eastern limit of the 11th-century churchyard coincides in position and alignment with the east end of the late medieval church and suggests that the early medieval church was in the same place and on the same alignment. The original northern extent of the lane to the east of the church corresponds to the northern boundary of the burial ground, suggesting that at this time there was no real development to the north. Subsequent timber buildings, built after c 1080 (period 10 phase 3 onwards), lay to the east of the lane and north of the churchyard, respecting the church boundaries and the field ditches, and reflecting the continued land ownership. It was not until the 1120s and 30s (period 10 phase 5) that the lane was extended to the north (following the alignment of the mid 11th-century ditch, S130) and this was perhaps brought about by the construction of the Guildhall in the 1120s. The field ditches and fences laid out in the third quarter of the 11th century (period 10 phase 1) may have had a short lifespan, but their alignment and location had a considerable influence on the later pattern of buildings and properties.

6.2 Treewrighting and woodland management in the 11th and 12th centuries

Damian Goodburn

Treewrighting

The range of woodworking techniques used for domestic buildings during the early medieval period in London has been given the term 'treewrighting', from the old English term for woodworker (*treow-wyrhta* or *trywwyrhta*: Bosworth 1882–98, 1013). Treewrighting involved working roundwood and timber with simple hand tools, following earlier traditions. Joints cut were simple and the degree of accurate prefabrication of

structures found in later medieval timber framing (or to some extent in earlier Roman work) was unknown. Timbers used in building were very rarely square or of uniform dimensions, and were produced by splitting (cleaving) and hewing techniques; saws were not used (Goodburn 1997b). The vast majority of buildings were built 'earthfast', that is, with their principal timbers set in the earth rather than on a sillbeam or pads well above ground as in later medieval English timber framing. The techniques of treewrighting, well exemplified at the Guildhall, were replaced – except in the very simplest of low-status structures – by the new techniques of timber-frame carpentry imported (along with most of the nomenclature) from France in the late 12th century.

Trees and woodland management

The study of the timber and roundwood used in the 11th- and 12th-century timber buildings at the Guildhall has thrown light on the woodland in which the parent trees grew. It is possible to reconstruct the parent tree for some of the building timbers by combining the recorded details with the tree-ring analysis. The timbers used in both the buildings and the burials are derived from different types of 'treeland', both wildwood or regrown wildwood and managed woodland and that on open land.

The wider radially-cleft wall staves, posts and wall boards were taken from straight old trees often as much as 1.0m in diameter and 200–350 years old (Fig 285). The vast majority of the cleft boards and planks found in the 11th- to 13th-century cemetery of St Lawrence also derive from slow-grown straight oak and to a lesser extent beech trees, many c 1.0m in diameter and in several cases much larger still. The widest radially-cleft board recorded was a boat-shaped bier (burial 39, Fig 363), at 0.58m wide implying a sound, straight parent tree of – at the very least – 1.2m diameter but more likely c 1.4m, a very large oak. Most trees used were clearly over 200 years old or older when felled; for example, burials 5, 6 and 14 included boards from oaks well over 350 years old.

These trees were of slow growth rate as measured in annual ring width (<2mm wide). The width of most modern English oak annual rings in stem timber today is typically 3–6mm as the trees grow in more open managed landscapes, not dark wildwood settings. These characteristics have been recognised as diagnostic of the extinct temperate wildwood woodland of north-west lowland Europe and elsewhere in the temperate zone (Goodburn 1992, 118; Peterken 1996, 149). This treeland could have been either uncleared wildwood or ancient regrowth on disturbed land. It may have been the *silva pastulis* of the Domesday Book, where swine and other animals were grazed, gradually thinning the tree cover. Current evidence shows that the last of this wildwood-type land was converted to open wood pasture or managed woodland by c 1250 in England (Rackham 1976, 39; Goodburn 1998).

Some boards, staves and posts were cut and cleft from smaller, faster-grown parent oaks and beeches, for example a radially-cleft post A[16753] cut from a parent oak log c 0.4m in diameter from a tree c 50–60 years old. Similar trees were used

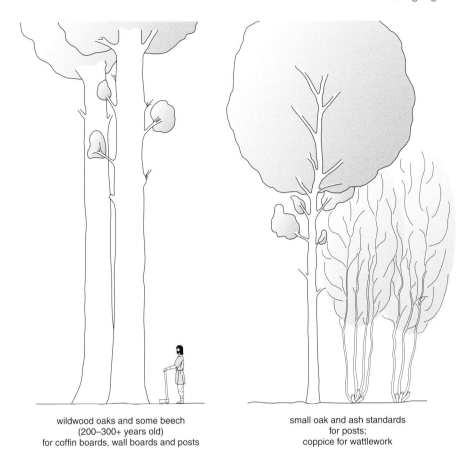

wildwood oaks and some beech
(200–300+ years old)
for coffin boards, wall boards and posts

small oak and ash standards
for posts;
coppice for wattlework

Fig 285 Model of two types of 11th- to 12th-century woodland – wildwood and young coppice – based on the evidence of timber used in buildings and coffins (scale c 1:100)

to make the boards used in some of the graves (eg burials 24 and 46). Such faster-grown parent trees could have come from more open woodland, like the managed woodland standards which can still be found in London woodlands today. Systematically managed coppice cut at various ages, most commonly to produce small-diameter rods only c 3 years old (or up to c 10 years old for heavier work) would also have been common close to the town. This is likely to be the *silva minuta* of the Domesday Book (Rackham 1976, 59), and in many cases it probably grew under spaced-out standard timber trees, the so-called 'coppice with standards' (Fig 285).

Origin of wattle

Most of the wattle identified (rods, sails and stakes) was not hazel but other species, dominated by oak, willow/poplar and alder, with hazel coming a relatively poor fourth and with some use of fruitwoods such as *Prunus* (sloe, cherry etc), Pomoideae (apple, pear, hawthorn) and beech (CD Table 10). The species diversity is less than in contemporary wattle found in the Fleet valley, another London site with good organic preservation (Tyers and Hibberd 1993). This presumably reflects the differing tree species in the understorey layer in woodlands in different parts of the London region. It follows that people were using the local woodlands, hedges and orchards as a resource, rather than trying to modify the species components by promotion of particular tree types and weeding out the others.

The larger samples of wattle show that within a structure composed mostly of a single species, there are nearly always some stems of a different species; this suggests a mixing of stems between harvesting and use. Sporadic peaks of hazel noted in the pollen analysis are likely to be associated with woodworking activity, such as the construction of wattle hurdles, and the importation to the site of harvested bundles. The excellent pollen preservation suggests the immediate springtime working of the hazel and rapid burial of the pollen-bearing deposits.

The impossibility of obtaining ring-counts from much of the wattle makes it impossible to produce evidence for size- or age-selection of the material. Nevertheless, it is self-evident (particularly from the oak material but also from the rest of the assemblage) that the sails were generally larger than the rods. It is thus clear that the stems were being selected according to diameter for construction purposes. Allowing for the variation in diameter along the length of the stems, the widespread appearance of both fast- and slow-growing stems of similar sizes in the oaks shows that size was the only important criterion for the builders.

The wattle could have been obtained from a managed coppiced landscape and/or from casually harvested trees (Fig 285). There is no hard and fast difference between the two types of landscape, and there are limitations to the data from the wattle samples that preclude further analysis. The bulk of the rods used had maximum diameters of 15–25mm and, if from a coppiced tree, had probably been cut on a fairly short cycle of c 3–5 years (contrasting with the c 9-year coppice typical of hazel used today). Very young rods have been found in wattlework from a number of sites in south-east England of prehistoric, Roman and medieval date (Goodburn 1994;

2003b; Goodburn in prep). Small rods up to c 20mm diameter have been recorded as impressions in burnt daub from Middle Saxon Lundenwic, where sails of 20–35mm diameter were also found (Malcolm and Bowsher 2003, 152). Thus, the practice of using relatively small whole rods was well established in the London area many years before their use at the Guildhall. However, heavier wattlework using older rods was also found in some instances, such as in Building 103 where the rods were up to 45mm in diameter and must have required great strength to weave.

Making timbers: log conversion methods

The methods used to make elements of the early medieval timber buildings and burial boards at the Guildhall site fall within what is becoming a well-known range of treewrighting techniques (Goodburn 1992; 1997a; 1997b; 1999) which are summarised here.

Some poles and small logs were used in the round, while others were hewn to a roughly rectangular shape with axes and used for wall posts, for example a boxed-heart ash post from Building 116 (period 10 phase 3) cut from a log c 200mm in diameter (Fig 286, a). Other posts were hewn to a roughly rectangular shape from a cleft half log of moderate size, for example a beech wall post from Building 100 (period 10 phase 3) from a log of c 200–250mm diameter (Fig 286, b). Posts were also made by radially cleaving much larger oak or beech logs into 1/8 and 1/16 sections, which were then hewn, for example a post from Building 116 cut from a log c 700mm in diameter (Fig 286, c). Some wide oak wall posts, staves and the bulwark planking were made from 1/32 sections, for example a grooved post from Building 116 which was cut from a log c 0.9m in diameter (Fig 286, d). The thin pales of oak or beech found in several structures must have been made by a further radial cleaving to 1/64 or even possibly 1/128 sections.

Fig 287 shows the width and finesse of manufacture of some of the burial boards. It is known from later medieval sources and experimental work that an average of c 30 boards could be split out of a large, straight-grained, fairly knot-free oak log (Goodburn 1992, 112). However, in one burial (burial 14) the boards were only c 10mm thick and had probably been trimmed down from 1/64 split segments taken from very straight-grained logs.

Jointing methods

The range of joint types and joint cutting methods recorded in the 11th- and 12th-century worked timber found at the Guildhall site was relatively simple and distinctive. The only types of joint recorded (whether on in situ or reused timbers) were a form of tongue-and-groove joint (Fig 288, a–b), a

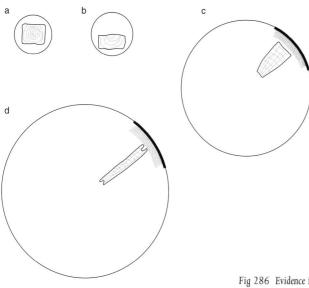

Fig 286 Evidence from building remains for log conversion methods and parent logs: a – boxed-heart ash post from Building 116; b – cleft and hewn box-halved beech post from Building 100; c – 1/16 split-section oak post from Building 116; d – 1/32 split-section grooved oak post from Building 116 (scale 1:20)

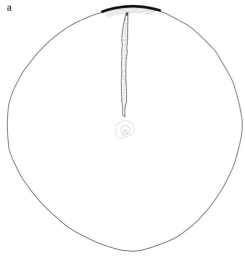

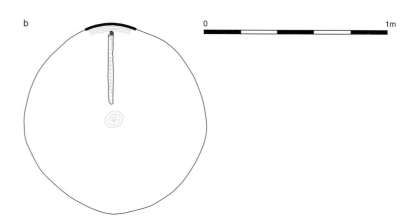

Fig 287 Evidence from burials for log conversion methods and very large parent logs: a – radially-split oak board from burial 39; b – radially-split oak board from burial 40 (scale 1:20)

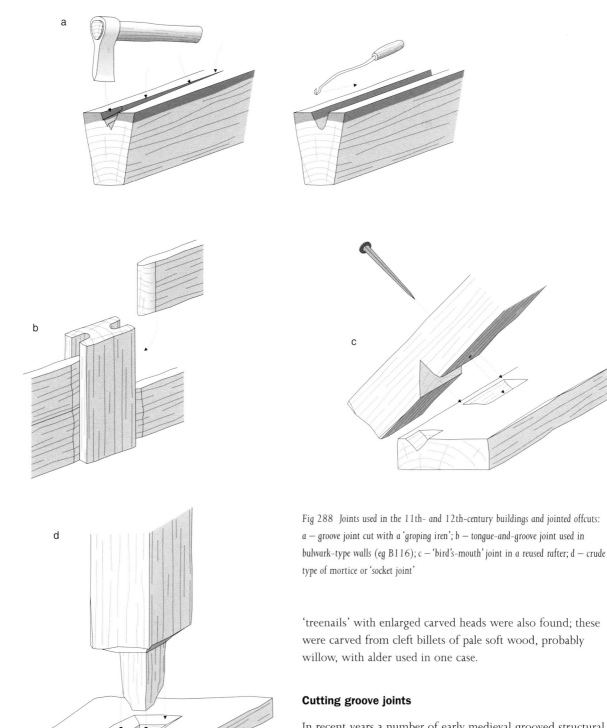

Fig 288 *Joints used in the 11th- and 12th-century buildings and jointed offcuts: a – groove joint cut with a 'groping iren'; b – tongue-and-groove joint used in bulwark-type walls (eg B116); c – 'bird's-mouth' joint in a reused rafter; d – crude type of mortice or 'socket joint'*

'treenails' with enlarged carved heads were also found; these were carved from cleft billets of pale soft wood, probably willow, with alder used in one case.

Cutting groove joints

In recent years a number of early medieval grooved structural timbers have been recorded in detail during excavations in London, including at the Guildhall site. The shape of the best-preserved grooves and the toolmarks inside them indicate that they were not made using planes, chisels and augers, as might have been expected, but cut out with small thin-bladed hachets (Fig 288, a). Then the jagged fibres in the bottom of the groove were sometimes cleaned up with a narrow hooked tool, presumably the mysterious tool referred to as the 'groping iren' in the famous anonymous medieval poem *The debate of the carpenter's tools* (Underhill 1986, 241). A freshly discarded end from a grooved post reused as a post-pad in Building 103 (period 11 phase 2) shows one way of cutting the joint whereby the groove was started by axe-cutting a shallow slope which was gradually deepened (Fig 288, a). In examples from

'bird's-mouth' joint in a reused rafter (Fig 288, c) and a crude type of mortice or 'socket joint' in a displaced post-pad (Fig 288, d). A fuller range of typical early medieval joints has been found on other London sites (Brigham et al 1992; Goodburn 1999; Goodburn in prep). Face pegging and, less commonly, nailing were also used as simple fastening techniques, such as between the secondary wall posts and boards in Building 116 (Fig 289). Fragments of typical early medieval pegs or

Fig 289 *View of partition wall in Building 116, from the east, showing grooved post in the foreground (0.2m scale)*

a well at 72–75 Cheapside (CID90; timber dated to AD 913), an auger hole was sometimes used to begin the groove (Goodburn 1993b; 1999, 50). The method of cutting groove joints has been put to the test experimentally with green oak and shown to work.

Cooperage finds

Stave-built tubs, buckets and casks must have been in common use at the site but relatively little evidence of them was found. Parts of three different sizes of stave-built wooden vessels were found, including parts of a barrel reused to line a well in Open Area 120 (Fig 290), parts of two tubs or small buckets discarded in Building 101, and two staves from a small coopered conical cup found in Open Area 109 (<A1535> and <1555>, Fig 291). The bucket elements were of local oak and the cask staves of French oak, while the cup staves were of silver fir which grows in central Europe, attesting some long-distance trade links in that quarter.

All the other cooperage was made of radially-cleft oak hewn and shaved to shape. Only in the barrel do the joint details on the end pieces survive (Fig 292), although the cup staves have two grooves in the outside faces to hold the hoops. The smaller vessel staves were slightly hollowed on the inside whereas the barrel staves were flat or even slightly convex. With all the elements, the edges had been 'jointed' with some form of plane. One of the barrel staves has a simple A-shaped mark, incised as a V-shaped line 3mm deep, which may have been a cooper's, merchant's or customs mark. The best-preserved staves survived up to c 1.2m long, with widths of 110–140mm and thicknesses of 18–22mm.

Fig 290 *View of barrel-lined well in Open Area 120 (0.2m scale)*

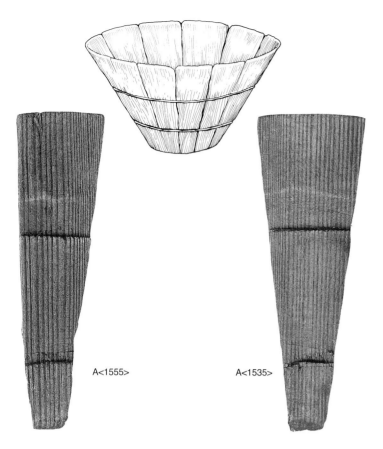

Fig 291 *Two staves from a rare, small coopered conical cup A<1535> and A<1555> (scale 1:1), along with a reconstruction of the vessel (not to scale)*

6.3 The 11th- and 12th-century timber buildings

Introduction

Then I gathered for myself staves and props and bars, and handles for all the tools I knew how to use, and crossbars and beams for all the structures which I knew how to build, the fairest pieces of timber, as many as I could carry. For I advise each of those who is strong and has many wagons, to plan to go to the same wood where I cut these props, and fetch for himself more there, and load his wagons with fair rods, so that he can plait many a fine wall, and put up many a peerless building, and build a fair enclosure with them; and may dwell therein pleasantly and at his ease winter and summer, as I have not yet done. (Whitelock 1955, 884)

Apart from this late 9th-century AD passage from King Alfred's preface to his translation of St Augustine's *Soliloquies*, contemporary documentary and pictorial sources are rare for early medieval wooden buildings, and our knowledge is largely derived from archaeological evidence.

The remains of at least 35 timber buildings were found at the Guildhall site, most (31) situated along the lane that ran north from Cat Street past the churchyard of St Lawrence Jewry and eventually on to the 12th-century Guildhall. With the sole

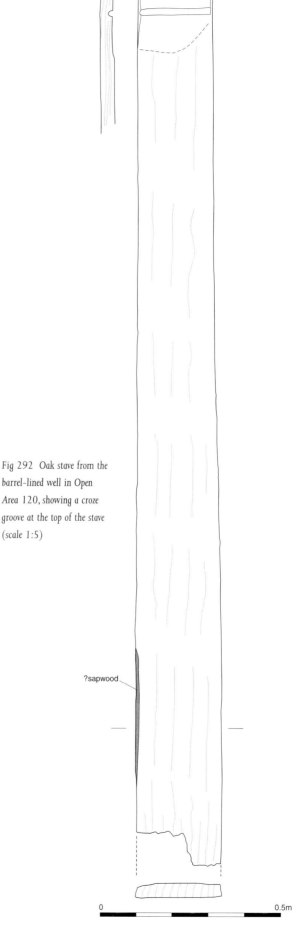

Fig 292 *Oak stave from the barrel-lined well in Open Area 120, showing a croze groove at the top of the stave (scale 1:5)*

?sapwood

0   0.5m

exception of a 10th-century AD sunken-floored building (Chapter 2.1, B134), the excavated timber buildings form a tightly-dated group ranging from c 1080 to c 1200 (periods 10 and 11). The study of these buildings complements and expands the current knowledge of early medieval timber buildings in London, which has been summarised by Horsman et al (1988), Milne (1992b) and Goodburn (1995). More recently, well-preserved Saxo-Norman buildings have been excavated along Cheapside (Hill and Woodger 1999) and a range of Late Saxon and early medieval buildings recorded at 1 Poultry (ONE94: Burch and Treveil in prep). Unlike many of these sites, at the Guildhall the excellent conditions for organic preservation and the absence of later cellared buildings allowed timbers and wattlework to survive. This presence of in situ timbers and wattlework has enabled some of the best-preserved buildings to be tentatively reconstructed, which contributes to the discussion of treewrighting and woodland management (above, 6.2) and allows comparison with timber buildings at York (Hall 1994), Dublin (Wallace 1992) and in Scandinavia (Clarke and Ambrosiani 1994). Detailed descriptions and illustrations of the individual buildings can be found in the chronological narrative (Chapters 3.1 and 3.2).

The timber buildings and the lane running north from Cat Street developed together in an organic and piecemeal fashion. The overall impression is that there was sufficient land available for buildings to be laid out, often leaving space between and around them. Most of the buildings fronted on to the lane, although the typical relationship and chronology is here reversed, in that the lane appears to develop in the space left between the buildings rather than the buildings developing along an already established street. The buildings initially lay both 'end-on' and with their long axis parallel to the lane. After the northward extension of the lane in the 1120s, in order for it to reach the new Guildhall, the long axis of all the buildings was orientated parallel to the lane in order to achieve the maximum street frontage.

This layout and development is what might be expected along a minor lane on the fringes of the town and is in stark contrast to the 11th-century timber buildings excavated along the street frontage at 1 Poultry (Burch and Treveil in prep). Here timber buildings were laid out against a principal street frontage that was already in the heart of the town, in an ordered fashion, mostly end-on to the street frontage and with little or no gap between neighbouring buildings.

Many property boundaries on the Guildhall site were marked by wattle fences (eg B115, B116 and B118). There are only two examples of a side alley or path leading away from the lane to the rear of the buildings, namely a cobbled surface (R101) running alongside Building 101 (Fig 298) and a cobbled path between Buildings 115 and 116.

A majority of domestic buildings in 12th-century London were of timber construction, as is evident in the archaeological record and from historical documents. Building regulations of the 1190s and c 1212 (Schofield 1999, 75–6; Barron 2004a, 247) encouraged citizens to build in stone rather than wood in an attempt to reduce the incidence of fires in the city, implying of course that most buildings were still of timber. In the study

area domestic stone buildings were first constructed along the nearby principal street frontages of Cat Street and Basinghall Street in the second half of the 12th century, although timber buildings continued to be erected along the lane leading north from Cat Street until the beginning of the 13th century. This presumably reflects the difference in wealth of the occupants of the properties; those along Cat Street and Basinghall Street at this time are though to have been Jewish-owned (below, 6.5).

Construction types

Nearly all the 11th- and 12th-century timber buildings found at the Guildhall site were constructed using earthfast methods, that is, the structural timbers were set directly in the ground in post-pits or wall trenches. A recent study recognised two main types of earthfast building, surface-laid and sunken-floored (Horsman et al 1988, 66). Unlike the late 10th-century AD sunken-floored building (B134), all the late 11th- to 12th-century timber buildings were surface-built with no indication of cellars or sunken floors. This conforms to the pattern recently observed elswhere in the City at 1 Poultry (Burch and Treveil in prep) and implies a development from 10th-century AD use of sunken-floored buildings to the exclusive use of ground-level buildings by the 11th century.

In some ways the use of earthfast construction allows for more flexiblity than later timber-framing systems and makes it comparatively easy for different walls of the same building to be built in different styles (Goodburn 1995, 48). Many of the wooden buildings at the Guildhall employed more than one construction technique, such as bulwark-style and post-and-wattle (eg B116) or post-and-plank and post-and-wattle (eg B122 and B126). A combination of different walling methods in the same building does seem to be relatively common in early medieval buildings in London and at other sites such as Hedeby (Haithabu, Germany), where bulwark and post-and-wattle walls have been found combined in one building (Goodburn 1997a, 252; Malcolm and Bowsher 2003, 153; Elsner nd, 31).

The earliest example of timber framing or 'carpentry' in London occurs in the late 12th century (Goodburn 1997b, 160–1; Milne 1992, 131), and at the Guildhall site there is no archaeological evidence for its use until the 13th century (Chapter 3.3, 'St Lawrence Jewry and its property: Tenement 1').

Size

Many of the buildings were rectangular in plan and about twice as long as they were wide (Fig 298). Of the few buildings whose full extent survived, Building 100 was 4.8m wide by at least 10.5m long, and Building 112 was 5.5m wide and 11.3m long. It is possible that these widths reflect the length of the tie-beams spanning the building: these could have used a standardised c 5.0m timber, perhaps reflecting the length of timber available (Building 117 was 4.65m wide and Building 103 was also 5.0m wide). The largest building with full measurements (B124) was c 7.5m wide and c 16.6m long; this width and that of Building 118 (7.1m) may suggest that there was another normative building width of c 7.5m. Although most of the buildings were rectangular in plan, a few had a more square plan: for example, Building 126 measured 4.2m x 5.8m and Building 118 was 7.1m wide and at least 7.9m long.

These dimensions are slightly larger than those found at Coppergate, York, where the average size of 9th-century AD post-and-wattle buildings was c 4.4m wide and at least 8.2m long (Hall 1994, 46), and of other contemporary buildings in London, where the majority were 4.0–5.0m wide and 6.4–10.1m long (Horsman et al 1988). The timber buildings at 1 Poultry are thought to have been somewhat smaller at c 3.0m wide and 6.0m or more in length; this may reflect the difference in pressure of space between the back lane of the Guildhall and the principal street of Poultry. The smallest building on the Guildhall site (B115) measured c 4.7m x 2.7m.

Foundations

The buildings had no separate foundations, and posts were usually set in individual holes occasionally packed with stones. Some posts had axe-cut tips indicating that they were driven (eg B118). A number of posts were set on the ground, supported on post-pads built of stone or timber offcuts; in most cases these were internal aisle posts (eg B103 and B118). The use of post-pads rather than postholes clearly implies that the posts were well braced.

The west walls of Buildings 123 (Fig 298) and 129 fronting on to the lane were represented by shallow trenches probably signifying a post-in-trench technique (with vertical posts set in a shallow trench) as some individual timber posts were still in situ while the rest had been robbed. Shallow slots (with some individual in situ posts) also defined all four external walls of Building 124 and suggest that the whole building was constructed in the post-in-trench technique (Fig 298). It has been suggested that this was a more advanced technique as it allowed a more accurate alignment of the posts (Horsman et al 1988, 71).

There was no evidence for the use of baseplates or sillbeams (whether laid in a slot or directly on the ground) nor for any foundation beds, techniques found in other Saxo-Norman buildings in London (Horsman et al 1988, 72–4). The use of mortised baseplates in early medieval timber buildings in London has recently been questioned, as none have been found in situ, and those found ex situ are plank-like in section and more likely to have been used as a top plate, sitting on top of the timber posts (Hill and Woodger 1999, 32, contra Brigham 1992, 86–7). There is, however, some evidence for the use of grooved baseplates for stave buildings in the second half of the 11th to 12th centuries in London (ibid, 90).

Roofs

Whether the roof load was principally carried on internal posts or the outer walls is a common topic of debate in the analysis of north European early medieval timber buildings. In many of the Guildhall buildings, the weight of the roof would certainly have been supported solely on the outer walls of the building. A number of the posts used for the external walls of Building 124 were associated with wedges or skids used to slide the post into position, which suggests that the posts were tall, heavy and used to support the roof. The same technique was used in the construction of a 10th-century AD building at Cheapside (Hill and Woodger 1999, 34, fig 32).

In some cases the roof was also supported by internal aisle posts of various types (eg B100, B101, B103, B124 and B113; Fig 298) and the outer walls merely enclosed the gap between the ground and the base of the roof. The roof timbers or trusses of Building 103 were supported on a line of posts set c 0.5–0.6m inside the walls and sitting on pads of stone and timber offcuts placed c 1.35–1.8m apart. Even though Building 100 used aisle posts to support the weight of the roof, the outer walls had to be reinforced with raking posts or buttresses. There was also evidence for the use of buttresses in Buildings 126 and 129. The use of aisle posts would have tended to obstruct internal movement whereas the use of external buttresses would have reduced external space. This must have been a key concern as London became more crowded and space more at a premium; interestingly, there was no evidence for the use of buttresses in contemporary timber buildings at 1 Poultry which lay closer to the centre of the town (Burch and Treveil in prep).

The use of buttresses in early medieval post-and-wattle timber buildings has been recorded at many sites in north-west Europe and is best-known from a 9th-century AD building in the Viking trading town of Hedeby/Haithabu (Clarke and Ambrosiani 1994, 142–7; Graham-Campbell 1994, 63). Recent work at Middle Saxon Lundenwic has also revealed an 8th-century AD post-and-wattle building with buttresses (Malcolm and Bowsher 2003, 73, 150). The overall form and scale of the buildings at Hedeby, Lundenwic and the Guildhall are similar, suggesting a long-standing building tradition.

Roof covering

The roofs of all the timber buildings were probably covered in material such as thatch, shingles or clapboard (overlapping horizontal boards). Six wooden shingles (found in a pit in OA114, period 11 phase 4) have peg holes 10–12mm in diameter and were made from radially-split oak (Fig 293). None appear to survive to their full length although two must come close at 310mm and 340mm respectively. The maximum thickness is 8–13mm, tapering to almost a feather edge, and the widths measure 110–160mm. The microstratigraphical study found no evidence for the use of turf as a roofing material (below, 'Walls').

The use of thatch for roofs would have been common in Late Saxon and early medieval London until after the fire of 1212, when regulations banned its use and roofs were to be covered in tiles, shingles or boards (Schofield 1999, 75). Sedges, rushes and spike-rush are well represented in the plant remains from samples, including those from floors and occupation deposits. The frequent association of these species with sea club-rush suggests that much of this material may have been collected from the Thames foreshore as this plant grows in shallow water at the muddy margins of tidal rivers (Clapham et al 1987). These plants may have been collected for use as flooring and roofing materials (both in houses and stables), with their regular occurrence in pit fills suggesting that they were deposited in these features after use, perhaps as a means of suppressing the foul odours from these pits. At other London sites of this period large seed numbers of sedges, rushes and spike-rush have also frequently been found (sometimes together with large amounts of wood), for example at Bull Wharf (BUF90: Giorgi 1999), at various 9th- to 12th-century AD City sites (Jones et al 1991) and at 1 Poultry (Davis, A, 2002).

Some of the charred plant remains may also indicate the presence of thatch, although it is very difficult to distinguish such residues from crop-processing debris used as fuel. Recent studies of smoke-blackened thatch material from 14th- to 16th-century buildings in southern England (Letts 2001; de Moulins in prep) have shown that all four cereals (often mixed) may have been used for thatch, although bread wheat and rye straw were used the most. Rivet wheat, however, also produced excellent thatching straw. These studies have also shown that a wide range of wild plants (seeds as well as whole plants including stems

and flowers) were present in thatch, with 42 different types being identified (ibid). Stinking mayweed and cornflower/knapweed were among the most common weeds, along with corncockle, charlock, docks, thistles, legumes (peas, broad beans) and their pods, and other plants not usually associated with arable fields, such as bracken, yellow rattle, carrot and greater plantain. In short, there is no specific indicator in archaeological deposits for the easy identification of thatch, although the incidence of rivet wheat or rye (grains and straw) and an unusually high incidence of legume pods and stems may point to its presence in medieval archaeological contexts.

Plant assemblages from several Guildhall samples can be considered for comparison with these studies (CD Table 52). Three contexts in Building 101 contained large amounts of charred (?cereal) stems, plus some grains (mainly oats), occasional rachis fragments, a range of weed seeds and bracken stems and leaf fragments. A cesspit fill (OA121) contained large numbers of rye grains (together with barley) and a large quantity of stems (possibly straw) although there were very few weed seeds, while Building 112 produced large amounts of charred stem fragments and grains (mainly of oats) plus rachis fragments of all four cereals as well as a wide range of weed seeds. These plant assemblages, however, do not provide any definite evidence for the presence of thatch when compared with the field survey data (Letts 2001). There is no definite rivet wheat in these samples, although rye is well represented in one sample, and straw of oat (the best-represented grain) could have been used if the plant was being brought on to the site for other purposes. In addition, the range of weed seeds is very similar to that in the field studies, with a good representation of stinking mayweed. The numbers of weed seeds in these Guildhall samples, however, are not particularly high and there is an absence of legume pods and stems, a characteristic of medieval thatch.

There is no evidence that the timber buildings used roof tiles, and it is more likely that tiled roofs were restricted to stone buildings (eg B120 and B121), which at this period would have housed London's more prosperous citizens, and other important buildings such as churches. Early medieval roofing tiles belong to the flanged and curved system, and were used in a similar fashion to Roman tegulae and imbrices. The evidence from the Guildhall suggests that the previous notion that both the flanged/curved and shouldered roofing tile types were introduced together after a fire in 1135/6 (Betts 1990, 221; Smith 1999a, 66) needs modification. It appears, rather, that the flanged and curved system was introduced somewhat earlier and that it was the shouldered peg system which was introduced around 1135/6 (Chapter 8.5). The Guildhall of the 1120s may have been one of the first London buildings to use the flanged and curved tiles.

Ceramic tiled roofs undoubtedly became more common towards the end of the 12th century when smaller, lighter and cheaper peg tiles replaced the earlier roofing tile types. This was due in part to pressure from the City authorities to replace thatched roofs. In 1212 it was recommended that inflammable thatch be replaced by ceramic tile, wooden shingles, boards, lead or plastered straw (Smith 1999a, 66; Schofield 1999, 75).

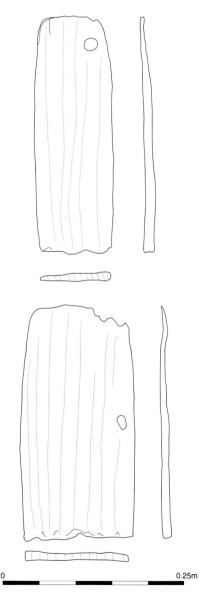

0   0.25m

Fig 293 Two discarded timber roof shingles (scale 1:5)

Walls

A majority of the walls of the timber buildings from the 11th and 12th centuries at the Guildhall were of post-and-wattle type: that is, constructed of earthfast posts to which wattle panels were attached or woven alongside (Fig 294, a). In some cases the wattle panels were prefabricated (eg B110) and the base of the panel secured in narrow slots. In others (eg B110 and B123) the wattle panels were supported by a post on the outside with a matching post on the inside to form a paired-post-and-wattle wall (Fig 294, b). The posts lay on the line of the wattle or sometimes the wattle was attached to the inside face of the posts. The wattlework usually took the form of a single panel or line (eg B100, Fig 295) although there are two examples (B102 and B111) of the use of a double line of wattle (c 0.15–0.22m apart), the gap presumably being infilled with daub or other material (Fig 294, c).

Woven roundwood wattlework – described by King Alfred in the 9th century AD as 'fair rods [to] plait many a fine wall' (Whitelock 1955, 884) – was in common use in medieval England and was widely used in the 11th and 12th centuries at the Guildhall. It was employed for a wide range of structures: internal and external walls, bench or bed revetting, animal pens, fences, pit linings, oven superstructures and portable hurdles. Portable hurdles can be distinguished by the neat weaving of relatively light rods and the winding of some or all of the rods around the end sails and back into the weave (eg from OA108, Fig 51). Details of the species selected and a discussion of the origin of the wattle are presented above (6.2).

All the rods and the vast majority of stakes were used in the round, without the halving by splitting common in recent hazel hurdles made in central southern and south-east England. The use of whole rods and uprights often in pairs or triples is more reminiscent of the recent willow wattlework of the Somerset levels. Light pliable rods and double sails have been found being used in a number of other fine wattlework structures from Saxo-Norman London, such as the woven floor surface at Vintry House (VRY89: Goodburn 1993a). The use of double sails is also seen in some of the Viking Age Dublin buildings (Wallace 1992, 177) and buildings in Anglo-Scandinavian York (Hall 1994, 31).

Sometimes small, cleft stakes or pales were also included in the weave, as in the internal bin or coop in Building 100. The weave was usually a plain alternating one, as in the south wall of Building 100 (Fig 38) and as used in an animal pen (S105, Fig 296). Sometimes the weave was more complex, as in the case of the three-rod wale used in the wall of Building 103 (Fig

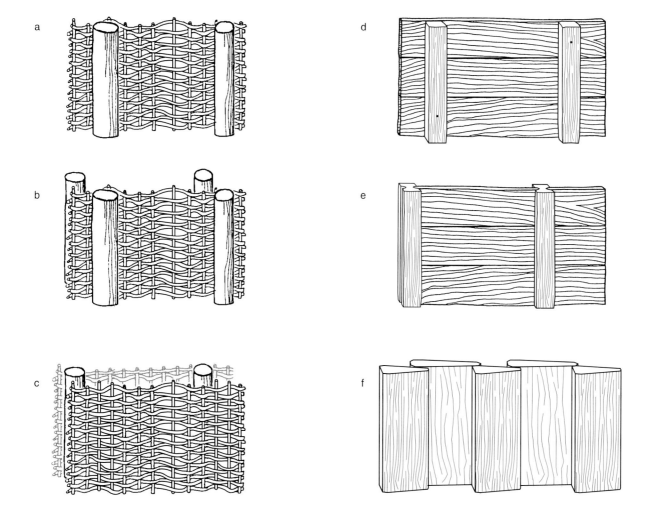

Fig 294 Schematic elevations of the main types of wall construction: a – post-and-wattle; b – paired-post-and-wattle; c – post-and-double-wattle; d – post-and-plank; e – bulwark; f – false board-and-muntin stave wall (after Horsman et al 1988, fig 70, and Goodburn 1995, fig 5)

Fig 295 *View of the south wall of Building 100 during excavation, from the south*

83); this produced a more robust wall, which may have been required if the building housed animals.

Two adjacent buildings (B126 and B122) showed the use of post- or stave-and-plank construction in their south walls and in some internal partitions (Fig 294, d). In Building 126 the staves were set with their centres 0.4–0.5m apart, with a number of planks laid on edge against the inside of the staves; at least one plank was nailed to an upright. In Building 122 the ends of the planks overlapped and were also laid horizontally on the inside face of the posts. The south wall of Building 129 was represented by an east–west line of collapsed planking and in situ staves; the use of the planking indicates a weatherboard-style wall. The occurrence of post-and-plank walls in early medieval buildings in London has hitherto been confined to sunken-floored buildings (Horsman et al 1988, 78; Hill and Woodger 1999, 30, 35; Burch and Treveil in prep), and this type of construction at the Guildhall is dated to the 12th century.

Bulwark-type wall construction describes walls with boards set on edge in the sides of grooved posts (Fig 294, e; Fig 297), as used in Building 116, in part of its replacement (B117) and

perhaps in Building 124. Its use extends back to at least the Bronze Age, being found for instance at Biskupin in Poland (Brunning 1995) and with a Late Iron Age example recorded at Glastonbury, Somerset (R Brunning, pers comm). The late survival of the bulwark technique in Denmark, southern Sweden and parts of north Germany does not indicate its origin, or anything other than that it was a fairly widespread north European technique. It was used in London by the early 10th century AD, as seen in the construction of a timber-lined well at nearby 72–75 Cheapside (Hill and Woodger 1999, 27–8, fig 24). Bulwark-type construction has also been recorded in an 11th-century sunken-floored building and timber-lined wells at Pudding Lane and in 12th- or 13th-century waterfront structures (Horsman et al 1988, 81).

It is clear that the investment of labour and materials in Building 116 was much greater than in the contemporary post-and-wattle building (B100) or indeed the later byre building (B103). More timber was required and it had to be more elaborately worked. Cutting long, deep groove joints in the post edges with a Saxo-Norman toolkit would have been a time-

Fig 296 *Detailed view of the wattle weave used in an animal pen (S105) (0.2m scale)*

consuming process even in comparatively soft green oak timber. Therefore, the cost per unit of space was higher for Building 116 than for Building 100.

An unusual wall construction technique used at the Guildhall consisted of alternating thicker and thinner vertical staves set slightly overlapping in a shallow trench (Fig 294, f) and was employed in internal partitions in Buildings 100 and 116. The builders thereby created the impression of a stave-and-muntin wall without the effort of cutting edge grooves in any timbers. Alternating thicker and thinner earthfast stave walls were used in 11th-century surface-laid buildings nearby at Ironmonger Lane (Horsman et al 1988, 75–6) and in an 11th-century building in Dublin (Murray 1983, 27–8). At the Guildhall there was no evidence for stave walls set on a baseplate, a technique used in the 11th-century waterfront at Billingsgate (BIG82) and a timber building at Pudding Lane (Horsman et al 1988, 76, fig 71).

The microstratigraphical study found no evidence for the use of turf walls. Comparisons were made with a turf roof on a plank-built building at the experimental farm at Baggböle (University of Umeå, Sweden), which had developed a specific micromorphological and pollen signature (Cruise and Macphail 2000; Macphail 2003). No such turf material was recognised at

Fig 297 *View of a grooved post set on a post-pad and forming part of a bulwark-type wall in Building 116; edge-set planks were slotted into grooves between two such posts (0.2m scale)*

the Guildhall, nor were typical turf lines, as described by Dimbleby (1985, 73) or as seen at the Overton Down experimental earthwork (Bell et al 1996; Crowther et al 1996). The archaeobotanical recognition of turf includes heather (roots, basal twigs and fragments), rhizomes, culm bases, mosses and a wide range of seeds of wild plants (Hall 2003). Samples taken from suspected turf used in walls of Buildings 111 and 115, however, contained little evidence for such material, with only wood, occasional grains, fruit seeds and wild plants of disturbed ground and wetland habitats suggesting mixing with other deposits. Heather was only recorded in a hearth and floor deposit in Building 100, while mosses were not identified at all.

It is likely that wattle walls were rendered with some form of daub, although unrendered wattle has been suggested for the Dublin wattle-walled buildings (Wallace 1992, 32). A number of buildings used double lines of wattle to form the wall, and the space between was most probably packed with earth (eg B111). In many cases the organic daub covering the walls would not have been visible in the archaeological record due to its similarity to the surrounding organic-rich deposits, while in other cases it was indicated by a slight change in the deposits along a band either side of the line of wattle (eg B115 and S102). Micromorphological study of the walls of Building 100 and Structure 105 suggests that stabling refuse (eg animal dung-rich material) was used to pack and cover the wattlework. This raises the possibility that many of the wattle walls were daubed with a very organic, light and insulating manure-based daub, rather than the brickearth-based daub used on some of the earlier Middle Saxon wattle-walled buildings in Lundenwic (Hughes 2004, 99–135).

Building interiors

Internal partitions

The internal space of buildings was sometimes divided by aisle posts (used to support the roof), where two rows of aisle posts created a central nave with two wider side aisles (eg B100 and B124, Fig 298). Some excavated early medieval buildings elsewhere also have a central nave narrower than the side aisles, for example most of the short-aisled buildings in Dublin (Wallace 1992, 16).

The interior of many of the buildings was also divided by internal partitions of the various construction types used for the external walls (eg Fig 298). It is assumed that these internal partitions rose at least to the same height as the external walls. Some buildings appeared to be divided into three rooms (eg B100, B117 and B129). This arrangement is typical in Viking Age towns such as Hedeby, Sigtuna and Lund, where the central room is interpreted as a dwelling space with a hearth, and the gable rooms as workshops or storage space (Clarke and Ambrosiani 1994, 142). Building 117 does have a hearth in the central room, while Building 100 has hearths in both gable end rooms and Building 129 has a hearth in one of them. Unusually, in the northern room of Building 117 a pit was dug, used (perhaps for storage) and backfilled during the life of the

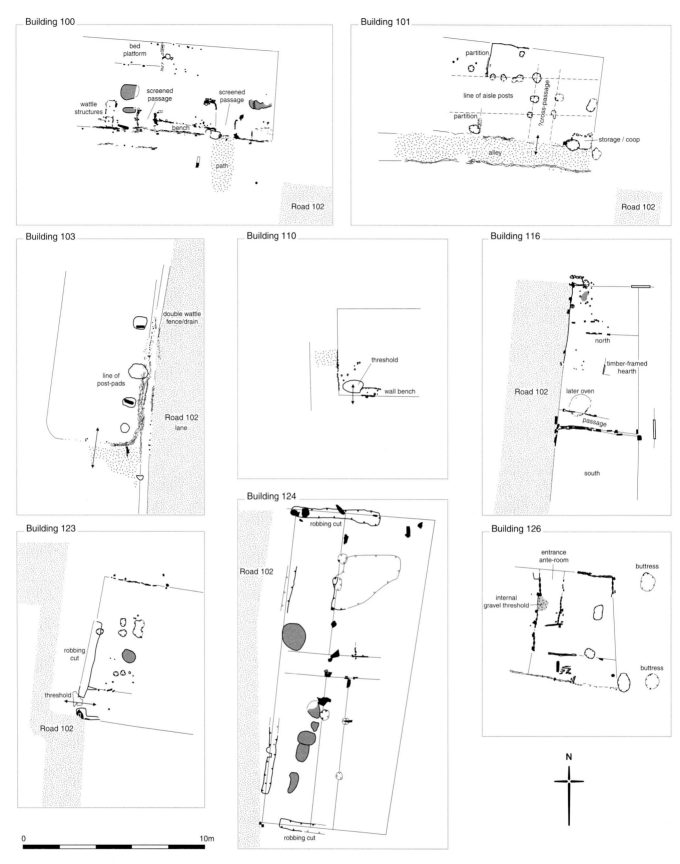

Fig 298 Plans of the best-preserved late 11th- and 12th-century timber buildings (B100, B101, B103, B110, B116, B123, B124 and B126) found alongside the lane leading north from Cat Street (R102) in periods 10 and 11 (scale 1:200)

building. Other buildings were divided into two unequal-sized spaces. The northern extension of Building 116 was divided into two (ratio 1:3), as was Building 126, while Building 124 was divided into two equal-sized rooms by a screened passage.

A number of other buildings (eg B100 and B116) had a screened passage running part-way across the building from the door, perhaps to protect the heated room from draughts and/or to divide the building into separate rooms (Fig 298). This type of feature may be a forerunner of the screened cross-passages seen in later medieval buildings. In recent vernacular dwellings in the south and east of Ireland a similar arrangement is found with a screen 'jam wall' running between the doorway and the room with a hearth (Kinmonth 1993).

No external porches were found. One building at the Guildhall (B126, Fig 298) had a room or enclosed area immediately behind the door, which may have acted as an ante-room to shelter the entrance, with another internal door at the opposite end of the space to give access to the rest of the building. Another building (B123, Fig 298) had an internal partition running part-way across the building, immediatley adjacent to the door and perhaps acting as a screen wall. Some buildings were also subdivided by short partitions that did not run the full length or width of the building.

Doors

Doorways are marked by gaps in the walls and doorposts (eg B100 and B126, Fig 298), indicating the use of a wooden door. In other cases, there was no doorpost associated with the gap in the wall, which perhaps means that the doorway was covered by something less substanial, such as a cloth curtain or a wattle panel. Doorways were also marked by timber threshold bars (eg B123, Fig 298) and/or layers of gravel found inside and outside the entrance (eg B110, B123 and B126, Fig 298). The doorways were c 0.7–0.8m wide, which is a similar width to an 11th-century wooden door found at Pudding Lane (Horsman et al 1988, 89–90). Doorways were usually positioned on the lane frontage or on the south side of the building.

Floors

Floors were commonly made of brickearth or beaten earth and rarely of chalk; organic materials, such as dung, were often used as preparation layers for brickearth floors. No high-status floors with plastered surfaces were found at the Guildhall (cf Dragon Hall, Norwich: Macphail 2001), nor was there any evidence for wooden floors like those found in two sunken-floored buildings at Pudding Lane and Watling Court (Horsman et al 1988, 85).

Brickearth was used as a flooring material both as very thin (minimum 1mm) 'spreads' and as substantial (40mm) 'slabs', and is found as burnt surfaces at and near hearths. Often there were several brickearth-type floors within a building that had been periodically replaced or repaired. Micromorphological study illustrates the complex nature of one of these floor sequences in Building 124 of period 11 phase 2 (Fig 90, {M820–1}). A brickearth floor composed of a very heterogeneous mixture of brickearth fragments, fine mortar inclusions and ubiquitous dung and bone was overlain by a series of prepared and beaten surfaces. For example, the succeeding 2mm thick beaten floor layer was sealed by a 1mm thick skim of brickearth, and this in turn was followed by a

25mm thick layer of dung and stabling refuse that may be interpreted as a preparation layer for a 30mm thick, good-quality (pure) brickearth floor. A 1mm thick beaten surface formed prior to a demolition episode which produced 40mm of very abundant wood charcoal, charred wood, wood and bark, burnt bone, and what may be partially-ashed bird coprolitic material. This was succeeded by another ubiquitous stabling deposit marking the disuse of the building.

Sedges, rushes and spike-rush are well represented in the samples from floors and occupation deposits and could have been used as floor-covering as well as roofing material. Other potential flooring or bedding material among the plant remains includes heather (eg B100) and bracken (eg B101, B115 and S105), although the charred remains of these plants may represent their use as fuel. Straw, found in a number of samples, was also used for bedding and flooring.

Hearths and ovens

Many of the buildings were provided with one or more hearths or open fireplaces, often periodically replaced in a similar position (Fig 298). Circular hearths, c 1.0m in diameter, tended to appear as scorched areas on a brickearth surface, whereas rectangular hearths were frequently contained within a shallow depression. The hearths were often accompanied by many thin deposits of ash and charcoal, the remnants of a wood fire.

A number of buildings (eg B116, B102 and B129) had timber-framed hearths (Fig 299), where a brickearth slab was contained within a revetment, which in one case was formed of planks laid on edge (B102). These hearths were usually square (c 0.8–1.2m²) and presumably were designed to raise the fire above the floor as a safety precaution and to facilitate their use. Such hearths are known from Middle Saxon Lundenwic (Malcolm and Bowsher 2003, 155) and from late 10th- to 11th-century AD London, for example at Peninsular House (Horsman et al 1988, fig 94). Like the surface hearths, the timber-framed hearths appear to have been for domestic use (cooking, heat and light), as was the case with similar hearths found in 11th-century Dublin buildings (Murray 1983, 96), although a 10th-century AD example from York appeared to have been used for metalworking (Hall 1984, 53, 55–6). Only one hearth within a building at the Guildhall (B113) had evidence to suggest that it was used for non-domestic purposes. This hearth may have been used by a smith, as some smithing slag was found in the rake-out and a small amount of slag and some vitrified hearth lining were recovered from the floor deposits.

At least four buildings had an enclosed oven (B100, B116, B118 and B123), perhaps used for baking bread and/or drying grain. One of the best-preserved examples was in Building 116, where the base of the oven was constructed in a shallow cut c 1.25 in diameter. This was filled with tile, ragstone and flint rubble which presumably acted as a heat reservoir, absorbing heat and releasing it slowly. Brickearth-type material was poured over the stones as a slurry to form the surface of the oven. The domed superstructure of the oven was then built, consisting of a wattle framework covered in daub, as evidenced

Fig 299 View of timber-framed hearth in Building 129, looking west (0.2m scale)

in the archaeological record by the remnants of wattlework found around the oven and the large quantity of burnt daub. Similar ovens have been found in late 9th- to 11th-century AD buildings in London (Horsman et al 1988, 98) and earlier, 7th- to 9th-century AD, buildings in Middle Saxon Lundenwic (Malcolm and Bowsher 2003, 155). Some open hearths (eg B109 and B124) and one timber-framed hearth (B129) featured similar rubble heat reservoirs but with no evidence for an enclosed oven above; similar examples have been found at Dublin (Murray 1983, 37) and York (Hall 1984, fig 155).

Hearths and ovens were also found outside buildings. An open surface hearth was found outside Building 100, and an enclosed oven was built on the lane immediately outside Building 123 and presumably used by the occupants of that house. Many hearths were constructed in the areas identified as the cookshop zone (OA132, OA133 and OA137, period 11; below, 6.4, 'Cookshops'). These were apparently built outdoors but are likely to have been protected by awnings or timber shelters. They were mainly open surface hearths, many with underlying rubble heat reservoirs, and a few were timber-framed hearths; enclosed ovens were not used.

Lighting

The building interiors would probably have been poorly lit, with natural light entering through the open door (which is presumably why many doorways were located in the south wall of the buildings). Any windows would probably have been small, unglazed, rectangular or triangular openings admitting minimal light. No evidence for windows or window glass survived on this site. A few fragments of window glass were found associated with an 11th-century building at Watling Court (Horsman et al 1988, 91–3). A 10th-century AD

clapboard recovered from Queenhithe was pierced by a small triangular opening thought to be a window (Goodburn 1997a, 255). A possible wooden window shutter was found in York (Hall 1984) and small window apertures have been observed in buildings at Hedeby (Wallace 1992, 33).

Smoke holes in the roof would also have let some light into the buildings, but rush lighting, candles or firelight would have been the main form of illumination for the majority of the population at this date. The occupants of some of the timber buildings also used ceramic lamps. Spike lamps or cressets, consisting of a small bowl surmounting a short, solid spike, were designed to be suspended in use and would have held a small quantity of oil with a floating wick. These were the most common ceramic lamp form found, although there are also a few examples of free-standing pedestal lamps (eg <P70>, Fig 300) and a ring-vase lamp. Lamps are relatively uncommon in London excavations, but here sherds from 30 different lamps in various fabrics were found in 12th-century contexts. An iron pricket candlestick <S119> is in a form known from the late 12th century in London and was most likely used in a nearby timber building.

Furniture

The remains of built-in benches along the walls were found in two buildings at the Guildhall (B100 and B110, Fig 298). They were marked by a line of wattlework within the building, running parallel to an external wall and serving to retain an earth-filled bench c 0.45m wide. In Building 100 the bench was situated between two screened passageways. Built-in benches are a common features against a screen wall in recent vernacular dwellings in south and east Ireland (Kinmonth 1993, 7). A second, wider version of a wall bench was also found in Building 100, measuring c 1.25m wide, and may be the remains of a bed platform. There was also evidence of other internal wattle structures (eg B100 and B101, Fig 298), perhaps storage bins or even coops for small livestock.

Built-in, often earth-filled furniture is a recognised feature of early medieval buildings in much of northern Europe and is perhaps best exemplified in the Viking Age buildings of Dublin, which have beds, alcoves and cupboards built in earthfast wattlework (Wallace 1992, 34–8). Traces of built-in earthfast furniture have also been found in a 10th-century AD sunken-floored building at Cheapside (Hill and Woodger 1999, 35) and 11th-century surface-laid buildings on Pudding Lane (Horsman et al 1988, 97) in addition to earlier examples in 7th- to 9th-century AD buildings in Middle Saxon Lundenwic (Malcolm and Bowsher 2003, 153). Narrow benches of a similar size to the Guildhall examples have been recorded in a 10th-century AD post-and-wattle building in York (Hall 1994, 59) and in a 9th-century AD building at Hedeby (Clarke and Ambrosiani 1994, fig 7.9)

Little evidence survived for the use of free-standing wooden furniture apart from the top of a three-legged stool from Building 115, a rare survival of simple domestic furniture (Fig 301). The stool had been made by hewing a radially-cleft oak

<P70>

Fig 300 *Pedestal lamp <P70> in St Neots-type ware (NEOT) (scale 1:1)*

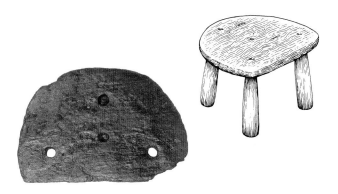

Fig 301 *Oak seat A[16691] from a three-legged stool found in a demolition layer overlying Building 115, and a reconstruction (width 0.33m)*

board 25mm thick to a D-shape 330mm across, chamfering the edges underneath and drilling three through-holes (c 18–20mm diameter) for the legs. The legs were set at a slight splay and the beginnings of another hole can also be seen in the middle of the original upper face. Fragments of one of the legs survived, and are of willow/poplar (Salicaceae) roundwood secured with an oak wedge, set across the grain of the oak top so as not to split it. It is very unlikely that the legs were over c 0.3m long as the leverage would soon have worked them loose if they had been any longer. Similar small stools have been found at other early medieval north European sites such as York (Morris 2000, 2303) and Hedeby (Elsner nd, 27).

Fire and the lifespan of buildings

With fire an ever-present danger confronting the closely neighbouring timber buildings with thatched or wooden roofs and open fires, it is perhaps surprising that few buildings showed signs of destruction by fire. There were no extensive site-wide fire destruction horizons, although destruction by fire was evident from the charred tops of *in situ* timbers of individual buildings. The relatively well-spaced timber buildings surrounded by open land at the Guildhall would have been less vulnerable to any town-wide fires than the more densely built-up areas of the town along Cheapside or the waterfronts.

A fire destroyed two contemporary adjacent buildings and an associated fence (B100, B116 and S103) at the Guildhall some time after c 1086. It is tempting to relate this episode to a fire of 1087 recorded in the *Anglo-Saxon Chronicle*, when the 'holy church of St Paul, the episcopal see of London, was burnt down, as well as many other churches and the largest and fairest part of the whole city' (Garmonsway 1972, 218). However, the fire that destroyed these two buildings did not affect the neighbouring buildings to the north (eg B115, B110 and B109), which suggests a more localised rather than town-wide fire, unless it marks the northern limit of this documented conflagration. Other localised fires seem to have taken place in the second quarter of the 12th century (by c 1140: period 10 phase 5) when one timber building (B127) may have been destroyed by fire. Another timber building (B126) was damaged and a sheep pen (S105) destroyed by fire in the last quarter of the 12th century (period 11 phase 2).

A series of severe fires which badly damaged the city are known from 1130–3 (Brooke 1975, 212, n4) and 1212 (Barron 2004a, 247). These fires gave rise to civic building regulations encouraging the use of stone. It has been suggested that it was the frequency of fires that led to the vernacular housing style employing the more temporary material of timber (Horsman et al 1988, 110). The nature of the buildings is, however, as likely to have been influenced by the wealth of the owners and the availability and cost of raw materials as by the common building traditions of the time.

The lifetime of a roundwood and timber building in Saxo-Norman London has been estimated at a minimum of 5–25 years and a maximum of 40 years (Horsman et al 1988, 109–10) and at Hedeby between 15 and 20 years (Clarke and

Ambrosiani 1994, 148). Many of the timber building on this site showed signs of long-term use; they were maintained, repaired and renovated, floors and hearths were periodically replaced, and the internal arrangements of the building were sometimes altered and doorways blocked. The two buildings destroyed by fire (B100 and B116) existed for less than ten years, while most buildings seem to have stood for between 20 and 40 years.

Use and status

A majority of the timber buildings appear to have had a domestic function, with people living, eating and sleeping in them. Many of them had one or more hearths for cooking, lighting and heat. There is no evidence that any of the buildings functioned solely as a workshop for craft activity. Rather, the evidence from discarded waste suggests that the craftworkers (eg leather workers, horn workers, metalworkers, butchers etc) pursued their trades alongside their living space.

The evidence from the stabling refuse indicates that some of the buildings were used for over-wintering of livestock, such as the possible cattle byre (B103). In other cases (eg B100) the microstratigraphy and pollen study suggest that the building was mainly for domestic use, but with stabling refuse trampled into the floor implying the proximity of animals. One wattle structure (S105) was definitely used to house animals, perhaps sheep or goats.

The composition of the botanical assemblages from different areas and buildings within the site was examined in order to establish the possible use or function of space across the site and over time. Domestic/human occupation is characterised by food residues – cereals, fruits (particularly cultivated species) and other potential economic plants, such as those used in textiles and medicine – while the presence of animals is indicated by hay or cereal fodder and/or stabling materials. However, the plant remains in the majority of the sampled features from the Guildhall, not only from buildings but also from open areas and structures, tend to consist of material indicative of a range of potential activities (domestic, economic and stabling), making it difficult to interpret the remains in terms of just one function. For example, the larger plant assemblages from buildings in period 10 allow a tentative interpretation of Building 118 as domestic accommodation, with a domestic and possibly stabling use of Buildings 101, 116 and 100, while in period 11 Structure 105 produced tentative evidence for both human and animal occupation. In addition, many of the plant assemblages are too small to allow any meaningful comment or interpretation, while a further complication is the possible mixing of plant material between deposits due to residual and intrusive activity.

Questions of social status and relative material wealth are notoriously difficult to explore on the basis of archaeological assemblages since there are so many imponderables to be balanced against what may appear, at face value, to be clear-cut evidence. It is possible to detect anomalous patterns in the data, and to see these as indications of exceptional status, but all such

interpretations must be tempered by caution in the light of what is absent from an assemblage and therefore can not be known, as well as what is present. This does not mean that the exercise is without value, but simply that the evidence may be open to more than one interpretation.

In the early medieval period, pottery was essentially functional, forming a basic component of everyday household equipment across the social spectrum. People needed pots in which to store, prepare, cook and serve food and drink, although other materials such as wood, metal, glass and horn were also used. In the context of ceramics alone, however, certain fabrics and forms are suggestive of greater affluence or higher social status, especially when they occur in larger numbers than usual. Setting aside the vagaries of archaeological survival, it is notable that there are relatively high proportions of both imported pottery and fine tablewares in period 10 (c 1050–c 1140). Among the imports, spouted pitchers in high-quality, wheel-thrown, glazed Andenne-type ware (ANDE) and decorated stonewares from the Rhineland (red-painted ware) are by far the most common finds across the site, as throughout London at this date. The overall quantities recovered, however, suggest that these, and other Continental finewares, were in more than casual or occasional use in the vicinity. How many households owned decorated Continental pottery, or how many vessels there were in any one household, is impossible to determine on present evidence, but it may be suggested that there were at least some higher-status households on the Guildhall site in the late 11th to early 12th centuries.

Just as there is a high proportion of early medieval imported pottery from the site, there are also numerous spouted pitchers in various fabrics. Whether they were made in imported fineware, or local pottery such as London-area greyware (LOGR) and early medieval grog-tempered ware (EMGR), most of them were decorated in some way (with applied thumbed strips, rouletting, combing, painting and/or glaze). This set them apart from the purely mundane pottery used to prepare meals, by giving them a place at the table. Andenne-type (ANDE), red-painted (REDP) and Stamford-type (STAM) wares in particular would have been most presentable, easily standing out from the drab utilitarian wares that formed the bulk of household ceramics. These were good-quality wares designed to be seen, not hidden away out of sight. The marked concentration of both imported pottery and serving wares may well have implications for the social status or wealth of those who discarded them.

Ceramics indicative of status, as far as it is possible to identify them, are most likely to be those that were brought into London from further afield than the main run of pottery vessels used in the capital. They were also likely to have been of higher quality than everyday coarsewares, and therefore more expensive and perhaps used for conspicuous display as well as for practical purposes. When found in reasonable numbers, the likelihood of their representing higher status or relatively wealthy households is increased. Continental imports in period 11 (c 1140–c 1230) account for 3.1% by sherd count and 3.9% ENV of all pottery, and mostly consist of ANDE and REDP from the Rhineland. Among the less frequently found imports are various glazed wares from northern France which were coming into the city during the 12th century, including north French unglazed ware and yellow-glazed ware (NFRE and NFRY), north French monochrome ware (NFM) and early Rouen ware (ROUE). These are good-quality, wheel-thrown vessels, mostly jugs, and would probably have been seen as more 'special' than locally-made glazed and decorated wares. Fine, glazed STAM too, although it is found from the mid 11th century onwards, is always less common than ANDE, which arrived in London via the wine trade. By analysing the distribution and quantities of northern French imports alongside the occurrence of STAM, particular concentrations can be seen in three areas of the site: Open Area 127 (the large block of land behind Basinghall Street), Open Area 109 (the yard on the south side of Building 102) and the large Building 124. The latter is especially interesting since it also yielded sherds from five lamps, as well as 26 sherds from at least 19 jugs or pitchers in STAM, ROUE, NFRE and NFRY, among which is a highly unusual STAM spouted pitcher with modelled birds (Nenk and Pearce 1994); there were also part of a STAM costrel and two bottles. It is highly likely that these vessels derived from a household or establishment of some wealth, in view of their number and quality. Other unusual items of interest that carry similar implications include a ring vase from Open Area 110 and a STAM lamp from Open Area 133.

Botanical remains may provide some indication of the status of the inhabitants of the site on the basis of the cost and rarity of particular foodstuffs in the archaeobotanical record. However, there was not a particularly large quantity of high-status foodstuffs, nor was there any particular concentration of such remains; thus, for instance, grape and fig are common on most early medieval London sites and can not be used as a reliable indicator. Peach, on the other hand, is rarely found but was present in Buildings 116 and 129 and Open Area 137. Mulberry, which occurs in a number of early medieval samples from the site, is another possible indicator of high status.

6.4 Life on the northern fringe of the city in the 11th and 12th centuries

Introduction

Most of the archaeological evidence for daily life comes, on this site, from the 11th- and 12th-century timber buildings and yards alongside the rear lane of St Lawrence Jewry which led north from Cat Street to the Guildhall. Good evidence was also found on the land between Cat Street and Basinghall Street (Chapters 3.1 and 3.2; periods 10 and 11). This section therefore concentrates on the significant data for the 11th and 12th centuries, with some late 10th-century AD (period 9) and 13th-century (period 12) evidence also discussed, where appropriate.

Daily life and possessions

Dress accessories and other decorative metalwork

The site produced relatively large quantities of lead/tin jewellery, including brooches (eg <S9>, <S12>–<S14>, Fig 302; Fig 384), a bead <S17>, finger rings (eg <S18>–<S19>), mounts (<S20>–<S22>, Fig 385) and pins with decorative heads (<S23> (Fig 302; Fig 386), <S24>–<S26>). These items were probably locally made, as many are identical to objects from a hoard found in 1838 in Cheapside (Guildhall

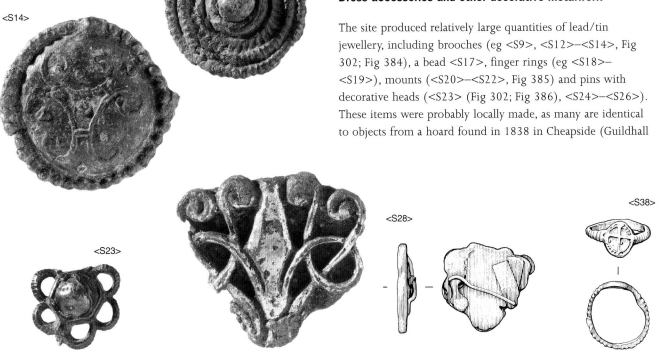

Fig 302 11th-century jewellery: lead/tin brooches <S9> and <S14>, decorative lead/tin pin head <S23> (with fragment broken off at the top), gilded copper-alloy brooch <S28>, and lead/tin finger ring <S38> (scale: line drawings 1:1, photographs c 2:1)

Museum 1908, 119, pl 54) and thought to be stock of a local 11th-century workshop. The Guildhall material is thus important as it gives the other side of the coin by representing the contemporary use and ownership of products from the same workshop (Chapter 8.8).

There is also a relatively large assemblage of other high-quality decorative 11th-century metalwork, including dress accessories such as copper-alloy brooches <S27> (Fig 26) and <S28> (Fig 302), a copper-alloy strapend <S139> (Fig 324), copper-alloy hooked clasps <S29>–<S34>, and lead/tin finger rings <S35>–<S37>, <S38> (Fig 302) and <S39>–<S41>. Other items include a book clasp <S82> (Fig 132), furnishing mounts probably used on caskets (<S42>–<S46>, Fig 314; Fig 387), and horse equipment <S47> (Fig 314) and <S48> (Fig 303). There are also several leather dress accessories including leather straps and a particularly fine 'hairslide' <L11> (Fig 408).

Fig 303 *Copper-alloy stirrup mount <S48> (scale c 1:1)*

Leather shoes

The large number of adults' and children's shoes illustrate changing fashions from the 11th to the 12th century (Chapter 8.15). The footwear covers a wide range of sizes from infant's through to adult's. The overall quality of the footwear is rather good, as attested by the large number of decorated shoes, where in some cases the embroidery material has been identified as silk thread. There are several examples of high-quality shoes with embroidered silk vamp stripes which could have been made by the same local manufacturer (below, 6.6, 'Leather working').

Domestic and leisure items

A number of domestic items (apart from the pottery) include bone and lead/tin spoons <S114>–<S117> (Fig 52; Fig 94) and wooden vessels <S118> (Fig 108). A bone die <S120>, antler gaming pieces <S121> and <S122> (Fig 304) and eight bone skates give a hint of more recreational pursuits, while a toy man carved from an antler (<S123>, Fig 304) was probably a child's plaything.

Musical instruments

Angela Wardle

Four fragments of stringed musical instruments were found in medieval contexts, comprising three bone tuning pegs and a wooden bridge. The three pegs (<S130>–<S132>, Fig 305) are identical in form and it is possible that – despite being found in dumps of different periods – they were used on the same instrument. The four fragments were found in 12th- and 13th-century contexts, and all come from the same general area of the site, to the north of St Lawrence Jewry. The wooden bridge <S133> (Fig 305) comes from the earliest context, dated to the early 12th century (period 10 phase 4, OA108). They differ from other medieval examples found in London

Fig 304 *Unfinished antler gaming piece <S122> and carved antler man <S123>, presumably a child's toy (scale 1:1)*

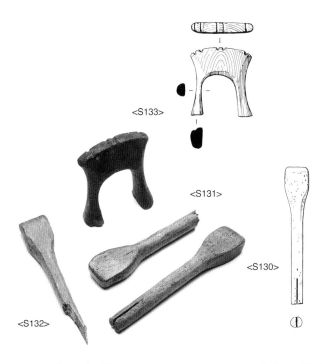

Fig 305 Three medieval bone tuning pegs <S130>–<S132> and a boxwood bridge <S133>, from 11th-century stringed instruments (scale 1:2)

(Wardle 1998, 285) both in the form of the head and the method of string attachment. Most of the London examples have a square-sectioned head, indicating that the peg was used with a tuning key (Lawson 1985, 152), but the Guildhall fragments all have heads of a broader spatulate form, which would be more suitable for turning by hand. There is only one example of this type of head among the Battle Abbey group (ibid, 153, fig 47, no. 33) and one from York (MacGregor et al 1999, 1978, fig 936, no. 8067), so they appear to be far less common than the square-headed form. The other major difference is the presence of a slot, rather than a perforation, at the lower end for the attachment of the string. Slots are also less common than circular holes and have not so far been recorded in London. Lawson (1985, 154) cites examples from Whitby in Yorkshire, Montgomery Castle in Wales and Wallingstones, Herefordshire. The narrow aperture of the slot through which the string was fastened indicates that the string itself was of thin gauge, and Lawson – in connection with the finds from Montgomery Castle – has suggested that it was of horsehair, made of several strands (Lawson 1980; 1993). It would clearly be easier to thread and tie the strands through a slot than through a small hole. Lawson has also observed that the slotted pegs (and therefore, perhaps, horsehair strings) occur more frequently on Welsh sites (G Lawson, pers comm) and, in discussion of instrument fragments from Winchester, cites a 14th-century poem which alludes to the horse-hair strings of the Welsh harp (Lawson 1990, 716, n16).

The type of instrument on which these pegs were used is uncertain, but the identification can be somewhat narrowed down. The placing of the string fastener at the lower end of the peg (type A: Lawson 1990, 712, fig 201) indicates that the instrument had an open frame, unlike the box-like psaltery,

where the string hole is in the head of the peg (Wardle 1998, 286, no. 944), and that it therefore belonged to the range of harps, lyres and simple lutes or fiddles current in the early medieval period. The clear colour differentiation on two of the pegs also indicates that they were inserted into a solid frame. The general arrangement of pegs on a variety of instruments, as visible in many contemporary illustrations, is summarised by Remnant (1986, 20, table 2; see also Lawson 1990, 712, fig 201). The width of the spatulate head on the three Guildhall pegs would seem to preclude their use on a multi-stringed harp, where the strings are closely spaced, and would be more suitable for the wider spacing on the neck of a simple fiddle such as the rebec. It should be noted, however, that these pegs are longer than any of the previously published examples from London and the other collections cited here, and the broad frame of the medieval harp would have required longer pegs, as would a longer-stringed base version of the fiddle. It has been suggested that they may be from a form of lyre, which would also have fairly widely-spaced strings (G Lawson, pers comm).

The boxwood bridge (<S133>, Fig 305) is an extremely rare discovery, with no direct parallels. Lawson (1990, fig 202) illustrates bone fittings which may be from castellated bridges from Hereford (Bewell House) and London (British Museum), both unstratified finds, and a bridge facing from a 15th-century context from Glimmingehus Castle, Skåne, Sweden (ibid; Lawson 1980, 212, no. 26, pl 31, a). Also illustrated is a smaller wooden bridge from Charavines (Isère), France, from an 11th-century context, which is of similar date and closer in form to the Guildhall find (Colardelle and Colardelle 1980, 196). The French bridge has notches for three strings which are asymmetrically positioned, perhaps suggesting two higher (melody) strings and a drone. The Guildhall bridge has five notches, which might represent five strings, perhaps one bass or drone string and two other pairs, but it is possible that the upper strings were repositioned for some reason and that only three were used. The curvature of the bridge suggests that it belonged to a bowed instrument and again, as for the tuning pegs, the range of possible candidates is fairly wide. However, in view of the early (12th-century) date, it is possible that it came from a form of bowed lyre similar to the Welsh crwth.

It is tempting to see the four fragments (pegs and bridge) as parts of the same instrument, and although this can not be proved, the pegs almost certainly are from the same instrument. The deposits in which three of the four items were found are dated to the first half of the 12th century or slightly later. Given that the objects are of an early type (quite unlike tuning pegs previously found in London) and that fragments of musical instruments are so rarely found in archaeological contexts at all, it might seem more plausible that these finds represent one, rather than two, 12th-century instruments. The question must remain open, pending further discoveries.

Pottery

The pottery from period 10 (c 1050–c 1140) is predominantly

domestic in character, with few, if any, observable differences in composition between assemblages from open areas and other parts of the site, either in fabric or in form. The broken pottery thrown away in pits and other cut features in the open areas provides as good an indication of domestic arrangements at the time as that stratified in or close to identified buildings. Very little industrial pottery was recovered from this period, constituting only 0.4% of all pottery by sherd count and 0.6% ENV (CD Table 35). Clearly, from the number of crucible sherds found (31 sherds/26 ENV, excluding intrusive material), metalworking was being carried out on a small scale in the vicinity at this date.

Cooking pots are by far the most common form in late 11th- to 12th-century contexts, as throughout the London area (84.3% by sherd count/81.9% ENV of all pottery assigned to period 10). Since the same forms could be used both for heating food and for storage, it is chiefly the presence or absence of sooting that indicates usage. This is not always easy to determine, especially if only the rim or upper body survives. In general, only vessels with no sign of sooting around the base have been classed as jars at the Guildhall, accounting for only 0.6% of pottery by sherd count (0.4% ENV).

Other vessels used for food preparation and serving consist mostly of bowls and dishes of various forms, some of them used to heat food, as shown by sooting around the base. As a functional class, they constitute only a small proportion of the pottery (CD Table 11), although in general open forms are relatively uncommon in early medieval contexts from London. Spouted pitchers are far more important in the Guildhall sequence, forming the second most common class of vessel at this date (10% by sherd count/11% ENV). This is a relatively high proportion of the total ceramic assemblage and higher than on some inland sites in the City, for example 1 Poultry (ONE94), where pitchers account for only 1% by sherd count/1.1% ENV of the identified forms dated between c 1050 and c 1150. At sites along the waterfront, a much higher frequency is usual, as at Bull Wharf (UPT90), where pitchers account for 13.9% by sherd count (19.2% ENV) of all forms at the same date. It may be that there were higher-status dwellings in the Guildhall area, where fine, decorative tablewares were relatively common. Fine pottery (and most of the pitchers found at this date were decorated in some way) was probably used in a domestic context, especially in the larger halls. There is no clear evidence that any of the pottery, apart from the metalworking vessels, was used in anything other than a household setting, whatever the size of the establishment may have been.

The great majority of the pottery recovered from features assigned to period 11 (c 1140–c 1230) is similar to the earlier material, being largely domestic in character (CD Table 12), with fabrics and forms typical of those used throughout the City during the 12th century. Industrial ceramics associated with metalworking account for only 0.4% of all pottery by sherd count and ENV, suggesting that this activity was carried out on a small scale at this date and that domestic occupation was the primary focus.

Health

Osteological evidence

Direct evidence for the health of the local population can be gleaned from the human bones recovered from the churchyard of St Lawrence Jewry dating from the 11th to early 13th centuries. They reveal no evidence of rickets (caused by a deficiency of vitamin D in the diet) or scurvy (caused by a deficiency of vitamin C). Pitting in the upper part of the eye sockets was seen in several children, and may be the result of a diet that was deficient in iron, aggravated by internal parasites.

Dental calculus accumulation on the teeth of the population was rather light, suggesting that there was some form of regular tooth-cleaning habit. Periodontal disease was rare, loss of teeth during life was fairly low (3.6%) and dental abscess formation was low (<1%). Dental caries infection was also very low. These figures are consistent with, or at the lower end of, the levels seen in other assemblages from Anglo-Saxon and early medieval England (Roberts and Cox 2003, 191–3, 259–3).

There was a high prevalence of osteoarthritis and other stress diseases of the skeleton. The level of trauma was also fairly high, with two instances of healed wounds to the skull and some healed fractures, especially of the ribs and extremities. A woman with a healed trepanation is the earliest known example of this surgical procedure from medieval London. Further details of the population's health, based on their bones, are discussed in Chapter 8.18.

Environmental evidence

Some of the insects present in the 11th- and 12th-century deposits (periods 10 and 11) have direct implications for human health, including the presence of internal parasites. It has been suggested that the flies and other insects breeding in this rubbish could potentially carry pathogens and the eggs of internal parasites such as *Trichuris* worms into human housing (Kenward and Hall 1995, 762). In particular, the two commonest species of fly present, the 'house fly' (*Musca domestica*) and the 'stable fly' (*Stomoxys calcitrans*), are seen as potential vectors for a range of detrimental pathogens such as salmonellosis, typhoid and diarrhoeal infections. It has also been suggested that they could be involved in the transmission of poliomyelitis (Oldroyd 1964; Smith 1973). The recovery of the human flea (*Pullex irritans*) suggests that the Saxo-Norman population of London carried the usual infestations of ecto-parasites.

The medicinal properties of plants were widely exploited in the past, although virtually every plant has such properties and it is therefore difficult to separate the residues of wild plants collected and used for medicinal purposes from the seeds of plants that may simply have been growing close by. The seed frequency of a species and its context may, however, provide some clue as to whether it was being deliberately exploited. Several plant species noted for their medicinal properties are well represented in some samples, including pit fills, from periods 9–11, namely black nightshade, henbane, hemlock and opium poppy.

Both black nightshade and hemlock were used to treat inflammations and ulcers while black nightshade was also used for shingles and ringworm (Culpeper 1653). Opium poppy has narcotic properties and was used to 'induce sleep, stray catarrhs and for hoarseness of the throat' (ibid, 205) while henbane was used as a hypnotic and brain sedative (Grigson 1987). Many of the fruits represented in the Guildhall samples also had medicinal properties; for example, blackberry juice was a remedy for swollen tonsils and gum ulcers, while damsons were used as cattle medicine.

Waste disposal

All of the 11th- and 12th-century yards were intensively used for digging pits for the disposal of rubbish, latrine waste and stable waste. The composition of the fills of the pits (a large number of which were sampled and analysed) suggests that they had multiple functions: they contained faecal remains (as evidenced by cereal bran and small fruit seeds), the residues of crop processing (weed seeds, chaff), the remains of food preparation (eg animal bone and fruit stones), burnt fuel (charcoal fragments) and construction materials including flooring (sedges, rushes, wood), as well as discarded or broken household items (pottery, wooden vessels and other artefacts).

The micromorphological studies have shown that stabling refuse was disposed of both in pits and by surface dumping. However, they also reveal that the stabling refuse found on the site is commonly stabling crust material, and that the more easily collected dung and fodder remains had been removed from the site, presumably as manure for the nearby fields. The generally good organic and pollen preservation on the site also implies that most of the stabling refuse observed had not remained long on a dungheap, where weathering processes and working by earthworms would have transformed the material into a poorly polleniferous 'moder' humus type (Bakels 1988; Mücher et al 1990). Although the amount of stabling refuse at the Guildhall may seem to be very abundant, it should be remembered that a cattle byre can be filled twice over during a single winter by the amounts of dung generated by just two cattle (P Reynolds and S Bottema, pers comm). It is therefore likely that most of the dung produced by stabled livestock was removed to manure local arable land (Engelmark 1992; Engelmark and Linderholm 1996; Viklund et al 1998).

Farming and food procurement

Local animal husbandry

There is ample evidence that stock animals were kept and bred by the people living along the lane leading north from Cat Street in the 11th and 12th centuries. Cattle and pigs were probably kept and to a lesser extent sheep or goats, along with horses. However, a large proportion of the meat supply would have been imported from farms further out in the hinterland of the town.

The keeping or stalling of animals within the settlement has

been confirmed by the presence of various deposits which can be interpreted as the remains of stabling waste, as well as by actual stalls, as seen within the suggested byre building (B103), animal pens (eg S105 and S109) and chicken coops (B100). Pollen analysis of the stabling refuse reveals a stall-fed winter diet, indicating that the animals were being stabled over the winter rather than overnight. On balance a stall-fed winter diet is favoured as an interpretation because a higher percentage of herbs might be expected if the animals were grazing freely in pasture during the day and being housed in pens or barns at night (Greig 1984; Moe 1983).

The relative uniformity of pollen assemblages shows that materials such as fodder and bedding were collected from the same areas (the settlement's hinterland) and brought on to the site. The lack of diversity in the pollen derived from the dung argues against a market situation, which would be reflected in a more varied and diverse pollen assemblage, representing both the environments from which livestock had travelled and grazing and browsing while being driven to market.

Unfortunately, the insect remains can not be used conclusively to prove that stabling material and deposits are common at this site, for while members of the 'indicator groups' of species that are thought to be associated with stabling material are present, they fail to dominate in any single deposit.

ANIMAL BONE EVIDENCE FOR HUSBANDRY

Kevin Rielly

There are a number of bones among the early medieval assemblages that clearly indicate a certain level of local production. This is shown by the presence of very young animals, which can be interpreted as infant mortalities and therefore as clear evidence of local stock keeping or breeding. A proportion of these youngsters could represent food imports and indeed a few of the bones do display butchery marks. However, many were clearly too young to be food animals, while some of the older individuals are represented by partial skeletons with no butchery marks, again suggestive of natural rather than deliberate mortalities. The great majority of these youngsters are sheep (CD Table 13); these bones were recovered across the site, with a notable concentration of 16 infant bones representing the remains of two individuals from a pit fill in Open Area 121. The distribution of similarly aged cattle, pigs and chickens is equally widespread, suggesting perhaps small-scale production of a variety of livestock within a number of households. Several buildings did in fact yield the bones of young individuals (eg B116, B103, B107, B113 and B124), with Building 124 producing young sheep, pigs and chickens.

With clear evidence for stalling, it can be assumed that local stocks were maintained by some local production, perhaps combined with the import of animals from the main production centres situated outside the town. Locally kept animals would have been useful for supplying milk products as well as fresh meat. The practice of keeping pigs within towns is well known (Hammond 1993, 40); they were generally culled when sufficiently fattened, as the so-called adult baconers, at about 2 years of age. There is a relatively large proportion of suitably aged pigs within the early medieval assemblages (CD Table 19) and it is possible that some or even all of these may have been locally fattened. Milk production would have required an infant cull, and it is possible that a proportion of the aforementioned calves and lambs may have been killed for this reason.

It would appear that non-food animals were also kept or stalled within the site area, as indicated by the recovery of three horse bones, probably from three different subadult individuals (two in period 10 and one in period 11). They were probably in their second year, at an age prior to the commencement of training for work purposes, which is generally taken to start at about 2 years old (Mortimer 1712, 146; Davis, S J M, 2002, 55). These younger animals may represent horses that had been locally bred or bought when young, in anticipation of being sold on for training purposes.

The great majority of the animals represented at this site were undoubtedly imported from the various production centres located in the hinterland of the town. These would have been provided from established herds, with the express purpose of providing meat for the townspeople. It is possible to deduce whether these animals were bred specifically for this purpose, or whether they represent surplus animals from, say, dairy- or wool-producing herds, by examining their age and sex structure.

For cattle, the evidence clearly demonstrates the very good survival of adult and old adult individuals (CD Table 14; CD Table 15), which would suggest that meat production was a secondary consideration. The representation of these two age groups across the site is, however, quite variable (CD Table 16). An obvious example of this variation is the inversely proportional change in emphasis of the Open Area 127 and Open Area 112 data. While there is a much smaller adult survival in Open Area 127 in period 10 compared to period 11, the opposite situation is shown by the periods 10 and 11 Open Area 112 epiphyses. It could be suggested that a portion of the observed variation may be an artefact of the very different quantities of epiphyses provided by these respective areas. Therefore, it may be more instructive to compare the overall results. Here, the major difference appears to have been a greater cull of young adults in period 10 than in period 11, with a corresponding greater survival of old adults in the latter period. This can be seen by comparing cattle age groups 4–6 (CD Table 14) and the percentage difference between the intermediate- and late-fusing groups (CD Table 15). In addition, a larger proportion of the older fraction in period 11 appears to have survived into old age (elderly), as shown by the vertebrae fusion proportions. It should be noted that some of the individual period 11 land uses, especially to the west of the lane (R102), have particularly high proportions of fused vertebrae, while most of the period 10 land uses produced smaller quantities of fused vertebrae.

The sheep/goat age structure tends to follow the cattle pattern in respect of the very good survival of adults, although the totals are smaller (at least on the mandible evidence) and clearly far fewer individuals survived to an elderly age (note the

single specimen in age group 6 (CD Table 14)). Essentially, the major culls appear to have occurred at the subadult and young adult stages, with perhaps a greater proportion within the latter age group (CD Table 17). This combined evidence masks the rather large variation noticed among those areas with suitably large sheep/goat assemblages. The age structures from the two areas described for period 10 (CD Table 18) could not be more different. The Open Area 127 assemblage has a very large majority surviving to adulthood, while Open Area 103 displays one of the smallest adult percentages. There is, perhaps, less pronounced variation among the period 11 areas, but it may be significant that Open Area 127 again has one of the highest adult percentages, as well as, again, a very good survival of older adults (percentage of fused late epiphyses). The overall proportion of older adults for periods 10 and 11, at c 35%, would suggest that a large proportion of the meat was provided by surplus milk- or wool-producing animals, but it is clear that the main emphasis was on meat production. It may be noted, however, that with the large proportion of young adults there was potential for the production of both these secondary products as well as relatively tender meat. The age structures within Open Area 127 (with the small number of subadults and the high count of old adults) may perhaps be indicative of waste from relatively poorer households. Obviously, this would conflict with the cattle age structure for this area, at least in period 10, where a higher than average count of subadults may point to a relatively high-status diet. What is clearly shown, particularly within period 10, is the very obvious dominance of young adults over subadults.

The presence of high counts of young adults is in fact a general feature of the period 10 and 11 assemblages combined, and can perhaps be viewed in terms of preference or as a result of economic pressures. It is well known that there was a dramatic increase in wool production during the medieval period in this country, possibly dating back to Late Saxon times (Maltby 1981, 178), and certainly from the 12th century onwards (Grant 1988, 151). The urban meat demand could have led to the supply of suitably young individuals, but it can be supposed that the demand for wool would have given rise to an economy where the need for both wool and suitable meat could be satisfied: hence the high proportions of young adults. There is certainly a strong possibility that the great majority of adult sheep dated to these periods (it can be suggested that most of the sheep/goat bones are actually of sheep) had been bred and used for their wool. The sexing evidence can not add very much to this conclusion. Based on the pelves, the sex ratio shows a majority of males, which probably include both rams and wethers. This ratio would include animals culled for their meat as subadults as well as those providing both wool and meat as adults. Both ewes and wethers can be used for their wool, being kept in separate flocks, with the wether apparently providing a heavier fleece (Maltby 1979, 85).

The vast majority of the pigs were culled when either immature or subadult, with just 15–20% surviving into adulthood in periods 10 and 11 (CD Table 14). There is perhaps a higher proportion of immature pigs in period 10, a feature which does not emerge from the epiphysis ageing data. In fact, both periods show a similar cull of first-year animals, of c 30%, which is then followed by a similar subadult cull of c 45–50% (CD Table 19). The sex ratio of the pigs from the maxillary and mandibular canines shows a dominance of males, both within the general population and also among the adult animals (CD Table 20). A generally high proportion of males is perhaps to be expected among an assemblage largely composed of pre-adults, where males tended to be culled in preference to females (Albarella and Davis 1996, 38), the females then being kept for breeding purposes. This does not, however, explain the equally high proportion of males among the adult animals.

There are some differences in the age structures for pig between the individual areas, but the most notable difference is between the period 10 and 11 assemblages from Open Area 127, with the earlier levels showing a better representation of first- and second-year (subadult) animals (CD Table 21). A greater number of younger individuals may point to a higher status of the local inhabitants, or conversely to a greater intensity of supply.

The overall evidence, however, clearly points to intensive pig production, accompanied by the supply of a lesser number of older individuals. The majority of these, within the young adult category, can be interpreted as adult baconers, while the remainder possibly represent surplus breeding stock. Contemporary sources refer to the fattening of pigs from about 18 months of age, these then being considered as suitable adult porkers or baconers when close to 2 years old (Trow-Smith 1957, 124–8; Maltby 1979, 57). This age would approximately correspond to the young adults. It is conceivable that a proportion of these adults were supplied by local production, either as kept and fattened animals or ones kept for breeding purposes. With the older animals confined to period 11, it can perhaps be suggested that the local breeding of pigs was a later innovation.

FODDER CROPS

John Giorgi

In addition to the residues of oats as potential fodder crops, a large number of the samples also contained a range of plants that may be indicative of the residues of hay fodder. During the medieval period there was a substantial trade in hay, while straw was sent to London for use as stable litter (Campbell et al 1993, 26).

Study of hay meadow plants (Greig 1984) suggests that the main seeds indicative of hay (and the most likely to be preserved as waterlogged remains because of their robust nature), and which are present in the Guildhall samples, are buttercups, self-heal, knapweed and hawkbit, while good preservation could extend this list to some of the Leguminosae, rushes, docks, ribwort and grasses.

Buttercup seeds are prolific in the samples, although this species may grow in other habitats including arable ground, while many of the *Centaurea* seeds, either cornflower or knapweed, could not be differentiated. It is also possible that some of the thistles (*Carduus/Cirsium* spp) in the samples may be

from grassland environments. However, most of the characteristic hay meadow plants are represented by small numbers of seeds in the Guildhall samples, although such plants do tend to produce much fewer seeds than their weedy counterparts and are therefore usually under-represented. Indeed, as Greig (1984) noted, sites most often produce floras consisting of a fairly small grassland component and a dominance of weeds of open land and/or sometimes wetland plants, showing characteristic hay meadow plants at particular times. Grassy material often becomes mixed in, especially when fed to animals with other food like grain, with the resulting dung itself being mixed with bedding before being dumped.

Other sites of this period have also produced evidence of the possible residues of hay fodder crops, for example in many samples from Bull Wharf (BUF90: Giorgi 1999) and Peninsular House (Jones et al 1991). It is not possible to establish what animals were being fed on the basis of the fodder available, although on demesnes around medieval London, oats were fed to carthorses for most of the year and to plough horses for six months of the year; unthreshed oats were sometimes fed to oxen, cows and calves during the winter, and the diet for the intensive sty husbandry of pigs included oats, barley and dredge, a mixture of the two (Campbell et al 1993, 42).

Hunting and fishing

Kevin Rielly

There is a considerable collection of game species represented among the animal bone from the early medieval deposits (CD Table 22; CD Table 23). These include several native species, such as red and roe deer, hare, teal, grey partridge, common crane, oystercatcher, woodcock, rock/stock dove and various passerines. Other birds may be added to this list, including goose and mallard, which could include a mixture of domestic and wild individuals. The same problem is applicable to the doves, where most or all of the remains may in fact represent domestic birds. In addition, there are the introduced species, fallow deer and rabbit. Mention should also be made, in the introduced category, of peacock, which was introduced into this country both for its meat and for ornamental purposes. None of these animals and birds is well represented, and they were recovered from most parts of the site. While they are generally regarded as high-status food items, with some – like the crane and peacock – rather more prestigious than the others, the low abundance and widespread presence of these species may in fact be indicative of infrequent purchases, perhaps for special occasions, rather than of local affluence. Certainly, the relative scarcity of such species found in these early medieval levels is in sharp contrast to their abundance in late 13th- and 14th-century deposits (periods 13 and 14), when this area was clearly home to some important citizens.

Several dogs were recovered from early medieval deposits, and it can perhaps be assumed, from their large size, that some may have been used for hunting purposes. Of particular interest is the partial skeleton recovered from a mid 11th-century ditch

(S130, period 10 phase 1). Although this skeleton was missing the skull, the long bones are very similar in both length and breadth to a modern-day greyhound (S Dyer-Hamilton, pers comm). A 'greyhound-type' was among the small number of known 'types' used by medieval hunters (Foulsham 2001). Medieval pictorial representations of such 'greyhounds' generally show them chasing hares, as for example in *The hunting book* by Gaston Phoebus, written in the 14th century. It may therefore be significant that a partially chewed and digested hare bone fragment was found in the same deposit, which could conceivably represent the remains of this dog's last meal.

Fish bones tend to be very common on medieval sites in London, clearly demonstrating that fish formed a staple part of the meat diet. The Guildhall site is no exception to this rule, with fish bones recovered from each one of the early medieval buildings and open areas. Another similarity with other medieval sites is the relative abundance of particular species or groups of species (CD Table 23; CD Table 24), revealing the most commonly exploited fisheries. The abundance of these particular groups is undoubtedly related to their availability and ease of capture, as well as, to a certain extent, their status as a relatively local food resource. This exclusive list represents freshwater, estuarine and, probably, inshore fisheries. In the first of these, both cyprinids and eels were caught in the Thames, often in large numbers, the former by angling or netting and the latter species with the use of nets or traps. Eels were caught either in spring, as elvers migrating up-river, or in midwinter, as somewhat older and larger fish migrating down-river and out to sea. The eels at this site clearly represent catches from the down-river migration, as shown by their generally large size. These fish were often caught in eel-bucks, set to face up-river and placed alongside weirs or watermills (Wheeler 1979, 61), according to a tradition going back to at least the 11th century (Hagen 1995, 163). Examples of another type of fish-trap, composed of a large V-shaped structure pointing downstream with a series of nets at the apex (similar in structure though somewhat smaller than the estuary 'kiddles' described below), have been found close to the riverbank at Isleworth, Putney, Barnes and Chelsea (Cowie and Blackmore in prep), all dating to the Saxon period. The positioning of the 'V' would suggest that these were also intended for catching eels.

The estuarine fisheries represented include those involving sprat (a member of the herring family), smelt, whitefish (cod and whiting) and flatfish (plaice/flounder). Each of these was commercially important in the Thames, with the first three operating in the winter months, catching sprat, whiting and young cod in the lower estuary and smelt in the upper estuary (Wheeler 1978, 150; 1979, 48, 76, 83). These would have been taken by netting or, in the case of cod, by line fishing. It should be noted that while sprat was not identified among the fish bones, those designated as clupeid (herring family) may well include this species, especially as sprat has been recovered from other medieval London sites, for example Winchester Palace (Locker 2006). None of the clupeid bones were sufficiently small to be identified as whitebait, representing another major Thames estuary fishery, this one operating in the summer months. The

absence of these fish is probably related more to the method of preparation (cooked and eaten whole) than to the non-exploitation of this important fishery. The presence of estuarine-caught whitefish is indicated by the good representation of whiting, cod and small gadids (CD Table 23), where it can be assumed that most of the latter belong to the two main whitefish species, and with a clear abundance of relatively young cod. There is, however, a problem with this interpretation, in that similarly-sized fish, both cod and whiting, may have been caught in coastal as well as estuarine waters (see below). Finally, from the estuary, there are plaice/flounder, which were caught by a variety of means, but mainly through the use of fish weirs (or kiddles). These were large V-shaped structures, often 100m to a side, positioned on the foreshore and pointing seawards, with nets or baskets at the apex of the 'V' intended to catch the fish as the tide receded. It seems that this method of capture, like the use of eel-bucks, was practised around the country and certainly in the Thames area since the Saxon period. A number of kiddles dating from this period were recently found on the Blackwater estuary in Essex (Denison 1999).

Marine fishing during the early medieval period was very much limited to inshore waters, with advances in shipbuilding that allowed the exploitation of more distant waters not arriving before the 15th century (Locker 2001, 43). In these coastal waters the main fisheries were based on herring and whitefish, mainly cod and whiting. Among the Guildhall assemblages are a number of larger gadids and cod, signifying older individuals, which could represent catches from this particular fishery. However, as mentioned above, there would appear to be a fine line between estuarine and coastal fishing for whitefish, especially as even the larger cod were to be found closer to the coast in winter (ibid, 45). Herrings were caught in large numbers off the East Anglian coast during their autumn migration, and in particular by the fishing fleets based at Great Yarmouth, which it appears had exploited this seasonal harvest from at least the 7th century AD (ibid, 39, 43). Here, unlike the freshwater and estuarine fisheries, there is the possibility that early medieval London may have relied, to a certain extent, on trade with coastal towns like Great Yarmouth for the provision of marine fish such as cod and herring. It can be surmised that a proportion of this trade dealt in fresh fish, depending on the season, while at other times such fish were bought either salted or dried (as stockfish) or pickled. Before the development of smoking in the 13th century and pickling in the 14th century, herring were salted whole and would not have kept for long (Wilson 1973, 33).

Arable agriculture

John Giorgi

CEREALS

All four cereals (free-threshing wheat, barley, oats and rye) present in the 11th- and 12th-century samples (periods 10–11) were grown in the London region in the early medieval period, with wheat being the most important and widely grown crop

(Campbell et al 1993, 24, 38). Oats, however, were also widely cultivated around London, and almost on equal terms with wheat because of their many uses and the consequent high demand. The respective grain acreage occupied by the four cereals on demesnes around London, with wheat accounting for 37%, oats 33%, barley 13% and rye just 10% (ibid), reflects fairly well their proportions at the Guildhall site.

In the medieval period around London, wheat and rye were either grown separately or sometimes together as 'maslin', while barley and oats were cultivated both as separate crops and together as 'dredge' (Campbell et al 1993, 38, 121). However, most of the Guildhall samples contain mixes of the different cereals, and where particular grains do predominate it is either as single cereals or as mixes that are unlikely to have been cultivated together, such as wheat and oats or rye and barley. Thus, it is likely that the different cereals only became mixed after harvesting or after being accidentally charred and discarded.

The areas of cultivation of the different cereals around London depended on their value and the cost of transporting them, as well as on the suitability of the soils. Thus, oats, which were the bulkiest and least valuable grain, were mainly cultivated and commercially produced closest to London (together with straw, hay and firewood) whereas wheat – which commanded the highest price per unit volume – was grown most extensively at some distance from the town (Campbell et al 1993, 113–15). Oats are more tolerant of heavy or waterlogged soils than the other cereals in the samples and so were grown in areas unsuitable for them, such as the coastal areas of the Thames, although they were not cultivated exclusively on such soils. Wheat is often associated with heavier clay and loam soils, while barley is a shallow-rooted crop best suited to light to medium silts and loams but not tolerant of excessive moisture. Rye is tolerant of poorer-quality, shallower and lighter soils, being well suited to light acidic sandy soils (too poor for wheat), although location was also important, and rye and rye mixture cultivation lay at a relatively low transport-cost distance from London.

The arable weed seeds in the samples reflect the range of soils used for growing the different cereals. It is possible that these weeds were also growing as plants of disturbed ground in the settlement itself, although this would not account for the variety of soils that these plants represent. The likelihood that these are cereal weeds is increased if they are found as charred remains and in association with large cereal deposits. Thus, stinking mayweed is one of the most frequent weed seeds in both the charred and waterlogged samples. This is a characteristic arable weed usually associated with cultivation on heavy clay soils and may have been imported with the wheat crop, although its distribution may have been more extensive in the past. At the other extreme is corn marigold, well represented in the samples and another potential arable weed, being associated with the cultivation of sandy soils. Wild radish, annual knawel and sheep's sorrel are also characteristic of acidic sandy soils.

In the Saxon and medieval periods, wheat, rye and winter barley were usually autumn-sown while spring barley and oats were mainly sown in the spring (Greig 1988, 125). It may be possible to establish the sowing times of the different cereals in the Guildhall samples by investigating the germination time of the associated weed seeds. Ellenberg (1988) has distinguished species within two classes, the Secalietea and Chenopodietea, as a means of differentiating autumn- and spring-sown crops respectively (although it is possible that some of these weeds may germinate in both seasons).

Of the species present in the samples from the site, corncockle, wild radish, cleavers, bromes and black bindweed occur most often in fields of autumn-sown crops, while chickweeds, fat hen, oraches, corn marigold and scentless mayweed are usually found growing among spring-sown crops. Again, however, no correlation can be made between these seeds and particular cereals in individual assemblages because of mixing, although the presence of these species may suggest that the cereals derive from both spring- and autumn-sown crops.

The large number of potential arable weeds in samples from the site, in conjunction with smaller amounts of other cereal debris (rachis fragments, stems and culm nodes), also points to crop-processing activities on the site, mainly involving the latter stages of cleaning by sieving the crops. The charring of some of this material suggests that it was then used as fuel.

PULSES

Legumes, including peas and horse beans, are poorly represented in the samples, although the documentary records suggest that legumes were extensively grown around London in the medieval period, albeit as a minority crop occupying c 5% of the sown acreage on many demesnes around 1300 (Campbell et al 1993, 134). Peas favour light soils whereas beans prefer heavier soils. Legumes were important, however, in restoring the levels of nitrogen in the soil, and took the place of fallows in the most intensive medieval rotations.

Fruit cultivation

John Giorgi

Of the fruits found in the samples, some may represent imported foodstuffs, while others were gathered from the wild or cultivated locally. For instance, grapes were cultivated in southern Britain in the early medieval period (Wilson 1991, 331) and hence the grape seeds in the samples may represent either home-grown produce, possibly cultivated in gardens on the site or nearby, or imported fruit. Figs can grow in this country but only produce infertile seeds, which means that the seeds in the samples are probably the residues of imported fruit. Figs and grapes were imported as dried fruit from southern Europe in the later medieval period (Cobb 1990).

Apples were one of the most widely cultivated fruits in the medieval period while pears appear to have been less commonly grown, judging by the documentary evidence (Greig 1988, 117). This is also reflected in the botanical record from the Guildhall sites, which shows a very poor representation of pear compared to apple. The cherry and peach stones may also come from locally cultivated fruit, with documentary evidence recording the planting of cherry and peach trees in the royal gardens at Westminster during the 13th century (Wilson 1991, 331). The plum stones may be from either wild or cultivated species. The other fruits – sloe/blackthorn, elderberry, blackberry/raspberry, strawberry and hazelnut – were probably all growing wild in woodland, hedgerow and scrub environments and gathered while in season, presumably from areas both within and outside the city walls.

Garden plants

John Giorgi

It is possible that a high proportion of the food and other economic plants represented in the samples were grown in gardens on the site or close by; medieval London contained many small gardens in which householders grew a few fruits and vegetables (McClean 1981, 64). Garden 'bedding trenches' were excavated on this site in an open area that seems to have been part of the garden of Warin de Bassingbourn's early 13th-century hall on Basinghall Street (period 11 phase 4, OA128). Cultivated plants grown in gardens like this would have included a number of those represented in the samples, such as apple and grape, opium poppy, the *Brassica/Sinapis* species and carrot, as well as (on a small scale) plants such as flax, hemp and weld used in fibres and dyes.

There are also several ornamental garden plants represented in the samples, such as rose and holly (from S130). Many of the wild plants represented in the samples could, however, also have been grown as garden plants. Garden areas on or near the site may also account for some of the nitrophilous weeds in the samples, such as sun spurge, fumitory, small nettle and fat hen, which are common weeds of gardens as well as waste places and fields.

Food consumption

The non-meat diet

John Giorgi

The botanical evidence for food plants in the early medieval samples consists mainly of the residues of cereals and fruits, with a small amount of evidence for the use of pulses and possibly other common vegetables.

CEREALS

Cereals are primarily represented by charred grains and a small number of mineralised grains, plus some cereal bran preserved by waterlogging. The definite consumption of cereals is shown by the presence of cereal bran in several samples from cesspit fills (eg OA109 and OA120) and a rubbish pit fill (OA127). The bran in the samples is extremely fragmentary (>2mm) and includes diagnostic wheat/rye cereals, which probably indicates human consumption.

Charred cereal grains were found in the vast majority of the samples, but the size of most of the assemblages is fairly small, amounting to less than one hundred grains; they were probably being charred accidentally while being prepared for consumption or during drying before storage and/or milling. Several large charred grain assemblages, however, suggest possible conflagrations or deliberate burning of spoilt crops.

The four cereals represented in samples are free-threshing wheat, barley, oats and rye. These cereals are the most common grains found on Saxon and medieval sites in Britain, albeit in varying quantities (Greig 1991, 315, 321). Examples in London include finds from 11th- to 12th-century deposits from the waterfront at Bull Wharf (BUF90: Giorgi 1999) and from several 9th- to 12th-century AD sites in the City (Jones et al 1991), as well as further west in 13th- to 14th-century deposits in Westminster (Giorgi 2006).

There are no significant differences in the relative representation of the cereals over time. The samples contain a mix of the different cereal grains, with oat being the best-represented, followed by wheat and then barley and significantly smaller amounts of rye. Oats are often the best-represented grain in samples from this period in London, for example at Bull Wharf (Giorgi 1999), in 13th- to 14th-century deposits at Shelley House to the west of the Guildhall (Giorgi 2004) and at Westminster, where both oats and free-threshing wheat were the two best-represented cereals (Giorgi 2006). Late Saxon to early medieval samples from 1 Poultry (ONE94) in the City produced all four grains, with each cereal dominant in at least one assemblage (Davis, A, 2002).

OAT

The predominance of oat at the Guildhall and many other London sites is not surprising given its many uses both for human consumption and as animal feed. Indeed, it was possibly the grain consumed in greatest volume during the early medieval period (Campbell et al 1993, 27). This is in contrast to Middle Saxon Lundenwic, for example at the Royal Opera House, where oats probably only occurred as weeds and the main cereals were wheat and barley (Davis 2003, 290).

Great quantities of oats were imported into London in the early medieval period, much of which was for fodder, especially for the horses upon which the city relied for haulage (Campbell et al 1993, 26). Oat was used in the grain mixes for a bread consumed by the less well-off households in London and in pottage, the common form of grain consumption in the countryside but possibly only eaten by the very poorest in the city (ibid, 27). It was also used in brewing, and a good proportion of the imported grain was employed for this purpose, with large quantities of ale being consumed in the Saxon and medieval periods.

The degree of cleanliness of the oat grains may indicate their use as either human or animal feed, since processing for fodder did not generally need to be so thorough. Thus, the proportion of weeds in a sample may indicate whether or not the grains were used as fodder. The general cleanliness of the oat grains in most of the Guildhall samples with good assemblages of this cereal (eg B100, B101 and OA103 (period 10), and B112,

B117, B124, B126, OA121, OA132, OA134 and OA137 (period 11)), suggests that most of the those assemblages represent residues of cleaned grains destined for human consumption. Among other contemporary sites in London, a 12th-century hearth deposit from Bull Wharf (BUF90) contained thousands of cleaned grains, including oat and barley, interpreted as human food (Giorgi 1999), while two large deposits of fairly clean oat grains from Westminster are also interpreted as human food (Giorgi 2006). There was no definite evidence for the use of oats (or barley) for brewing on the site because few grains in the cleaned cereal samples had sprouted.

On the other hand, several oat samples from the site include a large number of floret bases and weed seeds, and suggest that the grains represent the residues of fodder crops; for example, from Building 116 there are thousands of oat grains with florets and many weed seeds (especially grasses) from two hearth deposits, and a substantial quantity of the same material from a gully fill. This semi-cleaned grain may be the residue of a fodder crop (although possible mixing of plant remains can not be ruled out); many of the grains in these samples had sprouted so they may have been deliberately burnt as a spoilt crop. Similar deposits interpreted as fodder crops were recovered from a 10th-century AD oven at Peninsular House in the City, consisting mainly of oats plus barley (including sprouted grain) and a large number of weeds (Jones et al 1991), and from a 12th-century hearth at Bull Wharf (Giorgi 1999). Some of the unidentified cereal bran in the Guildhall samples may also be from animal consumption of cereals.

It is important to note that the relatively poor representation of oats as fodder compared to those probably intended for human consumption (as represented by charred grains) may be a reflection of processing rather than their relative importance on a site. Grains as fodder crops are consumed fresh, whereas cereals for human consumption are heated and therefore more liable to become charred.

WHEAT

Wheat is generally the second best-represented grain in the samples, with the rounded morphology of the well-preserved grains suggesting the presence of free-threshing wheats. Rachis fragments betray the presence of hexaploid bread wheat, which has also been identified at a number of other sites in Late Saxon to early medieval London, for example in 12th-century deposits from the National Gallery Extension (de Moulins 1989). Wheat was used for human consumption and (together with rye) was the main bread grain in the London region in the medieval period, producing high-quality white wheaten bread consumed by the more well-to-do. This cereal was also occasionally used in brewing as well as for pies and pastry (Campbell et al 1993, 24–6).

There are a number of very large assemblages of free-threshing grains in the Guildhall samples. Hundreds of grains of free-threshing wheat came from an occupation deposit in Building 118 (period 10 phase 5), while it is also well represented together with oats in a number of samples from period 11 (B126, OA134 and OA137).

Fig 306 *Emmer grains from Building 112 (scale c 2:1)*

The hulled wheat, emmer, was present in an occupation deposit in the period 11 phase 2 Building 112 (Fig 306) and occasional grains also came from Open Area 106 (period 10 phase 3) and Open Area 127; this cereal was also identified from a few spikelet forks. Present evidence suggests that emmer was probably not extensively cultivated in the post-Roman period, although hulled wheat grains (emmer and spelt) have recently been found in Middle Saxon samples from Lundenwic (Davis 2003) as well as in the lower Thames valley at Harmondsworth (Hinton 1996), while emmer grains have been identified in the middle and upper Thames valley (Pelling and Robinson 2000). It has been suggested that this cereal may have been brought into the country as seed-corn by Saxon groups from northern Europe (ibid). This grain would also have been used for human food.

BARLEY

Barley grains are also well represented in the samples although this is rarely the best-represented cereal in the larger assemblages. The well-preserved barley grains include twisted as well as straight grains, indicating the presence of six-row hulled barley. Barley was used for both human food (in bread mixes, pottage and brewing) and animal feed, although its inclusion in fairly clean deposits suggests that it was mainly intended for human consumption on this site. The only very large find was of hundreds of barley grains in a period 9 cesspit fill (OA121) together with the only large deposit of rye grains. It was also well represented, together with oats, in Open Area 105 (period 10 phase 2).

RYE

Rye is represented by only very occasional grains except from one cesspit fill (OA121, above). Rye makes dark and heavy bread which was consumed by the poor; it was rarely if ever used in brewing.

PULSES

There is little evidence from the Guildhall for common pulses, except for occasional charred peas in just two samples and horse beans in nine samples. Some of the indeterminate leguminous seeds including the *Vicia/Lathyrus/Pisum* species may also represent cultivated plants, although they could also be simply cereal weeds.

Pulses rarely survive unless charred and are only occasionally found in Late Saxon to early medieval samples from London; thus, for example, there is pea from Westminster (Giorgi 2006), horse bean from Bull Wharf (Giorgi 1999), pea and horse bean from a number of 9th- to 11th-century AD sites in the City (Jones et al 1991) and pea from Shelley House to the west of the Guildhall (Giorgi 2004). Legumes, however, were an important part of the medieval diet; they were widely used in pottage and stews, especially by the poor and in religious houses (Wilson 1991, 201), and were also ground up as flour and used with cereals in bread that was mainly eaten by the less well-off (Black 1985, 6). Peas and beans were also used as animal fodder (Wilson 1991, 202); for example, in the early 14th century beans were used to make bread fed to horses. Pulses are rich in protein and could be dried for use in winter and early spring when green vegetables were scarce.

COMMON VEGETABLES

There is a paucity of seeds of common vegetables from the Guildhall sites, probably because leafy vegetables are harvested before they set seed. The seeds of the *Brassica/Sinapis* group include common vegetables (eg cabbage, swede and turnip) but are difficult to identify to species and may be from wild rather than cultivated plants. These seeds are present in the majority of samples although usually only in small numbers. Some large quantities of seeds of this group occurring in features such as cesspits and refuse pits alongside other food remains may suggest that they are the residues of consumed plants (eg the exceptionally large numbers present in a cesspit in Open Area 109, and in other contexts such as Open Areas 112 and 132). A few carrot seeds were noted in 17 samples, although these may be from the wild rather than the cultivated species. Carrot has occasionally been found on other London sites such as Bull Wharf (Giorgi 1999). Common leaf and root vegetables were, nevertheless, widely consumed in medieval London in stews and pottage (Wilson 1991, 205) and were an important source of protein.

FRUITS

Fruits are the most common food remains in the early medieval Guildhall samples (periods 9–11), with a wide range of both wild and cultivated species (eg Fig 307; Fig 308) mainly preserved by waterlogging; there are also occasional mineralised remains (eg fig, grape and *Prunus* species), particularly in cesspit assemblages, and a few charred examples, in particular hazelnut shell and occasional grape seeds and fruit stones (eg sloe/blackthorn).

Waterlogged fruit remains include seeds of grape, fig, apple (also represented by endocarp fragments), pear, mulberry, bilberry, blackberry, blackberry/raspberry, strawberry and elderberry, stones of plum/bullace, sloe, cherry and peach, and walnut and hazelnut shell. Some of these fruits are obviously cultivated species (eg fig, grape, mulberry and peach) while the status of others is more difficult to ascertain (eg blackberry, plum and cherry). Some fruits would have been gathered from the wild (eg hazelnuts, strawberry, bilberry, sloe and elderberry).

The different species are present in varying abundance, although hazelnut shell and elderberry and blackberry/raspberry seeds are particularly prolific, occurring in large quantities in a large number of sampled features or areas. The

Fig 307 *Fruit stones from early medieval samples: plum/bullace, sloe/blackthorn, cherry and peach (scale c 1:1)*

Fig 308 *Fruit seeds from early medieval samples: grape, fig, apple, apple/pear, blackberry/raspberry and elderberry (scale c 2:1)*

fig, grape, apple, apple/pear, blackberry and wild strawberry seeds feature in moderate numbers of samples along with the plum/bullace, sloe and cherry stones (all of which, however, occasionally occur in very large numbers), while there are occasional mulberry seeds from five areas, apple endocarp fragments in four samples, walnut shell from about 13 areas, peach stones in three samples and bilberry and pear seeds in just one sample each. The best assemblages of mineralised and waterlogged fruit remains came from the pit fills in Open Areas 105, 114 and 127.

The various fruits in the assemblages would have had a

variety of uses, although some of the remains of wild fruits may simply represent plants growing in the vicinity rather than deliberately collected and used fruit. This is much less likely to be the case when such material is recovered in large quantities (together with other food remains) from pit fills, where it is most likely to be the residues of consumed fruit.

A wide range of fruit remains are commonly found (often in large quantities) on most Late Saxon to early medieval London sites because of the high number of excavated pits and the robust nature of this woody material. There is a similar range of cultivated and wild fruits from the Westminster sites (Giorgi 2006), from 10th- to 12th-century AD deposits at Bull Wharf (Giorgi 1999), from 9th- to 12th-century AD City sites (Jones et al 1991) and from Late Saxon to early medieval deposits at 1 Poultry (Davis, A, 2002).

Fruit in the medieval period would have had a wide range of uses, not only as food and drink but also in medicine and occasionally in industrial processes. As food, fruit was used in pottage, often cooked with spices, prepared in pies, pastries and puddings, and made into preserves (jams and jellies). Figs, hazelnuts and walnuts may have been dried and stored for consumption out of season. It has been suggested that it was considered unhealthy to eat fresh fruit because it was associated with common diseases such as diarrhoea and dysentery (Weinstein 1990). As drink, apples were used for making cider and verjuice, cherries for liquers and verjuice, and elderberries for wine, in addition to many other uses in syrups, jams, dye and also in the tanning industry.

Imported dried figs were used as a sweetener by the well-off, and by the poor in pottages and pies on festive occasions (Wilson 1991, 334), while home-grown grapes were used for verjuice (from unripe grapes, for pickling and cooking) rather than for making wine and eating fresh (McClean 1981). Grapes were also pickled, dried and stored for later consumption. The grape seeds from the Guildhall would represented the residues of consumed fruit unless vines were growing on the site.

Mulberry is only occasionally found in Late Saxon and medieval samples, for example from a 12th-century cesspit at Milk Street (Jones et al 1991) and from 13th- to 14th-century deposits at Westminster (Giorgi 2006). Mulberries were used in a pottage called murrey (Wilson 1991, 334) and for jams and jellies. Peach stones are also uncommon finds in deposits of this date, although they were found in 13th-century deposits at Billingsgate (BIG82: Pearson in prep), in 11th- to 12th-century deposits at Bull Wharf (Giorgi 1999) and in an early medieval deposit at 1 Poultry (Davis, A, 2002).

HERBS AND SPICES

Black mustard seeds are present in 15 samples, with moderate amounts in three samples from period 10. In the medieval period they were ground up and used in a liquid mixture (including honey and oil) described as 'more like a salad dressing' than today's thicker mustard (Mabey 1972, 147). These seeds have been found at a number of Late Saxon and early medieval London sites including Bull Wharf (Giorgi 1999). Other plants in the samples may have been used to flavour food: for example, poppy seed and linseed were used to enrich and flavour breads and pottages (Hagen 1992, 59).

WILD PLANTS

The leaves of wild plants represented in the samples, including the docks, goosefoots and oraches (rich sources of vitamin C), may have been collected and used in pottage or eaten as green vegetables. However, these are also common weeds, and it is difficult to determine whether they were gathered for food since they occur in mixed seed assemblages with other wild plants.

The meat diet

Kevin Rielly

FOOD PREFERENCE AND AVAILABILITY

A wide variety of food species were recovered from the medieval animal bone assemblages (CD Table 22; CD Table 23). The bulk of the meat requirement was clearly met by the major mammalian domesticates, although other food groups such as domestic birds, game species and fish made notable contributions (CD Table 25). The general pattern would suggest that the relative abundance of these food groups was roughly similar throughout the early medieval period. There are, however, some notable differences in the proportions of certain of these groups within particular areas. Conspicuously large collections of domestic birds (c 20% of the total hand-recovered counts), especially chicken, came from the various pit fills in Open Area 121 (period 10) and also Building 113, Road 102 and Structure 107 (period 11). Moreover, the domestic bird counts from certain pit fills in Open Area 121 constitute 40% and 30% of their respective hand-collected assemblages. Such concentrations may be indicative of a local meat preference or perhaps suggest the keeping of poultry in these areas.

Fish bones form the major part of almost all the recorded sample assemblages, but were particularly abundant (c 90% of the identifiable bones) in a series of period 11 deposits alongside the lane (R102). These include dumps in Open Areas 111 and 112, a cesspit in Open Area 138 and three hearth deposits, two from Building 124 and one from Open Area 132. Again, a meat preference within this general area may explain these concentrations. It is also of interest that large numbers of fish bones should have been found in hearth deposits, perhaps representing fish cooked and eaten nearby (below, 'Cookshops'). The fish bone assemblages from each of these deposits follow the general pattern of species representation (CD Table 23; CD Table 24), with a clear dominance of six species or species groups. There is some variation in the relative abundance of these groups, but essentially each period assemblage is largely composed of clupeids (mainly herring), with gadids (mainly cod and whiting) and plaice/flounder vying for second place. In terms of meat supply, judging by the typical size of these fish and assuming that they are all adult with the exception of most of the cod, it is likely that the herring may just have provided the greater quantity of meat (cf Locker 2001, 141).

Within the major food group, the mammalian domesticates,

there appears to be a decline in pig abundance and a corresponding increase in sheep/goat representation, culminating in quite similar proportions of cattle and sheep/goat in period 11 (CD Table 26). The rise in sheep/goat (or more likely of sheep: CD Table 22) is doubtless associated with the increasing importance of the woollen industry in the medieval period. The greater availability of sheep did not, however, radically diminish the popularity of beef, with cattle clearly satisfying the major part of the town's meat requirement (bearing in mind the relative size of the major domesticates as well as their relative abundance) throughout the early medieval period.

The good representation of pigs in periods 9 and 10 and their subsequent decline by period 11 could be explained by a change in preference and/or availability, with perhaps a greater number of households keeping pigs in the earlier periods. A larger number of very young pigs, probably infant mortalities, were recovered from period 10 than from period 11, but the numbers are perhaps insufficiently different to suggest an actual change in local pig-keeping. A very similar pattern is seen during the early medieval occupation at 1 Poultry (ONE94), where 10th- to 11th-century AD abundance again declines by the 12th century (Rielly in prep).

There are notable spatial variations in domesticate species abundance, whereby, for example, not all the period 10 areas yielded high counts of pig bones (CD Table 27). Here, it should also be mentioned that the large number of pig bones in period 10 was mainly derived from a major concentration of 'butcher's waste' in a pit fill in Open Area 127 (see below). It might be supposed that this unusual deposit may have skewed the figures towards pig abundance; however, this species was well represented in a number of other pits in this area, as well as in nearby features in Open Area 121. Pig is also well represented in period 11 (OA110) and sheep relatively abundant in period 10 (OA103), observations which contradict the general pattern. The Open Area 110 assemblage is also unusual for its good representation of sheep/goat, best viewed as 'epiphyses only' counts (Fig 309).

MEAT SUPPLY

This section is concerned with the redistribution of animal products, principally meat, following the assumption that most of the meat requirement was met by imported domestic livestock. Given a general mix of skeletal parts belonging to each of the three major domesticates throughout the site, it could be argued that animals were purchased by individual households and then slaughtered and butchered, and the waste disposed of nearby, or at least in accessible features or areas (eg the pitting in OA127). In this scenario, the killing and butchering may have been carried out by a designated member of the household or perhaps by itinerant professional butchers (Hagen 1992, 34). However, the site did produce a few deposits containing concentrations of head and foot bones, the so-called 'butcher's waste', which would suggest the local presence of butchers' establishments or markets. The best examples came from two pit fills in Open Area 127 (period 10), comprising butcher's waste collections of cattle and pig (Fig 310; Fig 311) in contrast to the typically mixed

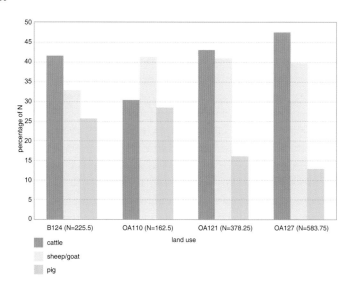

Fig 309 The representation of cattle, sheep/goat and pig in assemblages from selected 12th-century land uses (period 11) using the 'epiphyses only' method (N = hand-collected number of bones from the species combined; see Chapter 8.14)

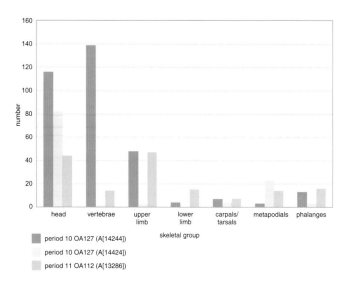

Fig 310 Comparison of cattle skeletal distribution from three 11th- to 12th-century deposits

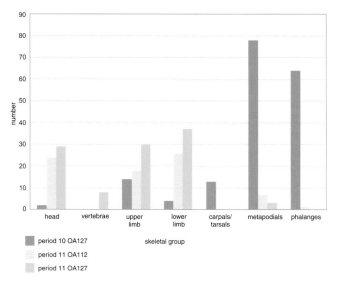

Fig 311 Comparison of pig skeletal distribution from three 11th- to 12th-century deposits

assemblages found elsewhere. It is interesting to note the differences between cattle and pig skeletal representation, with cattle dominated by head bones, vertebrae and pelves, and pig by metapodials and phalanges. These differences may arise from a number of factors, including the passing on of skins with certain bones still attached (below, 6.6, 'Horn working and tanning'); the defleshing/jointing pattern, which was probably based on the size of the respective species; and the use of particular parts, by the butcher, for the production of various cold meats such as brawn.

The general evidence would perhaps suggest the presence of markets within the local area offering either live animals, suitable for home slaughter and butchery, or portions of carcasses supplied by market-based butchers. There is clear evidence for such butchers in urban settlements from at least the Late Saxon period (Hagen 1992, 34). The relative importance of purchasing meat 'on the hoof' as against joints can not be adequately assessed on this evidence, although it can be assumed that an urban population is more likely to have made use of a butcher/consumer system. A major problem concerning the interpretation of this data is that the small number of 'butcher's waste' deposits can not be taken to indicate a relatively minor role played by market-based butchers. Such deposits are generally infrequent on archaeological sites, even those where butcher/consumer systems were obviously important, as for example in post-medieval London.

Cookshops

Most of the timber houses contained one or more hearths which would have been used for cooking, and some buildings also appear to have been provided with an enclosed oven presumably for baking food, for example bread (above, 6.3, 'Hearths and ovens'). These would have been for the private use of the household.

In the second half of the 12th century a zone of open-air hearths developed on the east side of the lane (R102) leading north from Cat Street (period 11 phase 2, OA133 and OA137) (Fig 312). These cookshops, some perhaps covered by awnings or with flimsy timber shelters, were used to prepare food for sale to passing trade. To the south, a similar intensity of hearths was found in a contemporary building (B124) and, following its demise, the site of the building was used for more open-air hearths (OA132). In the early 13th century this zone appears to have expanded to the west side of the lane, and soon after, by c 1230, the cookshops had disappeared and been replaced by the Guildhall yard.

William fitz Stephen gives a near-contemporary account of a cookshop on the riverbank in his 12th-century description of London: '... a public cookshop. There daily, according to the season, you may find viands, dishes roast, fried and boiled, fish great and small, the coarser flesh for the poor, the more delicate for the rich, such as venison and birds both big and little' (Douglas and Greenaway 1981, 958). Three later references from the beginning of the 13th century refer to the cookshops

in Vintry on the Thames, and it is suggested that they catered for river boatmen and dockworkers as well as travellers arriving by boat (Carlin 1998, 30).

Recent archaeological excavations in the Vintry ward at 29–30 Queen Street (QUS00) have located a cookshop as described by fitz Stephen (Telfer 2004). The cookshop dates from c 1135 and continued in use down to the 17th century, and is represented by a complex succession of numerous hearths and associated floors. As at the Guildhall, it is suggested that the 12th- and 13th-century hearths were essentially open-air but probably sheltered under some form of roof. Animal remains associated with the earliest hearth include the major domesticates, fish (eel, herring family and cod family) and birds (chicken, dove, goose, partridge and wild duck). Charred cereal grains (free-threshing wheat, barley, oats and rye) associated with a possible oven were either accidentally burnt during food preparation or came from straw used to fuel the oven.

Each of the suspected cookshop areas at the Guildhall produced thin scatters of bones, with some concentrations associated with certain hearths. These collections do not, however, compare with the wide range of foods documented by fitz Stephen, with the great majority of the archaeologically recovered bones identified as eel and clupeid (herring family). Neither can it be said that these bones are definitely related to cookshop activities, as vertebrae far outnumber head parts (allowing for the relative frequency of parts), which suggests general food waste rather than processing waste. However, it is possible that these food items had been cooked and eaten 'on the premises'. In addition, herrings may have been sold as fillets, cooked or preserved. Botanical evidence from samples provides a little more information about the possible food products: remains of wild and/or cultivated fruits include elderberry, peach and hazelnut, in addition to some horse beans and larger amounts of oats and wheat.

Discarded in one of the pits (OA136) was a large animal bone assemblage of cattle bones, mostly butcher's waste consisting mainly of mandibles. A weight <S57> (Fig 313) may have been used to measure the ingredients or cooked items on sale. It was found in the cookshop area (OA132) and appears to be somewhat makeshift, using iron nails driven into a lead disc to make a half avoirdupois pound (of 15 ounces). The chronological context of the weight (c 1200–30) is, however, earlier than the documented introduction of the avoirdupois system, shortly before 1270 (Egan 1998, 302–3).

Analysis of the pottery found in those open areas in which putative cookshops were identified has revealed somewhat ambiguous evidence for food preparation on a commercial scale. The best evidence comes from Building 124, where 287 sherds from some 11 cooking pots in early Surrey ware (ESUR) and south Hertfordshire-type greyware (SHER) were recovered, all in the same context and all sooted from use. The presence of SHER indicates a date of deposition after c 1170. The ratio of sherds to complete vessels suggests that they were discarded freshly broken and may have been used on the hearth or in the immediate vicinity. Only six sherds out of a total of 329 for the group do not come from cooking pots. It is possible, therefore,

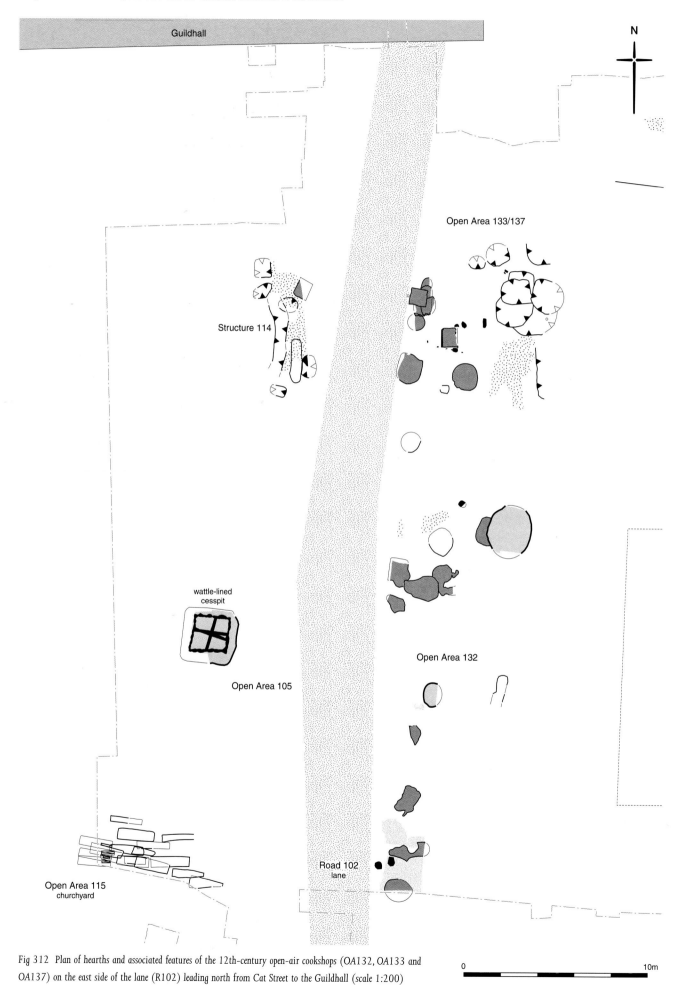

N

Guildhall

Open Area 133/137

Structure 114

wattle-lined
cesspit

Open Area 105

Open Area 132

Open Area 115
churchyard

Road 102
lane

Fig 312 Plan of hearths and associated features of the 12th-century open-air cookshops (OA132, OA133 and OA137) on the east side of the lane (R102) leading north from Cat Street to the Guildhall (scale 1:200)

0   10m

Fig 313 Lead weight <S57> (with iron nails) of half an avoirdupois pound, probably used in the cookshops (scale c 1:1)

that this find represents the remains of a commercial cooking establishment. There is, however, little comparable evidence to suggest that similar activities were taking place in Open Areas 133 or 137, although a group of four hearths in Open Area 132 yielded a relatively large number of decorated jugs in coarse London-type ware (LCOAR), with far fewer cooking pots. Whether these were also associated with commercial food preparation and the serving of beverages is uncertain, since these two forms are the most common vessel types found in London at this date and occur in large numbers across the site.

If the areas of hearths are correctly interpreted as cookshops, presumably they were set up to sell food to a transient clientele who visited them while making their way along the lane between Cat Street and the Guildhall. These 'fast-food outlets' may have grown up in association with a market, perhaps located to the east of the lane in what was an open space (eg OA127). They may have catered for workers engaged on nearby building projects such as the construction of the stone buildings along Cat Street and Basinghall Street or even work on the Guildhall building itself, as well as for visitors to the Guildhall or those attending the weekly Court of Husting.

Links with Scandinavia

It has previously been argued that aspects of the early medieval settlement at the Guildhall site indicate a significant Danish presence in this part of London and, in particular, a strong link with the Danish (now Swedish) town of Lund (Porter 1997; Bateman 1997; 2000). The evidence for this 'Anglo-Scandinavian' or Danish occupation is found, it has been claimed, in the 11th-century burial practices used in the churchyard of St Lawrence Jewry, in the dedication of the church to St Lawrence, in the architecture of the 11th- and 12th-century timber buildings, and in the name of the Court of Husting which was held in the Guildhall in the 12th century. It is suggested here, however, that there is little real evidence from the Guildhall site for distinctively Danish or Anglo-Scandinavian settlement. While the St Lawrence Jewry burial practices (particularly the use of hazel rods and staffs) do display parallels with Scandinavian practice (as seen, for example, on excavated early medieval sites at Trondheim (Norway) and Lund), it is argued below (6.12) that the range of burial practices can now

be seen as typical of English early medieval sites where the ground conditions allow preservation of organic material. The common link between the St Lawrence Jewry and Scandinavian examples is therefore taphonomic rather than cultural. A similar argument is advanced above (6.2 and 6.3) regarding the supposed Scandinavian traits in the timber architecture: as more English archaeological sites with good organic preservation are excavated, more examples of so-called 'Scandinavian' techniques are found. The range of building styles employed at the Guildhall site can now be viewed as part of an earlier English tradition seen, for example, in pre-Viking London at sites such as the Royal Opera House (Malcolm and Bowsher 2003).

Some of the Saxo-Norman decorative metalwork (Chapter 8.8) undoubtedly features Scandinavian-style ornament. It seems more plausible, however, to envisage local production among the native English population, influenced by imported art styles, rather than to see these pieces as manufactured by immigrant Scandinavians. Objects made in Scandinavia have indeed been found elsewhere in London, and there seems from the excavated evidence (from the City as a whole) to have been a high point of Danish fashion around the time of the reign of Cnut in England (1016–35). There is, however, no particular prominence of Scandinavian-made or Scandinavian-influenced objects at the Guildhall site, although objects with Ringerike style or derivative ornament are present, most notably a horse-harness pendant <S47> (Fig 314). Production by Norwegians,

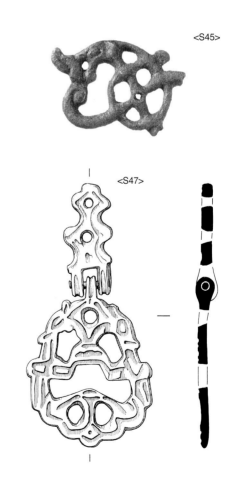

Fig 314 Objects with Scandinavian-style ornament: copper-alloy mount <S45> in Urnes style and horse-harness pendant <S47> in Ringerike style (scale 1:1)

whether in their homeland or in this country, of the few pieces of metalwork with late 11th- to early 12th-century Urnes style ornament found in London, like the mount <S45> (Fig 314), seems an unnecessarily complicated explanation for what was probably largely a matter of adopting fashions as part of a whole series of complex cultural influences. The evidence of the 11th-century pottery from the Guildhall site reveals a similar lack of Scandinavian traits: there is no evidence for Danish or Baltic pottery, in common with other sites across London. Various fabrics made within the area of the Danelaw are found in mid 11th- to 12th-century contexts (notably Stamford-type ware from Lincolnshire and Thetford-type ware from Norfolk), but much of this pottery was introduced after the Danelaw had ceased to be a separate political entity and so it has little 'cultural' significance.

Perhaps the most significant argument is that much of the early medieval occupation at the Guildhall site is now dated after the Danish rule of the first half of the 11th century. The church of St Lawrence Jewry seems to have been founded c 1050 (below, 6.11) and the houses along the lane (R102) to the north of the church date from c 1080–c 1200 (Chapter 3; above, 6.3). The other postulated links with Scandinavia can now be seen to be largely irrelevant: St Lawrence was a popular dedication of early Scandinavian churches but also of early English ones (Farmer 1997, 295–6). The name of the Court of Husting does preserve a Scandinavian element (Stenton 1970, 30–1) but this may simply date aspects of the court's development to the first half of the 11th century, during the reigns of Danish kings (Nightingale 1987, 566–7). It now seems that the Guildhall site presents evidence for 'ordinary' settlement of the 11th and 12th centuries, by Londoners who may have been exposed to cultural or even political influences from Scandinavia (and who conceivably had direct contact with the occasional Scandinavian merchant or immigrant in the area) but with no special Scandinavian connection.

6.5 Jewish occupation in the 12th and 13th centuries

The Norman Conquest led directly to the arrival of a Jewish community in London. According to the 12th-century historian William of Malmesbury, William I 'imported' Jews from the Norman community at Rouen (Hillaby 1994, 2), although it is unlikely that the London community was very large until after the massacre of the Jews of Rouen by crusading knights in 1096 (Roth 1949, 5–6). Their role was in large part to provide finance for William's capital projects, which was forbidden to Christians because of the medieval Church's laws concerning usury. The Guildhall study area lies towards the north of the medieval London 'Jewry', which extended south-west and south-east towards Cheapside (Blair et al 2001a, fig 1). The Jewry was simply an area with a relatively large Jewish population and not an exclusive ghetto of the type seen in early

modern European towns (Isserlin 1996, 36–7). The economic and political fortunes of the English Jews fluctuated: for much of the 12th century the community flourished but at the end of the century they suffered persecution during the reigns of Richard I and John, as well as heavy taxation in the following century under Henry III, before their final expulsion under Edward I in 1290 (Blair et al 2001b, 127–8).

Evidence for the Jewish occupation of the study area exists for properties on the Cat Street frontage, between the lane leading to the Guildhall on the west and Basinghall Street on the east (Tenements 8–11), and a single holding to the north on Basinghall Street (Tenement 13) (Fig 315). The actual property divisions on Cat Street probably developed by the early 12th century (Chapter 3.1) but the firm archaeological evidence for the houses within these properties first dates from c 1150 (Chapter 3.2). The principal archaeological evidence for the Jewish occupancy of one of these houses is the discovery of a ritual bath or mikveh at the rear of Tenement 8, probably dating from the time the house was built in the middle of the 12th century. We also have a roughly contemporary description of the neighbourhood as Jewish: the church of St Lawrence is described as 'St Lawrence in the Jewry' in c 1198 (HMC 1883, 14). Specific documentary evidence for Jewish occupancy of these properties is, however, slightly later, dating from the second half of the 13th century.

Evidence for 12th-century Jewish occupation

A sunken bath with steps leading down into it was discovered at the rear of a large 12th-century stone house in Tenement 8 on Cat Street and is described in more detail in Chapter 3.2. It is argued here and elsewhere (Blair et al 2001a; 2001b) that the form of the sunken bath is characteristically Jewish and, furthermore, that its identification as a mikveh is strengthened by its location (within the medieval Jewry) and archaeological context (dated to around the middle of the 12th century). Mikveh is Hebrew for 'a collection of water' and in this context it refers to a small subterranean bath filled with water collected by natural means. The function of a mikveh is to allow people to immerse themselves in order to achieve spiritual cleanliness or purity in various ritual contexts, for example after becoming ritually unclean through contact with the dead or defiling objects, or, in the case of women, through menstruation and childbirth. Leviticus 15 details the Mosaic Law of 'the uncleanliness of men and women in their issues and their cleansing' (Encyclop Jud, xi, 1533–44; xv, 751). A mikveh ought to contain a minimum of 40 seah (c 750 litres) of water, and the present example could have held about 2800 litres of water its (reconstructed) depth of 1.5m easily allowing an adult male to achieve full immersion. A second mikveh has more recently been discovered at 30 Gresham Street (GHT00), 120m to the south-west (Blair et al 2001b, 132–3).

Mikva'ot (plural) were often attached to synagogues, but could also be installed by wealthy individual Jews in the interests of privacy, much as they might worship in private synagogues created within their homes (Blair et al 2001a, 21, 31). There is

Fig 315 *Simplified plan showing medieval Jewish properties in the study area, combining 12th-century archaeological evidence and 13th-century documentary evidence (scale 1:1000)*

some archaeological evidence for the existence of a synagogue building on Basinghall Street in the 12th century, just a short distance to the north-east of the *mikveh*, although its identification as a synagogue derives from later documentary evidence. In 1256 Henry III gave to John son of Geoffrey the chapel of St Mary-in-the-Jewry which was contiguous to John's house and 'where there had once been a Jewish synagogue' (*synagoga Judeorum: Cal Close R 1254–6, 369–70*). The archaeological excavations in this location revealed a sequence of two 12th-century stone buildings (perhaps the same building partly rebuilt), which preceded the large stone hall later owned by John fitz Geoffrey (Chapter 3.2, 'Basinghall Street'). Because the buildings lay on the very southern edge of site A it is difficult to understand their form and development, but an architectural fragment <A20>, possibly a voussoir from a relieving arch, hints at the formal religious architecture that could have been associated with a synagogue. The buildings are dated by pottery to the last quarter of the 12th century and the tooling marks on the voussoir fragment can be broadly dated to *c* 1190–*c* 1275.

An important, but largely unfulfilled, aim of the research carried out for this publication was to examine the archaeological assemblages from the 12th- and 13th-century Jewish properties on Cat Street. Isserlin (1996, 37–42) has discussed the problems of identifying medieval Jewish material culture, by using either the presence of supposed 'marker' artefacts such as the tokens and lamps which have been postulated, rather unconvincingly, as indicating Jewish occupation (Pepper 1992, 5–6), or the absence of non-kosher foods (eg pork and eel). The present research therefore set out to compare actual assemblages of artefactual and environmental material (as opposed to individual items) from three complementary sets of properties: 12th- and 13th-century Jewish properties on Cat Street, 12th-century 'ordinary gentile' properties along the rear lane of St Lawrence Jewry, and the 13th-century aristocratic property (Tenement 12) on Basinghall Street. Unfortunately, the study proved inconclusive, largely because of the variable survival of evidence across the site. The 12th-century timber buildings along the rear lane of St Lawrence Jewry, apparently occupied by relatively humble gentiles, lay in an area of very good archaeological survival; but the other two groups of properties, Jewish and aristocratic, lay in areas closer to the modern street frontage and so suffered the

337

typical urban fate of heavy truncation by 19th- and 20th-century basements. As a result, the humble gentile properties produced much greater quantities and variety of pottery, other artefacts and dietary evidence (both animal and botanical). It would clearly be unsound to conclude from the surviving evidence that these households enjoyed a better standard of living than their wealthy Jewish or aristocratic neighbours.

There are hints that the Jewish occupants of Tenement 8, the property with the mikveh, were not strictly complying with dietary laws since pork, eel and oyster remains were found in the rear yard of this property (Chapter 3.2, 'Cat Street'). However, the animal bone assemblage was small and so the bones (and oyster shell) are just as likely to represent residual 11th- and 12th-century material (disposed of in the back yards by earlier non-Jewish occupants) as 'primary' refuse deposited by Jewish occupants in the second half of the 12th century. The other food remains from the Jewish properties were entirely typical of urban medieval assemblages, suggesting the consumption of a normal range of cereals and wild and cultivated fruits (including mulberry, a possible indicator of high social status). The most interesting material evidence from the Jewish properties is an assemblage of fine 13th-century tableware that seems to be related to the expulsion of the Jews in the 1290s (see below).

Evidence for 13th-century Jewish occupation

Jewish occupancy of the four properties in Cat Street (Tenements 8–11) in the 13th century is illustrated most clearly by a charter of 1280. In this, Roger de Clifford granted his property (Tenement 12) to the mayor and commonalty, describing his estate as lying between the lands 'late of Aaron son of Vives, [of] Slema lately wife of Peytevyn le Fort, [of] Belassez lately wife of Leo Preciose, Jews, and [of] Sir Matthew de Columbariis to the south, the lands of William son of Richard cissor and [of] the citizens of the City to the north, Basinghall Street to the east and the lands of the citizens to the west' (Cal Pat R 1272–81, 381). As Sir Matthew de Columbariis can be shown independently to have held Tenement 11, on the corner of Cat Street and Basinghall Street, this deed identifies Roger's four southern neighbours, in sequence from west to east, as:

Aaron son of Vives	Tenement 8;
Slema, widow of Peytevyn le Fort	Tenement 9;
Belassez, widow of Leo Preciose	Tenement 10;
Sir Matthew de Columbariis	Tenement 11.

A later grant of 1281–2 (CLRO, HR 13/58) further clarifies the property ownership details and some of the personal relationships. In a transaction whose intention is not entirely clear, the City granted Aaron a plot of land which, though the text does not expressly say so, plainly represented much of the southern portion of Roger de Clifford's former holding. Aaron must have been the grandson of Peytevyn and Slema (who had perhaps died as she is no longer mentioned) since he is described as 'son of Vives son of Peytennus le Fort'. Aaron was

amassing quite a sizeable property as he now held his grandmother's house (Tenement 9) and some of Roger de Clifford's estate (Tenement 12), in addition to his old property (Tenement 8). The 1281–2 grant also provides more detail regarding Belassez, who is described as 'Bellaset widow of Lenn, son of Precio'. We know the names of a few other occupants of these four Cat Street properties. A charter of 1308 (CLRO, HR 37/20) names the last Jewish owner of Tenement 10 as Abraham Motoun the Jew, who had presumably acquired it from Belassez. We know that Matthew de Columbariis had only acquired Tenement 11 in 1280, when it was confiscated by the Crown from Aaron Crespyn (Cal Pat R 1272–81, 389). The property had earlier been granted to Aaron Crespyn in 1271 by Manser, son of Aaron son of Abraham, and to Benet and Abraham, sons of Kok (Cal Pat R 1266–72, 533–4). The other Jewish-owned property in the study area (Tenement 13) lay on the west side of Basinghall Street, to the north of Blackwell Hall (Tenement 12). A grant of 1259, dealing with the property to the north, records its southern neighbour as the land 'once of Aaron Selegref' (CLRO, HR 2/32–3) but little is known of the layout of this holding, and it probably included a number of houses, not all of which were necessarily occupied by Jews.

Aaron son of Vives was a prominent member of the London Jewish community, who had close ties with the Cambridge community of Jews and a royal patron in Henry III's second son, Edmund Crouchback, Earl of Lancaster (Hillaby 1992, 146). We know that he purchased his original Cat Street property (Tenement 8) before 1271 because it is described then as 'adjoining the way leading to the Husting' (ie the Guildhall) when he bought it from Flora le Blund, who had previously acquired it from her brother, Samuel (ibid, 148). Five years later, Aaron proposed to rebuild his houses which had been destroyed 'during the last war in this realm' (ibid), presumably a reference to the civil strife of the 1260s, so perhaps he had bought the property in a damaged condition. Aaron was also responsible for establishing a synagogue on the south side of Cat Street, opposite the church of St Lawrence. Deeds of the 1330s and 40s relating to an adjoining property record the former existence of a schola Judeorum next door (CLRO, HR 63/99, 101; 75/31; Blair et al 2001a, fig 2).

In August 1279 Aaron's enemy Master Elias levelled against him formal accusations relating to coin-clipping, from which he was protected by Earl Edmund, who had already had to secure him against similar charges. The royal protection seems to have proved effective because his less fortunate neighbour in Tenement 11, Aaron Crespyn, was hanged for the same offence after a trial at the Guildhall (Hillaby 1992, 148–9; Cal LB A, 26).

The expulsion of the Jews in 1290

The London Jews seem to have suffered in the baronial wars of the 1260s as they were perceived as being on the royal side; their fortunes declined further with the passing of the Statutum de Judeismo in 1275, which severely limited their ability to carry out financial and property transactions (Blair et al 2001a, 16). In 1290, Edward I ordered that all Jews were to quit the realm by 1 November, the feast of All Saints, and up to 16,000 left for France and Belgium in October. A small number of London Jews, including Aaron son of Vives, were allowed the privilege of selling their property (rather than suffer confiscation) prior to departure. No record has been found of the fate of Tenements 8–10 in the immediate aftermath of the expulsion but Aaron's property (Tenements 8 and 9) does not appear in the official 'expulsion list' of the holdings of less favoured Jews, and he must therefore have been successful in finding purchasers (Hillaby 1992, 152).

An odd episode, almost certainly relating to the expulsion of the Jews, is revealed by the archaeological evidence for Tenement 9 (Chapter 4.1, 'Cat Street'). The rear of the house seems to have been demolished, and a large quantity of jugs and other fine tableware was buried in a hole dug into the old foundations (Fig 157). The pottery (which is not identifiably 'Jewish' in any way at all) is closely dated to c 1270–c 1300 and appears to have been deposited in a single episode. The tableware was originally owned by a household of some means, presumably that of Slema and/or her grandson Aaron, and which was clearly used to entertaining on a lavish scale. Aaron may have buried his goods for safekeeping, hoping to reclaim them if a reversal of the political situation allowed him to return, or this find may point to a darker episode, perhaps a bigoted ritual act by the new gentile owners who wanted to 'cleanse' the property.

6.6 Craft and industry

Introduction

Most of the archaeological evidence for craftworking comes from the 10th to 12th centuries AD (Chapters 2.1, 3.1 and 3.2), from material discarded in pits and dumps. Craftworking at this time would have been carried out on a household or domestic level alongside other activities such as animal husbandry and food preparation. From the early 13th century (Chapter 3.3), the evidence for craftworking within the study area diminishes due to the presence of the Guildhall and its precinct, and the increase in the density of housing in the surrounding streets. However, the one craft or industry that arguably did continue in the study area from the 10th to the 16th centuries AD was metalworking, which shows a strong association with this neighbourhood. Archaeological and documentary evidence has shown that the north-west of the City (north of Cheapside, around Cripplegate and the Guildhall) was closely associated with metalworking in the medieval period and later (Keene 1996, 99, fig 1; Pearce 2004, 104–5), and evidence from the Guildhall excavations suggests that this zone of the medieval City in fact extended further east. In addition to the metalworking, there is direct archaeological evidence for a number of other craft activities in the study area, including leather working, horn working and textile

production, many of which would have formed part of everyday life in the early medieval period. There is also indirect archaeological evidence for activities such as woodworking (debris and the timber buildings themselves) and itinerant butchers (from the animal bone evidence: above, 6.4).

In the later medieval period, the direct archaeological evidence of crafts is limited to cat skinning (for the fur trade) and the casting of copper-alloy dress accessories, probably by girdlers; both of these activities are discussed in this section. Land transactions recorded in the Husting rolls name a large number of individuals, and frequently describe their trades, providing ample evidence for a wide range of people's occupations within the study area. In the late 13th and early 14th centuries, mercers seem to have formed the largest trade group, with named individuals living at the southern end of Aldermanbury and the northern end of Basinghall Street, only a short distance north of the area known as the Mercery (Chapter 4.1, Tenements 4, 5, 6, 16, 17 and 19; Sutton 2005, fig 3.3). Metalworkers were also present in significant numbers, including goldsmiths in Aldermanbury (Tenements 1 and 5) and gold beaters, ironmongers and a copper beater (batur) in Basinghall Street (Tenements 16 and 17). The presence of a kettle maker, perhaps in Tenement 7 (the north yard of St Lawrence Jewry), is also suggested by the find of a 14th-century copper-alloy seal <S53> (Fig 316), although the precise dating of the object is uncertain. Both the mercantile mercers and the more craft-based metalworkers would probably have conducted their trades from their houses and tenements. The social character of the area was quite varied, though possibly in terms of localised concentrations rather than being truly mixed; the wealthier residents (including the mercers) seem to have been clustered at the north of Aldermanbury and the south of Basinghall Street, with more mixed properties of sublet tenements concentrated on Cat Street and the north of Basinghall Street (Chapter 4.1). Later in the 14th century and during the following century (Chapter 4.2 and 4.3) the diversity of trades of the people living in the study area seems to diminish, with

<S53>

Fig 316 Medieval copper-alloy seal <S53> of a 'kettle' maker, S. IOHIS KETELLARE (scale c 2:1)

noticeably fewer metalworkers but more people involved in the textile trades. The explanation for this is probably twofold: the presence of Blackwell Hall cloth market was naturally attracting wealthy merchants such as drapers and mercers, and the increasing use of the houses surrounding the Guildhall by mayors, aldermen and City office-holders means that wealthy merchants from the more successful guilds (including the Mercers and Drapers) are likely to have been well represented. The less wealthy mixed-use properties continued to exist on Cat Street and the north of Basinghall Street and, when good documentary records survive (eg for Tenement 17 in period 15: Chapter 4.3), a wide range of trades is recorded.

Boxwood working

There is limited evidence from a number of discarded boxwood offcuts (along with some boxwood objects and box leaves) for some small-scale craftworking in this material. Most of the boxwood items were found in the organic-rich deposits that were dumped in the churchyard of St Lawrence Jewry (OA108 and OA109) in the 12th century, and may derive from the refuse of the occupants of the buildings to the north of the churchyard, such as Buildings 101 and 102 (period 10 phases 4 and 5). These objects include a rare bridge for a stringed instrument (<S133>, Fig 305), a peg (A<1623>), a pin (A<1620>), a handle and the core (A<1609>) from turning a vessel on a lathe.

Boxwood in Britain grows very slowly and puts on thin annual rings, and the roundwood of young trees is very small. As a consequence, it is a hard, dense and close-grained wood, allowing very precise cuts in its end grain. Boxwood is a suitable material for making such items as small vessels, pegs, handles and musical instruments. It would have been cut with a small tenon-type saw as used by horn or bone workers, at a time when saws were not generally used in woodworking. It is even possible that they were the same workers. There appears to be no parallel for this boxwood working from contemporary London. There are two examples from York where boxwood was used for a lathe-turned vessel and a syrinx, a musical instrument often referred to as panpipes (Morris 2000, 2353, nos 9038, 8578), both of which are dated from c AD 975 to the early/mid 11th century. There is one example from Winchester, a small bowl dating from the second half of the 10th century AD (Keene 1990, fig 296, no. 3411). All three artefacts show that in the 10th and 11th centuries AD mature box trees were being selected to provide unusually large tangential boards or half sections for making musical instruments and turned vessels (Morris 2000, 2353). It is tempting to see a link between the rare boxwood musical instrument bridge (<S133>, Fig 305) and the boxwood working waste, and to view it as the product of a local woodworker's workshop rather than as simply a lost or discarded item.

There is evidence of woodworking in other types of wood from layers of wood chips, shavings and offcuts, although these could be debris from construction of the timber buildings. There is also evidence for turning wooden vessels on a lathe

from the discarded core A<1609>. Peaks of hazel noted in the pollen analysis are likely to be associated with woodworking activity, such as the construction of wattle hurdles, involving the introduction to the site of harvested bundles.

Leather working

Penny MacConnoran, with Alison Nailer

Almost six hundred pieces of waste leather were recovered from some eighty contexts. The waste is a mixture of thick bovine leather and thinner finely-dressed pieces (Fig 317). Three distinct types of waste – offcuts, trimmings and unusable discards (CD Table 28) – can be identified and indicate that new leather objects were being manufactured either on or in the vicinity of the Guildhall site. Larger quantities of leather-working waste from York have recently been reported on in detail (Mould et al 2003, 3245–54).

Over 60% of the Guildhall pieces are offcuts from pattern cutting. Many have a triangular or sub-triangular shape, the result of placing patterns as close together as possible. The curved edges of these pieces are indicative of the cutting-out of shoe soles, and there are also a small number of unused sole-shaped pieces. Some of the thinner pieces may be waste from shoe uppers. Several straight-cut pieces may point to the manufacture of other items such as straps. Also present are a variety of roughly square and other shapes of offcut whose origin can not be determined. The grain surfaces of numerous waste pieces retain traces of impressed guidelines from object outlines that had been marked on the hide to facilitate pattern cutting. A further 30% of the total waste pieces are trimmings from the final shaping of objects subsequent to pattern cutting. Most of these are narrow lengths and strips, and the curvature of a good number of them suggests shoe-sole shapes.

The unusable discards, which represent c 7% of the total, are from the unwanted parts of the hide and include edges and teats. There is also one large, thin, fine piece still retaining some animal hair. The discards are mostly small and not particularly coarse, and generally resemble the offcuts. Nine have peg holes, some of which show signs of having been stretched, indicating that the hides were pegged down and pulled taut. This was probably done in order to mark out object outlines on the hide prior to pattern cutting; the presence of cutting-out guidelines on some of the hide-edge discards supports this idea. The Guildhall leather workers may have received hides in a partly untrimmed state, cutting away the remaining unwanted parts at the same time as cutting out the object shapes. The York finds furnish evidence that leather workers purchased untrimmed hides (Mould et al 2003, 3245).

An intriguing feature on about eight offcuts is the presence on the grain surface of small teeth-like indents that resemble human bite marks (eg <L27>, Fig 317), with no corresponding marks on the flesh surface. These indents are somewhat square in shape and regular in appearance, set alongside each other in an arc shape. There are some previous examples from other London sites, and Mould has commented that they are known from

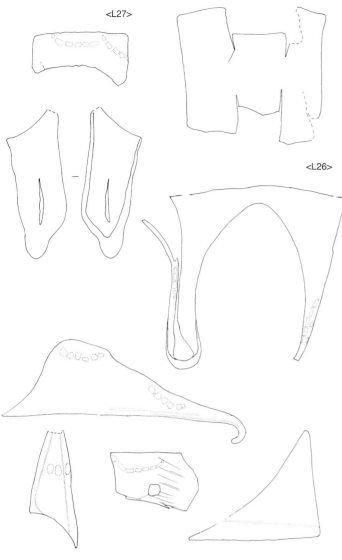

<L27>

<L26>

Fig 317 *Examples of waste leather, including an offcut of a reused item <L26> and an offcut with 'teeth-like' clamp marks <L27> (scale 1:2)*

other British assemblages. Examples from York have been identified as human teeth impressions (Mould et al 2003, 3264–5). It seems most likely, however, that the indents on the Guildhall examples are the marks left behind by some form of small iron clamp or similar tool whose purpose was to hold the leather taut, possibly while pattern cutting.

Over 68% of the waste came from period 10 (c 1050–c 1150) with the largest concentration from two quite substantial cesspits or refuse pits (phase 2, OA105) and itself representing 40% of the total assemblage (c 240 pieces). This group contains the highest incidence of each category of waste. Shoe-making offcuts and trimmings as well as other waste shapes are present, and both thick bovine and thin finely-dressed waste pieces occur. Clamp marks are present on some pieces. The homogeneous nature of the waste pieces and the paucity of other associated domestic leather objects suggests that this assemblage may be the result of direct dumping from a nearby workshop. However, it is unclear which particular building these pits served.

Other pits in Open Area 105 also produced 37 pieces of mixed waste including a hide edge with a peg hole. Numerous

other shoes and straps were discarded along with this waste, including six cut-up shoes and three clump repair pieces. Forty pieces of mixed waste, mainly offcuts, came from organic-rich deposits (period 10 phase 4, OA108) which extended over the churchyard of St Lawrence Jewry to the south of Buildings 101 and 102 and probably derived from refuse discarded by the occupants of these buildings. Some of these waste pieces are larger than usual, and both clamp marks and impressed guidelines occur on some fragments. A large number of shoes and other leather items occurred alongside this waste, including two repair clumps and eight cut-up shoes. Thirty-eight pieces of waste offcuts and trimmings were recovered from refuse pits perhaps used by the occupants of buildings fronting on to Cat Street (OA121) and lying beyond the limit of excavation. No other leather objects were found with this waste and it may represent primary dumping from a workshop in the vicinity. Building 117 (period 10 phase 5) yielded 25 pieces of mixed waste from a storage pit within the building. There were no associated leather shoes or other items, and it is possible that this too was a primary dump.

Just over 23% of the total waste assemblage came from period 11 (c 1140–c 1230). The largest concentration (66 pieces) came from a series of organic- and midden-rich dumps (phase 1, OA109). All classes of waste are represented, with some pieces having clamp marks, marking-out guidelines and peg holes. There is also an unused sole shape as well as one thin sheet-like piece with some animal hair still attached. The rest of the waste occurring in this period consists of very small scatters numbering no more than nine pieces from any one group. Among this widespread scattering there are further examples of hide edges with peg holes, offcuts with guidelines, clamp marks and some sole-shaped pieces (CD Table 28).

In conclusion, then, some of the dumps of waste may well represent direct discards from nearby workshops rather than secondary waste that had travelled and been redeposited. Examination of the offcuts and trimmings reveals that footwear manufacture was undoubtedly one of the local industries being pursued. Although other leather manufacturing trades can not be identified with any certainty, the variety of waste shapes and the presence of some finely-dressed pieces suggest that objects other than shoes may also have been made. The Guildhall leather workers did not necessarily work on untrimmed hides. The hides were brought into the town perhaps in a partly-trimmed state, the leather workers doing the final cutting-away of the unusable parts in tandem with their pattern cutting. While the presence and character of the leather waste indicates that the manufacture of new items was being carried out on or near the site during the 11th and 12th centuries, the quantity of the waste is rather meagre and does not in itself provide evidence for intensive industry. In this regard, the comments made by Pritchard in relation to the extensive quantities of waste one might expect from a busy workshop should be borne in mind (Pritchard 1991, 211).

In addition to the manufacture of new leather items, the presence of c 50 shoe parts and other unidentifiable items that had been cut up for reuse points to considerable recycling of old leather for use in the repair of shoes and presumably other items. The cobbler was responsible for both repairing shoes and salvaging old shoe leather to make reconditioned footwear. The thirty or so clump repair soles and repairs to numerous uppers also provide evidence for this activity.

Horn working and tanning

Kevin Rielly

There is clear evidence from the bones of the major domesticates for both skinning and horn removal, and it can be suggested that both horn working and tanning took place nearby in the 11th and 12th centuries (periods 10 and 11). The animal bone assemblage points to local horn workers, working with goat and sheep horn, who discarded the horncores mainly in pits (OA121 and OA122) situated to the rear of properties fronting on to Cat Street.

A number of cattle horncores were recovered, some still attached to the skull, but not in sufficient numbers – relative to the other skeletal parts – or in large enough concentrations to suggest a local industry. Conversely, there is a particularly good representation of sheep/goat horncores, 41 from period 10 and 124 from period 11, the great majority of which (37 and 96 respectively) belong to sheep. With both the sheep and goat horncores, there is a very clear bias towards male individuals (Fig 318; Fig 319). As this ratio is clearly at odds with what would be found in a breeding herd of either sheep or goats, it follows that these dumps, and the assemblages in general, feature a deliberate selection of horncores. The combined evidence therefore points to a local horn-working industry: the horncores had clearly been chosen for their size to produce the greatest quantity of raw material. Further evidence for this conclusion is provided by the recovery of two sawn goat horncores. As a rule, the saw was used during the medieval period by craftworkers rather than butchers. It is noteworthy that almost all the goat bones dated to the early medieval periods are either horncores or metapodials. Very similar goat assemblages have been found at a range of other medieval sites in London, for example at 1 Poultry (ONE94: Rielly in prep), and it can be suggested that these collections represent the remains of imported skins, with horns and feet still attached. These bones therefore represent specific craft waste from horn working and tanning, rather than food waste.

Cat skinning and the fur trade

Kevin Rielly

The preparation of the skins of smaller animals is shown by the concentration of cat bones recovered from various mid 12th-century dumps (period 11 phase 1, OA109; Fig 320). These bones represent the relatively complete skeletons of at least 24 animals, most of which were less than 8–12 months old (age of fusion after Smith 1969). Cuts to the skull clearly show that skinning took place, while the absence of parts of the hindpaw

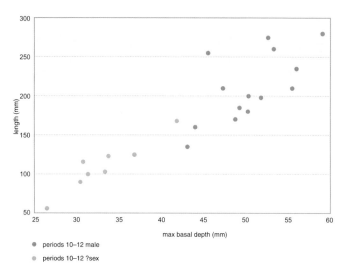

Fig 318 *Comparison of sheep horncore size by plotting length against maximum basal depth*

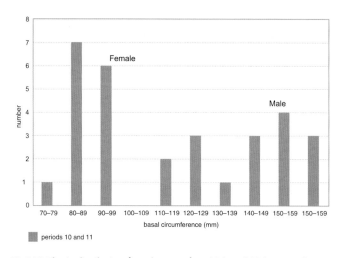

Fig 319 *The size distribution of goat horncores from 11th- and 12th-century deposits*

suggest that skins were removed with this part of the skeleton still attached. Clearly these bone assemblages represent skinning waste, and it can perhaps be suggested that the skins may then have been prepared at some nearby furrier's workshop. Significantly, a smaller collection of cat bones was also found nearby (period 11 phase 2, OA110), and these are also predominantly of subadult individuals. The age structure of the animals is interesting, with the bias towards youngsters perhaps suggesting a degree of selection, certain cats being chosen from various feral populations or else from stock kept and then culled for this purpose (CD Table 29). The latter interpretation has been suggested for a large quantity of cat bones from a 12th- to 13th-century deposit from nearby Northgate House (Drummond-Murray and Liddle 2003, 92). Cats were used for their skins throughout the medieval and early post-medieval periods (Serjeantson 1989, 131), and it may have been the case – certainly from the evidence gathered from these two London sites – that there was a preference for the skins of relatively young animals.

A similar assemblage of cat bones was found in a 14th-century context, dumped in the construction yard for the

Fig 320 *View of cat skeletons being excavated in Open Area 109*

Guildhall chapel (Chapter 4.1). This comprises at least 32 individuals, and features several skulls and two pelves with cut marks. The 14th-century examples differ from those of the 12th century in that no foot bones were recovered (an absence clearly not related to recovery bias). In addition, the proportion of individuals less than 1 year old is about 50%, compared to about 75–80% for the earlier remains. This evidence undoubtedly signifies a slight change in the method of skinning as well as, perhaps, in the method of supply and/or the market requirements. Comparative assemblages have been recovered from two other later medieval City sites: from part of the city ditch at King Edward's Buildings (Liddle 2007), dated c 1340–50, and from a pit at Wood Street to the west of the Guildhall and dated c 1300–50 (Howe and Lakin 2004, 85; Ainsley 2004, 106). Both of these collections contain bones with cut marks and both feature a mix of parts, including foot bones. The latter assemblage also represents a similar age pattern to the 14th-century Guildhall one.

The interests of those employed in the skinning of animals (other than for the leather trade) were overseen by the Company of Skinners. Although the Skinners' Company hall is not near the study area, the documentary evidence records skinners as being among the occupants of nearby properties in the 14th and 15th centuries (Chapter 4.2 and 4.3).

Walrus-ivory working

Of great interest was the recovery of two fragments of walrus maxilla <S134>–<S135> from later 12th- and early 13th-century deposits (period 11 phase 2 (B124) and phase 4 (S114)). The two bones are very similar, each comprising a small part of the tusk socket (canine alveolus) after the tusk had clearly been hacked out of the maxilla with a series of heavy chops (Fig 321; Fig 322). Both items were found on the east side of the lane (R102) and it can be suggested, given the rarity of such finds, the similar dating and the approximately similar location, that they represent waste items from a single ivory workshop. However, no walrus-ivory artefact has been recognised among the finds recovered from the site.

Similar walrus maxilla fragments have been found at other European sites, the nearest being the medieval Fishamble Street excavation in Dublin (Roesdahl and Wilson 1992, 384–5), with others from 13th- to 14th-century levels at Laukvik in the Finnmark area of Norway (C Amundsen, pers comm) and from medieval Novgorod in Russia (Smirnova 2001).

Textile production

There is some direct evidence of textile production on a small household scale, with several different activities attested, including thread spinning (evidenced by stone spindle whorls), embroidery, implied by needles (eg <S137> (Fig 323), perhaps a 'couching' needle for tapestries) and two glass linen smoothers (eg <S136>, Fig 323) used to impart a gloss in the

Fig 321 *Walrus maxilla <S134> from Building 124, showing how the bone was shaped around the tusk socket (scale c 1:2)*

Fig 322 *Lateral and interior views of walrus maxilla socket <S135> from Structure 114, showing heavy chops/shaping on the lateral side (scale c 1:2)*

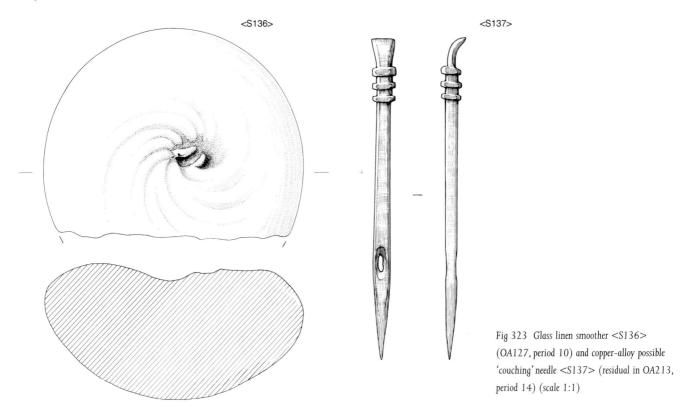

Fig 323 *Glass linen smoother <S136> (OA127, period 10) and copper-alloy possible 'couching' needle <S137> (residual in OA213, period 14) (scale 1:1)*

finishing of cloth by warming the glass and then sliding it over the cloth (Pritchard 1991, 173). There was no clear spatial focus to suggest a particular location for these activities.

Some of the plant remains from the 11th- and 12th-century buildings and yards along the rear lane of St Lawrence Jewry may be indicative of textile production. They include flax and hemp (although both types of seeds were also used in cooking and lighting) and weld/dyer's rocket. Dyer's rocket was exploited for its yellow dye used in textile manufacture, and one sample produced a large number of seeds, which suggests the actual use of the plant rather than the accidental inclusion of seeds from a plant growing as a weed.

A few sheep keds (ticks) were found in Open Area 126 and Building 102 (period 10 phases 4–5). The presence of large numbers of these has been taken as evidence for wool processing in the archaeological record (Buckland and Perry 1989; Kenward and Hall 1995).

Late Saxon metalworking

There is important evidence for copper alloy casting in the 10th or early 11th century AD, including part of a ceramic mould in a medieval fabric (<S138>, Fig 324). Copper alloy waste and slag fragments are unequivocal evidence for local manufacture and were found scattered across Open Areas 100 and 127 (within and around the old amphitheatre, Fig 12) in contexts dating to c AD 900–c 1050 (period 9) and the 1050s and 60s (period 10 phase 1). Two ceramic crucibles from these open

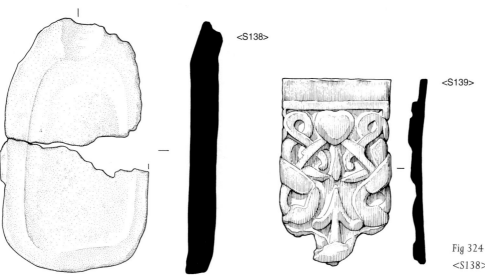

Fig 324 *Ceramic mould used for copper alloy casting <S138> and discarded waster of a Winchester style copper-alloy strapend <S139> (scale 1:1)*

areas (one found in the same pit as mould <S138>) are probably also associated with this early metalworking. The cast product of mould <S138> was perhaps a strapend with relief decoration. Most intriguingly, a discarded waster of a copper-alloy strapend <S139> (Fig 324) found in a slightly later context dated to the 1070s (period 10 phase 2, OA103) with accomplished Winchester style relief ornament could be the product of just such a mould. Chemical analysis has demonstrated that the copper alloy used was bronze, the most common alloy during the Late Saxon period (Chapter 8.9; Blades 1995). The style of the discarded strapend <S139> is commonly assigned to the 10th century AD and is perhaps the best evidence for the place of manufacture of some of the most admired small-scale English metalwork of that time.

There is also indirect evidence for metalworking in the form of nine bone trial pieces with incised linear designs, five of which are newly reported here (<S140> (Fig 325), <S141>–<S144>; Chapter 8.8) and the remaining four published by Pritchard (1991, 261–2). Only one of the pieces (<S140>) is from a definitely pre-Conquest context, while the remaining eight are from contexts dated by pottery to c 1050–c 1150 (period 10) and c 1150–c 1230 (period 11). However, this type of bone trial piece is usually seen as Late Saxon and most if not all of the nine obects probably date to the 11th century or earlier. A number of bone trial pieces have been found in contexts of this date along and to the north of modern Cheapside (ibid, 178–9; Hill and Woodger 1999, 38; Burch and Treveil in prep).

Such incised bones were probably practice items, with decoration ultimately intended for metalwork, although their precise role is uncertain (they often exhibit a range of competence on a single bone). Although some relatively straightforward motifs on other London finds of this category are closely comparable with motifs on items of metalwork, the notion that all such bone carvings were done as practice by metalworkers is difficult to reconcile with the least accomplished attempts, which could have been made by children imitating adults (so lacking in basic competence are the poorest ones) perhaps in a domestic rather than any commercial context. It is possible that the most common medium for such 'trial pieces' was wood, which would have been more easily carved, but much of this material may have perished. The bone carvings are mainly on cattle (or cattle-sized) ribs and mandibles but are also found on pig and horse bones; the bone was chosen primarily to provide a flat surface on which the patterns could be carved (Pritchard 1991, 178). The carvings include interlacing knots and rectangles, animal and human heads, interlacing panels and concentric circles. One of the pieces from site C (ibid, 184, no. 203) has a name inscribed on both sides. The two inscriptions are variations of what is probably the Old English male name Ælfbeohrt, although the female name Ælfburh is another possibility (Holder 1998, 86). In a further indication of the Saxon date of this piece (and possibly of the other items), the inscription uses a Roman script that is influenced by runic letter forms.

There are two main spatial foci of the Guildhall bone motif pieces. Four of the items (<S141>–<S144>) were recovered from two pits cut through, or adjacent to, the late 10th-century AD sunken-floored building (period 9, B134). It is tempting to see them as having been discarded by occupants of this building and subsequently disturbed by later pits. A further four bone motif pieces (Pritchard 1991, 262–2, nos 201–4) came from pits on the south side of site C, dating to the 11th or early 12th century (period 10); it is possible that they were carved by 11th-century occupants of a building or buildings along Cat Street.

Part of a possible ceramic cupel in early medieval coarse

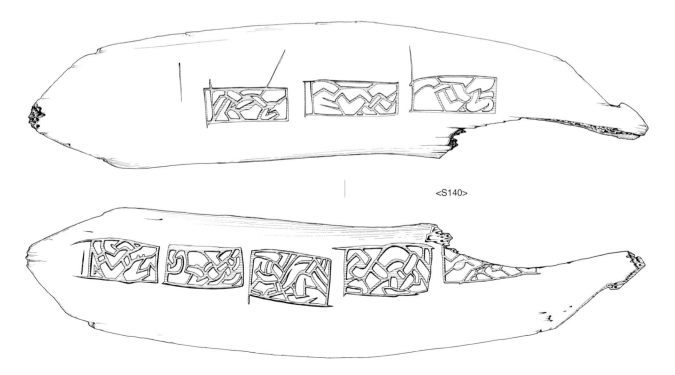

Fig 325 *Late Saxon bone trial piece <S140> with incised designs (scale 1:1)*

whiteware (EMCW) was found in a context dated to the third quarter of the 11th century (period 10 phase 1, OA100). Cupellation was the process by which precious metals were separated from base impurities; the metal to be refined was melted with an excess of lead on a small, shallow dish or cupel, effectively oxidising and dissolving any base metals present (Bayley 1992, 6). Ceramic cupels and potsherds used as cupels are known in groups of Middle and Late Saxon crucibles from various centres around England, including Lincoln, York and Winchester (ibid, 6, fig 7).

Late 11th- and 12th-century metalworking

Jacqui Pearce

There is evidence for a variety of metalworking activites taking place in the late 11th and 12th centuries, though for this period there is rather less evidence of the finished products. The evidence consists of mould fragments (including three Roman bricks reused as moulds for ingots: Bateman 2000, 60), copper alloy waste, galena (lead ore, eg Fig 326), litharge cake (a by-product of silver refining), copper-alloy and lead ingots, a lead 'cushion' for stamping a relief design on sheeting (<S155>, Fig 327) and contemporary ceramic crucibles. The archaeological evidence (albeit complicated by problems of the residuality of much of the material) would suggest that this metalworking is slightly later than that represented by the Winchester style strapend and the bone trial pieces, and that the focus of the activity had shifted further north, along the rear lane of the church of St Lawrence Jewry. The activities, carried out by the occupants of the late 11th- and 12th-century buildings along the lane, seem to have included copper alloy casting, lead refining and casting, and silver refining. Chemical analysis of the alloy droplets trapped in the crucibles reveals that a variety of copper alloys were used, ranging from purer copper to bronze and gunmetal (Chapter 8.9). It is unfortunate that no wasters were recovered, as they might have indicated the sorts of products being manufactured.

The best dating evidence for the metalworking is provided by ceramic crucibles. A relatively small number of metalworking crucibles were recovered from contexts dated to *c* 1050–*c* 1150 (period 10: 30 sherds from a minimum of 25 vessels) and much larger numbers came from contexts dated to *c* 1150–*c* 1230 (period 11: 106 sherds from a minimum of 70 vessels). This would suggest that the activity was mainly taking place in the 12th century, the time when occupation along the rear lane of St Lawrence Jewry seems to have been densest (Chapter 3.1 and 3.2). This dating accords well with that observed on sites in Gresham Street and Cripplegate (eg sites NST94 and NHG98), where large numbers of 11th- to 12th-century metalworking crucibles were found.

The ceramic crucibles occur in various fabrics, but mostly share the same small rounded form and are likely to have been used for melting copper alloys. Most crucible sherds were found in pits in the open areas, and the highest concentrations occurred in Open Area 127 to the east of the lane and in Open

Area 109, the churchyard at the south end of the lane (Fig 71). Early medieval coarse whiteware (EMCW) is the main fabric in which the crucibles were made, accounting for 77.4% of all examples from period 11 by sherd count (71.4% ENV). This fabric is one of the main Saxo-Norman types recognised in the City (Bayley et al 1991, 392–6; Pearce 2004, 102–4). The inclusions recall those found in Reading Beds clay, which was used in the main Surrey whiteware industries, although no specific sources are known for metalworking forms at this date. The ware is contemporaneous with the main early medieval coarsewares used in London from the mid 11th to mid 12th centuries, and may have continued in use into the 13th century. Related to EMCW is the finer medieval whiteware crucible fabric (MWCR), which has well-sorted, finer-grade, rounded inclusions. Although contemporaneous with EMCW, it appears to remain in use for longer into the 13th century, and accounts for 5.7% by sherd count (8.6% ENV) of all period 11 crucibles. All other crucible fabrics occur as more or less isolated examples. The recovery of part of a rounded crucible in Stamford-type ware (STAM) from Open Area 109 is of interest, since this type appears to have been preferred in London for melting silver on account of its strong, fine, thin-walled fabric

Fig 326 A piece of galena (lead ore) found on the site (scale c 1:1)

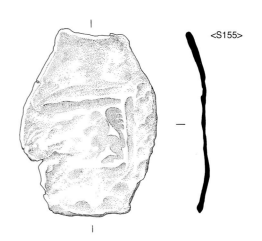

Fig 327 Lead 'cushion' <S155> for absorbing the force from a punch hammered on to sheet metal placed over it, used in the production of repoussé designs; the hind quarters of a stylised squatting animal on the right are probably from the final use (scale 1:1)

(Bayley et al 1991, 397–8, 403). In general, EMCW and the related MWCR appear to have been favoured for melting copper alloys. Several examples have traces of copper alloy deposits inside, and some also have thick slag in places. Many crucibles are sooted thickly, both inside and out, and most had clearly been strongly heated, resulting in vitrification of the fabric, glassy external surfaces and a distinct reddish colour in patches.

Nearly all the crucibles are of small or medium-sized rounded or hemispherical form, with a small, pinched pouring lip at the rim (eg <P79>, Fig 89). As far as it is possible to measure rim diameters from the generally small sherds that survive, these are in the range of 40–90mm, with most examples falling between 80mm and 90mm. Vessel thickness is variable, with 4–5mm the average. The one exception is part of a large, straight-sided, thick-walled crucible in late medieval/early post-medieval crucible fabric (LMCR) from Building 124. This type was previously thought to have been introduced in the 14th century (Bayley 1992, 5, fig 5), but evidence from the Guildhall suggests that it first came into use in London at around the same time as Kingston-type ware, c 1240. The example from Building 124, which is more than a single intrusive sherd, comes from a large context dated to c 1240–c 1300, and probably nearer the beginning of this range than the end. In later periods the number of LMCR crucibles rises sharply, as the quantity of smaller, rounded forms decreases.

An unusual vessel in coarse London-type ware (LCOAR) <P76> (Fig 328) was found in a context dated to the third quarter of the 12th century (period 11 phase 2, S107). The shape of the vessel resembles a distilling flask or cucurbit, a form usually associated with later medieval metalworking in which it was part of a still used to prepare strong acids to part precious metals (eg Pearce 2004, 104). If this is indeed its function, the 12th-century Guildhall vessel must be one of the earliest examples of the form known in London.

Smithing slag and vitrified hearth lining were found in one late 12th-century timber building (period 11 phase 3, B113) and may indicate the presence of a smith. The other slag material may derive from this building and other 12th-century buildings or yards; it is, however, possible that some of it is residual Roman material (Chapter 8.10).

14th-century metalworking

There is extensive archaeological evidence for metalworking in two parts of the study area in the late 13th to mid 14th centuries (period 13, Chapter 4.1): the north yard of St Lawrence Jewry (Tenement 7, OA219) and the south-east corner of the Guildhall yard (OA200). In both cases, there was evidence for the large-scale casting of dress accessories, producing articles such as buckles and strap loops. These accessories were designed to be attached to belts or girdles worn around the waist with one end dangling in front (Egan and Pritchard 1991, 35–7). The link between the objects, the manufacturing process and the place of manufacture is very clear: a number of foundry hearths were excavated in the St Lawrence Jewry workshop area, and three of this workshop's buckles were cast together and never separated (<S170>, Fig 329), while another buckle (<S157>, Fig 329) still had parts of the ceramic mould adhering to the metal.

The metalworkers would have bought in copper alloy, either as ingots or as scrap material; the morphology of the copper alloy slags from both areas shows that they are not in fact connected in any way with the smelting of raw copper ores (contra Thomas 2002, 77). A hypothetical ingot supplier could have imported refined copper and calamine ore (used to extract zinc) from the Low Countries or Germany, though it may well be the case that the imported supplies were supplemented by English copper and, perhaps more importantly, by recycled scrap copper-alloy objects (Blair and Blair 1991, 83–5). Chemical analysis of the artefacts, and of the crucibles used in their manufacture, shows that both workshop areas used copper alloys containing similar ranges of zinc, tin and lead, but that the composition of the Guildhall yard products is more commonly brass, whereas the St Lawrence Jewry products are more often in gunmetal (Fig 330), a popular alloy for medieval dress accessories (Heyworth 1991). The two areas may well have been parts of a single workshop, with the variation in composition simply indicating different batches of metal. Contemporary descriptions give the impression that the distinction between the various copper alloys (brass and gunmetal are used here in their modern senses) did not mean much in the medieval period, with most copper alloys described simply as 'latton' (Blair and Blair 1991, 81–4).

In order to obtain molten metal for the casting process, the

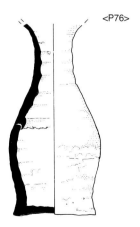

Fig 328 Coarse London-type ware (LCOAR) bottle or cucurbit (distilling flask) <P76> from Structure 107 (scale 1:4)

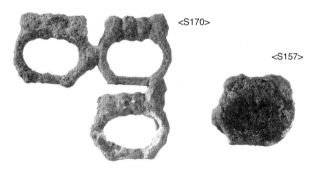

Fig 329 Three oval buckle frames still joined <S170> and a buckle <S157> still adhering to the mould, both produced in the 14th-century St Lawrence Jewry workshop areas (scale c 1:1)

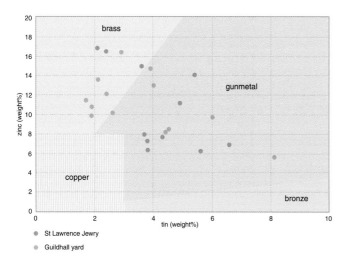

Fig 330 *Comparison of the composition of the copper-alloy products found in the St Lawrence Jewry workshop with those found in the neighbouring Guildhall yard*

copper alloy had to be heated in a hearth. Several hearths or furnace bases were uncovered in the excavations of the north yard of St Lawrence Jewry (though it should be noted that our understanding of the hearths is limited by the difficult circumstances of the early phase of the excavation of site A: Chapter 1.1) and a single small hearth was identified in the Guildhall yard (OA219 and OA200, Fig 148). There may have been three or four St Lawrence Jewry hearths in use by the workshop at any one time, and the stratigraphic evidence shows how these were rebuilt up to three times (a total of 13 hearth bases were recorded in the excavation). Unfortunately, only one of the hearths could be hand-excavated and recorded in more detail (Fig 331). The metalworkers first dug a shallow pit and then built a three-sided brickearth sill within the hollow. This low wall defined an internal 'kiln' space c 0.5m square. The base of the hearth consisted of tiles and ragstone fragments, with some tiles set on edge, upright, in order to allow heat circulation. The eastern side of the hearth may have been open, although stone and tile rubble was possibly the remains of the dismantled east wall. There was a narrow flue hole in the west wall, presumably to allow the insertion of bellows to provide enough oxygen to achieve the required temperature; the shallow cut containing the hearth was probably wider on its west side in order to allow better access for the bellows to pump air into the base of the hearth. The centre of the hearth was filled with burnt brickearth, ash and charcoal, presumably deriving from its final firing. The structure was probably originally capped with a brickearth dome since copper alloy requires a reducing atmosphere to prevent the metal from oxidising during heating (English Heritage 2001, 16). A rough wall represented by two kerb stones to the north of the hearth may have been designed to support a stone slab to form a working surface or table, and two postholes are probably evidence of a timber wind-screen or roof.

The copper-alloy ingots would have been broken into smaller pieces which were melted in ceramic crucibles placed in the hearths. These crucibles were of two main types (Fig 332): smaller rounded crucibles in medieval whiteware crucible fabric (MWCR)

or Kingston-type ware (KING) and deep, straight-sided, thick-walled crucibles in late medieval/early post-medieval crucible fabric (LMCR). The smaller rounded crucibles have a diameter of c 130mm at the rim and are up to 110mm in height (eg <P111>; <P130> is a shallower example); the larger crucibles (eg <P129>) are up to 200mm in diameter and perhaps had a similar depth (no complete profiles survived). These large crucibles could probably have held up to 5kg of copper alloy. This deep type of crucible was thought to have been introduced in the 14th century (Bayley 1992, 5), but the evidence from the Guildhall points to their use in the last quarter of the 13th century, or perhaps slightly earlier. All the crucibles from the site are highly vitrified from being subjected to intense heat, and usually have glassy external surfaces and large quantities of slag residues, especially on the outside and over the rim; these metallic residues are often as thick as or even thicker than the vessel walls (which were 10–25mm thick). The choice of crucible type does not appear to be significant; there was no clear correlation between the different types of crucible and the different copper alloys used, or the location in which they were found.

Once the metal had melted, the crucible could be removed from the hearth using metal tongs and the molten metal was

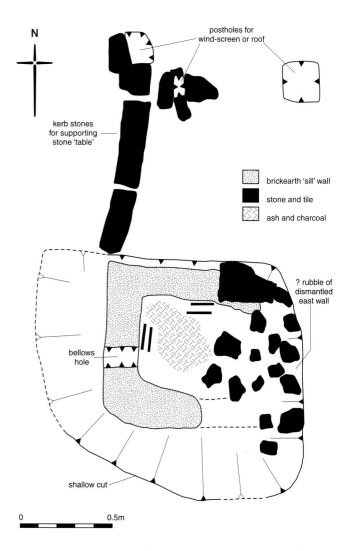

Fig 331 *Detailed plan of remains of a late 13th- or 14th-century hearth used for melting copper alloy in the St Lawrence Jewry dress accessory workshop area (scale 1:20)*

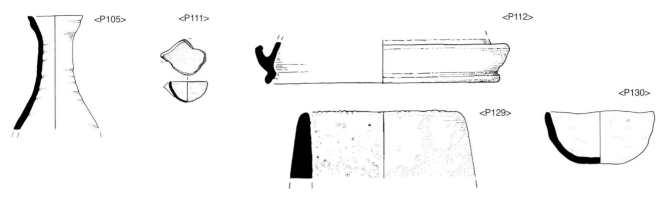

Fig 332 Medieval industrial pottery from the St Lawrence Jewry dress accessory workshop area (OA219) and the Guildhall yard (OA200/OA211/OA213): bottle or cucurbit in coarse London-type ware with calcareous inclusions (LCOAR CALC) <P105> (OA211), rounded crucibles in Kingston-type ware (KING) <P111> (OA219) and <P130> (OA213), alembic in London-type ware (LOND) <P112> (OA219) and deep crucible in late medieval/early post-medieval crucible fabric (LMCR) <P129> (OA213) (scale 1:4)

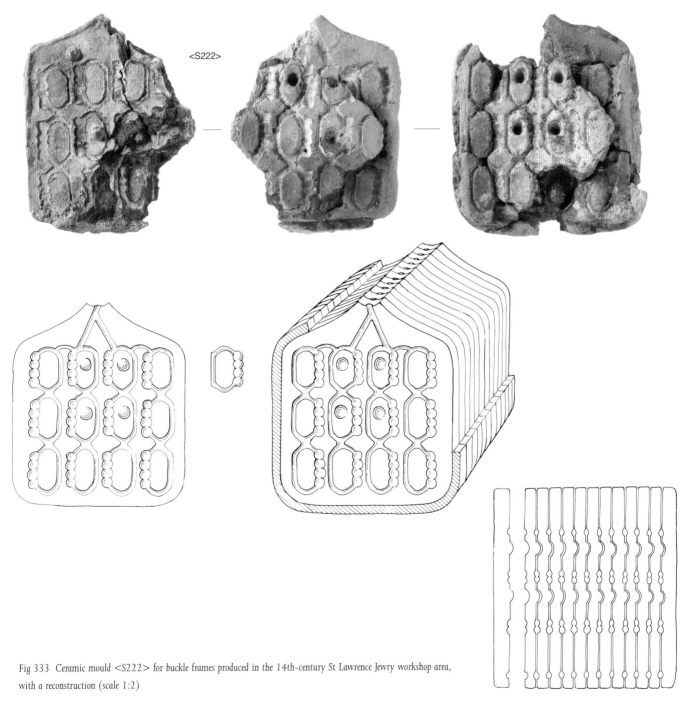

Fig 333 Ceramic mould <S222> for buckle frames produced in the 14th-century St Lawrence Jewry workshop area, with a reconstruction (scale 1:2)

then poured into the mould. Parts of a ceramic mould for buckle frames <S222> (Fig 333) were found in the St Lawrence Jewry workshop area, a unique survival of enough fragments to show that at least 144 identical products would have been produced at any one time using this mould. This particular mould seems to have developed a leak, probably through a crack brought about by thermic strain, and so it did not suffer the usual fate of being comprehensively broken to free the products once cast. Two other mould fragments were found on the site, one perhaps for producing 'forked-spacer' strapends (<S224>, from the St Lawrence Jewry workshop area) and the other for producing the frames for buckles or strap loops (<S223>, from the Guildhall yard workshop area). If all went well with the casting process, the cooled products would be removed from the mould and then finished by sawing, grinding and polishing with files ('fettling').

Wasters and other items found on the site allow at least 20 probable cast products to be identified (Fig 334). These were mainly small accessories for girdles and belts, such as buckles, strap loops, rivets and mounts, and are discussed in greater detail and illustrated in Chapter 8.8 (Figs 394–403). All these products, apart from finger ring <S210> (Fig 401), are of typical forms known from used examples found in excavations elsewhere in medieval London. The workshops can be securely dated to the late 13th to mid 14th centuries: comparanda found elsewhere in London for nearly all of the definable products mostly date from the 13th and 14th centuries (Egan and Pritchard 1991). This dating is reinforced on this site, where pottery from the hearths (and the other contexts in which the products and plant were found) is dated to c 1270–c 1350. A few of the products are otherwise known in London only from appreciably earlier contexts than this present foundry (eg strap loop <S178> (Fig 396) with a mid 13th-century parallel). This suggests that some of the fashions represented here were over a century old when the foundries were in production. Other possible products, particularly buckles like <S214>, were thought to be slightly later in date and so the dating of an example of this type of buckle to the 14th century is significant. From their metallurgical composition, the dress accessories produced here would have fulfilled the criteria laid down in the 1327 charter of the London Girdlers, which deplored the use of 'false work such as lead, pewter and tin' in girdle fittings and specified instead proper latton, copper, iron or steel (Egan and Pritchard 1991, 18).

There are hints of other products in addition to the dress accessories: purer copper and bronze wire was being used in the St Lawrence Jewry workshop area, and one of the Guildhall yard crucibles (A<4883>) contained copper alloy droplets with levels of arsenic and antimony that are commonly seen in large castings, such as cauldrons (Dungworth 2000a). Two ceramic bottles may have been employed in the distillation of strong acids, which could have been used for separating precious metals, rather than copper alloys. An alembic in London-type ware (LOND) <P112> (Fig 332), found in the St Lawrence Jewry workshop area, has a deeply flanged rim in an unglazed fabric and would have been an essential component of a still. Another unusual vessel that may relate to the workshops was

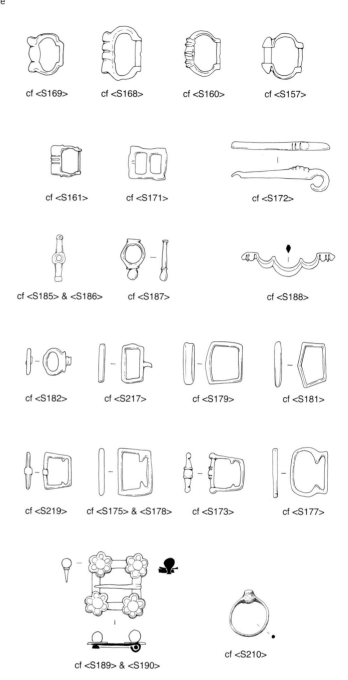

cf <S169>   cf <S168>   cf <S160>   cf <S157>

cf <S161>   cf <S171>   cf <S172>

cf <S185> & <S186>   cf <S187>   cf <S188>

cf <S182>   cf <S217>   cf <S179>   cf <S181>

cf <S219>   cf <S175> & <S178>   cf <S173>   cf <S177>

cf <S189> & <S190>   cf <S210>

Fig 334 Examples of the types of products made in the 14th-century metalworking workshop at St Lawrence Jewry and the Guildhall yard: buckle frames, clasp frames, strap loops, pendent loops and purse suspender (most of these illustrated examples are finished products found on other London archaeological sites; illustrations of the Guildhall items can be found in Chapter 8.8) (scale 1:2)

found in the 'little Guildhall garden' (OA211) a short distance to the east of the Guildhall yard. It must have been a bottle-shaped vessel with a long, narrow neck (<P105>, Fig 332) in unglazed coarse London-type ware with calcareous inclusions (LCOAR CALC). The vessel was clearly much larger than the usual form of bottle made in this fabric in the 13th to 14th centuries (Pearce et al 1985, 41) and it is quite possible that the form was produced specifically for industrial purposes, a suggestion based on parallels with later industrial bottles in early post-medieval redwares (Moorhouse 1972, 119–20, fig 33, nos 6–9).

The next best evidence for a similar foundry is from a secondary dump of waste at the Thames Exchange (TEX88) site on London's waterfront, where a more restricted range of material (no certain fragment of mould or kiln furniture has so far been identified from there) produced evidence of a somewhat wider range of products, with about 40 different accessories represented, perhaps a generation or more later in date than the Guildhall repertoire (Egan et al 1992, 112–14; Egan 1996b, 86–8, figs 2C and 3A; 2003). Comparison with much more limited evidence for casting dress accessories in other parts of London (Egan 1996b, 86–8; 2003), as well as in urban centres elsewhere such as Coventry (Wright 1987, 24–8, 84–8, fig 49, nos 3–7, 14–16), York (Mortimer 2002, figs 1322–3), Dublin (Hayden 2000, 105–7, fig 10), Toulouse, France (Barrère 1990, 277, nos 600–3) and Lund, Sweden (Bergman and Billberg 1976, 206, fig 149) shows that essentially the same technology was used across western Europe. The products, too, are remarkably similar over this wide geographical area. The basic technique is similar to that for the casting of copper-alloy domestic vessels and bells, as seen at Baltic House and 27–29 Whitechapel High Street (Egan 2002; 2005b), although these were the concern of a different guild. Hopes that chemical analysis would reveal a specific 'signature' alloy or alloys for the products of the St Lawrence Jewry and Guildhall yard complex have not been realised, perhaps because the somewhat 'dirty' copper alloys revealed by analysis are the result of a series of metal recyclings (Chapter 8.9). Analysis of the products of this workshop or workshops has, however, considerably enhanced our understanding of many previously unknown details of the medieval copper alloy foundry.

The archaeological evidence might suggest that the Guildhall yard workshop area had a slightly wider range of products than the St Lawrence Jewry area, although the similarities between the products found in the two areas are in fact much greater than the differences (Fig 335). The difference

in the copper alloys used, with gunmetal at St Lawrence Jewry and brass at the Guildhall yard (Fig 330), could be random, simply representing different batches of ingots. One possibility is that there were two separate workshops, with each one headed by a master, presumably a member of the Girdlers' guild, who employed apprentices and journeymen to do the finishing. Another scenario would be that the same master and workshop simply changed location (it would be difficult archaeologically to date the hearths, plant and products with enough precision to prove this) or that he was so successful that he needed more space. It is noticeable that the majority of the hearths were found in the St Lawrence Jewry property, so the two areas could have been used for different manufacturing stages, with the founding taking place there and the finishing carried out over the wall in the Guildhall yard. A final possibility is that the workers simply took advantage of the extensive building works taking place in the Guildhall yard (the construction of the new Guildhall and chapel in the late 13th and early 14th centuries: Chapter 4.1) to use the area as a convenient dumping ground for their waste.

The Girdlers' guild is first formally recorded in 1327, around the same time that the possibly two workshops were functioning. It is clear from the ordinances in the charters of 1327 and 1344 that the Girdlers saw themselves primarily as metalworkers: their main task was the manufacture of the dress accessories, which they fastened to girdles made by leather workers or weavers (Barker 1957, 1–27; Keene 1996, 98–9). The Girdlers were never a numerous body, but they seem to have been a moderately wealthy and successful guild. Their products were mass-produced but still good-quality items, even though they were excluded from working with the precious and more profitable metals (ibid). Girdlers seem to have been closely connected with the area of the Guildhall at this time (Chapter 4.1, 'Introduction and historical background'). Several girdlers are recorded as living within the study area in the late 13th and 14th centuries, including Ralph de Braughyng and Adam Throg in Tenement 5 (next door to the St Lawrence Jewry workshop area) and John Manyman in Tenement 9 (adjacent to the Guildhall yard). St Lawrence is depicted on the Girdlers' coat-of-arms and wealthy individual girdlers made significant bequests to the parish church of St Lawrence Jewry in the 14th century (ibid, 36–6; Schofield 1994, 78), and by the 15th century the Girdlers' Company hall lay only a short distance away on the east side of Basinghall Street.

Late 16th-century candleholder manufacture

Geoff Egan

An assemblage of material from the manufacture of copper-alloy candleholders, including foundry waste, crucibles and moulds (Fig 336), was found dumped in an outbuilding of the 16th-century Blackwell Hall cloth market (period 16, B204). It is possible to tie down the dating of this assemblage more precisely because pottery from the dumped material has a *terminus post quem* of 1580 and the building was burnt down in

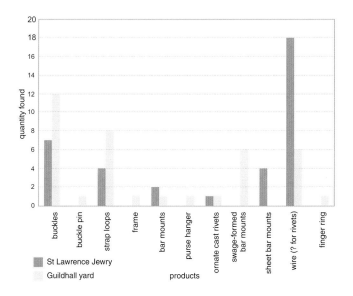

Fig 335 Bar chart showing types of dress accessory products/components (wasters and discards) made in the St Lawrence Jewry and Guildhall yard workshop areas in the late 13th or early 14th century

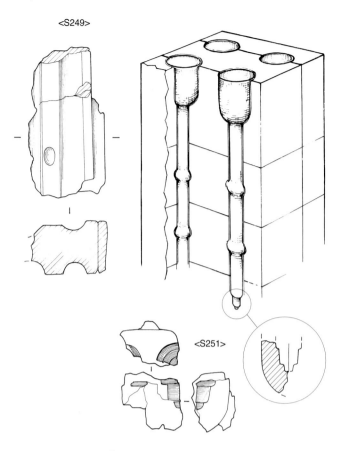

Fig 336 *Reconstruction of a candlestick mould, and selected mould stem fragments* <S249> *and* <S251> *used in the reconstruction (scale 1:2)*

1666. Furthermore, the stratigraphic evidence would suggest that the material was dumped in the building before it was extended to the south; this southern extension also has a *terminus post quem* of 1580 and was refloored on three occasions before the Great Fire of 1666. It can therefore be suggested that the candleholder material was probably dumped in the last quarter of the 16th century. There was no evidence at all of *in situ* hearths or other plant in or near this building, so the assemblage appears to be a dump from a foundry located elsewhere. The reason for dumping redundant waste material of this kind (which would have been of limited value even as hard-core) within a prominent civic building is not readily apparent. However, three moulds for similar candleholders <S273>–<S275> were found (dumped as floor make-up) in the vicarage of St Lawrence Jewry, which, by the late 16th century, had secular tenants; it may be that one of these tenants was involved in the manufacture of candleholders and simply took advantage of some building works going on a short distance to the east. A small assemblage of similar material has been found elsewhere in the City, at Riverplate House, Finsbury Circus (RIV87) to the north-east (Egan 1996b, 89–90, fig 5B), and limited waste from candlestick founding has been published from a site in Worcester which produced mainly cooking pots (Taylor 1996). Chemical analysis of the copper alloy droplets in the 16th-century crucibles suggests that the candlesticks were cast in gunmetal, and they show much less variation than the alloys used in the earlier copper-alloy

founding (Chapter 8.9).

The products, moulds and kiln furniture are catalogued and discussed in more detail in Chapter 8.8. The quantity of discarded kiln furniture and moulds is considerably greater than that of the actual products (including metal waste) of the foundry: four rather scrappy copper-alloy fragments <S276>–<S279> are the only items constituting near-finished products. The forms represented by the assemblage from the Guildhall site are plain cups and relatively plain, blade-knopped stems, with hints of a range of bases – trumpet-forms including domed, varieties of simple drums and skirted saucers, as well as somewhat more elaborate versions, including ?trilobed and ?hexagonal/octagonal. Most of these are well known, routine forms (cf Bangs 1995, 131–46, nos 105x–108 (the 17th-century 'English trumpet series') for some of the simpler bases, although for the stems there is a wider date span, from ibid, 68, no. 22, assigned to the 15th century, onwards). Overall, the products seem to have been at the plainer end of the known range, avoiding altogether the elaborate stem mouldings seen on many of the finest surviving contemporary candlesticks. If a date of deposition around the last quarter of the 16th century is proposed for the waste from the site evidence, this provides a useful fixed point for the reassessment of the development of English candlesticks (cf Koldeweij 2001 on metal ones). This was precisely the time when the first ceramic candlesticks were appearing on the market in England, presumably extending the popularity of this form of lighting appliance further downmarket than it had previously penetrated and stimulating an aspiration to the more expensive metal versions. Was the variety apparent in the foundry moulds itself something new – perhaps a response to this new rival medium?

6.7 The Guildhall and its precinct (*c* 1128–1999)

The Guildhall

The origins of the Guildhall

When the Guildhall was first established as the centre of corporate civic and commercial regulation, probably in the early 12th century, it is likely to have been located close to the existing agency of royal authority in the city, just as the Winchester *gihalda*, on its first appearance, occupied what had until very recently been part of the royal palace (Biddle 1976, 335–6, 423). Unfortunately, it is far from clear how that authority had previously been exercised in London, and there is only the occasional and casual reference to such royal officials as shire reeves or port (ie 'town') reeves or, after the Norman Conquest, to justices (Brooke 1975, 371–2). As at Winchester, the most obvious physical context was the royal palace, mentioned in several sources. This is a deeply problematic topic, for the sources in question are all more or less late in date, but it is nevertheless possible to discern an association between this north-western corner of the walled city and royal governance in one form or another, which is of direct relevance to the origins of the Guildhall.

The earliest evidence of this kind is the hall (*selde*) and reeve that over-kings of the late 7th century AD are known to have maintained in London to oversee the conduct of trade (Thorpe 1840, 14–15; Whitelock 1979, 395). The location of the hall is, however, much more likely to have been in the contemporary commercial centre of Lundenwic, to the west of the City in the Covent Garden area, though a palace or royal residence within the walled former Roman city, not far from the cathedral, would not have been out of place for ceremonial purposes. A palace specifically in the City is first recorded by the reliable early 12th-century chronicle of Florence of Worcester under the year 1017 when the maverick ealdorman Eadric Streona was murdered there at Christmas and his body thrown into the city ditch (ibid, 312). The reference is casual and incidental, and there is no reason to doubt it, especially as the existence in London at this date of a palace, or something approximating to one, would not be a matter of great surprise. More direct or more nearly contemporary evidence is lacking, however, no doubt largely on account of the completion of Edward the Confessor's new palace at Westminster c 1060, which must have resulted in the abandonment or demotion of its City predecessor.

There are, however, two other, quite specific, references to a pre-Conquest royal palace in London which, though deficient in several respects – not least in date – nevertheless agree that it lay in the Aldermanbury area, close to the later Guildhall. One of these is an allusion in St Paul's Cathedral building accounts of the early 1530s to the building of five 'tenements' on a Chapter property 'in Aldermanbury' which, the text claims, was once the palace of King Æthelberht of Kent, the cathedral's founder (HMC 1883, 1.44a; GL, MS 25191, fos 1–7 *passim*). The date of the accounts is of course irredeemably late, and the site is known to have been in other hands than those of St Paul's in the 13th and 14th centuries, but the genuineness of the Chapter's belief in the tradition is shown by its expression in an administrative document of purely confidential character that was never intended for outsiders' eyes, and its use merely for identifying the building work in question. But sincerity of belief is hardly enough, and the St Paul's 'tradition' could easily have been mistaken, and would count for little were it not for the existence of a second tradition of the same kind and import, this time emanating from the abbey of St Albans. This was recorded in the mid 13th century and drew on earlier abbey sources in stating that the parish church of St Alban Wood Street originally served as the chapel of the adjoining royal palace of King Offa of Mercia, the abbey's founder (*Gesta abbatum*, i, 55).

Some harsh criticism has been heaped on this source in recent years (Brooke 1975, 111, n1) on the grounds of St Albans' reputation (shared by many another religious house in the 12th century) for replacing lost genuine charters with forged ones while supplementing them with completely fictitious items. No charter is involved here, however, nor is there any suggestion that the abbey was laying any kind of

claim to the church, which it had indeed once owned but had long since exchanged with Westminster Abbey for other property. Most strikingly of all, and unaccountably overlooked until now, the passage goes on to speak of the palace as still surviving (ie in the mid 13th century) in a much reduced form: 'but by neglect and ambition of a succession of people … reduced to a small dwelling through unwarranted encroachment on the part of neighbouring citizens, though still retaining its ancient liberty.' Here was a simple statement of fact which, if false, would have readily been dismissed as nonsense by any contemporary familiar with the area.

Late and unsatisfactory as these two reports are, taken on their own, there is nevertheless a strikingly close coincidence between the indicated locations of the 7th- or 8th-century AD palaces they mention, Æthelberht's (according to St Paul's) and Offa's (according to St Albans) – something that can hardly be the result of collusion. Much later St Paul's records show that the five newly-built properties of the 1530s extended along the south side of Addle Street (eg Dean and Chapter accounts, 1548–9: GL, MS 25636, fo 3v). The church of St Alban Wood Street, on the north side of Love Lane (Fig 281), lay only a short way south of these properties, and the Offan palace adjoining it must have lain to its east or north, in exactly the same, quite restricted, area. Professor W F Grimes's post-war excavation work in the area suggested an 8th-century AD date for the earliest fabric of St Alban's church, but this has been challenged by Cohen (2001, 90–4), who proposed an 11th-century date, based on the dating evidence of the earlier contexts beneath the church which were of 10th-century AD or later date (ibid, 94, 98).

Grimes also noted the coincidence between the location of the hypothetical palace and the Roman fort at Cripplegate, which he discovered during the same excavation programme (Grimes 1968, 203–7). Recent reconsideration, taking account of the apparent early demolition of the fort's eastern walls, has played down the general significance of this association (Milne 2001), though part of the south wall did survive into the medieval period (Lyon 2004). There is, however, one other part of the fort circuit which is of especial interest in supplying a potential link between the palace of 1017, noted by Florence of Worcester and abandoned after 1060, and the emergence of the Guildhall in the early 12th century: the relation of the site of the fort's east gate to the Aldermanbury street frontage next to the church of St Mary. According to the earliest reliable map, Ogilby and Morgan's survey of 1676, immediately north of the church the frontage forms a conspicuous projection some 7.0m into the street, exactly at the point where it overlies the gate site (Fig 264; Fig 281; Dyson and Schofield 1984, 306). This would strongly suggest that the gatehouse had survived long after the circuit wall to either side of it, and the subsequent history of its site gives grounds for supposing that it may have accommodated the permanent royal official responsible for the governance of London in the king's absence, both before and after the establishment of the new palace at Westminster. Though itself too small to accommodate a palace, the gatehouse could plausibly have represented the surviving remnant of one, and in that way make better sense of the St Paul's and St Albans traditions pointing to palaces located immediately behind it – only a short distance from the city ditch into which Ealdorman Eadric's corpse was reportedly thrown at Cnut's lethal Christmas party of 1017.

By the early 12th century the east gate site, only some 100m from the Guildhall, was occupied by a highly distinctive early medieval property called, suggestively in the context, 'Aldermanbury'. The name signifies 'the fortified residence of the alderman' (Ekwall 1954, 195), and is first recorded c 1130 when it was applied to a soke, a private lordship comparable with a City ward (Davis 1925, 56–7, §6–7). As late as 1268 the ward soon to be known as Cripplegate was referred to as *Aldermanesgarde* (Rigg 1902, 46), strongly hinting that it originated, like other City wards, in a soke, and one that took its name from the official associated with the Aldermanbury property. The property itself gave its name both to the street and to the adjoining church of St Mary Aldermanbury, whose advowson it held and to which it was directly connected by means of a postern (eg GL, MS 25121/123, 1215, 1219). The arrangement indicates that the church was once an integral part of the property, serving it as a private chapel, and the relationship is made the more significant by the location of both at the very centre of the parish. This was clearly no ordinary property, and the range of legal privileges and jurisdictional rights still attached to it as late as 1247 (*Cart Antiq R* 13, no. 339) is unparalleled elsewhere in London. Of the terms used to describe it in successive deeds, *manerium* is perhaps the most significant, for it is indeed best seen as an 'urban manor', comparable in kind with the early 11th-century Godbegot at Winchester (Biddle 1976, 336–7, 342, fig 12), though superior in degree.

Privileges as comprehensive as this, placing the holders beyond the reach of all jurisdictions but the king's, could only have been attached to an establishment of exceptional status, such as might very likely have answered to the description of the 'small dwelling … still retaining its ancient liberty' that the mid 13th-century St Albans source regarded as the surviving remnant of Offa's palace. This is a context with which both elements of the name 'Aldermanbury' are fully compatible. The term '-bury' or *burh*, denoting a fortified place, would certainly have been applicable to a Roman fort gate, a prominent and robust masonry structure much less easily demolished than the adjoining circuit walls, and much more readily adaptable to other uses. There are closely comparable cases of the use of former Roman gatehouses put to good use in the early medieval period, such as at the *porta nigra* at Trier, occupied by a prominent individual and then by a church (Wightman 1970, 94–5). Much nearer to home, a district known as 'Earlsburgh' immediately outside the north gate (Bootham Bar) of York, was served by the church of St Olave which the eponymous earl, Siward of Northumbria, built before 1055 (YAT 1978, 13; Palliser 1978, 8). The parallel with Earl Siward surely lies near the heart of the matter, for his title of 'earl' was simply the Norse equivalent (*jarl*) of the Old English *ealdorman*, the other element of the name 'Aldermanbury'; both officials were the king's local or provincial governors. It is therefore entirely likely that the two *burhs*, at York and London, served similar purposes,

and that the name of the London *burh* similarly commemorated some very specific individual. Virtually all the medieval spellings of the name preserve the singular form 'alderman', and in one exception a genitive plural form of the Anglo-Saxon name was actually corrected (CLRO, HR 72/8), as if to uphold the integrity of the singular form in a milieu where authority had come to be vested in a plurality of aldermen.

If this insistence on the singular form referred to a quite particular ealdorman, there can be little doubt about the most celebrated holder of the office in London, and indeed in all Anglo-Saxon history. This was the Ealdorman Æthelred, the last leader of independent Mercia and the son-in-law to whom King Alfred entrusted London after its recapture from the Vikings in AD 886 (Keene 2003a). Under Æthelred's governorship the site of the Roman city began to be resettled after three centuries of virtual abandonment, and given new street layouts, renovated defences, markets and commercial facilities – all undertakings with which Æthelred was already familiar from his experience at Worcester and other Mercian towns. In London he was directly involved in the establishment of the great harbour known from the second quarter of the 12th century as Queenhithe but referred to, as early as AD 898, as *Æthelredeshithe* (Dyson 1990, 99–110) and located (it should be noted) at a point on the Thames due south of Aldermanbury. As a key partner of Alfred in the struggle against the Vikings, the Ealdorman Æthelred was a figure of national standing whose authority extended far beyond his base in London. He was much the most likely individual to have established a personal *ealdormannes burh* at Aldermanbury to serve as a civic and regional headquarters, and from which the palace recorded under the year 1017 was to develop. Whether or not the term 'ealdorman' was used by Londoners in commemoration of him to denote the successive royal officials appointed to govern the town, as distinct from the terms 'port-' or 'shire-reeve' employed by the king's scriptorium, the term became permanently attached to the premises on the gatehouse site.

Where the York analogy suggests how the gatehouse *burh* could have been pressed into service for the use of earls, ealdormen or reeves, the parallel with Winchester, where the guildhall (*gihalda*) first recorded in 1148 occupied a site on the High Street that until very recently had been part of the royal palace (Biddle 1976, 335–6, 423), emphasises the closeness of the physical relationship between royal and early civic government. It may even be possible to point to a yet more direct tie between Aldermanbury and the embryonic Guildhall. A Ramsey Abbey deed was witnessed 'before the entire London Husting at the house of Alfwin son of Leofstan' in 1123–8 (Davis 1925, 50), years in which the construction of the first Guildhall was either already under way or about to begin. Alfwin (or Ailwine or Æthelwine) was a member of a prominent and long-standing London dynasty of English origin (Brooke 1975, 246–7). His father Leofstan was very probably the reeve or sheriff recorded c 1108 and in 1114–15 (ibid, 372), and his son Henry was to become the first mayor of London at the end of the 12th century. Though not himself described as a sheriff, his family's record of involvement in the government of London makes it perfectly possible that he did so serve, for the list of incumbents for the 1120s is far from complete. If so, the house in which the aldermen were meeting pending the completion of the purpose-built Guildhall may well have been his nearby official residence at Aldermanbury, a possible further source of contact between the single ealdorman and the plural aldermen.

First referred to as aldermen in 1111 (Brooke 1975, 155), the leaders of the London wards would soon have felt the need for more spacious accommodation than had been required by the single alderman, of whom they may have fancied themselves the successors in function, dignity and, it would seem, in name. They represented the citizenry at large, and the size of the Guildhall shows that its primary concern was to accommodate sizeable numbers of Londoners in the Court of Husting, a body comparable with the hundred courts of the shires, in which the interests and concerns of the Londoners as well as those of the Crown could be ventilated and so far as possible reconciled. In this respect, one other early London institution may have had to be taken into account. This was the shadowy folkmoot, of which little more is known other than that it was summoned by bells to the north-east corner of St Paul's Cathedral precinct three times a year (ibid, 52, 209, 249; Stenton 1970, 29–30; Keene 2004, 20). The folkmoot has every appearance of an archaic popular assembly, perhaps superseded by the more exclusive Court of Husting. There is no further evidence of its meeting or functioning, and the surviving 13th- and 14th-century references to it in St Paul's records and in the City's custumals, the *Liber Albus* and the *Liber Custumarum*, smack of antiquarianism.

From the beginning, and long before the establishment of the Guildhall, the Husting's business seems to have been concerned with commerce, and probably with the adjudication of pleas of debt and land that later characterised it. Nominally at least, its origins lay in the 'husting of London' that was concerned with the definition of weights, according to an ostensibly late 10th-century AD Ramsey Abbey document (*Chron Ramsey*, 58; Kemble 1839–48, no. 973), although the reference to the husting may be an 11th-century interpolation (Nightingale 1987, 559–61). A document of 1032 (Kemble 1839–48, no. 745) speaks of 180 marks of white silver *be hustinges gewihte*, where the allusion is presumably to the husting of London, although the town is not named. Stenton pointed out that the term is of Scandinavian origin, signifying an indoor assembly of a lord's dependents (Stenton 1970, 30–1), and it has also been suggested as an 11th-century Danish term applied to an existing institution (Nightingale 1987, 559–63). Some of its functions may only have developed in the first half of that century, during the reigns of the Danish kings (1014–42) (ibid, 566–77; Brooke 1975, 21–5, 249), although little archaeological evidence of any distinctively Danish presence or influence has been found in the area of the future Guildhall (above, 6.4, 'Links with Scandinavia').

The new Guildhall of the 1120s could be seen as the physical manifestation of a growing civic consciousness, part of the developing 12th-century concept of urban liberty (Keene 2003b, 262), which was recognised by the increased civil privileges that appear to have been awarded during the reign of

Henry I (1100–35). Some doubt has been cast on the reliability of Henry's charter of 1130 to the citizens of London, but other evidence confirms that the citizens were given the right at this time to elect their own sheriffs, a significant change from the previous practice of appointment by royal authority (Brooke 1975, 31–3). The king and the citizens may have found it mutually advantageous to forge closer links at this time, perhaps to counterbalance the powerful baronial interests in their London fortresses at Baynards Castle and the Tower of London (Nightingale 1995, 49–50). The king would necessarily have retained an element of authority over the new Guildhall, and it has been suggested that in order to qualify for citizenship Londoners at this date would have needed to own property and pay the king's geld or tax, and that the new hall may therefore have come to be called the 'geld hall' (ibid, 44–7). If so, the new building may have combined fiscal, judicial and administrative functions from the outset, serving as 'geld hall', Court of Husting and office of the new sheriffs.

The origins of the 12th-century Guildhall thus lie in the relatively recent and radical institutional developments since the late 11th century, and may ultimately derive from the re-establishment of the intra-mural city of London by Alfred and the Ealdorman Æthelred in the late 9th century AD. The hall itself was clearly intended to house meetings of the Court of Husting, an existing body that seems to have been given new shape and direction, not least perhaps by the introduction, before 1111, of the body of aldermen who represented the citizenry at large. The hall itself has no antecedents on its site, despite the suggestion that the folkmoot, traditionally the City's most ancient assembly, may originally have convened within the remains of the old amphitheatre (Biddle 1989, 23–4). Though the 12th-century structure was indeed built on the site of the north bank of the Roman amphitheatre, the earthwork was completely levelled by this date (above, 6.1). The link between the amphitheatre and the Guildhall can now be seen as an intriguing topographical coincidence, and nothing more.

The 12th-century Guildhall

The evidence for the establishment of the Guildhall in the early 12th century is discussed in Chapter 3.1. Barron (1974, 15 and n2) showed that the City had a Guildhall by the 12th century; the key evidence is a rental document listing properties belonging to St Paul's Cathedral in c 1130, including one such property described as *terra Gialle*, apparently situated in Bassishaw ward (Price 1886, 18; Davis 1925, 57). This *terra Gialle* is probably to be identified with the Guildhall on linguistic grounds, since the form *Gialle* corresponds to other 12th- and 13th-century references to Guildhalls that all share a common orthographic feature, the elided medial '-ld-'. The 12th-century *terra Gialle* property is probably the same as the 13th-century description of the Guildhall yard as *partis exterioris de Gildhalla* (Barron 1974, 15) and is likely to be broadly similar to the well-defined Guildhall precinct of c 1300 (Chapter 4.1). The best evidence for this link between the separate property descriptions comes from the reference to the length of the property in the c 1130 document (132ft, or 40.2m), a dimension that matches the length of the Guildhall yard in the 13th century (period 12); one which is, admittedly, reconstructed, but which has been arrived at by an independent 'best fit' of the extensive cartographic, archaeological and documentary evidence for the surrounding streets and houses. Using the measurements given in the 1130s rental, the *terra Gialle* could be seen as including the northern part of the lane and the two houses on its east side (Fig 337; it is, of course, possible to suggest other reconstructions using these measurements). The construction of the Guildhall building would seem to date to the 1120s since the Court of Husting was still meeting elsewhere, in Alfwin's house – perhaps the fortified residence on Aldermanbury – in that decade. Archaeological excavation of the area just to the south of the later Guildhall (site A) has shown that a minor lane (R102) off Cat Street, originally laid out in the 11th century to provide access to the churchyard of St Lawrence Jewry, was gradually extended northwards in the second half of that century. The final extension seems to have occurred in the early 12th century (period 10 phase 5) when the lane was extended some 12m beyond the northernmost timber house. The reason for this final road extension must surely have been to provide access to the newly built Guildhall, an entrance that was, perhaps, secondary to a principal entrance leading from Aldermanbury, connecting the old Husting building on the west side of Aldermanbury to the new Guildhall on the other side of the

road. By the late 13th century the lane was described as the 'way leading to the Husting' (1271: Hillaby 1992, 146) or the 'way leading to the Guildhall' (1281–2: CLRO, HR 13/58) and, significantly, this was before the construction campaign on the new Guildhall began in the early 14th century.

What sort of building was this 12th-century Guildhall? The archaeological evidence is limited: the actual site of the Guildhall has not, of course, been excavated since the 15th-century Guildhall is happily still standing. There are, however, a few nuggets of archaeological detail that can inform us. During the reconstruction works of the 1960s, Peter Marsden (the archaeologist of the then Guildhall Museum) observed a plastered recess that had been blocked up in the wall of what is now recognised as the new Guildhall of c 1300 (Chapter 3.1, 'The Guildhall'). The plastered recess is most likely to have been a splayed window reveal and Marsden's suggestion that this feature was part of a 12th-century Guildhall is now even more plausible. It now seems that the new hall of c 1300 was simply an upward extension of the 12th-century single-storey hall, with the old windows of the hall having to be blocked by the new vaulting that supported the additional storey. Another element of archaeological evidence for the 12th-century Guildhall is a single fragment of stone capital <A19>, which may have been part of a blind arcade in the original hall. It was found in a 14th-century context, the date when the hall was rebuilt (period 13), but the architectural style is to be dated to c 1100–c 1200. The building is shown in the reconstruction painting (Fig 338) as a single-storey hall on a similar scale to the Court of Requests building in Westminster. It would be tempting to see the first Guildhall (like the 15th-century hall) as having been influenced by the far grander Westminster Hall, but this building was clearly of a more exalted status and size and, unlike the Guildhall, had high clerestory windows. The smaller Guildhall was probably still one of the largest secular stone buildings in the land, measuring (it is suggested) c 26.5m x 17.4m. It would have been something of a challenge in the 12th century to build a roof over that span and so it seems likely that it was an aisled hall, with timber posts or columns to support the roof trusses. The hall may have been similar to the original Westminster Hall in its combination of stone walls and timber aisle posts, but it is possible that it had two arcades of stone columns like the slightly later halls at Clarendon or Oakham (Wood 1965, 38). The simplified reconstructed cross-section (Fig 339, a) envisages timber aisle posts used to support a raised tie-beam that braces the roof. This type of roof would not have required unfeasibly large timbers of c 17m (for the full span of the building) but instead would have employed c 9.0m timbers for the raised tie-beam and c 8.0m timbers for the principal rafters (which could 'overlap' at the tie-beam). The only other archaeological evidence that might be connected with the first Guildhall is the discovery of a small quantity of 12th-century flanged roof tiles (curved like Roman tiles rather than flat like later medieval peg tiles) and some rare decorated ridge tiles (<T16> and <T17>, Fig 107). These tiles were found in the area just to the south of the hall and they suggest that the Guildhall of the 1120s may have been one of the first

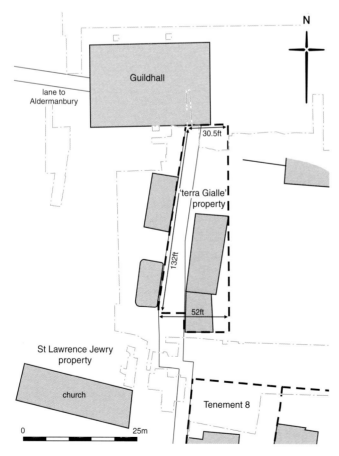

Fig 337 *Reconstruction of the Guildhall land, the terra Gialle, of c 1130 (scale 1:800)*

Fig 338 *Artist's reconstruction of the study area in c 1130 (Judith Dobie)*

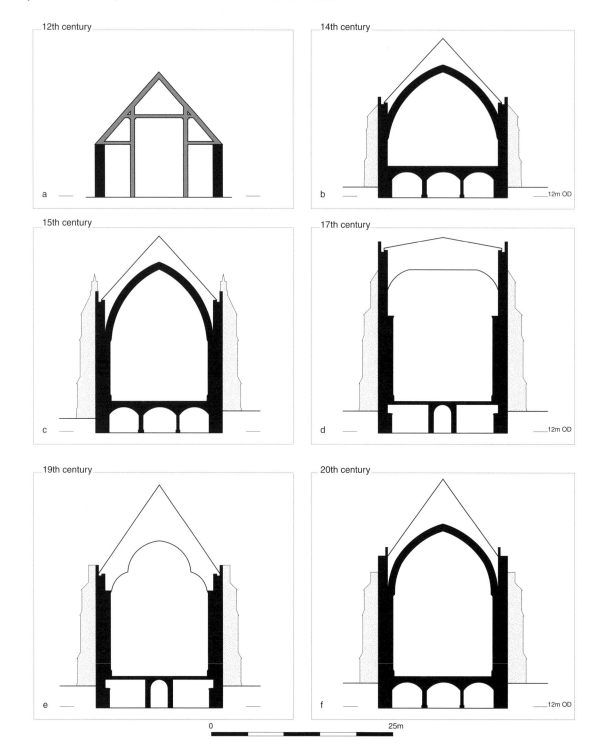

Fig 339 *Reconstructed cross-sections showing the suggested evolution of the Guildhall: a – the 12th-century aisled hall; b – the 14th-century hall with new upper storey; c – the greatly enlarged 15th-century building; d – the 17th-century adaptations including new clerestory and roof; e – the 19th-century Gothic roof; f – Scott's 20th-century restoration (the cross-sections are nominally drawn north–south along a line near the west end of the modern Guildhall; roofs are shown in simplified outline; buttresses are shown, stippled, in elevation in relation to the contemporary ground level; scale 1:500)*

tiled buildings in medieval London (Chapter 8.5).

The building may have begun to take on a wider political significance quite soon after its construction. By the second half of the 1130s England was in the grip of the civil wars that followed the death of Henry I, and Londoners largely supported Stephen rather than his cousin Matilda, Henry's daughter. Brooke (1975, 33–9) has emphasised the importance of the

mutual support sworn by Stephen and the leading citizens of London, and he speculates that the Londoners' declaration might have been accompanied by further concessions of power to the developing civic authority; Davis (1990, 54–6) suggests that this was, in effect, the first London commune.

The role of London's nascent government continued to grow during the reign of Henry II (1154–89). Henry granted the citizens a new charter confirming some of the City's judicial privileges, though it gives little detail about the administrative role of the City government (Brooke 1975, 40–4). In 1191 the Guildhall was the scene of some dramatic political events. With Richard I absent overseas, a dispute arose between the king's justiciar, William de Longchamp, and Richard's brother John, the future king (ibid, 44–9). By October, Longchamp was in his stronghold at the Tower of London and John was approaching the city. The citizens heard arguments for supporting both sides at the Guildhall, but eventually decided on loyalty to the king's relative rather than to his official; their reward from John was the granting of the London commune. In the late 11th and early 12th centuries a succession of northern French towns had secured guarantees of economic and political privileges from their feudal masters; these communes were associated with the granting of a charter, the swearing of oaths of support and the establishment of a town hall for the newly formed civic government (Fossier 1997, 371–3). These political developments, in contrast, had scarcely affected the 'Angevin empire' (including England, Normandy and Aquitaine) but Richard I did, in addition to London, grant communes in Rouen, Bordeaux and La Rochelle (ibid, 375). The London commune was the confirmation of its political and judicial privileges and was symbolised by the new post of mayor, a position held for the first twenty or so years by Henry fitz Ailwin, a leading London citizen who was probably the son of the Alfwin who was Henry I's sheriff when the Guildhall was first built (Brooke 1975, 245–8).

The 14th-century Guildhall

It has been argued (Chapter 4.1) that the impetus for the redevelopment of the Guildhall and its chapel at the end of the 13th century came from Henry le Waleys, who was mayor three times between the years 1273 and 1299, during Edward I's reign (Williams 1963, 245–62). Anne Sutton, in her investigation of the London Society of the Puy, has described the cultured Anglo-French milieu of the late 13th century that may have provided the inspiration for the new Guildhall precinct (Sutton 1992). She suggests that the London Puy may have been founded in the 1270s by wealthy merchants who had been welcomed at the hospitable and cultural meetings of the Arras Puy while conducting wool business in that city. The London Puy retained the musical interests of the Arras Puy, as well as its devotion to the Virgin Mary, and it seems to have developed into a significant, if short-lived, London confraternity at the end of the 13th century. Its members probably included prominent City merchants who held civic office, including the mayor, Henry le Waleys, and the Common Clerk, John de Bankwell. There is also good reason to suppose that Edward I was involved: he had attended meetings of the Arras Puy and several of the London members, including le Waleys, were trusted royal servants (ibid, 7, 10). The London Puy could therefore have served as a point of contact between the king and the few City officials he trusted, one of whom was le Waleys. The close involvement of the Society and le Waleys in

the development of the new Guildhall, or at least of its chapel, is firmly rooted in the documentary evidence. One set of statutes of the London Puy (recorded by the City's chamberlain, Andrew Horn, in the 1320s) may date from the late 1290s and they imply that the 'chapel of Our Lady near Guildhall' had been started, although there was not at that point sufficient endowment to provide a chaplain (ibid, 2–5; *Liber Cust*, ii, 579–94). In June 1299 le Waleys (who had just completed his final year as mayor) seems to have come to the rescue with an annual 5 marks quitrent to the Society to pay for a chaplain at the 'new chapel at Guildhall' (*Cal M Court R*, 44). The dates of these two documents point to 1298 as a likely commencement date for the redevelopment of the chapel, the Guildhall and the new precinct: it was in that year that the king handed back control of the City to the trusted le Waleys after a period of acrimonious direct royal control which began in 1285 (Williams 1963, 261–2). We might speculate that it was at a meeting of the Puy in 1298 (perhaps held in the old Guildhall or at le Waleys's hall in Stepney) that Edward and le Waleys discussed the latter's new mayoralty, looked forward to more harmonious relations and discussed the plan for the new civic precinct, including the chapel dedicated to the Virgin and managed by the Puy.

There is good reason to suspect that the new Guildhall chapel was started before the renovation campaign on the old Guildhall, as the surviving documentary evidence clearly suggests that it was the pious intention to create a new civic chapel that was paramount in the minds of le Waleys and the London Puy. However, work could have been carried out in tandem on the two adjacent buildings. It is possible that the west wing of Roger de Clifford's hall (period 13, B213) was acquired by the City in the 1280s as part of the preparations for the redevelopment project since the City would clearly have needed temporary meeting space while the Guildhall was being rebuilt. It is therefore possible that redevelopment work began on the hall as early as 1300, shortly after the beginning of the construction campaign on the new chapel. However, the surviving documentary evidence, analysed by Barron (1974, 21), would point to the 1330s as the time when the emphasis of the campaign shifted from the chapel (probably still not fully finished) to the old hall. This date would also make sense politically, as it was soon after the re-establishment of the City's liberties in 1327 under the young Edward III (Williams 1963, 297–300). A painted stone shield with the arms of Edward III was found reused in the wall of the 15th-century Guildhall, and it may originally have decorated the 14th-century hall (Fig 340); the shield is now on display in the Museum of London. In 1332 the mayor, the wealthy draper John de Pulteney, lent the sum of 10 marks for the repair of the hall (*Cal LB E*, 274) and it is possible that his actual financial contribution was much greater than this. Pulteney is known to have been a significant benefactor of London building projects during his life, particularly for the new College he added to the church of St Lawrence in Candlewick Street, thereafter known eponymously as St Lawrence Pountney (Harben 1918, 341). He clearly had an interest in contemporary architecture,

Fig 340 *Painted stone shield with the arms of Edward III which may have been part of the 14th-century Guildhall (height 630mm)*

spending a huge sum of money developing his newly acquired country estate at Penshurst, Kent, in the 1340s (Binney 1972). Reasonable sums of money were spent by the chamberlain on the hall in 1332–5 (£19 6s 10$^1/_2$d) and in 1343 (100s), although these are not nearly enough to account for all the necessary building works (Barron 1974, 21).

The evidence for the new building is discussed in Chapter 4.1, where it is argued that the new hall was built as an upward extension of the 12th-century hall, converted to have a lower ground-floor undercroft and additional first-floor chambers. The new hall can be seen in part as a response to the increasing specialisation of civic government which required separate chambers for the different functions of the administration. The Court of Husting probably met in the undercroft, essentially the same space it had used for two hundred years. The new undercroft was undoubtedly a lower-lying space than the old open hall but it was still well lit (by about eleven windows) and the five bays of plain quadripartite vaulting would have provided a solid and respectable civic courtroom, perhaps with a dais at the east end of the room. There is, unfortunately, little surviving evidence for the upper part of the hall, other than the fact that the new undercroft was clearly designed to support a taller upper space. Documentary evidence would suggest that the largest space of the new upper floor was used primarily by the Court of Common Council, the relatively new administrative body consisting of *probi homines*, 'good men', elected by the 24 City wards (Barron 2004a, 129–36). If this

chamber occupied four of the building's five bays it would have been a substantial room, measuring 18.9m x 14.9m (62ft x 49ft) and easily capable of seating the 150–200 Common Council members. In March 1386, for example, 179 Council members, 15 aldermen and the mayor attended the meeting (*Cal LB H*, 279–82). This room would have compared favourably with some of the contemporary first-floor great halls that were being built to enhance wealthy monastic or cathedral precincts, such as at Ely (Wood 1965, 25–6), or grand domestic halls such as de Pulteney's enlarged hall at Penshurst (Binney 1972). The upper floor may even have used one of the latest architectural innovations in its roof design, assuming the 15th-century roof copied its 14th-century predecessor. It is tentatively suggested that the roof was supported on great stone transverse arches (Fig 339, b) which would have created a broad hall, unencumbered by columns, and with a single hall-and-roof space like the new archbishop's palace at Mayfield, Sussex, of *c* 1325 (Wood 1965, 308–9, 324, pl 24). The third chamber of the new Guildhall was probably a single bay of the upper hall, adjacent to the Common Council room and used for the more exclusive meetings of the Mayor's Court and the Court of Aldermen. The Mayor's Court was the main commercial court, regulating the 'law merchant' and settling disputes concerning debt, apprenticeships and contracts (Barron 2004a, 154–6). The Court of Aldermen had a more executive than judicial role and, in this period, it formed the heart of civic government – sometimes clashing, in the 14th century, with the more radical Court of Common Council (ibid, 136–46). This smaller chamber measuring 4.5m x 9.8m (15ft x 32ft) could still seat at least 20 people (a typical meeting of the Mayor's Court might be attended by only 15 people: *Cal LB I*, 80) and it may also have housed the City's increasingly important archive of civic business.

The reconstruction painting (Fig 341) shows the hall at the end of the Guildhall yard, slightly set back and to the left of the more prominent chapel. The reconstruction of the hall has used the model of Penshurst Place, Kent, whose construction campaign almost certainly began while the Guildhall precinct development was still being completed, and a stylistic link between the two halls is an attractive idea given the important role of John de Pulteney in both buildings. As Barron (1974, 20) has pointed out, there is some similarity between the surviving elements of the two buildings and, moreover, they both seem to have been built upon earlier halls. The reconstruction features a crenellated parapet based on Penshurst (and which is a notable feature of the later Guildhall) and prominent outer arches enclosing two-light windows, a feature used at both Penshurst and Mayfield Palace (Wood 1965, pls X, b and 3).

It seems that a porch was only added to the hall later in the 14th century (Chapter 4.2). Steane (2001, 110–15) has described the symbolic and hierarchical significance of staircases, and it is possible that the approach to the upper hall from the Guildhall yard was perceived as somewhat disappointing, with the main public entrance squeezed in between the prominent chapel to one side and the precinct boundary wall on the other side (Fig 341). The solution was to enclose the 'dead' space between the chapel, the precinct wall and the hall in order to create a more decorative entrance, whose front was level with the main facade of the chapel (Fig 166). The archaeological evidence shows that the facade of the new porch was built in flint and Reigate stone, perhaps arranged in 'long and short' quoins to create a chequerboard effect and possibly echoing a decorative feature of the adjacent chapel.

The 15th-century Guildhall

The redevelopment of the whole Guildhall precinct in the years 1411–c 1450 (Fig 342) can be seen as part of a City-wide campaign of civic improvements, which had begun in the 1390s with work on London Bridge and the creation of Blackwell Hall cloth market, and continued in the mid 15th century with the Leadenhall complex, containing a market, granary, chapel and school (Keene 2003b, 263; Barron 2004a, 54–5). Like the Guildhall precinct development of a century before, its roots may have lain in a reconciliation that followed a time of political tension. London had witnessed some dramatic events in the late 14th century, with the Peasants' Revolt of 1381, the tension between king and Parliament in the late 1380s, and the suspension of the City's liberties – accompanied by the arrest of the mayor and sheriffs – by Richard II in 1392 (ibid, 13; Sheppard 1998, 97–8). The civic rebuilding projects that followed this difficult period might therefore be seen as a conscious assertion of civic pride, led initially by the charismatic Mayor Richard Whittington. As Keene describes, the mayor and his aldermen were becoming the king's representatives in a more formal sense and, like the king, wanted to be seen as patrons of architecture, the arts and music (Keene 2003b, 263). Whittington was the ideal candidate to initiate the new Guildhall project; he was an alderman, mayor, wealthy merchant and trusted royal servant (like de Waleys a century earlier), and he was well placed to supervise the project once it was under way because he was also involved in managing the improvement works taking place in Westminster Abbey in the second decade of the 15th century (Barron 1969, 219). He would therefore have had access to expert architectural advice and to the king's specialist craftsmen.

The 15th-century Guildhall has been extensively analysed by Caroline Barron (1974) and so the present account largely summarises her study of the building. Between 1411 and the late 1420s, the master mason John Croxtone built a new Guildhall, extending the existing building in height (for the second time) and in length. Croxtone retained the old undercroft, parts of which were by then nearly three centuries old, and built a new, grander undercroft on its east side. Rising majestically above both these vaulted chambers, he built the second-largest hall in the country, measuring nearly 50m in length (49.7m x 17.5m externally and 46.8m x 15.3m internally), and whose internal space rose up an impressive 21m to the roof (Fig 339, c; the height is reconstructed after Wilson 1976, figs 1–2). The inside of the hall, like its 14th-century predecessor, was one vast open space, without aisles or arcades, and with a roof that was probably supported on stone

transverse arches. In size the hall was second only to Wesminster Hall (an enormous 73.0m x 20.5m) and it was built in eight bays to give internal length to width proportions of 3:1. Christopher Wilson has defined an architectural style termed 'London Perpendicular', after the chapter house of St Paul's Cathedral (Wilson 1990, 212), which went on to become virtually standardised in the City's 15th-century churches. The interior of the Guildhall, with lower and upper levels of windows along the side walls and two great windows at each end, exemplified a developed form of this style, which included matching blind panels (where adjacent buildings prevented the use of windows) and two long walls covered with Perpendicular panel tracery. At each end of the building, below the great windows, wooden panelling and tapestries completed the decorative effect. The architectural purpose of the new hall can be seen as a stage for civic display, rather than a building with a specific 'office' function, since the Mayor's Court, the Aldermen's Court and (perhaps a little later in the 15th century) the Court of Common Council all had smaller, more practical chambers in which to meet. The new hall was, however, the main venue where citizens would experience civic justice. At the east end of the hall was the raised dais for the Court of Husting, still the main judicial court, though without the more governmental or administrative role it had had in earlier centuries (Barron 2004a, 127–9). At the other end, there were two smaller platforms on which were held the full weekly meetings of the Sheriffs' Court, dealing with civil and minor criminal cases (ibid, 163–4).

The relatively cramped space of the Guildhall property meant that Croxtone could not completely redesign the precinct as, for example, a town square with visible facades for all three major civic buildings on the site (the hall, chapel and cloth market). The presence of Blackwell Hall market and the Guildhall College meant that the hall had to remain at the north end of the built-up Guildhall yard cul-de-sac. In spite of its great height, the external facade of the building was therefore remarkably hidden, both from the yard and from the surrounding streets. Croxtone's solution to this problem was to design a grand porch (following the example set by the 14th-century Guildhall) in the only publicly visible space, the north end of the Guildhall yard. The recent archaeological excavations and archival research work have revealed new information about this grand porch; the building is described and illustrated in Chapter 4.3 (period 15), and the methodology of the reconstruction process is described in Chapter 8.3, together with a catalogue of the architectural fragments from the building that were recovered during the excavation. The following section discusses aspects of the medieval porch, including its construction and decoration.

The 15th-century Guildhall porch

Mark Samuel

The Guildhall porch represented the public face of the wealthy City of London corporation (Barron 1974, 27). The porch was a two-bayed or paired porch (Fig 343). The main porch leading to the great hall was part of the original design of the Guildhall. The eastern porch or 'screen', leading to the hall's east crypt and connecting the main porch to the adjacent chapel, must have been built either after or in tandem with the chapel and its spiral stair turret in the 1440s. The chronology of the reconstruction programme is discussed in Chapter 4.3 and the relationship between the hall, the porches and the chapel is illustrated on Fig 182. Stow assumed that the construction of the porch was the final act of building the Guildhall (Stow 1603, i, 272) and this implies a construction date in the late 1420s or 1430, a date which has been followed by most writers on the subject (Barron 1974, 26–7; Wilson 1976, 1). It is argued here that the hall and porch (or at least its principal western bay) are more likely to have been built at the same time. An inspection of the surviving hall buttresses within the first floor of the porch provides this evidence. Firstly, no keying between porch and hall ashlar is to be seen and, secondly, there is an internal relieving arch within one of the buttresses. Its purpose was to deflect weight from the first-floor porch door below, and this would surely imply that the porch door was built in advance of the upper part of the hall buttress. The main porch was thus probably built in the mid 1410s, and thirty years or so elapsed before the construction of the east porch.

If it is accepted that the main porch was weatherproof by the time work commenced on the roof of the great hall in 1418, it is possible to argue that it is the work of a hand other than Croxtone's. His role at the Guildhall has been called into question in the past (Wilson 1976, 14, n59) and it has been suggested that craftsmen who worked at Westminster Hall migrated to the Guildhall campaign (Barron 1974, n70). John Croxtone and the Westminster Hall master mason, Henry Yevele, are known to have had a mutual friend and colleague in Walter Walton (Wilson 1976, 14, n59; Harvey 1984, 314). He made the tabernacles in Westminster Hall in 1385 and may have designed the north facade there, and he was a sworn mason of the City in 1412. On the basis of these qualifications, we can speculate that to the older Walton was devolved the important task of designing the porch by his younger colleague. Given John Carpenter's role in the redevelopment of the Guildhall precinct (Chapter 4.3, 'Introduction and historical background') and his interest in classical learning, it is also possible that he had a role in the design of the porch, particularly in its combination of classical, Old Testament and New Testament motifs (Barron 2004b, 119–22).

The main porch was only two (tall) floors high; the stumps of buttresses above first-floor level are faced with ashlar and were clearly meant to be exposed. Surviving seatings show that the roof was pitched north–south, requiring a south gable end as in contemporary church porches. Croxtone probably flanked it with two pairs of spires (Barron 1974, plan 6), but there is no surviving pre-1666 pictorial evidence to corroborate this. The main hall buttresses would have been capped with pinnacles (Wilson 1976, 8, n27) or weatherings (as reconstructed in Fig 190).

The main gate of the porch was flanked by panels

incorporating paired statues of the Cardinal Virtues. The upper floor of the porch facade is only known from elevations and views of Christopher Wren and Robert Hooke's rebuilt upper floor, but it is probable that Wren broadly followed the original design in his 'Gothick' creation (Fig 244). The medieval facade echoed recently completed work at Westminster, such as the north porch of Westminster Hall (J Goodall, pers comm), with a continuous row of tabernacles at ground level and large detached tabernacles set in the plain wall at higher levels. Three such tabernacles could have accommodated the statues discussed below.

The main porch vestibule is vaulted while tracery was applied to the internal faces. A common motif of blind or panel tracery was used, employing triple panels with cinquefoil heads. The 'supermullioned with a split Y' pattern (Harvey 1978, 71) is employed here. The entire vestibule, including its vaulting and inner and outer portals, are unified by the same geometry; all arches and vaults spring from a level 2.85m above floor level. The vault web is c 5.52m above the (modern) floor at its highest point, and a detailed description of it can be found elsewhere (RCHME 1929, 26). The 'perch' (5.03m, or 16ft 6in) and its derivatives, as in the chapel, form a common yardstick of design. The vestibule is a perch wide (from panel to panel) and the same dimension separates the buttresses above the porch. The vault compartments are in plan 4.6m x 3.78m (15ft by three-quarters of a perch). The vault sweeps round the two-centred inner and outer entrances. Edward the Confessor's arms were represented in the lierne vault roof boss (Barron 1974, pl 11b), the spandrel of the outer opening (Nichols 1819, 3) and over the dais of the Court of Husting (RCHME 1929, 25), Edward's importance relating to a tradition that he granted London certain liberties. The chronicler Matthew Paris saw St Edward as the guarantor of the ancient liberties of the English people in an idealised past before the Norman Conquest (Binski 2005, 25), and as considering himself subject to the law (in marked contrast to Norman and Angevin kings). As such he was well suited to be the patron saint of the law courts of the fiercely independent 'barons of London'. By this date he was a political emblem of the elite, for the populace had already transferred their affections to St George as the patron saint of England (ibid, 27).

The form of the inner and outer entrances seems to show that they originally contained no doors; an inner door was probably an early modification. The stone benches could accommodate those waiting for cases at the Husting or Sheriffs' Courts. Record offices and official apartments could have been housed in the upper floor of the porch (Fig 192). A plan of the 1770s (Fig 259), the chief source of information about the upper floor, shows that the west wall had a great splayed fireplace, probably medieval; similar porches elsewhere used one of the steeples as a chimney (Howard 1936, 83). There is an extant (reconstructed) door at the north-east angle. A stair connected the chamber to the interior of the hall and served a secondary chamber over the east porch. The survival of parts of the east and west walls suggests that the interior was unaltered by Wren, and the west wall is still substantially intact (Fig 345).

The east porch or 'screen' connected the main porch to the chapel. It was only recognised in the 1960s when the entrance to the east crypt was revealed and restored (Barron 1974, pls 19, a–b). Wren and Hooke evidently carried out more extensive alterations to the east porch facade than had been thought (as revealed in Dance's elevations of 1788: Fig 371). A tall stair turret in the angle of the porch and chapel was recorded in early views (eg LMA, LCC/GLC 9600085) but was removed *c* 1774. The east porch led into a vestibule, with stairs leading down to the door into the east crypt, which may have been a dining hall (Barron 1974, 28). The lower entrance and surrounding facade were decorated in a similar manner to the exterior of the west crypt. It is likely that a door on the east side of the vestibule led into the light well along the south side of the Guildhall, giving access to the garden to the north (Fig 200). On completion, the east vestibule probably had an ornate timber ceiling forming the floor of a chamber above (illustrated in cross-section on Fig 197). Recovered fragments hint at the presence of a window in that chamber (window casement <A4>; Chapter 8.3). It was reached from a long mural stair rising from the hall (the third bay from the east: 'S6' in Wilson 1976, fig 3) and leading to the adjoining chamber over the main porch. Part of the corbelling that supported the staircase was recorded in the east angle of the surviving western bay of the porch in the 1960s (Barron 1974, pl 19, b).

The main porch featured a hierarchy of statues on the facade (Fig 190). On the ground floor, the Cardinal Virtues are shown beneath the revelations of the Old Testament on the first floor, which are in turn dominated by the New Testament revelation on the gable. The statues of the Cardinal Virtues were rediscovered in a Welsh garden in the 1970s through Professor Barron's detective work (Barron 1974, pl 9, b) and are now on display in the Museum of London (acc nos 2002.117/1–4). The Virtues – Justice, Prudence, Fortitude and Temperance – are from Plato's *Republic* and became Christian virtues in the Middle Ages (Hall 1979, 336). Taking the form of an armed virgin, each engages in single combat with a corresponding vice in the *Psychomachia* of Prudentius, written in the 4th century AD. After the 12th century, British craftsmen show them already triumphant and trampling on their fallen foe (Anderson 1971, 144). Until recently, only the verse by William Elderton, a 16th-century Sheriffs' Court attorney, quoted by Stow (1603, i, 272), provided any sort of identification of these statues. He identified them as Discipline, Justice, Fortitude and Temperance, and their arrangement *in situ* was depicted by Carter (Fig 344) and Schnebbelie (Fig 243).

In 1783 John Carter recorded these statues and two male figures from the upper storey, whom he identified as Moses (holding the tablets of the Law) and Aaron (usually shown with a flowering juniper staff and a censer) (GL, COLLAGE 3573, 3574). Aaron encouraged the Israelites to worship the golden calf (Hall 1979, 216) but was overruled by Moses and the Law. Moses is often paired with 'Synagogue', a veiled female with a broken spear and falling crown (eg at Canterbury, where four Cardinal Virtues also are depicted: Anderson 1971, 89). Synagogue represents the Old Testament religious practice (ibid,

103). Moses prevails over Aaron, the personification of Levite priesthood, as he usually does over Synagogue. In this location, therefore, there is a suggestion of both Civic Law and Canon Law being symbolised. In the reconstruction (Fig 190) Christ presents himself as the 'Alpha and Omega', blessing the onlooker (an English ivory diptych in the Victoria and Albert Museum forms the basis of the conjectural figure of Christ in Majesty: Alexander and Binski 1987, no. 520). The depiction of Aaron and Moses was considered an edifying motif for civic buildings, occurring in later contexts such as the Oude Griffie or record office in Bruges (1535–7), where Justice rather than Jesus is flanked by them (Blyth 1990, 28).

Elderton's identifications are not the 'correct' Cardinal Virtues (J Goodall, pers comm) and these errors have long been perpetuated. The mailed figure with a shield was misidentified by Carter as Justice but is correctly identified as Fortitude by Nichols (1819, 3). There was further confusion about the identity of the other three statues due to the intervention of the 18th-century sculptor Thomas Banks who was given them in 1794 (C Barron, pers comm). He reconstructed two of the figures traditionally identified as Discipline and Fortitude with the attributes of Temperance (a drinking vessel and pitcher of water) and Justice (a globe) respectively (GL, COLLAGE 3571). The figures have large metal crowns, a detail borne out by examination (J Goodall, pers comm). The figure traditionally identified as Discipline is dressed in a manner reminiscent of a nun, clothed in a long flowing undergarment and full-length cloak with a veil and a wimple (Grenville 2003). The rim around the head indicates that she once wore a crown, probably of metal. Whether this was a medieval detail or a later addition is not clear. The arms and the features of the figure beneath her feet have been smashed away. The revised identifications now proposed are (moving from left to right in the reconstruction drawing, Fig 190):

'Discipline' = Temperance (diluting wine with water);
'Justice' = Fortitude (holding a sword);
'Fortitude' = Justice (holding a globe);
'Temperance' = Prudence (holding a snake and a mirror).

It is unlikely that we will ever know who was responsible for these statues, but two names crop up. Firstly, there is Thomas Canon, a marble worker who carved the cycle of kings at Westminster (Harvey 1984, 44, 314). Recent cleaning has revealed his knowledge of French Gothic style (Hay 1995, 7, 11) and his ability to carve naturalistic draperies and gently swaying poses. Perhaps Canon (of whom nothing else is known) was young enough in 1385 to still be active *c* 1415 when the Guildhall porch facade was ready for his attentions. On the other hand, John Massingham senior, who was in London at the right period, is a possible candidate (Harvey 1954, 182–3). Massingham was the first English sculptor to adopt the new realism developed by Claus Sluter in the second half of the 14th century (Hay 1995, 200). The artistic context of these statues has yet to be fully understood.

The main porch front is in the tradition of portals

developed in cathedral construction, although the Guildhall portal represents a departure from the Decorated/Flamboyant style. The church of Saint-Nicaise in Rheims (Marne, France) was an early instance of placing figure sculpture within firmly delineated architectural settings (Wilson 1990, 135). Cycles of statuary were divided up by buttresses running the height of the west front of Beverley Minster, Yorkshire (c 1380–1420). The portal was thereby cut off from its architectural surroundings with only flanking pairs of tabernacles to accompany it. Like so much in the Perpendicular style, a stereotyped arrangement was eventually hit upon; for example, the late 14th-century west portal of Canterbury Cathedral shows most of the features familiar from the Guildhall (Harvey 1978, 463–5). A robust ground table framed coats-of-arms. Above the arms, a niche with a base weathering protected the statue and its polygonal plinth from the elements; the sheltering mouldings incorporated drips to disperse rainwater. The statue plinth would have had a moulded frame and sunken panels. A foiled canopy over the niche was ornamented with imitation rib-vaulting and flanking shafts connecting base with canopy. Obsolescent portals were sometimes replaced by this arrangement. The west front of Norwich Cathedral (Fernie 1993, pls 29–32) shows how such a porch was grafted on without regard for the surrounding 12th-century detail. As an entity, the Guildhall porch is best compared to the magnificent porches seen in contemporary 'wool' churches, a particularly fine example of which can be seen at Northleach in Gloucestershire.

The main porch front was solidly constructed using highly finished fine yellow limestone, very probably Caen stone, whereas Magnesian limestone was used for the later east porch/screen (Chapter 8.3). The side walls of the porch, which were never intended to be visible, are built from coursed ragstone random rubble (Fig 345) while light Reigate stone was used for the sheltered vault. The vault webs were probably also of Reigate stone. A crane and windlass or treadwheel would have lowered large blocks like the tabernacle base courses into position. The 'setter' trimmed the rear of each element to fit it to dressings already in position. Concentrations of vertical joints were carefully avoided, no two blocks being quite alike in shape (Samuel 1989, 132). Although the 'banker' mason cut the largest possible element from each expensive block of quarried stone, he was constrained by height. It was convenient to cut discrete features, such as capitals, to occupy single courses which ran uninterruptedly across the structure. The extant porch capitals correspond to the lower half of the tabernacle plinths (Fig 190) and these disparate dressings were therefore the same level and height. The rectilinear nature of the Perpendicular style was to some extent dictated by the need to maintain such through-courses.

The master mason probably used a tracing floor to sketch a full-size design that could be transferred directly to individual blocks already 'cut to square' on the bank. The relevant part of the porch 'plan' (which altered with each course) was scribed on both sides of each block. These scribed outlines were correctly related by using common axes of symmetry, the stone

then being cut away outside these 'controls'. Templates of wood or metal were used to ensure that uniform mouldings were cut between the two faces. At least two profile gauges would have been required to cut the tabernacle base element <A1> (Chapter 8.3). When it came to putting the blocks in place, 'setting-out' lines scribed on the surfaces allowed exact alignment relative to a taut cord. These cords were presumably attached to 'control points' on the timber scaffold.

Toolmarks show how the Caen stone blocks were supplied to the lodge in their quarried state. The first rough shaping or 'scappling' was done with a hafted adze. The banker mason then cut the block on bed with a clawtool and mallet. Toolmarks show that the moulding was roughed out with a sharp 30mm chisel before a tool called the 'comb' was used to polish the surface. Kentish ragstone required much harsher treatment, being cut with punches and 'pitchers' (bladeless chisels). Drafted margins were cut with the pitcher while the punch was used at a safe distance from the arris (edge) to prevent spalling (Samuel 1999, 168). A fine, hard, yellow mortar full of coarse sand was used to set dressings. The masons ensured that blocks were level: when setting a part of a superimposed niche on one of the statue corbels, they must have noticed a discrepancy and slid an oyster shell underneath to correct the level.

The Guildhall is comparable to town halls in other north European cloth-producing cities. England's wealth had derived largely from the export of wool, and economic connections with Flanders and Brabant were of prime importance but, by the 15th century, English woollen cloth was the major export and was being shipped in large quantities to Antwerp for distribution (Barron 2004a, 101–11). The much larger Brussels town hall (Fletcher 1943, 516) was built at roughly the same time as London's Guildhall. The constraints of the London site ruled out the level of external ornament used in the Low Countries, but visiting foreign merchants would have been suitably impressed when they emerged from the Cat Street gatehouse and saw the majestic porch. In 1440 the City aldermen duly rewarded Croxtone with an official apartment located above the Basinghall Street gatehouse overlooking the Guildhall (Chapter 4.3, 'The Basinghall Street gatehouse').

The later alterations to the Guildhall

The Guildhall building remained largely unchanged in the 16th and early 17th centuries (Chapter 4.4). The documentary evidence suggests that there was a campaign of repairs and maintenance in the late 1580s but that there continued to be problems with the roof into the 17th century. From the 1570s, the east crypt of the hall began to be used as additional storage space for Blackwell Hall market and in the 17th century it became known as the Welch Hall, after the provenance of the cloth stored there (eg 1667: CLRO, CCA 12, fo 207v). In the early 17th century the upper chambers of the porch housed the Irish Court, which oversaw the City's colonial interests in Ulster, where the City (as the Honourable The Irish Society) effectively acted as Crown agents.

The Guildhall was severely damaged in the Great Fire of September 1666, but the stone shell of the building survived (Chapter 4.5). Temporary works in October and November secured the medieval hall and the main reconstruction took place between 1667 and 1672. The damaged west crypt had to be rebuilt with substantial brick vaults (Fig 139; Fig 140) and the upper hall was raised by *c* 4.0m (internally) in order to create a new clerestory that allowed much more light into the building (Fig 339, d); this addition was probably very important as more of the ground-floor windows came to be blocked up as the surrounding yards and gardens were built on. A panelled timber ceiling was built over the clerestory, hiding the roof rather than exposing it (as had been the case with the medieval roof). These works have traditionally been attributed to either Christopher Wren or the City Surveyor, Peter Mills (Bradley and Pevsner 1997, 301), but it is suggested here that the works were carried out by one of the other City Surveyors, Robert Hooke, perhaps in conjunction with Wren. Wren and Hooke certainly worked on the repaired and enlarged Guildhall porch. The assymetrical, two-bay medieval porch was changed into a more symmetrical three-bay porch by opening up the Guildhall yard to the west (Fig 245). Wren and Hooke retained the medieval ground floor of the central and eastern bays, added a hybrid Gothic-classical first floor and capped the new porch with an ornate classical pediment featuring the royal coat-of-arms flanked by two griffins representing the City (Fig 244). The completely new west bay of the porch was designed to match this scheme and the full three-bay porch can be seen in Malton's aquatint of 1783 (Fig 266). Whereas the medieval decorative scheme seems to have been based on a hierarchy that began with classical motifs, continued with the Old Testament and rose to the New Testament revelation of Christ at the top, Wren and Hooke's new porch begins with Gothic on the ground floor, continues with a transitional 'Wren Gothic' on the first floor and culminates in a Baroque statement of royal and civic authority at the top.

Further modernisation of the hall took place in the 18th century. It was decorated with French and Bavarian standards captured in 1706 by the Duke of Marlborough at the Battle of Ramillies (Strype 1720, ii, 884), the end walls were repanelled in deal (CLRO, Misc MS 117/3, 1, 6) and lottery-drawing equipment (Fig 242) was installed so that the building could host revenue-raising state lotteries (Price 1886, 225–8).

In 1768 George Dance the younger took over from his father as the City's Clerk of Works and he soon began a major redevelopment of the Guildhall precinct (Chapter 5.1). This redevelopment saw relatively few changes to the hall itself but Dance began installing a series of monumental statues in the former windows and blind bays of the ground floor. His most important addition to the hall was his new porch of 1788 (Fig 346). He completely rebuilt the facade, removing both Wren and Hooke's work and the surviving medieval elements, but retained the medieval interior of the central bay. The new facade was mainly Gothic in its conception but he added some exotic Indian elements to create a design termed 'hindoo-gothic' by some contemporaries. Dance's porch marked the beginning of a

change in the spirit of work on the Guildhall. Whereas the 17th century changes were clearly intended as modernisation, this was the beginning of restoration. By the second half of the 19th century, medieval Gothic was firmly back in fashion and the restorers had clearly won the architectural argument. The City Architect, Horace Jones, attempted to return the hall to a more 'authentic' medieval state in the 1860s by lowering and 'Gothicising' the 17th-century clerestory, building a hammerbeam roof and adding medieval-style decoration to the external elements (Fig 339, e).

The Guildhall managed to survive the second 'Great Fire' that devastated the City of London on the night of 29/30 December 1940, although the German incendiary bombs destroyed its roof, leaving the building, once again, as a burnt-out stone shell. A temporary steel roof was erected and this had to last until 1953 when Giles Gilbert Scott began his restoration (Chapter 5.2). Scott's most dramatic decision was to support the new roof using transverse stone arches (Fig 339, f), almost certainly a more accurate restoration than Horace Jones's hammerbeam roof (though something of a compromise since he founded the new 'medieval' roof on the 17th-century clerestory, which he had to raise slightly). The Guildhall we see today thus reflects the efforts of many generations of architects, particularly Croxtone, Dance and Scott, but including elements of Horace Jones's 19th-century work and the unknown 14th-century architect whose west crypt still survives. Wren and Hooke's work in the 17th century is curiously invisible today (though their clerestory survives in an altered form), as are any traces of the 12th-century Guildhall (which may, however, survive in the core of the west crypt).

The Guildhall chapel and College

The 14th-century chapel and College

The evidence for the construction of the first Guildhall chapel is discussed in Chapter 4.1. The new chapel was probably the first component of an expanded Guildhall precinct and most likely formed the initial focus for this redevelopment, which was begun, it is suggested, in 1298 after Edward I handed back direct control of London to the City authorities. The construction project probably continued in the first decade of the 14th century, perhaps achieving partial completion at this time. However, documentary evidence would suggest that the building campaign restarted at the end of 1326 when another temporary period of royal control of the City ended with the accession of Edward III. The City, with the aid of the London Society of the Puy, could afford some important craftsmen including the king's master mason, Thomas of Canterbury (responsible for St Stephen's Chapel, Westminster), and the king's chief carpenter, William Hurley (who had collaborated on the new octagon lantern at Ely, in addition to his work at St Stephen's). According to the archaeological dating evidence, the chapel does not seem to have been finished until *c* 1350.

The archaeological excavations of the 1980s and 90s revealed the five bays of what is interpreted here as the south aisle of the chapel. The layout of the rest of the chapel is more a matter of inspired guesswork, but this is helped by some limited archaeological observations to the north where some pier foundations and an external buttress were exposed. The pier foundations fix the line of the arcade separating the south aisle and the nave of the chapel, and the external buttress probably defines the line of the northern arcade of the building (Fig 138). The plan of the building would therefore seem to take the form of a basilica, with a nave and two aisles of equal length, following the 14th-century fashion of Friars' churches such as Greyfriars, a short distance to the west in Newgate Street (Webb 1956, 171–2). The plan of the chapel shows that it was built as part of a planned redevelopment with the enlarged Guildhall, a programme lasting half a century. Though the buildings are offset, they were both built to the same module, with a bay width of 4.8m (15ft 9in, measured centre to centre) or 4.2m (13ft 8in, measured between the responds of the Guildhall). The chapel is illustrated in the reconstruction painting (Fig 341) with a basilican plan and with a superstructure based on Holy Trinity, Hull, another church built in the early 14th century following a 'refoundation' by Edward I (Alexander and Binski 1987, 228). The king's mason, Walter of Hereford, worked on both Holy Trinity, Hull (c 1295–1300) and Greyfriars (1306) (Harvey 1984, 126–7), and it is conceivable that he also had a role in the design and initial works on the Guildhall chapel. The layout of the interior of the Guildhall chapel could have been nearly as broad and well lit as Holy Trinity, with a relatively wide nave lit by both end windows and a clerestory. Some of the aisles of the Guildhall chapel could have functioned as separate chapels; three chantry chapels were dedicated in 1353 and there were five chantries later that century (Price 1886, 112; Cook 1947, 185). Archaeological evidence fills out a few details of the appearance of the interior of the building. The floor was almost certainly paved with floor tiles of the 'Westminster' type (named after their use in parts of Westminster Abbey), using a number of decorated designs, perhaps arranged in alternating straight or zigzag lines. Tiny fragments of window glass and some traces of dry paint pigment (the latter still adhering to their oyster-shell palettes) hint at a colourful decorative scheme using blue, green and yellow, with some red outlines painted on the glass. One of the most interesting archaeological discoveries consists of two statue fragments which hint at the quality of work that was carried out under Thomas of Canterbury's supervision. The two fragments seem to be from the lowest part of a life-size statue of a female saint, and the absence of paint might suggest that it once adorned the outside of the chapel (Fig 146). This might be all that remains of a statue of the Virgin or of Mary Magdalen (to whom the chapel was jointly dedicated), once occupying a prominent position on the west front.

The grand civic chapel, or at least this first incarnation, only lasted a century, for in 1411 it fell victim to an even more prestigious civic development scheme. The nave and north aisle were demolished that year (or soon after) but the arcade separating the south aisle from the nave must have been 'boarded up' with a wall so that the south aisle could be retained as a temporary chapel, an arrangement which was to last until c 1440 (Chapter 4.3). Not surprisingly, this temporary chapel was described in 1430 as 'small and ruinous' (Cal Pat R 1429–36, 57–8), a rather sad end to this once grand building on which so much time and money had been spent.

In the second half of the 14th century the chapel became part of a chantry college, known as the Guildhall College (Chapter 4.2). It lay within the civic precinct and was closely connected with the City, who appointed its warden, but independently managed its portfolio of property bequests. The College may not have been planned as part of the 1298 development scheme, since the accommodation building seems to have been inserted rather awkwardly as something of a topographic 'afterthought' on the south side of the chapel. Furthermore, the College clearly had a more formal religious structure than the pious but essentially secular confraternity of the London Puy who helped found the chapel at the end of the 13th century. Chantry chapels began in England in the 13th century as spaces within existing cathedrals and (later) churches where dedicated masses could be said for the souls of the dead (Daniell 1997, 179–80). Chantries were usually sponsored by members of the deceased person's family, guild or other fraternity, but the wealthiest donors could afford to pay for a number of priests, in other words a college, to celebrate the chantry masses (ibid, 15). The popularity of both chantries and colleges increased in the aftermath of the terrible plagues of the mid 14th century, and it is therefore tempting to see the Guildhall College as a response to the disaster that had struck London, a disaster which was commemorated by the survivors, who would also have wanted to insure themselves against future plagues. The new College was founded in 1353 by the mayor, Adam Fraunceys, and two other wealthy citizens, Peter Fanelore and Henry Frowyk (Cal Pat R 1350–4, 478; Price 1886, 112–18; O'Connor 1993, 52–5, 70). Mayor Fraunceys seems to have started something of a mayoral fashion with the establishment of the Guildhall College, for in 1381 William Walworth founded a college at St Michael Crooked Lane (perhaps in a rush of particular piety, having just defended the king by slaying Wat Tyler in the Peasants' Revolt) and in 1410 Richard Whittington established a college at St Michael Royal (Cobb 1989, 24). The College building at the Guildhall was literally attached to the chapel on its south side with at least one, and perhaps two, direct entrances leading into the chapel (Fig 347). The deep foundations suggest that it was at least a two-storey building, and this would have been the 'accommodation block' for the chantry priests, with its own latrine in the north-east corner.

The College became, in effect, a separate precinct within the larger Guildhall precinct, with a chapel, house and separate gatehouse on Basinghall Street to the east. The space between the accommodation building and the gatehouse was probably used as a garden, and the old 'chamber' on the south side (formerly private property but part of the Guildhall precinct since the 1280s) may also have formed part of the College precinct. Most of the surviving information about the Guildhall

Fig 341 Artist's reconstruction of the Guildhall precinct in the mid 14th century (Judith Dobie)

Fig 342 *Artist's reconstruction of the Guildhall precinct in the late 15th century (Judith Dobie)*

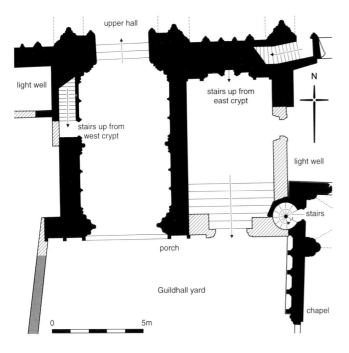

Fig 343 *Detailed plan showing the west and east bays of the 15th-century Guildhall porch (scale 1:200)*

College concerns its state in the late 15th and early 16th centuries, but by the time of the redevelopment of the College precinct in the first half of the 15th century, the institution had a warden and several priests who celebrated the various chantry masses in the chapel, and who managed the various property bequests that funded these masses (Barron 1974, 23–4, n67). The relationship between the Guildhall College and the City became even closer in the early 15th century when Mayor John Wodecock instituted a formal civic mass which immediately preceded the election of the new mayor; this first mayoral mass

of 1406 inspired the re-election of London's most famous mayor, Richard Whittington (Barron 2002, 88–9). The College and its chantry priests had both private and public roles for, in addition to celebrating chantry masses for the souls of the three founders and their families, they would do the same for the souls of the mayor, his sheriffs, the royal family and the Bishop of London (Price 1886, 113). The priests would also enhance the religious life of the Guildhall by increasing both the quantity and quality of the religious services in the chapel.

The 15th-century Guildhall chapel

Mark Samuel

A new Guildhall chapel was built as an important part of the enhanced Guildhall precinct of the 15th century. The remaining south aisle of the old chapel, which had lasted nearly thirty years as a temporary civic chapel, was finally demolished in *c* 1440 and work began on its replacement, after a financial 'kick-start' was provided by the bequest of 100 marks by Alderman John Wells (CLRO, JCCC 3, fo 24v). The building project suffered a few setbacks: the master mason of the Guildhall building, John Croxtone, began work on the chapel but was called away to work on the City's new development at Leadenhall in 1442; and his replacement, William Cliff, did not resume work on the chapel until 1444 (Cal LB K, 276; CLRO, JCCC 4, fos 14v, 16). The chapel project was complicated by the fact that an earlier benefactor, the former mayor Henry Barton, had placed an 'incentive clause' in his will, to the effect that his donation of church furniture would be annulled if the building was not finished within ten years of his death (Barron 1974, 38). The rather premature dedication of the chapel in 1444, eight years after Barton's death but before completion of the roof, was clearly designed to allow the provisions of the will to

Fig 344 *John Carter's drawing of the Guildhall porch in 1788, showing the two medieval porches after adaptation by Christopher Wren and Robert Hooke in 1672 Guildhall Library, City of London COLLAGE 3530)*

Fig 345 Photograph taken in 1968 looking south-east at the west wall of the Guildhall porch, showing the 15th-century masonry founded on the remains of the 14th-century porch (8ft (2.4m) scale) (GM145 1790.50)

Fig 346 View looking north-east, showing George Dance the younger's Guildhall porch of 1788, photographed during the reconstruction campaign of the late 1960s (GM145 1778.50)

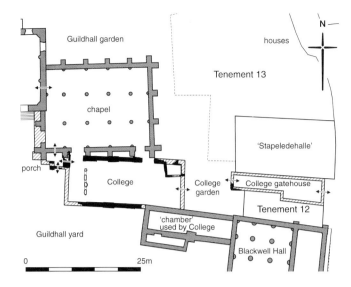

Fig 347 Simplified plan of the 14th-century College precinct within the larger Guildhall precinct (scale 1:800)

come into effect. These political manoeuverings, stalled initiatives and delays were recorded in minute detail in the City's official records, giving us a vivid impression of the complexities of the 15th-century civic administration (ibid, 35–9). The building itself no longer survives but, fortunately for us, it remained standing until the early 19th century when a series of important architectural drawings were made by John Buckler and Robert Schnebbelie (eg Fig 193). The foundations of the building were later mapped and recorded in the archaeological work of the 1980s (site A). These combined records allow a confident understanding of the chapel superstructure, the only real subject of conjecture being the roof. The construction process and the evidence for the appearance of the chapel are described and illustrated in greater detail in Chapter 4.3, and the methodology of its reconstruction and the rediscovery of its fabric are described in Chapter 8.3.

The new chapel was actually slightly smaller than its predecessor, though its overall length was greater, given its projecting chancel end. The nave and two aisles were lit by two impressive end windows, tall clerestory windows and the shorter windows of the aisles. The 'three persons in Trinity' which so appalled a visiting commission of Protestant ministers in 1643 (Barron 1974, n185) may have been depicted in the east window. According to the same source, the other stained glass showed 'Christ and the Virgin Mary in several forms, the prophets, apostles, pretended saints, popes, cardinals, monks, friars, nuns and such like' (CLRO, Repertory 56, fo 161). The building had wooden stalls, and the most important stalls may have been marked by painted portraits of the mayor and aldermen (a manuscript with the 25 portraits may be a design for these images: Payne 2003). The decorative scheme of the great east window alluded to John Wells, the building's most important donor, incorporating punning references to his name with hands projecting from wells bearing legends such as 'mercy' (Stow 1603, i, 274).

In addition to the pun on his name, the images may have reminded the 15th-century worshippers of another of his funded projects, the reconstruction of the water conduit at Cheapside, which featured images of wells embraced by angels (Barron 2004a, 257). The chancel of the new Guildhall chapel was therefore a prominent mausoleum for this important former mayor: Stow records how Wells was buried on the south side of the chancel above the vestry door and below a window (Stow 1603, i, 274), presumably in an alcove (Fig 198). The floor of the chancel was decorated with chequerboard marble altar paving (Nichols 1819, 62). The west front of the building was the most visible facade, and William Cliff employed the same style for it that Croxtone had used for the Guildhall and its adjacent porch. The facade was asymmetrical (as the north aisle was hidden behind the Guildhall porch) and was dominated by the seven-light window, probably flanked (? like the 14th-century chapel) by statues of the Virgin Mary and Mary Magdalen (Fig 197). A reconstruction drawing illustrates the westernmost bay of the chapel at clerestory level, showing the plan of the west window, the statue canopies, the clerestory windows and the aisle roofs (Fig 348). At ground level there were panels of blind tracery, of a similar type to the panels of the interior of the Guildhall, on either side of the main doorway. The conjectured reconstruction of the 15th-century chapel uses a hammerbeam roof form (Fig 199), although there is no positive evidence for this as the original roof was destroyed in the Great Fire of 1666, long before the detailed drawings of Buckler and Schnebbelie. The timbers of such a hammerbeam roof would have played an important role in enlivening the otherwise sober interior of the chapel. The roof was leaded (Barron 1974, n206), a fact which could suggest a lower-pitched roof than the one that has been reconstructed here. The copperplate map of *c* 1559 seems to illustrate the chapel with a battlemented parapet, and this may well have been a feature common to the Guildhall, chapel, library and perhaps some of the other precinct buildings.

The roofs were all reached by a spiral stair tower in the north-west angle of the chapel, which would have been removed during the redevelopment of the Guildhall porch following the local fire of 1776. The tower may well have doubled as the belfry, for bells are recorded (Barron 1974, n206) and the structure may have had a spire, perhaps visible in Hollar's distant view (Fig 189). A rood loft or pulpitum (ibid, n189) would have allowed communication between the north and south aisle roofs (reconstructed in the research archive: Samuel 2003). The vestry, perhaps a half-timbered building, probably fitted into the re-entrant between the south aisle and the chancel, but is otherwise unknown.

The execution of an entire new chapel in a single style and design was very much the exception in the City, where alteration of earlier fabric was the norm. It was entirely typical of the severe 'London Perpendicular' style favoured in the 15th-century City. Windows, glazing and, probably, the roof timbers and carved stalls formed the focus of attention, with the arcades no more than a backdrop. Wall faces were of plain Kentish ragstone rubble (minimising the need for expensive dressed stone by employing poured cement-like mortar) and the finished structure was probably rendered over and painted in imitation of stone. The window mouldings were of a standard form that stayed unchanged from the late 14th to the early 16th centuries. The chapel can be compared to the vanished Leadenhall chapel, one of Croxtone's final works in a 30-year career. This small single-cell chapel employed three-light windows, which appear

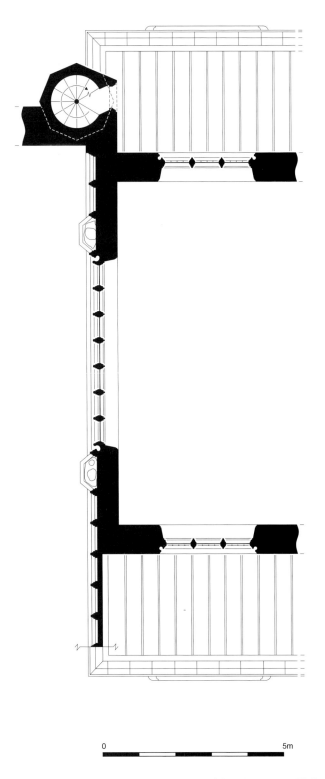

0   5m

again in the aisles of the Guildhall chapel, and a five-light east window (Samuel 1989, fig 11). At Leadenhall, the tracery is restricted to a row of uniform cinquefoil heads under the window arch. This type of window was to become the favoured type in London's parish churches, and surviving examples can be seen at St Olave, Hart Street. The five-light west and seven-light east windows were of what Harvey describes as a 'supermullioned gridiron with strong verticals' (Harvey 1978, fig 9), employing latticed transoms to create a filigree effect in which individual elements were barely visible (Fig 349). These are paralleled by the windows of St John Clerkenwell, the church of the Knights Hospitaller (the windows are restored but closely follow the originals). Harvey describes this as a relatively uncommon type of window, generally used in Suffolk, Oxfordshire and Gloucestershire (ibid, 72, map vi). The Guildhall chapel windows also incorporate a supertransom over the enlarged central light. The clerestory windows are a typical Late Perpendicular form, one of the most usual ways of providing tracery in a three-light opening: the supermullioned tracery with a split Y had an oculus split by a supermullion and there may have been an eyelet at the head (ibid, 70, fig 9). Identical and contemporary windows were employed at Farleigh Hungerford, Somerset, in 1443 (ibid, fig 12), but it would be rash to make much of this stylistic link. The west entrance was likewise typical, comparing with many surviving entrances where an outer rectilinear frame contains an arched opening flanked by several orders of pillar, one example being at Merton College, Oxford (Fletcher 1943, 445).

Harvey highlighted the 'heavily panelled' and 'rather pedestrian style' of the Guildhall chapel. He considered a mutual friend of Croxtone and Yevele, Walter Walton, important in determining the artistic 'success' of Guildhall (Harvey 1978, 154). Croxtone can not be blamed for a plain building: the adoption of a common style of Perpendicular had much to recommend it in terms of avoiding trouble and getting things done fast. The notion of a 'successful' or bravura individual performance was foreign to medieval thinking and it is almost impossible to distinguish one mason's work from another (Coldstream 1994, 169). Just because it is known that a particular mason was in charge, it does not mean that he imposed his ideals as a modern architect would (ibid, 165). A trusted confederate could be left to execute large areas of the building independently, and if the work fitted the general scheme, performed its role and came in under budget, the head mason was content.

An example of such deputising is well illustrated in the case of the Guildhall chapel. In 1442 William Cliff, who had previously been concerned with the City's new aqueduct (Barron 1974, 36), was the new mason in charge, and the Common councillor Thomas Knolles, who was commemorated in the building's foundation ceremony (Chapter 4.3, 'The chapel') continued to supervise the project on behalf of the client. A *magister* William Clyffe ran a workshop of carvers at Canterbury in 1450 (Harvey 1984, 62) and he may have been a Kent man (perhaps from St Margaret-at-Cliffe or Cliff near Rochester). Cliff was apparently given a free hand in finishing

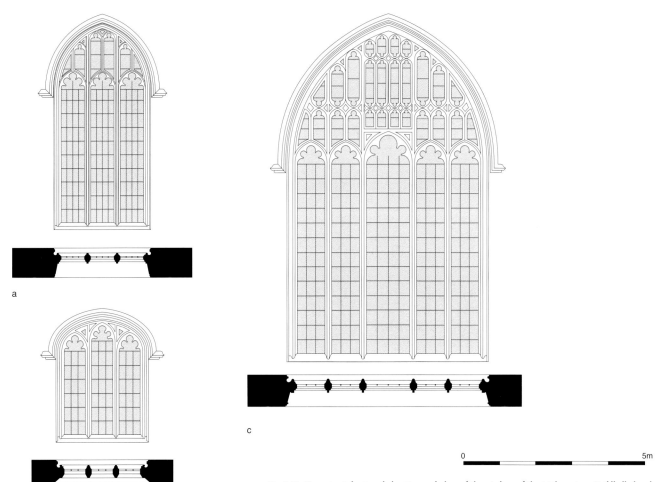

Fig 349 Reconstructed external elevations and plans of the windows of the 15th-century Guildhall chapel:
a – a clerestory window; b – an aisle window; c – the east window (scale 1:100)

the chapel by the aged Croxtone who was taken up with his swansong, the great garner and seld at Leadenhall. However, in 1446, four years after he left the chapel project to work at Leadenhall, Croxtone petitioned the City to double his wages and reimburse him for paying his workmen out of his own pocket (Baker 1970, 183). He had clearly remained involved in the chapel project, both in its overall supervision and in particular design aspects: he had been 'in attendaunce daily upon your werkes by vj yere and more about the fundamentez and reisyng of yo[r] chapelle at Guyldehalle and purveyng for the ourdenaunce and conseille of the mooldes thereof…' (Harvey 1984, 76). Croxtone's petition defines his role with exceptional clarity, by medieval standards. He certainly designed the moulds and must have determined the plan and elevations in detail prior to building the foundations and walls. Croxtone and Cliff may not have designed a masterpiece but the Guildhall chapel can be seen as a functional response to an underfunded brief, a project which clearly dragged on longer than intended (and which would have taken even longer if one of its main benefactors had not designed a will that gave an incentive for its completion).

The present study revealed some interesting details about the construction process. Croxtone, having demolished most of the superstructure of the (relatively new) 14th-century College house, decided to reuse its foundations (and lower courses) as the foundation for the nave of the new chapel. Parts of the reused foundations were in fact rebuilt, using below-ground arched 'flying buttresses'. The decision to make the fullest use of the existing foundations dictated much of the design of the new chapel. The length of the nave and chancel was therefore fixed and only the new aisles to the south and north required entirely new arched foundations, spaced to create an aisle width of half a perch (2.51m). The new foundation piers were up to 4.5m deep and rested on natural sands. The similar level of the foundation arches which linked the deep piers might suggest that some form of sighting level was used. Oddly, Croxtone seems to have decided to make the nave exactly two perches (10.02m) wide, even though this meant that the arcade piers did not sit squarely on the reused walls. The arcade piers were therefore placed on solid pads of Purbeck marble, which slightly 'overhung' the reused foundations. Like the Leadenhall garner (Samuel 1989, 142–3) the chapel was in essence a 'concrete' structure, and the wall facings and the dressed mouldings performed no structural role once the mortar had set. Purbeck marble was probably used for the piers, Reigate stone for the arcade arches and internal details, while Caen stone or Magnesian limestone was used for external mouldings and the west front facing. The walls were otherwise faced with coursed Kentish ragstone rubble with a core of mixed rubblestone and smashed chalk.

The 15th-century Guildhall College

As the rebuilding of the Guildhall had necessitated resiting the chapel, the new chapel in turn required a reorganisation of the College precinct since the chapel was built over the demolished College house (Chapter 4.3). The new accommodation house was situated less than 10m to the east of the chapel on Basinghall Street and was probably simply an enlargement of the 14th-century College gatehouse (Fig 350). There is no archaeological evidence of this new building but later documentary evidence shows that the College building was converted, after its dissolution in 1548, into two separate houses whose foundations, very fortunately, were surveyed in 1667. The College lost much of its garden space to the new chapel and house, but probably retained a small garden between the house and the chapel. The long redevelopment of the Guildhall, the chapel and the other buildings must have severely disrupted the religious life of the College in the first half of the 15th century.

Fortunately, a committed and highly educated civic official, John Carpenter, seems to have taken over Richard Whittington's role as the prime mover in the redevelopment of the Guildhall precinct and, in particular, of the College precinct. Carpenter was the City's Common Clerk between 1417 and 1438 (Barron 2004a, 364) and also one of Whittington's executors. He was connected with several aspects of the new College: he may have had a role in the design of the Guildhall chapel and porch (Barron 2004b, 119–22), the site of the new College accommodation block was granted by the City to him and the other Whittington executors (Cal LB K, 53), and he made bequests to fund a scholarship for four choristers (Barron 2002, 89; Cal Plea & Mem R 6, xix–xxi, 129–30). In particular, he was associated with the new library which he funded (in conjunction with Whittington's other executors and the executors of another mercer, William Bury) using a part of Whittington's wealth. Both Carpenter and Whittington had been members of what Anne Sutton has termed a 'circle of pious book-lovers', a group of wealthy mercers and others with common cultural interests (Sutton 2005, 167–8). Later, Carpenter bequeathed much of his own book collection to the library (Cal Plea & Mem R 6, ix–xiii; Brewer 1865, 143–4; Smith 1952; 1956; Bateman 2003). The library was in part a 'public' library (though it seems more likely that it was primarily used by the College priests, as well as being managed by the College) and it was one of an increasing number of libraries attached to monastic and secular religious establishments; there were perhaps as many as 15 such libraries in London in the 15th century (Barron 1996, 239–40). The library building was erected between 1423 and 1425 and, thanks to Stow, we know that it was built of stone with a slate roof, and that it had three chambers on the lower floor with the large main chamber above containing desks and chained books (Stow 1603, i, 274–5). The limited archaeological evidence for this building suggests that the main entrance (also described by Stow) was on the east side, facing the collegiate rather than the public part of the Guildhall precinct, since at the west end there was a large

latrine. The library is illustrated in the reconstruction painting (Fig 342) as a narrow two-storey hall, with the windows of the upper floor shown as illustrated in the copperplate map view of c 1559 (Fig 201) and with the east end based on the contemporary South Wraxhall Manor of c 1435 (Wood 1965, 64, pl X). Stow describes how the arms of Richard Whittington and the letters 'WB' for William Bury, the library's benefactors, were displayed above the doorway (Stow 1603, i, 274–5; CLRO, Repertory 12(1), fo 210v).

John Carpenter was also involved in another aspect of the College, the choir school. He left money in his will to support four boys, known as 'Carpenter's children', who would assist the priests in singing the masses in the chapel, and his will goes into some considerable detail as to their intended future welfare (Barron 2002, 89–90). They too were presumably housed and educated in the College house on Basinghall Street: 'such boys shall be boarders and shall eat, drink and live within the college of the said chapel, or in another place nearby' (Cal Plea & Mem R 6, xix–xxi, 129–30). The Guildhall College choir school was one of a number of 'song schools' attached to religious institutions in the 15th century (there was another newly founded song school at Leadenhall) and the four choristers would have been taught to write in English and Latin in addition to their music classes (Barron 1996, 224–5).

The College accounts show that the chapel, library and choir school were linked and constituted a separately administered entity within the Guildhall precinct (Cal Plea & Mem R 6, x). By the early 16th century, the College was a thriving institution with a particular strength in music, for, in addition to the warden and priests, there were the four choirboys, their tutor, two adult choristers and an organist/choirmaster (Barron 2002, 89–90). The enhanced importance of the Guildhall College may reflect the fact that the City's rituals were becoming increasingly religious in character; this trend may have begun with the new 'solemn mass' of 1406 which preceded the election of Richard Whittington as mayor, a

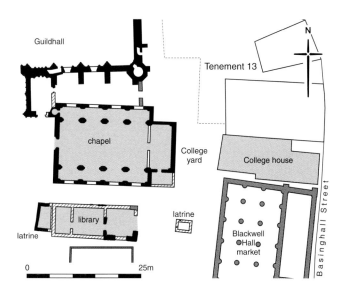

Fig 350 Simplified plan of the 15th-century Guildhall College within the larger Guildhall precinct (scale 1:800)

tradition which continued with every subsequent mayoral election (Barron 2002, 88–90).

The dissolution of the Guildhall College and the post-Reformation use of the chapel

By the late 1530s, the effects of the English Reformation – changes to the rites of the Mass, a different style of preaching and perhaps a vernacular Bible – would have begun to be felt in the Guildhall College and its chapel (Chapter 4.3). There may well have been physical effects on the fabric of the chapel in the 1540s, perhaps the whiting over of some painted images. In 1548, a decade after the Dissolution of the Monasteries, the Chantries Act of Edward VI brought about the confiscation of all the College property (both the precinct buildings and its endowed properties elswhere) and the majority of the fixtures (Barron 1974, 40–1). The library books do not seem to have been included in this official confiscation but William Cecil, secretary to Lord Protector Somerset, 'borrowed' them with the assent of the Court of Aldermen and they were never returned (CLRO, Repertory 12(1), fos 40v–41; Stow 1603, i, 275). To its credit, the City managed by 1549 to negotiate the repurchase of the chapel, the collegiate house and the library, though without the chapel's bells, plate and ornaments (Barron 1974, 41). In a businesslike manner, the City authorities pondered the best use of the former College buildings, perhaps in the light of the £456 13s 4d they had had to spend on its reacquisition (ibid). The library was converted into extra warehousing space for the highly profitable Blackwell Hall market (CLRO, Repertory 12(1), fos 164v, 207v) and the collegiate house on Basinghall Street was at least partially rebuilt as two properties, a rented house on the street frontage (providing a useful rental income of £10) and a house providing official accommodation for the hallkeeper (ie of the Guildhall, not Blackwell Hall market) on the west side (Chapter 4.4).

The chapel remained a private chapel for the civic authorities and on Michaelmas Day 1549 the mayor and aldermen attended a communion mass, no doubt a more sober and less musical service than previously, in the repurchased building (Barron 1974, 41). The chapel suffered the usual attrition of the remaining solid furnishings over the coming centuries, but this is better recorded than is often the case. In 1568 the Court of Aldermen ordered the dismantling of the upper part or 'carved work' of the roodloft (CLRO, Repertory 16, fo 386v) and in 1578 its ornate substructure (the pulpitum) was also destroyed (Barron 1974, n189). The main statues of the west front (presumably of the Virgin and Mary Magdalen) were probably removed in the 1620s, to be replaced by statues of Edward VI, Elizabeth and Charles I (Fig 221), perhaps the work of Nicholas Stone (Price 1886, 149–56). Other decorative changes were carried out in the early 17th century, reflecting the plainer, but not completely austere, spirit of the new Protestant religion: the reglazing of the west window in 1608 (CLRO, Repertory 28, fo 264), the redecoration of the choir in 1612 (CLRO, Repertory 31(1), fo 102) and the purchase of a new bell in 1630–1 (CLRO,

Repertory 45, fo 444v). During the Civil War, a stricter brand of Puritan Protestantism made itself felt in London, and in 1643 a visiting commission of ministers ordered the removal of the remaining medieval windows, and of the tombs and memorials with their pious Catholic inscriptions (CLRO, Repertory 56, fo 161; quoted above, Chapter 4.4, 'The chapel'). The task seems to have been efficiently carried out since no medieval tomb fragments from the 15th-century chapel have survived.

Following the Great Fire of 1666, the civic chapel was restored in a four-year programme beginning in September 1667 (Chapter 4.5). The works included a new roof and parapet, a coved ceiling, new windows and the replastering of the fire-scarred medieval masonry. The final repair may have been the painting of the Lord's Prayer and Creed over the communion table in December 1671 (CLRO, Misc MSS 135/22, 159/16). The City continued to maintain its chapel and in 1706–7 another campaign of improvements was carried out, including new wooden panelling, carving and whitewashing (CLRO, Misc MS 117/3, pp 3, 13). William Maitland's description of London gives a good impression of the chapel in the mid 18th century, describing the windows, the new gallery at the west end (which can just be seen on an 18th-century survey (Fig 259), the tapestries on the walls, and the new altar ('inclosed with Rails and Banisters'). He also describes the special seating for the mayor and aldermen including, in an echo of the medieval arrangements, the mayor's seat decorated with a cartouche (Maitland 1756, ii, 885). In 1782–3 the chapel was partitioned by George Dance for use as the Court of Requests, although one room was still retained for civic services (Chapter 5.1; Stroud 1971, 116–17). It is in this largely secular state that the chapel can be seen in a number of early 19th-century views (eg Fig 248). The 15th-century chapel was finally demolished in 1822, to make way for a new Courts of Law building, and the parish church of St Lawrence Jewry took on the role of civic chapel.

Burial in the Guildhall chapel

The interior of the Guildhall chapel was occasionally used for burials from soon after its construction in the late 13th century until about sixty years before its demolition in 1822. The chapel was always a private chapel of the Guildhall precinct, lying within the parish of St Michael Bassishaw. The majority of the evidence for burials in the Guildhall chapel is documentary, although a small assemblage of (reinterred) 18th-century burials was archaeologically excavated in 1987. For the medieval period, the main source is Stow's *Survey of London* (1603), supplemented by Weever's *Ancient funerall monuments* (1631). For the post-medieval period Hatton's *New view of London* (1708), Strype's 1720 updated edition of Stow, and Maitland's *History and survey of London* (1756) have been consulted. It is fortunate that before the chapel's demolition in 1822, a conscientious person (perhaps J B Nichols, the author of the 1819 history of the Guildhall) compiled a list of the surviving monuments (BL, MS 2879, transcribed by Lloyd 1978). According to Lloyd (ibid) there may once have been a burial register for the Guildhall chapel, kept at St Lawrence Jewry, but this had been lost by the late 19th century. The burial registers of the City parishes for which there is an *index locorum* (in the Harleian Society editions) have therefore been checked for references to burial in the Guildhall chapel. The evidence is summarised in CD Table 30.

In the 14th century at least three individuals were buried in the first Guildhall chapel (Chapter 4.1). Two of the burials may have been marked by grave slabs with square crosses (RCHME 1929, 67; Guildhall Museum 1908, 260) and one man, Godfrey the trumpeter, was buried in a Purbeck marble coffin decorated with two trumpets in relief and bearing a rhyming inscription in Norman French (Fig 143; Badham and Norris 1999, 134–5). It seems likely that Godfrey was connected with the Society of Puy, the group of merchants who were linked to the foundation of the chapel. The society was a typical medieval confraternity or 'mystery' (though the London Puy seems to have had a particularly wealthy and influential membership: Sutton 1992), whose members could practise piety, charitable works and the cultivation of music and poetry. Was Godfrey perhaps an important musical member of the society? No other burials were found in the south aisle of the chapel, but other early burials could have been transferred to the new chapel when it was built in the 15th century. Peter Fanelore, one of the three founders of the Guildhall College in the second half of the 14th century, had his own chantry in the chapel and so was probably buried here (*Cal Pat R* 1350–4, 478; Price 1886, 112; Steer in prep).

John Wells, a former mayor and a great benefactor of the rebuilt chapel, was buried in a wall tomb on the south side of the chancel of the newly rebuilt chapel in 1442 or soon after. However, in spite of this precedent only one other mayor, Thomas Knesworth in 1515, seems to have chosen to be buried here, the others preferring instead to be buried in their home parishes. The chapel does, however, seem to have been used as the main burial place of the College wardens and the other priests who celebrated chantry masses in the chapel and looked after the library; the wardens John Clipstone, Thomas Fraunces and Edmond Alison were all buried here, along with at least four other priests, and Stow's description of the burial monuments seems to imply that there were originally more than these seven (Stow 1603, i, 274).

Following the dissolution of the Guildhall College in 1548, the use of the chapel as a private burial ground virtually ceased now that there were no longer any collegiate priests to be buried there. In fact, only four burials seem to have taken place in the chapel in the century following the dissolution, though it can be argued that the tradition of civic burial in the chapel just survived the Reformation since in 1576 the former mayor John Langley was buried in a vault under Wells's tomb in the chancel. It seems quite likely that this tradition of burying important civic leaders in the chapel would have ended, had it not been for the Fire of 1666 and the consequent interruption to parish life as local churches were rebuilt. From 1669 to 1763, 41 people were buried in the chapel, although this is of

course a tiny number compared to the neighbouring parish churches (Chapter 4.5). Several of the individuals had held honorary or paid civic office, or were their relatives. For example, William Avery was a Town Clerk, and he and two of his children were buried here. Catherine Lightfoot died in 1674 and later both her husband William (an attorney at the Mayor's Court) and their son John were also buried in the chapel. Many members of the Man family were buried here, including William Man, the mayor's swordbearer for much of the 17th century, and Miles Man, the Town Clerk and perhaps William's son. Unusually, there was little archaeological evidence for family vaults (though these could have been entirely removed with the demolition of the chapel in 1822). The former mayor William Stewart was buried in a vault in 1723 and his heir and nephew also wanted to be buried there (CLRO, Repertory 160, p 293), but he did not die soon enough to join his uncle in the vault; there were concerns about the structural soundness of the old chapel (eg CLRO, JCLC 65, fo 184) and burials seem to have ceased in 1763.

The 1815 Act of Parliament that licensed the demolition of the chapel had stated that the floor and burials were not to be disturbed (Price 1886, 136). However, this early example of an archaeological 'planning condition' specifying preservation *in situ* was promptly ignored. The 1822 building contract for the works allowed the demolition of the chapel to a depth of 2ft below floor level (CLRO, CLD 334, no. 23). A pencil annotation in the Guildhall Library copy of Nichols's 1819 history of the Guildhall describes the effects of the demolition and ground reduction:

> The remains of mortality were collected into and formed a large tumulus of the etcetera's of Lord Mayors, Remembrancers, Town Clerks and [were] bricked up under the new buildings. The monuments were removed into St Lawrence's Church Jewry. (c 1822 pencil annotation on p 62)

Later, in 1889, the remaining archaeological deposits of the chapel (preserved beneath the 1822 Courts of Law building: CLRO, SCLB 290) were lowered again by approximately 1.5m in order to create a proper cellar as storage space for the new Art Gallery (ibid, 292: note pencil annotations). The 'preserved remains' of the chapel had thus been destroyed to a level at least 2.0m below the orginal medieval floor level by the time the chapel was archaeologically excavated in 1987 (site B). Large quantities of disarticulated human bone were recovered in the 1987 excavations (these remains have since been reburied in the East London Cemetery in East Ham) and six 18th-century coffins were also discovered (Chapter 4.5). These had presumably been reinterred under the Courts of Law/Art Gallery by either the 1822 or the 1889 contractors, perhaps in an attempt to avoid the trouble of moving them and reburying them elsewhere. The contractors might have perforated the formerly sealed coffins by accident and the resulting smell and leaking decomposition fluids would have encouraged them to rebury the coffins (against the south wall of the former nave) in some haste. The only positively identified individual among these six reinterments was Mary Warner, wife of Reverend John Warner, who was originally buried on 2 May 1753 (Hughes Clarke 1944, 127). Sadly, she had died during or shortly before childbirth, and she and her unborn baby were buried in a composite lead and timber coffin with a coffin plate giving her name. Three of the other excavated reinterments were of mature women aged approximately 26–45 who may be identifiable as Catherine Lightfoot (d 1674), Margaret Walker (d 1719) and Sarah Warner (d 1720).

The 1815 Act of Parliament also specified that the funerary monuments of the chapel were to be moved to the parish church of St Lawrence Jewry (Price 1886, 135–6). However, only two wall monuments seem to have been removed to safety by the time of the demolition, and at least twenty 17th- and 18th-century grave slabs remained in 1822 (Lloyd 1978). Most were presumably destroyed in the demolition process but two were reburied under the new Courts of Law building: the grave slab of William Lightfoot (Fig 251) was excavated in 1987 and that of John Bancroft (Fig 253) was found during the demolition of the chapel foundations in 1990 (both slabs are now in the Museum of London). Fortunately, both the wall monuments that were moved to St Lawrence Jewry (of William Stewart (Fig 249) and Catherine Lightfoot (Fig 252)) survived the severe damage to the church in the Second World War, and they have been re-erected inside the vestibule of the rebuilt church.

The evolution of the Guildhall precinct

From its earliest beginnings in c 1130, the Guildhall building was part of a larger property which is termed here the 'Guildhall precinct'. The use of the term 'precinct' might perhaps seem more appropriate for a religious institution; however, the term evokes the enclosed topography of the Guildhall and, furthermore, it was used in the medieval period to describe enclosed secular institutions such as Oxford colleges (Kurath et al 1956–99, vol P, 1193). Assuming that we have correctly interpreted its name, the *terra Gialle*, the original 12th-century precinct, was rented from St Paul's (Price 1886, 18; Davis 1925, 57). If this Guildhall land or yard lay on the south side of the hall (as it did later on), it may have included two of the houses that lay alongside the lane, the 'way leading to the Husting', and the tenants of these mid 12th-century houses (period 11 phase 2, B124 and B129; Fig 351, a), would presumably have paid rent to the Guildhall as the lessee of the land. In the second half of the 12th century, the land to the south of the Guildhall seems to have been gradually cleared of houses and a number of fast-food 'cookshops' were established alongside the lane to the Guildhall, presumably serving the aldermen, merchants and petitioners using the Guildhall and the Court of Husting. By c 1230, the cookshops had also disappeared (perhaps moving on to Cat Steet) and there appears to have been a large open area surrounding the south-east, east and north sides of the Guildhall (Chapter 3.3; Fig 351, b). The size and shape of this yard can be defined to a reasonable degree, particularly on its east side because dimensions are

recorded for the property to the south-east (Tenement 12) and for one of the properties to the north-east (Tenement 17). The property was clearly very secluded, and it was described as a yard (*curia*) in 1271–2 (CLRO, HR 4/122). The yard had virtually no street frontage apart from its entrances on Cat Street (the 'lane leading to the Husting') and Basinghall Street.

The size of the precinct increased slightly in the 1280s when the 'chamber' (B213) and part of the garden (OA128) which formerly belonged to Roger de Clifford's hall were acquired by the City (Chapter 4.1). We know that a gatehouse was added to the Cat Street entrance by 1303 (*Cal LB C*, 239) and these changes might imply that the major works on the hall and chapel (beginning c 1298) were in fact part of a grander planned scheme to redevelop the whole precinct. The addition of a gatehouse and a substantial precinct wall (surrounding the yard and gardens) would seem to mark the transition of the precinct from an open space situated at the end of a public lane to a close that could be secured and from which the public could, if necessary, be excluded (Fig 351, c). This emphasis on security may in part be explained by the turbulent events of the 1250s and 60s when the political tensions of the baronial civil war spilled out on to the streets surrounding the Guildhall (Chapter 3.3). Having passed through the two gatehouses, the visitor to the Guildhall would have entered the main yard and seen the grand new chapel at its north end. The precinct also had two, more private, garden areas. The larger garden to the north (behind the hall and chapel) may have contained an orchard and/or formally laid out trees, although the archaeological evidence for this is very uncertain. The 'little Guildhall garden' to the east included a 'fountain', which might indicate a private piped water supply like the 13th-century system at the monastic precincts of St Mary Spital (Thomas et al 1997, 43) or perhaps a simple well (two barrel-lined wells were found in the garden). At the south-east of the precinct there was an industrial zone (OA200), used for the manufacture of brass dress accessories; this area of the precinct may simply have been sublet to girdlers on a temporary basis to provide useful income during the lengthy construction process. The 14th-century civic precinct would thus have resembled a cathedral close (though rather smaller than the St Paul's precinct: Keene 2004, 19), very different from the more 'open' 14th-century town halls situated by public squares, market places or rivers, a model seen at York, Norwich or, further afield, in Germany and Flanders (Steane 2001, 205–11, 217–23). Were the mayor and aldermen of the late 13th century simply so confident of London's economic prosperity and importance that they did not need to flaunt it by purchasing a new site for an urban town hall on Cheapside? Perhaps the topographic model to which they were instead aspiring was the urban royal palace at Westminster, with Mayor Henry le Waleys seeing himself as Edward I's 'baron', ruling over London, the wealthiest 'manor' of England. This walled manor is shown on London's communal seal of the 13th century, which illustrates the city, the London martyr Thomas Becket and St Paul, while naming the 'barons of London' (ibid, 227–8; Barron 2004b, 113–15). Le Waleys and the barons of

Fig 351 Simplified phased plan of the evolving Guildhall precinct from the 12th to the 20th century (scale 1:2000)

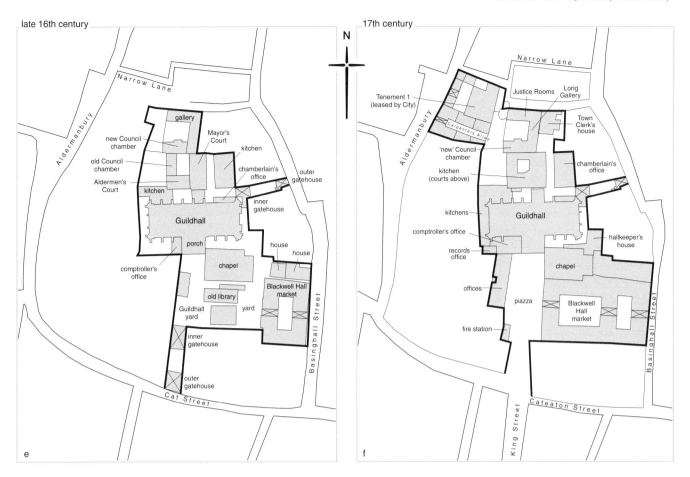

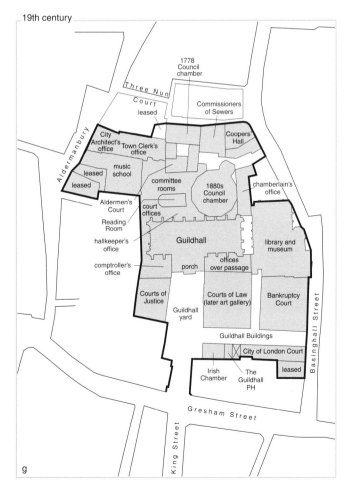

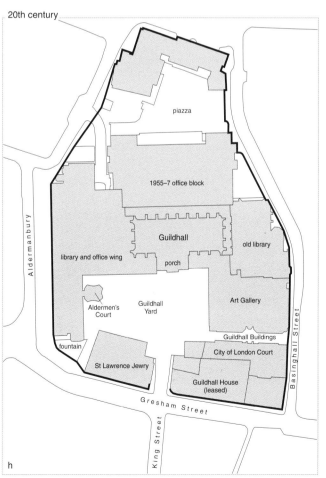

London thus created a walled precinct with both private and public elements, with the hall, chapel and yard forming a 'stage' for the private and public rituals that were an increasingly important part of civic life (Keene 2003b, 263–4).

A century after le Waleys, the aldermen of London, perhaps led by the mayors Richard Whittington and/or Thomas Knolles, seem to have initiated a redevelopment of the Guildhall precinct (Chapter 4.3). The architectural inspiration may have been to create a more dramatic 'landmark' secular building worthy of comparison with the town halls of Flanders or the Duchy of Brabant, whose merchants were among London's principal trading partners (Barron 2004a, 100–11). For example, the very elaborate Bruges Hôtel de Ville was built around the end of the 14th century (c 1376–1420: Blyth 1990, 26–8) and it would have been known to many of the London merchant aldermen. However, London was densely built up by the early 15th century and it was perhaps impractical to resite the new Guildhall in a more public location. Similarly, the constraints of the existing Guildhall site allowed little opportunity for such external display, but John Croxtone (if he was the actual designer) certainly built an impressive new hall which dominated the closed site of the precinct and whose central towers may just have been visible from busy Cheapside to the south. The intention may also have been to create a more uniform and modern precinct, with the facades of the porch and chapel (and perhaps the library as well) forming a more architecturally unified whole. This desire for architectural uniformity may have been influenced by royal precincts of the second half of the 14th century, such as at Vincennes and the Hôtel Saint-Pol in Paris (Whiteley 2005), or the new collegiate precinct at New College, Oxford (Wilson 2003, 105). The old Guildhall precinct with its large areas of open space became more differentiated in the 15th century, perhaps as a combination of planning and evolution (Fig 351, d). The new precinct had a more public area (entered from Cat Street, with the grand hall forming its symbolic heart), a separate religious precinct to the east (with the chapel, library and College house clustered around another yard) and the more private and secluded administrative area to the north (with the Mayor's Court, Aldermen's Court and Council chamber), where the actual administrative and judicial business was carried out). There was also an important fourth component, the economic zone of Blackwell Hall market on Basinghall Street, whose cloth sales provided much of the revenue to finance the other three parts.

In the second half of the 16th century, the biggest change to the Guildhall precinct was the conversion of the former religious precinct of the Guildhall College to serve as enlarged space for Blackwell Hall cloth market (Chapter 4.4). The rebuilt market, its outbuildings and its yard now occupied a substantial area, entered directly from Basinghall Street and increasingly separated (both physically and administratively) from the Guildhall precinct to the west (Fig 351, e). The public face of the Guildhall and its yard remained largely unchanged but, to the north, the more private 'local government' precinct became increasingly built up with administrative, executive and judicial

buildings to serve the developing bureaucracy. The most impressive new building was the 'Long Gallery', built in the 1620s on newly acquired land just to the south of the church of St Michael Bassishaw (Fig 351, f). This was explicitly built as a private, recreational and decorative building, 'fit and convenient for the beautifying and adorning of the Council Chamber' (CLRO, Repertory 35, fo 226v). The two new gallery wings, together with the earlier Council chamber, formed a three-sided building surrounding a garden, a Jacobean belvedere built as a 'retiring place' (CLRO, Repertory 34, fo 226v) for the mayor and aldermen. The principal part of the gallery was presumably at first-floor level, its windows facing inwards to the secluded garden. This building was no doubt influenced by Tudor galleries in aristocratic houses, for example at Bridewell Palace, a short distance to the south-west in the City (Gadd and Dyson 1981, 51–4, 58, figs 1–5). After the Great Fire the rebuilt gallery was usually called the 'Matted Gallery', presumably referring to tapestries and rugs, but in its original state it may have been decorated with timber panelling, perhaps like the 'linenfold' panelling used on the 16th-century gallery at The Vyne, Hampshire (Marks and Williamson 2003, 286, cat no. 148). The other significant change in the 16th century, and continuing into the 17th century, was the increasing emphasis on entertainments and banquets which necessitated the construction of a series of kitchen facilities. In the 15th century the Guildhall College house could have provided some limited catering facilities for civic functions but the first proper civic kitchen seems to have been initiated by Mayor John Shaa in 1501–5. The new kitchen on the north-west corner of the Guildhall (Fig 351, d) was probably part of a decision by Shaa and the aldermen no longer to rely on the halls of livery companies for banqueting facilities (Chapter 4.3; Barron 1974, 32). The first kitchen became known as the 'roasting kitchen' when a large new 'great kitchen' or 'boiling kitchen' was built on the north-east side of the hall in the second half of the 16th century (Fig 351, e; Chapter 4.4). In the second quarter of the 17th century, a brick vault was built under the main Guildhall yard (one of the few remaining free spaces in the precinct) as a storage cellar for keeping drinking vessels, jugs (large quantities of which were found abandoned in the cellar) and, one assumes, food, drink and other vessels used in the banquets. These facilities appear to mark a change of emphasis in the City's role; in the medieval period the City authorites had laid on extravagant City-wide pageants and processions to celebrate, for example, royal weddings (Barron 2004a, 18–22), but in the 16th and 17th centuries the emphasis seems to have shifted to equally grand but more localised banquets which took place within the Guildhall precinct itself. The mayor and aldermen were presumably emulating the increasingly elaborate courtly and aristocratic banquets that were developing in the 'London season' (Sheppard 1998, 131–2). One such mayoral banquet took place in 1641 in honour of Charles I, who was shortly to experience something of a change in the manner in which he was treated by the City (Price 1886, 190–1). The Guildhall, and the monumental approach to it from the south, remained of great symbolic importance in the life of the City, but the practical business of running the City and administering justice was increasingly taking place in more modern (and better-heated) buildings in the more private areas of the precinct.

The Guildhall precinct, like much of the old medieval City, was severely damaged in the Great Fire of 1666 and the process of rebuilding the civic precinct can be seen as a model for the rebuilding of the whole City. In both cases the initial plans for radical rearrangement of the ground plan seem to have quickly given way to a more pragmatic reconstruction largely following the medieval layout (Chapter 4.5). Much of the precinct, like the City as a whole, was simply rebuilt on existing foundations using, in some cases, more modern, classically-influenced brick facades that had been becoming fashionable earlier in the 17th century. The Guildhall, the chapel, the Long Gallery and the Mayor's and Aldermen's Court buildings were all rebuilt using as much of the medieval fabric as could be saved. However, because the City authorities were the owner of their precinct, they were able to alter more aspects of its topography than of the City as a whole. The biggest change was the reordering of the public face of the Guildhall – the porch and the Guildhall yard – by Christopher Wren and Robert Hooke. They added a third bay on the west side of the porch to create a symmetrical three-bay facade that blended new classical design with the surviving Gothic elements (mainly at ground-floor level) of the two medieval bays. The old medieval yard was expanded westwards (to accommodate the new third bay of the porch) and was transformed into a classical piazza by the addition of a colonnaded office building on its west side (Fig 351, f), designed, surely, in emulation of Inigo Jones's Covent Garden piazza (there is, however, no direct evidence of Wren or Hooke's involvement in the building). On the east side of the new piazza, Blackwell Hall market was greatly extended with a west wing, probably with the City Surveyor Peter Mills as its architect. On the south side of the piazza one of the City's few completely new roads, King Street, led south towards the new quay facilities on the Thames. There almost certainly was an element of grand civic 'townscape' planning to unify these various elements: the visitor walking north from Cheapside along King Street would see the new Guildhall facade – south-facing and therefore bathed in sunlight – symmetrically positioned at the centre of the perspective along the new street.

New office buildings for the Town Clerk, the hallkeeper, the chamberlain and the comptroller were added in the gaps between existing buildings or on newly acquired land to the north. An interesting component of the new piazza was Wren and Hooke's fire station (a valuable addition given recent events) which was built in the south-west corner, and was an intriguing two-storey building which incorporated a new church burial vault underneath. Although the new precinct was not the complete overhaul imagined by Wren and others in the immediate aftermath of the Great Fire, it was a more radical departure from the medieval topography than seen elsewhere in the City. Furthermore, the new precinct (particularly its modern public piazza) symbolised the transformation of the old 'black

and white' medieval City (of timber, plaster and stone) into a more classically-influenced 'red and white' town built of brick and stucco. Of course, as elsewhere in the City, the precinct retained much medieval fabric hidden away behind the new brick facades and tiled roofs.

The precinct remained largely unchanged in the late 17th and 18th centuries, until the appointment in 1768 of the energetic George Dance the younger as City Surveyor, following the retirement of his father (Chapter 5.1). Dance largely kept to the existing post-Great Fire topography of the precinct, but he built a number of important new administrative and judicial buildings including a new Guildhall porch facade, a new Council chamber (for the Court of Common Council) and a new chamberlain's office, which featured new office space for his own use (Fig 351, g). By the end of the century, Dance and the important City Lands Committee (a sub-committee of the Common Council) were considering a more radical overhaul of the precinct. The first stage of this overhaul was the replacement of the classical colonnaded building on the west side of the Guildhall yard with a sober Georgian office block in 1795. The more radical revisions came about in the 1820s when both Blackwell Hall market and the old medieval chapel were demolished, to make way for new buildings for administration and the judiciary. Wren and Hooke's great classical piazza only lasted 150 years (the old medieval Guildhall yard had lasted rather longer). The new precinct was a densely built-up local government complex, less elegant than Wren and Hooke's classical reorganisation, but more practical in its response to the ever-increasing need for office space. Further important changes to the layout of the precinct occurred in the 19th century, though their architectural form was increasingly conservative. The City Architect Horace Jones designed a new library and a new Council chamber, both using Perpendicular Gothic elements in order to echo the newly 'medievalised' old Guildhall. By the late 19th century, the precinct had acquired an important cultural role, in addition to its more practical administrative and judicial office space: there was a public library, a museum and an art gallery (Fig 351, g). Baddeley's new guidebook, first published in 1898, described these cultural buildings and the history of the Guildhall itself; in addition to its other more practical roles, the civic precinct had now become a tourist destination for the cultured visitor.

The most wide-ranging changes to the precinct since its late 13th- or early 14th-century inception came about with the redevelopment that followed the severe damage of the Second World War (Chapter 5.2). Giles Gilbert Scott and his son Richard rebuilt the precinct as a pair of town piazzas, with a more public southern square dominated by the restored medieval Guildhall and a more administrative northern square serving the principal civic office block (Fig 351, h). Interestingly, the precinct retains some functional elements of its 15th-century predecessor, including the Guildhall (now largely ceremonial), a 'private' chapel (the parish church of St Lawrence Jewry), a library (the public rather than collegiate Guildhall library), the public space of the enlarged Guildhall Yard, and the more private office space to the north.

6.8 The evolution of Blackwell Hall (*c* 1200–1396)

It has been established from the archaeological evidence that a large masonry hall was constructed on the west side of Basinghall Street *c* 1200, about half a century before the earliest documentary reference to the building in 1256 (Chapter 3.2). The early property consisted of a principal north–south building along the street frontage, with a large walled courtyard to the rear, probably containing stables and other outbuildings (Fig 352). The archaeological evidence for this building is largely confined to the foundations excavated on site A, but the excavations also produced some architectural fragments including a vaulting rib, a clustered pier and some painted stones (Fig 111; Fig 112), which suggest that the hall was an imposing two-storey building with a distinctive slate-covered roof. In the reconstruction painting (Fig 341), the early north–south wing of the hall (fronting directly on to Basinghall Street) is based on Boothby Pagnell manor house, Lincolnshire, a building of similar size and date with a vaulted ground floor and a principal first floor housing the hall and private chamber (Wood 1965, 19, pl IV). There is also archaeological evidence for a garden to the west (OA128), which the (slightly later) topographic evidence would suggest was part of the hall's property.

This hall was known as Blackwell Hall in the 14th century, after the then owner John de Bankwell, but for whom was the early hall built? It has been pointed out that the building is clearly earlier than its 14th-century name suggests (Schofield 2003a, 159–60). In 1256 it was in the ownership of John fitz Geoffrey (*Cal Close R* 1254–6, 369–70) but a later document (relating to the grant of a small house to the north in 1299) names the property as 'once of Warin' (GL, MS 7531/2, item 8). We know that the hall passed from John fitz Geoffrey to Roger de Clifford and then to de Bankwell, so Warin must have been a previous owner. In the early 17th century John Stow described, from memory, coats-of-arms carved and painted in the old Blackwell Hall as 'a Gerond [gyronny] of twelve points, gold and azure' and he believed them to be the arms of the Basing family (Stow 1603, i, 287). Kingsford, editing Stow's volumes in the early 20th century, took issue with this, correctly noting that the Basing family's coat-of-arms is 'or, five eagle displayed sable, two, two and one, a canton ermine' (ibid, ii, 337). He went on to suggest that the arms Stow describes were in fact of the Clifford family, probably depending more on their documented ownership of the hall than on their actual arms. The Clifford arms, while also azure and gold (Fig 353), do not match Stow's detailed description, which reveals his good memory and his understanding of the terminology. It seems more likely that Stow wrote Basing meaning Bassingbourn, which he also names in his discussion, referring to the village of the same name in Cambridgeshire. According to *Papworth's ordinary of British armorials*, there are two versions of the Bassingbourn coat-of-arms, which would appear to represent different members or branches of the family. A 'Gyronny of eight Or and Azure' (Fig 353) is given as belonging to Garin de Bassingburn (identified in documents of

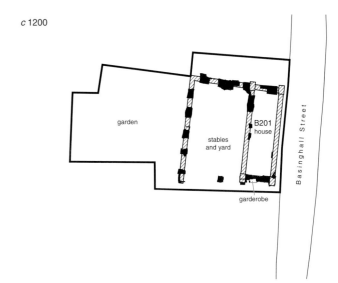

c 1200

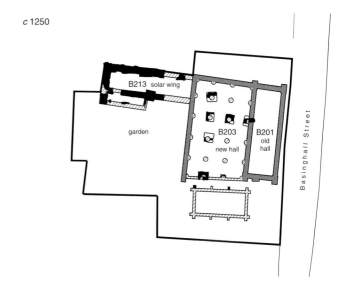

c 1250

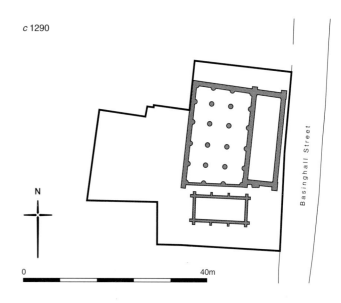

c 1290

N

0   40m

Fig 352 *Phased plan comparing Warin de Bassingbourn's hall of c 1200 with the enlarged hall of John fitz Geoffrey of c 1250, and John de Bankwell's hall of c 1290, later known as Blackwell Hall (scale 1:800)*

c 1256–66) and a 'Gyronny of twelve Or and Azure' is given as that of Warin Bassingborne (in documents of c 1262–92) (Papworth 1874, 899–901); similar arms are recorded in seals of the family from the late 13th and 14th centuries (Birch 1892, 470–1, nos 7200, 7204). Is this second 'Warin Bassingborne' to be identified with the 'Warin' named in the late 13th-century document, perhaps the son of the original founder of the hall?

Gerald Paget's account of the Bassingbourn family (BL, L.R. 301.bb.12, family no. 32) indicates that there were three men identified as 'Warine de Bassingbourn' between the late 12th and mid 13th centuries. The first Warin was sheriff of Cambridge in 1170–6 and seems to have died before 1199. His son Wymar and grandson Warin both supported the barons against King John, and the family's extensive lands in Cambridgeshire and Lincolnshire were seized in 1216 but returned to Warin the following year. He died in October 1229, with his son and heir, Warin, still a minor. The younger Warin later fought in Gascony and Wales, and was a staunch adherent of Henry III against the barons; in the 1260s he held many positions of high rank including those of the lordship of Knockainy, Co Limerick, and constable of Northampton Castle, but retained a residence at Bassingbourn. The only direct evidence of a London property of the Warins, according to Paget, is a reference to the younger Warin's widow, Isabel, who in 1287 had to sue the abbot of Sawtry concerning 'her dower in London' (ibid, citing *Cal Pat R* 15 Edw I, m9d). It seems a strong possibility, therefore, that our hall of c 1200 on Basinghall Street was built by the second Warin de Bassingbourn (or perhaps by his father Wymar or even his grandfather Warin) as his London residence. The building was

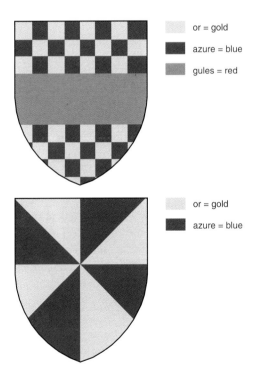

or = gold

azure = blue

gules = red

or = gold

azure = blue

Fig 353 Comparison of the coats-of-arms of the Clifford family (checky or and azure a fess gules) and the Bassingbourn family (gyronny of eight or and azure), from Glover's roll of c 1253–8 (after London 1967); the latter more closely matches Stow's description of the arms inside Blackwell Hall

quite capable of meeting the requirements of an early 13th-century baron, with a grand house on the street frontage that would stand out from others, together with secure stabling, outbuildings and a garden to the rear. The garden, with its formal arrangement revealed by the excavated 'bedding trenches', reflects the status of an important town house and its use as a domestic property. The property would also have been a convenient political and administrative base in London, close to the administrative centre of the Guildhall. If our interpretation is correct, Warin de Bassingbourn's hall of c 1200 would be one of the earliest known lay 'great houses' of London (most of which seem to have been acquired or built after 1250), serving as 'office', private hostel and more public social centre for its aristocratic owner (Barron 1995, 4–5). The superficial similarity of 'Bassishaw' (in the name of the ward and parish) and 'Bassingbourn' may simply be coincidence: Ekwall cites a 12th-century mention of the parish name and he argues for an Anglo-Saxon origin of the place-name (Ekwall 1954, 94).

By the mid 13th century the hall had become the property of John fitz Geoffrey. Fitz Geoffrey was born after 1205 and was the son of Geoffrey fitz Piers, fourth Earl of Essex (BL, L.R. 301.bb.12, family no. 220). Besides belonging to a wealthy family, a branch of the Mandevilles, John fitz Geoffrey acquired the lands of Gilbert de Lacy through the dower of his wife in 1234, and in the early 1250s he was granted lands in Ireland. He occupied prominent political offices, having been admitted to the Privy Council in 1237, becoming justiciar of Ireland from 1245, as well as being sheriff of Yorkshire. He probably purchased the hall as a useful London residence for his official duties, perhaps after 1237 and certainly by 1256. The archaeological evidence for an enlarged hall points to a date in the mid 13th century, that is, under the ownership of fitz Geoffrey, although the direct archaeological dating evidence for this is limited (Chapter 3.3, 'Tenement 12'). He retained Warin's hall on the Basinghall Street frontage and expanded it to the rear, building a large extension within the former courtyard area, and an additional solar wing (Fig 352). The main part of the new hall was a large building with a vaulted undercroft and at least one upper floor. To the west, a smaller wing is interpreted as the more private great chamber or solar, again probably of two storeys, and furnished with a large garderobe. Architectural fragments recovered from the demolition material in the garderobe pit include part of a window sill with a rebate for an iron window bar (<A26>, Fig 126) and a roof louver to allow smoke to escape (<T18>, Fig 127). In the reconstruction painting (Fig 341), the two new buildings are based in part on the (slightly later) private wing in the lower bailey of Chepstow Castle (Wood 1965, 125–6, pl XII). South of the solar wing lay the garden, now smaller than Warin's garden, and botanical samples produced evidence of cultivated fruits (figs and grapes) and wild fruits (blackberry/raspberry, elderberry, strawberry and hazelnut), some of which were presumably grown in fitz Geoffrey's garden. The final addition to fitz Geoffrey's hall was a private chapel situated to the south (Fig 352), built on the site of a former synagogue, and tentatively reconstructed as a four-bay building (Chapter 3.3, 'Tenement 12'). There is little archaeological evidence for the chapel apart from two fine buttresses of its north wall, but its location is reasonably certain given the topographical description in the document of 1256 (*Cal Close R* 1254–6, 369–70). The enlarged hall, with its public and private wings, a garden and a chapel, would have been a substantial property suitable for conducting fitz Geoffrey's affairs of state.

Fitz Geoffrey was one of the seven barons, including Simon de Montfort, who confronted Henry III over his excessive expenditure in 1258. He died that year and his eldest son John, though still a minor, took over his father's estates (BL, L.R. 301.bb.12, family no. 220). John fitz John inherited his father's allegiances and joined the barons against Henry III, commanding a division of the baronial army at the Battle of Lewes. However, he was wounded and taken prisoner at the Battle of Evesham in 1264, and all his lands were granted to Gilbert, Earl of Gloucester, and Roger de Clifford. The property that de Clifford acquired must have included the hall on Basinghall Street, which he granted to the City in 1280 (*Cal Pat R* 1272–81, 381). De Clifford was a member of one branch of the Clifford family (BL, L.R. 301.bb.12, family no. 134) and was on the royal side in the baronial wars. He held a number of important positions, including those of constable of Hereford Castle and sheriff of Gloucester, and his role in the wars earned him new titles and confiscated estates.

In the 1280s the property was transferred to John de Bankwell, in a complex series of land transactions involving the City (Chapter 4.1, 'Tenement 12'). De Bankwell was not a feudal baron like the hall's previous owners but seems to have been a wealthy and successful member of the City mercantile community, being an alderman, Common Clerk of the City and later holding royal office as seneschal of Ponthieu. He appears not to have acquired the whole property, losing the western half of the garden and the former solar wing to the City's newly expanded precinct (Fig 352). The property seems to have been specifically granted to de Bankwell as a reward for good civic service (*Cal Chart R* 1257–1300, 434; CLRO, HR 22/55–6) and this grant was hereditary, unlike the later grants of civic accommodation which only applied during the period of office, or to the widow of a deceased office-holder. After de Bankwell died in 1308 in unfortunate circumstances – crowd congestion at the coronation of Edward II led to a wall collapsing on him (*ODNB*, iii, 727) – the property remained in his family throughout most of the 14th century, and there is little evidence for any change to the hall and other buildings (Chapter 4.2, 'Tenement 12'). The City reacquired the property in 1395–6 in order to house a new cloth market, known as Blackwell Hall market (below, 6.9). The name of the hall had evolved between the late 13th century (when the de Bankwells appear in the documentary records with various alternative spellings such as *Banquell* and *Bauquell*: Chapter 4.1, 'Tenement 12') and the 14th century (when the family name is generally given as *de Bacwell* or simply *Bakwell(e)*: Chapter 4.2, 'Tenement 12'). After its acquisition by the City, the market buildings seem to have been called both *Bakwellehalle* (*Cal Pat R* 1396–9, 13) and *Blackwelhalle* (CLRO, LB I, fos 2, 6), but it was the latter version that became the standard name. In summary, during the two centuries after its construction, 'Blackwell Hall' changed from a

modest baronial London residence to a particularly grand and impressive hall (larger, in 1250, than the adjacent Guildhall), then changing to a hereditary civic 'apartment', before ending up as a regulated civic marketplace.

6.9 The development of Blackwell Hall cloth market (1396–1820)

The medieval market

The City bought the Blackwell Hall property in 1395–6 and it is likely, though not certain, that it was specifically acquired with the intention of creating a regulated marketplace for the sale of woollen cloth. The documentary evidence for the acquisition is discussed in Chapter 4.2, where it is described how a committee of aldermen and civic office-holders saw this process through to completion. Barron argues that the creation of the new market was part of a process of economic expansion and City development that began some twenty years earlier with the establishment of a supervised wool market at Woolwharf (Barron 2004a, 52–5); these supervised marketplaces for 'foreigners' (ie non-citizens) and 'aliens' (ie foreigners) became an economic success story of the late medieval City. The secure and central accommodation of the new market at Blackwell Hall attracted both the English producers (and their distributing merchants) and the cloth-purchasing merchant exporters (whether English, Italian or German); the City of course benefited from the fees and from the use of the port of London for the export of the cloth. Cloth exports, already increasing in the 14th century, quickly became the dominant London export and a major source of the City's wealth, a vindication of its strategic decision to invest in the new market. In the early days of the market fewer than 20,000 cloths per year were being exported through London, but by the end of the 15th century this had risen to about 50,000; by the mid 16th century the number was nearly 100,000 (ibid, 97–111, fig 5.4). During this time, London's share of the national wool cloth export trade rose from about 50% to a virtual monopoly of nearly 90% (ibid, fig 5.5).

The ordinances which regulated this new market were issued by Mayor Richard Whittington in 1398–9 (*Cal LB H*, 449) and a keeper was appointed to run the market for the City (Kingsford 1916, 49), who, from 1405, was nominated by the Drapers' Company (Barron 2004a, 54). The Company owned two houses in the property to the north of the market which were probably used by the keeper and other market officials (Chapter 4.3, 'Tenement 13'). The Drapers formed one of the principal components of the national production and exchange chain for cloth, and were the controlling force in the London market (Bateman 2004, 6–7). The cloth was bought from rural producers, brought to Blackwell Hall and sold at the market to exporting merchants who shipped and re-sold the cloth in the Netherlands at the great fairs of Antwerp and Bergen-op-Zoom. These exporting merchants were often Italian or from the

Hanseatic League in the early days of Blackwell Hall market, but the trade was increasingly dominated in the 15th century by the English Merchant Adventurers, merchants specialising in risky overseas trade who had come to form 'cells' within the older guild companies of which they were members, such as the Drapers or Mercers (ibid; Barron 2004a, 101–11).

The large spaces of the 13th-century hall may have been seen as increasingly out-of-date and unsuitable for domestic occupation but would have been ideal as warehouse space for the cloth. The undercroft spaces of the building could have been easily converted to storage rooms by adding chambers or chests (Barron 2004a, 53) and the upper floors would presumably have been the better-lit trading areas. The different spaces of the market became known by names such as Devonshire, Colchester or Worcester, describing the origin and type of the cloth and the merchants who sold it (Bateman 2004, 6). There is little archaeological evidence for changes made to the former private hall of the Bankwell family (Chapter 4.2, 'Blackwell Hall market') but the new market had approximately 360m² of warehouse space on each floor of the old medieval hall. In addition, it seems likely that the market acquired the use of the timber building (B204) just to the west; there is no other documentary explanation of its function and the later market was built over the footprint of this building. Adding the (presumably) two floors of this building would give a total warehouse space of about 860m². The market also retained the old chapel of St Mary-in-the-Jewry (John fitz Geoffrey's private chapel of the 13th century) which may have retained its religious use in the early period of the market. The old hall garden was perhaps metalled over to create a yard for the carts that brought and took away the cloth. The early market was held every week between Thursday and Saturday (Barron 2004a, 53). The collection of the important 'aulnage' duty from the cloth-selling merchants was supervised by the alnagers, who measured cloth by the aulne or ell (1.1m); this duty was paid to the king on all cloths sold (*Cal LB E*, 53). The alnagers also examined the quality of woollen goods and stamped them with a seal of approval. The only archaeological evidence of the alnagers' activity were three relatively uninformative lead cloth seals <S282>–<S284> (Fig 354) found during the excavations. By the 16th century, the alnagers had a separate office, rented from the property on the south side (Chapter 4.4, 'Tenement 11').

The market in the 16th century

From the second half of the 16th century the market was administered by Christ's Hospital, an orphanage and school in Newgate Street founded in 1552. The relationship between the two institutions had begun with a charitable civic donation: 500 marks of the annual market profits had already been assigned in 1548 to St Bartholomew's Hospital, and in 1557 any further profits were earmarked for Christ's Hospital (Allan 1937, 1–7; Jordan 1960, 190–1). The involvement of Christ's Hospital in the actual administration of the market greatly increased in the 16th century and this was probably a mutually convenient relationship; the City was freed from another administrative

burden, and Christ's Hospital received at least a quarter, and probably nearer a third, of its annual income this way (Manzione 1997, 57–8, 77–9, 82, 87–8). In a typical year, 1564–5, the orphanage received £607 4s 4d for an operating cost of £182 13s 11d, thus making a tidy profit of £424 10s 5d (ibid, 82; these figures combine Manzione's calculations for 'Blackwell Hall' with those for 'Worsted Hall' and 'Bay Hall', which must surely have been separately-accounted parts of the same market). The City, the market and the orphanage remained closely connected; the records of both the Court of Aldermen and the Common Council show that the City continued to keep a close eye on the affairs of the market, and most of the governors of Christ's Hospital were ex-mayors, aldermen or leading guild members (ibid, 121–37). In 1613 the Court of Aldermen granted a petition from the Hospital for the 'free nomination, placing, deputation and appointment of the keepers of Blackwell Hall and of all others porters and officers', as well as the proceeds of the business (CLRO, JCCC 29, fo 50). This was clearly a major concession, giving the Hospital a larger measure of autonomy in its management of the market. But the City still retained a general supervision of the market; in 1616, for example, it ordered that the keepers at Blackwell Hall should keep the doors shut so that no goods be removed from the premises except on designated market days (CLRO, Repertory 32, fo 267).

The Merchant Adventurers managed to survive the slump in the cloth export trade in the mid 16th century by moving the cloth export 'staple' from Antwerp to Hamburg, creating new markets for English cloth in the Baltic and the New World. The changing economic and financial conditions meant that the old Merchant Adventurers began to lose ground to newer 'joint stock' companies such as the Levant Company, founded in 1592, and the East India Company, founded in 1600 (Bateman 2004, 8). The continuing success of the market led to an increasing demand for warehouse and administrative space. In

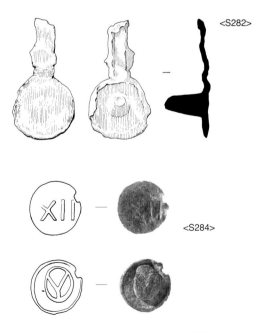

Fig 354 *Lead cloth seals dating from the 14th century <S282> and the early 16th or 17th century <S284> (scale 1:1)*

1523 the keeper of the market, the draper Thomas Cremour, was given improved accommodation, and the evidence would suggest that this consisted of rebuilding or adding another storey to the market chapel (Chapter 4.3). The dissolution of the Guildhall College in 1548 was used as an opportunity to increase the size of the market by converting the library into extra warehousing space, but the relentless pressure for space continued (Chapter 4.4). By the late 16th century, the market was using the east crypt of the Guildhall (known as the 'Welch Hall' after the provenance of the cloth stored there) and the vestry of the Guildhall chapel for extra storage. The market authorities still had to extend both the old library (with a shed described as the 'new storehouse', B219) and build a new extension to the timber building (B204), doubling its size. Including the rented alnagers' office in the property to the south, the warehouse and administrative space had increased to c 1820m^2, more than double its size in the 15th century (this figure does not include the new market keeper's house in the converted market chapel). The market was now arranged as three ranges of buildings around a yard (Fig 355).

The documentary evidence makes it clear that this was not an entirely successful arrangement. The age of the medieval buildings on the east side of the market was certainly beginning to show in the second half of the 16th century, and the conversion of the other buildings to the west and north may not have provided ideal accommodation. Complaints were made by the market users, and so surveys and repairs of the various buildings were carried out in the 1560s and 70s (Chapter 4.4). In 1587 it was decided to build a brand new building to meet the needs of the market. We are very fortunate that the 1587 building specification prepared by the Court of Aldermen has survived (CLRO, Repertory 21, fo 500v) because, in conjunction with the limited 16th-century archaeological evidence, it shows that the new building of 1588 was largely reused as the east wing of the 1660s building, for which detailed survey evidence survives. The reconstructed plan of the 1588 building is shown in outline on Fig 355 and in greater detail on Fig 219. The detailed measurements contained in the 1587 building specification have also been used to reconstruct the eastern facade of the new market building, where it fronted on to Basinghall Street (Fig 230). The masonry building had two upper storeys above the ground floor, with a central doorway leading through a covered passage into the central courtyard. A second passage led from the new courtyard into the old market yard to the west. In 1589, therefore, the improved market had at least 2800m^2 of storage and administrative space, a significant increase on the capacity earlier in the 16th century (the figure assumes that the east crypt of the Guildhall and the vestry were no longer used by the market but that the buildings on the west side of the yard were). The rooms of the market were presumably still divided according to the origin of the cloth, as had been the case in the 15th century, and as continued to be the case in the rebuilt market of the 17th century.

If Stow was correct in saying that the new market building cost £2500 (Stow 1603, i, 289), there was only a 14% overspend

compared to the budget set by the Court of Aldermen, and the enterprise can therefore be seen as a rather impressive example of local government budgeting and project management. The City only paid £50 towards the project (and this was intended as a loan) while the merchant taylor Richard May had donated £300 (CLRO, Repertory 21, fo 505v; Stow 1603, i, 289; Jordan 1960, 204). The bulk of the money was raised by an extra charge of a penny on the sale of every cloth, a temporary levy that was to apply for only two years (CLRO, JCCC 22, fo 141r).

The market in the 17th century

In the 17th century new 'joint stock' companies such as the Levant and East India Companies were increasingly dominating the cloth export trade. Though Christ's Hospital remained the market administrators, a new group of merchant middlemen, known as the Factors of Blackwell Hall, gained control of the market in the second half of the 17th century, effectively taking over from the older Merchant Adventurers. The Factors filled much the same role as the medieval Drapers, linking the rural cloth manufacturers with their customers, the London-based exporting merchants (Bateman 2004, 11–12). At the start of the 17th century they had sold the cloth on commission as agents of West Country and Yorkshire clothiers but within two or three generations they controlled the market more fully. The Factors bought the cloth and then had it finished, dyed and packed for export by new joint stock companies such as the Levant Company. Though the relative value of woollen cloth as a proportion of national exports was declining, the cloth trade was still hugely important, accounting for c £3m (out of a total export value of c £6.4m) in the early 18th century (ibid, 11; Sheppard 1998, 144).

The market was severely damaged in the Great Fire of 1666 but a new market building was begun the following year and completed by 1670 (Chapter 4.5). The new market was on a huge scale, consisting of ranges of warehouses surrounding two internal courtyards (Fig 355). The 16th-century building on Basinghall Street was rebuilt (with the new facade built slightly further out, reducing the width of the street) and a complete new wing was added to the west, land having been acquired from the properties to the south (Chapter 4.5, 'Tenement 8' and 'Tenement 9'). The new building had four storeys with a grand classical facade on the Guildhall yard (Fig 261) and, one presumes, another significant facade on Basinghall Street. The architect of the new building may have been Peter Mills, the City Surveyor (English Heritage 1988, 8; Colvin 1995, 655–7), and it is argued here that elements of the design of the west facade influenced Wren and Hooke's work on the new Guildhall piazza. The new market had double the space of its predecessor, with approximately 5800m^2 of floor space. A surviving market minute book for 1698–1761 (GL, MS 12851) gives some detail of the internal organisation of the buildings, with individually named warehouse 'halls' continuing to reflect the origin or type of the cloth for sale: Devonshire, Gloucestershire, Worcestershire, Kentish, 'Medley', 'Spanish' and 'Blanket'.

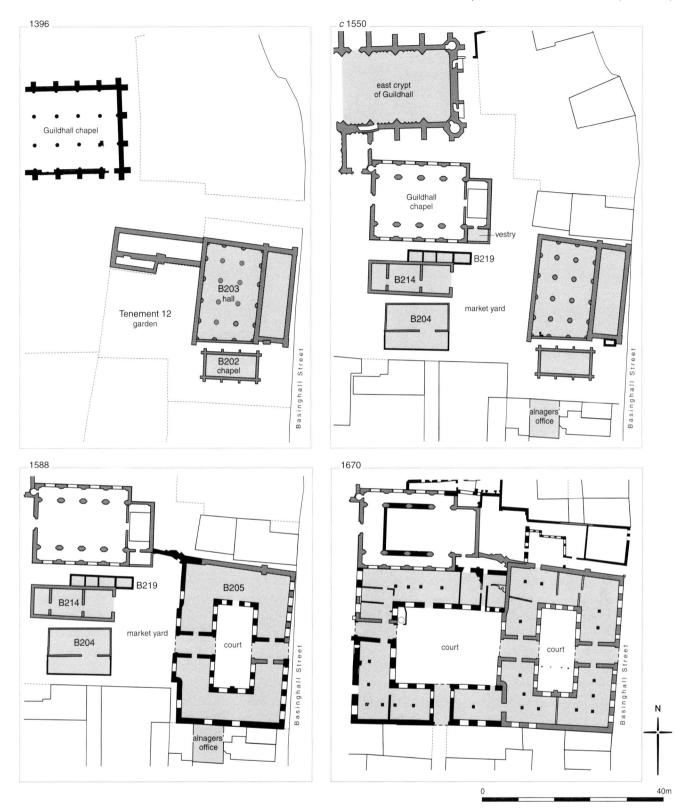

Fig 355 *Phased plan showing the evolution of Blackwell Hall market from 1396 to the 17th century (scale 1:800)*

The decline of the market in the 18th century

The Industrial Revolution significantly changed the pattern of cloth manufacture and export in the 18th century, with new industries and expanding ports arising in the north of England, reducing both the turnover and profitability of Blackwell Hall market (Bateman 2004, 12–13). The old medieval market was

becoming something of an anachronism and so parts of the building were put to alternative uses; in 1785 the Commissioners of Land Tax for the City of London rented part of the ground floor, paying Christ's Hospital a useful rent of £52 10s (CLRO, CCA 64, p 37). Plans to demolish the market in the 1790s were not immediately put into effect and it was not until 1820 that the building was finally demolished (Chapter 5.1). The remaining goods and fixtures, together with those of the old Guildhall chapel, were sold by auction (CLRO, JCLC 112, 20) and the site of the old market was replaced by a new Courts of Law building in 1822 (Fig 278). Curiously, in the 1860s there were plans for a new market related to the wool trade, just north of the old Blackwell Hall; the Coopers' Company was asked if its company hall on Basinghall Street (Tenement 17) could be used for auctions of imported wool, but the scheme did not materialise and the new Wool Exchange ended up in Coleman Street (Foster 1961, 109; Smith, T, 2002).

6.10 Inns and taverns on Cat Street from the 15th to 17th centuries

Barron has shown how commercial inns began to appear in London in the 14th century, taking over the role of earlier private 'inns' as temporary London bases for visiting aristocrats or important merchants (Barron 1995, 12–14). In some cases there was a direct process of 'commercialisation', whereby a private aristocratic 'great house' was sold or leased as a commercial inn. The first mention of an inn on Cat Street comes at the end of the 14th century with The Saracen's Head, and from the 15th to 17th centuries a small part of the Cat Street frontage between the church of St Lawrence Jewry and Basinghall Street was dominated by this and three other inns (The Three Tuns, The Maidenhead and The King's Arms), together with a number of smaller 'offshoots'. The Saracen's Head and The King's Arms were on the sites of 12th-century Jewish 'great houses' but in both cases the old buildings had probably been demolished. None of the Cat Street inns can therefore be shown to have been the successor of a medieval private inn. Instead, the inns were sited here from the late 14th century in an advantageous position towards the north of the City, close to both the seat of civic government at the Guildhall and the commercial centre of Blackwell Hall market. It would be possible to see the 'cookshops' of the late 12th century, which probably also catered for visitors to the Guildhall (above, 6.4), as precursors of the Cat Street inns (although at least a century and a half separates the 'cookshops' and the inns).

It is perhaps unfortunate that so little of these medieval and early modern inns survived in the archaeological record. Parts of The Saracen's Head, The Three Tuns and The Maidenhead lay within site C, but no medieval ground levels survived on this site due to truncation by 19th- and 20th-century cellars. Nor, unfortunately, have any historic images been located, showing Cat/Cateaton Street with, for example, the late 17th-century Three Tuns or King's Arms. Most of this section is therefore based on documentary sources, and the inns are reconstructed in Fig 356 with as much detail as the sources allow (see Chapter 8.2).

The study area also includes another medieval inn, The Swan, situated further north on Basinghall Street (Fig 174). This inn is first recorded in the early 15th century and was later the site of the Coopers' Company hall (Chapter 4.3, 'Tenements

16–18'; GL, MS 7531/2, item 30; Foster 1961, 13; Lillywhite 1972, 536, no. 14209). There is evidence in the study area for a brewery in Aldermanbury in the mid 14th century, and parts of the same property were later acquired by another brewer and by a vintner (Chapter 4.1, 'Tenement 5'; Cal Wills 1, 552; CLRO, HR 76/198; 97/140–1; 146/9).

Only two of the inns were rebuilt after the Great Fire of 1666, The Three Tuns and The King's Arms, the former surviving until 1919 as The Guildhall Tavern. The decline of the Cat Street inns was due, in part, to a specific desire by the civic authorities to banish inns from the environs of the Guildhall and its precinct (specific, but ultimately unheeded, instructions not to reopen an inn were issued to the owner of The Three Tuns property immediately after the Fire). The reasons for the decline of the Cat Street inns may also lie in the growth in popularity of coffee-houses in the second half of the 17th century. The first coffee-house was opened in London in 1652 in St Michael's Alley, Cornhill, and numerous rival establishments were quickly set up in different parts of London, so that by the end of the century it was estimated that the coffee-houses of London numbered nearly three thousand (Lillywhite 1963, 17–27).

The Saracen's Head

The first mention of The Saracen's Head occurs in March 1403 when Thomas Guldeford junior granted to Thomas Whythorn and his wife Idonea the tenement called le Sares Inne Hede on the hoop with a shop and houses (CLRO, HR 132/7). It was situated between the tenement belonging to the parish church to the east (Tenement 9), the entrance to the Guildhall (introitus Gyhalde) to the west, Cattunstrete to the south and the tenement which Thomas and Idonea already held to the north (Fig 356, a). The inn may have been established slightly earlier, in May 1397, when Guldeford first granted the (unnamed) property to Whythorn and Idonea (CLRO, HR 128/77). In this earlier transaction, Whythorn is described as a brewer (pandoxator) and his wife is named as the grantor's daughter. The property had been owned by the Guldefords since the mid 14th century (Chapter 4.2, 'Tenement 8'). In 1463 the inn seems to have been owned or managed by John Pemberton and John Humberston, vintners (CLRO, HR 192/23); since the document does not mention any houses on the street frontage that were not part of the inn (unlike the earlier documents), this might indicate that the inn occupied more of the street frontage of Tenement 8 (Chapter 4.3). In 1553 the inn was owned by John Smyth, innholder (who had been the leaseholder since 1544), and his wife Margaret (CLRO, HR 246/74; Repertory 11, fo 99; Chapter 4.4). The property has been reconstructed (Fig 356, a) using the description and measurements in a viewers' investigation of 1521 (Loengard 1989, no. 49) and in a later deed of 1553 (CLRO, HR 246/74). The actual inn seems to have been next to the outer gatehouse of the Guildhall (with some other houses to the east which did not form part of the inn). There were stables in a courtyard to the rear (presumably accessed through a covered passage from Cat Street), a facility

Fig 356 *Phased plan showing the development of the inns on Cat Street between the 15th and 17th centuries (scale 1:1000)*

shared with The Three Tuns according to the 1553 document (Chapter 4.3). The inn appears to have been a typical London 'courtyard inn', and its tight urban layout, maximising limited street frontage and sharing rear facilities with the adjacent inn, resembles that of a pair of late medieval Oxford inns, The Star Inn and The King's Head (Pantin 1961, 175–6).

The only archaeological evidence for The Saracen's Head comes from a 16th-century latrine in the rear courtyard, in which large numbers of storage jars, serving vessels and drinking vessels had been thrown away (Chapter 4.3; Fig 212; Fig 213). Most of them date to c 1480–c 1550 and the fineware drinking vessels suggest that the inn was relatively prosperous. The presence of partridge bones in the latrine, in addition to the usual beef, mutton and pork waste, provides evidence of fine dining. The latrine, like the stables and courtyard, could have been a shared facility with The Three Tuns. Part of a glass alembic <S281> suggests that distillation was also taking place in the inn. Surprisingly few other medieval tavern assemblages have been found in London and so this one is of some importance.

In the second half of the 16th century there is no further mention of The Saracen's Head, which may simply have changed its name to The White Lion (Fig 356, b), first described in this location in 1596 (CLRO, CLGB 1, fo 30r; cf Repertory 1, fo 52 and CLGB 1, fos 163, 165). It could, perhaps, have been this change of ownership which prompted the disposal of some of the inn's old tableware in the mid 16th century. The inn seems to have been rebuilt in 1600 and a 25-year lease on the 'White Lion near unto the Guildhall Gate' was granted in 1603 to Richard Bridger, vintner, at an annual rent of £3 (CLRO, Repertory 25, fo 34; CLGB 1, fo 68r). The last named tenant was the alderman William Flewellin (later buried in the Guildhall chapel: CD Table 30) who paid £4 rent for a 40-year lease in 1640 (CLRO, CCA 3, fo 110v). The inn is referred to as the 'White Lion in Catteaton Street' or the 'White Lion in Guildhall gate' in the 1640s and 50s (Lillywhite 1972, 648–9, nos 16376, 16397). It was not rebuilt after the Great Fire of 1666 because the damaged building was demolished to enlarge the entrance to the Guildhall yard from the newly built King Street (Fig 356, c; Chapter 4.5).

The Three Tuns

The Three Tuns seems to have been founded at the beginning of the 16th century, no later than 1512, and is the earliest recorded use of this popular inn name deriving from the barrels on the arms of the Vintners' and Brewers' Companies (Lillywhite 1972, 585–7, no. 15147). In 1542 the owners, the Mercers' Company, leased 'the three tounes next the Guyldehalle' to Jane Wynke, widow of Robert Wyncke, vintner, for 15 years for a rent of £5 per annum (MC, First register of leases, fo 174). The inn lay behind The Saracen's Head, next to the inner gatehouse of the Guildhall, and must have fronted on to the Guildhall yard (Fig 356, a). A lack of space meant that it had to share a courtyard and stables with the earlier inn, The Saracen's Head. A small part of the cellar of The Three Tuns was archaeologically excavated on site D (Chapter 4.3, 'Tenement

8'). The Company had been forced to sell the inn in 1550 in order to raise money (Sutton 2005, 374–5) and in 1569 Richard Betenson of London, gentleman, leased the 'Three Tonnes near the Guildhall gate' at the rather higher annual rent of £42 1s 5¹/₂d (CLRO, MD 82, no. 17). The Three Tuns was referred to as a favourite haunt of Ben Jonson in a poem of the 1620s or 30s by Robert Herrick (Shelley 1909, 57–8; Lillywhite 1972, 587) and the inn is also mentioned by Samuel Pepys in his diary entry for 11 February 1660, when it was General Monck's temporary headquarters:

> Thence we took coach for the City to Guild-hall, where the hall was full of people expecting Monke and Lord Mayor to come thither, and all very joyful. Here we stayed a great while; and at last, meeting with a friend of [Mr Chetwind], we went to the Three Tun tavern and drank half a pint of wine. (Latham and Matthews 1970–83, i, 50)

The inn continued in use until the Great Fire of 1666, following which the City purchased part of the site of the damaged inn in August 1669 for £650 in order to enlarge both the approach to the Guildhall yard and Blackwell Hall market (CLRO, CLD 30, no. 3). The authorities seem to have decided that there should be no more inns in the area of their new piazza, for the owner of The Three Tuns was ordered not to allow the house to be used 'for a public house as selling ale, beer, wine, coffee, or other tipple or victual' (Cal Fire Court 2, vi–vii). However, in 1678 a new building on the remaining part of the inn site (described as in King Street near the Guildhall and 'over against the east end of St Lawrence Church') was called 'the new Three Tuns tavern' (Fig 356, c) and was occupied by Thomas Dewhurst, victualler (ibid).

The inn probably continued into the 18th century, apparently changing its name to The Crown, for in 1699 the City Cash Accounts record the annual payment of £1, compensation for the fact that the new Three Tuns encroached slightly on the Guildhall yard (CLRO, CLGB 7, 25; CCA 23, fo 25v); and these payments continued as late as 1740 when the tenement is described as 'lately called the Crown Tavern in Guildhall Yard' (CLRO, CCA 40, fo 43). There may well be a link between The Crown tavern, The Crown coffee-house (recorded with no date in 'King Street Guildhall': Lillywhite 1972, 135, no. 1726) and The Guildhall coffee-house, which is first mentioned in the 1670s and was located at 23 King Street, immediately north of the new Three Tuns/Crown (Fig 356, c; ibid, 257, no. 510; Lillywhite 1963, 252–4). The windows of The Guildhall coffee-house are just visible on the right of Fig 261. The Guildhall coffee-house was known as The Guildhall Coffee-house and Tavern in the 19th century and it lasted, as the enlarged Guildhall Tavern, until 1919 (Lillywhite 1972, 257, nos 510, 8169; Wagner 1924, 106).

The Maidenhead

The Maidenhead is first mentioned in 1523 (Lillywhite 1972, 349, no. 10230), and in 1549 Roger Andrewes was the tenant innholder of 'the Mayden Hed' (Loengard 1989, no. 237). This viewers' investigation provides useful details and measurements of the inn (Chapter 4.4, 'Tenement 9') which have been used to reconstruct the property (Fig 356, b). The inn was only one part of the densely occupied property (with other private houses to the rear) and there may not have been much space for stabling. There was a passage with a gatehouse above on the west side of the inn, and it seems likely that the inn enjoyed the use of at least part of the small courtyard which lay further to the rear. Andrewes bought the property in 1556 for £50 (CLRO, HR 248/85). The inn passed to Andrewes's son, John, and then to his son William who, in 1582, sold it to John Nicolles, girdler, and his wife Ellen for £466 13s 4d (CLRO, HR 265/74). The sale document (even if much of it is a standard property description) describes the inn as including cellars, solars, chambers, lodgings, rooms, yards, gardens, stables, wells and ways. Subsequent property transactions refer to the leasing of the inn to Thomas Funstone, gentleman, in 1590 and back to William Andrewes in 1591 (CLRO, HR 271/6, 38). On 18 March 1597 Edward Maxey, an agent of Sir Robert Cecil, Principal Secretary of State, excused a delay in his visit to Portsmouth from his lodging at the 'Mayden Hedd at Yeeldhall gate in London' (HMC 1899, 118). The inn continued into the 17th century, being mentioned in a description of the adjoining property in 1612 (Schofield 1987, site 11), and it may still have been in use at the time of the Great Fire. The damaged property was leased to the City (who needed the rear in order to enlarge Blackwell Hall market) in 1668, when the burnt inn was described as in the tenure of Thomas Ward and his wife Barbara (CLRO, HR 340/82). This document also mentions two other small inns in the property, perhaps separate parts of The Maidenhead, called The Unicorn and The George (perhaps the 'George in Cateaton Street' of the 1650s to 60s: Lillywhite 1972, 206, no. 6923). Neither The Maidenhead nor The Unicorn/George seem to have been rebuilt after the Great Fire, although there was another Maidenhead in King Street in 1706 (ibid, 349, no. 1994).

The King's Arms

The King's Arms inn is first attested in 1574 when John Tucker (a pewterer who had bought the property from St John's College, Oxford) sold it to Roger James, 'beerbrewer', for £80 (CLRO, HR 259/67; Chapter 4.4, 'Tenement 11'). The inn is not, however, actually named until 1612 (when the next-door property was surveyed), at which time the tenant was Rowland Wilson (Schofield 1987, site 11). It is possible that the name of the inn was influenced by a previous owner of the tenement, Thomas King the blacksmith (Salter 1931, 98, no. 9), rather than referring to the royal arms. This inn name usually refers to the Stuart arms and is not used in London before 1603 (Lillywhite 1972, 310). The inn may briefly have been called The Jesus since in January 1603 George James sold to Thomas Draper, beerbrewer, 'half the messuage called the Jesus now or late in the tenure of William Atmere, pewterer, abutting on Cateaton Street on the south' (GL, MD 20518). The inn was the principal component of the property, consisting of a large building fronting on to Cat Street and a courtyard to the rear, the latter probably accessed from Basinghall Street rather than via a covered passage through the inn (Fig 356, b). At the time of the Great Fire of 1666, The King's Arms was owned by a Mr Crispe, and it is Mills and Oliver's post-Fire surveys that allow the reconstruction of the property (Mills and Oliver 1666–7, ii, 30; iv, 8, 22, 40, 65v, 82, 176, 179v).

The property included a number of separately let houses on Basinghall Street, one of which was described in 1572 as 'the three tuns in Basing Haule', clearly not the same as The Three Tuns on Cat Street/Guildhall yard (Salter 1931, 93–4, no. 3). This may be the same inn as The Bluecoat, 'the sign of the Bleewcoate' mentioned in 1667 (Mills and Oliver 1666–7, iv, 22). This inn would appear to have been situated in the former alnagers' office of Blackwell Hall market (Fig 219), a fact that might explain the name, which refers to the school uniforms of the boys of Christ's Hospital in Newgate Street (which managed Blackwell Hall market, immediately adjacent to this inn).

The King's Arms does appear to have been rebuilt after the Great Fire, using the original walls as far as possible (Chapter 4.5). The inn apparently remained here until the mid 18th century (Lillywhite 1972, 311, no. 9351), and earlier that century it had been described as a 'House of a very good Trade' (Strype 1720, i.iii, 68).

6.11 The parish churches of St Lawrence Jewry and St Michael Bassishaw

The study area of the modern Guildhall precinct lies in three parishes: St Mary Aldermanbury to the north-west, St Michael Bassishaw to the east and St Lawrence Jewry to the south-west. The church of St Lawrence Jewry lies on Gresham Street (historic Cat Street) at the south of the modern Guildhall precinct and St Michael Bassishaw lay at the north of the study area until its demolition at the end of the 19th century. The church of St Mary Aldermanbury lay outside the study area on the west side of Aldermanbury. It was heavily damaged in the Second World War and the whole site was archaeologically excavated by Professor W F Grimes in 1967–8, with the results recently re-analysed and published (Milne 2001, 70–86). This study therefore concentrates on the two churches of St Michael Bassishaw and St Lawrence Jewry. St Michael Bassishaw has been excavated on two separate occasions, once in the 1890s as the church was being demolished and a second time in the 1960s during the redevelopment of the northern part of the Guildhall precinct (Chapter 1.3, sites PRG1027 and GM13). Ivor Noël Hume made some archaeological observations during the rebuilding of St Lawrence Jewry in the 1950s following its extensive wartime damage (site GM200), and the Museum of London excavated the north-east re-entrant of the church in the 1990s (site A). Bateman and Miles (1999) proposed a development sequence for the church, based on an analysis of its plan-form and supported by some documentary information, and this model is largely followed here. The evolution of the churches is discussed in more detail for each archaeological period in the chronological narrative (Chapters 3 and 4).

In addition to the two parish churches, there were also at least three private chapels within the study area. The most important of these was the Guildhall chapel, founded at the end of the 13th century (above, 6.7), which had a size and status superior to most parish churches. In the mid 13th century, John fitz Geoffrey, the owner of the large hall later known as Blackwell Hall, added a private chapel to his property which became known as St Mary-in-the-Jewry (above, 6.8). The earliest documentary reference records that it was built on the site of a former synagogue (*Cal Close R* 1254–6, 369–70) and the limited archaeological evidence comprised two well-finished Reigate stone buttresses whose positioning seems to indicate a three- or four-bay chapel (Chapter 3.3). In the early 15th century the alderman William Estfeld, who was soon to be mayor, built a small private chapel at the rear of his property on Basinghall Street (Chapter 4.3, 'Tenement 13').

The origins of the churches

The church of St Lawrence Jewry is dedicated to St Lawrence, a 3rd-century AD Roman deacon and martyr who is supposed to have been roasted on a gridiron over a slow fire (Farmer 1997, 295–6). The church is referred to as 'St Lawrence in the Jewry' in *c* 1198 (HMC 1883, 14) and as 'St Lawrence in Old Jewry' in 1318 (*Cal LB E*, 98), reflecting the long-standing Jewish association with the area until their explusion in 1290. The church was presumably originally known as plain St Lawrence; the topographic suffix of 'in the Jewry' can not pre-date the establishment of the London Jewish community in the 1070s and it may only have become necessary once there was a second St Lawrence, St Laurence Pountney, in the south-east of the City, even though this church is not evidenced before the 13th century (Harben 1918, 341). Archaeological evidence for St Lawrence Jewry has demonstrated that its foundation must date to before the Norman Conquest, probably *c* 1050, as the earliest horizon of burials in its churchyard is dated by dendrochronology to the 1050s and 60s (Chapter 3.1, 'St Lawrence Jewry'). There is no archaeological evidence for this Late Saxon church but it is shown in the reconstruction painting (Fig 282) as a timber church based on the model of Greenstead, Essex.

The evidence would suggest that St Michael Bassishaw was founded slightly later, in the 12th century (Chapter 3.2, 'St Michael Bassishaw'). The dedication to the archangel Michael may have been influenced by the famous Norman shrine at Mont-Saint-Michel, although the saint was already popular in pre-Norman England and Wales (Farmer 1997, 348–9). The church is first documented in 1196 when it was called 'St Michael de Bassishaghe' (Harben 1918, 408), but Newcourt's *Repertorium* records a plausible tradition that the church was given to the priory of St Bartholomew by a Bishop Gilbert of

London (Newcourt 1708–10, i, 477), who could be variously identified with bishops serving in 1127–34, 1163–87 or 1313–16 (Fryde 1986, 258). The archaeological evidence would also point to a date in the 12th century; Marsden's excavations in the 1960s showed that the church overlay rubbish pits containing pottery dated to *c* 1080–*c* 1150. His excavations did also reveal a few postholes which were earlier than the first masonry church but not enough to make a convincing argument for a timber church. The most plausible conclusion is that a stone church was founded on a new site in the second or third quarter of the 12th century.

It can be seen, therefore, that the two churches have 'typical' London origins, as the majority of London's churches were established between the late 10th and 12th centuries AD and developed into parish churches by *c* 1200 (Brooke 1975, 122–43; Schofield 1999, 31–2). But by whom were these two churches founded? London churches seem to have originated in one of at least three ways: as a private chapel on a prominent tenement, as neighbourhood churches, or as an establishment founded by a group of traders (Brooke 1975, 131–6; Schofield 1994, 35). It may be the case that St Michael Bassishaw was the first type of private foundation. Both the ward and the parish contain the same place-name and occupy the same area, which is unique in London. Furthermore, evidence for the foundation of the important Blackwell Hall estate on Basinghall Street, the principal street in the ward, seems to point to an early association with the Bassingbourn family in the 12th century (above, 6.8) and this might suggest the foundation, or at least the early 'sponsorship', of the church by the family in the 12th century. St Lawrence Jewry may also have been a private foundation, perhaps as part of an estate granted by William I to the abbey of St Salvius at Montreuil (Chapter 3.1), although a more communal origin seems equally plausible. The archaeological evidence suggests that the church had the parochial function of burial from an early date. St Lawrence Jewry was right on the periphery of the growing city in the third quarter of the 11th century, and so it may simply have been founded by residents north of Cheapside on available land at the end of a built-up road (later known as Lawrence Lane) leading north out of the city from Cheapside. By the 14th century the church was financially supported by girdlers (Bateman and Miles 1999, 112), who also rented its property to carry out their trade (above, 6.6), but it might be stretching the evidence to postulate their involvement in the foundation or early maintenance of the church some 250 years earlier.

The medieval development of the churches

The postulated Late Saxon timber church of St Lawrence Jewry seems to have been replaced by a new stone-built church in the 1070s, perhaps because of damage suffered in the London fire of 1077 (period 10 phase 2). The excavation of the churchyard to the north of the church provided very good dating evidence for the construction work, although the form of the actual church is not known. It is suggested that the early 12th-century church was of a simple Norman type (Fig 357), whose plan is

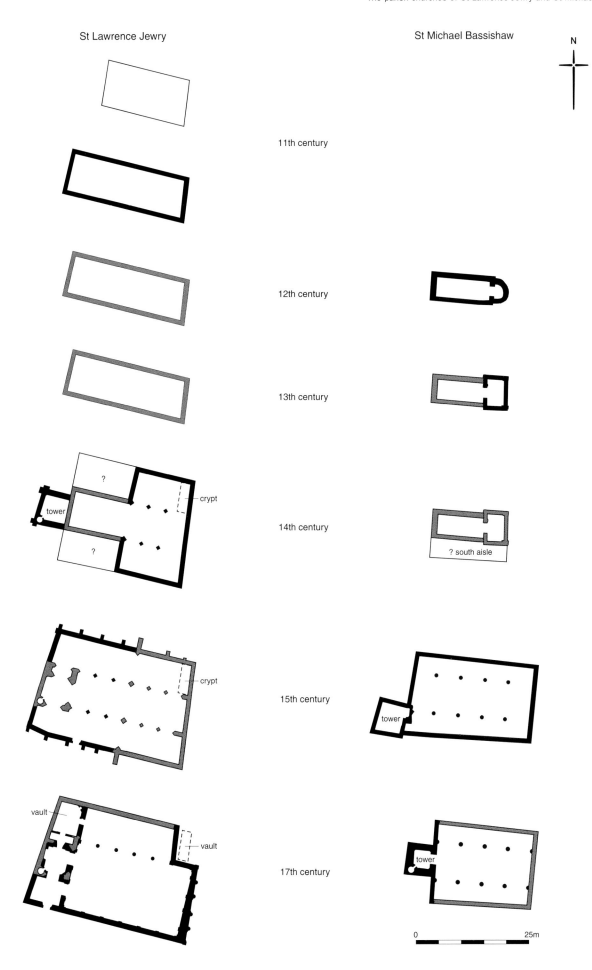

St Lawrence Jewry

St Michael Bassishaw

N

11th century

12th century

13th century

14th century

15th century

17th century

tower

crypt

?

?

crypt

tower

? south aisle

vault

vault

tower

0   25m

Fig 357 Phased plans illustrating the suggested development of the parish churches of St Lawrence Jewry and St Michael Bassishaw from the 11th to 17th centuries (scale 1:800)

'preserved' as the nave of the later medieval church, which was surveyed soon after the Great Fire of 1666 (Fig 233). The stone church may have reused part of the southern entrance to the Roman amphitheatre for its east wall; it was certainly topographically influenced by the position of the (just) surviving bank and entrance earthwork (above, 6.1). In the reconstruction painting (Fig 338) the church is modelled on the two-celled church of Hales, Norfolk (Cook 1954, 246, pl 55) though with a square east end. The plan of the early stone church of St Michael Bassishaw is better known, particularly its apsidal east end which was excavated by Marsden in the 1960s (Fig 120; Fig 121). This type of simple rectangular two-cell plan with an apsidal east end would appear to be typical of early Romanesque London churches and is seen at St Bride Fleet Street, St Martin Orgar and St Pancras (Schofield 1994, 44–5). The length of the church is uncertain but must have been less than 19m, suggesting that it was smaller than St Lawrence Jewry (Fig 357). The limited artefactual evidence might also suggest that St Lawrence Jewry had a higher status: a rare ceramic floor tile <T1> (Fig 380; Chapter 8.5) and a Caen stone voussoir <A13> (Chapter 8.3) almost certainly derive from the early stone church of St Lawrence Jewry. Hints of the church's interior decoration were also found: two shell palettes <S73> (Fig 358) and <S74> still bore traces of red and blue pigment, and their archaeological context would suggest that they were used in the decoration of the first masonry church.

The archaeological and documentary evidence would seem to indicate that both churches were enlarged in the 13th century, perhaps in part as a response to the increasing population (Chapters 3.3 and 4.1). A number of decorated floor tiles of 'Westminster' type were found in the St Lawrence Jewry property and point to improvement works taking place in the second half of the 13th century (Chapter 8.5). In situ archaeological evidence from site A showed that a barrel-vaulted crypt, probably a charnel crypt, was added on the north

side of the nave (Fig 160). The dating evidence for this is not certain but a date in the first half of the 14th century seems likely (Chapter 4.1). The earliest documentary evidence for charnel crypts in London churches is from the 15th century, but this late date is probably more a result of limited surviving pre-Reformation churchwardens' accounts, and a 14th-century date for some crypts is plausible (Harding 1992, 128, n53; Schofield 1994, 49–51, 61–2). The below-ground crypt that survived in the archaeological record at St Lawrence Jewry must originally have been built below a north chapel or a north aisle, and it seems a reasonable guess that this included a Lady chapel as at St Bride's; a south chapel and/or aisle could well have been added at this time (Bateman and Miles 1999, 128–9). The documentary history of St Lawrence Jewry is reasonably clear in the 13th century; the church passed from the abbey of St Salvius in Montreuil to a canon of St Paul's in 1247, then to a canon of St Martin le Grand in 1284–5 and finally to Balliol College, Oxford, in 1294, in whose ownership it remained until the 18th century (Chapters 3.3 and 4.1). The redecoration of the church floor could well pre-date the acquisition of the church by Balliol College but the major works of the Lady chapel and charnel crypt probably started after 1294. The rebuilding was aided by considerable financial bequests from rich merchants and, in particular, individual girdlers (Schofield 1994, 78; Bateman and Miles 1999, 112).

The more prosperous central location of the parish of St Lawrence Jewry ensured that it continued to have a grander church than its neighbouring parish to the north. There is, however, evidence for the enlargement of the east end of St Michael Bassishaw, although the dating remains uncertain (Chapter 4.1, 'St Michael Bassishaw'). Excavations in the 1960s found five pier bases that do not fit the original apsidal form of the church and which seem to indicate an enlarged square chancel or sanctuary, entered through a new chancel arch (Fig 357; see also Fig 136). These developments were dated to the late 12th or early 13th century by Cohen (1994), and it is argued here that the work is probably 13th-century. There is also evidence for further enlargement works in the 14th century, probably adding additional side chapels. Some architectural fragments of this date were recovered in the excavations of the 1890s (and the limited excavation records suggest a south aisle or chapel of this date) and there is documentary evidence for a chapel of St Mary by 1347 (Chapter 4.1).

The two parish churches had therefore become more complex spaces by the 14th century, with more separation between laity and clergy (expressed at St Michael Bassishaw by the more 'closed' chancel) and greater segregation of the social classes of the laity (expressed at St Lawrence Jewry, and perhaps at St Michael, by the additional Lady and/or chantry chapels). It would of course be interesting to know more about the decorative schemes of the churches, and it is unfortunate that none of the medieval architectural fragments seen in the 1890s excavation of St Michael Bassishaw (including, apparently, some elements in the Decorated style) survive today.

The two churches underwent further enlargement and

<S73>

Fig 358 Shell palette containing red pigment <S73>, probably used during the decoration of the interior of the first masonry church of St Lawrence Jewry (scale c 1:1)

improvement in the 15th century (Chapter 4.3). Bateman and Miles (1999, 129) suggest that the west tower of St Lawrence Jewry might have been added towards the end of the 14th century, with the aisles being extended west to meet the tower in the 15th century (Fig 357). Further modifications in the 15th century are noted in a later inscription (dated 1618), which stated that the alderman Sir William Eastfield financed the glazing of a window in the church in 1442 (Strype 1720, i.iii, 43). The church of St Michael Bassishaw seems to have been more completely rebuilt in the 15th century, thanks to generous endowments from the mercer John Barton (Chapter 4.3). The new church was built on a much larger rectangular aisled plan (Fig 357), although the interior may well have had a 'closed' appearance, resulting from aisles separated into chapels (as opposed to the more 'open' plan of a 14th-century friary church). The new church seems to have reused little of the earlier church, apart from the foundations of the old south wall and south arcade. The new tower was curiously offset at the south-west angle of the new church, and was perhaps constrained by the topographic requirement to allow a lane to pass round the north of the church to connect Aldermanbury with Basinghall Street (Fig 216). Evidence for a staircase within the tower would suggest access to a clerestory gallery or rood-loft. The 1890s excavations produced evidence of the tiled floor and the plain octagonal columns of the arcades. The two churches thus ended up with broadly similar plans in the 15th century, although probably arrived at by different means: accretion in the case of St Lawrence Jewry, and more or less complete rebuilding in the case of St Michael Bassishaw. Both churches were probably well decorated in the Perpendicular style, with generous areas of stained glass and 'panelled' bays defined by arcade columns rising from the floor to the clerestory and up to the roof. The masons' and carpenters' work would have been paid for at St Michael Bassishaw largely thanks to the investment of John Barton, and at St Lawrence conceivably by donations from some of the 20 wealthy citizens who paid for funerary monuments in the 15th century (Steer in prep). In addition to the large number of funerary monuments, the stained glass and the painted decoration, there would also have been more 'portable' religious art in the form of plate, manuscripts and altar panels, of which a few tantalising examples with a London provenance survive, including a 15th-century missal from St Lawrence Jewry (Ker 1964, 221; Schofield 1994, 62–6; Marks and Williamson 2003, nos 135–6, 143).

The churches after the Reformation

Beginning in the late 1530s, the parishioners would have witnessed the arrival of vernacular bibles, new Protestant preaching and changes in the rites of the Mass (Sheppard 1998, 148–52). The effects of the Protestant Reformation on the interior of the two parish churches can be appreciated from the example of well-studied churchwardens' accounts from two other London parish churches, St Michael Cornhill and St Andrew Hubbard (Schofield 2003b). These two churches

underwent a rapid succession of alterations in the 1540s and 50s, with painted images whitewashed, then repainted during Mary's reign, and covered up once again in Elizabeth's reign. Both St Michael Bassishaw and St Lawrence Jewry were redecorated in the early 17th century, perhaps in a reaction to the earlier iconoclasm, and the changes almost certainly included new timber galleries. The churches may well then have undergone another phase of iconoclasm in the 1640s, which perhaps finally removed the medieval stained glass and any remaining statues (ibid, 317). One aspect of continuity was the use of prominent church burial structures in both churches after the Reformation, for example that of John Gresham in St Michael Bassishaw (1556) or that of his relation Richard Gresham, the former mayor, in St Lawrence Jewry (1548) (Steer in prep). Harding has termed the continuing use of church monuments 'a paradigm of centrality and marginality, inclusion and exclusion', with the spatial order of the church continuing to reflect the social hierarchy by means of an individual's inclusion in the church after death, or exclusion to a series of less desirable burial locations (Harding 2002, 11, 118–24).

Both churches were severely damaged in the Great Fire of 1666 (Chapter 4.5). St Lawrence Jewry was lavishly rebuilt between 1671 and 1677, broadly following the medieval plan but combining the old south aisle and nave to form a wide and open Protestant preaching space (Fig 357). Fortunately, the RCHME volume on the City recorded the Wren interior in great detail before the church was bombed in the Second World War (RCHME 1929). Work on St Michael Bassishaw was carried out between 1675 and 1679 and seems to have been a more conservative (and much cheaper) rebuild of the medieval plan, retaining the nave and two aisles. The west end of the church, including the projecting medieval tower, was demolished and a new tower was added on to the west end of the four remaining bays (Fig 357). In the early 18th century the tower was rebuilt and a vestry added to the south-west re-entrant. The involvement of Robert Hooke in the reconstruction of the City churches, in addition to Christopher Wren's important role, has received increasing attention in recent years (Jeffery 1996; Cooper 2003; Jardine 2003), and it is argued here that Hooke played the dominant role in the design and execution of St Michael Bassishaw and that he also had an important hand in St Lawrence Jewry. One previously unknown feature of St Lawrence Jewry revealed in the archaeological excavation is an extraordinary building occupying the north-east re-entrant of the church (and partly explaining why the church was rebuilt with this 'missing' corner). Hooke and Wren appear to have designed an ingenious compromise building to satisfy both the civic and parish leaders, featuring a below-ground burial vault (accessed from the churchyard to the north) capped by a civic fire station whose doors led out on to the Guildhall yard to the east (Chapter 4.5, 'The Guildhall yard, new piazza and fire station'). There was a second burial vault under the north-west angle of the church.

After the severe damage of the Second World War, St Lawrence Jewry was rebuilt and largely restored to its 'Wren and Hooke' state in the 1950s (Chapter 5.2; Bradley and

Pevsner 1997, 229–30). The church is now more of a 'private chapel' to the Guildhall than a parish church, though it is of course frequented by its 'daytime' parishioners working in the City. The parish now includes the old parish of St Michael Bassishaw, whose church was demolished in the 1890s due to structural problems (probably attributable to the poor work of the 17th-century builder, John Fitch, rather than to any failing by the designer, Robert Hooke).

6.12 The churchyard of St Lawrence Jewry

The topography of the churchyard from the 11th to 19th centuries

Archaeological excavation of the north-east corner of the churchyard of St Lawrence Jewry gives an insight into the development of a parish cemetery, and by incorporating information from property transactions and historic maps (Chapter 8.1 and 8.2) a model of the development of the churchyard from c 1050 to c 1850 has been developed (Fig 359). The church property was much larger than the churchyard itself, and archaeological excavation and documents from the 14th century onwards show that the northern part of the property was never used for burial but was built up, with a vicarage and houses (Chapter 4.1). This northern area is described in the various archaeological periods in Chapter 4 as the 'north yard' of St Lawrence Jewry; this section only deals with the southern part of the property, the part used for burial. A detailed catalogue of the burials is given in Chapter 8.17, and the osteological evidence is presented in Chapter 8.18.

The archaeological excavations only took place in the north-east corner of the churchyard and so the reconstructed model of the whole churchyard (Fig 359) involves a good deal of conjecture. The excavations provided a good idea of the evolving northern boundary of the churchyard, while its eastern extent is well defined by the excavated road and by the later Guildhall precinct. The southern boundary was always Cat Street (modern Gresham Street) and the historic road layout can be reconstructed with a reasonable degree of confidence (Chapter 8.2). The weakest aspect of the model concerns the western boundary, where the reconstruction is largely based on 17th-century evidence.

The rare feature of this archaeological site is that the contemporary medieval ground levels survived, allowing an unusual range of evidence to be excavated. In most excavations of urban churchyards, the archaeological deposits have been truncated by more recent cellars and basements (eg St Nicholas Shambles, London: White 1988, 9), or the intensity of later medieval or post-medieval burials has reduced any contemporary land surfaces or deposits to a homogeneous 'cemetery soil' (eg St Mary Spital, London: Thomas et al 1997). Archaeological evidence here has shown that the early medieval

churchyard was not used exclusively for burial. Throughout the 11th and 12th centuries large quantities of domestic refuse and soil were disposed of in the churchyard and, in the 12th century, a number of timber buildings (fronting on to the lane to the east) encroached on it. However, the original northern boundary of the churchyard was re-established on a number of occasions, suggesting that the church had the power to enforce its property rights, even if it was not able to 'police' the churchyard at all times. It has been suggested that the use of churchyards for refuse disposal 'may be more a lack of clear boundary definition, or temporary encroachment on an unused section of the cemetery, rather than a true dual function' (Gilchrist and Sloane 2005, 45). At St Lawrence Jewry the boundaries are well defined, and the scale and duration of refuse disposal in the churchyard suggest that there may have been a more formal financial relationship between the church and those using the land, perhaps the tenants of the church in the houses to the north. By the end of the 12th century this practice seems to have stopped, though it is not clear if this reflects an increasing exercise of authority by the church.

Prior to the foundation of the church, the land around the old Roman amphitheatre was grassland used for keeping livestock and for the disposal of domestic refuse (Chapter 2.1). It is argued here that the foundation of St Lawrence Jewry took place by the middle of the 11th century and that the churchyard was being used for burials (Fig 412) before the Norman Conquest (period 10 phase 1; above, 6.11). The churchyard boundary was marked by wattle fences, probably serving as much to keep out animals as to define the churchyard itself (Fig 359, a). There were also internal fences defining burial plots within the churchyard, perhaps areas for the burial of particular groups of people of differing status or family groups (Fig 20). The archaeological evidence suggests that the lane on the east side of the churchyard was contemporary with the first church and churchyard; it may simply have evolved in order to allow access to the burial ground and it stopped abruptly on the line of the northern limit of the churchyard. A smaller gravel path led from the lane into the two enclosed burial areas. It is suggested that the eastern boundary of the north part of the churchyard probably continued the line of the east end of the early church, although there is no direct evidence for this. A small strip of open land, c 6.0m wide, lay between the lane and the churchyard fence; it was presumably owned by the church but was never used for burials.

The reconstructed 11th-century churchyard had a surface area of c 1500m^2 (excluding the church itself), if the large open space to the south of the church is included. If, however, it is assumed that only the northern part of the churchyard was used for burial (the part furthest from the road), the actual burial ground area would have been c 650m^2. This is still considerably larger than the contemporary London parish cemetery of St Nicholas Shambles, estimated at 163m^2 (White 1998, 8).

For a twenty- to thirty-year period at the end of the 11th century (c 1070–c 1100; period 10 phases 2–3) the north-east

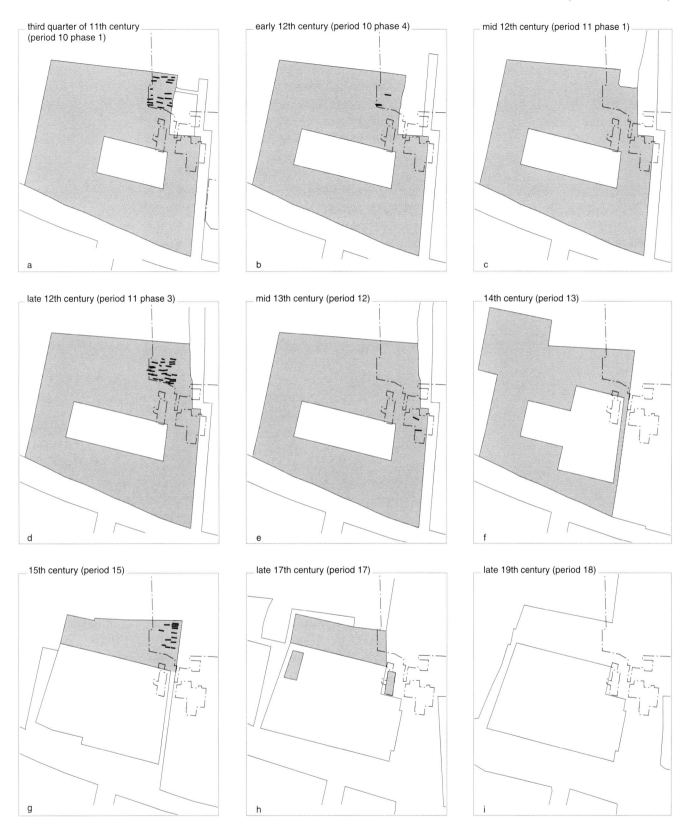

third quarter of 11th century
(period 10 phase 1)

a

early 12th century (period 10 phase 4)

b

mid 12th century (period 11 phase 1)

c

late 12th century (period 11 phase 3)

d

mid 13th century (period 12)

e

14th century (period 13)

f

15th century (period 15)

g

late 17th century (period 17)

h

late 19th century (period 18)

i

Fig 359 Reconstructed model of the churchyard of St Lawrence Jewry from the 11th to 19th centuries; the boundaries for which there is good evidence are shown as a thicker line (scale 1:1000)

part of the churchyard was not used for burials, perhaps because the old timber church was being rebuilt in stone (above, 6.11). Normal burial may well have continued in other parts of the churchyard during this time, and a few isolated burials (Fig 418) did take place in the north-east corner at the very

beginning of the 12th century (period 10 phase 4; Fig 359, b).

During the 12th century the lane on the east side of the churchyard was widened and extended to the north, apparently to allow access to the Guildhall, and it became increasingly built up (Chapter 3.2); some of the buildings on the west of

397

the lane encroached on the churchyard (eg B103 which trims the very north-east corner of the churchyard on Fig 359, c). The occupants of the building clearly used the churchyard for access, for digging cesspits and for disposing of their domestic waste. The southern extent of this building coincided with the line of the mid 11th-century internal fence which marked one of the earlier burial plots; this might suggest that the encroachment of Building 103 came about as a formal rental arrangement with the church, rather than as an opportunistic piece of 'squatting'.

Towards the end of the 12th century, c 1170, the north-east part of the churchyard was once again used exclusively for burials after a hiatus of some seventy years, and the northern boundary was re-established on its original 11th-century line (period 11 phase 3; Fig 359, d). The graves were laid out in formal rows (Fig 419), with the northern extent of the actual burials still on the line of the 11th-century internal division. The eastern limit of the burials lay some 3.0m west of the lane, leaving an open strip of land between the grave rows and the lane. The strip could have been set aside for a particular group to be buried in, but never actually used, or it might have been for ceremonial use; processions outside the church could include the annual marking of the churchyard boundaries (Gilchrist and Sloane 2005, 36). The north-east corner of the churchyard continued to be used for burials until c 1230 (period 11 phase 4); the northern extent of the burials lay further south and the intensity of burial increased (Fig 423). It is possible that the apparent lack of care taken by the gravedigger (which manifests itself in the archaeological record as 'intercutting' graves, the earlier graves being disturbed by the later ones) reflects a change in religious belief. As the church increasingly emphasised Purgatory rather than the Day of Judgement, it may have become less imperative to preserve the whole body in the ground until Judgement Day (Daniell 1997, 146). The intercutting of graves could, however, simply reflect the increasing size of London's living and dead populations.

Two burials of the mid 13th century (period 12; Fig 359, e; Fig 424) show that the eastern boundary of the churchyard had a 'dogleg', a topographic anomaly which is assumed to have been an original feature of the churchyard. Additions to the church and the redevelopment of the Guildhall precinct decreased the size of the churchyard in the 14th century to c 1150m², or c 500m² if only the northern part is included (period 13; Fig 359, f). The church may have gained some space in the north-west corner of its churchyard; the evidence for this is based on a grant of 1333 which describes two newly constructed shops 'in the corner of the northern part of the churchyard of the church' (CLRO, HR 62/106). The church itself was enlarged with a new chapel, perhaps a Lady chapel, which was built over a small charnel crypt. The chapel encroached on the churchyard and its construction would undoubtedly have disturbed many earlier burials; and it may have been this that necessitated the new charnel crypt.

In the late 14th century (period 14) the churchyard was further reduced in size. A combination of the enlargement of the church and the increasingly built-up Cat Street frontage

meant that the whole of the southern part of the old churchyard was now virtually unusable. There remained a narrow strip of land between the church and the street which was probably not used for burial, and two narrow paths leading to the remaining part of the churchyard on the north side of the church. The churchyard was now only c 330m² in area. It was in the 15th or 16th century that its north-east part began to be used once again for burials (period 15; Fig 359, g) after a hiatus of some two centuries, although the dating evidence is uncertain. The northern boundary of the churchyard and the northern limit of the grave rows (extending to a short distance south of the boundary) lay in almost exactly the same positions as in the 11th century. A number of the 16 archaeologically excavated graves were stacked multiple graves with, in one case, as many as seven bodies interred in the same narrow grave. Like many urban parish churches, the parish authorities of St Lawrence Jewry were in a difficult position: the rising population in the 16th century was increasing the need for burial space, just as the same pressure was leading to greater urban density and more limited churchyard space. The parish burial register shows that the annual burial rate rose from 10–15 burials a year in the mid 16th century to 20–25 per year for most of the late 16th and early 17th centuries (Hughes Clarke 1940, 111–69). This increased pressure on space required the establishment of a 'new churchyard' in 1659 (ibid, 163) but its location and size are uncertain.

With the redevelopment of the Guildhall precinct and the reconstruction of the church after the Great Fire of 1666, the churchyard was reduced to a narrow strip on the north side of the church (Fig 359, h). An attempt to gain more burial space was made by the creation of two brick burial vaults (which in theory could achieve higher burial density by stacking of coffins), a 'Great Vault' under the north-west of the church and a 'Little Vault' outside the church in its north-east re-entrant, in the same location as the earlier charnel crypt (Chapter 4.5). The total space available for burial was now only c 250m², although this figures does not include a number of small private vaults within the church.

The churchyard of St Lawrence Jewry was finally closed, after eight hundred years of continual use, under the Burial Act of 1853, which allowed the closure of small urban parish churchyards and the creation of larger municipal cemeteries on the edges of towns and cities. The final entries in the burial register bear that date, and many of the early 19th-century burials in the 'Little Vault' were archaeologically excavated; the vault had been sealed up and forgotten, to be rediscovered during the archaeological excavations in the 1990s (Bateman and Miles 1999, 131). The churchyard became 'fossilised' as an open space on the north side of the church, a wider part of the alley leading west from the Guildhall yard towards Gresham Street (Fig 359, i). The old churchyard later became part of the enlarged Guildhall Yard of the second half of the 20th century (Fig 280).

An understanding of the excavated burial assemblages can perhaps be enhanced by considering what proportion they represent of the total numbers of people who were buried in the churchyard. Various attempts have been made to estimate the changing population of medieval and early modern London (eg Harding 1990; Barron 2004a, 237–42) and, by assuming that the parishes were broadly equal in population (rather than size), it is possible to guess at annual burial rates. Taking a broad estimate of 20,000 for the population of London in the late 11th century (ibid, 237, n1), the number of parishes at that time (c 95: ibid) and a 'pre-modern' average annual London mortality rate of c 3% (calculated after Harding 2002, 14–18), we might expect there to have been an average of about five or six burials a year in the parish at that time (or perhaps fewer since St Lawrence Jewry was then a peripheral parish). The 17 archaeologically excavated burials interred in a c 20-year period between the 1050s and the 1070s (period 10 phase 1; Chapter 8.17, burials 1–17) could therefore represent as much as 10–20% of the burials made at that time. If one assumes that the northern half of the churchyard was gradually filled up at the sort of density and rate indicated by the excavated burials (17 burials occupying c 75m², interred over c 20 years), it ought to have taken about 175 years to fill up. The archaeological evidence roughly agrees with this figure: the grave rows of the late 12th century overlay those of the third quarter of the 11th century, suggesting that the gravediggers had run out of space and gone back to the north-east corner after an interval of approximately 150 years.

The excavated assemblages of 13th-century and later burials are less significant as they must represent much smaller percentages of the total numbers of interments at the church, given the increase in London's population (Barron 2004a, 237–42). The burials of the late 12th and early 13th centuries (period 11 phases 3–4; Chapter 8.17, burials 21–63) form a reasonably large assemblage (43 burials) but they could represent as little as 5% of all those buried in the churchyard at this time. The 26 interments of the 15th to 16th centuries (period 15) clearly represent an insignificant sample, perhaps as little as 1% of those buried in that period.

Medieval burial practice in the churchyard

The following discussion concerns the archaeologically excavated group of 72 people who were buried in St Lawrence Jewry churchyard between the 11th and 13th centuries. A group of 15th- or 16th-century burials in the churchyard was also excavated, but this assemblage is much less significant due to both the difficult circumstances of their excavation (Chapter 1.1) and the lack of organic survival. A group of 19th-century burials from the 'Little Vault' of the church has already been published (Bateman and Miles 1999). It was therefore decided to concentrate here on the nationally important sample of 11th- to 13th-century burials. It should be noted that the element 'Jewry' in the name of the church reflects only the Jewish occupation of the district, and that the Jewish cemetery for London was at Cripplegate, just outside the walled city (Blair et al 2001a, 19). The details and location of individual burials are given in Chapter 8.17 and summarised in CD Table 31, while the osteological information is presented in Chapter 8.18.

The highly organic nature of the deposits within the churchyard and the lack of subsequent truncation by later cellars permitted the remarkable survival of timber boards, coffins and roundwood used in the burials. This excellent preservation, combined with the many tree-ring dates, gives a unique insight into the use of timber in burials in 11th- to 13th-century London and adds considerably to the small corpus of such material from the rest of Britain. Even within this relatively small sample, there is a wide variety of timber coffins and other grave furniture used to transport and house the dead.

In contrast to the great variety of coffins, the alignment and attitude of the bodies was very consistent. All the burials were laid out west–east in a supine position with the head at the west end. Arms were positioned either at the sides of the body or flexed with the hands together in the pelvic region.

The people

Although this group of skeletons is too small to provide a statistically significant set of results, some general demographic conclusions are nevertheless possible. In particular, this early medieval population was characterised by a high adolescent mortality and by few adults surviving beyond 45 years of age, the exceptions being two men (burials 18 and 64). There are roughly equal numbers of men and women, and their stature (mean height 1.71m and 1.57m respectively) is comparable to data from other medieval sites.

There was no evidence to suggest family plots in the cemetery, nor that the individuals in the multiple graves were necessarily blood relatives. There was a high prevalence of osteoarthritis and other stress diseases of the skeleton. The level of trauma was also fairly high, with two instances of healed wounds to the skull and some healed fractures, especially of the ribs and extremities. A woman with a healed trepanation (Fig 426) is the earliest known example of this surgical procedure (perforating the skull, presumably to relieve pressure on the brain) from medieval London. Further details of the health of the population are discussed in Chapter 8.18.

Preparing, transporting and housing the dead

Although the survival of the timber was excellent, there was little survival of textile to indicate whether any of the bodies were wrapped in shrouds or windings sheets, or clothed at the time of burial. Only one burial (burial 39, Fig 363) produced direct evidence of textile: a few fragments of coarse cloth were found on the torso and between the upper and lower legs, and impressions of textile were visible where the base and cover boards had been in contact with the body; these may be the remnants of a shroud. The complete lack of shroud pins at St Lawrence Jewry does not preclude the use shrouds, as it has been suggested that such pins were temporary ties used when stitching the shroud and should be considered as accidental losses (Gilchrist and Sloane 2005, 110). The analysis of the attitude of the bodies at St Lawrence Jewry has suggested that many of them may have been buried in a shroud for which no direct evidence, in the form of textiles or pins, survives (see below).

The graves were dug to size to accommodate the individual(s) to be buried and were quite shallow, no more than c 0.6m deep, which is in line with the range (c 0.4–0.7m) for graves from medieval monasteries (Gilchrist and Sloane 2005, 131). Evidence for the use of a coffin or boards was found in 46 (64%) of the burials. In 12 of these the timber was too decayed to ascertain their original form. In the remaining 34 cases, however, the survival of the evidence was good, and the various coffins and boards used in the graves can be divided into several categories (Fig 360).

COVER BOARD ONLY

For 13 burials, the body was placed in the grave and then simply covered with a board or boards (Fig 360, a). The board may have been supported on soil 'ledges' in the grave-cut or on soil backfilled around the body (neither method left any trace); in one case (burial 54) the boards were supported on stones laid alongside the head and one side of the body. In the double burial (burial 24) of a woman and child laid side by side, four branches or poles were laid across both bodies and supported four short oak boards used to cover the bodies (Fig 360, b; Fig 361). A more elaborate form used two boards pitched at c 45° over a 2-year-old (burial 4) to create a roof effect as seen on a

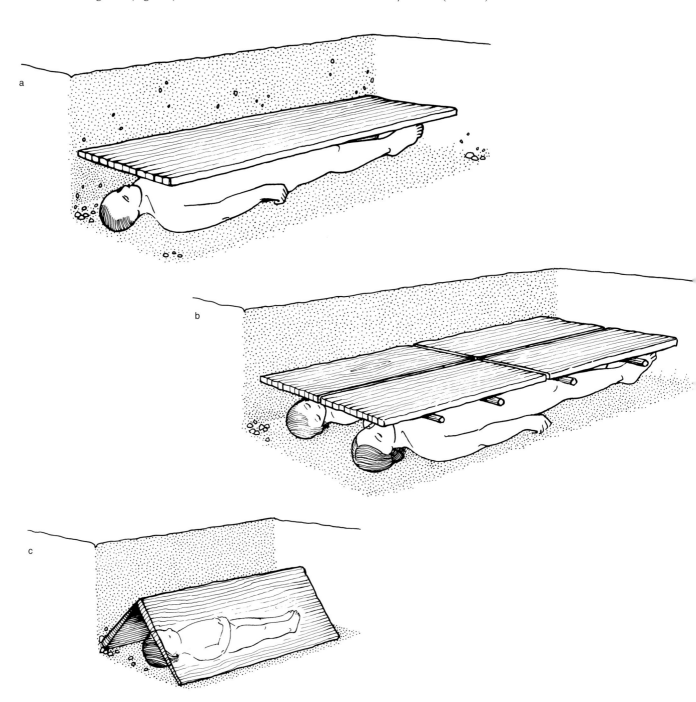

Fig 360 Schematic reconstruction of the types of coffins and boards used in the 11th- and 12th-century burials, based on excavated examples: a – cover board only (burial 40); b – cover board only supported on branches or poles (burial 24); c – cover boards creating a roof effect (burial 4); d – cover board and base board (burial 5); e – unfastened coffin without end board (burial 2); f – unfastened coffin with cover boards supported on regularly spaced sticks (burial 18); g – fastened coffin using pegs (burial 12) (Faith Vardy)

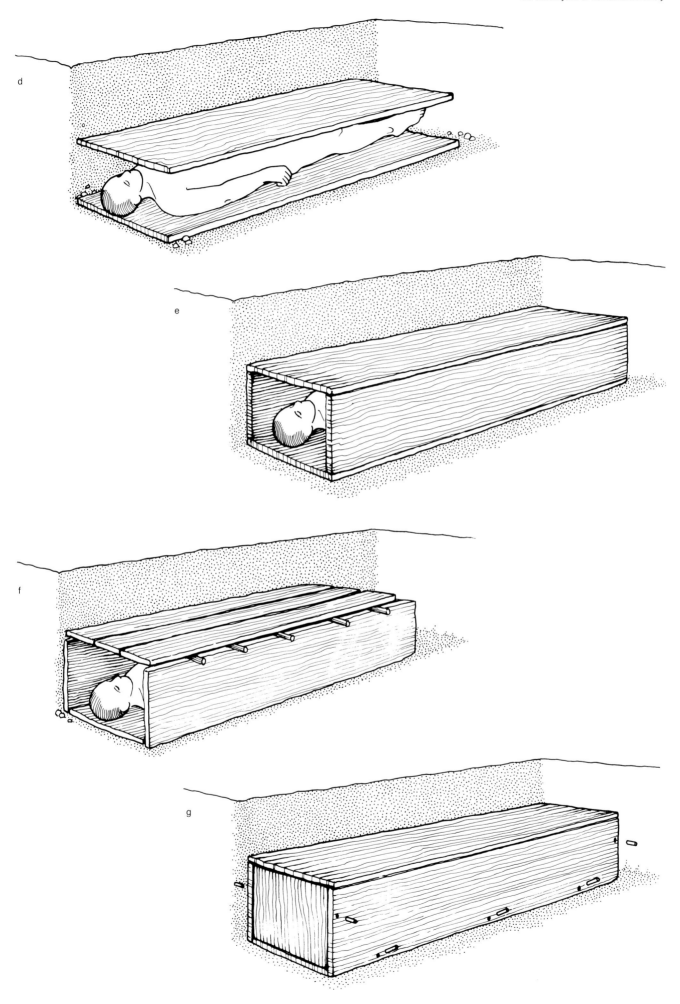

d

e

f

g

a

b

Fig 361 *Views of the burial of a woman and child (burial 24), from the north-east: a — four short oak boards covering both bodies; b — the boards removed, showing the four poles that supported them*

medieval illustration (Fig 360, c; Fig 362). The use of a cover board with a similar method of support was found in the eastern exterior cemetery of Bordesley Abbey, Worcestershire. Here the earliest graves used cover boards supported by short wooden cross-pieces, with one of these burials producing a tree-ring date of *c* 1150±9 (Astill et al 2004, 126). The use of a simple cover board was also observed in a burial found in the cloister walk at Sandwell Priory, Staffordshire (Hodder 1991, 100). At Merton Priory, Surrey, *c* 20 burials of the 12th to 14th centuries were also covered by a plank; some of these timbers were reused and at least one was significantly older than the date of burial (Miller and Saxby 2007, 154–5).

The intention appears to have been to cover the entire body, as was the case with all these burials apart from one (burial 30). This was a double (side by side) burial of an adult and child, and the cover board did not cover either of their heads or the entire body of the child, presumably just reflecting the timber available at the time of burial.

This method was used for both men and women, as well as for a high proportion of children (*c* 46%), where there was less need for a base board to carry the body. The use of a cover board only may have a chronological correlation since, with the exception of one burial (burial 4), this usage was not practised

in the 11th century and only occurs after *c* 1170 (period 11 phases 3–4). All recorded boards used were of radially- or tangentially-cleft oak.

COVER BOARD AND BASE BOARD

In five burials the cover board was used in association with a base board (Fig 360, d). The body was presumably lowered into the grave either on the base board or after it had been put in the grave, and then covered with another board. In two cases (burials 39 and 52) the base board was definitely used to transport the body to the graveside. The most elaborate burial of this type (burial 39) used a wide boat-shaped base board with augered holes regularly spaced around the edge (Fig 363). The body was lashed to the bier with fine willow rods, and after the body on its bier was placed in the grave it was covered by a rectangular board. A similar case (burial 52) used a rectangular board tapering towards the feet. The woman was tied to the board using fine willow rods threaded through regularly spaced holes around the edge of the board. Once placed in the grave the body was covered with another board. It is likely that in the three other burials of this type the base board was similarly used as a means of transport, even if the method of lashing the body to the board left no trace.

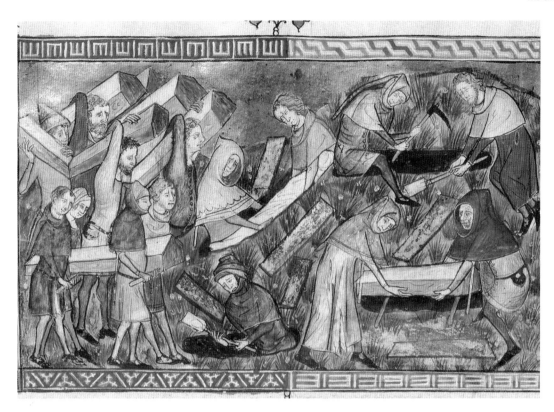

Fig 362 14th-century illustration of coffins being interred (Royal Library of Belgium, MS 13076 77, Chronique et annales de Gilles le Muisit, fo 24v)

Fig 363 A woodwork specialist cleaning a bier used to transport and then lower a body into the grave (burial 39)

In two of these burials, the cover board appeared to be supported by stones laid beside the head (burial 5, Fig 360, d; Fig 367) or placed either side of the head, knees and feet (burial 13). Presumably, as with the 'cover board only' type, the boards in the other burials were supported on a stepped grave-cut or on soil backfilled around the body.

The use of a cover board and base board is found in a burial of 1250–1450 in the south chapel at Sandwell Priory, in which the body lay between two planks (Hodder 1991, 100). This method was used at St Lawrence Jewry for adolescents and adults of both sexes but not for children, perhaps because the lightness of a child's body did not require a carrying board. This type of burial is recorded from c 1050 (period 10 phase 1) to c 1230 (period 11 phase 4).

UNFASTENED COFFINS

Six of the burials used four or more boards to create the appearance of a coffin within the grave, with a base board, cover board (lid), sides and sometimes even end boards, but there is no evidence of these elements being fastened with, for example, pegs or nails (Fig 360, e–f). These have been termed 'unfastened coffins' and must have been assembled once the body had been placed in the grave, and not used to transport the body to the graveside. The similar use of loose boards has been found in a pre-Conquest burial at St Peter's church, Barton-upon-Humber (Rodwell and Rodwell 1982, 291).

The impracticality of these unfastened coffins for carrying the body is also indicated by the fact that one of the burials (burial 20) had no base board, and for three of the burials the base board could not even have functioned as a bier as it was made from a number of loose planks (burial 14 (Fig 364) and burial 18), and/or the base board was too short for the body and ended below the knees (burials 6, 14 and 18). The intention with these burials appears to have been to cover the entire body, as was indeed the case with all of them (where a full body survived) apart from one (burial 18) where boards only covered the body from the head to above the ankles.

The cover board was supported in four of these burials by stones and/or tiles placed beside the head (burials 2, 14 and 18) or beside the head and feet (burial 6, Fig 367). A more elaborate method of supporting the cover board(s) over the body was employed in burial 18 (Fig 360, f; Fig 365), by creating a framework of five or six regularly spaced sticks laid across the body and resting on the side boards; this in turn supported three thin beech boards that covered the body. A similar method was used in a double burial (burial 24) but of the 'cover boards only' type. The differing size of the cross-members in these two burials presumably reflects the different weight of the boards placed over the bodies. This method of burial was only used for adult men and women, and its use is restricted to period 10 phases 2 and 4 (c 1070–c 1120).

FASTENED COFFINS

There were ten excavated examples of fastened coffins from the churchyard (Fig 360, g). Seven burials were contained in pegged wooden coffins, and some of these coffins definitely tapered towards the feet of the body (eg burials 7 and 11). The pegs were of willow/poplar, cleft oak or squared oak. The timber used in some of these coffins was quite thick and allowed pegs to be inserted through the face of one board into the edge of the adjoining board (burial 11, Fig 414). Other coffins were lighter and constructed from thinner boards (burials 12, 15 and 19), which required the pegs to go from face to face (skew-pegged). One of the skew-pegged coffins (burial 12, Fig 360, g; Fig 366) is remarkably similar to the coffin from a pre-Conquest burial at St Peter's church, Barton-upon-Humber (Fig 415; Rodwell and Rodwell 1982, fig 11) and to a 10th-century AD coffin from Beverley Minster, Yorkshire (Johnson and Allen 2004, 37). These lighter coffins may not have been able to travel any great distance.

Stones and tiles had been placed at the head and foot end of the lid of two of these coffins (burials 12 and 17) perhaps to warn a future gravedigger of their presence and thus avoid disturbance. Within one these coffins (burial 12) fragments of stone and tile had also been placed across the legs and either

a

b

Fig 364 *Views of a burial in an unfastened coffin (burial 14), from the east: a – with cover board in position; b – the cover board removed, showing the collapsed sides of the coffin (0.2m scale)*

Fig 365 *View of a burial in an unfastened coffin (burial 18), with regularly spaced sticks across the body to support the cover board, from the south (0.2m scale)*

Fig 366 *View of a pegged coffin (burial 12) under excavation, from the east*

side of the head. This form of burial was used for both sexes and all ages (including a baby of 6 months) but was restricted to c 1050–80 (period 10 phase 1) apart from one slightly later burial of c 1100–20 (burial 19, period 10 phase 4).

In three burials (burials 7, 8 and 19) a single rod or stick was found immediately under the base board, while one burial (burial 10) had three sticks, one of willow/poplar and two of oak (*Quercus*). All four of these burials were contained in pegged

or pegged and nailed coffins (half of all the examples of this type of burial) and it is possible that these sticks are the remnants of dowel-rods used in the construction of the coffin, as seen at Barton-upon-Humber (Fig 415; Rodwell and Rodwell 1982, fig 11) rather than having some symolic meaning.

There was only one example of a coffin that used both pegs and nails (burial 8). The side boards were nailed through into the end of the foot board and skew-pegged at an angle through to the base board. Perhaps this reflects the different thicknesses of the boards or the strength required of the coffin. This adolescent burial took place in c 1050–80 (period 10 phase 1).

The use of 'nailed only' coffins is rare at St Lawrence Jewry, being represented by only two burials (burials 9 and 57). In one such coffin (burial 9) the sides were nailed through to the base and the foot board, and in the other coffin (burial 57) the sides and lid were nailed through to the foot and head boards. These two coffins were used, respectively, for an adult in c 1050–80 (period 10 phase 1) and an adolescent in the early 13th century (period 11 phase 4).

NO COFFIN

No evidence for the use of a coffin or boards was found in 26 (c 36%) of the burials, but the actual number originally without a coffin is likely to be considerably lower as many of these burials were the most truncated and any evidence may not have survived. However, all but one of the burials without evidence for a coffin date from c 1170–c 1230 (period 11 phases 3–4) onwards and this may be a genuine pattern.

TREEWRIGHTING TECHNIQUES USED ON THE COFFINS AND BOARDS

Damian Goodburn

The boards and planks were mainly cleft from large, slow-grown straight oak trees, with a smaller number of beech used. A large proportion of the boards used were second-hand and partially worn from their first use; some were clearly of great age when they were used as burial furniture; for example, burial 14, which is dated to c 1066–92, included two boards with a tree-ring sequence of the 5th–7th centuries AD. Although they could be the inner fragments of unusually long-lived trees (c 600 years old), the evidence may indicate that they were reused. At Bordesley Abbey, Worcestershire, many of the timbers used to cover the burials were also reused from earlier buildings or furniture, and it is suggested that the timbers derived from buildings of some special importance to the community (Astill et al 2004, 126). In the case of St Lawrence Jewry, it is unlikely that the timbers derive from an early version of the church itself, which probably only dates from the mid 11th century. Perhaps there was another important early timber building in the neighbourhood that also supplied the 9th-century AD timbers used in the 11th-century Building 116 (Chapter 3.1).

The woodworkers who made the timber elements used in the graves (coffins, boards, covers and biers) employed the same comparatively simple techniques as used in the other contemporary woodwork. It is likely that the range of techniques employed in making the more elaborate box-like coffins were also used to make simple boxes and crates for other purposes such as the transport of goods and household storage. Some of the contemporary treewrighting techniques used in the timber buildings were more elaborate and required greater care and skill than the grave furniture. It does not appear that these Londoners were considered in any way prestigious, if judged only by the quality of woodwork. All three types of joining used (face-to-edge pegging, skew-pegging and nailing) were quick and easy methods. There was no evidence of sawn planking or carpentered joints even in the late 12th- and 13th-century coffins and boards, which date to after the introduction of more advanced carpentry. For example, the boards used in burial 49 (with a felling date after 1222) were still radially-cleft like those of nearly two hundred years earlier; craftsmen working on contemporary London buildings were using more advanced techniques such as sawn planking.

An interesting aspect of the assemblage of boards used in the burials is that they often had very little edge trimming as the treewrights were trying to leave the boards as wide as possible. This means that the inner heart side 'feather edge' and outer bark side wane or 'bark edge' were often left almost intact, giving long tree-ring sequences and providing considerable insights into contemporary woodland types in the region during the Saxon and Norman periods (above, 6.2).

The toolkit needed to make the rough boards consisted of an axe, wooden wedges and a large wooden mallet or 'maul' (for a description of timber conversion methods see above, 6.2). Once the boards had been obtained, only a few additional tools were required. Where the boards and planks had been further smoothed and trimmed a broader-bladed smoothing axe might have been used. The largest recorded axe facets on the boards were those on the boat-shaped bier board (burial 39, Fig 363) where the axe used must have had a fairly broad blade of c 200mm. A measuring stick and one or two small augers, for making peg and withy-lashing holes, together with

a form of gimlet for boring the occasional nail pilot hole, probably completed the toolkit required. The boards may have been simply trimmed by relatives of the deceased rather than by any specialist worker.

The coffins and boards are characteristic of London's 'treewrighting period' and quite distinct from later medieval carpentry traditions (Goodburn 1997b). The recently excavated simple plank coffins from the western cemetery of Roman London (Goodburn 2003a, fig 86) look superficially similar but can be easily distinguished by the use of sawing to prepare the planks and of substantial nails rather than pegs or small nails for the fastenings. The parent trees used were also much smaller, faster-grown oaks than any used for burial timbers in the 11th- to 13th-century St Lawrence Jewry cemetery.

Overall the raw materials and workmanship of the coffins and other boards do not imply any great expenditure, judging by the documented prices of similar raw cleft boards of comparable size used for shipbuilding in the 1290s. In detailed accounts the smallest 6ft (1.84m) boards seem to have cost just under a penny each, around three quarters of a day's pay for labourers working in the shipyards (figures from shipbuilding accounts cited in Friel 1995). Presumably smaller and second-hand boards would have been even cheaper. Clearly the box coffins would have required four principal boards and offcuts for the end boards, as well as perhaps half a day of a treewright's time to smooth and cut the boards and fit the peg fastenings. The coffins may therefore have cost about five or six times as much as the simple grave cover boards or roughly the equivalent of a master shipwright's daily pay in the 1290s.

BODY ATTITUDE AND THE EVIDENCE FOR SHROUDS
Although all the burials at the Guildhall show a similar body attitude (supine, extended, legs together and arms at the sides) there are subtle differences. The Guildhall burials have been analysed in accordance with a study carried out on the 10th- and 11th-century AD graveyard at Raunds, Northamptonshire, where two body attitudes, parallel-sided and non-parallel-sided, were recognised (Boddington 1987, 36, fig 4.9). Parallel-sided bodies have their arms pressed closely to the body (often with a 'hunching' of the shoulders), hands tight against or over the pelvis and feet together, whereas non-parallel-sided bodies have their legs splayed and arms lying further away from the body.

Of the 72 bodies at St Lawrence Jewry, 46 could be classified according to the Raunds categories (Fig 367), and of these the vast majority (39) were parallel-sided. At Raunds the parallel-sided position was linked to the constraining effect of a coffin and/or a shroud and the absence of clothes (Boddington 1987, 41); its distribution appeared to be spatially significant within the cemetery (ibid, 36–7). At St Lawrence Jewry there does not appear to be a correlation between the use of a coffin and parallel-sided burials, as c 31% of these showed no evidence of a coffin or other boards, a similar proportion to all the burials (c 36% of which showed no evidence for a coffin). It appears that at St Lawrence Jewry this body position (feet together, elbows and hands tucked into the sides of the body) is very suggestive of being wrapped and constrained in a shroud, irrespective of

Fig 367 View of examples of parallel-
sided (burial 5, on the left) and non-
parallel-sided (burial 6, on the right)
burials, from the east (0.2m scale)

whether the body was also contained within a coffin or boards.

Some of the burials at St Lawrence Jewry exhibited some form of 'bone tumble', where the bones (commonly the vertebrae and ribs) appear somewhat displaced and chaotic to varying degrees. This characteristic has been recognised and analysed on other sites, for example the 12th- to 13th-century Jewish burial ground at Jewbury, York (Brothwell 1987), the 10th- and 11th-century AD graveyard at Raunds, Northamptonshire (Boddington 1987) and the eastern cemetery of Roman London (Barber and Bowsher 2000). The burials from St Lawrence Jewry have also been classified according to the presence or absence of this feature, and of the 45 burials (out of 72) that could be classified, only seven (c 15%) exhibited bone tumble. Various explanations have been put forward for this pattern of disordered bone. In the eastern cemetery of Roman London the presence of bone tumble was correlated with grave depth and the presence of a coffin, with the agent of displacement likely to have been groundwater (ibid, 88–9). At Jewbury, York, it is taken to indicate a significant delay between death and burial, allowing partial decomposition above ground prior to the coffin being moved (Brothwell 1987, 26). At Raunds the occurrence of bone tumble may be due to the delay between death and burial (in a coffin), where death occurred at a distance from the cemetery or the funeral was delayed to allow a gathering commensurate with the individual's importance (Boddington 1987, 41). The relatively low number of burials at St Lawrence Jewry showing bone tumble compared to Raunds (32%) may indicate that in most cases there was little delay between death and burial, as might be expected for an urban parish churchyard. There is a 100% correlation between bone tumble and the presence of some form of coffin (whether fastened or unfastened) at St

Lawrence Jewry. The coffin would maintain a space around the body while it decayed, and so the trunk could collapse after the loss of muscle and other soft tissue. In the case of a body without a coffin, the surrounding soil would prevent displacement during the decomposition process. However, many coffined bodies showed no evidence of bone tumble, and these may indicate the use of a shroud within the coffin. In summary, of the 45 burials in coffins or with boards that could be classified (out of 72), as many as 38 may have been wrapped in a shroud.

HEAD AND FOOT SUPPORTS

There was no evidence for the use of 'pillow' stones placed under the head but stones and tiles were placed on either side of the head and/or the feet in nine of the burials (c 13%). These included adult men and women and one child, and all date from c 1050–c 1120 (period 10 phases 1–4) except for one that dates from c 1170–c 1200 (period 11 phase 3). Two of the burials were in pegged coffins, four in unfastened coffins, one with a cover board only, and one with a base board and cover board. In the case of the unfastened coffins and board burials, the stones and tiles may have been used to support the unattached cover board and stop it resting on the face of the deceased. This would, however, have been unnecessary in the two pegged coffins and in an unfastened coffin whose cover board (lid) was supported by sticks across the body (burial 18, Fig 365); in these instances the stones could have been used to support the head in an upright position. In three of the burials, stones were also found placed along one side of the body or legs (burials 12, 13 and 54).

The use of stones as head supports is known from the 12th to 16th centuries but is more common in the 11th and early

12th centuries (Gilchrist and Sloane 2005, 125). For example, the use of stones placed on either side of the head is seen in over 12 burials from St Peter's church, Barton-upon-Humber (Rodwell and Rodwell 1982, 301) and in 22 cases at St Nicholas Shambles, London (Schofield 1988, 18), in both coffined and uncoffined burials. Apart from a functional explanation for the use of the stones, they may have served to keep the face upright, so that on Judgement Day the resurrected body would be looking east towards the risen Christ (Daniell 1997, 161).

GRAVE MARKERS

There was little surviving evidence for the use of grave markers apart from the mound of soil marking the backfilled grave, which must have remained visible in order for subsequent burials to form rows. There is a single possible example of the use of a timber headboard (burial 13). Here, in addition to the base and cover boards, a board was set on end at the head end of the grave and appeared to have projected upwards, and may have functioned as some kind of grave marker. The top of the board had rotted away and its original height is lost along with any decoration. A similar grave marker set vertically in the ground was represented by a rectangular void at St Peter's church, Barton-upon-Humber (Rodwell and Rodwell 1982, 292).

ITEMS PLACED IN GRAVES

Very few items were found placed alongside the burial in the grave or coffin. An iron padlock A<236> was found in the lower torso region just above the pelvis of a ?woman aged 26–45 (burial 35) with no surviving evidence for a coffin. This is most likely a residual find, although padlocks have been found in other medieval burials, including three found in the pelvic area of adult women, and may symbolise chastity or sexual purity (Gilchrist and Sloane 2005, 178). A copper-alloy buckle A<3564> recovered from the fill of burial 15 could derive from a belt, but this is a common category of find and it does not seem to have been found close to the body.

A small copper-alloy bell A<1165> (Fig 368) was found at the end of a bundle of four thin wooden rods placed along the right side of a woman aged 26–45 years covered with a plank (burial 40). This may be a sacring bell, rung when the Host was elevated and perhaps at other important points during religious services. Two other bells, possibly deliberately placed, have been found alongside monastic burials at Merton Priory, Surrey, and at Barnstaple Priory, Devon (Gilchrist and Sloane 2005, 177); such bells may have been used in the burial ceremony or procession (Daniell 1997, 44).

The body of a man aged 26–45 years (burial 39) was accompanied by a roundwood pole or staff c 60mm in diameter and 1.58m long, with one axe-cut end, placed beside the bier in the grave on the right-hand side of the body. The man, buried in the late 12th century (period 11 phase 3), was lashed on to a boat-shaped bier and covered with a rectangular plank. Three burials at St Lawrence Jewry had one or more short flimsy sticks or rods, usually (where identified) of willow/

poplar (Salicaceae), placed alongside them. One stick was placed on the base board alongside the upper leg of a woman aged 36–45 years (burial 6). In the case of an adult of unidentified sex (burial 20), one stick was placed along the leg and two sticks lay on the other side of the upper body (Fig 369). In the third case, of a woman aged 26–45 years (burial 40), a bundle of four thin rods (c 6–8mm in diameter and c 0.55m long) was placed along her right side.

The presence of a staff in a grave may signify that the dead person had undertaken a pilgrimage during their lifetime. For example, this is the explanation given for the five burials accompanied by staffs at Hulton Abbey (Klemperer 1992, 85) and at Sandwell Priory, both in Staffordshire, where more than twenty burials were accompanied by wooden rods, many of which could be interpreted as functional staffs. The size of the Sandwell full-length staffs (c 1.35–1.96m long and 22–40mm in diameter) is similar to the St Lawrence Jewry example, and one is contemporary, from a burial dated c 1150–c 1250, while the others occur in periods dated between c 1250 and 1524 (Hodder 1991, 111–13). Another example of a full-length staff was found in a 15th-century burial in Worcester Cathedral interpreted as that of a pilgrim (Lubin 1990). Further afield, full-length staffs have also been found in Scandinavia, and it has been suggested that the earliest use of hazel sticks placed alongside burials is to be found at Lund (formerly Denmark, now Sweden) where in one churchyard nearly half the burials included hazel sticks and date from c 1000 (Gilchrist and Sloane 2005, 173).

Similar thin, short sticks to those found in burials at St Lawrence Jewry have been found alongside three burials at Sandwell Priory (Hodder 1991, 111) and in a pre-Conquest burial at St Peter's church, Barton-upon-Humber, where a pair of hazel 'wands' were placed by the right leg (Rodwell and Rodwell 1982, 312). At Bordesley Abbey, one skeleton in the eastern cemetery was accompanied by a willow wand c 1.5m long (Youngs and Clark 1982, 186). These flimsy sticks seem less likely than the longer rods to represent a pilgrim staff. They could be a symbol of office such as that of the wand- or rod-

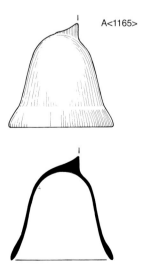

A<1165>

Fig 368 Copper-alloy bell A<1165> found alongside burial 40 (scale 1:1)

Fig 369 *View of a burial with short sticks placed on either side of the body (burial 20), from the north (0.2m scale)*

bearers mentioned at Westminster Abbey whose task was to control crowds. A more likely use, according to Daniell, was as symbolic grave goods, possibly to represent the Resurrection or power of Christ (Daniell 1997, 167–8).

MULTIPLE BURIALS

Six graves contained more than one body. In the most common type of multiple burial two (or in one grave three) bodies were placed side by side and all head to head in the same grave (burials 22, 24, 30 and 45). Two of these multiple burials had a cover board and two contained no form of coffin or boards. In the less common type one body was placed on top of another (head to head) in the same single-sized 'stacked' grave, simultaneously and with little or no gap between the bodies (burials 29 and 38). In one of these cases both bodies were contained in some form of coffin, and in the other a child was buried on a base board with a cover board and an adult above was buried in some form of coffin. There appears to be no age or gender pattern to the people buried together, and they include men, women, adolescents and children in various combinations.

Multiple burials occur exclusively in c 1170–c 1200 (period 11 phase 3) and account for 40% of the people buried in the excavated part of the churchyard at that time. Although these people were bound together in burial there is no indication from the osteological anlaysis that they were blood relatives. The practice of multiple burial may have been expedient and resorted to when there was an increased mortality rate in the parish population, perhaps due to a local epidemic or famine. Multiple burials may also indicate the relative poverty of those interred in this way. Along with the large mass burial pits found at St Mary Spital, London (Thomas 2004, 50) were many

smaller multiple side by side burials with two or more bodies in the same grave (C Thomas, pers comm). Four multiple burials (each with two or more) at St Andrew Fishergate, York, dating to the late 10th to 12th centuries AD, are thought to be 'battle casualties' as all are men and many exhibit blade injuries (Stroud and Kemp 1993, 158).

CHALK BURIALS

There was one example of an adolescent laid on a thin layer of fine white chalk-like material that covered the base of the grave-cut (burial 36). The body was then covered with a single oak plank. This form of basal lining, although rare, is known from other medieval cemeteries and may relate to the visual appearance of the grave; the use of white chalk surrounded by dark soil might have been seen as comparable to a white shroud (Gilchrist and Sloane 2005, 143).

Conclusions

The burial assemblage from St Lawrence Jewry churchyard provides a fascinating glimpse of burial practice in 11th- to 13th-century London. Many of the burials were contained within some form of wooden coffin or arrangement of timber boards. The coffins and some of the base boards would also have been used to transport the body from home to church and then on to the graveside, before being buried with the body. Burials with no coffin or base board, or short or multiple base boards, must have been transported on biers or coffins to the graveside and the body removed and placed in the grave. For most parish churches the coffin was a communal, reusable resource (Gilchrist and Sloane 2005, 111).

In spite of the poorer preservation and increased truncation of the later burials there does appear to be a trend away from the use of unfastened coffins and pegged coffins. Unfortunately, this is matched by a rise in the number of coffins too decayed to ascertain their original form.

The unfastened coffins were assembled after the body had been placed in the grave, as were the cover boards, and are not related to the transport of the body to the graveside. The intention appears to have been to enclose or cover the body with a pseudo-coffin, which was doubtless a cheaper method than using a true coffin. The need to cover the body could have been as a mark of respect for the dead or to avert the gaze of the living from the dead.

The variety of the use of timber seen in this churchyard could well be typical of contemporary parish churchyards in the City, although it might possibly indicate the presence of a particular ethnic or cultural group residing in the parish of St Lawrence Jewry. There are, unfortunately, few contemporary excavated parish cemeteries in the City for comparison. At the parish church of St Nicholas Shambles in the north-west of the City, 234 bodies dating from the 11th to 12th centuries were excavated (White 1988). However, there was no organic survival and thus little evidence for coffins or any other use of timber remained. The burials were categorised into six types: I, simple burial, perhaps in a coffin; II, with a stone pillow; III, grave with a floor only of chalk and mortar; IV, a cist of mortared stones, or simply lined with chalk and mortar; V, charcoal burial; and VI, grave lined with dry-laid tile or stone (ibid, 18–25). The burials from St Lawrence Jewry are statistically compared with those from St Nicholas Shambles in Table 3.

The comparison shows that many of the burial types are broadly similar at St Lawrence Jewry and St Nicholas Shambles (the lack of evidence for timber coffins at St Nicholas Shambles is simply due to the poor organic preservation). The most significant difference may be the lack of mortared cists (type IV) and lined graves (type VI) at St Lawrence Jewry. This appears to represent a real difference in local burial traditions – and

between two parishes which were not very far apart – but whether this is due to the status or the ethnic/cultural affinities of the local population is unclear. The only other excavated contemporary cemetery in the City is that of the mid 11th-century churchyard of the church of Syredus, which became the cemetery of the priory of Holy Trinity Aldgate in the 12th century (Schofield and Lea 2005, 135–9). Burials relating either to the earlier church or to the priory (it was not possible to distinguish two clear 'phases' of burial) were of type I or IV. The absence of mortared cists at St Lawrence Jewry is again the main difference between these two burial assemblages.

The choice of using a stone coffin, a stone-lined grave, a wooden coffin or simple wooden boards may reflect the status of the deceased person, since the different types of grave furniture would have incurred different costs. The most expensive option would have been the stone coffin, but a fastened timber coffin would also have been relatively expensive in terms of raw materials and labour (Daniell 1997, 161). Stone-lined graves may have been perceived as a cheaper form of stone coffin (White 1988, 23), just as the graves with cover boards or the unfastened coffins may have been cheaper versions of full timber coffins. It has been suggested that the choice of material to 'house' the burial may have mirrored the actual house of the deceased person (Daniell 1997, 162).

Many of the variables in burial practice evident at St Lawrence Jewry (such as the presence of coffins, boards, wands, staffs and head supports) are seen in the cemeteries of a wide range of religious institutions in England (Barton-upon-Humber, Sandwell Priory, Bordesley Abbey, Merton Priory, Hulton Abbey etc) and in Scandinavia (Lund, Trondheim: Gilchrist and Sloane, 173). The connection between these sites is their date and the fortuitous high levels of organic survival. What is remarkable about the St Lawrence Jewry burials is that they may reflect the most genuinely typical range of burial practice used in an 11th- to 13th-century urban parish cemetery; it is the luck of having such superb organic survival that is rare.

Table 3 *Comparison between 11th- to 13th-century burials at St Lawrence Jewry and 11th- to 12th-century burials at St Nicholas Shambles, according to the typology used at St Nicholas Shambles (White 1988, 18–25)*

	Type I simple burial (? with coffin)	Type II with stone 'pillow'	Type III grave with chalk 'floor'	Type IV stone cist	Type V charcoal burial	Type VI lined with tile/stone
St Nicholas Shambles	80.0%	9.0%	4.0%	3.5%	0.5%	2.0%
St Lawrence Jewry	80.0%	13.0%	1.0%	–	–	–

7

Conclusions

7.1 Future research

The publication of a large-scale archaeological project such as the Guildhall excavations is inevitably partial and selective. There is, therefore, the opportunity for future research, and a large body of unpublished information lies in the four individual site archives and in the combined research archive (Chapter 1.2). It is hoped that future researchers will make use of this data. For example, the catalogue of accessioned finds (Chapter 8.8) is highly selective, with relatively large numbers of artefacts not included, particularly later medieval and post-medieval items (since the analysis concentrated on the 11th- and 12th-century artefacts and on items associated with the Guildhall or with Blackwell Hall market). Similar selection criteria have been applied to the animal bones and plant remains, and the relevant archaeological research archives contain more detail on the later medieval and post-medieval remains. The unpublished research archive also contains much more detail of the medieval and later histories of the properties along Aldermanbury, Cat Street and Basinghall Street.

The architecture and the churchyards of St Lawrence Jewry and St Michael Bassishaw have been discussed in Chapter 6. However, there are surviving vestry minutes and churchwardens' accounts for both churches, dating back to 1556 in the case of St Lawrence Jewry (GL, MS 2590/1 and /2; MS 2593/1 and /2) and 1617 for St Michael Bassishaw (GL, MS 2598/1; MS 2601/1); further study of these documents might throw light on some of the changes taking place at the time of the Reformation (at St Lawrence Jewry) and could inform our understanding of the post-Fire reconstruction campaigns. There may also be records of structural changes to the churches in some of the St Paul's Cathedral archives, now held by the Guildhall Library (eg the dean's and bishop's registers in the DCPC Muniment Books series, or the DCPJ City Churches Rebuilding series). The important assemblages of early medieval human remains from the churchyard of St Lawrence Jewry are discussed in Chapters 6.12, 8.17 and 8.18, but it is perhaps regrettable that no comparable group of late medieval or post-medieval graves could be excavated from the same graveyard. A large part of the parish cemetery lies preserved under the south-west corner of the modern Guildhall Yard, and this group of unexcavated burials is an important archaeological resource which, one day, could yield significant new information, particularly when combined with parish records and existing archaeological information. A new programme of archaeological excavation monitoring refurbishment work in the Guildhall's north piazza, the north block and the old library began in 2006 (site code GHN06). Although the works are small-scale, they may reveal new information about the layout of the churchyard of St Michael Bassishaw and the houses along Basinghall Street.

The Guildhall itself may still have a few secrets to give up in the future. The walls of the hall contain recycled architectural fragments from the earlier Guildhalls, some of which were observed during rebuilding works in the 1860s (RIBA 1865,

177–85). Sally Jeffery, the former architectural historian of the Corporation of London, has shown that there is a wealth of unpublished information on the hall in the 17th, 18th and 19th centuries (CLDTS, Jeffery archive). Much could be learnt from a future architectural study of the early modern fabric of the building, since Barron (1974) and Wilson (1976) concentrated their studies on the medieval hall. There may even be some work for future archaeologists if evidence for the elusive 12th-century hall lies buried beneath the crypts of the Guildhall.

7.2 The results of excavation and research

The City of London Corporation (formerly known as the Corporation of London), the local government body for the City of London, has a long history of co-operation with archaeologists, and the excavations of the 1980s and 90s were the culmination of a century of archaeological sponsorship by the (then) Corporation. London's first official archaeological rescue excavation took place in 1882 when the Corporation asked Henry Hodges to record the old Mayor's Court and chamberlain's office before their demolition. Hodges drew elevations and views of the buildings, conducted a watching brief during their demolition and recorded earlier archaeological features. He published the results within four years, and his archaeological report – beautifully illustrated with phased watercolour plans – was included at the end of J B Price's illustrated history of the Guildhall (Price 1886, 253–6). Hodges's successors at the Museum of London (which remains linked to the City of London Corporation) have attempted here to follow his fine example, and this publication is the result of a long campaign of archaeological excavation and post-excavation research, very generously supported by the City of London Corporation.

The research aims for this publication were first defined in 1997 (Bateman and Porter 1997) and refined two years later (Bateman et al 1999). The approach of this book has been to respond to those research aims using the integrated model of archaeological publication first used by the Museum of London for St Mary Spital (Thomas et al 1997), and which has evolved in a number of publications over the following years. This form of archaeological publication aims to integrate, as far as possible, the various strands of archaeological and historical evidence into a single narrative. An important aspect of this approach that has been developed in the present report is the use of historical map regression techniques to create a series of base maps on to which the pieces of archaeological, architectural and documentary information could be placed. To give an example, a plan showing the Jewish houses on Cat Street in the 12th century (Fig 78) takes its overall form from various 17th- to 20th-century maps (used in the map regression), adds details from a 16th-century survey of one of the houses, shows the excavated medieval foundations (which

were dated to the 12th century by analysis of stratigraphic and pottery evidence), and adds the evidence for tenement boundaries (deriving from 13th-century and later property descriptions). This type of mapping is used to enhance the purely archaeological evidence, and illustrates individual dated periods in Chapters 2–5. Simplified versions of the maps are then repeated in Chapter 6 in order to illustrate a more 'vertical' slice of time, showing, for example, the development of Blackwell Hall market through the centuries as a sequence of plans.

An important area of interest concerns the time between the Roman amphitheatre (Bateman et al in prep) and the Late Saxon activity, a period that might be described as something of a 'holy grail' for archaeologists working in the City of London. This report, perhaps somewhat disappointingly, concludes that there is an almost complete lack of archaeological evidence between the end of the Roman period and the 10th century AD. There are intriguing hints of activity in the form of a Merovingian buckle <S1> (Fig 283) lost on the site of the old amphitheatre, but the impression is that this area remained largely unused grassland for nearly five hundred years. The evidence suggests that the reoccupation of this area began in the 10th century AD when small farmsteads were established beyond (north of) the expanding Late Saxon town. Furthermore, the results of the excavations show that by the 11th century the old amphitheatre was barely visible, even as an earthwork. By the time the first Guildhall was built in the 1120s, virtually all traces of the amphitheatre had vanished, and so the situation of the Guildhall, directly over the north bank of the old amphitheatre, can now be seen as an interesting topographic coincidence, but without any further significance.

The discovery in the 1992 excavations of a graveyard and a number of well-preserved timber buildings of the 11th and 12th centuries was immediately recognised as one of the most significant aspects of the archaeological evidence. The initial interpretation was that the graveyard and buildings were part of a defined settlement with evidence for links with Denmark (Porter 1997; Bateman 1997), and the occupation was thus dubbed 'Anglo-Scandinavian' (Bateman et al 1999). An important aspect of the post-excavation research project has therefore been to investigate the nature of this settlement. If previous studies of the Guildhall sites understandably emphasised the special nature of the archaeological evidence, here it is argued that it is the scale of the excavations and the degree of organic preservation that are exceptional; the wealth of evidence uncovered is surely typical of ordinary life and death in 11th- and 12th-century London. Furthermore, it is argued that the occupants of the area were Londoners without any particular Scandinavian connection (Chapter 6.4).

The archaeological evidence presented in Chapter 3.1 and 3.2 shows that the important change to the area came around the middle of the 11th century when the church of St Lawrence Jewry was founded on the northern edge of the town. By the 1080s, when the expanding town seems to have reached this far north, a number of timber buildings were constructed at the end of a path that ran along the east side of the church. In the

12th century the path developed into a town lane as more buildings were erected on either side. The houses were relatively small, single-storey timber structures built using traditional English timber techniques of earthfast posts supporting the main weight of the roof, with the walls infilled between the principal posts in a variety of ways. The houses were vulnerable to both fire and rot, and the occupants had to rebuild them roughly every 20–30 years (Chapter 6.3). The occupants kept their livestock both in the adjacent fields and in their yards, and they also kept some animals in their houses over the winter. They brought in their arable crops from nearby fields for processing and consumption, and they used much of their domestic waste and animal dung to manure the fields (Chapter 6.4). The occupants of the town lane also practised a number of small-scale craft activities: there were shoemakers and less-skilled cobblers, boxwood workers who used this fine-grained wood to make items such as musical instrument components, metalworkers who cast small objects in copper alloys, and skinners who provided the raw material for furriers, using cats which were probably bred for this purpose (Chapter 6.6). The men, women and children who lived and died along this lane were probably buried in the adjacent churchyard of St Lawrence, and the archaeological excavations provided a mass of detailed evidence concerning the burial traditions and treatment of the dead (Chapter 6.12), as well as providing physical evidence for the health, age and status of the local population (Chapter 8.18). The lane seems to have been abandoned by the beginning of the 13th century when the residents were apparently forced out by changes to the area brought about by the building of the Guildhall, and perhaps also by the arrival of wealthier neighbours to the south and east.

An important new research theme was opened up in 1990 when the Museum of London archaeologist Richard Sermon interpreted a stone-lined pit on one of the Guildhall sites (excavated in 1985) as a mikveh or Jewish ritual bath (Pepper 1992, 4). This was the catalyst for an examination of the evidence on this site for the medieval London 'Jewry', a topographic term that was also applied to the church of St Lawrence (in the) Jewry. Along Cat Street and Basinghall Street, wealthy Jewish merchants were building large town houses and synagogues in the second half of the 12th century; one of these town houses contained the mikveh in an outbuilding at the rear (Chapter 6.5). The property was still in Jewish ownership a century later, and the documentary evidence has allowed us to track the fortunes of the Peytevyn family as they weathered the civil unrest of the 1260s, only to face expulsion in 1290 along with the entire Jewish population of England. A further aspect of the research was an attempt to build on the archaeological and documentary evidence and define an archaeological 'signature' of Jewish occupation; but it did not, in this case, prove possible to categorise 'Jewish' assemblages of artefacts or food residues. However, an important group of Jewish-owned artefacts was identified, namely the tableware belonging to Aaron the grandson of Peytevyn (although there is nothing intrinsically 'Jewish' about the actual pottery). In an odd episode, it appears that Aaron left at least some of the family tableware behind in 1290 and that the next occupants of the property deliberately buried the set in the foundations of the demolished building, perhaps with the intention of ritually 'purifying' the property.

London archaeologists have long been studying the evidence for medieval churches, particularly those that no longer exist, and work has included a wide-ranging survey (Schofield 1994) and a detailed study of two churches close to our study area, St Alban and St Mary Aldermanbury (Milne 2001). This example has been followed here, with an examination of the churches of St Lawrence Jewry and St Michael Bassishaw combining information from excavations with a study of documentary evidence and an analysis of their plan-form. Their histories are compared in Chapter 6.11, that of St Lawrence Jewry beginning around the middle of the 11th century and continuing to the present day, while St Michael Bassishaw originated slightly later, in the 12th century, and was demolished in the 1890s.

An unexpected result of the documentary research for this volume has been the evidence for a cluster of late medieval and early modern inns on Cat Street. Public inns have been seen as developing from the private inns or 'great houses' that were temporary London bases for aristocrats or wealthy merchants (Barron 1995, 12–14). The evidence studied here suggests that the Cat Street inns developed more as a market-led response, providing hospitality to visitors to the Guildhall and Blackwell Hall market (Chapter 6.10). The archaeological evidence for the inns is somewhat disappointing but the documentary and cartographic evidence has allowed a study of four main inns, with the earliest (The Saracen's Head) dating from the late 14th century and the latest (The Guildhall Tavern) surviving until 1919.

Excavations in the north-west part of the City of London have often found evidence for medieval metalworking. On the Guildhall site there seems to have been a local tradition of copper alloy working that began in the 10th century AD with the casting of small dress accessories including items of a type known as 'Winchester style'. The tradition continued in the 11th and 12th centuries, and re-emerged in the 14th century with the large-scale production of dress accessories, apparently by members of the Girdlers' guild (Chapter 6.6). Less significant evidence for the manufacture of candlesticks in the 16th century was also found.

In 1993 the team of archaeologists uncovered a series of massive chalk foundations on the east side of the site, near Basinghall Street. The initial research showed that these must relate to the medieval hall known as Blackwell Hall that gave its name to the 14th-century cloth market, an institution which survived as late as 1820. Building on important published work (Bateman 2004), the archaeological evidence is here combined with some important documentary evidence (in particular a 16th-century building specification and an 18th-century survey) to suggest a model for the development of a baronial hall into a civic market (Chapter 6.8 and 6.9). Blackwell Hall was probably founded by the aristocrat Warin de Bassingbourn who built a new town house along Basinghall Street in c 1200, which the baron John fitz Geoffrey then enlarged in the mid

13th century. The building became known as Blackwell Hall after the alderman and merchant John de Bankwell who was granted the property (perhaps as a reward for his service as the City's Common Clerk) in the 1280s. The hall was repurchased by the City at the end of the 14th century in order to create a market for the sale of woollen cloth; the enterprise proved highly successful, and the market buildings were further enlarged and improved in the 16th and 17th centuries.

The Corporation of London (renamed in 2006 the City of London Corporation) is probably England's oldest surviving local government institution and the Guildhall has been at the heart of this government for nearly nine hundred years. The evidence for the Guildhall and its administrative precinct therefore forms one of the core subjects of this volume. By adding new archaeological information to existing historical and architectural studies, it has been possible to chart for the first time the development of the precinct from the early 12th century to the end of the 20th century (Chapter 6.7). Eight main phases in its history are illustrated (Fig 351), beginning with the construction of the first Guildhall in the 1120s. Right from the beginning it combined fiscal, judicial and administrative functions, serving as 'geld hall' (for payment of the king's 'geld' or tax), Court of Husting and as an office for the newly appointed civic sheriffs. This separate civic institution thus emerged during the reign of Henry I, evolving from an existing London royal administrative base which, it is argued here, may have been situated a short distance to the north-west in Aldermanbury. The Guildhall seems, like its predecessor, to have been controlled in the early years by a prominent and long-standing London dynasty, whose 'rule' culminated in Henry fitz Ailwyn becoming the first mayor of London at the end of the 12th century. Subsequent reorganisations of the Guildhall and its precinct are then charted, beginning under the mayors Henry le Waleys at the end of the 13th century and John de Pulteney in the early part of the 14th century. Le Waleys, with the support of Edward I, built a new civic chapel and de Pulteney continued the works with the enlargement of the Guildhall itself. Following the Black Death, a College of priests was founded at the Guildhall to serve in the Guildhall chapel. The next big rebuilding campaign came at the

beginning of the 15th century, perhaps initiated by London's most famous mayor, Richard Whittington, and at least partly administered by the City's Common Clerk, John Carpenter. The master mason John Croxtone carried out the works, rebuilding the Guildhall and its chapel, and the City went on to erect a series of new buildings, both for the religious College (including the library) and the secular administration. One of the more important aspects of this publication is the architectural reconstruction of the main facade of Croxtone's new Guildhall, in particular the porch on its south side which was the most visible part of the new hall. The precinct was not drastically altered again until after the Great Fire of 1666, although the surviving medieval open spaces had been gradually filled in during the 16th and earlier 17th centuries. The reconstruction programme of the late 1660s seems to have been directed by Christopher Wren and Robert Hooke, and it included an enlarged Guildhall porch, a 'lost' early work of Wren that is reconstructed here for the first time. The later alterations to the Guildhall, studied in less detail in this book, included a major campaign of improvements by the City Surveyor, George Dance the younger, beginning in the 1770s, and further works carried out in the 1860s by the City Architect, Horace Jones.

The most radical change to the Guildhall and its precinct came about as result of what has been called the 'second Great Fire of London', the firestorm resulting from the German bombing of London on the night of 29/30 December 1940. The architects Giles Gilbert Scott and his son Richard completed a campaign of reconstruction and reorganisation for the Corporation of London, with the restored medieval Guildhall (its full length visible for the first time) dominating the enlarged Guildhall Yard. It was this long campaign of restoration and redevelopment − the fifth major rebuild since the 1120s − that provided the opportunity for the series of archaeological excavations which are reported on here. From the public open space of the new Guildhall Yard many elements of the site's long history can now be appreciated, beginning with London's Roman amphitheatre (marked out with black paving), continuing with the restored medieval Guildhall itself, and finishing with the Scotts' dramatic 20th-century precinct buildings.

8

Specialist appendices

8.1 Documentary sources

Tony Dyson

The full documentary survey underpinning the present publication was intended to complement Caroline Barron's *The medieval Guildhall of London* (1974) in two ways. Firstly, it took account of the properties fringing the Guildhall and its precinct on Aldermanbury, Cat Street and Basinghall Street, and on Church Alley to the north, in the hope of throwing further light on the topographical and other relationships between them and the precinct, as well as on their own layout and the character and trades of their occupants. Several of these adjoining properties came to be acquired by the City and effectively absorbed into the precinct. The same documentary information also provides a context for the numerous peripheral archaeological excavations and observations that have taken place since the 1950s, in addition to the major Guildhall Yard excavations of the 1980s and early 1990s. Secondly, the survey extended the coverage of the entire area, both precinct and adjoining properties, beyond *c* 1600, where Barron's study terminates, to the early 19th century, and thus covers the building programmes of the 1610s and the late 1660s and 70s following the Great Fire, as well as the comprehensive alterations and improvements of the 1770s and 80s. Limited time precluded examination of the vastly increased documentation generated by the radical and extensive rebuilding schemes of Victorian and later date. The research archive (Dyson 2003) gives a full account of the documentary work and recounts the histories of the properties fringing the Guildhall precinct in greater detail than is possible in this volume.

For the period up to *c* 1550 much the most important single source consists of property title deeds. These provided the mainstay of the survey, enabling the street-frontage tenements surrounding the precinct to be reconstructed and so establishing a basic topographic framework for the entire area. The deeds derive from the surviving archives of livery companies, religious houses, parishes and other large property-holders, but the largest collection by far is preserved in the City's Husting rolls, where many deeds and wills relating to property in the City were registered. The special importance of deeds is that, as well as providing details of ownership, they usually record the names of neighbours or streets on all four sides, making it possible both to identify material specific to individual properties, and to chart the physical relationship of those properties one to another on the ground. Measurements, which would be of still greater value in this respect, are only rarely recorded.

Coverage of individual properties by deeds can vary disconcertingly, as can be seen from the blank record of Tenements 5 and 6, 10 and 11, 16 and 19 after the 14th century (Chapter 4.2). This is partly explained by their acquisition by institutions which subsequently held on to them, precluding further changes of ownership and the production of the deeds that would have documented them. Less straightforward was the identification of the institutions in question, for a search of the likeliest sources in the available time proved unproductive. In this respect, it is ironic that the City commonalty, having established a deed registration service by the mid 13th century, did not itself make more use of it. With the exception of those for the predecessors of Blackwell Hall (Tenement 12), the City's own early title deeds do not appear to have survived, in the Husting rolls or elsewhere. The likeliest explanation of this omission would be their separate inclusion in a special deed register now lost, stolen or otherwise unavailable. Whatever the reason, the circumstances of the acquisition by the City of Tenement 13 in *c* 1400, of Tenement 19 at some entirely unknown date, and of portions of Tenement 3 as recently as 1790, remain obscure.

Sources other than deeds in these earlier periods, being largely concerned with legal infractions, tend to be sparse, though often of great value where they do occur. They include the City's own records, including the Letter Books, Mayor's Court and Plea and Memoranda rolls, and records relating specifically to property, such as the Assize of Nuisance, Possessory Assizes and Viewers' Certificates. The prepotent influence of the City corporation in the study area appears to have all but eclipsed that of the state: Crown records such as Patent, Close and Charter rolls only rarely concern themselves with these properties. In the mid 16th century, Particulars for Grant, which often provide invaluable information about the recently confiscated properties of dissolved religious houses (as indeed they do in the case of the former Guildhall chapel and College properties) are of no help with tenements in lay ownership. Lacunae such as these compound the problems of linking the medieval properties with their post-medieval successors, when they next emerge in the records, often no earlier than the post-Fire surveys of Mills and Oliver.

Although very little new evidence can be added from contemporary sources to Caroline Barron's account of the medieval Guildhall, the retrospective value of evidence from later periods is demonstrated by the light thrown on the layout of the medieval precinct by post-medieval sources, notably on the extent of the garden to the north of the Guildhall, the western part of which can now be seen to have been fully taken up by Croxtone's continuing building programme of the 1420s (Chapter 4.3), and whose precise plan is clearly apparent from an 18th-century City plan (Fig 209).

After *c* 1550 the character and coverage of the sources change fundamentally. With the increasing disuse of enrolment in the Court of Husting the evidence relating to Tenements 1–6 and 8–19 diminishes, save in those cases where properties were acquired by identifiable institutions whose records survive: Tenements 2 (the City in the 1590s), 10 (the Clothworkers' Company in 1587) and 17–18 (the Coopers' Company in 1490 or soon after). Many properties are documented only in the records generated by the accident of the Great Fire, and some not even there. At the same time the City's own records were becoming ever more comprehensive, especially the Repertories of the Court of Aldermen, though for present purposes these are still less helpful than they might have been. Little attempt was made, for example, to outline the findings of the innumerable inquiries

initiated by the Court, even though the appointments are assiduously recorded. They, or at any rate the indexes to them, become noticeably less comprehensive during the 18th century. From 1633 the City Cash Accounts provide a vital source of information about the date and nature of the City's building works (among other matters), although their value is often diminished by the practice of recording as total sums payments made to contractors in respect of more than one project.

These records were soon supplemented by those of various ad hoc rebuilding committees set up immediately after the Fire, their somewhat fragmentary surviving records petering out altogether after the late 1680s. During this brief post-Fire period they complement the records of the City Lands Committee, whose records are of prime importance. Its Grant Books and Lands Deeds were largely confined to leases of properties (such as Tenements 2, 3, 13 and 19) previously purchased by the City, rather than applying to the civic buildings, but the voluminous Journals and Papers cover both, and constitute the main source for the construction, repair and maintenance of the civic buildings from this period onwards. Limitations of time have meant that the use of these records has been highly selective, the most effective approach to them being through the City Cash Accounts, which succinctly identify the key periods of expenditure on major building operations.

8.2 Cartographic reconstruction

Nick Holder

A number of topographic plans showing the Guildhall area over a thousand-year period were created using an updated version of the methodology of cartographic reconstruction outlined by Johns (1989). The authors of the present book enjoyed the advantages of modern computer software, in particular AutoCAD. Using the modern digital 1:1250 Ordnance Survey (OS) map as a starting point, plans of the earlier archaeological periods were created using computer-based map regression techniques. For the period 1770–1939 (Chapter 5.1), the relevant portion of the 1929 OS map was the starting point. The 'raster' data of the scanned map (a series of dot or pixel images) was converted into more useful 'vector' data by digitising (ie creating digital outlines of) the buildings, yards and streets using AutoCAD software. The digitised 1929 map was fitted to the modern OS map by using the 'align' and 'scale' functions of the software, having defined some common points on both maps (the corners of St Lawrence Jewry church and the Guildhall). The 1929 map fitted almost perfectly on to the modern OS map; the discrepancies were of the order of 0.1–0.5m, and the modern OS map is not necessarily the more accurate of the two (indeed, the Guildhall itself was more accurately surveyed on the earlier map).

For the period 1666–1770 (Chapter 4.5), a detailed 1770s survey of the Guildhall (Fig 246), and Ogilby and Morgan's map of 1676, were scanned, digitised and located using the same methodology of matching common points on these maps and the 1929 map. The 1770s survey fitted very well: when distances between the churches of St Lawrence Jewry and St Michael Bassishaw and the Guildhall were compared, there was less than 1.0m discrepancy over a range of c 100–150m. (The variation was not constant so it could not be attributed to a scaling error.) Much of the Ogilby and Morgan map fitted satisfactorily (with discrepancies of 1.0–2.0m) but it became apparent that the west side of the Guildhall had been inaccurately drawn. It would appear that the cartographers' surveys carried out along the *frontages* of Aldermanbury, Cateaton (now Gresham) Street and the Guildhall yard were very accurate; however, the surveys had not been tied together well at their meeting points at the *rear* of the properties and, furthermore, the angles of street junctions were not always accurately surveyed (cf Johns 1989, 57–8). A better fit of the Ogilby and Morgan data was obtained by locating it in 'blocks' of houses in several stages around the edges of the (better-quality) 1770s Guildhall survey. The resulting digital map was then checked against the archaeological data; there was less than 0.5m discrepancy for Blackwell Hall and the Guildhall chapel, although the chamberlain's office (north of the Guildhall) had to be rotated slightly (by up to 1.5m) to fit the excavated evidence. Having reconstructed a map of the study area in the late 17th and 18th centuries, the property holdings defined by the documentary survey (Tenements 1–20) could be added.

The only accurate map for the period 1550–1666 (Chapter 4.4) was John Leake's survey of the ruined City, commissioned by the mayor and aldermen after the Great Fire of 1666 and published in 1667 (BL, Add MS 5415 art 56). Although it lacks the detailed accuracy of Ogilby and Morgan's later map, the Leake survey is the only map to show the pre-Fire road layout, and the manuscript version even has road widths indicated. The 'copperplate' map of c 1559 (Saunders and Schofield 2001) and Faithorne and Newcourt's map of 1658 (Margary 1981) are map-views rather than proper surveys but they are useful for giving an impression of the street frontages. A combination of this cartographic, documentary and archaeological evidence was used to inform decisions about 'retaining', editing or deleting the streets, buildings and yards from the post-Fire map. The Guildhall precinct could be reconstructed relatively easily thanks to the large number of older buildings that were mapped on the 1770s survey (Fig 246). The southern part of the study area was also relatively easy to reconstruct thanks to the large number of archaeological interventions. The houses on the street frontages of Cat (later Cateaton) Street, Basinghall Street and Aldermanbury were reconstructed by 'tiling' the individual Mills and Oliver surveys of Fire-damaged properties (Mills and Oliver 1666–7) on to the reconstructed tenement outlines that had been defined for the post-Fire period (Chapter 4.5). The raw survey evidence and/or the tenement outlines were adjusted by up to one metre to achieve a 'best fit', and the evidence from the archaeological sites GM3 and GM4 on the Aldermanbury frontage was also used. Other surveys and documentary descriptions allowed further reconstruction; for example, Tenement 11 has a series of detailed measurements

and Tenement 10 was surveyed by Ralph Treswell in 1612 (Schofield 1987, 54–5).

The methodology was continued for the earlier periods, although it became increasingly difficult to reconstruct buildings or yards where there was no archaeological information. The property outlines could generally be retained or edited with some confidence thanks to documentary information that sometimes included measurements. A working assumption was that the property outlines would become simpler the further back in time.

In some cases (eg for Tenement 7 (St Lawrence Jewry) in the 15th century: Chapter 4.3) a reconstruction of individual buildings and yards was attempted given the detailed description of their relative locations. In other cases, a combination of archaeological and documentary evidence was used. For Tenement 11, for example, the location of the street frontage had already been defined (in periods 16 and 17, Chapter 4.4 and 4.5) and the width of the stone house had been defined in the early 17th century (period 16, Chapter 4.4), but archaeological evidence was used to map the rear of the building as it was in the 12th century (period 12, Chapter 3.3).

It should be noted that there is a lack of firm data relating to the medieval street layout and the street frontage of the buildings. With the exception of the southern part of Basinghall Street (whose west frontage was archaeologically excavated), the medieval streets were defined by the 'best fit' of the 17th-century maps, and these street frontages were then carried back into earlier periods. An 'educated guess' was made to simplify the street frontage further back in time; for example, it was decided that the lane leading to St Michael Bassishaw was probably no earlier than the church itself. In other respects the reconstructed early road layout largely follows Milne and Cohen's analysis (Milne 2001, 122–5).

8.3 Architectural reconstruction, architectural fragments and petrological analysis

Mark Samuel, with Desmond T Donovan and Kevin M J Hayward (petrological analysis)

Introduction

Detailed architectural research and analysis concentrated on two buildings, the Guildhall porch and the Guildhall chapel. The results of the analysis, including both text and figures, have been integrated into the main chronological narrative for the medieval Guildhall chapel (Chapter 4.3), and for the medieval and later Guildhall porches (Chapter 4.3 and 4.5). There are also essays considering the structural techniques as well as the art-historical context of the medieval porch and chapel (Chapter 6.7); a fuller account is provided in the research archive (Samuel 2005). The 'process' of reconstructing the porch and chapel has to be justified by the available surviving evidence. The reconstruction of the chapel relies on combining old views and accounts with 20th-century archaeological data; fortunately, an accurate survey made just before its demolition provides a vital link between the two sets of evidence. There is better material evidence of the porch, not least its partially surviving structure. Furthermore, architectural fragments reused in the foundations of the 18th-century porch tell us much about parts of its earlier phases.

Stones have been included in the catalogue if they derive from a known building on the site. The only group which allows reconstruction are the stones from the Guildhall porch. The research archive (Samuel 2005) contains a comprehensive record of each architectural fragment, including 1:1 and 1:2 scale drawings, and describes the process of architectural reconstruction. The archive also includes a detailed bibliography of the antiquarian plans, elevations and views of the porch and chapel.

Catalogue entries include the catalogue number, accession number and context number, the latter two with the relevant site letter-prefix (Chapter 1.3; Table 1). Dimensions given are treated as if the viewer was facing a notional wall in which the stone is set: 'H' is course height, 'W' is width and 'WD' is 'wall depth' (distance from the viewer). In the case of the two grave slabs, 'W' is maximum width. Rough dating is usually based on the tools employed for finishing. Moulding evidence, where present, occasionally refines this down to a 50-year date span. Building dates are derived from the wider analysis presented in the chronological narrative (Chapters 3 and 4). Petrological analysis was limited to addressing specific research questions, namely the types of stone used in the 14th-century chapel, the 15th-century porch and its 17th-century successor.

Architectural reconstruction of the Guildhall chapel (1440–55: Chapter 4.3)

Many features of the Guildhall chapel are poorly known; the vestry, roof, gables and wall crestings were destroyed in the Great Fire of 1666, and the belfry turret and west gable end were removed in the 1770s. The remaining building survived into an era of developing national feeling for the past. John Chessel Buckler recorded the west elevation and several internal details (Barron 1974, pls 26, 28, a–b) in an early act of 'rescue archaeology' perhaps sponsored by the unknown 'E.T.C ' (Anon 1820). Robert Schnebbelie shadowed him, producing a complementary series of records (Fig 193; Fig 248). Written descriptions were also made about this time (Nichols 1819; Anon 1820). Barron (1974) garnered a wealth of documentary evidence about the 15th-century chapel, right down to the furnishings and glass. Finally, between 1987 and 1996 the basic plan and the foundations were recorded during the excavation of sites A and B.

The published reconstructions (west elevation (Fig 197), longitudinal cross-section (Fig 198), lateral cross-section (Fig 199), bay plan at clerestory level (Fig 348) and window plans/elevations (Fig 349)) are 'hybrid', drawn in pencil on film

using an AO drawing board with parallel motion and set square. This 'low-resolution approach' allowed rapid cross-reference between plans and elevations. The pencil drawings were subsequently scanned and redrawn digitally for publication.

The excavated remains provided only a fixed outline of the foundation. The 1770s plan of the Guildhall precinct (Fig 246) was made when the chapel was still used for services and includes important details such as the stair turret/belfry in the north-west angle. An accurate survey by the City's Office of Works was made shortly before the chapel's demolition in 1822 and this plan exactly fits the excavated foundations (Fig 370). Further details of the chapel are given in Schnebbelie's 1819 sketch-plan (GL, COLLAGE 3675), which picks out blocked medieval windows and the quadripartite vaulting of the aisles, and in Buckler's superb series (GL, COLLAGE 3644, 3656, 3682). It is quite possible that additional material related to his survey is held in the 89 volumes of Buckler's drawings in the British Library (BL, Add MSS 36356–36443), which were not consulted.

The west front can be pieced together from a variety of records of different quality. There was no accurate measurement of heights of the chapel, other than those recorded on Buckler's precious elevations. Buckler's superb view of the west front (Barron 1974, pl 26) can be 'corrected' using the Office of Works plan (Fig 370) which shows features common to both. This allows the width of the west window to be estimated. Its sill height is shown on the elevation of the west door (GL, COLLAGE 3644). This chain of inference is continued by using another view, a drawing made to record a statue of Edward VI (GL, COLLAGE 3674), since the corbel on which it rests is said to be original in a 19th-century description (Anon 1820, 117). George Dance the younger made a scaled 'presentation' elevation of the adjacent porch in the 1780s (Fig 371). A view of the subsequent demolition of this porch (GL, COLLAGE 3546) is the only tolerably accurate view of the medieval screen and chapel together and as such allows the height of the west window to be roughly measured. The exterior of the east window was recorded by Buckler and the interior by Schnebbelie (GL, COLLAGE 3654, 3671). Buckler also recorded the clerestory windows from the north (GL, COLLAGE 3655), and the aisle windows are recorded in that view and in the measured drawing of the nave arcade (GL, COLLAGE 3682). The same drawing also records several 'datums' that link the interior of the chapel to the exterior (the cinquefoil heads of the ground-storey niches share the springing line of the arcade, presumably because it was convenient for the builders to make such changes at a common datum).

Features destroyed in the Reformation or the Great Fire pose the worst problems of reconstruction. The west gable end is a case in point and the existence of a crenellated parapet is wholly reliant on the 'copperplate' view of c 1559 (Fig 201). The inferred gable destroyed in the Great Fire was probably adorned with blind tracery (Fig 197). A roof of hammerbeam construction would best cope with the large span of the nave and the rationale for this part of the reconstruction is explained in Chapter 4.3. The turret at the north-west angle draws on the

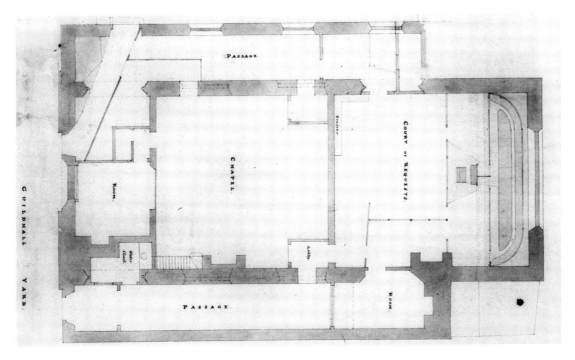

Fig 370 Survey of the Guildhall chapel by the Office of Works of the Corporation of London, carried out shortly before the demolition of the chapel in 1822 (London Metropolitan Archive – CLRO, SCLB 16)

somewhat better evidence of the 1770s survey (Fig 246) and Malton's engraving (Fig 266). Such details as the corbelled wallwalk connecting the turret with the battlements are guesswork, but the need for roof access would have made something of this nature necessary. The rood loft was probably similarly employed to provide access to the aisle roofs.

Architectural reconstruction of the Guildhall porch

The analysis here combines visual information with the excavated plan data, modern surveys and the evidence of the reused moulded stones to reconstruct Croxtone's 15th-century porch and Wren and Hooke's 17th-century porch. The interior of part of the medieval Guildhall porch has survived to the present day. Until the excavations of the 1990s (site A), the 700-year evolution of the porch was unknown. A simple open passage to the Guildhall's upper floor in the early 14th century (Chapter 4.1) became a covered, gated passage in the second half of the 14th century (Chapter 4.2). This porch was then rebuilt as part of the new Guildhall built by John Croxtone in the 15th century (Chapter 4.3). It largely survived the Great Fire to be remodelled by Christopher Wren and Robert Hooke in antiquarian style (Chapter 4.5). Their use of defective stone probably prompted George Dance the younger to replace the entire facade in 1788 (Chapter 5.1); his work has in turn needed renewal on two occasions (Chapter 5.1 and 5.2).

Wren and Hooke's involvement with the porch is known from a single record (CLRO, Repertory 76, fo 248) when the design met with approval on 16 September 1671. The Repertory entry implies that these very busy men were acting in a supervisory rather than a direct capacity, although Wren's hand

has been detected in the design (Wilson 1976, 8, n22). It was, however, generally assumed that the porch survived in its medieval form until 1783 and this led to misinterpretation of post-Fire images of the porch. Archaeology has, however, confirmed that Wren and Hooke's work was far more extensive than previously realised.

The chief documentary sources for the porch were published by Barron (1974, 26–7). George Dance's 'presentation' elevations (CLRO, SCLB 81–3) are the most accurate record and the most significant is reproduced here as Fig 371. Dance was commissioned to repair or replace the entire facade after a fire in 1783 (Stroud 1971, 117). He presented three different options for the City Lands Committee (ibid, 119) that record all the extant medieval fabric. The additional 17th-century west wing had been destroyed in the 1783 fire and is therefore not shown in Dance's elevation but it is shown in outline in Malton's engraving of 1783 (Fig 266). There are several drawings by John Carter (Fig 344; GL, COLLAGE 3573–4) and Jacob Schnebbelie (Fig 243) which show the facade after the removal of the burnt west portion. This information is complemented by the archaeological excavation of the porch which revealed *ex situ* moulded stones that had been cut up and reused in the foundations of Dance's 1788 porch.

An ambiguous caption to John Carter's 1788 view (Fig 344) has long misled researchers:

…on the spouts are this date 1669. the year when the Hall was repaired after the fire of London. (The addition above the gothic window[s] are in the roman style, a clumsy design rais'd on the fine gothic work below, instead of which there should have been replac'd woodwork in the manner of Westminster Hall.)

Barron assumed, on this basis, that only the classical pediment of the main porch was 17th-century work (Barron 1974, 27). However, the mention of Westminster Hall suggests that it is the new roof of the Guildhall that is being castigated, not the porch.

During the reconstruction work of 1985–6, a total of 56 architectural fragments were recovered from the Dance foundations. Of these, 23 were recognised as medieval on the basis of the marks left by finishing tools. Analysis of the Dance elevations allowed 11 fragments to be identified as parts of the ground floor of the main porch (c 1415–18) or the associated east porch/screen (c 1444–5). Caen stone was used for the former and Magnesian limestone for the latter. A further 11 fragments were cut from a soft glauconitic limestone and differed in style and toolmarks from the medieval material. Detailed recording allowed four of these to be identified as parts of the pediment and coping of the later porch recorded by Dance (Fig 371). These fragments proved that Dance, almost by accident, had recorded a lost early work of Christopher Wren and Robert Hooke.

Fig 371 *Survey of the Guildhall porch (1788), probably by George Dance the younger, showing the mixed medieval and 17th-century work of the central portion and the east screen (right) and Dance's original proposal for rebuilding the west wing of the porch (left), following damage in a fire of 1783 (scale c 1:100) (London Metropolitan Archive – CLRO, SCLB 81)*

The medieval porch (main porch *c* 1415–18, east porch/screen *c* 1444–5: Chapters 4.3 and 6.7)

The archaeologically recovered mouldings almost all derive from paired tabernacles flanking the main portal. A composite three-dimensional reconstruction of a pair of tabernacles was achieved through a series of steps that exploited the very precise geometrical framework originally employed by Croxtone (Fig 373). The tabernacles were then related to the extant gate jambs and ground floor of the porch, which had to

be re-surveyed for this purpose. Work could then begin on the two-dimensional reconstructed elevation of the whole porch, using the sources discussed in the previous section. The identifiable mouldings are described below and their original locations are illustrated on the elevation drawing Fig 372. Two mouldings could not be located but may derive from the much-altered embrasure of the first-floor window, which survived in its medieval form despite external refacing and enlargement. The reconstructed facade, including the tabernacles, is discussed in Chapter 6.7. The four surviving

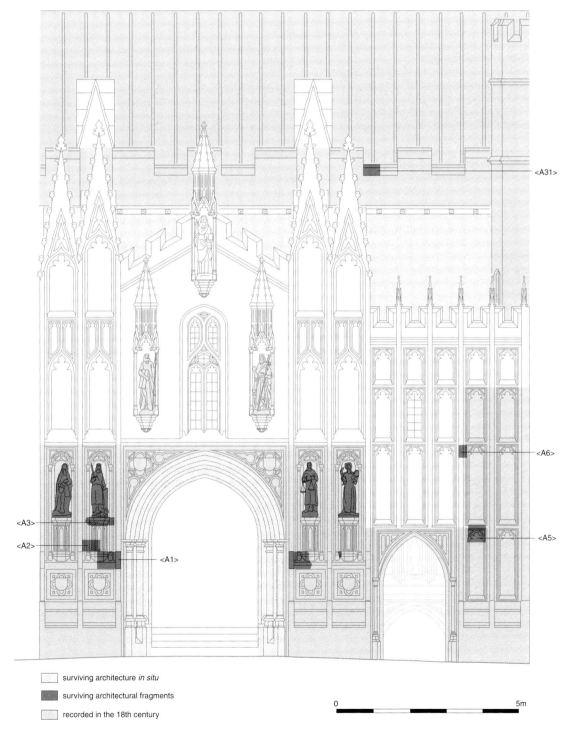

surviving architecture *in situ*

surviving architectural fragments

recorded in the 18th century

0   5m

Fig 372 Simplified reconstructed elevation of the 15th-century Guildhall porch, showing the evidence for the full reconstruction drawing (Fig 190) and the suggested original location of the recovered architectural fragments (indicated by catalogue nos) (Mark Samuel) (scale 1:100)

states of the Cardinal Virtues (Museum of London acc nos 2002.117/1–4) are discussed in Chapter 6.7 and are not catalogued here.

<A1> Tabernacle base course from main porch (Figs 372–4)
A<6593>, A[21101]
H 450mm, W 649mm, WD 700mm. This is a near-complete tabernacle base element which supported one of the polygonal plinths of the statues of the Cardinal Virtues. A 'mirror-image' block was also recovered (A<6605>). Four such elements were coupled up to form a single course 0.448m high (Fig 373, a) with joints displaced from the midline of each tabernacle. The width can, however, be measured from other fragments. This block represents the union of four distinct mouldings: the polygonal plinth of the statue base (Fig 373, b), a weathering/drip-mould and two polygonal colonnette bases. Each tabernacle was exactly a yard wide measured from the inner reveals of each pair of buttresses (the corbel <A3> allows the bay to be accurately measured). They resembled the smaller tabernacles that flank the east crypt entrance (Barron 1974, pl 19, a). The more heavily weathered areas were apparently chiselled and stained red. The north porch of Westminster Hall uses a continuous row of ground-storey tabernacles, and these and the larger separate raised statue niches on corbels can be seen as a direct influence on the Guildhall porch. These were quite probably the work of Walter Walton who prepared internal tabernacles there and who was a mentor of Croxtone (Harvey 1984, 314).

<A2> Tabernacle plinth from main porch (Fig 372; Fig 373)
A<6597>, A[21101]
H 320mm, W 378mm, WD 510mm. The Dance elevations show the panelled statue plinths that rested on the base course. A single battered fragment was found representing about a quarter of one plinth and part of the niche behind it; it was nonetheless sufficient for a reconstruction. The plinth was formed from two courses and the lost upper course made a full height of c 0.7m. This height and the cinquefoil heads are known only from Dance's elevations. It rested on the base course <A1> as illustrated (Fig 373, b). The plinth met the back of the niche at an acute angle, requiring an elaborate stop which survived. The general treatment is a widespread type, being seen in the western portal of Westminster Abbey (Cocke 1995, fig 65) and the tabernacled reredos at St Cuthbert's, Wells, Somerset (Cook 1954, 166, pl 98).

<A3> Tabernacle corbel course from main porch (Figs 373–5)
A<6601>, A[21101]
H 210mm, W 790mm, WD

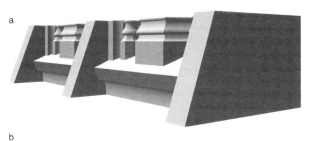

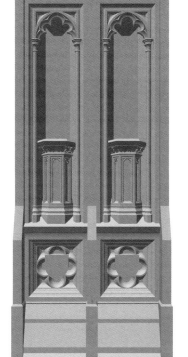

Fig 373 *Series of three-dimensional computer drawings reconstructing a paired tabernacle of the 15th-century Guildhall porch: a – base element <A1> was used to reconstruct a complete course of the tabernacle; b – plinth fragment <A2> was used to create the full plinths over the tabernacle bases; c – corbel block <A3> was placed over the plinth; d – the full paired tabernacle could then be completed, using Dance's elevation drawing (Fig 371)*

Fig 374 *Fragment of tabernacle base <A1> (0.5m scale)*

Fig 375 *Detail of tabernacle corbel fragment <A3>, showing the pairs of vine leaves*

570mm. A corbel coursing block was shattered in the 18th-century demolition, but the central corbel could be reassembled from three fragments. The coursing block, when complete, must have incorporated the entire niche including its shafts (also known from the base course <A1>). The corbel rested on the tabernacle plinth <A2> as illustrated (Fig 373, c) and its surface was keyed for mortar to secure a statue. The bases of the actual Cardinal Virtue statues were measured and they fit this polygonal area; the bases on which they currently sit (as recovered from the north Wales garden and as displayed in the Museum of London) must derive from some other source. The outline of the niche is indicated by a mortar scar on this surface and setting-out lines mark the axis of symmetry. The corbel's sharp drip-mould (now greatly damaged) protected a casement ornamented with deeply undercut vine leaves arranged in pairs across each face (Fig 375). Tabernacle corbels in the pulpitum screen (c 1410) at Canterbury Cathedral are ornamented in the same way. The vine is a common symbol of the Christian faith from its use in biblical metaphor: 'I am the true vine…' in John 15:1–17 (Hall 1979, 322).

<A4> Window casement ? from embrasure of main porch window (not illustrated)
A<6594>, A[21101]

H 243mm, W 283mm, WD 347mm. This window casement was cut back and altered in situ, perhaps to allow the insertion of a timber window frame. A coat of plaster was applied to the altered moulding. This may well be part of an original window over the main porch. The changes can therefore be attributed to Wren and Hooke's alterations. The medieval window probably employed a 'trademark' Croxtone motif of paired panels over an ogival arch (as reconstructed in Fig 372).

<A5> Cinquefoil from panel of blind tracery in east (crypt) porch/screen (Fig 372; Fig 376)
A<6603>, A[21101]

H 432mm, W 545mm, WD 285mm. This important survival can be identified from Dance's elevation (Fig 371) as part of the east porch and proves that part of it was of 15th-century date. The relatively intact cinquefoil head was framed by an ogee. Other surviving elements (the screen buttress <A6> and screen fillet <A7>) allow the centre-to-centre spacing of the dividing buttresses to be accurately reconstructed (Samuel 2005). This 'interval' was 0.865m wide with a clear space between buttresses of 0.74m. It is probably no accident that this dimension roughly conforms to the corresponding width (0.72m) of the surviving tabernacles of the crypt doorway. The 'repeat' of the bay conforms well to the known width of the east porch. It is

therefore likely that additional blind panelling of this type ran over the east crypt outer door as shown in the reconstruction (Fig 372).

<A6> Buttress from east porch (Fig 372)
A<6604>, A[21101]

H 432mm, W 230mm, WD 326mm. This fragment allows the screen to be better understood. The slender 6in (152mm) buttress projects 0.21m and incorporates a sloping offset weathering (which may be a post-Fire alteration, although it can not be seen in the Dance elevation (Fig 371); the common presence of an ogee mould links this to <A5>. The altered fragment may have flanked the enlarged post-Fire window over the doorway; one side had been cut away and plastered over to create a smooth reveal. It is probable that at this time the surfaces were roughly tooled clean, allowing a maroon stain to be directly

applied to the bare stone.

<A7> Window casement ? from first-floor window of east porch (not illustrated)
A<6606>, A[21101]

H 260mm, W 223mm, WD 285mm. This appears to derive from the internal casemented embrasure of a window. The casement met the chamber with an elaborate ogival moulding, heavily modified at a later date. After the mould was altered it was stained a maroon tint. At least eight coats of paint were subsequently applied.

<A8> Vertical moulding ? from interior of one of the first-floor chambers (not illustrated)
A<6607>, A[21101]

H 230mm, W 132mm, WD 320mm. This 'axial termination' (a fillet flanked by ogees separating sunk ashlared fields) probably derives from the interior of one of the chambers over the west or east porch.

Christopher Wren and Robert Hooke's Guildhall porch of 1672 (Chapter 4.5)

Christopher Wren and Robert Hooke rebuilt the upper storeys of the medieval paired porch and built an additional west screen to create a broadly symmetrical three-bayed porch. The design featured a prominent pediment with the royal and City arms. The window of the chamber above the medieval gate was enlarged with French windows and a balcony was constructed. The soft limestone proved defective and the parlous nature of the stonework must eventually have decided Dance on demolition, although this is not mentioned as a factor (Stroud 1971, 118). The original locations of the architectural fragments identified below are illustrated on Fig 377; analysis of the fragments shows that Dance's elevation (Fig 371) was simplified in its details.

<A9> Voussoir from the entablature of the pediment (Fig 377)
A<6595>, A[21101]

H 272mm, W 742mm, WD 518mm. This represents the 'common' form of voussoir in the entablature. The extrados is 'blown', probably by frost damage, but the protected curved soffit indicates an arch centre at a distance of c 1.53m (?5ft). The convergence of the 'radiant' joints gives a very different value (2.27m distant) which has been employed

in the reconstruction (Fig 377). The complete arch had a thickness or wall depth of at least 0.52m.

<A10> Voussoir from the entablature of the pediment (Fig 377)
A<6596>, A[21101]

H 277mm, W 797mm, WD 326mm. The moulding is destroyed but the stone can be pinpointed on the right-hand side of the entablature (Fig 371). Rapid deterioration led to at least one in situ repair. One of

Fig 376 Cinquefoil head of a panel of blind tracery <A5> from the east bay of the 15th-century Guildhall porch (0.5m scale)

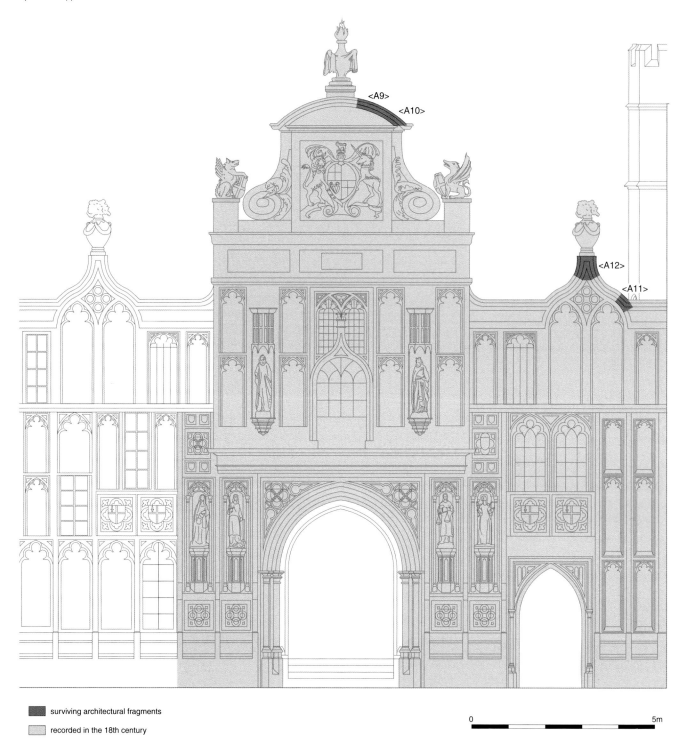

surviving architectural fragments

recorded in the 18th century

0   5m

Fig 377 Simplified reconstructed elevation of Wren and Hooke's Guildhall porch of 1672, showing the location of the moulded stones in the catalogue (the full elevation is shown on Fig 244) (Mark Samuel) (scale 1:100)

the joint surfaces is 'radiant' but the other cuts across the moulding at an acute angle, demonstrating that the arch was segmental. The soffit curvature indicates an arch centre at a distance of *c* 2.21m. Dance's record of this curvature is questionable but his depiction of the overall width of the pediment seems accurate.

<A11> Voussoir of ogival decorative feature (Fig 377) A<6598>, A[21101] H 250mm, W 540mm, WD 400mm. Two blocks can be recognised as parts of the large ogival structures that adorned the cresting of the side facades. Dance recorded the east one in a simplified form. Despite the usual loss of moulding detail,

this block is recognisable as a voussoir and shares the finial base moulding of <A12>. It marks the point where the east side of the ogival structure met a flat parapet coping. The arch centre was *c* 0.93m (?1 yard) distant from the soffit. This measurement assists the accurate reconstruction of the ogival feature.

<A12> Finial base on ogival decorative feature (Fig 377) A<6602>, A[21101] H 636mm, W 512mm, WD 393mm. The severely weathered but complete block marks the apex of the ogival arch and shares the same moulding as <A11>. The flat surface bears an elaborate channel for the pouring of molten metal to form a secure joint

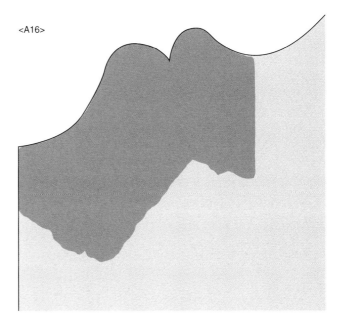

between dressings. Jacob Schnebellie's 1788 view (Fig 243) shows details omitted from Dance's view (Fig 371) such as the massive garlanded and flower-filled stone urn that rested on the apex. It is probable that the metal was poured into a channel in the urn to spread at the bed, the radiating channels allowing the air to escape. The ogee arch seems to have been wholly ornamental, with brick-filled cinquefoil panels below.

Architectural fragments from other medieval buildings

Church of St Lawrence Jewry (*c* 1080, with later modifications)

It is suggested that the first stone church was built c 1080 (Chapter 3.1) and was subsequently modified and extended in the late 13th or early 14th century (Chapter 4.1), in the late 14th century (Chapter 4.2) and again in the 15th century (Chapter 4.3). Fragments of worked stone were found reused or dumped in the churchyard and the north yard of the church property (Tenement 7).

<A13> Voussoir (not illustrated)
A<1737>, A[10746]
Dimensions not recorded (fragment inaccessible). An intact but featureless voussoir of Caen stone, dating to c 1100–c 1275, was found in a cesspit to the north of the church that was used in the early 13th century (Chapter 3.2, OA114). The voussoir may have been left over from the building campaign of the first stone church.

<A14> Grave slab (Fig 131)
B<1118>, B[3067]
H 175mm, W 122mm, WD 110mm. Fragment of raised grave slab, dated to c 1275–c 1400, presumably disturbed during the building works of the early 14th century.

<A15> Grave slab (Fig 131)
D<30>, D[71]
L 1760mm, W 520mm, Th 125mm. The complete slab was reused in the party-wall on the west wall of the Guildhall gatehouse (Chapter 4.1, B208). The sharp taper is typical of the Purbeck school. The rock is grey-green, hard and brittle, with superficial characteristics of Purbeck marble. The recumbent gravestone stood proud of the ground and its small size suggests that it was not used for an adult. It is bordered by two hollow chamfers that meet to form a sharp 'blade'. The top of the slab carries a cross staff with a heraldic cross botonée. The foot is ornamented with a stepped or cross calvary motif. A 'pill' separates the cross from the shaft. The slab can be dated stylistically to c 1250–c 1350 (S Badham, pers comm); the archaeological context refines this to the second half of the 13th century. The grave slab was left roughly tooled, being perhaps unfinished. The slab was split on its natural bed and the reverse was left in this quarried state. A clawtool was used to cut the field, the blade being held parallel to the long axis of the grave slab. The hollow chamfers were dug out with a point, and the arrises were created with a pitcher forming distinctive drafted margins. A light cutting compound used with an abrasive polishes Purbeck marble readily; in the 1220s vinegar was used (Alexander 1995, 118–19).

<A16> Arcade pier with double ogee moulding (Fig 378)
B<1136> B<1140> B<1146>, B[3071]
H 225mm, W 298mm, WD 288mm. Three fragments form part of the moulding of an arcade pier similar to piers from the Guildhall chapel (Barron 1974, pl 28, a), but the findspot suggests that it derives from St Lawrence Jewry. The stones were found

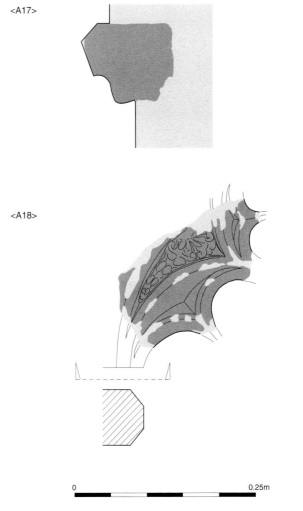

Fig 378 *Worked stone possibly derived from St Lawrence Jewry: three fragments <A16> that form part of the moulding of an arcade pier, a possible associated fragment of octagonal capital <A17>, and a decorated moulded element <A18> perhaps from a tomb canopy (scale 1:5)*

425

during the 'tunnelling' phase of excavation of site B, but they almost certainly derive from post-medieval, perhaps post-Great Fire, demolition deposits in the north yard of St Lawrence Jewry (Chapter 4.5, Tenement 7). ?15th century.

<A17> Octagonal capital (Fig 378)
B<1137>, B[3072]
H 256mm, W 125mm, WD 105mm. Fragment of octagonal capital, perhaps originally capping the arcade pier <A16>. ?15th century.

<A18> Complex moulded element from blind arcade, recess or monument (Fig 378)
B<1138>, B[3072]
H 242mm, W 145mm, WD 85mm. Decorated moulded element with foils but no glazing slot, perhaps from a funerary monument such as a tomb canopy. The structure was of late medieval date, being not earlier than c 1400.

The Guildhall of the 1120s (Chapter 3.1)

<A19> Capital, probably from blind arcade colonnette (not illustrated)
B<1261>, B[117]
H 105mm, W 170mm, WD 110mm. This barely recognisable fragment may derive from a blind arcade colonnette. Since the original Guildhall was largely rebuilt between 1298 and c 1350 (Chapter 4.1), the evidence of its findspot (found in 14th-century fills of a masonry cesspit: Chapter 4.2, S216) and its stylistic dating to c 1100–c 1200, suggest that it was used in the original 1120s Guildhall.

Possible synagogue building of the late 12th century (Chapter 3.2, B120 or B121)

<A20> Relieving arch of window (not illustrated)
A<4251>, A[19661]
H 144mm, W 125mm, WD 77mm. This is probably part of a relieving arch of a window, datable by tooling to c 1190–c 1275; the archaeological context points to a date in the last quarter of the 12th century.

Large stone hall of c 1200 later known as Blackwell Hall (Chapter 3.2, B201) with additions of c 1250 (Chapter 3.3, B203 and B213) and c 1396 (Chapter 4.2, B203)

Worked stones were discovered in the foundations and demolition debris of the later buildings (B205, B206 and B207) that replaced the original 'Blackwell Hall' (B201 and B203). Two moulded stones were found in the backfill of the latrine of the west wing (added to the original hall, c 1250) and may have been used in this building.

<A21> <A22> Vault rib (Fig 111)
<A21> A<3769>, A[19269]
<A22> A<2750>, A[19167]
H 84mm, W 90mm, WD 85mm (<A21>); H 103mm, W 77mm, WD 75mm (<A22>). These are parts of roughly cut Reigate stone vault ribs dated to c 1180–c 1220. Both seem to have been reused in the medieval period, perhaps in a new vault in the c 1250 hall. <A21> has lateral chamfered beaks.

<A23> Clustered pier (Fig 111)
A<2859>, A[19501]
H 88mm, W 85mm, WD 110mm. Probably part of a clustered pier formed from a single continuous wave mould, dated c 1200–75.

<A24> Painted ashlar (Fig 379)
A<2833>, A[19513]
H 252mm, W 150mm, WD 167mm. This presumably formed part of the border of a larger painted scheme. It bore a distinctive semicircular hollow flanked by fillets, a motif used from the 12th to the 14th century (Morris 1992, 13). The fragment was subsequently reused on a different orientation. A total of 27 painted Reigate stone ashlars, featuring various red on white patterns (eg Fig 112), were found, perhaps used in the earliest hall of c 1200, and/or in the extension to the west of c 1250, according to the approximate dating of the tooling marks. Most bear traces of whitewash painted with a regular pattern of false ashlar joints: double lines with a simple flower in each painted 'ashlar'. One block A<2828> indistinctly shows a more complex foliated or cusped pattern below the whitewash.

<A25> Vault rib (Fig 379)
A<2763>, A[19035]
H 110mm, W 62mm, WD 144mm. This ogee-moulded vault rib fragment is difficult to date stylistically but the use of a comb suggests after c 1350. It could date to c 1396 when Blackwell Hall was acquired by the City for use as a cloth market.

<A26> Window sill (Fig 126)
B<910>, B[176]
H 175mm, W 258mm, WD 166mm. Fragment of a window sill with a rebate for an iron window bar, perhaps from the 'great chamber' of the west wing (B213).

Guildhall chapel of c 1298–c 1350 (Chapter 4.1)

<A27> Window tracery (not illustrated)
B<909>, B[176]
H 165mm, W 190mm, WD 130mm. This fragment can be dated to c 1275–c 1350 but not orientated; it probably derives from the first Guildhall chapel.

<A28> Window surround (Fig 147)
B<901>, B[117]
H 85mm, W 130mm, WD 88mm. This Reigate stone fragment incorporates a casement hollow shaded by a roll moulding. It probably formed part of a window surround, perhaps of the Decorated style. It may derive from the first Guildhall chapel.

<A29> <A30> Statue fragments (Fig 146)
Museum of London inv no. 2004.143
H 632mm, max W 300mm

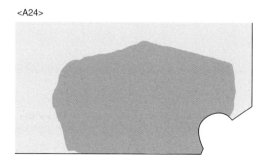

<A24>

<A25>

Fig 379 Painted ashlar <A24> and a vault rib <A25>, probably derived from the large stone hall of c 1200 later known as Blackwell Hall (scale 1:5)

0   0.25m

(<A29>); H 670mm, max W 310mm (<A30>). Two fragments of a medieval statue sculpted from friable yellow limestone (probably Caen stone) were recut to form plinth elements for a buttress of the 15th-century Guildhall, probably at the east end of the building. The fragments were found during restoration works in 1995 and are now in the Museum of London collection (Samuel 2003). They are from the bottom of a sculpture, which portrays a draped life-sized figure standing on a bundle of cloth (formed by the drapes) with a draped foot pointing forward. Later recutting prevents the fragments rejoining, but they show that the statue, which appears to have been an unpainted exterior figure, was carved in the round. Similar drapery is found in 14th-century works such as the much smaller female saint at St Andrew's church, Pickworth, Lincolnshire, dated to c 1320 (Alexander and Binski 1987, 420). This dating, and the fact that it was reused in the 15th-century Guildhall, suggests that the statue was part of the first Guildhall chapel.

The Guildhall c 1415–24 (Chapter 4.3)

<A31> Coping stone of parapet (Fig 372)
<6599>, A[21101]
H 290mm, W 192mm, WD 458mm. After the Great Fire, the medieval Guildhall's crenellated parapet was replaced with a higher parapet over a clerestory. This weathered coping stone was presumably dislodged at the time and like the extant ashlar is cut from Kentish ragstone. It was incorporated in the 1788 porch but may have been initially reused in the fabric of Wren and Hooke's porch. These coping mouldings were highly stereotyped: a large central cresting roll threw rainwater down a weathering to fall free of the outer wall face. The element survives to its full length of 18in (0.458m). The (separating) crenellation rather than the cap of the (raised) merlon seems to be represented. The parapet was only 0.229m thick and was implicitly of solid ashlar. Two elements such as <A31> were apparently employed to make each crenellation a yard (0.914m) wide. Ten elements filled the space between each buttress (4.625m) to create two crenellations with one free and two engaged merlons (Fig 372). The c 1559 'copperplate' map (Fig 201) shows this arrangement but this may be coincidental because the view is highly stylised.

Other worked stone fragments and ashlars from the east window of the Guildhall were recorded in 2003, along with a significant assemblage of iron ties (Samuel 2003). The ironwork is discussed in Chapter 4.3.

Guildhall library of c 1423–5 (Chapter 4.3, B214)

<A32> Cornice (Fig 203)
A<2437>, A[10664]
H 276mm, W 240mm, WD 220mm. A fragment of a substantial Reigate stone cornice, deeply coated with whitewash, which served to jetty an internal wall face inwards. It was found in the demolition debris in the backfill of the latrine at the west end of the library.

16th-century additions to the medieval vicarage of St Lawrence Jewry (Chapter 4.4, B223)

<A33> <A34> <A35> <A36>
Tudor fireplaces (Fig 235)
<A33> B<1124>, B[3084]; H 275mm, W 165mm, WD 118mm
<A34> B<1125>, B[3086]; H 244mm, W 230mm, WD 125mm
<A35> B<1127>, B[3085]; H 245mm, W 175mm, WD 135mm
<A36> B<1129>, B[3078]; H 280mm, W 325mm, WD 140mm
All four fragments are parts of stone fireplace surrounds, apparently from three separate fireplaces. Fireplace <A33> features a 'Tudor rose' design and <A34> is based on a four-centred arch. The elements <A35> and <A36> are broadly similar but the mouldings do not quite line up.

Petrological analysis

Four samples of stone were selected for thin-section microscopic analysis in order to define the building stone used in two buildings.

Guildhall chapel of c 1298–c 1350

Desmond T Donovan

Three stone samples from the south wall of the Guildhall chapel (Chapter 4.1, B220) were analysed. The building stone almost certainly derives from the initial building campaign of c 1298 or soon after.

A{33}, A[11016]
This is a highly calcareous, slightly glauconitic, poorly sorted sandstone. Subrounded quartz grains range in size from about 50μ to 1mm. The matrix consists largely of sparry calcite and there are small shell fragments. The rock is likely to be in the Lower Cretaceous, probably from the south-east of England.

A{35}, A[10961]
The rock is a calcareous, glauconitic sandstone. The quartz grains are angular to subangular in form and range in size between about 200μ and 600μ, with rare larger grains up to 1mm. The glauconite grains are in the size range of c 100–250μ, occasionally larger. The rock is from the Lower Cretaceous, probably from the Lower Greensand formation; it is probably Kentish ragstone from north Kent.

A{36}, A[9999]
This sample was taken from an in situ buttress of the south wall of the chapel. The rock is a fine-grained, pale cream limestone of uniform appearance. It gives a very strong reaction with dilute hydrochloric acid. The average grain size is c 250μ and there are also abundant crinoid ossicles. The rock can be identified as Caen stone from the Middle Jurassic rocks in the region of Caen, Normandy.

The east screen of the Guildhall porch of the late 1440s

Kevin M J Hayward

One stone sample was taken from a catalogued medieval moulded stone that had been reused in the foundations of George Dance's Guildhall porch of 1788. Architectural analysis of the fragment suggests that it derives from the interior of a window casement, probably from the east screen of the medieval porch.

<A7>, A<6606>, A[21101]

A worked stone in a very light, quite powdery, homogeneous carbonate limestone with no fossils. Fine microcrystalline dolomite dominates the rock, removing the primary fabric. There are occasional dedolomitic patches of coarser low ferroan calcite. One example of a Shagariniid foraminifera microfossil was observed. Dolomitic rocks of low density are typical of the Upper Permian Magnesian Limestone. In particular it bears a strong resemblance to the Sprotborough Member of the Cadeby Formation (Kaldi 1986, 93). This narrow outcrop runs northwards from Nottingham up to Teesside and was exploited extensively for building stone. The recognised use of Magnesian limestone for fine carved stonework in medieval London is rare, with Reigate stone and Caen stone seen more frequently. However, little attempt has been made to distinguish it from Caen stone.

Although no formal identification of the (presumed) Caen stone used for the main porch has been made, the fine hard yellow limestone is certainly not the same as this more pallid building stone. The screen element (<A5>) firmly associates this Magnesian limestone with the east porch/screen. The apparent switch to Magnesian stone in the 1440s also affected the building of Eton College (begun in 1442) and was due to the deteriorating relationship between Britain and France (Parsons 1990, 9). The switchover at the Guildhall seems to confirm this rather neatly.

8.4 Microstratigraphy: soil micromorphology, chemistry and pollen

Richard Macphail (soil micromorphology, microprobe), with John Crowther (chemistry) and Gill Cruise (palynology)

Introduction

The Guildhall site (site A) first became the focus for a microstratigraphic study in 1992 because of the potential for substantial dark earth deposits being present above the Roman amphitheatre (Bateman 1997; Bateman 2000; Macphail 1981; Macphail and Courty 1985; Macphail et al 2003b). During excavation and through a series of analytical assessments that combined geoarchaeology and palynology (1992–7), it became clear that the site offered opportunities to investigate the dark earth to early medieval transition, and early and later medieval stratigraphy, as well as the underlying pre-occupation Roman soils, the Roman amphitheatre, and dark earth (Bateman et al in prep; Macphail and Cruise 1995).

The investigation of the medieval Guildhall was carried out in the context of other London site investigations where the natural soils and Roman, dark earth, Saxon and medieval levels have been studied. These investigations had mainly been carried out through soil micromorphology but with inputs

from bulk analytical studies and occasional palynology. They include the Middle Saxon sites of Bruce House and Jubilee Hall (Macphail 1988), the dark earth and Norman site of King Edward Buildings (KEB92: Macphail and Cruise 1993; Watson 1998) and 1 Poultry (ONE94: Macphail and Linderholm in prep). The analysis of microstratigraphic signatures for Saxon and medieval deposits is also an ongoing international research topic (Cruise and Macphail 2000; Engelmark and Viklund 1986; Gebhardt and Langohr 1999; Guélat and Federici-Schenardi 1999; Macphail and Cruise 2001; Simpson et al 1999; Viklund et al 1998).

At the Guildhall, 50 thin sections, 48 bulk samples and 31 pollen samples were studied during the post-excavation investigation of the earlier and later medieval sequence. The same samples were utilised to achieve a totally integrated microstratigraphic approach that employed soil micromorphology, chemistry, magnetic susceptibility and palynology, in order that consensus interpretations would be available to contribute to the cultural and environmental reconstruction of the medieval Guildhall site (Macphail and Cruise 2001). The authors have previously carried out interdisciplinary studies on the Experimental Earthworks Project and Butser Ancient Farm, both of which provide valuable analogues for investigations at the Guildhall (Bell et al 1996; Crowther et al 1996; Cruise and Macphail 2000; Macphail et al 2003a). These have yielded insights into the recognition of uses of space that have been reported from both prehistoric and historic sites across Europe, in conjunction with ethnological studies and experiments (Cammas 1994; Kenward and Hall 1995; Lawson 2000; Macphail et al 1997; Matthews et al 1997; Reynolds, 1979; 1987; Viklund et al 1998). The aims and objectives, as listed in the assessment document, have been addressed through this approach.

Samples and methodology

Monolith and bulk samples, and subsampled monoliths, provided 50 thin sections (soil micromorphology, microprobe), 48 bulk samples (chemistry) and 31 pollen samples (palynology).

Soil micromorphology

Thin sections were viewed at a number of magnifications from x1 up to x400 under the polarising microscope, employing plane polarised light (PPL), crossed polarised light (XPL), oblique incident light (OIL) and fluorescence microscopy using blue light (BL). The combined use of these different forms of illumination permits a large number of optical tests to be made, enabling more precise identification of materials (Bullock et al 1985; Stoops 1996). Archaeological microfeatures and materials were also identified from published and unpublished archaeological and reference studies, with semi-quantitative counting and microfacies analysis based upon Bullock et al (1985) and more recent developments (Courty 2001; Courty et al 1989; 1994; Goldberg et al in prep; Macphail and Cruise

2001, table 1). Fifty-six types of natural and anthropogenic inclusions, structural features and pedofeatures were counted (Macphail et al 2003c, table 2).

A Jeol JXA8600 electron probe micranalyser (EPMA) was used at the Institute of Archaeology of University College London to carry out microprobe analyses of soil microfabrics and features, which included materials in four samples ({687-4}, {687-5}, {879-2b} and {977-1}). This work was carried out on uncovered thin sections. These were first examined under a scanning electron microscope (SEM), and a number of features were chosen for line or grid analysis. Amounts of Si, Al, Fe, Mn, Ca, K, Mg, Na, P, and S were measured, with some samples also being analysed for Cu, Pb and Zn (reported as mean % in Macphail et al 2003c, table 3).

Chemistry

Analysis was undertaken on the fine earth fraction (ie <2mm) of the samples. LOI (loss-on-ignition) was determined by ignition at 375°C for 16 hours (Ball 1964) – previous experimental studies have shown that there is no significant breakdown of carbonate at this temperature; pH (1:2.5, water) using a standard calomel electrode (Avery and Bascomb 1974); and Pb, Zn and Cu by atomic absorption spectrophotometry following extraction with 1N HCl. An indication of the carbonate content was gained by observing the reaction when 10% HCl was added (Hodgson 1997). Phosphate-P_i (inorganic phosphate) and phosphate-P_o (organic phosphate) were determined using a two-stage adaptation of the procedure developed by Dick and Tabatabai (1977) in which the phosphate concentration of a sample is measured first without oxidation of organic matter, using HCl as the extractant (P_i); and then on the residue following alkaline oxidation with NaOBr (P_o). A Bartington MS1 meter was used for magnetic susceptibility measurements. χ_{max} was achieved by heating samples at 650°C in reducing and then oxidising conditions. The method used broadly follows that of Tite and Mullins (1971), except that household flour was mixed with the soils and lids placed on the crucibles to create the reducing environment (after Graham and Scollar 1976; Crowther and Barker 1995).

Pearson product moment correlation coefficients were used to examine the relationships between the various properties analysed, and analysis of variance (using the Scheffé procedure) was undertaken to compare the mean values for individual groupings of soil microfabric types (SMTs), as identified (Macphail et al 2003c, table 1). Analysis of variance was only carried out on groupings with four or more samples. In cases where the data for individual properties had a skewness value of ≥1.0, a log_{10} transformation was applied in order to increase the parametricity. Statistical significance was assessed at $p = 0.05$ (ie 95% confidence level).

Pollen

Samples were removed from column and box samples prior to sample impregnation for thin section manufacture. Pollen samples were prepared using HCl, KOH, HF and acetolysis as described in Moore et al (1991) with the addition of microsieving to facilitate removal of fine particles. Estimates of pollen concentrations and pollen preservation characteristics are based on the methods and criteria outlined by Stockmarr (1971), Cushing (1967), Havinga (1984) and Delcourt and Delcourt (1980). Pollen counts are a minimum of 300 pollen and spores with the exception of samples from {822/823} where counts of a minimum of 100 were made. All slides were scanned for pollen types which may have been missed during routine counting and these were recorded as single occurrences. Pollen nomenclature is based on Moore et al (1991), Stace (1991) and Bennett et al (1994).

Results

The results of this extensive analysis of individual land uses are integrated into the chronological narrative (Chapters 2–4). More general discussion of the use of buildings, local environment, stabling waste and livestock keeping is included in the thematic chapter (Chapter 6.3 and 6.4). Given the constraints of space, necessarily much of the technical details, procedures, tables and figures that underpin the more general conclusions of this study are confined to and available from the research archive (Macphail et al 2003c).

Soil micromorphology

Eighty-seven contexts and layers were identified, described and counted to produce microstratigraphic data that were later combined with bulk and palynological information to produce linked soil microfabric types (SMTs) and microfacies types (MFTs) (Macphail et al 2003c, table 2, figs 1, a–l). Full details are available in the research archive (ibid, tables 1–3). A number of materials and their provenance were identified on the basis of their soil micromorphology.

Chemistry

The results are presented in the accompanying tables in the research archive: analytical results for individual samples (Macphail et al 2003c, table 3); overall summary statistics for the 48 samples (ibid, table 4); Pearson correlation coefficients for the relationships between the various soil properties (ibid, table 5); and comparisons of the results for individual soil properties for different groupings of context types (ibid, tables 5–13). A general overview of the results is given in the research archive, focusing on the general character of the soils/sediments and the key anthropogenic indicators (ibid).

The 48 bulk samples display very wide variability in terms of the key anthropogenic indicators assessed. Many of the phosphate-P concentrations are very high, some exceptionally high (indicative of the presence of bone as well as phosphates derived from the decomposition of phosphate-rich organic materials); and many samples show clear indications of enrichment with organic matter, Pb, Zn and Cu, and of magnetic susceptibility enhancement.

There are strong direct correlations between phosphate and heavy metal concentrations, and between the different heavy metals. However, magnetic susceptibility enhancement is much less strongly correlated with the chemical properties, which suggests that the circumstances leading to chemical enrichment are not necessarily the ones associated with burning.

In general, SMTs 1a, 1b, 1d and 4a/b/c appear to have been less affected by human-related activities than SMTs 4d, 4e/f/g, 5a/b/c, 7a/d/f, 10 and 11. In the majority of cases there are statistically significant differences in the mean values of the various chemical and magnetic properties between SMT 4a/b/c and SMTs 4e/f/g, 5a/b/c, and 7a/d/f, but not between the latter three SMTs.

On the basis of their chemical and magnetic susceptibility properties, it is clear that the various contexts sampled from the different SMT groupings exhibit quite marked variability. For example, sample {BD979c} from the brickearth flooring (SMT 1d) stands out as showing much stronger signs of anthropogenic effects than the other samples from this SMT. Such variability may furnish valuable insights into the nature of the environment in which particular contexts developed.

Pollen

Full results of the palynological investigation (eg pollen diagrams) are presented in the research archive (Macphail et al 2003c). The main palynological characteristics were identified and found to be associated with the major soil microfabric types (ibid, table 2). The list of samples and related soil microfabrics are outlined in tabular form (ibid, table 6).

8.5 Ceramic building material (and slate)

Ian M Betts

Introduction

A vast quantity of medieval and post-medieval building material was recovered, comprising ceramic roofing tile, slate roofing, brick, floor tile and a number of rare types. It provides much valuable new information, particularly on the early development of ceramic roofing tile during the 12th and early 13th centuries. The material is recorded by fabric type, with fabric code numbers referring to the ceramic building materials fabric reference collection held by the Museum of London Specialist Services (MoLSS). Full details of the codes can be found in the research archive (Betts 2003); details of the illustrated ceramic building material are given in Table 4.

Medieval ceramic building material

Early use of ceramic roof tile

Post-Roman ceramic roofing tiles were formerly believed to have been first used in London *c* 1135/6 (Smith 1999a, 66), but their presence in small quantities in period 10 (*c* 1050–*c* 1140) at the Guildhall suggests that they could be somewhat earlier. Vast numbers of early shouldered peg, flanged and curved roofing tile (together with the occasional early peg and ridge tile) were found in contexts dating to period 11 (*c* 1140–*c* 1230). Unexpectedly, many flanged and curved tiles are directly associated with pottery dated *c* 1080–*c* 1150, and this also suggests an earlier date for their first use. Previously, it had been thought that roofing tiles were first introduced into London following a serious fire in the first year of King Stephen's reign (1135/6), but it would seem unlikely that so many flanged and curved tiles could have been nailed on to roofs and then taken down and discarded in just 15 years. It is probable, therefore, that the flanged and curved system started somewhat earlier in the 12th century. Most of these tiles were found in open areas to the south of the Guildhall, which might suggest that the Guildhall of the 1120s (Chapter 3.1) was one of the first tiled buildings in London. It is worth noting that a number of roofing tiles from the foundation trench of the chapter house at Battle Abbey, Sussex, may be as early as *c* 1100 (Streeton 1985, 95).

These early medieval roofing tiles belong to the flanged and curved system, and were used in a similar fashion to Roman *tegulae* and *imbrices*. A solitary shouldered peg tile (A[12194]) was also recorded, although it is possible that this was actually the centre of a flanged tile (where no edges survive, as in this case, it is not always possible to tell them apart). The majority of the early medieval flanged and curved roofing tiles are made from a fairly coarse sandy clay (fabric 2273) and many have a partial glaze covering. On the Guildhall site another set of flanged and curved early roofing tiles was recognised for the first time in London. These tiles, which were made with a finer sandy clay (fabric 3228), seem to date to the same period as the other flanged and curved tiles. Their lack of glaze suggests, however, that they were made at a separate tilery.

Developing this argument on the dating of the use of tiles in the 12th century, it can now be suggested that it was shouldered peg tiles that were first introduced *c* 1135/6. Certainly most shouldered peg tiles on the Guildhall site were found with pottery dated no earlier than *c* 1140–70. The dating would certainly accord with the documentary evidence, which reveals that following the 1135/6 fire some of London's more wealthy citizens covered their houses with 'thick tile' (Betts 1990, 221). This reference to 'thick tile' better fits a description of shouldered peg tiles (which can be up to 24mm thick) than flanged tiles, which are generally thinner (11–19mm). The majority of shouldered peg tiles are in the same coarse sandy fabric (fabric 2273), sometimes with frequent small white calcium carbonate inclusions, possibly shell (fabric 2272). A tile kiln making shouldered peg tiles in fabric 2273 was found at Niblett Hall, Temple Lane in 1991 (GeoQuest 1993). The absence of flanged

Table 4 Details of illustrated ceramic building material

Cat no.	Context	Acc no.	Description	Land use & period found	Building from which item may derive	Fig no.
<T1>	A[13929]	A<1329>	floor tile	OA9, period 11	St Lawrence Jewry (period 10)	380
<T2>	A[19211]	A<3256>	decorated floor/roof tile	S234, period 15	-	381
<T3>	B[178]	B<780>	floor tile (Betts 2002a, type W22)	OA213, period 13	Guildhall chapel (B220, period 13)	144
<T4>	A[21501]	A<6264>, A<6265>	floor tile (Betts 2002a, type W30)	OA202, period 13	Guildhall chapel (B220, period 13)	144
<T5>	A[19150]	A<2759>	floor tile (Betts 2002a, type W41	B204, period 14	Guildhall chapel (B220, period 13)	144
<T6>	B[410]	B<462>	floor tile (Betts 2002a, type W55 or W56)	OA213, period 13	Guildhall chapel (B220, period 13)	144
<T7>	A[19251], A[19319]	A<3257>, A<4050>	floor tile (Betts 2002a, type W74)	OA200, period 13	Guildhall chapel (B220, period 13)	144
<T8>	A[19252]	A<3258>	floor tile (Betts 2002a, type W92)	OA200, period 13	Guildhall chapel (B220, period 13)	144
<T9>	-	MoL no. 17803	floor tile (Betts 2002a, type W95)	unstratified (found 'at Guildhall', perhaps during works in late 19th century)	Guildhall chapel (B220, period 13)	144
<T10>	A[19026]	A<2613>	floor tile (Betts 2002a, type W104)	B206, period 17	Guildhall chapel (B220, period 13)	144
<T11>	A[19252]	A<3258>	floor tile (Betts 2002a, type W114)	OA200, period 13	Guildhall chapel (B220, period 13)	144
<T12>	B[349]	B<183>	floor tile (Betts 2002a, type W119)	OA213, period 13	Guildhall chapel (B220, period 13)	144
<T13>	A[19313]	A<4048>	floor tile (Betts 2002a, type C)	OA200, period 13	Guildhall chapel (B220, period 13)	144
<T14>	A[19206]	A<3758>	decorated floor tile	B204, period 14	Guildhall chapel (B220, period 13)	144
<T15>	B[3053]	B<761>	decorated floor tile	unstratified ('GUY88' tunnelling phase of site B)	St Lawrence Jewry (Tenement 7, period 13)	382
<T16>	A[21549]	-	top of decorated ridge tile	OA119, period 11	1120s Guildhall (period 10)	107
<T17>	A[21563]	-	top of decorated ridge tile	OA133, period 11	1120s Guildhall (period 10)	107
<T18>	B[176]	B<1254>	louver	S216, period 14	John fitz Geoffrey's mid 13th-century solar wing (B213, period 12)	127
<T19>	B[3086]	B<1203>	tin-glazed floor tile	unstratified ('GUY88' tunnelling phase of site B)	vicarage of St Lawrence Jewry (B223, period 16)	236
<T20>	B[3082]	B<1206>	tin-glazed flower wall tile	unstratified ('GUY88' tunnelling phase of site B)	vicarage of St Lawrence Jewry (B223, period 16)	236
<T21>	B[3085]	B<1216>	tin-glazed landscape wall tile	unstratified ('GUY88' tunnelling phase of site B)	vicarage of St Lawrence Jewry (B223, period 16)	236
<T22>	B[3086]	B<1231>	tin-glazed landscape wall tile	unstratified ('GUY88' tunnelling phase of site B)	vicarage of St Lawrence Jewry (B223, period 16)	236
<T23>	B[3063]	B<1080>	tin-glazed landscape wall tile	unstratified ('GUY88' tunnelling phase of site B)	vicarage of St Lawrence Jewry (B223, period 16)	383
<T24>	D[1]	D<51>	tin-glazed flower wall tile	S212, period 18	first-floor apartment above the Guildhall gatehouse (B208, period 16)	226

and curved tiles suggests that this roofing system had fallen out of use slightly earlier (c 1200) than the use of shouldered peg tiles, which seems to have continued until c 1220.

It is not clear when 'normal' peg tiles were first used on roofs in London. The newer peg tiles were smaller and lighter compared to shouldered peg tiles and probably cheaper too. With the exception of one dated c 1080–c 1150, probably intrusive, all the other early peg tiles are dated c 1140–1220/1300. This would suggest that these peg tiles were first used around the mid to late 12th century, which is similar to their date of introduction in the Cheapside area of the city (Betts 1990, 223). Ceramic tiled roofs undoubtedly became more common towards the end of the 12th and in the early 13th century, in part due to pressure from the City authorities to replace thatched roofs. In 1212 it was recommended that inflammable thatch be replaced by ceramic tile, wooden shingles, boards, lead or plastered straw (Smith 1999a, 66).

It is very difficult to say with any certainty which buildings in the area of the Guildhall had tiled roofs. Most of the roofing tile that survived was found associated with the floors, hearths and walls of small 12th-century timber buildings, and there were no collapsed roof deposits. This is in part because when buildings were demolished or rebuilt the valuable tiles would have been taken down and reused. Thus, negative evidence of roofing tile does not necessarily imply that the timber buildings were not tiled; but, on the other hand, it seems likely that many relatively low-status timber buildings during the 12th century would have been thatched or have had roofs of wooden shingles (examples of which were found discarded in a pit: Chapter 6.3, 'Roofs'; Fig 293). It is more likely that tiled roofs were restricted to important stone buildings such as the Guildhall of the 1120s, or the houses of London's more prosperous citizens, such as the mid 12th-century Jewish properties on Cat Street (Chapter 3.2, B107, B114, B135).

Floor tile

Saxon polychrome relief-tile

Fabric type: 3244

These tiles have been found on nine sites in England, where they are believed to have been made some time between the mid 10th and late 11th centuries AD (Keen 1993, 67; L Keen, pers comm). The Guildhall tile (<T1>, Fig 380) is one of only three such tiles known in London, each of which is decorated with a different design. This tile and an example from Westminster Abbey have already been published (Betts et al 1995, 165–70) and a further example has recently been found nearby at 10 Gresham Street (GSM97 <120>). All the London tiles, which are made from the same distinctive sandy clay, closely match similar Saxon tiles found in Winchester and, significantly, certain pottery and roofing tiles made in the Winchester area. Based on fabric, it would seem reasonable to suggest an origin in the Winchester area for the London examples. The Guildhall tile was probably part of a batch used in the church of St Lawrence Jewry, either in the masonry church of the 1070s or already in its timber predecessor (Chapter 6.11).

Possible early glazed floor tile

Fabric type: 2273

A number of glazed and unglazed tile fragments in roofing tile fabric 2273 were unusually thick (25–31mm). Definite floor tiles in this fabric have been found at both Bermondsey Abbey, where they are unglazed (Betts in prep a) and St Mary Stratford Langthorne, where they are glazed (Smith 2004, 138). It is therefore possible that certain of these tiles could have been used as flooring rather than roofing. However, on most tiles there are no conclusive signs of wear, and their edges are sanded rather than knife-trimmed to a bevel which was the normal practice with floor tiles, although it is worth noting that the Bermondsey Abbey floor tiles have similar sanded edges. The only exception is a fragmentary tile found dumped in period 17 (D[1]) which has vertical, partially trimmed edges and a slightly worn green-glazed upper surface.

What may be a decorated early floor tile (<T2>, Fig 381) was found in a later cesspit fill (S234, period 15). It includes parts of two deeply incised semicircles below a brown glaze. Again the surviving edge is sanded rather than knife-trimmed, so there is no certainty that it was used for flooring and it may be a decorative early roof tile. If it is flooring – and there does appear to be evidence of slight wear – then it presumably belongs to a small group of 12th- or early 13th-century inscribed floor tiles in the same fabric already known from Bermondsey Abbey (Betts in prep a) and St Mary Stratford Langthorne (Barber et al 2004, 24, fig 16). The floor tile could perhaps have been used in the 12th-century Guildhall (period 10 phase 5 to period 11) – it was found in a later context within the Guildhall precinct – but it would also be possible to suggest other contexts, perhaps one of the 12th-century Jewish houses along Cat Street (eg B114, period 11), or the hall of c 1200 of Warin de Bassingbourn (B201, period 11).

'Westminster' tiles

Fabric types: 2199, 3081

The majority of floor tiles are of 'Westminster' type made in London during the second half of the 13th century. These have been the subject of a special study by the author (Betts 2002a)

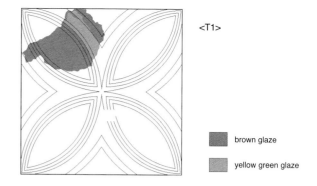

Fig 380   11th-century polychrome relief tile <T1> (scale 1:3)

brown glaze

yellow green glaze

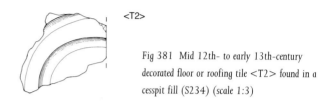

Fig 381   Mid 12th- to early 13th-century decorated floor or roofing tile <T2> found in a cesspit fill (S234) (scale 1:3)

so only brief details will be given here. The 57 'Westminster' tiles are a mixture of plain brown, green and yellow and decorated types. There are a total of 29 decorated examples with 19 different design types (ibid, designs W21, W22, W30, W31, W34, W41, W47, W48, W55 or 56, W72, W74, W92, W95, W104, W106, W114, W115, W119, W144). Particularly notable is design W22, showing two lions, which is known only on a single tile found at the Guildhall (<T3>, Fig 144).

Four tiles belong to the thin 'Westminster' group (designs W74 and W114), which may have been made after the main period of 'Westminster' tile manufacture, during the late 13th or early 14th century (Betts 2002a, 25). A further probable 'Westminster' tile, which may belong to the thin 'Westminster' group, has another design (ibid, design C) only found on a single Guildhall tile (<T13>, Fig 144).

None of the Guildhall tiles was found in situ in a floor but it is possible to suggest their likely original provenance, based on their findspot (CD Table 32). Fourteen of the tile types were probably used in the Guildhall chapel (B220, period 13), built between 1298 and c 1350; four of these were actually found in the construction site area (OA213 and B211) that seems to be associated with the second phase of construction work on the chapel, dated to c 1326–50 (Fig 152). It is also possible that some of the tiles were used in the more or less contemporary Guildhall. Seven of the tile types may have been used in the church of St Lawrence Jewry, probably put in during the second half of the 13th century.

Eltham Palace/Lesnes Abbey group

Fabric types: 2317, 2324

There are two tiles in slightly sandy fabrics similar to those used to make tiles of the Eltham Palace/Lesnes Abbey group. One is decorated (<T14>, Fig 144) while the other is plain light green in colour. The latter is 131mm in breadth by 23–24mm in thickness, the same as definite members of this group from

Merton Priory (Betts 2007, 203–7). If the Guildhall tiles belong to this group they would date from the late 13th to early 14th centuries, and thus they too may have been used in the Guildhall chapel (Chapter 4.1).

Penn tiles

Fabric types: 1810, 2894

There are 15 Penn tiles dating to the second half of the 14th century, all but one of them decorated. Penn tile pavements seem to have used only limited numbers of plain tiles, mainly in single tile borders between decorative panels, as in the Norman Gate south tower at Windsor Castle (Betts and Cromwell in prep) and the Bloody Tower at the Tower of London (Keen 2002, 227), or alternating with decorated examples as in the Aerary pavement at Windsor Castle (ibid, 220–5).

There are ten different designs from the Guildhall, all but one of which have been published by Eames (1980) in her catalogue of medieval tiles in the British Museum (Eames design types 1398, 1846, 2107, 2230, 2334, 2409, 2535, 2870, ?2834). The remaining decorated tile (<T15>, Fig 382) has an unpublished design type and may have been used in the church of St Lawrence Jewry. It seems reasonable to assume that some of the other tiles were used in floor repairs in the Guildhall or its chapel; there are certainly many buildings in London with 'Westminster' tile floors where Penn tiles were added a century later, perhaps as repairs or during rebuilding.

Dieppe, France

Fabric type: 3241

Decorated floor tiles imported from the Dieppe area of Normandy have been found on various sites along the coast of southern England, as well as in Ireland and at a single site, Cowick Manor, in northern England. Dieppe group tiles were also brought up the Thames to London where they are found in small quantities associated with various churches and monastic sites (Norton 1993, 87–8). They date to the last quarter of the 14th and possibly into the beginning of the 15th century. There is only one example from the Guildhall, an unstratified tile (B<762>) decorated with Norton's design type 46.

Low Countries

Fabric types: 1678, 2497, 2504

Plain glazed floor tiles from the Low Countries (often referred to as 'Flemish' tiles) are common on many London sites, although there are surprisingly few from the Guildhall. There are two types of medieval Low Countries tile present. The first is a smaller variety of plain dark green glazed tile with either nail holes in two diagonally opposite corners or four round nail holes, one in each corner (all 1.5mm diameter). These measure 114–116mm square by 24–25mm thick (A[10760], A[19037]) and are probably 13th- to mid 14th-century in date. Secondly, there is a larger tile (A[14010]), possibly dating to the second half of the 15th century, again green-glazed with four nail holes (only three distorted holes still survive) and measuring 138mm in breadth by 27mm in thickness. The smaller type are almost

<T15>

Fig 382 Mid to late 14th-century decorated Penn floor tile <T15> (scale 1:3)

identical in size to the decorated 14th-century Penn tiles used to pave at least one building in the Guildhall area, suggesting that they could have been used together in the same floor.

Wall tile

Fabric type: 3092

Found associated with Building 124 was a small fragment of plain green-glazed wall tile of Norman date. It is in a distinctive fine micaceous fabric which is quite different from the clays used for the manufacture of early roofing tile. Wall tiles of this type are known elsewhere only from Westminster Abbey, Newgate Street (Betts 1996, 19–20) and more recently from Northgate House (MRG95), where they were found with medieval features dating to the period c 1050–c 1150 (Betts 2002b).

Two areas of in situ walling at Westminster Abbey show that the tiles were set at a 45° angle alternating with lighter-coloured stone blocks to produce a decorative chequerboard effect (Betts 1996, pl 3). Their rarity (they were not used outside London) would suggest that the Guildhall tile came from a prestigious Norman masonry building, possibly the nearby church of St Lawrence Jewry.

Roofing tile

Flanged, curved, shouldered peg and ridge tile

Fabric types: 2272, 2273, 3228

At least some of the 12th- to 13th-century buildings would have had ceramic tiled roofs. These would have used either the flanged and curved or shouldered peg tile system, both of which would have had the ridge of the roof covered by curved or specially made ridge tiles. There are two small fragments of decorated ridge tile (<T16> and <T17>, Fig 107) which were probably used on the roof of the 12th-century Guildhall. They show certain similarities to examples used in the Cheapside area (Betts 1990, 225).

The Guildhall site is significant because it has produced clear evidence of two distinct groups of flanged, curved and ridge tiles: a glazed coarse sandy type (fabric 2273), some with calcium carbonate inclusions (fabric 2272), and an unglazed finer sandy type (fabric 3228) that had never previously been recognised in London. Both seem to be of similar date, although they almost certainly originate from different tileries. All the shouldered peg tiles are of coarse sandy type.

433

Two sizes of shouldered peg tile (both fabric 2273) were used at the Guildhall, a wider type measuring 190–215mm at the base (thickness 19–21mm) and a smaller type 158–160mm at the base (thickness 14–18mm). Only one tile preserves its complete length of 324mm and is of the wider type. Interestingly, the smaller type have a single round nail hole (12–14mm diameter) while the wider type have two round nail holes of similar size. Shouldered peg tiles of similar size were found in early medieval deposits at Swan Lane (SWA81: Pritchard 1982) and here too both single and twin nail hole types are present. A green or brown glaze covers the bottom third of each tile.

Only one complete flanged tile has ever been found in London, at Bury Court, St Mary Axe. It is 357mm in length and has tapered sides measuring c 260mm at the top edge to c 220mm at the bottom edge (Pritchard 1982). This is exactly the same width estimated for the top edge of a tapered flanged tile from Open Area 133 (A[21663]). A substantially complete tile from the same open area (A[21578]) is somewhat smaller, measuring 330mm in length. More significantly, the sides are not tapered, giving a more uniform width of 236–247mm. The thickness of both types (all fabric 2273), excluding the flanged area, is in the range 16–20mm.

All flanged tiles seem to have had a single nail hole located in the middle of the tile near the top edge. Most tiles in fabrics 2272 and 2273 also have a strip of green or brown glaze running down their centre. They, along with other early roofing tile types, were attached to the roof by iron nails, the remains of which are occasionally found in situ in the nail hole, as in a flanged tile from Open Area 127 (A[19763]). Wooden pegs may also have been used although these normally decay to leave no trace.

No substantially complete curved tiles survive, although they were presumably similar in length to the flanged tiles with which they were used. Pritchard (1982) noted that there are two sizes of curved tile based on the width of the upper end. Both Pritchard's types were present at the Guildhall, one with a width of c 144mm and the other with a width of c 176mm. There is also a bottom edge, probably belonging to the smaller type, measuring 180mm wide. Curved tiles have a single round nail hole in the crest near the top edge with, in the case of fabrics 2272 and 2273, glaze covering much of the lower two thirds of the tile.

No complete or even substantially complete flanged and curved tiles survive in the finer sandy fabric type 3228. They are, however, generally thinner (10–13mm) than those in fabrics 2272 and 2273, which suggests that they may have been slightly smaller in size.

Peg and later ridge tile

Fabric types: 2271, 2277, 2537, 2587, 2816, 3090, 3091, 3204, 3216

From the 13th century onwards most buildings in the Guildhall area would have had peg-tiled roofs. The date when such tiles were first used in London is uncertain, although they first appear in mid to late 12th-century contexts and seem to have

superseded the earlier roofing tile types some time during the early 13th century. The vast majority of these peg tiles were made using sources of clay different from those used to make flanged, curved and shouldered peg tiles, suggesting that different tile makers were involved in their manufacture.

Along the crest of the peg-tile roofs would have sat curved ridge tiles, but unlike the earlier examples in fabric 2273 they seem to have been undecorated. The vast majority of both peg and ridge tiles are in local London area fabrics (2271, 2277, 2537, 2587, 2816, 3090, 3216) with only occasional (<0.1%) silty fabric tiles from kiln sites thought to be located further away (fabrics 3091, 3204). The peg tiles are almost all of the type with two round nail holes, with in many cases a splash or a more uniform coat of glaze covering the bottom third. A notable exception is a peg tile from a masonry garderobe pit (S216, period 14) which has a single central round nail hole 12mm in diameter and is 157mm wide and 9mm thick (A[11475], fabric 2586 near 2271). Single peg hole tiles are occasionally found in London, such as at Swan Lane (Pritchard 1982), but their rarity suggests that they were a relatively short-lived type.

There are a considerable number of partially complete tiles (their sizes are tabulated in the research archive), but disappointingly few with complete lengths.

Tapered peg tile

Fabric type: 2273

The tile makers producing the shouldered peg and flanged and curved roofing tile systems seem to have switched to the manufacture of peg tiles, perhaps due to competition from other tileries operating around London. There are no complete peg tiles in fabric 2273, but two fragments (A[21613] and A[23032]) indicate that they had slightly tapering sides. Tapered peg tiles are very rare in London, although they were present at Swan Lane in the same fabric (Pritchard 1982). Their rarity may reflect the fact that the production of tapered peg tiles does not seem to have extended much beyond the early 13th century, as 80% of peg tiles in fabric 2273 are found in period 11.

Louver

Fabric type: 2274 (LOND)

Louvers were placed on the roofs of buildings in order to allow smoke to escape from the interior or to provide ventilation. The manufacture of louvers and finials, another kind of roof furniture, seems to have been the responsibility of potters rather than tile makers.

The four Guildhall examples were made by London-type ware (LOND) potters during the 13th to mid 14th centuries. All have parts of their outer surface covered by a green glaze but none shows signs of sooting, which suggests that they were used for ventilation. According to Moorhouse (1988, 45) many louvers found in Britain seem to have been used for this purpose. One of the Guildhall louvers (<T18>, Fig 127) may have been used in the roof of the solar wing added to John fitz Geoffrey's hall (B213, period 12) in the mid 13th century. Others may originally have been used in the early 14th-century

Guildhall (period 13): three fragments were found (but as residual finds in later contexts) in the Guildhall yard area, to the south of the Guildhall.

Finial

Fabric type: 2274 (LOND), 3228

A small globular ornamental finial B<1275> was found unstratified. It has a light green glaze covering a white slip and is probably similar in date to the louvers. Part of a London-type ware (LOND) green-glazed finial B<1270> was found on the same site. There is no slip but the surface had been decorated by the application of lines of scales. There is a published example of a similar LOND finial from London (Pearce et al 1985, 119, no. 442).

Markings on roofing tile

A small number of peg and shouldered peg tiles have single diagonal finger marks in the top left- or right-hand corner. A flanged tile bears part of a similar mark, which seems to have been in the form of a single line running parallel to the top or bottom edge. These are believed to be some sort of batch mark used to identify groups of tiles ready for firing. The most common type of mark on the Guildhall tiles is a diagonal sloping line in the top right-hand corner of peg tiles in fabric 2271.

Slate roofing

At least one early medieval building seems to have had a slate roof at some period during its life. Slate was being exported from south Devon and Cornwall in the late 12th century, and this was almost certainly the quarry source of the slates used in medieval London.

At the Guildhall, roofing slate first appears in period 11 and is present in small quantities throughout the medieval period. It has been noted that in Sussex ecclesiastical buildings, manor houses and other high-status buildings were twice as likely to have had slate roofs than more humble buildings (Holden 1989, 76). The presence of slate indicates that at least one important building in the Guildhall area had a slate-tiled roof, perhaps the early Blackwell Hall building of c 1200 (B201, period 11 phase 4).

Slate roofing tiles rarely survive intact, and no complete dimensions survive on the Guildhall examples. A few do, however, have nail holes remaining, which are mainly round (8–13mm diameter) although one slate is unusual in having a rectangular hole (8 x 11mm).

Medieval brick

Fabric types: 3031, 3040, 3043, 3046

There are a small number of medieval bricks, most of which are described as Flemish-type as they are believed to be probable Flemish, or more accurately Low Countries, imports (Ryan 1996, 33–4). They were probably brought into London for use in minor structural work such as chimneys, fireplaces and flooring. Three probable Low Countries brick types have been identified by Ryan: a 'cream type' (often yellow or occasionally pale brown in London: fabric 3031), a 'grass-marked type' (fabric 3040) and an 'estuarine silty type' (fabric 3043), although only those of cream type were used in any quantity in London. All have been dated to the early 14th century in Essex, although in London the dating evidence suggests a broader, mid 14th- to mid 15th-century date range.

A later group of what may be London-made bricks (fabric 3046) were used in Structure 224. These have a distinctive length of 270–271mm, which places them firmly in the late 15th century. The sizes of these and other brick types are tabulated in the research archive.

Post-medieval ceramic building material

Floor tile

Low Countries

Fabric types: 1813, 2318, 2497, 3075

Floor tiles arriving in London from the Low Countries after c 1480 are generally larger in size and many are in distinct silty fabrics. They were initially plain-glazed in the medieval fashion, but there was a switch to the use of unglazed tiles possibly as early as the late 16th and certainly by the early 17th century. Both types seem to have been used in a building or buildings in the Guildhall area.

There are only two substantially complete post-medieval Flemish tiles. The first is a glazed tile (fabric 2497) which measures 151–153mm square by at least 28–31mm in thickness, the top having been removed by wear (A[14010]). At least four, and possibly five, round nail holes are present in the top surface. The second is a later unglazed tile 250–252mm square by 30mm thick with square nail holes (c 2mm square) in two diagonally opposite corners (A[10760]).

Tin-glazed

Fabric type: 3067

There is evidence for the use of decorative flooring in at least one building in the Guildhall area in the late 16th to mid 17th centuries. Five tiles of this date survive. A small fragment painted in blue on white, but probably part of a polychrome design (<T19>, Fig 236) may have been used in the vicarage of the church of St Lawrence Jewry (B223, period 16). This may be a variant of a 'foliate cross' pattern that occurs on both Dutch and English tiles. The tile thickness (18–19mm) suggests a late 16th- or early 17th-century date. Foliate cross tiles were made in the Netherlands in 1570–1660 (Pluis 1997, 300, A.01.27.43) while in London they were made at Pickleherring in Southwark from 1618 to c 1630 (Tyler et al in prep). The Guildhall tile could be from either source.

Also found were a polychrome tile and a worn blue on white tile each with one quarter of the same 'Tudor rose' design (A<1580> and B<1205>). They were almost certainly made in London as this was one of the most common designs painted on London floor tiles during the first half of the 16th century. Their thickness (12–17mm) and the way the colours are applied suggests that they may be from the delftware factory at Pickleherring, Southwark.

A polychrome tile showing a geometric floral pattern D<49> is probably Dutch. There is a published complete tile from London with a similar design (Britton 1987, 174, no. 195). A badly blackened Dutch polychrome tile with a central floral pattern D<50> belongs to a type dated c 1600–20 (Pluis 1997, 276, A.01.21.04). These two tiles may have been used in the first-floor apartment of the inner gatehouse leading into the Guildhall yard (period 16).

Tin-glazed wall tile

Fabric types: 3064, 3067, 3078
Another indication of the internal decoration of the buildings on the site is provided by the presence of a small but diverse group of 17th- and 18th-century wall tiles. Tiles of this type decorated fireplace surrounds, washbasin recesses and, to a lesser degree, kitchen and basement areas. The main types are described below. There are a small number of other polychrome and blue on white tile fragments but these are too small to allow their decorative pattern or origin to be determined.

i) Three tiles with polychrome multi-leaf flower designs with prominent 'barred ox-head' corners (<T20> (Fig 236), B<1283>, B<1284>, B<1294>). Similar multi-leaf flowers were produced by the tile painters at Rotherhithe, while there is a flower vase design with almost identical corners from Pickleherring, Southwark. They also display certain similarities to Dutch tiles dated 1630–40 (van Dam 1991, 66, no. 72). The Guildhall tiles were probably used in the vicarage of St Lawrence Jewry (B223, period 16) and were almost certainly made in London, probably at either Pickleherring or Rotherhithe, in the period c 1630–66. Two of the tiles show heat damage, with one having an almost totally black surface. Similar blackened delftware tiles have been found at Billingsgate (BIG82: Betts 1991) and the nearby site of Monument House (BPL95: Betts and Smith in prep); in the case of these examples the blackening was due to heat damage sustained in the Great Fire of 1666, and the same is almost certainly true of the Guildhall tiles.

ii) Purple, blue on white landscape tiles with a distinct 'open box' type border (B<1215>, <T21> (Fig 236), B<1219>, B<1285>, B<1286>, B<1287>). They are Dutch, and the border decoration is dated 1660–80 (Pluis 1997, 520, B.01.00.34).

iii) Blue on white landscape tile set in a circular border with a wide, plain white margin (<T22>, Fig 236). The lower left corner has been cut away to allow the tile to fit around an obstruction. There is also evidence of slight glaze discolouration, again possibly the effect of heat during the Great Fire of 1666. The tile, which is Dutch of mid 17th-

<T23>

Fig 383 Late 17th- to 18th-century Dutch tin-glazed wall tile with landscape design <T23> (scale 1:2)

century date, has corner motifs of the 'spider's-head' type. The partially complete corner motif on the Guildhall tile is comparable with those on Dutch tiles dated 1650–1775 (Pluis 1997, 556, C.08.00.09). Another smaller fragment of blue on white tile with a figure in a landscape (B<1089>) also shows discolouration. This is Dutch and may be of similar date.

iv) A series of four blue on white landscape tiles with identical barred ox-head corners (B<1080>, <T23> (Fig 383), B<1104>, B<1220>). The clarity and detail of the painting and the style of the barred ox-head corners indicate their Dutch origin. Tiles with this corner design can not be closely dated; in the Netherlands their date range is 1680–1830 (Pluis 1997, 552, C.07.00.27–8), but the Guildhall examples show certain similarities to Dutch landscape tiles of the early to mid 18th century.

v) Blue on white tulip design (<T24>, Fig 226) with unusual leaf-head corner motif. This tile is Dutch, from a pit fill associated with pottery dated c 1630–80. It may have been used in the first-floor apartment above the Guildhall gatehouse (B208, period 16).

vi) Two small fragments of blue on white tiles with landscape set in a circular border (B<1079>, B<1282>); both have a slight pinkish tinge, suggesting that they may be from the same tile. Probably 18th-century English.

Peg and ridge tile

London-made peg and plain ridge tiles continued to be the dominant form of roofing in periods 15–17. These are similar to their medieval counterparts, although they are no longer glazed and a variety of different nail hole shapes are present in addition to round ones. The more complete examples are listed in the research archive.

Pantile

Fabric type: 3202
There is no evidence for the presence of pantile roofs (Smith

1999b) in the Guildhall area, although a couple of fragments were found in period 17 (A[13026], A[14311]), possibly from tiles used in rebuilding Blackwell Hall market (B206, period 17).

Brick

Fabric types: 3032, 3033, 3035, 3042, 3046, and 3065
Brick was used for a variety of purposes in the Guildhall area, chiefly in wall foundations, cellar walls and floors, and as the lining of cesspits. The various types and their sizes are given in the research archive.

The majority of earlier bricks are of bright red 'Tudor type' (fabrics 3033, 3042, 3046, 3065) although they were actually used in London from the second half of the 15th century until at least the Great Fire of 1666. Most of the Guildhall bricks probably date from the 16th to mid 17th centuries. The brick used after the Great Fire tends to be darker red (fabric 3032), sometimes with a slight yellowish tinge on the sides. These bricks continued to be used in London until yellow London 'stock' bricks (fabric 3035) from Kent became increasingly fashionable from the mid 18th century.

8.6 Clay tobacco pipes

Kieron Heard

Methodology

The clay tobacco pipes are dated and classified according to the 'Chronology of bowl types' (Atkinson and Oswald 1969, 171–227) or (for some of the 18th-century pipes) the 'Simplified general typology' (Oswald 1975, 37–41). The prefixes AO and OS are used below to indicate which typology has been applied. Some of the stem fragments can be dated approximately, based on an estimation of the stem bore diameter. The pipes have been quantified and recorded according to guidelines proposed by Higgins and Davey (1988). The record sheets form part of the site archive and the pipes are also recorded on the MoLAS Oracle database.

The assemblage

Of the 290 fragments recovered, 186 are from bowls and 99 from stems; seven pipes are marked and one is decorated. Some 20% of the pipes came from the make-up and backfill of a brick vaulted cellar in the Guildhall yard (S223, period 16). Eleven pipe bowls of types AO13 and AO15 were recovered from the make-up for the relaid cellar floor and suggest that this relaying of the floor took place after c 1660. The backfill of the vault contained a larger group of pipes with the same date range. Some 71% of the pipe bowls from

the site were recovered from tunnelled deposits excavated on site B; these pipes are in effect unstratified, but many of them may derive from the same brick vault. The remaining pipe fragments occurred as small groups in a range of deposits and features.

The whole assemblage is almost entirely of 17th-century date. In fact, 91% of the pipe bowls are dated to c 1660–80. There is a small number of pipes in the date range c 1610–60, two pipe bowls dated c 1680–c 1710 and two that are of 18th-century date. The 17th-century pipes are typical of pipes made in the London region during that period and almost all of them conform to the established typology for London pipes (Atkinson and Oswald 1969). Only two of the 17th-century pipes are marked with the makers' symbols (B<469>, B<1291>) but this is to be expected given that most of them were made during the period c 1660–80, when marking was rare in London. Of the pipe bowls dated c 1660–80, 89% are of type AO15, featuring bulbous bowls with blunt spurs and with milling around the rims. Again, this is to be expected since that bowl form tends generally to predominate over contemporary forms AO13, AO14 and AO18.

There are a small number of pipe fragments that might have derived from kiln debris, although no pipe kiln structures were found on the site. Broken pipes were used to reinforce pipe kiln muffles (the clay vessels in which pipes were stacked for firing) and such pipes can be recognised from the patches of fired clay that adhere to their surfaces.

Moulded marks

<CP1> Clay tobacco pipe B<1217>, unstratified
WD. Bowl type unknown. The seam of the pipe is decorated with an oak leaf/acorn motif. This suggests that it is type AO28 (c 1820–40) or AO29 (c 1840–80).

<CP2> Clay tobacco pipe A<6913>, A[10409]; period 16, S223
IS. Bowl type OS12 (c 1730–80). This pipe was found in the upper backfill of the 17th-century brick vault, in conjunction with a medium-sized group of pipes dated c 1660–80; it is assumed to derive from later consolidation of the backfilled structure. The pipe has a common mark that seems to occur most frequently in Southwark. The maker is unknown.

<CP3> Clay tobacco pipe B<1109>, unstratified
IS. Bowl type OS12, AO27 (c 1780–c 1820) or AO28 (c 1820–40).

<CP4> Clay tobacco pipe B<1032>, unstratified
TW. Bowl type unknown.

<CP5> Clay tobacco pipe B<1209>, unstratified
Flower symbol. Bowl type unknown. The pipe is of 18th- or 19th-century date.

Stamped marks

<CP6> Clay tobacco pipe B<469>, unstratified
Horseshoe symbol. Bowl type AO5 (c 1610–40).

<CP7> Clay tobacco pipe B<1291>, unstratified

Sun symbol, enclosed in a heart-shaped frame. Bowl type AO10 (c 1640–60). This is a fairly common style of mark, possibly reflecting contemporary tavern signs. The maker is unknown.

8.7 Pottery

Jacqui Pearce

Introduction and methodology

All pottery was recorded in accordance with standard Museum of London Specialist Services (MoLSS) procedure and entered on to the Oracle database. Minimum quantification by sherd count and estimated number of vessels (ENV) was carried out, with '1' recorded as the minimum for collections of non-diagnostic body sherds. Fabric, form and decoration codes are those in current use. Fabric and form codes and their expansions are listed in Table 5, Table 6, CD Table 33 and CD Table 34.

A total of 42,955 sherds of medieval and later pottery from a minimum of 25,052 vessels were found in 2551 contexts from all sites included in this publication. Most contexts are small in size (fewer than 30 sherds), with larger contexts defined as medium (30–99 sherds) and large (100+ sherds). Small context size tends to hinder chronological refinement, which is best achieved in larger and more statistically viable contexts, particularly when these show little sign of subsequent disturbance.

A breakdown of the number of medieval and later contexts recorded is given in Table 7 by period. This reveals a heavy concentration of finds in the earlier medieval period (c 1050–c 1230, periods 10 and 11), dropping markedly in the middle decades of the 13th century (period 12), with larger quantities of pottery and a number of notable groups surviving from the period c 1270–1411 (periods 13 and 14). Details of illustrated pottery are given in Table 8.

The medieval period

The 10th to mid 12th centuries AD (periods 9 and 10)

Relatively small quantities of Late Saxon pottery were recovered from contexts assigned to period 9, following the dark earth accumulation, and can be dated broadly to c AD 900–1050/1100. The main fabric is Late Saxon shelly ware (LSS), which dominated London's ceramic supply during the 10th century AD and continued in use well into the 11th century. Other hand-made coarsewares began to be introduced c AD 970–c 1000 (early medieval sandy ware (EMS) and early medieval sand- and shell-tempered ware (EMSS)). All the sherds recovered come from fabrics and forms common during this period, and are typical of everyday 10th- to early 11th-century AD domestic pottery, with no evidence for industrial activity. The main form is the cooking pot or jar, and there is a limited range of bowls and dishes. No Continental imports were identified. Although there are too few finds in period 9 to allow further conclusions to be drawn, the available evidence suggests that there was domestic occupation in the area on a small scale during the 10th century AD.

Period 10 contexts are broadly dated by the latest pottery present to c 1050 or later, with many dated to c 1080+ by the presence of London-type wares. Relatively few small contexts (70 out of 603) are dated to the 10th to early 11th centuries AD and include sherds of Late Saxon shelly ware (LSS). Fifteen small contexts are dated to the late 10th century AD by the presence of early medieval hand-made coarsewares. However, the main period of activity on the site appears to have begun in the third quarter of the 11th century, with 93.7% of the contexts in period 10 dated to c 1050–c 1200 (including those with a *terminus post quem* of c 1080). This was clearly the time at which the earliest post-Roman activity took place over much of the site, including much of the structural work.

The period 10 ceramic assemblage is dominated by early medieval hand-made coarsewares (84.6% by sherd count/83.9% ENV), which were coming into use in London from c AD 970 onwards as the market for Late Saxon shelly ware (LSS) began to break down. Early Surrey ware (ESUR) is by far the most common fabric found in period 10, accounting for 33.3% of all pottery by sherd count (32.4% ENV). It quickly gained a sizeable share of London's ceramic market during the second half of the 11th century and remained popular well into the 12th century, going into decline only after c 1140 with the introduction of locally made, wheel-thrown shelly-sandy wares. This pattern can clearly be seen in the pottery from the Guildhall. Jars or cooking pots are the main form found in this early whiteware, and there are also sherds from spouted pitchers, which sometimes have simple incised decoration. Early medieval sand- and shell-tempered ware (EMSS) is also common, as it is across the City. It was introduced into London c 1000, continuing in use alongside ESUR until the mid 12th century and remaining one of the main fabrics for everyday domestic usage throughout period 10.

London-area greyware (LOGR) was first used in London c 1050 and appears to have gained an important hold on the market by the end of the 11th century, making it one of the most common fabrics in period 10 contexts, along with ESUR and EMSS. There is a notable similarity in fabric with wheel-thrown London-type wares, which first appear in the archaeological record at the end of the 11th century (Vince 1991b, 267). Spouted pitchers of similar form are found in both LOGR and coarse London-type ware (LCOAR), alongside cooking pots, in late 11th- to early 12th-century contexts at the Guildhall. LCOAR is the most common of the London-type fabrics in 12th-century contexts, but is poorly represented on the site by comparison with early medieval hand-made wares (CD Table 35). The finer London-type ware (LOND), which entirely replaced LCOAR by the beginning of the 13th century, is even more rare at this date (0.4% by sherd count/0.3% ENV).

There are a relatively large number of spouted pitchers in early medieval grog-tempered ware (EMGR) in period 10, accounting for 3.1% of all pottery by sherd count (3.4% ENV). The ware now appears to be more widespread than was previously thought (Vince and Jenner 1991, 80), first occurring in mid to late 11th-century contexts and continuing in use until the mid 12th century. The Guildhall finds suggest that spouted pitchers were far more common than other forms

Table 5 Medieval pottery fabric codes, their expansions and date ranges

Fabric code	Expansion	Date range AD (approx)
ANDA	Andalusian lustreware	1250–1450
ANDE	Andenne-type ware	1050–1200
ANDE SPP1	Andenne-type ware type 1 spouted pitcher (collared rim, rouletting and rounded spout)	1050–1100
ARCH	archaic maiolica	1270–1350
BADO	Badorf ware	900–1200
BLGR	blue-grey ware	1000–1200
BRIM	Brill/Boarstall ware	1250–1500
CBW	coarse Surrey-Hampshire border ware	1270–1500
CHEA	Cheam whiteware	1350–1500
DEVS	developed Stamford-type ware	1150–1250
DUTR	Dutch red earthenware	1300–1650
EARL	Earlswood-type ware	1200–1400
EGS	early German stoneware	1250–1300
EMCH	early medieval chalk-tempered ware	1050–1150
EMCR COAR	early medieval coarse crucible fabric	1000–1200
EMCW	early medieval coarse whiteware	1000–1150
EMFL	early medieval flint-tempered ware	970–1100
EMGR	early medieval grog-tempered ware	1050–1150
EMIS	early medieval Surrey iron-rich sandy ware	1050–1150
EMS	early medieval sandy ware	970–1100
EMSH	early medieval shell-tempered ware	1050–1150
EMSS	early medieval sand- and shell-tempered ware	1000–1150
ESHER	early south Hertfordshire coarseware	1050–1200
ESUR	early Surrey ware	1050–1150
HUY	Huy-type ware	875–925
KING	Kingston-type ware	1240–1400
KING HD	Kingston-type ware in the highly decorated style	1240–1300
KING METCOP	Kingston-type ware metal copy jug	1270–1350
KING NFR	Kingston-type ware with north French-style decoration	1240–1300
KING POLY	Kingston-type ware with polychrome decoration	1240–1300
KING RIL	Kingston-type ware rilled baluster jug	1310–1400
KING SBOSS	Kingston-type ware with stamped boss decoration (except wheat ear)	1270–1350
KING SMR	Kingston-type ware small rounded jug	1310–1400
KINGSL	Kingston-type slipware	1250–1400
LANG	Langerwehe stoneware	1350–1500
LCALC	calcareous London-type ware	1080–1200
LCALC EAS	calcareous London-type ware with early-style decoration	1140–1200
LCGR	Low Countries greyware	1350–1500
LCOAR	coarse London-type ware	1080–1200
LCOAR CALC	coarse London-type ware with calcareous inclusions	1080–1200
LCOAR EAS	coarse London-type ware with early-style decoration	1140–1200
LCOAR GRIT	coarse London-type ware with gritty inclusions	1080–1200
LCOAR ROU	coarse London-type ware with Rouen-style decoration	1170–1200
LCOAR SHEL	coarse London-type ware with shell inclusions	1080–1200
LIMP	Limpsfield-type ware	1150–1300
LLON	late London-type ware	1400–1500
LLSL	late London-type slipware	1400–1500
LMCR	late medieval/early post-medieval crucible fabric	1240–1480
LMHG	late medieval Hertfordshire glazed ware	1340–1450
LOCO	unsourced London-area coarseware	1080–1200
LOGR	London-area greyware	1050–1150
LOND	London-type ware	1080–1350

Fabric code	Expansion	Date range AD (approx)
LOND BAL	London-type ware baluster jug	1180–1350
LOND EAS	London-type ware with early-style decoration	1140–1200
LOND FLAR	London-type ware flared baluster jug	1240–1350
LOND HD	London-type ware in the highly decorated style	1240–1350
LOND NFR	London-type ware with north French-style decoration	1180–1270
LOND PELL	London-type ware with pellet decoration	1140–1220
LOND POLY	London-type ware with polychrome decoration	1240–1350
LOND ROU	London-type ware with Rouen-style decoration	1180–1270
LOND TUL	London-type ware tulip-necked baluster jug	1270–1350
LOND WSD	London-type ware with white slip decoration	1240–1350
LSS	Late Saxon shelly ware	900–1050
MAGR	Mahgrebi ware	1270–1350
MG	Mill Green ware	1270–1350
MG COAR	Mill Green coarseware	1270–1400
MG POLY	Mill Green ware with polychrome decoration	1290–1350
MG WSD	Mill Green ware with white slip decoration	1290–1350
MISC	miscellaneous unsourced wares	900–1500
MORAN	Midlands late medieval orange ware	1400–1500
MORG	organic ware (with voids)	1000–1200
MPUR	Midlands purple ware	1400–1500
MWCR	medieval whiteware crucible fabric	1150–1500
NEOT	St Neots-type ware	970–1100
NFM	north French monochrome ware	1170–1300
NFRE	north French unglazed ware	900–1200
NFRY	north French yellow-glazed ware	900–1200
NMDX	north Middlesex ware	1050–1200
NORG	Normandy glazed ware	1050–1250
NORM	Normandy gritty ware	1050–1250
REDP	red-painted ware	900–1250
REDP BUF	red-painted ware with buff fabric	900–1250
REDP OLV	red-painted ware with olive fabric	900–1250
REDP WHT	red-painted ware with white fabric	900–1250
RHGR	Rhenish Tiel-type greyware	900–1100
ROUE	early Rouen ware	1170–1300
SAIG	Saintonge ware with even green glaze	1280–1350
SAIM	Saintonge ware with mottled green glaze	1250–1650
SAIN	Saintonge ware	1250–1500
SAIP	Saintonge ware with polychrome decoration	1280–1350
SATH	sandy Thetford-type ware	1000–1150
SCAR	Scarborough ware	1200–1350
SHER	south Hertfordshire-type greyware	1170–1350
SHER COAR	coarse south Hertfordshire-type greyware	1170–1350
SHER FINE	fine south Hertfordshire-type greyware	1170–1350
SHER FL	south Hertfordshire-type flint-tempered greyware	1170–1350
SIEG	Siegburg stoneware	1300–1500
SPAM	Merida-type micaceous ware	1270–1650
SPGR	Spanish green-glazed ware	1250–1500
SPOA	miscellaneous unsourced Spanish amphorae	1200–1500
SSW	shelly-sandy ware	1140–1220
STAM	Stamford-type ware	1050–1150
THET	Ipswich-/Thetford-type ware	900–1100
THWH	white Thetford-type ware	1050–1150
TUDG	'Tudor Green'	1350–1500
VALE	early Valencian lustreware	1380–1450
VALM	mature Valencian lustreware	1430–1500

Table 6 Post-medieval pottery fabric codes, their expansions and date ranges

Fabric code	Expansion	Date range (approx)
BORD	Surrey-Hampshire border whiteware	1550–1700
BORDG	Surrey-Hampshire border whiteware with green glaze	1550–1700
BORDO	Surrey-Hampshire border whiteware with olive glaze	1550–1700
BORDY	Surrey-Hampshire border whiteware with clear (yellow) glaze	1550–1700
CHPO BW	Chinese blue and white porcelain	1590–1900
CREA	creamware	1740–1830
CSTN	Cistercian ware	1480–1600
DUTR	Dutch red earthenware	1300–1650
DUTSL	Dutch slipped red earthenware	1500–1650
EBORD	early Surrey-Hampshire border whiteware	1480–1550
ENGS	English stoneware	1700–1900
ENPO	English porcelain	1745–1900
FREC	Frechen stoneware	1550–1700
LANG	Langerwehe stoneware	1480–1550
LMCR	late medieval/early post-medieval crucible fabric	1480–1700
LONS	London stoneware	1670–1926
MART	Martincamp-type ware	1480–1650
METS	metropolitan slipware	1630–1700
MISC	miscellaneous unsourced pottery	1480–1900
MOCH	mocha ware	1780–1900
MORAN	Midlands orange ware (oxidised Midlands purple ware)	1480–1600
MPUR	Midlands purple ware	1480–1750
NIMS	north Italian marbled slipware	1600–1750
PEAR	pearlware	1770–1840
PEN	Peninsular House ware	1650–1700
PMBL	post-medieval black-glazed redware	1580–1700
PMBR	London-area post-medieval bichrome redware	1480–1600
PMFR	post-medieval fine redware	1580–1700
PMR	London-area post-medieval redware	1580–1900
PMRE	London-area early post-medieval redware	1480–1600
PMSR	London-area post-medieval slipped redware	1480–1650
PMSRY	London-area post-medieval slipped redware with clear (yellow) glaze	1480–1650
RAER	Raeren stoneware	1480–1610
RBOR	Surrey-Hampshire border redware	1550–1900
SAIN	Saintonge ware	1480–1650
SIEG	Siegburg stoneware	1500–1630
SPAM	Iberian red micaceous ware	1480–1650
SPGR	Spanish green-glazed coarseware	1480–1650
SPOA	miscallaneous unsourced Spanish amphorae	1480–1500
STSL	combed slipware	1660–1870
SWSG	white salt-glazed stoneware	1720–1780
TGW	English tin-glazed ware	1570–1846
TGW C	tin-glazed ware with Orton type C decoration (plain white glaze)	1630–1846
TGW D	tin-glazed ware with Orton type D decoration (polychome painted)	1630–1680
TGW F	tin-glazed ware with Orton type F decoration ('Chinamen in grasses')	1670–1690
TPW	transfer-printed ware	1780–1900
TPW2	transfer-printed ware with type 2 decoration (stipple and line)	1807–1900
WEST	Westerwald stoneware	1590–1900

Table 7 Post-Roman pottery by period, by sherd count, estimated number of vessels (ENV) and size of context (S = <30 sherds; M = 30–99 sherds; L = 100+ sherds)

Period	Date range	Sherds	ENV	S	M	L	Total
9	to c 1050	142	55	19	1		20
10	c 1050–c 1140	7249	4479	559	42	8	609
11	c 1140–c 1230	22874	14464	1065	119	32	1216
12	c 1230–70	2052	963	51	18	3	72
13	c 1270–c 1350	6432	2866	289	29	12	330
14	c 1350–1411	2616	1341	107	9	7	123
15	1411–c 1550	394	185	41	2		43
16	c 1550–1666	615	346	44	3		47
17	1666–c 1770	472	258	63	5		68
18	c 1770 onwards	109	95	23			23
Total		42955	25052	2261	228	62	2551

Table 8 Details of the illustrated medieval and post-medieval pottery (see Table 5 and Table 6 for expansion of fabric codes)

Cat no.	Site	Context	Period	Land use	Form	Fabric	Fig no.
<P1>	A	[14170]	9	OA127	BOWL FLAR	LSS	17
<P2>	A	[14170]	9	OA127	DISH FLAR	LSS	17
<P3>	A	[20403]	10	OA103	PTCH	LCOAR	35
<P4>	A	[20350]	10	OA103	LAP SPIKE	NFRE	35
<P5>	A	[13348]	10	OA105	PTCH	REDP OLV	32
<P6>	A	[20258]	10	OA105	BOWLDISH	ESUR	32
<P7>	A	[23469]	10	OA105	BOWL	ESUR	32
<P8>	A	[23630]	10	OA105	CP	EMSS	32
<P9>	A	[23630]	10	OA105	CP	EMS	32
<P10>	A	[17486]	10	OA108	BOWL SPOUT	EMSS	54
<P11>	A	[17396]	10	OA108	CP	EMSH	54
<P12>	A	[23305]	10	OA117	PTCH	REDP BUF	57
<P13>	A	[23236]	10	OA117	SPP	EMS	57
<P14>	A	[23305]	10	OA117	PTCH	NFRY	57
<P15>	A	[11417]	10	OA127	SPP	ESUR	67
<P16>	A	[11677]	10	OA127	CP	ESUR	67
<P17>	A	[14078]	10	OA127	JAR ST	THET	67
<P18>	A	[14126]	10	OA127	JUG	STAM	67
<P19>	A	[19951]	10	OA127	CP	EMSS	67
<P20>	A	[23459]	10	S130	CP	ESUR	29
<P21>	A	[23464]	10	S130	CP	EMSS	29
<P22>	A	[23465]	10	S130	CP	EMSH	29
<P23>	A	[23463]	10	S130	SPP	ESUR	29
<P24>	A	[23447]	10	S130	SPP	EMGR	29
<P25>	A	[23258]	10	S130	PTCH	REDP OLV	29
<P26>	A	[23355]	10	S130	SPP	STAM	29
<P27>	A	[20042]	10	R101	CP SM	EMSS	50
<P28>	A	[21815]	10	R102	CP/SPP	LOGR	61
<P29>	A	[21815]	10	R102	JUGPTCH	LCOAR	61
<P30>	A	[13908]	11	OA109	BOWL	ESUR	72
<P31>	A	[17097]	11	OA109	SPP	LCOAR	72
<P32>	A	[17098]	11	OA109	LAP SPIKE	LCOAR	72
<P33>	A	[13815]	11	OA109	PTCH	ANDE	72
<P34>	A	[13578]	11	OA110	VASE RING	LCOAR	-
<P35>	A	[13398]	11	OA110	JUG	NFRE	85
<P36>	A	[13133]	11	OA112	JUG	LCOAR	97
<P37>	A	[13133]	11	OA112	BOT	STAM	97

Table 8 (cont)

Cat no.	Site	Context	Period	Land use	Form	Fabric	Fig no.
<P38>	A	[13388]	11	OA112	LAP SPIKE	SHER FL	97
<P39>	A	[13286]	11	OA112	TPTCH	LOND	97
<P40>	A	[13458]	11	OA112	PIP	LOGR	97
<P41>	A	[17326]	11	OA120	CP	SSW	100
<P42>	A	[20127]	11	OA120	FRYP	ESUR	100
<P43>	C	[631]	11	OA121	SPP	ESUR	114
<P44>	C	[300]	11	OA121	JUG ERND	LCOAR	114
<P45>	C	[1241]	11	OA121	JUG RND	LCOAR	114
<P46>	C	[1008]	11	OA122	TPTCH	LCOAR EAS	-
<P47>	C	[283]	11	OA122	SPP	EMSH	118
<P48>	C	[1194]	11	OA122	BOWL RND	LOGR	118
<P49>	C	[1196]	11	OA122	CP	LCOAR	118
<P50>	A	[10750]	11	OA114	JUG ERND	LCOAR	105
<P51>	A	[11295]	11	OA127	BOWL	LCOAR SHEL	109
<P52>	A	[11296]	11	OA127	BOWL SP	LCOAR	109
<P53>	A	[11372]	11	OA127	CP FT	LCOAR SHEL	109
<P54>	A	[11119]	11	OA127	JUG	LCOAR	109
<P55>	A	[19533]	11	OA127	TPTCH	LCOAR	109
<P56>	A	[19528]	11	OA127	DJ	LCOAR	109
<P57>	A	[14146]	11	OA127	JAR	SSW	109
<P58>	A	[19862]	11	OA127	DISH	SSW	109
<P59>	A	[19717]	11	OA127	DISH	LOGR	109
<P60>	A	[19533]	11	OA127	CP	ESUR	109
<P61>	A	[19760]	11	OA127	PTCH	STAM	109
<P62>	A	[19496]	11	OA127	JUG	DEVS	109
<P63>	A	[17341]	11	OA130	TPTCH	LCALC	92
<P64>	A	[17341]	11	OA130	CP/SPP	LOGR	92
<P65>	A	[17357]	11	OA130	BOWL HAND	LOGR	92
<P66>	A	[17095]	11	OA130	LAP PED	LCOAR	92
<P67>	A	[13775]	11	OA132	CP	LCOAR	106
<P68>	A	[13068]	11	OA132	SPP	LOGR	106
<P69>	A	[21796]	11	OA133	SPP	LOGR	93
<P70>	A	[21795]	11	OA133	LAP PED	NEOT	93, 300
<P71>	A	[21636]	11	OA133	DISH	ESUR	106
<P72>	A	[23101]	11	OA133	LAP SPIKE	LCOAR	93
<P73>	A	[32044]	11	OA133	LAP SPIKE	STAM	93
<P74>	A	[10797]	11	OA136	CURF	LCOAR	101
<P75>	A	[10797]	11	OA136	BOWL	LCOAR CALC	101
<P76>	A	[13829]	11	S107	CUCU	LOND	328
<P77>	A	[23051]	11	B111	JUG	LCOAR	76
<P78>	A	[21803]	11	B112	LAP SPIKE	LOGR	89
<P79>	A	[21940]	11	B112	CRUC RND	EMCW	89
<P80>	A	[21756]	11	B113	SPP	EMGR	98
<P81>	A	[13881]	11	B124	SPP	LOGR	92
<P82>	A	[17158]	11	B124	SPP	LOGR	92
<P83>	A	[17026]	11	B124	SPP	LOND	92
<P84>	A	[13848]	11	B124	COST	LCALC	92
<P85>	A	[13825]	11	B124	MISC	NFRY	92
<P86>	A	[17026]	11	B124	JUG	STAM	92
<P87>	A	[13001]	12	OA202	BOWL	LCOAR SHEL	124
<P88>	A	[11370]	12	OA128	CP FT	SSW	130
<P89>	B	[309]	12	OA128	CP	SHER FL	130
<P90>	A	[13087]	12	OA216	JUG	LOND HD	134
<P91>	A	[13087]	12	OA216	CAUL	SHER	134
<P92>	A	[19301]	13	OA200	JUG	KING	151
<P93>	B	[3125]	13	OA202	JUG ZOO	KING	151
<P94>	A	[19336]	13	OA202	DISH DRIP	KING	151
<P95>	A	[19336]	13	OA202	BOWL HAND	LOND	151
<P96>	C	[31]	13	OA205	JUG RND	SHER	157
<P97>	C	[31]	13	OA205	CP FT	SHER	157
<P98>	C	[31]	13	OA205	JUG FLBAL	LOND TUL	157
<P99>	C	[31]	13	OA205	JUG FLBAL	LOND FLAR	157
<P100>	C	[31]	13	OA205	JUG PEAR	LOND HD	157
<P101>	C	[31]	13	OA205	JUG PEAR	LOND HD	157
<P102>	C	[31]	13	OA205	JUG CON	LOND HD	157
<P103>	A	[11521]	13	OA128	JUG TULBAL	LOND TUL	154
<P104>	A	[11292]	13	OA128	CURF	LCOAR	154
<P105>	B	[833]	13	OA128	BOT	LCOAR CALC	332
<P106>	A	[20735]	13	OA219	JUG RND	LCOAR	161
<P107>	A	[17131]	13	OA219	FRYP	LOND	161
<P108>	A	[9997]	13	OA219	CP	CBW	161
<P109>	A	[9997]	13	OA219	JUG	MG	161
<P110>	A	[10638]	13	OA219	CURF	SHER	161
<P111>	A	[10680]	13	OA219	CRUC	KING	332
<P112>	A	[20738]	13	OA219	ALEM	LOND	332
<P113>	C	[512]	13	S206	DJ CON	LOND	159
<P114>	B	[192]	13	S216	JUG BAL	LOND ROU	130
<P115>	B	[435]	14	B211	JUG BAL	LMHG	151
<P116>	B	[166]	14	B214	FRYP	DUTR	204
<P117>	A	[19352]	14	OA202	JUG ANTH	KING	171
<P118>	A	[23588]	14	OA202	JUG	LOND	171
<P119>	A	[19154]	14	OA202	BOWL	LIMP	171
<P120>	B	[423]	14	OA213	JUGPTCH	LOND	151
<P121>	B	[177]	14	OA213	DISH COND	LOND	151
<P122>	B	[177]	14	OA213	JUG	KING	151
<P123>	B	[385]	14	OA213	JUG	KING HD	151
<P124>	B	[182]	14	OA213	JUG	CBW	151
<P125>	B	[384]	14	OA213	JUG	SHER	151
<P126>	B	[385]	14	OA213	JUG	SHER	151
<P127>	B	[423]	14	OA213	JAR	SHER	151
<P128>	B	[182]	14	OA213	JAR	SHER COAR	151
<P129>	B	[182]	14	OA213	CRUC STR	LMCR	332
<P130>	B	[177]	14	OA213	CRUC DISH	KING	332
<P131>	C	[1011]	14	S206	JUG CON	MG	172
<P132>	A	[11000]	14	S217	JUG	SHER	170
<P133>	B	[208]	14	S217	BOWL FLAR	LIMP	170
<P134>	C	[841]	15	S210	JAR SHL	PMRE	213
<P135>	C	[841]	15	S210	TROU	PMSRY	213
<P136>	C	[841]	15	S210	DJ RND	EBORD	213
<P137>	C	[841]	15	S210	CUP NECK	CSTN	213
<P138>	C	[841]	15	S210	CUP NECK	CSTN	213
<P139>	C	[841]	15	S210	POSS	CSTN	213
<P140>	C	[918]	15	S210	PIP	CHEA	213
<P141>	C	[949]	15	S210	JUG ZOO	LMHG	213
<P142>	A	[10907]	16	S223	JUG RND	FREC	225
<P143>	A	[10907]	16	S223	JUG BART	FREC	225
<P144>	A	[10907]	16	S223	TYG	PMBL	225
<P145>	A	[10907]	16	S223	JUG BART	FREC	225
<P146>	A	[10907]	16	S223	JUG BART	FREC	225
<P147>	A	[10907]	16	S223	JUG BART	FREC	225
<P148>	A	[10907]	16	S223	JUG BART	FREC	225
<P149>	A	[99996]	16	S224	JUG BART	FREC	227
<P150>	A	[10719]	16	S225	LID	RBOR	237
<P151>	A	[11481], [11483]	12	OA128	JUG BAL	ROUE	130

made in EMGR. Indeed, there is a relatively high proportion of spouted pitchers in all fabrics (both locally made and imported finewares) in period 10 (10% by sherd count, 11% ENV), which may suggest the presence of a number of large households or establishments in the area, in which decorative tablewares were a notable element.

Continental imports account for 8.3% of all period 10 pottery by sherd count (9.1% ENV), while wares made in parts of England outside the London area are less common (1.5% by sherd count/1.9% ENV). The chief imports are Andenne-type and red-painted wares (ANDE and REDP), from the Rhineland and Meuse valley (CD Table 35; cf Vince 1991b, fig 7).

Cooking pots are by far the most common form in period 10 contexts, as they are across London (84.4% by sherd count/82.2% ENV of all pottery). The same forms could also be used for storage, and it is not always easy to determine usage from body sherds, although sooting is taken to indicate cooking. Very few large cooking pots were identified in any fabric, and most vessels are of more or less standard size, as used by households across London at this date. Other vessels used for food preparation and serving consist mostly of bowls and dishes of various forms, some of them sooted and used to heat food. They constitute only a small proportion of the pottery from period 10 (CD Table 36), and spouted pitchers are far more important in the Guildhall sequence. There is no clear evidence that any of the pottery, apart from the metalworking vessels, was used in anything other than a household setting, whatever the size of the establishment may have been. Very little industrial pottery was recovered from this period, constituting only 0.4% of all pottery by sherd count (0.6% ENV) (CD Table 11), although metalworking was clearly being practised on a small scale in the area, only becoming important later in the 12th century (period 11). Crucible sherds were found across the site, although most come from open areas. All are in early medieval coarse whiteware (EMCW), the main fabric used for ceramic crucibles in London between c 1000 and c 1150, and all have the round-bottomed profile typical of the form at this period. Most show evidence of having been used to heat metals.

Mid 12th to early 13th centuries (period 11)

The latest pottery from period 11 features dates to the second half of the 12th century, although a considerable quantity of early medieval hand-made coarsewares was also recovered. These represent the main kinds of pottery used by Londoners in the post-Conquest period, and account for 69.6% by sherd count of all pottery from period 11 (68.8% ENV) (CD Table 37). The hand-made tradition continued to provide the bulk of the capital's everyday household pottery at least until the middle of the 12th century, when wheel-thrown, unglazed shelly-sandy wares began to take a hold on the market, probably made within the London-type ware industry (Blackmore and Pearce in prep). However, certain hand-made fabrics continued in production and were used alongside wheel-thrown pottery well into the second half of the 12th century, especially early Surrey

ware (ESUR) and London-area greyware (LOGR), the two most common fabrics in period 11 (CD Table 38). Cooking pots are the main form made in both (CD Table 39). Spouted pitchers were also made in LOGR, similar in form to early 12th-century London-type ware examples and usually bearing incised decoration of some kind (eg Pearce et al 1985, fig 21, nos 40, 42). Bowls and dishes are relatively uncommon in LOGR, although body sherds can be difficult to distinguish from other forms. The only other form recognised in LOGR from period 11 is the spike lamp, of which 11 examples were recorded. ESUR was still common in London in the second half of the 12th century, mostly as cooking pots and spouted pitchers with combed decoration.

By the end of the 12th century, wheel-thrown, unglazed south Hertfordshire-type greyware (SHER) had begun to appear on the London market, gaining popularity as a source of durable and practical everyday kitchen pottery, mostly as cooking pots/jars and jugs. At the same time, wheel-thrown shelly-sandy ware (SSW) was also flourishing and is found in similar proportions to SHER in period 11 contexts (CD Table 38).

After early medieval hand-made coarsewares, London-type wares are the second most common fabric group found in period 11 contexts, with the coarse type (LCOAR) and its variants outnumbering the finer type (LOND), which finally displaced all coarser fabrics in the early 13th century. By the end of the 12th century LOND was at least as common in the City as LCOAR. Since this is not reflected in the period 11 material, the bulk of the pottery may well have been deposited around the middle of the 12th century, before LCOAR had begun to decline and while hand-made wares were still in everyday use. The main forms, found in similar proportions, are jugs and pitchers, and cooking pots, although from the 13th century onwards jugs began to outnumber cooking pots as other industries (eg SHER) took over the supply of kitchen wares.

Continental imports form a relatively small proportion of the period 11 pottery, with spouted pitchers in Andenne-type ware (ANDE) and red-painted ware (REDP) the most common types (CD Table 38). Other imports include spouted pitchers and jugs from northern France, in north French monochrome, unglazed and yellow-glazed wares (NFM, NFRE and NFRY) and early Rouen ware (ROUE), first appearing in London at the end of the 12th century. There are also sherds from several vessels in Stamford-type ware (STAM) from Lincolnshire, including decorated spouted pitchers, bottles, a spike lamp and a crucible. Sherds from 30 different lamps in various fabrics were found in contexts assigned to period 11, most of them spike lamps or cressets in LOGR and LCOAR, as well as EMS, EMSS, SHER and LOND.

There is some evidence for metalworking activity during period 11, in the form of 106 sherds from a minimum of 70 crucibles mostly in early medieval coarse whiteware (EMCW) and mostly of the same small rounded form, and probably used for melting copper alloys. Most crucible sherds were found in pits and dumping in the open areas, especially Open Areas 109 and 127. Related to EMCW is the finer medieval whiteware crucible fabric (MWCR), which appears to remain in use for longer into the 13th century. Part of a rounded crucible in STAM from Open Area 109 may be indicative of silver working, for which its fabric was preferred (Bayley et al 1991, 397–8, 403). In general, EMCW and the related MWCR appear to have been favoured for melting copper alloys, and abundant evidence for such use has survived on the Guildhall examples.

Mid 13th century (period 12)

A very high proportion of the pottery from contexts assigned to period 12 consists of early medieval hand-made coarsewares, with early Surrey ware (ESUR), London-area greyware (LOGR) and early medieval sand and shell-tempered ware (EMSS) the most common, as in period 11 (together, 57.4% by sherd count/40.1% ENV) (CD Table 40). By the beginning of the 13th century these wares were no longer in contemporary use in London and must be seen as residual in period 12. In the course of the 12th century, London-type wares, shelly-sandy ware (SSW) and south Hertfordshire-type greyware (SHER) came to dominate London's ceramic supply. Cooking pots are the only forms represented in SSW and the most common type in SHER, although the greywares also include a few sherds from bowls, a cauldron leg and several jugs.

London-type wares are the second most common fabric group found in period 12 contexts, although 12th-century fabrics (coarse London-type ware (LCOAR) and its variants) and styles of decoration (notably the 'early style') are the main types present (CD Table 40) and probably residual. However, there are also sherds from jugs decorated in the north French and Rouen styles, which appear to have been introduced c 1170 (Vince 1991b, 268), alongside the introduction of the French forms that inspired them (Pearce et al 1985, 28–9). Both styles of decoration continued in production throughout the first half of the 13th century. The highly decorated style developed out of these early French-influenced styles in the mid 13th century, but is not well represented in period 12 (four sherds). Jugs are by far the most common form made in London-type wares of all kinds and dates found in period 12, with cooking pots far less common, probably because they were largely supplied in other wares (eg SSW and SHER). There are a very few bowls, and sherds from a finial and two louvers.

Kingston-type ware (KING) was first used in London at the beginning of period 12. This is the earliest glazed Surrey whiteware fabric recorded in London and it rapidly gained a major hold on the London market, providing good-quality jugs, frequently decorated, as well as cooking pots, bowls, dishes and many other forms. The overall quantity of KING found in period 12 contexts at the Guildhall is very small (13 sherds: CD Table 40), and it probably dates from early in the life of the industry, before it had gained a substantial hold on the market.

Continental imports in period 12 are again dominated by 11th- to 12th-century types, with Andenne-type ware (ANDE) and red-painted ware (REDP) by far the most common, as they are across the City up to the late 12th or early 13th century.

From the last quarter of the 12th century an increasing number of French wares began to enter the capital, and from c 1170 sherds from high-quality, decorated jugs in north French monochrome ware (NFM) and early Rouen ware (ROUE) are occasionally found in stratified contexts, these wares continuing to enter London into the 13th century. Several sherds from three finely decorated jugs in ROUE were recovered from Open Area 211 and would very likely have been seen as valuable items, suitable for display as well as for serving.

Cooking pots are by far the most common form recorded in period 12 (CD Table 41), a consequence of the large number of early medieval coarsewares recovered, although they are also found in London-type ware (LOND), KING, SSW and SHER. Jugs and spouted pitchers are the next most common form (20.9% by sherd count/32.1% ENV), mostly in LOND and later in KING as well, with decoration becoming increasingly elaborate during the 13th century. By comparison with cooking pots and jugs, all other ceramic forms identified in the various industries represented in period 12 are of minimal importance.

There is proportionately less ceramic evidence for metalworking from period 12 than from period 11. Crucibles account for only 0.4% by sherd count (0.7% ENV) of all forms recorded in period 12. All are small rounded crucibles in either early medieval coarse whiteware (EMCW) or medieval whiteware crucible fabric (MWCR), the main fabrics in use during period 11. Used largely for melting copper alloys, they seem to be replaced during the middle decades of the 13th century by the larger, thick-walled, straight-sided crucibles in late medieval/early post-medieval crucible fabric (LMCR), none of which were found in period 12, and the EMCW and MWCR rounded crucibles are most likely residual by c 1240–70.

Late 13th to mid 14th centuries (period 13)

In the last quarter of the 13th and the first half of the 14th century, there is still a high proportion of residual 11th- to 12th-century pottery (31.8% by sherd count/38.7% ENV), including Late Saxon pottery, early medieval hand-made coarsewares and imports, and all 12th-century London-type wares (CD Table 42). Excluding all fabrics and forms that are clearly out of production by c 1270, London-type wares are by far the most common source represented across the site at this date, totalling 36.3% by sherd count (28.7% ENV) of all period 13 pottery (CD Table 42; CD Table 43). As in other periods, jugs are the most common form made in London-type ware (LOND). French-inspired decoration continued in production until the middle of the 13th century, by which time it was evolving into the 'highly decorated style', which represents the most elaborate form of London-type ware decoration. All these French-inspired styles are found at the Guildhall in period 13, with the north French style and highly decorated jugs the most numerous.

During the second half of the 13th century the London-type ware industry moved towards the production of very plain, standardised flared and tulip-necked baluster jugs in various sizes. These are the most common London-type ware jugs found in period 13 (6.3% of all pottery by sherd count/2.2% ENV). They are functional vessels, made specifically for holding and serving wine – and possibly other beverages – in large quantities, and are part of a move towards the manufacture of more practical and utilitarian jug forms. The number of cooking pots recorded in LOND at the Guildhall in period 13 is very small by comparison with jugs, with other forms such as bowls, dishes and pipkins much less common again. To a large extent, this can be accounted for by the widespread use of these forms in other fabrics, especially south Hertfordshire-type greywares (SHER and its variants) which account for 9.2% of all period 13 pottery by sherd count (8.8% ENV), mostly in the form of cooking pots.

By comparison with London-type wares, Surrey whitewares are much less numerous in period 13, although together they are the second most common kind of non-residual pottery (CD Table 42). Throughout the 13th century, Kingston-type ware (KING) (Miller and Stephenson 1999) was the main whiteware used in London, and coarse Surrey-Hampshire border ware (CBW) is poorly represented by comparison with KING in period 13 (3.1% by sherd count/3.4% ENV as opposed to 8.8% by sherd count/10.2% ENV). Jugs of various shapes are the main type found in KING at this period, although there is a higher proportion of cooking pots than in all contemporary fabrics other than SHER. By the mid 14th century, CBW provided the bulk of London's cooking pots, and south Hertfordshire-type greywares were in decline, a trend that is clearly reflected at the Guildhall. Many of the KING jugs are decorated, mostly in the north French or highly decorated styles typical of the mid to late 13th century, although there are also plainer, undecorated forms. Apart from a small number of bowls and dishes, other forms found in KING at this date include dripping dishes, crucibles and part of a lobed cup.

Mill Green ware (MG and MG COAR), made at kilns around Ingatestone in Essex, was first used in London c 1270 (Pearce et al 1982), although it was never as common as LOND or KING, remaining in use in the capital for a fairly short period up to the mid 14th century. At the Guildhall in period 13 Mill Green ware accounts for only 2.7% of all pottery by sherd count (3.6% ENV).

Continental imports in the late 13th to mid 14th centuries are dominated by French wares, although these are rare at the Guildhall. Small amounts of late 12th- to mid 13th-century north French monochrome ware (NFM) and early Rouen ware (ROUE) were found (six and four sherds respectively). From c 1270, high-quality jugs in Saintonge ware from south-west France began to appear in London, and there are examples from the Guildhall with mottled green glaze (SAIM: 13 sherds) and with polychrome decoration (SAIP: nine sherds). However, a far higher proportion of the imported pottery found in period 13 consists of residual 11th- to 12th-century wares.

Cooking pots continue to dominate the forms identified at the Guildhall in period 13 (CD Table 44), again largely on account of the high proportion of residual 11th- to 12th-century pottery found at this date. However, jugs are the most common vessel type in all the main fabrics (44% by sherd count/45.7% ENV of all period 13 pottery), with baluster and rounded forms the most frequently found. Crucibles are the next most common form found in period 13, accounting for 5% of all pottery by sherd count (2.8% ENV). All other forms are of minor importance only. A total of 430 crucible fragments from a minimum of 111 vessels were recovered from contexts dated to period 13, which makes a marked contrast with period 12. By the late 13th century, deep, thick-walled crucibles in late medieval/early post-medieval crucible fabric (LMCR) had largely replaced the small rounded whiteware forms in early medieval coarse whiteware (EMCW) and medieval whiteware crucible fabric (MWCR). The former comprise 92.3% by sherd count of all crucibles found at the Guildhall at this date (CD Table 45). All recorded examples from the site are highly vitrified from being subjected to intense heat, usually having glassy external surfaces and large quantities of slag residues. These large, heavy crucibles were clearly made to hold a far larger quantity of molten metal than the small rounded crucibles found in periods 11 and 12. The contrast with the smaller and somewhat less frequent rounded crucibles found in earlier periods appears to indicate a change in the nature and scale of industry on the site, from small-scale metalworking to a more organised and larger-scale casting activity.

Late 14th century (period 14)

With the exception of a handful of intrusive post-medieval sherds, most open areas, buildings and other structures assigned to period 14 produced pottery dated at the latest to c 1350– c 1500, or somewhere in between. Overall, a fairly large quantity of residual pottery was found in period 14; 11th- to 12th-century pottery alone accounts for 10.6% by sherd count (17.3% ENV) of all finds at this date (CD Table 46).

Surrey whitewares are the most common type of pottery in period 14, with Kingston-type ware (KING) by far the most abundant (35.6% by sherd count/16.9% ENV). Jugs are again the main form, with examples in the 13th-century north French and highly decorated styles. Cooking pots are common in KING from period 14, and sherds from crucibles and a cup were also found.

There is appreciably less coarse Surrey-Hampshire border ware (CBW) present in period 14 contexts than there is KING (14.9% by sherd count/17.4% ENV). Finds include large rounded or bunghole jugs, with broad strap handle, thumbed base and sometimes red-painted decoration, and large cooking pots or jars with broad, flat-topped rims and often with applied vertical strips around the body. Jugs are much plainer and less varied in form and decoration, part of a general trend reflected in other contemporaneous ceramic industries in the London area. Cheam whiteware (CHEA) is represented by one sherd only; it is first found in London c 1350 and remained in production up to c 1500. There are also two sherds from cups and one from a jug in 'Tudor Green' (TUDG), which was made at the various Surrey whiteware production centres almost as a sideline from the late 14th century onwards.

After Surrey whitewares, 13th- to 14th-century London-type wares are the next most common type of pottery found in period 14 (13.1% by sherd count/18.2% ENV of all pottery) (CD Table 46). Evidence from the waterfront sequence shows that the London-type ware industry was no longer in production by c 1350, and that there was apparently a hiatus between its demise and the introduction of late London-type ware (LLON) c 1400 (Pearce et al 1985, 135). The London-type wares found at the Guildhall in period 14 were, to a large extent, no longer being made when the period starts and much of the material must therefore be considered residual, along with other contemporary 13th- to early 14th-century fabrics and forms. Jugs are the main vessel type found, including tulip-necked and flared baluster types.

South Hertfordshire-type greyware (SHER) is less common than the glazed wares in period 14, accounting for 4.7% by sherd count (7.8% ENV) of all pottery; this figure could well include some residual sherds. Cooking pots and jars are the main forms represented. There are also sherds from at least two bowls in the comparable east Surrey-made Limpsfield-type ware (LIMP), a fabric that is far more common in south London than in the City. Fine-quality jugs in Mill Green ware (MG), from Essex, and in late medieval Hertfordshire glazed ware (LMHG), probably from the St Albans area, are also found in period 14 at the Guildhall. Continental imports in period 14 account for only 0.9% of all pottery by sherd count (1.7% ENV). Most of these are residual by the 14th century, but there is also one sherd of Langerwehe stoneware (LANG), imported from the Rhineland during the late Middle Ages.

Overall, jugs are by far the most common vessel form found in period 14 contexts, figuring prominently in all the main glazed wares in use in London in the 13th and 14th centuries (CD Table 47). Cooking vessels constitute the second most common functional category and consist principally of cooking pots. Industrial vessels (crucibles) are the next most common form at this date (9.7% by sherd count/7.9% ENV), showing that industrial activity continued into the early 15th century at least. The main crucible fabric in period 14 contexts is late medieval/early post-medieval crucible fabric (LMCR), made in the form of large, thick-walled, straight-sided vessels. All fragments recorded are highly vitrified and copper alloy slag residue is found on most examples.

The transitional period

The 15th to mid 16th centuries (period 15)

In all, only 14 contexts out of 54 (26%) assigned to period 15 have a *terminus post quem* after c 1400, and most include sherds that are clearly residual by period 15. Residual medieval pottery occurs in reasonable quantities (14.5% by sherd count/21.2% ENV), although this is a lower proportion of the assemblage than in earlier periods.

By the 15th century Surrey whitewares dominated London's ceramic supply, with coarse Surrey-Hampshire border ware (CBW) the most common fabric found in all major assemblages from c 1350 onwards. At the Guildhall in period 15, Surrey

whitewares account for 37.4% of all pottery by sherd count (33.6% ENV), with CBW the most common fabric on the site (26% by sherd count/20.8% ENV) (CD Table 48). Jugs, including a number of large rounded or bunghole forms, cooking pots, bowls and dishes are the main forms, and the vessels are noticeably lacking in decoration. There is much less Kingston-type ware (KING) at this date (6.2% by sherd count/10.6% ENV) as it was not being supplied to London after c 1400. Cheam whiteware (CHEA) was first used in London c 1350, but there are only three vessels represented in period 15, including a near-complete pipkin. Two sherds of 'Tudor Green' (TUDG) were found, as well as eight sherds from three drinking jugs in early Surrey-Hampshire border whiteware (EBORD), a fine whiteware made at Farnborough Hill in the period c 1480–c 1550, and probably at other centres too, and used principally for good-quality drinking vessels (Pearce 1997, 52–3). No later Surrey-Hampshire border whitewares, made after c 1550, were found in period 15.

Late London-type ware (LLON) first appears at the beginning of the 15th century after a hiatus in production in the London ceramic industry between c 1350 and c 1400. Only three sherds of LLON were found at the Guildhall in period 15. Thirteenth- to 14th-century London-type wares are less common in period 15 than CBW, and plain tulip-necked or flared baluster jugs are the main type found. More decorative jugs are found in Mill Green ware (MG), residual by 1400, and late medieval Hertfordshire glazed ware (LMHG), including 70 sherds from a remarkable tall baluster jug with zoomorphic decoration.

The development of early London-area post-medieval redware (PMRE) at the end of the 15th century is marked at the Guildhall in period 15 by the presence of a number of sherds from cauldrons, pipkins and jugs. These utilitarian redwares were sometimes slip-coated or given bichrome glazing (PMSRY, PMBR). Together, London-area red earthenwares account for 3.4% by sherd count (6.2% ENV) of all period 15 pottery. There are also sherds from drinking vessels in Cistercian ware (CSTN), brought into London from the north of England.

Imported pottery at the Guildhall in the 15th and early 16th centuries included Siegburg stoneware (SIEG) drinking vessels, but no Raeren stoneware (RAER), which is the main type found in early 16th-century contexts in London. Overall, Continental imports account for 8.9% by sherd count (8.4% ENV) of all period 15 pottery, and also include Martincamp-type ware (MART) flasks from Normandy, a Dutch slipware (DUTSL) carinated bowl, part of a starred costrel from the Seville area, and an albarello in mature Valencian lustreware (VALM).

Jugs are the most common forms of vessel found in period 15, made mainly in late medieval fabrics such as CBW, LOND, KING, MG and LMHG, and with large numbers also made in the 16th-century local redware industry. Cooking vessels are the next most common functional group identified in period 15 (31.3% by sherd count/27.4% ENV) (CD Table 49), mostly late medieval cooking pots in CBW and residual earlier fabrics, such as LOND and KING. There are also cauldrons and pipkins in the 16th-century PMRE. Drinking vessels, including CSTN cups and

EBORD and SIEG drinking jugs, are more common than in earlier periods on the site, although all other forms occur in relatively small numbers, including bowls and dishes.

Sherds from at least eight large, straight-sided metalworking crucibles in late medieval/early post-medieval crucible fabric (LMCR) were found in period 15 contexts; they are similar to those found in period 13 and may be residual by this date.

The post-medieval period

Mid 16th century to the Great Fire (period 16)

About half the contexts assigned to period 16 (25 out of 53) have a *terminus post quem* of 1550 or later. The remaining contexts have all been dated between *c* 1050 and *c* 1500, so a high proportion of the pottery recovered from period 16 features on the site (34.1% by sherd count/42.9% ENV) was no longer being made by the 16th century, and would certainly have been out of use by 1550.

Once all residual pottery has been excluded, the breakdown of major fabric sources (CD Table 50) shows that imported pottery accounts for an astonishing 33.6% of all contemporary wares in period 16, with Essex fine redwares the second most common source by ENV at 7.2% (11.2% by sherd count). This unusual pattern is explained by the large cellar deposit (S223), which included 218 sherds from at least 133 Frechen stoneware (FREC) *bartmann* jugs and 58 sherds from a minimum of 25 post-medieval black-glazed redware (PMBL) tygs, probably associated with the Blackwell Hall market. These dominate the period 16 assemblage when viewed as a whole, and little contemporary imported pottery other than German stonewares was recorded in period 16. There are isolated sherds of Dutch red earthenware (DUTR) and north Italian marbled slipware (NIMS), as well as 27 sherds from a jar in Peninsular House ware (PEN), probably imported from the Iberian peninsula and associated especially with deposits of the Great Fire period.

Surrey-Hampshire border wares are relatively well represented and occur in the usual range of forms, mostly tripod pipkins but also including part of a stool pan. London-area redwares are less common, accounting for only 3.9% of all period 16 pottery by sherd count (4.8% ENV); bowls and cauldrons or pipkins are the main forms. There are only four sherds of tin-glazed ware or delftware, all dating to the mid 17th century, a time when this decorated pottery was becoming increasingly popular. The only other fabric that is reasonably well represented is Midlands purple ware (MPUR), found in London in 17th-century contexts almost exclusively as tall, cylindrical butter pots used for transporting and storing dairy produce.

Late 17th to late 18th centuries (period 17)

Only two of 57 contexts assigned to period 17 are dated after the Great Fire. All remaining contexts have a significantly earlier *terminus post quem*, so a very high proportion of the pottery from period 17 features is residual. The main period of use represented by the residual wares is the 13th to mid 14th centuries. When all residual pottery is discounted, only three sherds of post-Great Fire pottery remain. The only definite 18th-century pottery recovered is a sherd of white salt-glazed stoneware (SWSG), which was made, largely in the Midlands, between *c* 1720 and *c* 1780. Two sherds from English brown stoneware ginger beer bottles date to the 19th century.

8.8 Accessioned finds

Geoff Egan, with Angela Wardle (musical instruments)

Introduction

The majority of the medieval (including Saxon) items found on the site are included in the catalogue that follows, though it remains a selective catalogue because of the limited space available. The focus of the catalogue is on the significant assemblage of 11th- and 12th-century artefacts found associated with the timber buildings on a 'back lane' of the medieval town. Some previously published items are not catalogued here, for example four 'trial piece' animal bones with incised linear designs (from site C), which have been discussed by Pritchard (1991, 261–2, nos 201–4).

The medieval deposits on this site were characterised by a high degree of reworking, mixing earlier material in with contemporary items (as is often found on intensively occupied urban sites). Such is the degree of residuality, based on known dating for a range of objects among those recovered, that any hopes that analysis of the sequence would allow a number of 11th-century objects to be assigned firmly to one side or the other of the 1066 watershed (or indeed straddling that divide) have not been realised. Considering the volume of deposits excavated, and at site A screened by metal detecting, there is remarkably little among the non-ceramic registered finds from the Saxon period (period 9) that is recognisable as contemporary. The great majority of items recovered from these layers are residual Roman or very likely to be. Similar problems continue through the later medieval sequence, although material from two sizeable copper alloy casting assemblages, from the production of dress accessories and candlesticks, is relatively readily distinguished in the few instances where single items have strayed into later deposits.

More positively, there are many objects of great intrinsic interest compared with typical medieval assemblages away from the waterfront. Particularly for the earlier end of the post-Roman sequence, there are a number of individual and group highlights. Objects of metal are generally very well preserved. This is particularly valuable for the unique insights the assemblages permit into life in a different part of the town, where patterns of discarding were not the same as those beside the Thames (with its extensive reclamation requirements). The residuality/mixing problem, however, means that assigning objects to specific structures is fraught with difficulty.

At the individual level, a very significant item is a Merovingian (?6th-century AD) buckle <S1> (Fig 283), which was found in a domestic deposit of the late 12th to early 13th centuries. Many other items have their own particular significance, despite the divorce of the majority from their likely original contexts.

The majority of the later medieval finds from the site are from the extensive 'open area' deposits in the back yards of the 11th- and 12th-century houses; a large proportion of them appear to be residual. An attempt to give some focus was made by considering the identified, non-residual registered items in relation to the specific buildings and yards in which they were found. Unfortunately, this analysis produced little significant correlation between particular types of artefact and particular buildings, yards or areas. A few of the buildings yielded multiple finds of lead 'tokens' in some early periods, but the uncertainty of the function of these objects at this early date means that their significance is not clear. There are concentrations of metalworking waste in several of the medieval buildings, but again it is in no instance certain that this is anything more than residual, background material. It is difficult to resist the notion that the considerable mixing of deposits has irretrievably obscured the majority of any significant groupings there once may have been.

The most profitable way of looking at the majority of this assemblage is thematically rather than by location. The significant location can in fact be seen as the whole site: a developing 'central place' in the administration of the City, with a church lying to the west and the main market for the most significant national product – Blackwell Hall for cloth – to the east. Even though the excavated sequence of Blackwell Hall market encompasses the entire period of its history from the late 14th to the early 19th century (during which the market developed from a regional to the unrivalled national cloth market, and went on to become the central commercial premises for the international cloth trade with all parts of the emerging, world-wide Empire), just three, relatively uninformative, cloth seals are the sole specific artefacts that bear archaeological witness to this massive enterprise (Fig 354). The important assemblages of late 13th- to early 14th-century dress-accessory founding material, and of 16th-century candlestick manufacturing waste, are considered in separate sections.

Through much of the medieval part of the sequence, there are numerous well-preserved objects of lead/tin alloy, a material which is usually so vulnerable in London soils away from the waterfront that it tends not to survive well, if at all. Several of these items are also notable for their high degree of decoration or other surface detail, inevitably the first part to succumb to any corrosion. The different, presumably more individual discard mechanisms in this area of the City, distinct from the large-scale dumping at the waterfront, potentially give these rare survivals added value. As if to demonstrate just how precarious their survival is, the peculiar environmental conditions of large parts of the Guildhall sites, while kind enough to preserve much more finely detailed lead/tin than is usual at this height in the City, have not preserved all items of these alloys in good condition: ampulla <S85> and spoon <S117>, for example, having both gone some way towards illegibility.

The following abbreviations are used in the catalogue: Diam (diameter), H (height), L (length), Th (thickness), W (width), Wt (weight).

Saxon finds

There are remarkably few non-ceramic items definitely of this date. Furthermore, the majority of the Saxon finds were recorded as residual items in later contexts, reflecting the highly mixed nature of the medieval deposits. Two of the Saxon items were discovered as 'intrusive' finds in late Roman contexts; this is explained by practical problems of archaeological excavation (the nature of biological 'reworking' of soils and the consequent difficulty of distinguishing late Roman 'dark earth' from early medieval soil deposits) rather than indicating any transitional late Roman to early medieval occupation on the site. However, the discovery of the Merovingian-type buckle <S1> (if it was discarded in its own day and 'reworked' through the archaeological sequence) is a unique indicator of a Continental (or at least Kentish) visitor to the ruins of the amphitheatre during the opaque centuries of the city's abandonment. The evidence for Late Saxon (10th- and 11th-century AD) metalworking is catalogued separately.

Dress accessories

<S1> Copper-alloy buckle (Fig 283)
A<5826>, A[21756]; residual in period 11, B113
Heavy oval frame with narrowed bar, 21 x 29mm; subcircular-sectioned outside edge and sides have rebated line of beading; groove with beading (blurred at ends) along outside edge; rebated bar has central, angular knop; frame is worn from missing pin.

This form of robust buckle, with a relatively small aperture compared to the frame's thickness, is characteristic of the pagan Saxon period (5th or 6th century AD), or, since the closest parallel is from grave 36 at Saint-Denis near Paris (Fleury and France Lanord 1998, 105 and front cover), of the Merovingian period (6th century, possibly early 7th century AD). There are a couple of similar finds from France in the British Museum (B Ager, pers comm), one thought to be from the Herpes (Charente) cemetery in the south-west (inv no. 1905, 5–20, 373) and

another, which retains a club-shaped pin, probably from the Marne region (inv no. ML3523).

Another Merovingian-style buckle, but of iron and forming part of a belt suite found with a burial in the Saxon settlement of Lundenwic to the west of the City (Scull in prep, J<1>), has a much more readily explicable context. Further, typologically much closer, parallels in England (many from burials and mostly assigned to the 6th century AD) include one with similar beading decoration, though in a different configuration, from near Chichester, Sussex (Marzinzik 2003, 23–4, pl 14, no. 1).

Objects from this period are notoriously elusive in the area of the old Roman city, almost to the point of non-existence (following upon the Billingsgate bathhouse brooch and glass beaker fragment, usually dated to the AD 400s). The closest items found previously are a couple of 4th- to early 5th-century AD buckles of broadly comparable form of the kind associated with 'Germanic federates' and three imported ?northern French ceramic vessels assigned to the late 6th or 7th century AD (Vince 1990, 12, fig 5). The context of the present object remains isolated and poorly understood.

<S2> Copper-alloy buckle (Fig 33) A<3665>, A[20320]; period 10, OA105
Corroded; 33 x 33mm (25 x 22mm); ornate, flared frame and robust, folded subrectangular plate (rebated towards pin) are openwork (with drilled holes); ?wrought pin survives. The frame and plate are bent together (as found).

Probably for horse equipment as the style of cast then drilled-hole ornament is that of many Saxo-Norman stirrup mounts (Williams 1997), but there seem to be far fewer buckles (Williams 1996, 172, fig 6, no. 37, from Surrey). No precise parallel has been traced.

<S3> Copper-alloy strapend (Fig 13) B<429>, B[986]; intrusive in period 8, OA9
Corroded; 28 x 19mm; oval with pair of holes for attachment in bilobed end; engraved with stylised (beast) in main panel. 10th century AD (G Thomas, pers comm). Cf Malcolm and Bowsher 2003, 268 and <S29>–<S34>.

<S4> Copper-alloy hooked clasp

A<6125>, A[23385]; period 10, B110
Plain, oval panel, L 29mm, W 14mm, with pair of holed loops for attachment; recurved hook. 11th century (G Thomas, pers comm). Cf Malcolm and Bowsher 2003, 192, fig 145, and 266.

<S5> Copper-alloy brooch (Fig 13) A<3174>, A[17907]; period 10, OA105
Nummular form; corroded sheet disc, Diam 23mm; small, central cross pattée, <u>A</u>EDE(L..I)AN REX ANGLOR' around (underlined A on its side).

Apparently in the name of Athelstan, first king of all the English (AD 924–39), this particular design seems to be based on that of the obverse of his 'circumscription-cross' type penny (though to[tium] Brit[annorum] or Saxonum were the phrases used rather than Anglor[um] on this issue and on Athelstan's other coins that give his longer title: cf North 1975, 93, pl 9, no. 16). London was among 20 mints that issued circumscription-cross pennies.

The form is comparable to slightly later coin-brooch finds from the London waterfront site of Thames Exchange (TEX88). This one has lost the backing plate with the pin and securing mount. Presumably residual as found, as it seems unlikely that such a specific reference would still have been significant over a century after Athelstan's death.

Horse equipment

<S6>–<S8> Iron horseshoes (<S6>, Fig 18) A<3348–9>, A<6890>, A[20266]; period 9, OA100 A<3355>, A[20290]; period 9, OA100
These four scrappy fragments from the same area of the site are the earliest of a category of find represented by a total of over eighty from the subsequent

sequence (together these four pieces amount to about a single shoe). They are all of the rounded (plain-edged), relatively broad type 1, which Clark assigns to the 10th century AD (Clark 1995, 85–6, 92, fig 75); the first, comprising one branch (L c 105mm, W 30mm) and with three rectangular-headed nails surviving, is the most complete.

Comparanda for the 11th-century Cheapside hoard of pewter jewellery

The well-known manufacturer's hoard found in the early 19th century (Guildhall Museum 1908, 119, pl 54; Clark 1991,

155–6, no. 408) was, until very recently, an isolated discovery with no known parallels – from actual use – for its distinctive brooches, beads and finger rings. Finds from the Guildhall, along with others from Bull Wharf (BUF90: Ayre and Wroe-Brown in prep) and 72–75 Cheapside (CID90: Hill and Woodger 1999, 40), provide a limited series of comparanda from London (which for the first time allow this material to be assessed in the context of consumption), along with several analogous contemporary items not present in the manufacturing group. The site produced three parallel forms of brooch, along with four arguably related ones, one bead, and a couple of comparable finger rings; thus five categories in the Cheapside hoard can be paralleled by finds from the present site.

The hoard itself can now begin to be seen as comprising only part of a fuller repertoire of almost certainly contemporary accessories (several of these, including mounts, which were not present in the hoard, are listed in this section, following the specific comparanda under each category). This material arguably stands at the beginning of a tradition that was to continue, via brooches and decorative pins (again not present in the hoard itself) into the 'highly decorated' series of later Norman dress accessories, spoons and candlesticks (Egan 2000). The site provides no evidence for production before the mid 11th century of items similar or analogous to those in the hoard, but pervasive residuality means that this is not a definite indication that the tradition only started after 1066.

Specific comparanda for items in the Cheapside hoard are marked * in the following catalogue.

Brooches

The first three brooches listed are circular, with concentric rings with transverse hatching around glass stones (Fig 384). They are similar to Guildhall Museum 1908, 119, nos 11–26, pl 54, no. 12; Clark 1991, 155, no. 408 (smaller size); and to a brooch from excavations on Cheapside (Hill and Woodger 1999, 40, <251>). A scrap of textile on <S9>, the only complete example, may begin to explain the absence of pins from all of these accessories (despite loops surviving on the backs of several, formerly interpreted as having held lost pins). The overall similarity of <S9>–<S12> perhaps masks their variety at a detailed level.

<S9>* Lead/tin brooch (Fig 302; Fig 384) A<6373>, A[23414]; period 10, B126
Diam 19mm; yellow glass stone in recess with raised, concentric-circle border; three more outer concentric circles, the first shallow and delimiting a ring of transverse hatching, the outer two more prominent and overlain by further rings of transverse hatching (undamaged); textile fibres through the integral loop at

the back may represent an alternative means of fixture following loss of the pin itself.

<S10>* Lead/tin brooch A<3482>, [17876]; period 10, B100
Diam 16mm+; the neater of the two incomplete smaller ones, with three concentric rings surviving, and green glass stone.

<S11>* Lead/tin brooch A<5413>, A[20730]; residual in

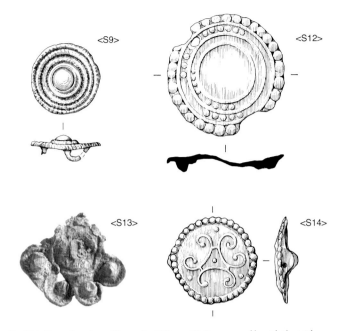

<S9>

<S12>

<S13>

<S14>

Fig 384 *Pewter brooches* <S9> *and* <S12>–<S14>, *comparable with the 11th-century Cheapside hoard of pewter jewellery (scale 1:1)*

period 13, OA219
Similar to <S10>; corroded with incomplete border; Diam 17mm; green stone.

<S12>* Lead/tin brooch
(Fig 384)
A<5931>, A[23370]; period 10, OA100
Corroded (fragments missing from edge); broadly similar to the above but Diam 31mm; device on central, raised circle is illegible, surrounded by three rings of beads/pellets (becoming increasingly large towards the perimeter) alternating with concentric raised circles; a small hole near one of the missing

fragments could perhaps represent provision for a replacement pin. Cf Clark 1991, 155, no. 408 bottom right (larger size), though that one is clearly from a different mould.

<S13>* Lead/tin brooch
(Fig 384)
A<2549>, A[17900]; period 10, OA105
Battered and incomplete; Diam c 30mm; four surviving roundels (of original eight, judging from parallels) with false stones around central ?plain boss. Cf Guildhall Museum 1908, pl 65, nos 6–7 (both eight-lobed); Clark 1991, 154, no. 408 bottom left.

The following three brooches are not represented in the Cheapside hoard, but recent finds from Bull Wharf (BUF90), as well as the present items, suggest that they are likely to have been part of the contemporary range of pewter jewellery available in London.

<S14> Lead/tin brooch (Fig 302; Fig 384)
A<5654>, A[23079]; period 11, B126
Diam 22mm; domed roundel with outline triskele-type motif with recurved arms, central pellet and three radiating, obliquely hatched bands, each with a pellet near the perimeter; border of pellets; pin missing. Variant of BUF90 <946>.

<S15> Lead/tin brooch
A<2382>, A[17689]; period 10, B102
Incomplete, Diam 22mm; border band with (originally six) circle-and-pellet motifs, separated by paired-ladder motifs transversely, all around domed centre (cf false stone), which is defined by two bands of cross-hatching. Cf Egan and Pritchard 1991, 253–4, no. 1332, now thought to be residual as found.

Comparable with BUF90 <1501> and <1757>.

<S16> Lead/tin brooch
A<5931>, A[23370]; period 10, OA100
Corroded, with two areas of edge missing; Diam 32mm; raised centre (distorted, motif unclear – parallels suggest a triskele), surrounded by two concentric circles of beading, all within pelleted border; original pin was probably replaced by one for which a new attachment hole was pierced, but this second one too is missing. Comparable with BUF90 <422> and <946>.

Bead

The tradition of lead/tin beads, though not prominent, arguably continued from the relief-decorated Cheapside hoard examples to the late medieval period (Egan and Pritchard 1991, 315–16, nos 1584–5, assigned to the early 15th century) although the latest ones appear to have been much plainer.

<S17>* Lead/tin bead
A<1513>, A[13910]; probably residual in period 11, OA109
Distorted; L 15mm, max Diam

c 8mm; longitudinally lobed. Cf Guildhall Museum 1908, pl 65, no. 13; Clark 1991, 154, no. 408 (with different decoration).

? Finger rings

These have two-ply twisted wire frames. They could probably have been used as either brooches or finger rings. Since none so far is known with a pin, they are listed as the latter. Cf Guildhall Museum 1908, pl 65, nos 3, 8–11; Clark 1991, 154, no. 408 top right.

<S18>* Lead/tin finger ring
A<1028>, A[13447]; period 11, OA138
Distorted, almost in a knot in its present state; ? 13 x 7mm.

<S19>* Lead/tin finger ring
A<6411>, A[21985]; period 11, B126
Diam ? c 25mm.

Mounts

All have integral, single rivets. The site dating for these items firmly places them earlier than what must now be regarded as a 14th-century revival in the use of lead/tin for mounts, following an apparent hiatus (rather than their first usage, as suggested by the excavated finds previously available: Egan and Pritchard 1991, 18–19, 25, table 3). It will be difficult without further finds to define when the earlier series, as represented by the present items and a few others from different sites, declined (and indeed whether there was actually a complete cessation of their use). The indications from the items below and others is that they were probably current in the 12th century and perhaps the early 13th, leaving origins uncertain (? possibly in the late 11th century). No relationship between any of these and the items in the Cheapside hoard (which did not include mounts) is demonstrable, despite the similar site dating.

<S20> Lead/tin mount (Fig 385)
A<4258>, A[20621]; period 10, OA102

Circular, domed; Diam 10mm; rebate at base with beaded border.

449

<S21> Lead/tin mount (Fig 385)
A<5336>, A[21812]; period 11,
OA133
Domed lentoid, 4 x 14mm;
possibly unused.

<S22> Lead/tin mount (Fig 385)

A<2360>, A[13665]; period 11,
OA110
Rectangular, 6 x 8mm; the
pyramidal form is
emphasised by saltire ridges;
raised linear border; integral
rivet.

<S25> Copper-alloy pin
A<1716>, A[17273]; period 10,
B101
L of shaft 45mm; yellow glass
head.

<S26> Copper-alloy pin
A<1287>, A[13824]; period 11,
S105
L of shaft 50mm; green glass
head.

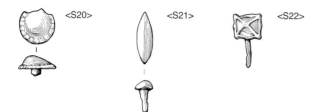

Fig 385 Lead/tin mounts <S20>–<S22> (scale 1:1)

Pins with decorative heads

There is a significant point of comparison, for the first item
listed, with some Cheapside hoard brooches with their green or
yellow glass stones, even though there were no pins at all in
the hoard. It is possible that this tradition continued among
pins later than among brooches, as some of the simple glass-
headed pins may date from as late as the second half of the
12th century (Egan and Pritchard 1991, 300, 304, nos 1468–
9, pl 7E). So far, a combination of ornate lead/tin and glass in
the head is known only from <S23>; <S24> may never have
had a separate gem, arguably placing it in another category.
Further finds are needed before it is possible to confirm the
proper place, relative to each other and to the Cheapside finds,
of the different strands of the tradition.

<S23> Lead/tin pin head (Fig
302; Fig 386)
A<1825>, A[17199]; period 10,
OA108
Head only; openwork sexfoil,
Diam 12mm, with central green
glass stone; the missing shaft
would presumably have been of
copper alloy (cf <S24>).

<S24> Lead/tin pin head
A<5955>, A[23355]; period 10,
S130
Head only; openwork roundel,
Diam 17mm; apparently two
similar motifs in the mould parts
(differentiated by the failure of
the metal to flow during casting
at different points on each

respective side), brought together
to enclose the copper-alloy pin
shaft (part of which survives);
a border of pellets surrounds a
diametrical moulded bar (which
should have encased the pin),
from which symmetrical, moulded
branches spring towards the base,
with two ?horizontal struts near
the top end, flanking a couple of
raised rings laterally on each face.
 This botched casting, with
bubble voids as well as the two
sides of the mould out of register,
probably does not convey
adequately the intended design,
which may perhaps have included
a glass stone set into each of the
four rings (cf <S23>).

<S23>

Fig 386 Decorative lead/tin pin head <S23> with green glass stone (scale 1:1)

Saxo-Norman decorative metalwork of the 11th and 12th centuries

If residuality had not been so high on the site, the recovery of
an unusually large number of notably high-quality, decorative
items stylistically from the period just before or immediately
following the Conquest might have helped pin down whether
or not there was any rapid change in fashions with the advent
of the Normans. As it is, in view of the wider picture of
deposit reworking on the site, the post-1050 contextual dating
assigned to the following objects can not be regarded as
certainly indicative of their time of manufacture. These items,
nevertheless, together with some of the earlier and later finds,
arguably constitute the most impressive assemblage of Saxo-
Norman decorative metalwork from any site in the City so far.
(For a discussion of the implications of items with
Scandinavian-style ornament, see Chapter 6.4.)

Dress accessories

BROOCHES

<S27> Copper-alloy brooch
(Fig 26)
A<5949>, A[23447]; period 10,
S130
Cut quarter sheet brooch disc, 10
x 12mm, with repoussé 'short-
cross' design (probably based on
the reverses of Cnut's 'pointed
helmet' coinage issue of 1023–9
(North 1963, 118, pl 11, nos
14–18) with the dash and broken
annulet enclosing a pellet
simplified to a separated dash and
annulet, in the same way as the
legend has become little more
than a series of radiating dashes
with an occasional one at right
angles); roughly pierced near cut
edge.
 The context in which this was
found may be only about a

quarter of a century later than the
coin issue the design is based on.

<S28> Copper-alloy brooch
(Fig 302)
A<5539>, A[20730]; residual in
period 13, OA219
Triangular sheet backing plate, 22
x 30mm, to gilded, curvilinear
motif with four spiralling
terminals (?originally symmetrical
openwork of delicate wires
flanking a trapezoidal central form
– a small fragment is broken off
one side as found); separate wire
pin and catch.
 The gilded motif is probably
a broken-off pin head (J Graham
Campbell, pers comm), too
attractive to discard, so reused in
this accessory.

HOOKED CLASPS

All have two holes for attachment. For other London finds of
this category, see <S4> and cf Murdoch et al 1991, 106, nos
13–14; Malcolm and Bowsher 2003, 266.

<S29> Copper-alloy hooked clasp
A<2050>, A[17396]; period 10,
OA108
L 19mm, Diam 10mm; three
punched circles.

<S30> Copper-alloy hooked clasp
A<2963>, A[20061]; period 10,
S120
L 18mm, Diam 12mm; three
punched circle-and-dot motifs.

<S31> Copper-alloy hooked clasp
A<3313>, A[20422]; period 10,
OA105
Incomplete; L 15mm+, plate
10mm+; three punched circles.

<S32> Copper-alloy hooked clasp
A<3323>, A[20441]; period 10,
OA100
L 15mm, Diam 13mm; saltire
bands and central, short-armed
cross.

<S33> Copper-alloy hooked clasp
A<5762>, A[23430]; period 10,

OA100
Surviving L 15mm, Diam 17mm;
three punched circle-and-dot
motifs; hook broken off.

<S34> Copper-alloy hooked clasp
A<2010>, A[13334]; period 11,
B129
Distorted and corroded; L c 20mm,
W 15mm; triangular plate has
line of engraved rectangles along
perimeter, but main device
(probably a stylised animal) is
illegible; broken off at one of two
attachment holes.

Lead/tin finger rings

This highly decorated series is distinct from the Cheapside
hoard tradition of twisted-wire finger rings. There is nothing
in the site dating to confirm the suggestion made from
evidence elsewhere that this category post-dates that one
(indeed, such hints as there are from the Guildhall reverse the
expected chronology). These more familiar designs for finger
rings do, nevertheless, continue more widely on London sites
up to at least the mid 15th century (Egan and Pritchard 1991,
332–5).

Two categories may be distinguished, based on the position
of the casting seams, which may run around the hoop
horizontally, or appear on opposite sides of the hoop vertically.
There is, again, little difference in dating from the Guildhall
sites for these two forms of seam. Two of the three examples of
the latter have the same phasing as ones with the former trait,
although the wider picture from finds beyond the site suggests
that those with vertical seams are a later grouping, continuing
into the late medieval period.

WITH MOULD SEAM HORIZONTALLY

<S35> Lead/tin finger ring
A<3403>, A[17879]; period 10,
OA126
Incomplete and distorted; three
round bezels; surviving L 31mm.

<S36> Lead/tin finger ring
A<1465>, A[13910]; period 11,
OA109
Incomplete; surviving L 16mm;
transversely hatched hoop

with two round bezels, one
with radiating lines and the
other with a hatched centre
surrounded by oblique
hatching.

<S37> Lead/tin finger ring
A<1475>, A[13963]; period 11,
B117
Scrap consisting of little more
than one bezel survives.

WITH MOULD SEAM VERTICALLY

<S38> Lead/tin finger ring
(Fig 302)
A<6026>, A[23443]; period 10,
S130
Diam 19mm; round bezel with
cross-and-pellets motif defined
by ring with transversely
hatched border; transversely
hatched loop. Despite the

similarity of the motif to that
on long-cross sterling pennies,
there can be no connection as
this accessory is earlier than
the coin series by over a
century.

<S39> Lead/tin finger ring
A<2560>, A[17767]; period 10,

OA105
Strip from hoop; surviving L
26mm.

<S40> Lead/tin finger ring
A<1343>, A[13927]; period 11,
OA109
Diam 13mm; transversely
hatched hoop; round false stone

in round bezel.

<S41> Lead/tin finger ring
A<1668>, A[17119]; period 11,
OA109
Diam c 18mm; transversely
hatched hoop flanks bezel in form
of a daisy-like flower (partly
deficient in metal).

Furnishing mounts

These may all be from caskets.

<S42> Copper-alloy furnishing
mount (Fig 387)
A<6793>, A[11544]; period 10,
OA127
Incomplete; three non-contiguous
cast fragments (mostly flat-backed
though parts are hollow here),
overall at least 65 x 75mm
originally; in Romanesque style
with high-relief, curvilinear
openwork intertwined ?dragon
(characteristically bent leg, part of
body, and perhaps a wing survive)
and serpent (small, leonine head
with an arc of ?saliva/venom
droplets, and tail survive); both
creatures appear to be scaled and
the saliva droplets are echoed by
similarly shaped fins on the tail;
traces of gilding and three holes
for attachment survive.

Even in its present state this
piece has some claim to be
among the most impressive items
of metalwork in this style
excavated in London.

<S43> Copper-alloy furnishing
mount (Fig 387)
A<2671>, A[20078]; period 10,
OA100
Elaborately moulded mount, L
40mm, W 8mm; flat area at one
end for one of two attachment
rivets (both survive), heavily
stylised animal head and
longitudinally grooved ?body,
ending at second rivet, then
second, similar animal, the head of
which forms the terminal (the part
occupied by this beast arches up
from the flat plane of the back of
the rest of the object at a defining
transverse ridge); apparently
complete. This is presumably one
component of some kind of clasp
or catch plate (perhaps too robust
for a dress accessory).

<S44> Copper-alloy furnishing
mount (Fig 387)

A<2956>, A[20400]; period 10,
OA100
Elaborately moulded mount, L
65mm; at one end a rectangular
frame, 12 x 15mm, with
transverse ridges; decoration
includes animal head adjoining
spatulate housing for one of the
two attachment holes; the back
is flat.

Several of these distinctive
items are known from about the
same period. They may be some
kind of casket clasp (there is no
provision for a buckle-type pin on
the frame). It seems unlikely that
these would go with components
like the preceding one (at least
these two seem irreconcilable,
even though they came from the
same series of deposits).

<S45> Copper-alloy furnishing
mount (Fig 314)
A<1297>, A[13378]; period 11,
S112
Incomplete (broken off at right);
surviving fragment 37 x 24mm;
flat-backed and asymmetrical;
curvilinear openwork
prominently-snouted, gaping-
jawed serpent, whose horn
develops into a circle, the head
being balanced by a spiral-ended
band from the right; hole for
attachment. This accomplished
piece is one of the few items
from London in Urnes style (ie
the latest of the Scandinavian
styles defined in Britain, dated to
the late 11th to early 12th
centuries).

<S46> Lead/tin foil furnishing
mount (Fig 387)
A<6419>, A[21958]; period 11,
OA133
Strip (found folded up, in two
pieces); combined surviving L
93mm, W 25mm, with (incised)
herringbone pattern between

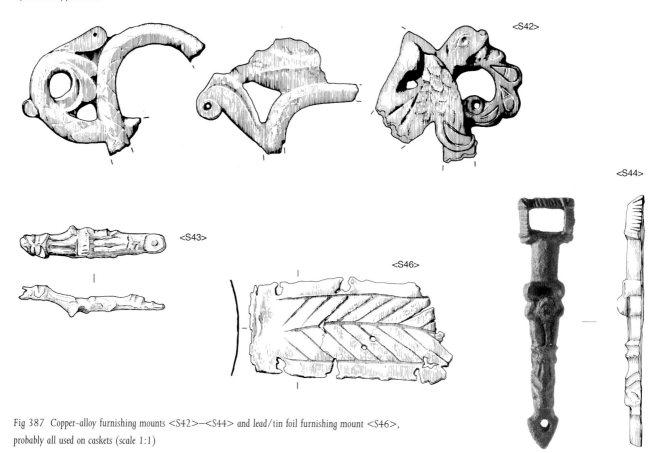

Fig 387 Copper-alloy furnishing mounts <S42>–<S44> and lead/tin foil furnishing mount <S46>, probably all used on caskets (scale 1:1)

border lines; torn off original object to which it had been mounted by tacks. Perhaps set on the outside of a casket. Several analogous fragments with more recognisably Saxo-Norman stamped motifs have been found at the waterfront, such as at Bull Wharf (BUF90 <898> and <1714>). Later medieval, plain pieces of lead/tin foil were probably used to line caskets (eg Egan 1998, 86–7, nos 233–4, 236).

Horse equipment

<S47> Copper-alloy harness pendant (Fig 314)
A<2639>, A[17924]; period 10, OA100
Ornate pendant and holder, both with elaborate outlines and detailing executed as grooves; tripartite, moulded suspender, 14 x 29mm, with two central drilled holes, holding heavily stylised, openwork motif (45 x 35mm) of opposed dragons, whose wings are folded and whose gaping mouths flank a pierced lozenge.

The style is familiar among stirrup mounts of the 10th and 11th centuries AD (Williams 1997), but pendants are not so common.

<S48> Copper-alloy stirrup mount (Fig 303)

A<5913>, A[20730]; presumably residual in period 13, OA219
Lozenge-shaped plate, 29 x 42mm, with oblique grid on solid ground, and pierced terminal loop; the flange at a right angle at the other end has an iron rivet which holds a fragment of an iron strip with which the mount was connected to the stirrup.

Cf Williams 1997, 69–71, type 12 'closed' version (ibid 73–4, no. 322 is an 'open' version of the present design from the waterfront in London); also very similar to Biddle 1990, 1116–17, fig 362, no. 4270 (unidentified in text; unusually, the complete iron strip survives on this one, which is from a deposit assigned to the mid 11th century).

Central place objects: commercial and institutional items of the 11th–13th centuries

A few finds stand out by reason of their significance for international relations with regions from Scandinavia to Italy and Constantinople, or for aspects of trade within England or perhaps just in London. Arguably, they reflect the development of the Guildhall area as a central place within the City's organisational infrastructure, and so they are grouped together with other items that help characterise the economic high status and importance of this part of the City.

Continental bowl mount

<S49> Copper-alloy bowl mount (Fig 388)
A<2519>, A[17820]; period 10, OA126
Sheeting with punched decoration; semicircle, Diam 50mm, continuous with strip, 78 x 13mm; both with beading and linear borders; the former has the upper half of a facing king with a linear moustache and angled crown (with a tripartite finial including a central loop) and wearing a robe on his back (fastened at the neck by a possible central brooch and a cord having two round tags), holding up two fruiting vine branches (each with three bunches of grapes); the strip bears repeated palmette motifs.

This distinctively shaped mount is characteristic of ones set on 11th- or 12th-century German vessels. Similar mounts were affixed on the inside of a copper-alloy bowl (or Schale) now in the Staatliche Galerie Moritzburg in Halle, Germany (Fig 389; Weitzmann-Fiedler 1981, 132–3, no. 188, figs 147–9) and on the outside of the lid of a double cup made of wood, now in the church of St Godehard in Hildesheim, Germany (ibid, pl 22) (for an example from Italy see von Hessen 1984). They were presumably

Fig 389 *Reconstruction drawing of a sheet copper-alloy bowl or Otto-Schale in Halle, Germany, with mounts similar to <S49> (see Fig 388) (after Weitzmann-Fiedler 1981, fig 188, a)*

Fig 388 *Copper-alloy mount <S49>, probably originally set on an imported bowl such as the Otto-Schale (see Fig 389) (scale 1:1)*

intended to enhance the appearance and value of what were already expensive vessels. The mounts are set in fours as radii on the walls of these two Continental vessels. Those on the first surround a central roundel with a bust labelled OTTO, previously variously interpreted as one of the Emperors Otto I–III, but recently and more persuasively as Bishop Otto of Bamberg (c 1063–1139); hence the term *Otto-Schale* has been applied to that vessel and to another in Riga, Latvia, with four surviving (of five) similar roundels (ibid, 132, fig 187). Both of these vessels are regarded as highly prestigious containers, perhaps with direct episcopal associations (potential links with royalty are now out of favour). The parallels have foliate scrolling along the main stem and, in the case of the two in Germany, in the semicircular terminal of each mount.

The Guildhall mount is presumably of Continental, probably German, origin (as would have been the copper-alloy bowl on which it was most likely set). In the absence of any candidate from the site for an accompanying central roundel, it is not possible to say whether it was from a further *Otto-Schale*, with all that that might imply. The unparalleled regal figure in the semicircular terminal has proved difficult to identify, 'king-of-the-vine/grapes' being a fair description but devoid of further inference. He could be a *Mai-König* (May-king) from German folklore (N Stratford, pers comm): the grapes might symbolise wine, perhaps drunk from the vessel to which this mount was attached (although they could perhaps point to a season of the year other than spring).

Many *Schalen* were originally connected with religious institutions and others come from aristocratic residences; the Guildhall mount therefore raises several questions about its ownership. The mount was discarded in a small ditch or pit c 1100, some years before the construction of the Guildhall in the 1120s (period 10 phase 4, OA126). The open area in which the object was found was part of the St Lawrence Jewry property by the 13th century (Chapter 4.1,

Tenement 7) and it may already have been owned by the church at this earlier date. However, the church of St Lawrence seems on the face of it to have been a poorer foundation than might be expected to own such an object. The original context of the vessel represented by this find remains open to speculation.

Byzantine lead seal

<S50> Lead seal (Fig 390) A<6021>, A[23444]; period 10, OA105
A weakly struck circular lead seal for a document, Diam 34mm, with hole horizontally for an attachment cord: tabular legend, including 'ΓENIKON' // [B motif integral with casting] bearded ?saint, legend to right.

Enough of the incompletely registered devices are legible to show that the lettering is Greek (though a B-like character on one side, integral from the casting of the blank, is more prominent), and to reveal the seal as coming from the *genikon*, the central Byzantine imperial department of finance at Constantinople. Eight different seals, all from this same administrative centre, are now known in London, and those which are identifiable were used by a variety of its officers in the narrow period c 1040–90 (Egan in prep a). The dating of both the object and the context in which it was found pre-date the establishment of the Guildhall in

Fig 390 *11th-century Byzantine lead seal <S50> (scale 1:1)*

the 1120s and so the artefact may not have any primary connection with the emerging civic administration. Speculation as to the significance of the flurry of official communications to London from the very centre of the Byzantine Empire that is implied by these finds is unresolved, but they may possibly relate to the hiring of mercenaries ('Varangians') from among the native English population which found itself dispossessed of appropriate opportunities for advancement in the aftermath of the Norman Conquest. (Thanks to M. J-C Cheynet (Collège de France) for identifying this item.)

Trade seal

<S51> Lead trade seal (Fig 133) A<5638>, A[21512]; period 12, OA216
Single ovoid disc with hole horizontally through middle for attachment provision, Diam 12mm; bearded king's head facing // TT (lombardic lettering).

Presumably to identify a specific variety of Continental goods. The stamps are very similar (virtually identical) to the two central devices on grosso coins of the Italian city of Lucca issued by the German Emperor Otto IV from 1209 (on which the TT motif, together with the surrounding circle of pellets, stands for his name: Hoffman 1970, 318, no. 321). This very close parallel is surely more than coincidence – Lucca was a centre for the manufacture of silks, for which small, lightweight seals would be suited, and it is these internationally traded, luxury textiles that may be suggested as the most likely goods for the seals to have been attached to. These would, in this case, be the earliest lead cloth seals so far known in what became the western European tradition, possibly following on from pre-millennium Byzantine issues from Constantinople (cf Endrei and Egan 1982, 49–51, fig 2). The present example is the first to be identified.

Several of these seals are now known from London (eg Swan Lane (SWA81 <632>) from a deposit assigned to the late 14th century and Thames Exchange (TEX88 <8000>)). Some, like the latter, have in place of the TT motif a mounted knight wearing a cylindrical close helm and holding a shield, with different arms: one has ?three stars along the left and part of a cross on the rest, another just a fleur-de-lis; the former arms may possibly in turn relate to those on a series of somewhat later cloth seals occasionally encountered in London (eg Egan in prep b, no. 691).

Whatever the significance of the tiny differences between them, with at least five finds of such seals in London, they suggest a significant volume of trade, the most likely goods being silks from Lucca. There are actual discoveries in London of silks of similar date, which comprise early plain-woven textiles and, from the late 14th century, patterned ones (Crowfoot et al 1992, 88–9, nos 337–52, and 112–26). The Royal Wardrobe accounts include details of the import of Lucchese silks (cf merchants of Lucca living at the 1 Poultry (ONE94) site: Burch and Treveil in prep). While the seals are probably unconnected with royal purchases, they suggest a much wider circle of customers in London for these exotic textiles in the next century. There is documentary evidence for mercers, who would have been involved in the silk trade, in Tenements 4, 5 and 6 (only about 20m to the west of the seal's findspot) along Aldermanbury; that evidence dates, however, from the late 13th century (Chapter 4.1).

Seal matrices

Both those recovered are late medieval in date and for personal seals. A large one of lead ostensibly relates to an aristocratic woman, while a later, small one of copper alloy features a privy mark.

<S52> Lead seal (Fig 391) B<2>, B[205]; residual in period 16, B219
Rough plano-convex disc, abraded, ?hammered, and cut by blade (not obviously for cancellation): Diam 74mm, Th 6mm; griffin capturing a fleeing quadruped, with legend in two rings: outer (+)SI..I(L)…(ALI)…N(I)…V..(?O RIS); inner +FILII COMITIS (P)ICARDI – Sigillum Al(i)..n(i) uxoris filii comitis Picardi ('seal of [?Alianor etc – variant of Eleanor], wife of the son of the count of Picardy', or 'wife of Count fitz Richard') all in lombardic lettering (the other side is plain). The style is comparable with that of several 12th- to13th-century seals. The individual referred to has not been traced.

This has a relatively aggressive motif for a medieval woman's seal. It seems most unlikely to have been a matrix intended for the use of the French aristocrat it purports to name (perhaps particularly in such a cumbersome form apparently amounting to '[name], daughter-in-law of the count of Picardy'), and the metal it is made of is also far too lowly. It could perhaps be a sample of engraving for the approval of prospective customers in general, if it is not simply some kind of elaborate doodle. It does not obviously go with the other evidence for metalworking in the vicinity, and its very manufacture was hardly a wise path to tread in case it was misconstrued or fell into the wrong hands to be used illicitly. The archaeological context of the seal does not help its interpretation, as it was found within a 16th-century storeroom of Blackwell Hall market. The findspot of the object lies within the area of the old aristocratic property, Tenement 12, and it might therefore be possible to argue that the seal belonged to the wife of one of the owners, Warin de Bassingbourn, John fitz Geoffrey or Roger de Clifford (Chapter 6.8). However, the impression that the object is not a genuine aristocratic seal would argue against this.

<S53> Copper-alloy seal (Fig 316) A<5580>, A[23086]; period 17, S227
Circular, Diam 24mm, with holed lateral tab; device consisting of opposed motifs each like a letter 'S' on its side, flanking conventional privy mark, +S'IOHIS KETELLARE (lombardic lettering) around.

Ketellare presumably means 'kettle maker', or maker of hammered-sheet vessels (there is unlikely to

<S52>

Fig 391 Medieval lead seal <S52>, purporting to be that of an aristocratic woman but which may be an engraver's sample (scale c 1:1)

be any connection with the 14th-century dress-accessory foundry (Chapter 6.6)). The object is medieval (though found in a later context) but there is no documentary record of a kettle maker in Tenement 7 (the medieval property in which the object was found) or, indeed, in any other property in the study area.

Weights

As is usual with medieval weights (cf Egan 1998, 301–9), it is difficult to suggest definite standards represented by all the following items; nevertheless, the avoirdupois system may be represented by two of the four. From 1357 avoirdupois weights were checked at the Guildhall for accuracy, and if found to be of true weight were duly stamped (Statute 31 Edw III st 1 c 2). It is not possible to suggest that any of the rather anonymous listed items (which are of appropriate date) was lost while in the area for this regulatory purpose, and none of them is marked.

<S54> Lead weight
A<3361>, A[20288]; period 10, OA105
Rough disc; Diam 17mm, Th 6mm, Wt 12g.

<S55> Lead weight
A<6097>, A[23419]; period 10, OA105
Plano-convex; Diam 22mm, H 8mm, Wt 25g. About 2% light of the standard ounce of the period.

<S56> Lead weight
A<147>, A[11587]; period 11, OA127
Corroded disc; Diam 52mm, Th 10mm, Wt 187g; some scratches; abraded.

<S57> Lead weight (Fig 313)
A<2323>, A[13419]; period 11, OA132
Discoid; Diam 45mm, Th 32mm, Wt 211g; ?seven iron nails of various forms roughly hammered in, both partly and fully (heads all on one face; one shaft has gone through to the other side and been bent over there); probably a half avoirdupois pound (of 15 ounces), of which the measured weight is less than half of one percent light.

The avoirdupois system is recorded for certain only from c 1280 onwards, and though it may have been in existence a little earlier (Egan 1998, 302–3, table 14) the gap of at least two generations separating it from the date assigned to the deposit in which this object was found seems an inexplicably long one.

The nails may have been to make up the standard weight (this particular practice is, however, unparalleled).

<S58> Lead weight
A<5631>, A[21536]; period 13, OA202
Rectangular with convex sides; corroded in one area; c 12 x 12mm, Th 6mm, Wt 5g.

<S59> Lead weight
A<6564>, A[20730]; period 13, OA219
Hammered discoid; Diam c 20mm, Th c 4mm, Wt 14g. ? One half ounce avoirdupois (just over half of one percent light).

Scales

These suggest transactions involving small amounts of valuable materials, perhaps in manufacture (see the contemporary fragments of litharge cake) or, perhaps more prosaically, the accurate checking of the weights of coins, which at this date would have been silver.

<S60> Copper-alloy scales
A<1659>, A[14751]; period 9, B134
Stirrup fragment; top, L 15mm, and one side, L 50mm.

<S61> Copper-alloy scales
A<225>, A[14310]; period 10, OA127
Stirrup; H 59mm, span 11mm; suspension loop at top broken off.

<S62> Copper-alloy scales
A<6372>, A[23415]; period 10, B110
Arms, distorted; sheet tubing with hole pierced at each end, L c 90mm; separate pointer broken off at hole for attachment.

<S63> Copper-alloy scales
A<5707>, A[23246]; period 11, OA134
Folding arms and pointer (found folded); L of arms 34mm, L of pointer 13mm.

Gold thread

These very scrappy, and at this stage undiagnostic, fragments could relate either to ecclesiastical vestments or to high-status garments worn by the governing classes of Saxon and Norman London.

<S64> Gold thread
A<4342>, A[17870]; period 10, R102

<S65> Gold thread
A<6275>, A[20320];

period 10, OA105

<S66> Gold thread
A<6274>, A[17118]; period 11, OA109

Ecclesiastical or Guildhall institutional items (including clerical and religious objects) of the 11th–14th centuries

Window glass

These medieval fragments are all incomplete panes and it is difficult to say much about the original grand designs. The fact that five of the fragments (<S67>–<S71>) were found in the area just to the south of the first Guildhall chapel of c 1300 (Chapter 4.1) would suggest that they were originally used in that building, which was demolished to make way for the new chapel in the early 15th century. Unsurprisingly, most of the pieces were recovered from demolition contexts much later than their date of original manufacture and use.

<S67> Window glass (Fig 145)
B<152>, B[423]; period 14, OA213
Decayed; trefoil against cross-hatched field.

<S68> Window glass (Fig 145)
B<151>, B[423]; period 14, OA213

<S69> Window glass
B<149>, B[34]; period 16, B219
Blue; thick (up to 7mm), 55 x 50mm; one side grozed, with surface decay.

The following have reddish paint:

<S70> Window glass
B<204>, B[229]; period 17, B216
Pale green; series of ?border lines, pair of slightly curved hair lines to one side.

<S71> Window glass (Fig 145)

Decayed; band with outline and in reserve paired annulets flanking large roundel.

B<847>, B[315], unstratified
Decayed; border lines, meeting at corner with a trefoil, from which curved lines or foliate stems diverge, against cross-hatched field.

<S72> Window glass
B<1163>, B[3082], unstratified

Patchy, yellowish, in painted outline. Possibly part of a

letter in an inscription; ?late medieval.

Shell palettes with pigments

The palettes <S75>–<S78> were all found in 14th-century contexts in the Guildhall yard, and the range of pigments recorded here could have been used in wall painting either in the Guildhall itself or its chapel, or, conceivably, for manuscript illustration in the Guildhall College. Palettes <S73> and <S74> were recovered from slightly earlier contexts in close proximity to St Lawrence Jewry and so may be associated with wall painting in the first masonry church, built around the end of the third quarter of the 11th century (period 10 phase 2). These types of palette are unusual finds away from major religious and secular institutions (note that these colourants are not associated with dyeing textiles, which in any case would not have been carried out at Blackwell Hall cloth market). They may be compared with two shell palettes assigned to the 12th century, neither obviously from an ecclesiastical site (Pritchard 1991, 171, 260, fig 353, nos 184–5).

<S73> Shell palette (Fig 358)
A<2668>, A[20014]; period 10, S101
Oyster shell and red pigment; Raman-spectroscopy analysis indicates vermilion.

B113
Blue material.

<S74> Shell palette
A<5759>, A[21685]; period 11,

<S75> Shell palette
A<2669>, A[19338]; period 13, OA200
Wt c 2g; blue pigment. Raman-spectroscopy analysis indicates azurite with chalk.

None of the following has been analysed:

<S76> Shell palette
B<212>, B[495]; period 13, OA211
Oyster shell with red contents.

<S77> Shell palette
B<29>, B[204]; period 14, OA213

Oyster shell with blue contents.

<S78> Shell palettes
B<783>, B[385]; period 14, OA213
Two oyster shells with green contents.

Glass vessels

These tend to be found at the sites of institutions such as religious houses in the Middle Ages. It is uncertain whether the urinal fragment <S79> is institutional or domestic (from the vicarage or one of the other private sublet houses in the north yard of St Lawrence Jewry).

<S79> Glass vessel
A<2070>, A[17152]; period 13, OA219

Urinal walling fragment; pale green.

Styli

These bone implements for writing on wax tablets are characteristic finds from religious houses (Egan 1998, 109,

table 14, category H) but they also occur in other contexts. The following small assemblage could reflect record keeping at the civic administrative centre of the City, and/or clerkish pursuits connected with the Guildhall College. However, the styli were found in closer proximity to St Lawrence Jewry (<S81> was found in the vicarage) which might suggest that they are linked to the medieval parish church. Three from the sites in question have already been published (Bateman 2000, 83). All are turned, with bulbous, collared heads.

<S80> Bone stylus
D<59>, D[62]; period 13, R200
L 60mm; presumably re-carved to a point following loss of the original metal one.

<S81> Bone stylus
A<71>, A[10636]; period 14, B223
L 68mm; trace of iron point.

Book fittings

The findspots of a book mount and a book clasp would seem to link these objects to the church of St Lawrence Jewry rather than the Guildhall.

<S82> Copper-alloy book clasp (Fig 132)
D<45>, D[112]; presumably residual in period 11, R102
Dimensions 35 x 22mm; accomplished, relatively heavy cast openwork with a menacing beast with prominent wings and head forming the terminal (pierced for the lost securing lace, which it appears to bite); the central hole was probably for a corresponding pin, with a separate rod for attachment to strap at inner end. An early, very ornate version of what

became a relatively common item in the later medieval period (Egan 1998, 277–80); probably from a bible.

<S83> Copper-alloy book mount (Fig 132)
A<974>, A[13166]; period 12, OA216
Crude, roundel with three lobes; Diam c 45mm; central dome has two concentric, herringbone-tooled very rough circles around (almost making a spiral), and three collared, projecting lobes, each holed for attachment.

Pilgrim souvenirs or related items

The survival of these two finds away from the waterfront, in relatively poor condition, is of significance for the overall distribution of these items across London. The soil conditions away from the waterlogged deposits along the Thames are generally inimical to the survival in recognisable form of thin objects of lead/tin, and only the water-retaining environment within the body of the Roman amphitheatre has so far allowed even the partial preservation of items like these. The only other souvenir from this higher part of the City seems to be a severely corroded Becket ampulla (of a different design from <S85>), from the nearby site of 72–75 Cheapside (CID90 <35>).

<S84> Lead/tin rood (Fig 58)
A<6387>, A[23296]; period 10, OA117
Incomplete; transverse arms, each with two attachment loops, and

part of lower shaft; relatively crude rendition of Christ's bare arm and abdomen against obliquely hatched field; reverse has paired rows of alternately blank and obliquely hatched triangles.

Unless this fragment was intrusive as found, it pre-dates the main, high medieval European tradition of lead/tin souvenirs from notable shrines, which seems to have developed its early momentum in the 12th century. If this were a later pilgrim badge (and the presence of decoration on both sides would be another unusual trait for such an item), the loops would suggest a Continental origin. Lucca is a possibility (Spencer 1998, 254, nos 254, f, h) but its later rood souvenirs, like those of Bermondsey Abbey in London, have Christ wearing the long-armed, seamless coat; alternatively, it could possibly be Scottish (cf a stone mould with two versions of cruder roods from north Berwick: Yeoman 1999, 61, fig 39, d). An Italian origin might make identification as one of the very earliest pilgrim badges just about conceivable, otherwise (at the date suggested) it is best considered as simply a religious trinket in the 'highly decorated' Norman-period tradition, and one that happens to anticipate mass-produced pilgrim souvenirs in several ways.

<S85> Lead/tin Becket ampulla (Fig 162)
A<6174>, A[20735]; period 13, OA219
Rectangular, L 53mmm, H 51mm; flattened and corroded; archbishop facing // ? murder scene. Most closely comparable with Spencer 1998, 60–1, nos 17, b, c, although the detail differs from both these. This item is probably of 13th- or perhaps early 14th-century date.

Coins and other numismatic items, mainly of the 11th and 12th centuries

A large number of coins were recovered, particularly at site A where metal detecting was routine, but the space available precludes full publication here. A small sample of the coins from the site follows. The quasi-numismatic items are given greater overall prominence as they are felt to be of greater significance for the fresh perspectives they provide. Lead pieces stamped by official coin dies continue the series published by Archibald (1991). Perhaps most important are the lead/tin items that are termed '?early tokens.' If this basic identification is accepted, the well-stratified series presented below significantly extends the period of use of such items, familiar from the 13th century onwards, back towards the time of the Norman Conquest (Egan in prep d).

Official coins

<S86> Silver coin (Fig 27)
A<2656>, A[17924]; period 10, OA100
Cnut cut halfpenny: diademed bust // short cross; moneyer …rte on Sta… (? Swart on Stamford); issued 1029–35.

<S87> Silver coin (Fig 27)
A<2950>, A[20431]; period 10, OA100
Edward the Confessor London penny: radiate // small cross type; moneyer ?Swetman on

Lund; issued 1044–6.

<S88> Silver coin (Fig 392)
A<1798>, A[17497]; period 11, OA109
William II penny: facing bust // cross in quatrefoil; issued 1090–3.

<S89> Silver coin
A<1223>, A[13586]; period 11, B103
Henry I penny: profile // cross fleury; issued 1100–35.

'Roundels' struck on lead/tin with official coin dies

Cf Archibald 1991, where 61 such items are noted, ranging in date from the 8th century AD to the 1150s. The majority of

Fig 392 Silver William II penny <S88> (issued 1090–3) and Edward the Confessor penny stamp on a lead/tin rolled sheet <S92> (issue of 1056–9), both found in slightly later (period 11) deposits (scale c 1:1)

these, 36 or 37, are known to be from London and 21 are from elsewhere in England, while the others have no known findspot. Those listed below are from 11th- and 12th-century archaeological contexts, and they comprise coin types from only the last decade of English rule and the first quarter century of the Norman era.

<S90> Lead/tin 'roundel'
A<4253>, A[20288]; period 10, OA105
Harold II penny: 'PAX' type; moneyer Wulfwine on [?Camde] (?Camulodunum); issue of 1066.

<S91> Lead/tin 'roundel'
A<2546>, A[17864]; period 10, OA105
William I Lincoln penny: profile // cross and trefoils; issue of 1083–6.

<S92> Lead/tin 'roundel' (Fig 392)
A<1249>, A[13723]; period 11, OA138
Edward the Confessor London penny on rolled sheet: sovereign // eagles; issue of 1056–9.

<S93> Lead/tin 'roundel'
A<1349>, A[17016]; period 11, OA109

William I penny (Diam 25mm): sword // cross over quadrilateral (fleury at angles); issue of 1080–3.

<S94> Lead/tin 'roundel'
A<1546>, A[17119]; period 11, OA109
William I penny (offcentred): profile right // cross and quatrefoils; issue of 1083–6; angled perimeter from cutting out flan.

<S95> Lead/tin 'roundel'
A<1094>, A[12312]; intrusive in period 8, OA9
Broken half (estimated Diam c 20mm): cross and trefoils reverse of William I penny, obverse unclear (the former would officially have gone with the 'profile' issue, as in <S94>).

Early tokens

Over a hundred potential medieval tokens were recovered from site A, including a number of early examples, many of which lack obvious devices. They are divided into cast ones, which have devices from moulds on one or both sides, and 'blanks' (which include ones with imprints from wooden and textile surfaces). The former are a familiar phenomenon, at least from the 13th century onwards (eg Mitchiner and Skinner 1983, 33), while the latter have not previously been published in any detail and their function is debatable. The earliest of both categories, found in archaeological contexts of the 11th and 12th centuries, potentially extend the known usage of unofficially produced tokens in this country into the first half of the 12th century, and perhaps even further back towards the Norman Conquest.

While a few of the items with cast devices have become worn in some way, the majority seem not to have received such sustained treatment. The cast tokens may without great difficulty be seen as an extension of the familiar high medieval tokens into an earlier period. The question of function is, however, particularly difficult for the blanks. In this uncharted territory, it may be worth recalling that the so-called 'Winetavern' series from the late 13th century is sometimes accompanied in assemblages by marginally larger, cast blank flans, which could be seen as analogous to these earlier items. The questions raised here are unlikely to be resolved beyond doubt, and some of the cruder items currently archived as blank tokens may not command universal agreement on this point. The emergence of a previously unrecognised phenomenon of a range of very rough lead/tin discs in the period leading up to the earliest cast tokens of these alloys, is in any case established by these finds, whether or not they had some quasi-numismatic function.

WITH CAST DEVICES

These are apparently the earliest tokens in the usual sense so far known in England. It would be easy without the contextual dating to confuse some of them with ones from three or more centuries later, or even post-medieval versions.

<S96> Lead/tin token
A<2410>, A[17748]; period 10, B118
Damaged edge; Diam 21mm+; worn; short cross and pellets, with border of radiating strokes on both faces.

<S97> Lead/tin token
A<3837>, A[19440]; period 11, OA127
Irregular flan; Diam 14mm; bubble hole; folded over at one side; double-headed bird displayed, beaded border // 12-petalled rosette, beaded border.

<S98> Lead/tin token
A<3826>, A[19441]; period 11, OA127
Crude; Diam 19mm; radiating lines // similar with pellets between.

BLANKS

Several different methods of production are evident among these. Some appear to be blobs rolled out flat (which might explain the imprints from wooden and perhaps textile surfaces), while others are more or less carefully cut out of sheeting, and others again are apparently made of two layers of sheeting which is sometimes evident at the edges or when they come apart. Besides the recognised surface textures (imprints from wood can be very subtle) it is possible that some of these items might originally have been coloured with pigments to aid differentiation, if indeed that was a requirement. Item <S104>

had been rolled on a wooden surface, <S107> may also have been, and <S102> has textile imprints; <S103> may have a weakly registered device (in which case it should be in the previous category) and <S108> has a simple scratched device.

<S99> Lead/tin ?token
A<6065>, A[23434]; period 10, OA105
Flan partly irregular; Diam 12mm; irregular surfaces.

<S100> Lead/tin ?token
A<1752>, A[17239]; period 10, OA108
Diam 13mm; slightly irregular surfaces.

<S101> Lead/tin ?token
A<2479>, A[17696]; period 10, B118
Irregular flan; Diam 13mm; flat surfaces.

<S102> Lead/tin ?token
A<2928>, A[17929]; period 10, OA104
Incomplete flan; Diam 14mm; imprint from textile on both faces.

<S103> Lead/tin ?token
A<2537>, A[17780]; period 10, OA126
?Blank; Diam 14.5mm; series of cuts around perimeter evident from shaping; possible weak registration of pointed-canopy type motif on one face.

<S104> Lead/tin ?token
A<2483>, A[17800]; period 10, OA126
Irregular flan; Diam 15mm; ?imprint from being rolled on wooden surface (at different orientations) on one face.

<S105> Lead/tin ?token
A<3055>, A[20074]; period 10, B116
Diam 15mm; series of cuts around perimeter evident from shaping.

<S106> Lead/tin ?token
A<3192>, A[20502]; period 10, OA103
Irregular hexagon; Diam 15mm.

<S107> Lead/tin ?token
A<2407>, A[17748]; period 10, B118
Diam 20mm; series of cuts around perimeter evident from shaping; slightly irregular surfaces probably from rolling.

<S108> Lead/tin ?token
A<5566>, A[21958]; period 11, OA133
Diam 19mm; folded in half; simple scratched cross on visible face.

<S109> Lead/tin ?token
A<5739>, A[23419]; period 10, OA105
Diam 19mm; apparently two discs stuck together to make one item.

<S110> Lead/tin ?token
A<5606>, A[21914]; period 11, B126
Diam 22mm; apparently folded over near middle.

<S111> Lead/tin ?token
A<5445>, A[20730]; ?residual in period 13, OA219
Diam 13mm; apparently folded over.

Jettons

There are surprisingly few of these ubiquitous, copper-alloy accounting counters among the finds from what was a commercial area. Perhaps they were not much used in the cloth trade at Blackwell Hall (Chapter 6.9), although this seems unlikely. A couple that are particularly well preserved are catalogued here.

<S112> Copper-alloy jetton
A<59>, A[10638]; period 13, OA219
English issue; Diam 23mm; king's head facing // three pellets in centre, bounded by three concave lines, with crown in each outer area, border of pellets on both sides. ? Edward II issue. (Cf

Mitchiner 1988, 101–2, nos 129–32, with no precise parallel.)

<S113> Copper-alloy jetton
A<5578>, A[23086]; period 17, S227
Nuremberg issue; Diam 27mm; ship on a sea, trefoil GLV(E)…

around // lozenge with four fleurs-de-lis, three annulets along each side, (VOI: VOI)… around (lombardic lettering, nonsense legends). Early 16th-century 'ship' issue. (Cf Mitchiner 1988, 369–75, nos 1152–65, 1168–86.)

Domestic items of the 11th and 12th centuries

Spoons

BONE SPOONS

<S114> Bone spoon
A<2659>, A[17305]; period 10, OA108
Overall L 170mm; pointed-oval bowl, 52 x 22mm, has carved opposed, open-topped heart motifs; stem with pointed end and knop in middle. An unusual find, although probably relatively common in its time (cf Ward-Perkins 1940, 127–8, pl 25; Kjølbye-Biddle 1990).

HIGHLY DECORATED LEAD/TIN SPOONS

These early pewter utensils with their sometimes enigmatic decoration were widespread in Norman and later London, perhaps up to the late 13th century. The discovery of three in an area with suitably preservative soil conditions is no surprise (over fifty are now known from the City). At present they seem simply to have been a branch of the domestic pewterware that was superseded by the fashion for plain versions, rather than having had any special religious or other significance.

<S115> Lead/tin spoon (Fig 52)
A<1563>, A[17239]; period 10, OA108
Bowl, 54 x 33mm, cut roughly in two and the pieces folded together as found; decorated with fish internally, and externally with a cross of, vertically, opposed-hatched lozenges and, horizontally, similar triangles alternating with plain ones; and there are concentric arcs (variously hatched) in the upper fields and rough, feline heads (of somewhat mournful aspect) in the lower ones.

<S116> Lead/tin spoon (Fig 94)

A<5721>, A[21992]; period 11, OA133
Corroded bowl, 48 x 27mm; crudely decorated with fish internally, and externally with vertical stripes variously hatched and with dot motifs; a transversely hatched band divides these from a multiple-chevron motif at the top, all within a hatched perimeter band.

<S117> Lead/tin spoon
A<6025>, A[23246]; period 11, OA134
Handle only, surviving L 98mm; longitudinally grooved, with terminal male figure.

Wooden vessels

<S118> Wooden vessel(s) (Fig 108)
B<379>, B[733]; period 11, OA127
Several fragments, probably from more than one vessel: ?narrow, vertical-sided cup and broad-rimmed, footed bowl (the latter includes one heavily knotted piece, probably *Acer* sp, from a burr).

Apparently a rare instance of the 'Saxon' tall cup (cf Pritchard 1991, 240–1, fig 3.126, no. 368) and the 'later' medieval tradition of broad drinking bowls occurring together.

Lighting equipment

<S119> Iron candlestick
A<1917>, A[13778]; period 11, OA110
Corroded (described from X-ray); pricket candlestick with lateral scrolls flanking main spike; L *c* 70mm. The form is known in London from the late 12th century (Egan 1998, 140–1, nos 377–84).

Leisure

DIE

<S120> Bone die
A<1332>, A[13992]; period 11, B124
Dimensions 11 x 10 x 10mm; 'regular' layout (ie opposite sides total seven), variant 2 (Egan 1997, 3, fig 2; Bateman 2000, 58). This is one of the 16 possible variants for regular dice (no preference seems to have come to the fore until the 16th century).

BONE SKATES

The discovery of eight skates some way from the Thames (but close to Moorfields) seems to underline the popularity of these common items of leisure equipment (Bateman 2000, 60; cf Pritchard 1991, 208–9, fig 3.91).

GAMING PIECES

<S121> Antler counter
A<1345>, A[13992]; period 11, B124
Antler disc; Diam 52mm, Th 9mm; ring of circle-and-dot motifs around central hole (Diam 10mm). (Bateman 2000, 58.)

<S122> Antler counter (Fig 304)
A<12953>, A[17296]; period 10, OA101
Antler disc; Diam 36mm, max Th 8mm; plain but for turned groove near edge; signs of burning on same face; more cancellous material is abraded away on opposed sides. The reason for abandoning this piece soon after the start of carving is unclear.

CHILD'S PLAYTHING

<S123> Antler toy man (Fig 304)
A<3942>, A[20074]; period 10, B116
Incomplete; adapted antler, probably of roe deer, but possibly red deer; H 155mm, surviving W 37mm; a bearded face is carved on the side near the trimmed proximal end, so that the main stem serves as the figure's body and the tine prongs act as limbs.

This significant find is notable for the clever use of the natural form to produce the impression of a body and limbs more or less to scale, in what would at a later period (in wood) be termed a peg doll. This late 11th- or early 12th-century plaything, if correctly identified, may be the earliest post-Roman toy from London. Like the only other medieval toy identified from before *c* 1300 from the city, a bird made from sheet lead (Egan 1996a, 1, fig 1), it is a one-off, individual manufacture, probably made by someone well known or closely related to the particular child, in contrast to the mass-produced commercial ones made after that date.

Weaponry

Scabbard chapes

It is possible but unlikely that the first four were for domestic implements rather than weapons. This form has few published parallels; see Goodall 1984, 344–5, fig 193, no. 192, for one

459

(not identified in the text) from Exeter, residual in a late medieval deposit.

SIMPLE

<S124> Copper-alloy scabbard chape (Fig 393)
A<3270>, A[20067]; period 10, OA105
Folded-sheeting triangle, tapering to base, with two arms, each having a hole for missing rivet near end; L 52mm, W 12mm; leather survives from scabbard.

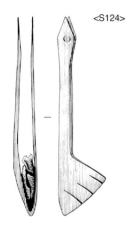

Fig 393 Copper-alloy scabbard chape <S124> (scale 1:1)

OPENWORK

<S125> Copper-alloy scabbard chape (Fig 113)
A<18>, A[11181]; period 11, OA131
Oblique-angled, bent, two-sided ?cast frame, 30 x 23mm; openwork dragon with tooling on body; strips with holes for rivet at terminals.

<S126> Copper-alloy scabbard chape
A<1428>, A[13764]; period 11, OA110

Corroded; 45 x 28mm; openwork has tooled, parallel lines (?hand motif) and expanded attachment terminal.

<S127> Copper-alloy scabbard chape
A<1440>, A[13992]; period 11, B124
Fragment of openwork, surviving 20 x 19mm; with tooled, parallel lines and holes for two missing rivets.

CAP FORM

<S128> Copper-alloy scabbard chape (Fig 25)
A<3318>, A[20431]; period 10, OA100
Cast; L 30mm, W 33mm; curved end with knop terminal; ornate

inside edge has two openwork circles flanking central trifoliate motif; tooled lines follow the upper profile; the two rivets survive. A high-quality fitting, presumably for a sword.

Sword

<S129> Iron sword
A<2071>, A[17147]; period 11, R102
Corroded (details taken from X-ray); tang and top part of blade, surviving L 140mm; separate, oval

pommel with angled ends, 63 x 27mm; a fragment of wood alongside the blade could perhaps come from the scabbard. A high-quality weapon. (Cf Ward-Perkins 1940, 22, 24, pommel type III.)

Musical instruments (11th or 12th century)

Angela Wardle

<S130> Bone tuning peg (Fig 305)
A<680>, A[13166]; period 12, OA216
Complete; L 73mm, W of head 13mm, Diam of shaft 6.5mm. Long-bone midshaft fragment. Expanded spatulate head, with rectangular section, well worn, set on a parallel-sided circular-sectioned shaft, with a sawn slot through its centre at the lower end (L 14mm) for attachment of the string. The peg has been made by hand and slightly irregular knife cuts can be seen on the shaft. There are very faint wear marks – ridges observable under the microscope – in the area of the slot, where the string has been wound around the shaft. The central part of the shaft is much lighter in colour than the slot and handle, which is very shiny and may have been 'polished'. The lighter section would have been protected from light and dirt by the frame or finger board through which it passed, suggesting that the frame was at most 25mm in width. There are also wear marks on the central part of the shaft, caused by its rotation within the frame.

<S131> Bone tuning peg (Fig 305)
A<1824>, A[13926]; period 11, OA109
Incomplete; surviving L 57.5mm, W of head 14mm, Diam of shaft 6.5mm. Long-bone midshaft fragment. The head and shaft are similar to <S130> and the head is highly polished, presumably through use. There are toolmarks on the shaft, which is broken at the top of the slit, and the central part shows colour differentiation where it was covered by the frame of the instrument.

<S132> Bone tuning peg (Fig 305)
A<1826>, A[13927]; period 11, OA109
Incomplete; surviving L 70mm, W of head 13.5mm, Diam of shaft 6.2mm. Long-bone midshaft fragment. Identical in form and manufacture to the examples above; the shaft is broken at the lower end, where one side of the

slit can be seen. Judging from the surviving length of the object and the position of the upper end of the slit, this would have been similar in length to <S130>. There is slight colour differentiation on the central part of the shaft and very clear wear marks, where it has been turned within the frame.

<S133> Wooden bridge (Fig 305)
A<1556>, A[17239]; period 10, OA108
Complete; H 37mm, W 34mm, Th (at top) 6mm. Boxwood (*Buxus sempervirens*) bridge from a stringed instrument, with high arched feet, each oval-sectioned at the base. The surface of one foot is very smooth, but the other appears to have been roughened deliberately, perhaps suggesting that it required some adjustment for a secure fit to the body of the instrument. The bridge, which has a markedly curved upper edge, carried up to five strings, represented by shallow notches on the upper surface, but these are not placed symmetrically. From left to right the strings are set at 3mm, 16mm, 19.5mm, 28mm and 31.5mm, giving an asymmetrical arrangement of one, two in the centre, and two. The groove on the extreme right (second pair) is less well defined and it is possible that only one groove was utilised, giving a symmetrical arrangement, but there are no obvious wear marks that might clarify this. It is also possible that both the 'double' notches were created by adjustment of the position of the strings on the bridge and that originally there were only three.

The curvature of the top edge of the bridge suggests that it was used on a stringed rather than a plucked instrument, and there are parallels for double stringing on a variety of ancient instruments, allowing for combinations of plucking and bowing or other effects. Sympathetic strings, which were allowed to vibrate while the parallel string was played, are also known, but the form of the instrument for which the bridge was designed remains elusive (Chapter 6.4).

Craft production (not including metalworking) in the 11th and 12th centuries

Walrus bone waste

Both pieces are from the animal's skull, and have the original surface pared away (species identification by P Kertesz). These exotic items are presumably waste discarded from the carving of walrus ivory, a material used for carving prestigious objects in England in the Saxo-Norman period (Beckwith 1972). No walrus-ivory artefact has been recognised among the finds recovered from the sites.

<S134> Walrus bone (Fig 321)
<->, A[21598]; period 11, B124
Small part of the tusk socket (canine alveolus) hacked out of the walrus maxilla.

<S135> Walrus bone (Fig 322)
<->, A[13930]; period 11, S114
Small part of the tusk socket (canine alveolus) hacked out of the walrus maxilla; partly burnt.

Cloth processing

The following items are two of a range of tools from the sites that are relevant to textile processing. From thread spinning, evidenced by stone spindle whorls, to embroidery, implied by needles, several different stages of production are attested. No clear focus for these has emerged to suggest a specific location for particular textile processing activity.

<S136> Glass callender (Fig 323)
B<131>, B[398]; period 10, OA127
Decayed; incomplete plano-convex head; Diam 70mm, Th 33mm; worn from use; handle missing. This object was presumably an expensive item in its day because of the material from which it is made. Cf Pritchard 1991, 173–4, fig 3.54, nos 186–8, and a previous find of a linen smoother of glass, from nearby Basinghall Street, in the Museum of London curatorial collection.

<S137> Copper-alloy textile tool (Fig 323)
B<3>, B[182]; period 14, OA213
Rectangular-sectioned shank with triple-reel moulding defining curved, spatulate end; L 83mm; expands for ?gouged eye near point. Presumably of c 12th-century date in view of the following parallels. Cf Biddle

1990, 814–15, nos 2523–4, suggested to be 'couching needles' for the embroidering of tapestry, and discussed in ibid 807–10, where this activity is seen as an upper-class pastime rather than routine work; no. 2523 has a Romanesque-style animal-head terminal with a curved underside comparable to the basic form of the present item, but it lacks the well-defined, almost blade-like end; the explanation proposed for this arguably similar but more robust tool – that it was for sewing document parchments together – seems unlikely for the present item, the curved, flat end of which suggests more a scraping function than no. 2524 from Winchester's ?smoothing/polishing (no. 2523 has a completely different, ?non-functional terminal). Two further parallels from London are cited (ibid, 809, nos 1, 7).

Late Saxon (10th- and 11th-century AD) metalworking

MOULD AND STRAPEND

<S138> Ceramic mould for copper-alloy casting (Fig 324)

A<203>, A[14020]; period 9, OA127

Fragmented end or top piece, 67 x 40mm, including ingate, for ?shield-shaped product (an accompanying piece is probably from the other element in a two-part mould); flattish-faced product from surviving face, 52 x 30mm; the fabric is comparable with that of later, locally made medieval moulds rather than Roman ones. Energy dispersive X-ray fluorescence (EDXRF) analysis showed the presence of small amounts of copper and zinc, but not enough metal survives to allow a satisfactory alloy analysis for comparison with surviving, potentially contemporary objects (below, 8.9).

The product was perhaps a cast strapend with relief decoration on the face mainly missing from the recovered mould pieces (see <S139>, below). Any part of an item in complex relief was likely to have had the corresponding mould become greatly fragmented in releasing the product, whereas a flat surface would be much more likely to survive in sizeable fragments.

<S139> Copper-alloy strapend (Fig 324)
A<3268>, A[20403]; period 10, OA103
Identified by metallurgical analysis as bronze or leaded bronze (Dungworth 2003). Heavy, subrectangular 'relief-decorated' plate with accomplished Winchester style relief design, although the surface is rough and the outline uneven; the rebate at the inside edge lacks the attachment holes that are an essential feature of these accessories (in other finds there are between two and four: eg Pritchard 1991, 145–7, fig 3.26, no. 97, a London find which is assigned to the 10th century AD); the terminal is deficient in metal from the casting (below, 8.9).

This is undoubtedly a waster, discarded unfinished from the

mould because of some accident in the casting. This is evident from its rough state (quite apart from the absence of attachment holes), particularly when compared with a very close parallel from Winchester assigned to the early to ?mid 10th century AD and which has relief on both faces (Hinton 1990, no. 1056). This parallel is described as having 'a scalloped acanthus leaf growing a central plant stem with three paired tendrils, on which perch two backward-turned, biting dragons' and at the bottom an animal mask, from which 'issues a symmetrical plant with a central, scalloped bud'; the animals are given detailing by tooling, and the drill that made the rivet holes was probably also used for the openwork. In the light of the finished example it is possible to interpret a very similar design for the Guildhall piece, including dragons, a possible mask (deficient in metal) at the base, and plant motifs, and to see where the drill would have been applied to create the openwork. This piece could be described in very similar terms, save that there appears to be a second mask in the centre at the top, the foliage is somewhat abbreviated by comparison – to two pairs of leaves – and the creatures, with their heads at the bottom, are more bird-like and face outwards, rather than inwards towards each other.

This find is significant in indicating that the place of manufacture of at least some objects in the renowned 10th-century AD Winchester style (this term must surely now be taken less literally than it has sometimes been) was London (cf mould <S138>, above, the surviving part of which was perhaps for the back of a comparable strapend, although this was found in a deposit assigned to period 9, in a different part of the site).

BONE TRIAL PIECES

Nine bone trial pieces or 'motif pieces' with incised linear designs could well relate to metalworking (and are therefore catalogued here); five are newly reported and four others are already published (Pritchard 1991, 261–2, nos 201–4). The possible use of these trial pieces by metalworkers is discussed in Chapter 6.6.

<S140> Bone trial piece
(Fig 325)
A<4946>, A[22107]; intrusive in period 7, OA8
Fragment of ox-sized rib, surviving L 168mm, with three ?uncompleted motifs on one face and five (one broken off) on the other, all in rectangular frames; while there are some basic resemblances to knotwork beasts, a number of illogicalities mean that these are from the hand of a very inexperienced worker.

<S141> Bone trial piece
A<106>, A[11556]; period 10, OA127
Ox lower-right mandible upper-part fragment; ?external (three motifs): quadruple knot, uncompleted subrectangular panel, ?knot (part broken off).

<S142> Bone trial piece
A<106>, A[11556]; period 10, OA127
Ox rib; external (six motifs): four triple knots (one illogical), two illogical interlaces (uncompleted) // internal (six motifs): five triple knots, one animal head.

<S143> Bone trial piece
A<67>, A[14163]; period 11,

OA127
Ox lower-right mandible; external (15 motifs): two conjoined interlace panels, four animals and two uncompleted heads, four triangles plus ?another broken off, one complete animal head, one ?human face // internal (three motifs): one uncompleted interlace panel, concentric subcircles, tiny motif.

<S144> Bone trial piece
A<67>, A[14163]; period 11, OA127
Ox lower-left mandible fragment; external (14 motifs): four interlace rectangles, three knots in squares, one triple knot, three quadruple knots (two similar, one of which is uncompleted), one complex knot, one unfinished motif // internal (13 motifs): four rectangular interlace panels (two adjacent to each other and an uncompleted one, the fourth adjacent to a rectangular outline), three squares with knots, one adjacent to another with an uncompleted motif, another square outline, one triple knot, hints of two sets of parallel lines. Generally more accomplished than the motifs on the preceding items.

Metalworking in the 11th and 12th centuries

The 11th- and 12th-century deposits (periods 10 and 11) produced a variety of metalworking evidence: copper alloy casting, lead refining and casting, and silver refining. These activities seemed to be particularly concentrated in Open Area 100, a small field or enclosed area of the third quarter of the 11th century situated just to the north of the church of St Lawrence Jewry. Metalworking is discussed in Chapter 6.6.

Galena (lead ore)

<S145>–<S146> Galena
A<3264>, A[17993]; period 10, OA100
A<5412>, A[20731]; period 10, OA100
Two pieces of galena, weighing respectively 107g and 102g, have been identified and it is possible that they derive from a single, unlocated silver-refining enterprise (cf the scattered finds of litharge cake, below). These seem so far to be the sole pieces of unrefined lead ore identified in London (although it is

possible that they are residual Roman pieces). They must have been brought from one of the highland zone locations where this material outcrops naturally, presumably in the Mendips or Derbyshire. The logistics of transporting such a heavy material in the raw state more than a hundred miles overland (or even further if by sea) rather than refining it at the site of its occurrence, presumably made sense to contemporaries involved in the refining and subsequent

working of silver in London. To take this course suggests a very undeveloped stage of silver extraction (significantly less rationalised than in the Roman period).

Roman bricks reused as moulds for ingots

These have all previously been published (Bateman 2000, 60).

<S147> Brick mould
A<4877>, A[19951]; period 10, OA127
Incomplete, triangular-sectioned slot, surviving L 67mm, W 10mm.

<S148> Brick mould
A<4876>, A[19874]; period 11, OA127
Triangular-sectioned slot, L 135mm.

<S149> Brick mould
A<5861>, A[21563]; period 11, OA133
Triangular-sectioned cross, c 40 x 55mm. A similar find in a late 11th-century deposit at a site on Milk Street was interpreted as T-shaped (cf Thor's hammer) but was perhaps for a cross (Pritchard 1991, 166–7, no. 175).

Ingots

<S150> Copper-alloy ingot
A<3805>, A[19441]; period 11, OA127
Hammered rod with unevenly tapered ends; L 18mm, section 7 x 6mm.

<S151> Lead ingot
A<2063>, A[17199]; period 10, OA108
Sub-round, plano-convex with edges roughly trimmed and series of cuts and scratches on surface; Diam c 58mm, Th 9mm, Wt 423g.

<S152> Lead ingot
A<4717>, A[19951]; period 10,

OA127
Flattish, subrectangular; 19 x 10mm.

<S153> Lead ingot
A<3684>, A[20400]; period 10, OA100
Irregular, plano-convex roundel; 22 x 18 x 15mm.

<S154> Lead ingot
A<5983>, A[23376]; period 10, OA105
Rounded fragment with two cuts at right angles (ie roughly a quarter-circle with projected Diam c 30mm); Th 6mm, Wt 3g.

Litharge cake

This is the characteristic leady waste product from silver refining. A potential focus might be suggested in Open Area 100, although there were no multiple finds in single contexts. The 14 fragments were recovered from contexts assigned to periods 10 and 11. They vary in weight from 2g to 129g, and include a D-shaped piece and fragments with straight and rounded edges; full details are available in the relevant research archive (Dungworth 2003). No hint of specific post-Roman silver products was recovered from the sites, unless a lead 'cushion' (<S155>, below) was used for sheeting of this metal.

Waste copper alloy

This was very widespread in earlier medieval deposits. However, neither strapend <S139> nor mould <S138> was accompanied by a clear focus of other metal waste, and so the location of the industry or industries these items represent is unknown. It did not necessarily lie within the area of the site.

Lead 'cushion' for stamping design on sheeting

<S155> Lead 'cushion' (Fig 327) A<1868>, A[17519]; period 11, OA109
Rectangular lead sheet-like pad, 35 x 48mm, with partial, multiply registered impression of a quadruped in a linear frame (the rear quarters, on the left side and presumably from the last use, have come out most clearly; very little detail is legible elsewhere, probably because multiple, superimposed registrations have each left a partial trace); the crouching animal is in mainstream Late Saxon style.

The soft metal pad distributed and absorbed some of the force behind the production of repoussé designs from a punch hammered on to sheet metal placed over it, ensuring that the sheet did not split and that the design was registered crisply. (Cf Hinton 2000, 71–4, figs 46–8, no. 117 for a lead pad perhaps used for a similar purpose from an Anglo-Saxon smith's grave of c AD 660–70; Arwidsson and Berg 1983, 16, pls 10 and 22, no. 85, publish another from a smith's tool chest found in Sweden.) The finds recovered give no definite indication whether base metals (cf lead/tin foil <S46> from period 11) or precious ones, or both, were being worked in this way.

Copper-alloy dress accessory founding in the late 13th or 14th century

A medieval foundry is represented by both excavated plant and waste material. This evidence for copper-alloy dress accessory manufacture seems to be by far the fullest so far uncovered in England and indeed more widely in Europe (Egan 2003). The industry, and its possible links to the Girdlers' Company, is discussed more fully in Chapter 6.6. The range of cast products (with comparanda drawn from Egan and Pritchard 1991) includes six forms of buckles (ibid, nos 288 (cf 298, 301), 289, 292 (cf 302, 318), 297, 437, 444), four forms of strap loops (ibid, nos 1249, 1258, 1261, 1262), one form of bar mount (ibid, no. 1158), two forms of purse hanger (ibid, nos 1192, 1198), one form of ornate rivet (ibid, no. 314 (buckle) or no. 1343 (brooch)) and one form of finger ring (comparable to ibid, no. 1620).

Products

All the following are likely to be wasters; * after the catalogue number denotes a more definite waster. The annotations (GY) and (SLJ) after the land use number indicate in which of two areas, the Guildhall yard or the north yard of St Lawrence Jewry, the item was found.

BUCKLES

<S156>* Copper-alloy buckle (Fig 394)
B<445>, B[297]; period 13, OA211 (GY)
Distorted, sub-oval frame, 15 x 23mm; sheet pin; Wt 3g. The curious frame has much in common with ones of wrought iron, with its distinct asymmetry and discernible marks apparently from having been hammered – a most unusual method of manufacture for this metal, which it is difficult to parallel.

<S157>* Copper-alloy buckle (Fig 329)
A<6154>, A[20735]; period 13, OA219 (SLJ)
Oval frame, 21 x 18mm; outside edge has two knops and is narrowed for missing roller; frames blocked; sprue to one side; Wt 6g. Cf Egan and Pritchard 1991, nos 288, 298 and larger no. 301, assigned to the early 13th and late 14th centuries.

<S158>* Copper-alloy buckle (Fig 394)
A<5613>, A[21543]; period 13, OA202 (GY)
Fragment of oval frame with offset, recessed bar; deficient in metal; Wt 2g. Several potential parallels, including <S159>, below.

<S159>* Copper-alloy buckle
A<6679>, A[23612]; period 13, OA202 (GY)
Tiny fragment of moulded frame; deficient in metal; Wt 2g. See

<S160>, below.

<S160>* Copper-alloy buckle
A<6679>, A[23612]; period 13, OA202 (GY)
This fragment could be part of <S159>, above; Wt <2g. ?Variant of Egan and Pritchard 1991, no. 297, assigned to the late 14th century.

<S161>* Copper-alloy buckle (Fig 394)
A<6605>, A[23605]; period 13, OA202 (GY)
Oval frame fragment, 14 x 11+mm; ornate outside edge has three grooves near centre and lateral knop; deficient in metal; Wt <2g. Cf Egan and Pritchard 1991, no. 437 (with plate), assigned to the late 14th century.

<S162>* Copper-alloy buckle (Fig 394)
A<6615>, A[23607]; period 13, OA202 (GY)
Frame fragment with central pair of bulbous swellings; deficient in metal; Wt <2g. No precisely comparable item in Egan and Pritchard 1991.

<S163>* Copper-alloy buckle
A<6633>, A[23611]; period 13, OA202 (GY)
?Oval frame side scrap; deficient in metal; L 11mm, Wt <2g. (See below, 8.9, for chemical analysis of this item.)

<S164>* Copper-alloy buckle (Fig 394)

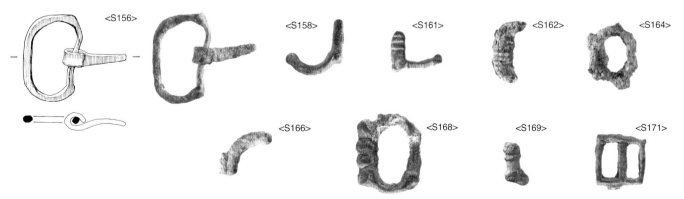

Fig 394 Copper-alloy buckle wasters <S156>, <S158>, <S161>, <S162>, <S164>, <S166>, <S168>, <S169> and <S171> found in the 14th-century metalworking areas (scale 1:1)

B<190>, B[146]; period 14, OA213 (GY)
Corroded; oval frame, 13 x 15mm, with three knops and two ridges on outside edge, and side sprue; Wt <2g.

<S165>* Copper-alloy buckle
B<421>, B[385]; period 14, OA213 (GY)
Incomplete, angled frame with multiple knops, deficient in metal, at least 15 x 17mm; Wt 2g. Form apparently not in Egan and Pritchard 1991; this could be a brooch rather than a buckle. (See below, 8.9, for chemical analysis of this item.)

<S166>* Copper-alloy buckle
(Fig 394)
A<6759>, A[19302]; period 14, OA202 (GY)
Fragment of rounded/oval frame with offset ?outside edge; Wt 2g. Too little survives to determine the precise form.

<S167> Copper-alloy buckle
B<198>, B[114]; period 14, OA213 (GY)

Square frame, 15 x 13mm; thick outside edge; perhaps discarded from the mould without filing; possibly a waster; Wt 4g.

<S168>* Copper-alloy buckle
(Fig 394)
A<5535>, A[21518]; residual in period 17, S227 (SLJ)
Oval frame, 20 x 18mm, with four knops on outside edge; Wt 3g; this is the form represented by mould <S220>, below. Cf <S170>, below, and Egan and Pritchard 1991, no. 292 assigned to the mid 13th century, no. 302 assigned to the late 14th century, and (with plate) no. 318 assigned to the same period.

<S169>* Copper-alloy buckle
(Fig 394)
A<5898>, A[21518]; residual in period 17, S227 (SLJ)
?Oval with moulded, knopped and multiply ridged edge; deficient in metal; Wt 2g. ?Variant of Egan and Pritchard 1991, no. 289, assigned to the mid 13th century.

<S170>* Copper-alloy buckle
(Fig 329)
A<5581>, A[23086]; residual in period 17, S227 (SLJ)
Three oval frames still joined, each 18 x 20mm, with four knops on outside edge; combined Wt 12g. Comparanda as for <S177>, below.

<S171>* Copper-alloy buckle

(Fig 394)
B<189>, unstratified (?SLJ)
Square frame with central bar; 9 x 8mm; with sprue; Wt 2g. Cf Egan and Pritchard 1991, no. 444, assigned to the late 14th century. (B<192>, also unstratified, is a similar item, with no indication of being a waster.)

BUCKLE PIN

<S172>* Copper-alloy buckle pin
(Fig 395)
A<2424>, A[19150]; period 14, B204 (GY)
With grip near loop; uneven

shaft; deficient in metal; L 49mm, Wt 3g. Cf Egan and Pritchard 1991, 115–16, nos 541, 547; the form is usually found on circular buckles assigned to the 14th century.

STRAP LOOPS

The rivets on these strap loops are external, except for <S179>, in which it is lacking (it was presumably intended to have a separate, internal one).

<S173>* Copper-alloy strap loop
(Fig 396)
A<124>, A[10676]; period 13, OA219 (SLJ)
Rectangular slide with central and corner knops; 21 x 17mm; the X-ray plate shows a crack in the frame; Wt 6g. Presumably a waster. Cf <S218>, below, and Egan and Pritchard 1991, no. 1261, assigned to the mid 14th century.

<S174>* Copper-alloy strap loop
(Fig 396)
A<129>, A[10676]; period 13,

OA219 (SLJ)
As <S173>; frame incomplete through deficiency of metal on one side but blocked on the other with excess; Wt 2g.

<S175>* Copper-alloy strap loop
(Fig 396)
A<125>, A[10676]; period 13, OA219 (SLJ)
Rectangular slide; Wt 3g. Cf Egan and Pritchard 1991, no. 1258, assigned to the mid 13th century.

<S176>* Copper-alloy strap loop

<S172>

Fig 395 Copper-alloy buckle pin waster <S172> (scale 1:1)

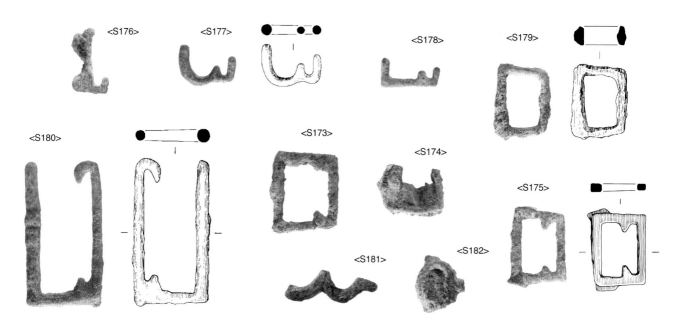

Fig 396 Copper-alloy strap loop wasters <S173>–<S182> found in the 14th-century metalworking areas (scale 1:1)

(Fig 396)
A<6623>, A[23601]; period 13,
OA202 (GY)
Slide-form base only; L 17mm;
deficient in metal at top, two
sprues; Wt <2g. ? As <S175>.

<S177>* Copper-alloy strap loop
(Fig 396)
A<6680>, A[23612]; period 13,
OA202 (GY)
Curved top, ?slide; deficient in
metal; Wt 2g. Cf Egan and
Pritchard 1991, no. 1262,
assigned to the late 14th century.

<S178>* Copper-alloy strap loop
(Fig 396)
A<12925>, A[23612]; period 13,
OA202 (GY)
Subrectangular slide, H 16mm;
deficient in metal; Wt <2g; with
projection. Cf Egan and Pritchard
1991, no. 1258, assigned to the
mid 13th century.

<S179>* Copper-alloy strap loop
(Fig 396)
A<5560>, A[20945]; presumably
intrusive in period 10, B116
Rectangular frame (no rivet), 18
x 15mm; Wt 3g; chemically
analysed (below, 8.9). Cf Egan
and Pritchard 1991, nos 1247,
1249, assigned to the early 13th
and late 14th centuries; of
similar form is no. 1235, a still-
joined group of four from a site
some way to the east of the
Guildhall yard (Armitage et al

1981), while Northgate House
(KHS98) <18> is a similar
group of three (Drummond-
Murray and Liddle 2003, 89, 91,
fig 5).

<S180>* Copper-alloy strap loop
(Fig 396)
B<436>, B[410]; period 14,
OA213 (GY)
Rectangular slide, 38 x 19mm;
central pair of knops on outside
edge; one side missing through
deficiency of metal; Wt 6g. Not
precisely paralleled in Egan and
Pritchard 1991, but can be seen
as a longer version of no. 1269,
assigned to the late 12th to early
14th centuries.

<S181>* Copper-alloy strap loop
(Fig 396)
A<5536>, A[21518]; intrusive in
period 17, S227 (SLJ)
Pentagonal; top only of one loop,
W 19mm, with part of adjacent
one; sprue to other side; Wt 2g. Cf
Egan and Pritchard 1991, 231–2,
fig 147, no. 1252, assigned to the
late 14th century.

<S182>* Copper-alloy strap loop
(Fig 396)
B<458>, unstratified (?SLJ)
Oval with integral rivet; frame 13
x 9mm, blocked with excess
metal; Wt 2g. Cf Egan and
Pritchard 1991, no. 1230,
assigned to the late 13th to early
14th centuries.

FRAME OF UNCERTAIN FORM

<S183> Copper-alloy frame
B<420>, B[385]; period 14,
OA213 (GY)
?Surviving edge and side only,
with ?knops (unless these are

excess metal); 13 x 12mm; Wt
<2g. Could be part of a buckle or
a strap loop (not certainly a
waster).

BAR MOUNTS

<S184>* Copper-alloy bar mount
(Fig 397)
A<2172>, A[17142]; period 13,
OA219 (SLJ)
Three-lobed with hole in centre
(terminal lobes apparently not
pierced for attachment); 18 x
7mm, Wt <2g.

<S185>* Copper-alloy bar mount
(Fig 397)
A<2863>, A[19329]; period 13,
OA200 (GY)

Two; complete one L 29mm, with
three lobes; combined Wt 6g. Cf
<S186> and Egan and Pritchard
1991, no. 1158, assigned to the
late 13th to early 14th centuries.

<S186>* Copper-alloy bar mount
(Fig 397)
A<6164>, A[20735]; period 13,
OA219 (SLJ)
Two; each L 26mm, with three
lobes; combined Wt 4g. Cf
<S185>.

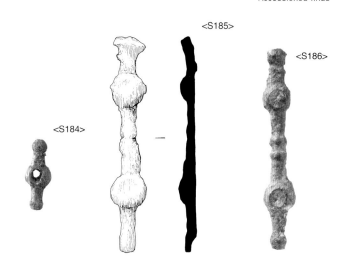

Fig 397 Copper-alloy bar mount wasters <S184>–<S186> (scale 1:1)

PURSE HANGERS

<S187>* Copper-alloy purse
hanger (Fig 398)
A<6466>, A[23572]; intrusive
in period 10, OA100
Knopped suspension loop with
lateral sprues; L 21mm, Diam
11mm, Wt <2g. Similar to Egan
and Pritchard 1991, no. 1192,
assigned to the late 14th century.

<S188>* Copper-alloy purse
hanger

A<5748>, A[20995]; residual
in period 15, OA202 (GY)
Incomplete hanger; multiple-
arched (two of intended
?three of these); L 24mm, Wt
<2g; deficient in metal. Cf
Egan and Pritchard 1991,
223–4, no. 1198, assigned to
the early 15th century, and
A<751>, a similar fragment
(?unphased) which appears
broken.

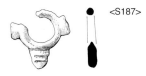

Fig 398 Copper-alloy purse hanger waster <S187> (scale 1:1)

CAST RIVETS AND ANALOGOUS ITEMS

These have knopped heads (cf those on Egan and Pritchard
1991, brooch no. 1343 and perhaps those on the plate of
buckle no. 314, respectively assigned to the mid 13th and late
13th to early 14th centuries).

<S189>* Copper-alloy rivets
A<101>, A[10679]; period 13,
OA219 (SLJ)
Two, with collared knops on
spikes; each Diam 7mm, L 15mm;
combined Wt 4g.

<S190>* Copper-alloy rivet
(Fig 399)
A<2797>, A[19211]; residual
in period 15, S234 (GY)
Two, similar to <S189>; each
Diam 8mm, L 17mm;

combined Wt 7g.

<S191> Copper-alloy rod with
knops
B<324>, B[325]; period 14,
OA213 (GY)
Smaller and neater than the
preceding items, almost like three
beads on a wire; Wt <2g. Cf
Thames Exchange (TEX88)
<8155>, also from a foundry
assemblage, for a more closely
comparable item.

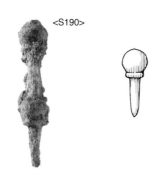

Fig 399 *Copper-alloy rivet waster <S190> and reconstruction of single rivet (scale 1:1)*

SWAGE-FORMED BAR MOUNTS

<S192>* Copper-alloy end-piece from bar for mounts (Fig 400) D<23>, D[65]; period 13, R200 (GY)
Bar; L 40mm, W 3.5mm; plain along most of length but with arched profile and edge grooves near one end, on one side with a hint of raised-triangle decoration. Not cast but shaped from a hammered rod or bar in a swage and then cut into short lengths for individual mounts (see <S221>, below).

<S193> Copper-alloy bar mount (Fig 400)
A<2811>, A[19307]; period 13, OA200 (GY)
Six, two variants: plano-convex, 5 x 9mm, 5 x 10mm, 5 x 12mm and 5 x 15mm, each with holes for two rivets; similar, 6 x 13mm and 7 x 9mm, both with raised triangles along edges and holes for two rivets.

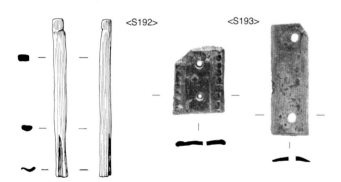

Fig 400 *Copper-alloy swage-formed bar mounts <S192> (scale 1:1) and <S193> (scale c 2:1)*

SHEET BAR MOUNTS

<S194>* Copper-alloy bar mount A<91>, A[10679]; period 13, OA219 (SLJ)
Ridged centrally and with domed, lobed ends; 5 x 19mm; rivet holes marked, but apparently not pierced through. Cf Egan and Pritchard 1991, no. 1149, assigned to the late 13th to early 14th centuries.

<S195>* Copper-alloy bar mount A<89>, A[10679]; period 13, OA219 (SLJ)

Three lobes, the central one holed (lacks terminal holes for attachment); 20 x 8mm.

<S196>* Copper-alloy bar mount A<92>, A[10679]; period 13, OA219 (SLJ)
Incomplete; surviving L 15 x 4mm, with one of terminal lobes (apparently lacking attachment hole); pronounced arched profile.

<S197> Copper-alloy bar mount A<90>, A[10679]; period 13,

OA219 (SLJ)
Lobed ends with holes for attachment; 16 x 4mm; arched profile. Not obviously a waster.

WIRE

The larger gauges are suitable for making plain rivets for buckle plates and the like. Wire was a common find in later medieval contexts at the sites. The following items are from deposits with manufacturing evidence.

<S198> Copper-alloy wire A<6622>, A[23601]; period 13, OA202 (GY)
Three; hammered, square-sectioned bars altered to round-sectioned wire towards one end; L 37mm; combined Wt <2g. Perhaps strictly discarded working ends rather than wasters. Item A<3893> from the same site is somewhat similar (L 43mm), although it is from A[19604] which is assigned to period 11.

<S199> Copper-alloy wire A<128>, A[10676]; period 13, OA219 (SLJ)
L 30mm, gauge c 1mm.

<S200> Copper-alloy wire A<93>, A[10679]; period 13, OA219 (SLJ)
L 77mm, gauge c 1mm.

<S201> Copper-alloy wire A<94>, A[10679]; period 13, OA219 (SLJ)
Corroded; thin strip wound around shaft; L 101mm, gauge c 2mm.

<S202> Copper-alloy wire A<95>, A[10679]; period 13, OA219 (SLJ)
Three; corroded; total L 12mm, gauge c 1mm; hints of spiralling.

<S203> Copper-alloy wire A<96>, A[10679]; period 13, OA219 (SLJ)

Two; corroded; total L 146mm, gauge c 1.5mm; one piece has spiralling end with point.

<S204> Copper-alloy wire A<99>, A[10679]; period 13, OA219 (SLJ)
Two; gauge c 0.75mm (one with possible drawing knop marking distinction between this and gauge c 1.25mm; cf <S201>).

<S205> Copper-alloy wire A<12>, A[10441]; period 13, OA219 (SLJ)
Two; L 36mm and 41mm, gauge c 1.25mm.

<S206> Copper-alloy wire A<121>, A[10639]; period 13, OA219 (SLJ)
L c 55mm, gauge c 1mm.

<S207> Copper-alloy wire A<122>, A[10643]; period 13, OA219 (SLJ)
Corroded; L 27mm, gauge c 2mm (possibly a lace chape).

<S208> Copper-alloy wire A<127>, A[10680]; period 13, OA219 (SLJ)
Three; L 58mm, 65mm and 70mm, gauges c 0.75mm and 1mm.

<S209> Copper-alloy wire D<12>, D[75]; period 13, R200 (GY)
Several; L 23–141mm, gauges c 1–1.25mm.

FINGER RING (POSSIBLE PATRON)

<S210> Copper-alloy finger ring (Fig 401)
B<434>, B[410]; period 14, OA213 (GY)
Finger ring with integral oval 'stone' in tapering, round (slightly asymmetrical) bezel and circular-sectioned hoop,

Diam 31mm; all in a single casting; Wt 3g. Possibly a patron (master form) for making moulds (the integral 'stone' would of course be reproduced at any subsequent stage; or a part of the mould for making the void for a stone was omitted).

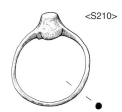

Fig 401 14th-century copper-alloy finger ring <S210> (scale 1:1)

SHEET-LIKE ITEMS CAST WITH BUCKLE FRAMES IN LOW RELIEF

These enigmatic objects, the only ones of their category known so far (except for <281> from the GPO site, Newgate Street (POM79)), look at first sight like castings from mispairings of mould elements, one for the buckle frame, the other perhaps for some kind of plate-like item (or perhaps the first mould was simply distanced about 1mm away from a flat surface); the central cut-out could perhaps represent a hopeless attempt at salvaging something usable from this error. Alternatively, they might, when in relatively well-defined relief (this applies to the first but not to the second item), be used (?ideally in combination) as a master-form to impress the basic frame shape into the still-wet clay of a mould, the central hole perhaps being to channel the excess upwards, where it could be scraped off. None of these explanations is particularly convincing.

<S211> Copper-alloy object
B<307>, B[353]; period 14,
OA219 (SLJ)
Oval buckle (with narrowed inside and thickened outside edges, c 12 x 28mm) in half relief, on overlapping, sheet-like ?cut-out pentagonal outline, 16 x 26mm, with irregular, rectangular hole; Wt 3g. The buckle form is halfway between Egan and Pritchard 1991, 68 and 70, fig 42, nos 274 and 277, assigned to the late 13th to late 14th centuries.

<S212> Copper-alloy object
(Fig 402)
B<110>, B[353]; period 14,
OA213
Similar to <S211> but slightly dished, cut sub-rectangle, 22 x 16mm, and central aperture appears integrally cast to match the buckle form; 'frame' (in lower relief than in <S211>) is less clear, of basic oval form, 12 x 18mm, with knops flanking narrowed bar; Wt 4g. The buckle form is difficult to parallel. ?Intrusive.

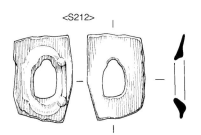

Fig 402 Copper-alloy sheeting with buckle-frame form <S212> (scale 1:1)

Possible discards and other accessories (apparently usable items from production-deposits sequence)

The following accessories from the same sites, in some cases found in the same group of deposits as foundry waste, show no definite indication of themselves being wasters. It is possible that some of them were discards, as they lack the exceptional preservation that would have allowed any that might not have been file-finished directly after casting to be defined from

rough surfaces, like several from the Thames Exchange (TEX88) waterfront site (Egan 2003, 248).

BUCKLES

<S213> Copper-alloy buckle
A<12932>, A[23612]; period 13,
OA202 (GY)
?Oval frame fragment; part of one side and offset and narrowed bar.

<S214> Copper-alloy buckle
A<264>, A[10808]; period 13,
OA219 (SLJ)

Corroded, incomplete; oval buckle frame with forked spacer, c 25 x 16mm. An early occurrence if from the very end of the period indicated (elsewhere these are late 14th-century onwards: Egan and Pritchard 1991, 78–80). Perhaps intrusive; nothing indicates that this is a waster.

STRAP LOOPS

<S215> Copper-alloy strap loop
A<3784>, A[19336]; period 13,
OA202 (GY)
Rectangular frame, 14 x 13mm;
?separate rivet missing.

<S216> Copper-alloy strap loop
A<2868>, A[19333]; period 13,
OA200 (GY)
Rectangular slide with central and corner knops; 18 x 19mm. Cf Egan and Pritchard 1991, no. 1261, assigned to the mid 14th century.

<S217> Copper-alloy strap loop
B<193>, B[216]; period 14,
OA213 (GY)
Rectangular frame with integral rivet. Cf Egan and Pritchard 1991, no. 1236, assigned to the late 13th to early 14th centuries.

<S218> Copper-alloy strap loop
B<6>, B[128]; period 14, S216
(GY)
Rectangular slide with central and corner knops. Cf <S182> and <S183>.

<S219> Copper-alloy strap loop
B<233>, B[204]; period 14,
OA213 (GY)
Rectangular slide with knop. Cf Egan and Pritchard 1991, no. 1257, assigned to the early 13th century.

<S220> Copper-alloy strap loop
B<117>, B[14]; unstratified
(?SLJ)
Pentagonal frame (lacks rivet), 21 x 11mm; hint of corrosion on one side.

CAST BAR MOUNT

<S221> Copper-alloy bar mount
A<3839>, A[19440]; intrusive in period 11, OA127

Three knops, with terminal curved loop; total L 17mm. (For ? purse hanger.)

Moulds

<S222> Ceramic mould (Fig 333)
B<939>, B[4625]; period 13,
OA219 (SLJ)
For oval buckles with four knops; two main parts, presumed to be from the same mould: ie at least 12 layers (possibly more) each of 4x3 identical frames, to produce a minimum of 144 products simultaneously. There are two main parts, one with no trace of metal (comprising seven layers, surviving H 45mm), the other with degraded metal in place (five

layers, surviving H 33mm), and several further, small fragments (both with and without metal), some from topmost, outer layer; suggested original dimensions 114 x 98 x c 80mm+; combined Wt of surviving portions 778g. Each product would be 18 x 24mm, oval with four knops on the thickened outside edge and a recessed bar (as Egan and Pritchard 1991, 72–4, no. 292, which is 18 x 25mm and assigned to the mid 13th century; a range of slightly different sizes is known for buckles of this form from across England).

This unique survival seems to have sprung a leak, to be discarded with only part retaining the metal. Estimated weight of metal needed for 144 frames: c 450g (446.4g based on 3.1g per frame as measured for one of those found at Meols, Cheshire (Egan in prep c), which is slightly wider than the London ones). Buckle wasters or discards <S168> and <S170> are also of this form.

<S223> Ceramic mould
A<2667>, A[19255]; period 13, OA200 (GY)
Two small, non-joining fragments from multiple-layered mould for ?rectangular frames for buckles or strap loops; combined Wt 8g.

<S224> Ceramic mould
A<4148>, A[10643]; period 13, OA219 (SLJ)
Fragment, 19 x 41mm, from a plate in a multiple mould, with 30mm long, parallel grooves for ? prongs of a forked-spacer strapend 10mm apart; Wt 6g. No corresponding metal item has been recognised among the wasters from the site (forked-spacer buckles are thought to date from the late 14th century onwards, although strapends can be earlier).

one side when it was folded, and this was only noticed while the holes for rivets were being drilled, at which point the item was discarded. An apparently routine folded plate of this form, D<14> (28 x 16mm) came from D[75], which also produced foundry waste.

<S232> Copper-alloy sheet waste (Fig 403)
A<124>, A[10676]; period 13, OA219 (SLJ)
Irregular strip offcut, c 11 x 36mm; one straight edge, the other with a series of cutouts from small circles, Diam 5mm

(? or multi-lobed objects – the arcs left from the circles seem too close to have each produced a complete roundel).

<S233> Copper-alloy sheet waste (Fig 403)
B<293>, B[435]; period 14, B211 (GY)
Offcut, 20 x 9mm, with outline of small, circular (? or multi-lobed) objects as for <S232>. (Compare this and <S231> and <S232> with Egan 1996b, 88, fig 3, a (top); possibly from making roves, apparently not otherwise present in this manufacturing assemblage.)

Non-definite waste

CASTING WASTE (AMORPHOUS)

<S225> Copper alloy casting waste
A<130>, A[10676]; period 13, OA219 (SLJ)
Runnel; Wt 6g.

<S226> Copper alloy casting waste
A<6624>, A[23601]; period 13, OA202 (GY)
Unidentified fragment; rough, D-sectioned rod, L 12mm, section 5 x 3mm, thickened at one end; Wt <2g. Possibly a sprue or from a length intended to be made into bar mounts.

<S227> Copper alloy casting waste
A<6604>, A[23605]; period 13, OA202 (GY)
Wt <2g.

<S228>–<S230> Copper alloy casting waste
D<18–19>, D<46>, D[75]; period 13, R200 (GY)
Several fragments; combined Wt 39g.

SHEET WASTE

<S231>* Copper-alloy sheet waste (Fig 403)
A<98>, A[10679]; period 13, OA219 (SLJ)
?Mis-cut, incomplete buckle-plate sheeting; 23 x 17mm; one of the original two folded loops extant (the loss of the other may be recent damage); a pair of holes are drilled through both thicknesses, and a further one goes through only one; Wt 2g. It looks as if a plate intended to be 13mm wide was not trimmed on

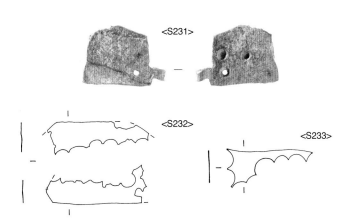

Fig 403 *Copper-alloy sheet waste <S231>–<S233> (scale 1:1)*

Copper-alloy candlestick casting waste from the 16th century

An assemblage of copper-alloy candlesticks, together with a larger quantity of kiln waste and moulds, was found reused as floor make-up in a building in the Guildhall yard (B204). The building was probably an outbuilding of Blackwell Hall cloth market and it is suggested that the assemblage dates to the final quarter of the 16th century. The evidence for the founding and casting is discussed in more detail in Chapter 6.6 along with a reconstruction of a mould (Fig 336); the kiln furniture (<S234>–<S241>), the moulds (<S242>–<S275>) and the casting waste are catalogued here. Four rather scrappy copper-alloy fragments <S276>–<S279> are the only items that are finished or near-finished products.

Kiln furniture

<S234> Furnace slab
A<2762>, A[19025]; period 16, B204
Two furnace slab fragments; one with right-angled corner; Th 42mm; combined Wt 517g.

<S235> Furnace slab
A<2606>, A[19040]; period 16, B204
Fragment of furnace slab; Th 22mm; Wt 126g.

<S236> Furnace slab
A<6841>, A[19040]; period 16, B204
Right-angled corner of refractory clay luting around multiple mould slabs; Wt 57g.

<S237> Furnace slab
A<2761>, A[19040]; period 16, B204
Refractory ceramic ?slab, Th c 15mm, with flat surface; other ceramic material adhering; Wt 66g.

<S238> Furnace slab
A<6894>, A[19040]; period 16, B204
Several fragments of buff-orange clay, mostly lacking form through breakage, but some with single, flattish surfaces and/or rounded concavities running their surviving length; occasional traces of melted copper alloy; total Wt 368g.

Kiln furniture with mould

At least 1.837kg of kiln furniture with mould was recovered from contexts associated with candlestick founding. These heterogeneous aggregates hint at possible structures within the furnace.

<S239> Kiln furniture with mould
A<2724>, A[19040]; period 16, B204
As <S240>–<S241> but no structures evident; Wt 1.242kg.

<S240> Kiln furniture with mould
A<12949>, A[19040]; period 16, B204
Agglomeration of roof tiles held together as three sides of a box or channel by ceramic, with copper alloy waste; Wt 121g.

<S241> Kiln furniture with mould (Fig 404)
A<12951>, A[19040]; period 16, B204
Four fragments of mould or kiln furniture, including fragmented ring and voided-squared structures (Diam of apertures c 35mm) fused with copper alloy waste; total Wt 474g.

Fig 404 Kiln furniture with mould <S241> (scale c 1:2)

Mould fragments

FOR CUPS

At least 171g of mould fragments for cups was recovered from contexts associated with candlestick founding.

<S242> Mould fragment for cup
A<12924>, A[19040]; period 16, B204
Cup core, Diam 15mm (central rod 5mm), in copper alloy slag; combined Wt 27g.

<S243> Mould fragment for cup
A<12950>, A[19040]; period 16, B204
As <S242>; Diam c 21mm (central rod 7mm); Wt 15g.

FOR STEMS

At least 523g of mould fragments for stems was recovered from contexts associated with candlestick founding. These, along with the preceding moulds for cups, seem to be unique survivals. (See Egan 2005b, no. 337, for a mid 16th-century brass candlestick in which the former for the central hollow became displaced prior to casting.)

<S244> Mould fragments for stem
A<2710>, A[19040]; period 16, B204
Two fragments for at least two layers (one rounded mortise survives) each of two slightly tapering, plain stems (Diam 9–12mm, surviving L 75mm); the bright orange colour may imply that the main surviving parts were not fully fired; Wt 83g. (Previously published in Egan 1996b, 90, fig 5B.)

<S245> Mould fragment for stem
A<2710>, A[19040]; period 16, B204
Corner fragment for four products, L 80mm+, Diam 12–13mm; Wt 26g; most not reduced (? not fully fired).

<S246> Mould fragments for stem (Fig 405)
A<2721>, A[19040]; period 16, B204
Fragmented former-rod for inner void; four lengths (three for stem, Diam 10mm tapering to 6mm, surviving total L 98mm; one for cup, Diam 16mm, L 24mm+); combined Wt 17g.

<S247> Mould fragment for stem
A<6847>, A[19040]; period 16, B204
For two products ? with bladed knops; surviving L 50mm, Diam c 15mm; Wt 73g. This piece would have been flanked by at least one more to each side.

<S248> Mould fragments for stem
A<6895>, A[19040]; period 16, B204
Two stem-hollow former plug pieces, embedded in slag; Diam 10mm; Wt 10g.

<S249> Mould fragments for stem (Fig 336; Fig 405)
A<6897>, A[19040]; period 16, B204
Several; for at least four cast together, some with oval 'tenons'; Wt 326g.

<S250> Mould fragments for stem
A<6905>, A[19025]; period 16, B204
Four; one for two products; Wt 36g.

<S251> Mould fragments for stem (Fig 336)
A<12973>, A[19040]; period 16, B204
Two; for doubly rebated stem bases; Wt 18g.

<S252> Mould fragments for stem (Fig 405)
A<12975>, A[19040]; period 16, B204
Two; L between knops c 40mm; Wt 43g.

<S246>

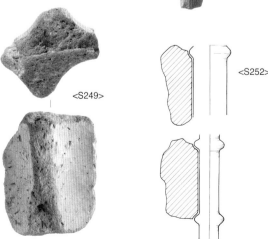

<S249>

<S252>

Fig 405 Mould fragments for candlestick stems <S246>, <S249> (scale 1:1) and <S252> (scale 1:2)

FOR BASES

At least 1.023kg of mould fragments for bases was recovered from contexts associated with candlestick founding.

<S253> Mould fragment for base
A<612>, A[19025]; period 16, B204
Plain, flat base; Wt 8g.

<S254> Mould fragment for base
A<6900>, A[19025]; period 16, B204
Several cope fragments, for ?domed bases; Wt 300g.

<S255>–<S256> Mould fragments for base
A<6901>, A<6906>, A[19025]; period 16, B204
Two core fragments; different basal-skirt profiles; Wt 72g.

<S257> Mould fragments for base
A<6903>, A[19025]; period 16, B204

Two cope fragments, for drum bases; two different profiles (one piece has a vertical seam); Wt 64g.

<S258> Mould fragments for base
A<6904>, A[19025]; period 16, B204
Two ?cope fragments, for ?trumpet-shaped bases; Wt 13g.

<S259> Mould fragment for base
A<6909>, A[19025]; period 16, B204
Damaged piece, for ?edge of a

tray; ? from uppermost piece in a stack; Wt 3g.

<S260> Mould fragment for base (Fig 406)
A<6907>, A[19025]; period 16, B204
Core, for bifacially bevelled base; Wt 23g.

<S261> Mould fragment for base (Fig 406)
A<6842>, A[19040]; period 16, B204
End, for flat base, Diam c 100mm; Wt 77g.

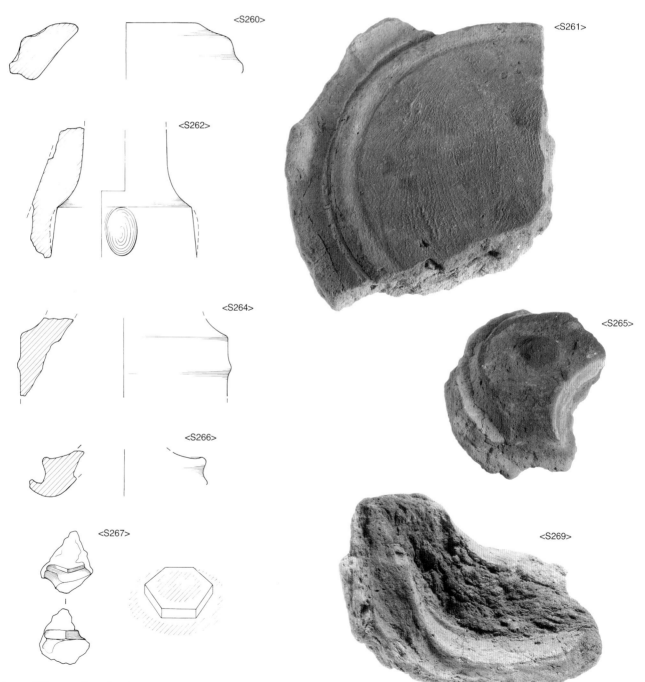

Fig 406 Mould fragments for candlestick bases <S260>–<S262>, <S264>–<267> and <S269>–<S272> (scale 1:2, photographs at c 1:1, reconstruction of <S267> not to scale)

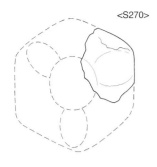
<S270>

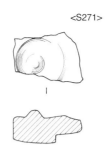
<S271>

<S272>

<S262> Mould fragment for base
(Fig 406)
A<6843>, A[19040]; period 16,
B204
Cope, for trumpet base with oval
boss on vertical side; Diam
c 80mm, surviving H 60mm;
Wt 58g.

<S263> Mould fragment for base
A<6844>, A[19040]; period 16,
B204
Fragment from stack; for ?two
differently angled bases, Diam
c 80mm; Wt 43g.

<S264> Mould fragment for base
(Fig 406)
A<6846>, A[19040]; period 16,
B204
Core, for horizontally ridged basal
drum, Diam 140mm, surviving H
40mm; Wt 36g.

<S265> Mould fragment for base
(Fig 406)
A<6848>, A[19040]; period 16,
B204
End corner with tenon, for
product Diam ? c 40mm; Wt 27g.

<S266> Mould fragment for base
(Fig 406)
A<6849>, A[19040]; period 16,
B204
Core, for basal skirt H 15mm,
Diam c 85mm; Wt 21g.

<S267> Mould fragment for base
(Fig 406)
A<6850>, A[19040]; period 16,
B204
Core, for ?hexagonal, rebated
?base at least 70mm broad, H
15mm+; Wt 10g.

<S268> Mould fragment for base
A<6851>, A[19040]; period 16,
B204
Fragment, from between

?polygonal bases; Wt 7g.

<S269> Mould fragment for base
(Fig 406)
A<6854>, A[19040]; period 16,
B204
Corner fragment, from stack for
two ?hexagonal bases with
rounded corners; surviving H
6mm, Diam ? c 100mm; Wt 59g.

<S270> Mould fragment for base
(Fig 406)
A<6857>, A[19040]; period 16,
B204
Core, for ?hexagonal base,
possibly with horizontal, lobed
foot; surviving H 10mm, Diam
? c 80mm; Wt 13g.

<S271> Mould fragment for base
(Fig 406)
A<6858>, A[19040]; period 16,
B204
For ?trilobed base; central knop-
tenon; Diam 50mm+; Wt 13g.

<S272> Mould fragments for
base (Fig 406)
A<6898>, A[19040]; period 16,
B204
Several fragments for drum
bases with horizontal ribs, most
of them including vertical seams;
Wt 280g. Vertical seams are
normally very elusive among
mould pieces, perhaps because
they were particularly vulnerable
to damage when the mould was
broken to free the cast object.

<S273>–<S274> Mould fragments
for base
B<1212>, B[4479]; period 16,
B223
Two fragments of cope for
different skirted bases: (a) max
Diam c 160mm, narrowing with
three or four rebates; (b) max
Diam c 180mm, with curving

profile between two rebates;
combined Wt 42g.

<S275> Mould fragment for base

B<1292>, B[4479]; period 16,
B223
For ?octagonal, skirted base;
Wt 17g.

FOR INDETERMINATE PRODUCTS

At least 2.485kg of indeterminate mould fragments was
recovered from contexts associated with candlestick founding.
They include fragments of probable base moulds, cores and
copes; full details are available in the relevant research archive.

Copper alloy casting waste

At least 416g of copper alloy casting waste was recovered from
contexts associated with candlestick founding, including just
four rather scrappy copper-alloy items <S276> and <S277>–
<S279> that are the only finished or near-finished products.

<S276> Copper alloy casting
waste
A<2636>, A[19025]; period 16,
B204
Vessel wall (or ? sheet trimming);
Wt 55g.

<S277> Copper alloy casting waste
A<2818>, A[19037]; period 13,
OA200
? Candlestick base fragment
(possibly a runnel that solidified
in a mould); Wt 16g.

<S278> Copper alloy casting waste
A<2471>, A[19040]; period 16,
B204
Cast candlestick or vessel walling
fragment, c 15 x 25mm, with a
slight curvature; Wt 7g.

<S279> Copper alloy casting waste
A<4564>, A[19040]; period 16,
B204
Fragment of cast walling (? slight
curvature), Th 3mm; could be
from basal skirt or bell; Wt 6g.

Finds from 16th-century inns

Glass vessels

Two glass vessels, including an alembic <S281> used in
distillation, were found in a 16th-century latrine in a yard to
the rear of two inns on Cat Street, The Saracen's Head and The
Three Tuns (Chapters 4.3 and 6.10). A large number of ceramic
storage jars, serving vessels and drinking vessels had also been
thrown away in this latrine.

<S280> Glass vessel
C<69>, C[944]; period 15, S210
?Lamp fragment; corroded.

<S281> Glass vessel
C<70>, C[841]; period 15, S210
Alembic rim fragment; corroded.

Blackwell Hall market and the cloth trade: late medieval to early modern items

Cloth seals

The only items in the recovered assemblages that may relate directly to the business of the biggest and most important cloth hall in England, which came to serve the known world with textiles that passed through it, are three relatively uninformative, incomplete cloth seals (Endrei and Egan 1982; Egan 1995; cf Egan 2001, 51–2). These may all be from the 16th or early 17th century (despite one apparently disparate, impossibly early context dating). See Egan 1995, 40–2, nos 61–8, for cloth seals thought to have been put on cloths at or under the auspices of Blackwell Hall, although documentation of details of the practice followed in this place are remarkably elusive.

It is one of the vagaries of archaeological survival that the many cloth seals found at the locations of dyehouses on the Thames waterfront in London (Egan 1991, 16–17) and the relatively large numbers of London seals found in Salisbury (Egan 2001, 44, 51–2) are both indirect testimony of the range of the capital's textile trade, almost all of which would have gone through Blackwell Hall, while the actual site of this institution could only produce the following few, unimpressive scraps. Without the documented background, these three items would hardly have been taken to represent such a significant phenomenon in the development of the City's early modern economy.

<S282> Lead cloth seal (Fig 354)
A<3402>, A[17924]; period 10, OA100
Disc one only, Diam 18mm; no indication of use (rivet still upstanding). Recovered from a deposit of Saxo-Norman date, this must be from the late 14th century at the very earliest, and quite probably, from its form, from the early post-medieval period.

<S283> Lead cloth seal
A<2591>, A[19188]; period 17, B206
Disc two only, Diam 18mm;

?portcullis with legend around. Presumably a late 16th-century crown-over-portcullis county seal (Egan 1995, 9; 2001, 50, 54–5, 60, nos 3, 30, 39, 78–90); the place-name is illegible.

<S284> Lead cloth seal (Fig 354)
B<160>, B[44]; period 17, S220
Disc one only, Diam 14mm; XII // (on rivet) (V – could be part of a letter or privy mark, etc). Stamp giving dimension of a cloth, as measured by the weaver/clothier or alnager. ?16th or early 17th century.

8.9 Metallurgical analysis

David Dungworth

Introduction and methodology

The samples submitted for analysis included crucibles, moulds, hearth lining and copper-alloy artefacts. The samples were visually inspected and the most promising were analysed in order to determine their chemical compositions. Eleven crucibles were examined in order to define the nature of the clay used; the crucibles were also inspected for copper alloy droplets trapped in the vitrified surfaces, and 35 droplets (from 16 crucibles and one mould) were analysed (cf Dungworth 2000b). Thirty-three stratified copper-alloy artefacts were analysed to characterise the range of alloys used in the manufacture of the products. The samples were quantitatively analysed using an energy dispersive spectrometer attached to an electron microscope (cf Dungworth 2001). The copper alloy droplet and artefact samples were assigned to the four main alloy types (brass, gunmetal, bronze and copper) according to the levels of zinc and tin present (Bayley 1991). Strictly speaking, the copper category is in fact 'fairly pure copper', that is, alloys containing less that 8% zinc and less than 3% tin (since pure copper is only used very rarely during the medieval period). Full details of the chemical analysis are presented in tabular form in the research archive (Dungworth 2003).

Evidence for medieval metalworking on the site was concentrated in three or four broad phases: the 10th to 12th centuries AD (periods 9–11), c 1270–c 1350 (period 13) and c 1550–1666 (period 16). The earliest metalworking may in fact be further divided into 10th- to 11th-century AD and 12th-century phases (Chapter 6.6). There was some evidence of both the manufacturing processes and the products in all these periods of manufacture. The products manufactured in the 10th to 12th centuries AD probably included strapends in the Winchester style, made in leaded gunmetal. The best evidence was for the large-scale manufacture of copper-alloy dress accessories in the 14th century, and the chemical analysis helped to define two slightly different types of 14th-century production. The 16th-century material consisted of waste products from the manufacture of gunmetal candlesticks.

Results

Crucibles

The earliest crucibles are clearly associated with activity in periods 9–11 (c AD 950–c 1230). The fabric of the vessels, early medieval coarse whiteware (EMCW), is dated here to c 1000–c 1150. The crucibles were rather small, thin-walled (<10mm) vessels and of rounded or hemispherical form with a small lip. The analysis showed that the clay used to make the crucibles had relatively low levels of aluminium oxide.

The late 13th- to 14th-century crucibles used in period 13 (c 1270–c 1350) were fairly large and thick-walled vessels (with rim diameters of c 100mm and walls 10–20mm thick) having straight sides and rounded bases. These crucibles could have held up to 5kg of molten copper alloy. The outer surfaces of these crucible fragments were often heavily vitrified and in many cases had added outer layers applied (cf Bayley 1992, 3–4). Such outer layers were added to protect the crucible fabric from thermal shock and to help keep the contents of the crucible molten when the vessel was taken out of the hearth and the metal poured into moulds. These crucibles are made in late medieval/early post-medieval crucible fabric (LMCR), which is generally dated to c 1240–c 1480.

The 16th-century crucibles are very similar in size to the 14th-century ones and appear to be in the same fabric, suggesting that, on this site at least, it continued in use into the 16th century. The chemical analysis did, however, reveal slight differences between the 14th-century and the 16th-century crucibles, with the later ones having noticeably higher levels of aluminium oxide. Full details of the chemical composition of the ceramic fabrics of the metalworking crucibles are available in the research archive (Dungworth 2003).

Vitrified ceramic hearth lining

Two fragments of vitrified ceramic hearth A<2782> from period 13 (OA200) were analysed. The ceramic structure of the hearth would in places have been subjected to temperatures in excess of 1000°C, which has resulted in a black glassy inner surface. The outer surface remains an oxidised maroon colour.

Copper alloy slag

Two fragments of copper alloy slag A<5757> from period 13 (OA202) were analysed. Such slags form as a result of reactions between the fuel ash, crucibles, molten metal and any fluxes that may have been used. The morphology of the slags shows that they are not connected in any way with the smelting of copper ores but result from the melting and casting of copper alloys.

Ceramic moulds

The surviving half of a two-piece mould <S138> (OA127, period 9) was examined using scanning energy dispersive X-ray fluorescence (EDXRF) analysis (Scott 2001). The mould had been used to cast a subrectangular object, and the size and shape of this mould are similar to the Winchester style strapend <S139> recovered from the site (Fig 324). The EDXRF technique has been used successfully to determine the shape of copper-alloy objects cast in ceramic moulds even where relatively little relief survived on the mould (Dungworth 2001, 16–17, fig 13). The technique is based on the fact that zinc in the copper alloy that had been poured into the mould would have diffused into the ceramic mould and be concentrated in those parts of the mould that were in contact with the metal. Scanning EDXRF analysis allows the mapping of element distribution across the surface of an object. The analysis of mould <S138> did show the presence of small amounts of copper and zinc, though in this case the zinc was evenly distributed across the surface of the mould and the copper levels were too low to allow scanning. The surviving mould fragment is therefore likely to be for the undecorated reverse side of an object such as a strapend.

Comparison of the chemical composition of the artefacts and the trapped metallic droplets

The copper alloy droplets trapped in the vitrified surfaces of the crucibles contain varying levels of copper, zinc, tin and lead. Not all copper alloy droplets in a single crucible share the same chemical composition; for example, crucible A<4883> contains three copper droplets, one bronze droplet and one gunmetal droplet. The degree of vitrification on the surface of many of the crucibles shows that they were reused many times and so if the composition of the copper alloys melted varied with each reuse, then the copper alloy droplets would also vary. In addition, a copper alloy droplet trapped in a vitrified layer would be subjected to heat and oxidation with each reuse of the crucible. While the thermochemical properties of many of the elements in a copper alloy vary widely, zinc, tin and lead are all more volatile and more easily oxidised than copper. Thus, copper alloy droplets maintained at high temperatures under oxidising conditions will tend to be transformed into copper, and then copper oxide (Dungworth 2000a). The low levels of zinc, lead and tin in the copper alloy droplets compared to the contemporary artefacts suggests that the droplets have been transformed by exposure to high temperatures. This makes any comparison between the droplets and the artefacts problematic.

Nevertheless, there are some differences between the droplets and the contemporary artefacts that are difficult to explain in this way. Nickel was detected in only a single artefact but in over a third of the droplets. This element has similar thermochemical properties to copper and is unlikely to be depleted or enriched by exposure to high temperatures and/or oxidising conditions. In addition, arsenic and antimony were detected more frequently in the droplets than the artefacts. These two elements should behave in similar ways to zinc, lead and tin and should be progressively removed by exposure to high temperatures and/or oxidising conditions. Thus, despite the difficulties in comparing the compositions of the artefacts and the droplets trapped in the crucibles, it is possible that the crucibles were not actually used to melt the copper alloys used in the manufacture of the dress accessories, but for melting copper alloys for the production of larger objects than these.

8.10 Iron slag

Lynne Keys

Introduction and methodology

Nearly 46kg of iron slag was recovered from post-Roman deposits (all from site A), both hand-collected and from bulk environmental samples. No specific sampling was carried out for the recovery of micro-slags (eg hammerscale) during the excavations.

The slag assemblage was examined by eye and categorised

on the basis of morphology. Each slag type within each context was weighed but in the case of smithing hearth bottoms each example was individually weighed and measured. Full details of this analysis are available in tabular form in the research archive (Keys 2003).

Results

The diagnostic slags indicate secondary smithing activity, the hot working of an iron shape by a smith to turn it into a utilitarian object or high-temperature welding to join two pieces of iron. These activities generate bulk slags, the most characteristic being the smithing hearth bottom and micro-slags such as hammerscale. There was little evidence for a specific location of a smithy; the material was recovered from across the site and some is undoubtedly reworked from earlier Roman deposits. The only possible location identified was Building 113 (period 11 phase 3).

8.11 Timber

Damian Goodburn

The Guildhall project yielded a very large number of detailed written and drawn records of worked timber and roundwood which are available in the research archive. The preservation of the roundwood, timber buildings and wood used in the graves varied due to differing levels of later truncation, differential decay susceptibility or damage by ancient fires. Thus work here was concentrated on those best preserved, while still trying to provide representative coverage of the types of building styles and grave assemblages encountered. There are also other small groups of early medieval woodwork worthy of presentation here, such as domestic furniture and cooperage finds.

Much of the detailed recording and sampling of the early medieval woodwork was carried out on site using the methodology described in the Museum of London archaeological site manual (Museum of London 1994, 3.4). Initial post-excavation work provided brief selective assessment of the worked wood. During the analytical phase of the work all the timber specialist records were scanned and the best-preserved material was selected for further study, concentrating on in situ material from buildings and graves. The results of this work are incorporated in the chronological narrative (Chapter 3), thematic sections (Chapter 6.2 and 6.3) and burial catalogue (below, 8.17).

Since the late 1980s archaeologists from London have been carrying out systematic experimentation in ancient woodland on the edge of Greater London involving the use of replicated early medieval type tools, techniques and materials (Goodburn and Redknap 1988). The work has followed on from detailed recording and has often been targeted at investigating and testing specific hypotheses about early medieval woodworking

practice. Some of this work was prompted by evidence excavated at the Guildhall such as the well-preserved grooved timber offcuts (Goodburn 1993b). This experimental work with green (fresh) oak timber and native species of roundwood has provided practical insights into the raw materials, logistics, techniques and tool use of the time.

8.12 Wattle

Ian Tyers

Introduction

A total of 870 samples of timbers from 51 groups of wattle walls, hurdles, fencing and the like from site A were examined, and 332 of these from 20 groups were studied in detail. Most of the material was sampled in accordance with the then recommended London excavation procedure (Museum of London 1994, 3.4.3). This consisted of taking a short length from each horizontal and each vertical element and bagging each of these sampled elements separately but grouped within a single bag for each wattle structure. Some of the material was too fragmentary to recover in this way. At the time of the excavations a major attempt to systematically recover and record similar material from a central urban medieval London site had just been undertaken at the Fleet valley excavations (Tyers and Hibberd 1993). The Guildhall wattling clearly represented another large assemblage of such material, and it was hoped that sampling and analysis of this material would not only furnish information of direct relevance to the Guildhall excavations but also provide corroborative data for the interpretations of the Fleet valley evidence and give a more realistic regional overview of the use of small roundwood in medieval London.

The material was sampled in 1992–5 but not examined until 2003. The intervening decade had not been kind to the samples; some had dried out and shrunk beyond reliable recording, and much had acquired (or presented at the outset) a curious mixture of mineralised centre rings and de-lignified outer rings, making the creation of microscopic slide sections all but impossible. It was decided that an extended assessment would be undertaken on some of the material.

Methodology

Five parameters were originally recorded for each of the Fleet valley stems, although it was concluded afterwards that two of these were of little interpretative value (the season of felling, and the minimum diameter of non-circular material). The state of the Guildhall material has meant that the recording of the remaining three parameters (species, maximum diameter and ring count) is uneven. About 30% of the material no longer allowed for the cutting of good microscope cross-sections suitable for reliable identification, 20% were too soft to be able to record a reliable diameter, and 60% were too spongy to obtain cross-sections good enough to count the rings. In all three categories the data is probably biased towards the oak stems which tended to be better preserved. The assemblage as a whole does not lend itself to statistical analysis.

For each context analysed the following data were recorded: 'spec', maximum diameter and ring count. 'Spec' is an encoding of the botanical name for the species, genus or family of the timber; 'species' is not the correct term for the range of identification levels appropriate to the material. A review of freshly broken or razored ends under a low magnification (x7–x40) binocular microscope was used to isolate the *Quercus* material and the material too deteriorated to identify reliably. Thin sections of the rest were then made into temporary glass slides and identified using a high magnification microscope (x100–x400) and the key provided by Schweingruber (1990), being categorised as:

unidentified – examined but too poorly preserved to section;
Quercus (oak) – but may include *Castanea* (chestnut) which may be indistinguishable in immature material;
Alnus (alder) – in poorly preserved immature material may overlap with Salicaceae and/or *Corylus*;
Salicaceae (willow/poplar family) – likewise may overlap with *Alnus* and *Corylus* in immature or poorly preserved material;
Corylus (hazel) – may overlap with *Alnus* and Salicaceae in immature or poorly preserved material;
Prunus (fruitwoods: sloe, cherry etc);
Pomoideae (fruitwoods: apple, pear, hawthorn);
Fagus (beech) – somewhat unusual as roundwood.

The larger diameter was measured except where very squashed, and any material that was not a full cross-section or was very mushy was not measured. The count of the rings (number of years) was only recorded for the ring-porous species (*Quercus* only), as this is not reliable for many of the diffuse porous material without complete microscopic cross-sections and was impractical with this poorly preserved material. A summary table of the species identified (CD Table 10) along with a discussion of the results is given in Chapter 6.2. The full details of the material analysed are available in the research archive (Tyers 2003).

8.13 Plant remains

John Giorgi

Introduction

During the excavations at the Guildhall a total of 822 bulk environmental soil samples were collected from post-Roman deposits for the potential recovery of biological material. This included the retrieval of botanical remains for providing information on the nature of economic and/or human activities on the site and the character of the local environment, both from a spatial and a temporal perspective.

Sampling and processing methodology

Virtually all the post-Roman samples were partly or fully processed. A standard sample size of between 10 and 50 litres was collected from the main phase of excavations (site A) with occasional large samples of up to 200 litres collected from particularly large or potentially interesting deposits; samples of less than 10 litres were taken from small features that were 100% sampled. The volume of the samples from the earlier excavations at sites B and C was much smaller, often less than 10 litres.

Samples were processed according to the potential level of organic preservation. Those samples which contained well-preserved organic remains by survival in an anoxic environment were subsampled (500g) and wet-sieved to 0.25mm. Other samples were processed in a flotation machine using sieve sizes of 0.25mm and 1mm for the recovery of the flot and residue respectively. Part of the flots from these samples was also stored wet (in case of organic remains) while the remaining part was dried. Unprocessed soil of up to 10 litres was retained from organic-rich samples for further processing or in case of the presence of other biological remains such as insects that require different recovery methods. The sample residues from the processed flotation samples were dried and sorted.

Assessment

A total of 210 samples (c 26% of the processed samples) were selected for assessment on the basis of representativeness by period, area, group and feature type. The samples were assessed using a low-powered binocular microscope, and preservation, abundance and species diversity of botanical and other biological remains were noted. An assessment report with recommendations for analysis was then prepared (Giorgi 1997).

Analysis

On the basis of the assessment a total of 334 samples were selected for analysis of the plant remains. The intention of the selection was to analyse a representative sample from different feature types, areas and buildings within each period.

The richest periods in terms of sample numbers collected and analysed are period 10 with 107 samples and period 11 with 185 samples (32% and 55% of all samples); far fewer samples (less than 20) were recovered from each of the other periods (periods 9 and periods 12–17). These samples are from a range of feature types (25), with different pit fills being the best-analysed feature with 126 samples (38%), followed by occupation/floor deposits (56 or 17%), hearths (36 or 11%) and external dumps (33 or 10%).

Identification and recording

For the detailed analysis, the plant remains were separated into different size fractions for ease of sorting and scanning, and identified using a low-powered binocular microscope together with modern seed reference collections and reference manuals (Anderberg 1994; Beijerinck 1947; Berggren 1969; 1981). Charred plant remains (with the exception of charcoal) were extracted and quantified in absolute numbers while waterlogged and mineralised material was only scanned and abundance of individual species recorded (CD Table 51; CD Table 52). The results are tabulated and summarised by land use for each period, although details of individual samples are available in the research archive (Giorgi 2003). Ecological information is based mainly on Clapham et al (1987) and Stace (1991).

Preservation

A large quantity of botanical material was recovered from the samples although there was variation in the quantity and quality of the recovered remains. The earliest material (periods 10 and 11) produced the best-preserved and richest plant assemblages with the highest species diversity. Most of the plant remains were preserved by waterlogging (survival in an anoxic environment) although there were also charred plant remains (with occasional large assemblages) and some mineralised plant remains, in particular from cesspits.

The range of botanical material

The charred plant remains consist mainly of fragmented charcoal, with other remains comprising primarily cereal grains with smaller quantities of chaff (florets, rachis, glume bases) and stem fragments. There are moderate numbers of charred weed seeds and a few other economic plants preserved by charring (eg fruits and nuts). Mineralised plant remains are much less common and restricted largely to fruit remains, although much of this material was poorly preserved and could only be reduced to genus (eg *Prunus* fruit stones) or family. The waterlogged plant remains include seeds and fruits, which are the most common and easily identifiable of the remains, representing both economic (mainly fruits) and wild plants; however, more fragile material, such as moss, leaf, cereal bran and stem fragments, was also present in samples with good organic preservation.

Economic or food plants represented in the samples consist mainly of cereals and fruits; identified cereals are oat (*Avena* spp), including cultivated oat (*A sativa*) identified from floret bases; wheat (*Triticum* spp), both free-threshing – including hexaploid bread wheat (*T aestivum*) identified by rachis fragments – and the hulled wheat, emmer (*T dicoccum*); six-row hulled barley (*Hordeum vulgare*); and rye (*Secale cereale*). There is less evidence for pulses except for occasional charred peas (*Pisum* sp) and beans (*Vicia faba*).

Fruits comprise the most abundant food plant remains, partly because of the high number of samples analysed from cesspit or rubbish pit fills and partly because the woody nature of much of these remains enhances the survival potential. A wide range of cultivated and wild fruits are represented by mainly waterlogged and occasional charred and mineralised remains, with elder (*Sambucus nigra*), blackberry/raspberry (*Rubus fruticosus/idaeus*) and hazelnut (*Corylus avellana*) shell being the most frequent remains. Other fruit seeds include grape (*Vitis vinifera*), fig (*Ficus carica*), apple (*Malus* sp, including endocarp fragments), pear (*Pyrus* sp), apple/pear (*Malus/Pyrus* sp), mulberry (*Morus nigra*), bilberry (*Vaccinium myrtillus*), blackberry (*Rubus fruticosus*) and wild strawberry (*Fragaria vesca*). Fruit stones of plum/bullace (*Prunus domestica*), sloe/blackthorn (*P spinosa*), cherry (*P avium*) and peach (*P persica*), as well as walnut (*Juglans regia*) shell, are also present.

Other potential food plants include common vegetables, possibly represented by some of the *Brassica/Sinapis* seeds and by carrot (*Daucus carota*) seeds; spices, for example black mustard (*Brassica nigra*); and potential textile plants such as hemp (*Cannabis sativa*) and flax (*Linum usitatissimum*) – also potential food plants – and dyer's rocket (*Reseda luteola*). A large number of the wild plants also had various other potential uses, for example for medicinal purposes and as building or flooring (including stabling) materials. Other wild plants point to the potential presence of hay fodder residues.

A significant proportion of the disturbed-ground plants in the samples are potential arable weeds (both of fields and gardens), with the most frequent species being stinking mayweed (*Anthemis cotula*), corncockle (*Agrostemma githago*), hairy buttercup (*Ranunculus sardous*) and corn marigold (*Chrysanthemum segetum*). Other common arable weeds represented are wild radish (*Raphanus raphanistrum*), cornflower (*Centaurea cyanus*), knotgrass (*Polygonum aviculare*), persicaria (*P persicaria*), pale persicaria (*P lapathifolium*) and black bindweed (*Fallopia convolvulus*), fool's parsley (*Aethusa cynapium*), spiny-milk/-sow thistle (*Sonchus asper*), small nettle (*Urtica urens*) and several grasses (mostly as charred seeds) of brome (*Bromus* spp), rye-grass (*Lolium* spp) and fescue (*Festuca* spp). These are not all necessarily imported arable weeds because many also grow as weeds of waste places; it is more likely, however, that the charred weeds of these species are by-products of crop processing used as tinder.

A number of the disturbed-ground plants are species that require or prefer soils with high levels of nitrogen, with the best-represented of these species being various goosefoots, especially fat hen (*Chenopodium album*), red/glaucous goosefoot (*C rubrum glaucum*), nettle-leaved goosefoot (*C murale*), maple-leaved goosefoot (*C hybridum*), oraches (*Atriplex* spp), stinging nettle (*Urtica dioica*), black nightshade (*Solanum nigrum*), hemlock (*Conium maculatum*) and elder (*Sambucus nigra*). These plants are frequently present on rubbish tips, dungheaps and well-manured gardens, and reveal the presence of rotting organic matter in the form of middens and dungheaps. Henbane (*Hyoscyamus niger*) and white horehound (*Marribium vulgare*) are two other frequent waste-ground species in the samples, being moderately high nitrogen-level plants found in fairly dry environments on roadsides, as well as on walls and on relatively undisturbed waste ground.

Wetland plants include both bankside or marshland species and aquatic or semi-aquatic plants; bankside or marshland plants are the best-represented species, particularly sedges (*Carex* spp), rushes (*Juncus* spp) and spike-rush (*Eleocharis palustris/ uniglumis*); of the aquatic plants, sea club-rush (*Scirpus maritimus*) and celery-leaved crowfoot (*Ranunculus sceleratus*) are the most frequent. Other fairly well represented wetland plants are water pepper (*Polygonum hydropiper*), gypsy wort (*Lycopus europaeus*) and hemlock.

Hedgerow, shrub or woodland species are represented mainly by wild fruits, particularly elder, brambles and hazelnut shell, although these may be imported food residues rather than reflecting the local environment. There are few other woodland plants except for occasional finds of bryony (*Bryonia dioica*) and hop (*Humulus lupulus*).

Grassland plants are also represented in the samples, albeit by much smaller numbers of seeds; however, such plants are generally under-represented in the archaeobotanical record because they are not such high seed producers. The grassland plants include a range of species often associated with hay meadows and shed light on the potential import of hay fodder on to the site.

Interpretation

The interpretation of plant remains in urban contexts is problematic because it is often difficult to identify seeds and fruits to species level, and thus ecological information from the wild plants may be limited because species within a genus can have significantly different habitats. Indeed, the most frequent plants in the Guildhall samples are docks (*Rumex* spp), buttercups (*Ranunculus acris/repens/bulbosus*) and sedges, species of which may grow in a number of habitats. Moreover, many species may grow in more than one habitat; thus, for example, sheep's sorrel (*Rumex acetosella*), a fairly common plant represented in the samples, grows in both grassland environments and as an arable weed of sandy soils.

Another problem is that of distinguishing wild plants growing on or near the site from those that may have been imported for use as food, fodder, building materials or raw materials for crafts and industries, or as weeds of imported plants. This problem is exacerbated by the mixing of plant residues from various sources and activities, which is frequent in urban contexts. In virtually all the samples, the assemblages are made up of wild plant remains from a number of habitats together with the residues of different food or economic plants. It is also often difficult to establish the actual use of cultivated plants and sometimes of wild ones.

A number of approaches have been used in this analysis to resolve or at least limit these problems. With regard to environmental information, the association of various plants within a single sample assemblage may shed light on the origins of the material and the possible habitats that they represent (which may of course be several in each instance). Other specific studies can also facilitate the interpretation of assemblages of wild plant remains from the samples. These include studies on the recognition of turves (Hall 2003), hay meadow plants (Greig 1984) and thatching residues (Letts 2001; de Moulins in prep). The possible use of a wild plant may also be determined by its frequency and the context from which it was retrieved. Thus, it could be argued that a high seed frequency of a wild plant in an assemblage with a low species diversity of wild plants and/or a high diversity of economic plants is evidence for the use of that plant, particularly if it is found in a disposal context such as a cesspit or rubbish pit fill. This reasoning has been used to suggest that high frequencies of *Brassica/Sinapis* seeds and seeds of potential medicinal plants in pits at the Guildhall are more likely to be the residues of used plants. Finding similarly high frequencies of seeds of sedges and rushes in occupation deposits increases the likelihood that they represent flooring materials.

Discussion of the plant assemblages is included in both the chronological narrative by land use (Chapters 2–4) and the relevant thematic sections (Chapter 6). It has not been possible to present all details of individual botanical assemblages from each analysed sample, although the research achive (Giorgi 2003) contains detailed information on the remains from each individual sample, as well as providing more detail for the later medieval and post-medieval samples (periods 13–17).

8.14 Vertebrate remains

Kevin Rielly

Methodology

Recovery

The sampling procedure carried out at each site involved the selection of a variety of deposits, more commonly from deeper features like pits or wells, but also from various horizontal layers such as floors and middens. Sample sizes tended to be in the region of 10–30 litres. The recovery strategy was to wash the sample, using a Siraf tank, through a 1mm mesh. The resulting residue was dried and hand-sorted to recover any archaeological artefacts and environmental items. The importance of sampling is not merely to recover the smaller species such as birds, fish and small rodents, but also to enhance the recovery of the major domesticates, in particular the smaller parts, such as phalanges, and all parts of very young individuals. However, the general sampling strategy was very much aimed towards the recovery of small mammal, fish and bird bones, a policy intended to augment the material provided by hand recovery. An unfortunate consequence of this policy is that samples rarely contain larger bones, these having been removed from the area to be sampled prior to the soil being deposited in the sample bucket. Obviously, this non 'whole-earth' sample approach will tend to bias the sample against the recovery of – in particular – the larger domesticates such as cattle and horse, and to a certain extent the smaller domesticates as well, including sheep, goat, pig and possibly chicken and goose.

Selection

Analysis focused on those assemblages that either provided the largest collections of bones or produced bones of particular interest. As well as quantity, other selection criteria included state of preservation, good dating and large assemblage size, ideally with a high proportion of bones which could provide age, sex and/or size data. Samples were generally chosen if they had been taken from a selected hand-collected assemblage, but otherwise a major consideration was the presence of identifiable fish, bird or small mammal bones. The relevant information for this site and context selection process was taken from the assessment report (Rielly 1997) as well as from an in-depth post-assessment review of the stratigraphic and dating evidence.

The selection process resulted in the choice of a number of hand-recovered and sample assemblages from each of the three major sites (sites A–C). Most of the bones, and therefore most of the selected assemblages, are dated to periods 10 and 11, but attempts were made to introduce deposits from each of the major occupation periods and from most areas of the site. Clearly, the spatial analysis would work best where the quantities of bones were greatest, as in periods 10 and 11. Some periods produced rather poor quantities of bones, and the analysis was therefore largely limited to periods 9–14, with a particular emphasis on the significant 10th- to 12th-century AD assemblages of periods 9–11. While all aspects of the data from periods 9–12 are discussed (with the exception of size; see above), the periods 13 and 14 data are limited to species representation and a discussion of aspects related to local industries or crafts.

Recording

All bones that could be identified to species were fully recorded using a database divided into various headings: species, skeletal part, fragmentation (the proportion of the skeletal part represented), sex, age (a general age if possible, as well as teeth eruption/wear and epiphyses fusion), size, and various modifications such as butchery, working and pathology. The tooth eruption/wear data employ the method devised by Grant (1975; 1982), while the measurements are essentially taken from von den Driesch (1976). A bone was deemed to be measurable if it was a whole limb-bone (bird and mammalian domesticates) or if it included an epiphysis that could be classed as belonging to an adult.

Some of the species identifications need explaining. Thus partridge is the common or grey partridge; small passerines are those smaller than the thrush family, and large thrush is blackbird-sized; while crow refers to either carrion crow or rook. Regarding the identification of Gadidae (cod family),

when dealing with a postcranial skeletal part, a distinction is made between large and small gadid. Essentially, the former is defined by vertebrae larger than c 10mm in diameter, probably representing fish of about a metre in length. Such large fish are most likely to be cod, as this species tends to mature at a greater size compared to other gadids such as haddock.

Sexual distinctions noted during recording include the following: cattle pelves (after Grigson 1982, 8); sheep pelves (after Prummel and Frisch 1986, 576); chicken spurs (after West 1985) and medullary bone (after Driver 1982); and from reference collections, pig canines and sheep and goat horncores.

Use of data

Quantification was undertaken on two levels: the total fragment count and a weighted method involving a modified epiphysis-only count (after Grant 1975). The latter method involved the production of counts based on the number of epiphyses (with whole bones counted twice, with the exception of phalanges) and the maximum occurrence of a particular zone for a selection of the remaining skeletal parts. The latter include the skull, maxilla, mandible, atlas, axis, sacrum and astragalus. Counts for the maxilla and mandible involved the representation of particular teeth, while the vertebrae counts were indicated by the presence of articular surfaces. The skull was quantified by counts of certain key areas such as the orbit, horncore, occipital and temporal condyles, occipital crest and zygomatic. Within the final count for skulls, the maximum numbers of all these parts, as well as the maxilla, were taken into account. A further consideration, when calculating species abundance, was the expected frequency of particular skeletal parts. These were calculated for all species, with atlas and axis multiplied by two and, for pig, metacarpals and metatarsals divided by five. The two methods were mainly used to compare the representation of the major mammalian domesticates, the aim being to reduce the inherent bias within hand recovery and achieve a better representation of the larger species, that is, cattle in comparison to sheep/goat and pig.

Studying exploitation strategies relating to the major animal and bird domesticates uses the data available from the teeth and epiphyses. All the epiphysis data has been combined into three age groups: Early, Intermediate and Late (CD Tables 15–19; CD Table 21). Cattle vertebrae are also used, here noting the fusion of the anterior and posterior epiphyses of the centrum. The mandibles are similarly divided into different age groups, for cattle, sheep and pig (CD Table 53).

The mandibular and epiphysis fusion data are compared with reference to certain broad age categories, which have been extrapolated from those used by O'Connor (1989) specifically for mandibular data, as follows:

juvenile – unfused early group epiphyses;
subadult – unfused early and intermediate group epiphyses with worn second adult and unworn third adult molar;
adult – fused intermediate group epiphyses with worn third mandibular molar;

young adult – the difference between fused intermediate and fused late group epiphyses;

older adult – fused late group epiphyses and third adult molar in full wear (corresponding to mandible wear stage 12 or 'g' of Grant 1982).

The ages equated with the various stages of tooth eruption and wear, as well as those ascribed to the epiphyses fusion, are taken from a collation of information from a variety of authors as described in Schmid (1972).

The size data presented in this report are essentially used to determine the sex ratios of the major domesticates. No attempt has been made to discuss the relative size of the various domestic animals and birds represented among the bone collections from the Guildhall. However, they are comparable in size to those recovered from contemporary deposits at other City sites such as 1 Poultry (ONE94: Rielly in prep).

8.15 Leather items

Penny MacConnoran, with Alison Nailer

Introduction

The Guildhall leather assemblage consists of *c* 180 accessioned items of which just over 140 are shoes. In addition, there are over 300 fragments of odd shoe parts and moderate amounts of waste from leather working (CD Table 28). Although the majority of the footwear assemblage is in a fragmentary condition, certain stylistic and constructional trends can be distinguished.

Non-footwear leather items

The most common items are straps and belts. Fragments of ten straps of varying widths and thicknesses can be identified. Most are plain and made of thick leather, with some examples having the leather folded lengthways and seamed at the back in a variety of stitching techniques (<L1> and <L2>, Fig 407). Item <L2> has been cut at one end, presumably to salvage the buckle. There is just one decorated strap end (<L3>, Fig 407) which has its terminal cut into a large fleur-de-lis shape, with a rivet or mount hole in the centre. The design has been inexpertly cut out and looks like a home-made modification.

Many of the non-shoe items can not be reliably identified, partly due to their torn and fragmentary state and also because some (such as <L21>) have been cut up, presumably to salvage reusable leather. There are two large pieces of sheet leather (<L14> (Fig 28) and <L15>) with a variety of seams and awl holes, which are made from finely-dressed, fairly thin leather and which would seem to be parts of garments although their precise function has not been ascertained. One of the few recognisable items appears to be part of a bag or purse (<L13>, Fig 73) with a zigzag arrangement of stitch holes which suggests an embroidered pattern.

There are two objects, both elliptical in shape with longitudinal slashes, which are thought to be hair accessories. One of these (<L11>, Fig 408) is very well made and has a large awl hole at both ends, presumably for the attachment of a pin. The other (<L12>, Fig 408) is clumsily made and could be

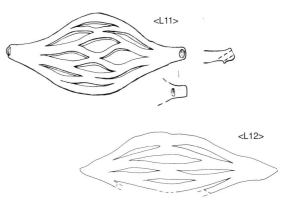

Fig 408 Leather hair accessories <L11> and <L12> (scale 1:2)

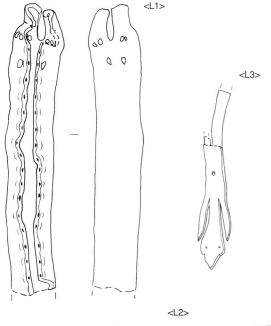

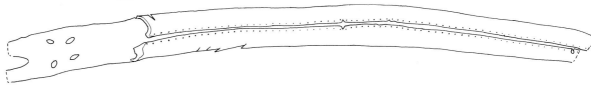

Fig 407 Leather straps <L1>–<L3> from Open Area 105 (scale 1:2)

a home-made version. A small number of examples were previously known from London, including Hosier Lane (HSN99) <12> and Bull Wharf (BUF90) <1935>. Other examples have been found on Continental sites, including Trondheim (Marstein 1989), where they have been interpreted variously as missile slings for use in hunting and sport and also as toys. Numerous variations of these objects are known from York, where their function has yet to be satisfactorily explained (Mould 2003, 3408–11). An example from the High Street excavations in Dublin has also been identified as a hair ornament (Q Mould, pers comm).

Footwear

The majority of the shoe assemblage dates from the late 11th to early 12th centuries, with a relatively small number of items dating from before and after this time. This is consistent with trends noted in other London assemblages of similar date, particularly New Fresh Wharf, Seal House, Billingsgate and Swan Lane (Pritchard 1991). Practically all of the sufficiently complete uppers indicate that the footwear type is that of an ankle shoe composed of a main one-piece wraparound upper usually with one or more small inserts to make up the desired shape. The uppers have varying numbers of thong slots around the quarters through which a fastening thong was passed to close the upper at the front of the shoe in a drawstring fashion. The shoes are all of turnshoe construction (Grew and de Neergaard 1988, 46–7) and over one third are embellished with an embroidered stripe on the vamp. The shoes range in size from tiny children's shoes to large adult size. Where possible, the more complete shoes have been ascribed to a general category of size such as 'child' or 'small adult' rather than to a specific modern shoe size. The post-conservation shrinkage of the leather in general has been a minimum of 10%.

The 10th to early 11th centuries AD

A small group of ankle shoes was discarded in pits in Open Area 127 (period 10). As is consistent with footwear of this date, the uppers and soles are joined by thonging. The group includes three of the most complete shoes from the site (<L36>–<L38>, Fig 68). The uppers are made from stout bovine leather. The two larger shoes <L36> and <L37> are so similar that they could have been made by the same craftsman. Each has a simple vamp stripe marked by a row of tunnel stitching. Both shoes have the unusual feature of a small rectangular tab at the throat and also show signs of having been modified, presumably for comfort reasons. Parallels with throat tabs from 1 Poultry (ONE94 <3075>) are of similar date. The third shoe <L38> is a child's ankle shoe with a faint vamp stripe that appears to have been impressed rather than stitched. It had been modified around the throat where a deep U-shape had been cut away, presumably to make the shoe more comfortable for the child.

Late 11th to early 12th centuries

The vast majority of the footwear came from contexts that have a pottery date range of c 1050–c 1150 and is mainly represented by uppers. One of the most striking aspects of the assemblage is the very large number of shoes with embroidered stripes on the vamp. The Guildhall examples of this shoe style more than double the number hitherto known from London (Grew and de Neergaard 1988, 75–9). There are 50 shoes with embroidered decoration, of which 19 come from contexts that are dated to c 1050–80, indicating that this style of footwear was well established in London in the later 11th century and continued into the 12th century.

Pritchard has written an account of the embroidery techniques used to create the vamp stripes found on previously excavated London shoes (Pritchard 1988). Similar techniques are found on the Guildhall footwear. In addition, a large number of vamps have a pronounced raised stripe where the leather was pinched up or folded in two before being embroidered (eg <L47>–<L48> (Fig 409) and <L49> (Fig 53)). Colour would have been a key element of the stripe although no trace of pigment remains on the surviving embroidery. Items <L47>–<L49> are also the only cases where stitching material survives, here identified as silk. By contrast, wool embroidery was used on an example from Coventry (Thomas 1980, 55, fig 6).

Many of the embroidered uppers are of thin, finely-dressed leather. Hide types have been identified as sheep or goat and also deer. It has been suggested that finely made shoes with vamp stripes might have been limited to indoor use (Grew and de Neergaard 1988). In view of the quantities that have now been excavated from London sites, this would seem unlikely. It is assumed that silk-embroidered shoes would have been considered to be quality accessories. Ankle shoes with vamp stripes of similar date to the Guildhall examples are known from many sites across Europe and Britain including Gdansk, Vlaardingen, Haithabu, Trondheim, Oslo, Dublin and York (Mould 2003, 3341–3).

Other forms of ornament on the footwear include the addition of decorative top bands of which there are two detached examples (<L123> and <L119> (Fig 34)). The latter may have held a decorative thong or braid possibly in the style of a shoe from Vlaardingen (Goubitz et al 2001, 52, fig 22, b). There are also two late 11th-century uppers with a row of multiple slots just below the top edge of the quarters (<L92> (Fig 53) and <L98>) through which a drawstring would have been threaded, creating a decorative effect as well as serving to close the shoe. This technique was previously recognised on a similarly dated shoe from London (Pritchard 1991, 229, fig 3.114) and is also found at York (Mould 2003, 3297, fig 1625) and Trondheim (Marstein 1989, fig 4, b).

A small number of shoe uppers appear to have had an external appliqué patch attached, as evidenced by the presence of carefully arranged fine grain/flesh stitch holes (<L120> (Fig 34), <L124> and <L125>). One shoe upper (<L121>,

<L47>

<L48>

Fig 409 Silk stitching on two leather shoes <L47> and <L48> from Open Area 108 (scale c 1:1 except detail of <L48> (left) not to scale)

Fig 410) that had been cut up for reuse retains an arrangement of fine grain/flesh stitch holes for a triangular patch. This is somewhat similar to a shoe from Seal House, which has been interpreted as having decorative appliqué work on the heel part of the upper (Pritchard 1991, 232, fig 3.121 no. 343). It is possible that the separate toe-piece of <L126> is itself an appliqué patch. The fine stitching on the vamp of one shoe (<L54>, Fig 73) suggest an external patch. Such patches appear to be functional as well as decorative.

Of interest is an upper with a small circular cutout (<L52>, Fig 410) which is edged with a binding seam. A similar feature occurred on another early 12th-century example from Seal House in London (Pritchard 1991, 235, fig 3.120, no. 342). A

small number of shoes from York have similar small holes cut out of their quarters, and it has been shown that they are more probably indicative of repairs than decorative cutouts (Mould 2003, 3345–6).

A good deal of the footwear shows considerable signs of wear in the usual places at tread and heel (eg <L159>, Fig 34). Numerous soles display evidence of repairs, with some clump repair patches still held in situ by thonging (eg <L162>). There are also numerous detached repair clumps throughout the assemblage (eg <L163> and <L165>).

Of particular interest is a child's sole (<L160>, Fig 411) with a large repair sole thonged to the underside of the original worn sole. The repair sole had been cut from a shoe vamp, part

481

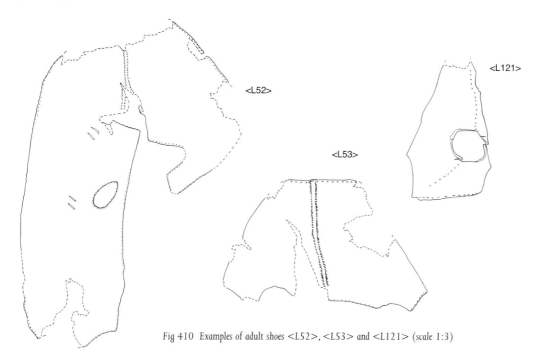

Fig 410 *Examples of adult shoes <L52>, <L53> and <L121> (scale 1:3)*

of the decorative stripe of which still remains. The small semicircular cutaway on one vamp (<L51>, Fig 34) is unusual; it may represent a very neat repair or have held an insert that was part of the original design.

There are a number of children's and adults' shoes which display signs of what may be home-made modifications, usually in the area around the vamp throat which has been cut lower to achieve a more comfortable fit (eg <L93> (Fig 53), <L94> (Fig 73), <L99> and <L95> (Fig 73)). The repairs and modifications to the numerous small shoes in the Guildhall assemblage suggest an adult population attentive to the comfort of its children's feet.

Toe shapes in the late 11th-century shoes are gently rounded, becoming more gently pointed into the 12th century. Heel shapes are either round or V-backed with straight waists. There are just two early 12th-century shoes which have exaggerated toes; one is a sole (<L159>, Fig 34) and the other is an upper (<L100>) whose outward-curling toe had been stuffed with moss to retain its shape. There are similar examples of early 12th-century date from Swan Lane (Grew and de Neergaard 1988, 11). This is a toe shape which remained in vogue only fairly briefly at that time.

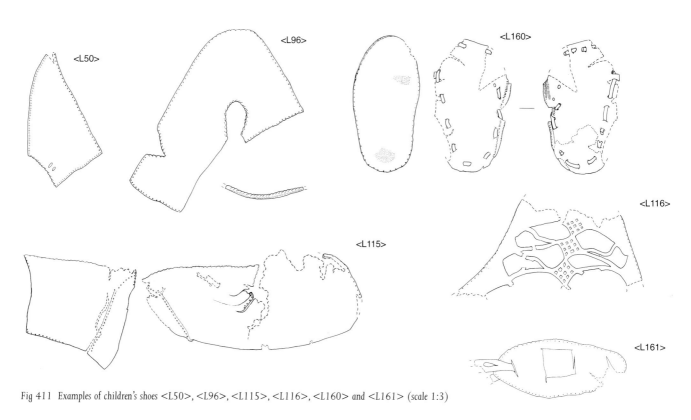

Fig 411 *Examples of children's shoes <L50>, <L96>, <L115>, <L116>, <L160> and <L161> (scale 1:3)*

While nearly all the footwear conforms to the ankle-shoe style with drawstring fastening, there are a few exceptions. One example is an adult shoe or slipper whose deerskin upper has extremely low-cut sides, and decorative cutouts and slashes on the vamp and quarters (<L114>, Fig 34). Its unique features set this shoe apart from the general trends of the time. The jagged and straight slashes are very roughly done and may be home-made modifications. The sole shape is normal, with a straight waist.

Another variant is a small ankle shoe in poor condition (<L115>, Fig 411). This has two pronounced diagonal stripes on the quarters which may have been of similar effect to a vamp stripe. It is equally possible, however, that they were merely a different technique for attaching a V-back heel, a feature which died out in the early 12th century.

The vamp fragment from a slipper or sandal (<L116>, Fig 411), though very incomplete, resembles an early 12th-century example from Trondheim (Marstein 1989, fig 14). Swann has commented on the 'window tracery' effect of such footwear (Swann 2001, 55) of which she says there are occasional examples from Oslo and Trondheim. Previously, the earliest London example of footwear with openwork decoration dated from the first half of the 13th century (Grew and de Neergaard 1988, 79–81, fig 115, a). This shoe comes from external dumping associated with Building 126, but there have been some difficulties in ascribing this building to a period. Nevertheless, the associated pottery dating of *c* 1050–*c* 1150 makes this a very early example of an openwork shoe from a London site.

Catalogue of illustrated leather

Only the illustrated leather items appear as full entries in this catalogue; a complete catalogue of all the leather items is provided on the accompanying CD-ROM. Abbreviations used in the catalogue are as follows: Diam (diameter), L (length), W (width). Incomplete dimensions have been placed in brackets. A glossary of leather terms can be found in another volume in this series (Egan 2005a, 242–3).

Straps

<L1> Leather strap (Fig 407)
A<4392>, A[17548]; period 10, OA105
Incomplete; L (157)mm, W (25)mm. Thick leather, folded to centre-back butt seam with single row of awl holes on both edges. One end has four large grain/flesh stitch holes to anchor a buckle, with a slot for the buckle pin. Other end missing.

22mm. Thick leather folded along both long edges to centre-back butt seam. Unusually, the flesh side faces outwards. Four nail or rivet holes for holding a buckle and a slot for the buckle pin at the surviving original end; the other end has been cut off. The back of the strap has been cut away at the buckle end, possibly to salvage the buckle.

<L2> Leather strap (Fig 407)
A<4394>, A[17548]; period 10, OA105
Incomplete; L (335)mm, W

<L3> Leather strap (Fig 407)
A<4327>, A[17611]; period 10, OA105
Incomplete; L (98)mm, W 10mm.

Fragment, fairly thick leather, laminated and cut. The terminal is inexpertly cut into a foliate or fleur-de-lis shape with a single rivet or mount hole.

<L4>–<L10> Leather straps: see CD-ROM

Hair accessories

<L11> Leather hair accessory (Fig 408)
A<4375>, A[17238]; period 11, OA109
Complete; L 98mm, W 38mm. Leaf-shaped item of thick leather now laminated into two layers. The design has been made by cutting slashes into the leather and expanding it sideways. There is a large awl hole cut transversely into both extremities and emerging on the flesh side. These holes probably held a wooden pin or similar in place. There are previous examples from London, including Bull Wharf (BUF90) <1935> and Hosier Lane (HSN99) <12>, and several similar examples from Coppergate in York dating from the mid 10th to late 13th centuries AD (Mould 2003, 3408–11). There are also Continental examples, including some from Trondheim (Marstein 1989, fig 63, a–d), while a comparable example to <L11> comes from High Street, Dublin (National Museum of Ireland acc no. E711:5193; Q Mould, pers comm).

<L12> Leather hair accessory (Fig 408)
A<4420>, A[17867]; period 10, OA126
Complete; L 110mm, W 32mm. Laminated. Similar to <L11> (above) but looks like a home-made or unfinished version as it is roughly made, with uneven edges.

Garments or unidentified items

<L13> Leather unidentified item (Fig 73)
A<4550>, A[17119]; period 11, OA109
Incomplete; L (130)mm, W (78)mm. Sheet fragment, torn and cut up. Fairly thick leather. Single row of grain/flesh stitch holes along both surviving original adjoining edges. Further stitch holes in large irregular zigzag pattern along longer edge. Backstitch (or similar) has been used in all rows. There appears to be a pair of vertical thong slots towards the centre of the item but there is also damage here. The object seems to have been deliberately shaped and suggests a pocket, purse or bag flap.

<L14> Leather garment (Fig 28)
A<6309>, A[20731]; period 10, OA100
Incomplete; L (515)mm, W

(305)mm. Panel of finely-dressed, fairly thin leather possibly from a garment. There are six fragments in all, four of which join. A wide curving V-shape is cut into one end with a fine binding stitch along these edges. The other original edges all have grain/flesh stitching; at least one of these is an overlapped seam. In the body of the panel are four short parallel rows of thong slots which suggest that a lace or similar was once present. There is impressed ornament in the form of two concentric circles (one Diam 32mm), each of which has two further circles within. The piece is similar to <L15>.

<L15> Leather garment: see CD-ROM

<L16>–<L25> Leather unidentified items: see CD-ROM

Waste

<L26> Leather waste (Fig 317)
A<6289>, A[23258]; period 10, S130
L 75mm, W 66mm. Offcut

fragment, probably from a reused item. Cut into a rough H-shape.

<L27> Leather waste (Fig 317)

A<4396>, A[17239]; period 10, OA108

L 52mm, W 28mm. Small offcut fragment, laminated. There are two sets of impressions of 'teeth-like' clamp marks on the grain surface. Several other pieces of waste have similar marks.

<L28>–<L35> Leather waste: see CD-ROM

Shoes

THONG-STITCHED SHOES

<L36> Leather shoe (Fig 68) A<6588>, A[15930]; period 10, OA127

Partly complete; L (250)mm, W (105)mm. Virtually identical to <L37> (below). Nearly complete upper with toe end missing and fragment of sole, now detached. Adult-size ankle shoe. Sole is straight-waist shape and has a round back. Toe shape is round. The upper is of very thick bovine leather and has laminated into two layers; the sole is also laminated. Wraparound one-piece upper with near-vertical side seam at right side of ankle, suggesting left foot. Lasting margin and side seam are thong-stitched with some thonging still in situ. There is a single thong slot in the quarters at each side of the ankle. The top edge of the upper appears to have been cut from around the sides of the quarters and down to the vamp where a short lengthwise slash has been made, presumably to make the shoe a better fit. At the centre of the throat is a small rectangular tab with a butt seam around its three edges. This feature occurs on a small number of shoes from 1 Poultry (ONE94, eg <3075>), and may be part of a fastening arrangement (Nailer and Reid in prep). A decorative stripe runs down the centre of the vamp marked by a row of horizontally-cut small tunnel-stitch holes; these do not penetrate through to the flesh surface. A thong-stitched shoe with vamp stripe came from Swan Lane (SWA81: Pritchard 1991, 285–6); other examples are known from Bull Wharf (BUF90).

<L37> Leather shoe (Fig 68) A<6589>, A[15930]; period 10, OA127

Partly complete; L 250mm, W across tread 90mm. Near-identical to <L36> (above).

Adult-size ankle shoe with fragmentary sole and nearly complete upper still joined together by thonging. Thick leather. Wraparound one-piece upper with vertical seam at the right of the ankle, suggesting left foot. Round toe. Toe end of upper detached. Sole is straight-waist shape with round back (indicated by shape of upper). There is a large vertical thong slot at each side of the quarters for a fastening thong. The top of the quarters adjoining the vamp may have been modified by cutting. There is a rectangular tab at the throat, with edge/flesh seams on all three sides of the tab, and a vamp stripe similar to <L36>. See <L36> (above) for comparanda. Both could have been made by the same shoemaker.

<L38> Leather shoe (Fig 68) A<4330>, A[11716]; period 10, OA127

Nearly complete; L 160mm, W at waist 54mm. Child's ankle shoe. Left foot. Gently pointed toe. Wraparound upper and sole. Worn at toe and heel. Thong-stitched lasting margin. Small triangular insert at the side seam on the right side of the ankle. Fairly low on each side of the ankle is a single thong hole, stretched and worn, to hold a fastening thong. The top edge of the vamp is quite crudely finished and it may have been modified for greater comfort; thus, the vamp has been cut low over the instep and the throat is cut away. There is a faint vamp stripe which appears to have been impressed rather than stitched. Though not identical, this shoe has similarities to <L36> and <L37> (above).

<L39>–<L46> Leather thong-stitched shoes: see CD-ROM

UPPERS WITH VAMP STRIPES

<L47> Leather shoe (Fig 409) A<4252>, A[17396]; period 10, OA108

Incomplete; L from throat to toe 127mm, W (135)mm. Vamp only. Adult-size ankle shoe. Left foot. Round toe, worn. Very finely stitched lasting margin. Butt seams at vamp wing and throat. One pair of small thong slots very close to right throat edge. There is a small C-shaped flap cut into the leather at the right toe end of vamp. Embroidered vamp stripe with good survival of in situ silk thread in apparent plait stitch covering raised fold in leather. Deer hide.

<L48> Leather shoe (Fig 409) A<6285>, A[17305]; period 10, OA108

Incomplete; L (65)mm, W (126)mm. Upper fragment, torn. Stitched lasting margin. Central vamp stripe composed of two rows of embroidery stitching with silk thread in situ flanking a raised central fold of leather; a row of tiny horizontal awl cuts lies outside each of the silken rows.

<L49> Leather shoe (Fig 53) A<4328>, A[17489]; period 10, OA108

Incomplete; L (238)mm, W (190)mm. Incomplete wraparound upper, torn. Small adult-size ankle shoe. Small regular stitch holes on lasting margin. Vertical edge/flesh butt seam to left near back of heel and butt seam to left of throat for (missing) insert. Binding stitch along top edge. Vamp stripe formed by two rows of very fine grain/flesh stitch holes with some of the silk embroidery thread surviving at the toe end. Small thong slots are aligned in a single row for drawstring fastening.

<L50> Leather shoe (Fig 411) A<4435>, A[17820]; period 10, OA126

Incomplete; L (118)mm, W (45)mm. Vamp fragment from small shoe. Fine stitching on lasting margin. Butt seam to side; binding seam around throat edge. Very fine stitching along cut edge indicates that vamp was originally in two parts, overlapped and seamed down centre to create a vamp stripe. Pair of thong slots at side of vamp suggests drawstring fastening.

<L51> Leather shoe (Fig 34) A<6292>, A[23429]; period 10, OA105

Incomplete; L (107)mm, W (110)mm. Upper vamp fragment, torn. Round toe. Vertical edge/flesh butt seam at left side of vamp, binding seam along throat edge. Vamp stripe at centre composed of four lines of stitch holes which do not penetrate through to flesh surface. There is a butt seam to a small semicircular (missing) insert on one side of the toe. The pattern of the vamp suggests that this was a left shoe, in which case the insert would be over the little toe area. The insert is extremely neat and appears to be an original element of the design rather than a repair.

<L52> Leather shoe (Fig 410) A<4326>, A[17593]; period 10, B102

Incomplete; L (270)mm, W (150)mm. Fragment of wraparound upper and a small fragment of sole (may not belong). Ankle shoe. Leather of upper is rigid and in poor condition. Butt seam on right side, suggesting left foot. Regular stitch holes on lasting margin. Butt seam, probably for missing insert, at throat. Binding seam on top edge. Four pairs of small thong slots arranged in a single row for drawstring fastening. Vamp stripe at centre marked by two rows of stitch holes each side of a raised fold in leather. The oval openwork cutout on left quarters, edged with a binding seam, is probably a repair. This is very similar to an early 12th-century example from Seal House (Pritchard 1991, 273, fig 3.120, no. 342).

<L53> Leather shoe (Fig 410) A<6310>, A[23463]; period 10, S130

Incomplete; L (96)mm, W (170)mm. Vamp fragment. Very small regular stitch holes on lasting margin. Butt seams at right of vamp wing and along throat edge. The toe end is cut straight across and has a row of grain/flesh stitch holes along edge, indicating a separate toe piece or a repair. Vamp stripe marked by two rows of very fine awl holes.

<L54> Leather shoe (Fig 73)
A<4553>, A[17119]; period 11, OA109
Partly complete; L 240mm. Almost complete wraparound upper. Small adult-size ankle shoe. Right foot. Gently rounded toe. Regular stitch holes on lasting margin. Vertical edge/flesh butt seam at left of ankle. Edge flesh seam on left vamp wing; grain/flesh stitch holes on right vamp wing. Butt seam to missing insert at vamp throat. Binding stitch along top edge. Five pairs of small, widely-spaced thong slots arranged in single row around quarters for drawstring fastening. One large (stretched) thong hole at corner of top edge and vamp throat for fastening over instep. Pronounced vamp stripe is marked by raised fold in leather flanked by grain/flesh stitch holes. A slash or tear next to the side seam has been repaired with binding stitch. On the left side of the toe a slight bulge in the shoe is marked by a semicircle of fine grain/flesh stitches, probably for an external patch. There are a number of very small tunnel

stitches within the patch area and the leather is torn. The bulge may be the result of a bunion. Two further rows of fine grain/flesh stitch holes meet diagonally across the toe, suggesting a second external patch there.

<L55> Leather shoe (Fig 28)
A<4428>, A[20400]; period 10, OA100
Incomplete; L (300)mm, W across instep 160mm. Nearly complete wraparound upper and detached insert, torn. Adult-size ankle boot. Right foot. Round toe. Leather is rigid. Small regular stitch holes in lasting margin. Butt seam on left side of quarters and to insert at vamp throat. Insert is small and rectangular and has two butt seams with binding stitch on the opposing sides. Narrow vamp stripe formed of two rows of fine stitch holes which do not go through to flesh side; some thread survives in situ. Six (very narrow) pairs of small vertical thong slots arranged in a single row for drawstring fastening, three each side of ankle. One small lace hole to right of vamp throat and another on the insert near the top edge.

<L56>–<L91> Leather uppers with vamp stripes: see CD-ROM

UPPERS WITH PLAIN VAMPS

<L92> Leather shoe (Fig 53)
A<4371>, A[17396]; period 10, OA108
Incomplete; L (260)mm, W (190)mm. Wraparound upper fragment: vamp and part of quarters, torn. Adult-size ankle shoe. Right foot. Vertical edge/flesh butt seam on left of quarters. The lasting margin has regular stitch holes and an angle in the margin towards the heel suggests a V-back. Unusually, there are edge/flesh stitch holes across the toe, for a missing insert or repair. The low-cut wide vamp throat is edged with binding stitch. Just below the top edge of the quarters is a horizontal row of small, closely-spaced, vertical thong slots for drawstring fastening.

<L93> Leather shoe (Fig 53)
A<4415>, A[17239]; period 10, OA108

Incomplete; L 322mm, W 190mm. Wraparound upper. Adult-size ankle shoe. Right foot. Gently pointed toe. Very thick leather. Lasting margin with small regular stitch holes. Edge/flesh butt side seam to left with a small triangular insert (missing) at the base. There is a diagonal butt seam across the toe to another insert (missing). The vamp throat is a low-cut semicircle and the top edge is cut with no binding stitch. A single pair of thong slots on each quarter, the left pair divided by the side seam, for a drawstring fastening.

<L94> Leather shoe (Fig 73)
A<4549>, A[17119]; period 11, OA109
Nearly complete; L 140mm, W at waist 48mm. Child's ankle shoe. Left foot. Gently rounded toe. One-piece wraparound upper and sole with toe end missing. Sole is

straight-waist shape with rounded heel. Sole leather is thin and delaminated, and a second layer of thin leather has been used inside the seat, probably as a combined reinforcement and comfort piece; this seat-shaped piece is cut straight across at the waist and is grain-side down; edge/flesh stitching survives. The vamp throat has been cut in an oval. Near-vertical butt seam at right side of quarters. A single pair of short slots for drawstring fastening survives on each side of the ankle.

<L95> Leather shoe (Fig 73)
A<4268>, A[17096]; period 11, OA109
Incomplete; L (110)mm, W (64)mm. Upper vamp and part of left side of quarters. Small child's or baby's ankle shoe. Rounded toe. Finely-stitched lasting margin; butted edge/flesh seam to side; binding seam on top edge (detached). Throat cut low (binding seam on edge), then made lower by cutting out a

curved shape, leaving throat edge raw, presumably to make the shoe a more comfortable fit. One pair of small vertical thong slots each side of ankle.

<L96> Leather shoe (Fig 411)
A<4442>, A[17768]; period 10, R101
Nearly complete; L 95mm, W at waist 45mm. Baby's bootee. Complete wraparound one-piece upper with vertical butt seam at side. Sole missing. Fairly thin leather. Left foot. Round toe. The stitch holes of the lasting margin are very fine and closely-spaced. The rear of the quarters is cut into a V to accommodate a sole with a V-shaped heel. A detached piece of top band (L 65mm) fits the vamp throat whose edge has fine binding-stitch holes. There is no evidence for a binding around the top edge of the upper, which is straight-cut.

<L97>–<L113> Leather uppers with plain vamps: see CD-ROM

SHOES WITH UNUSUAL FEATURES

<L114> Leather shoe (Fig 34)
A<6308>, A[23386]; period 10, OA105
Partly complete; L 270mm, W at waist 80mm, W at tread 93mm. Low shoe or slipper. Complete sole and four upper fragments consisting of part of toe end of vamp and right side and back of quarters. Adult-size shoe. Right foot. Gently pointed toe. Sole is straight-waist shape. Regular stitch holes on lasting margin of upper. The wraparound upper is torn and fragmentary, and is cut from thin leather which has been identified as deer hide. The upper is very low-cut, the top edge coming close to the lasting margin at the side of the foot. The side seam to left of heel is an edge/flesh stitched butt seam. There are no other seams and no binding stitch on any of the cut edges. The heel is the best-preserved part of the upper. The upper rises at the quarters to form a triangular tab on each side of the ankle. There is a further rounded tab at the back of the heel. Each ankle tab has a pair of long slashed slots, the rounded

heel tab having oval slots. Beneath the slots on the heel tab is a long decorative slash edged with crudely cut slashes forming 'teeth'. The surviving portions of vamp suggest that the instep was entirely cut away, only the toe area being covered. The surviving toe-end fragments of vamp show two long, crude, transverse slashes across the toes; above these are two further horizontal slashes with similar jagged 'teeth' edges to those on the heel.

There are no close parallels for this shoe from other London excavations. The nearest are probably the one-piece openwork shoes from 1 Poultry (ONE94: Nailer and Reid in prep), but these are technologically very different. The reduction in size and crude slashing of the upper is probably the owner's modification of an already unusual but plain shoe. The sole is worn but not greatly so. The fragile leather of the upper combined with the shoe's odd appearance suggests that it was probably limited to indoor use.

<L115> Leather shoe (Fig 411) A<6294>, A[23160]; period 10, OA117
Incomplete; L (175)mm, W (80)mm. Partly complete upper, two pieces: most of vamp and quarters, torn. Child's ankle shoe. Rounded toe. Right foot. No fastening evidence survives. Thread-stitched lasting margin with traces of small tunnel stitches at the right forepart presumably for repair piece. Butt seams to edges. Binding seams along top edges. An unusual feature at the back of the heel consists of two pronounced stripes, similar to vamp stripes, formed from two rows of grain/flesh stitch holes. These apparently decorative details start high behind the centre heel and fall at an outward slant to the lasting margin. There are traces of irregular grain/flesh stitch holes between the stripes and the cut edges. This, coupled with different colouration and wear

characteristics between the stripes and the cut edges, suggests that the stripes were only partly decorative. Their main function was probably to anchor a large V-back heel piece.

<L116> Leather shoe (Fig 411) A<6296>, A[23414]; period 10, B126
Incomplete; L (90)mm, W (148)mm. Portion of decorated vamp from slipper. Very insubstantial item with openwork straps and decorative cutouts. It is the only example of its type from the assemblage. The two surviving edges have fine edge/flesh butt seams, suggesting that there may perhaps have been inserts between vamp and sole. This shoe resembles a Norwegian example of early 12th-century date from Trondheim (Swann 2001, 57, fig 56).

<L117>–<L118> Leather shoes with unusual features: see CD-ROM

OTHER UPPER PARTS

<L119> Leather shoe (Fig 34) A<4387>, A[17548]; period 10, OA105
Incomplete; L (322)mm, W 10mm. Decorative top band from shoe upper. Folded strip of leather with edge/flesh seam along one long edge and a binding seam along the other. A single row of fine awl holes runs along the length of the binding through both thicknesses of leather; the wear pattern indicates that a lace or similar was woven through the length of the strip. This type of top band is not common in London.

<L120> Leather shoe (Fig 34) A<4382>, A[17577]; period 10, OA105
Incomplete; L (55)mm, W (96)mm. Vamp fragment, torn and laminated. Toe only. Finely-stitched lasting margin. Two parallel lines of fine grain/flesh stitch holes, with the impression of running stitches on the flesh side, are arranged in a chevron over the end of the toe. Possibly for the attachment of an appliqué patch.

<L121> Leather shoe (Fig 410)

A<12936>, A[20263]; period 10, R100
Incomplete; L (110)mm, W (65)mm. Upper fragment: vamp/quarter, cut up for reuse. Finely-stitched lasting margin. Fine, even grain/flesh stitch holes for the attachment of a triangular appliqué patch on the outside of the shoe. There is similar appliqué work on an ankle shoe from Seal House (Pritchard 1991, 230, 236, fig 3.121).

<L122> Leather shoe (Fig 34) A<4450>, A[20375]; period 10, OA105
Incomplete; L (170)mm, W(65)mm. Upper fragment: quarters. Binding/butted seams along four edges. No surviving lasting margin but four large grain/flesh stitch holes along lower edge may suggest a repair. A doubled thong is tightly interwoven through a horizontal row of ten short vertical slots. The thonging is anchored at one end of the slots and broken off at the other. The slots graduate in height from 4mm to 8mm. This type of thong fastening is a mid 11th- to mid 12th-century feature and is

known on other shoes from London.

Soles

<L159> Leather shoe (Fig 34) A<4388>, A[17548]; period 10, OA105
Incomplete; L 300mm, W 98mm. Complete sole. Adult-size shoe. Right foot. Straight waist. Exaggerated toe curling to right, suggesting right shoe of 'scorpion's tail' style. Regular stitch holes on lasting margin. Very worn with a mixture of tunnel and grain/flesh stitching for repair pieces at heel and tread. Similar to early 12th-century examples from Seal House (Pritchard 1991, 232, figs 3.117–18, nos 338–9).

<L160> Leather shoe (Fig 411) A<4325>, A[17750]; period 10, B101
Incomplete; L 110mm, W at waist 50mm, W at tread 55mm. Child's complete shoe sole with repair pieces. Right foot. Round toe. Straight waist. Worn at heel and beneath big toe. Edge/flesh seam around sole has fine stitch holes. A repair piece covering the entire sole had been stitched with a

thong, still in situ, to the missing upper. This repair piece had been cut from the vamp of a shoe upper, as indicated by the remains of a vamp stripe formed by at least two rows of very fine stitch holes along one side. The leather of this repair is sheep or goat hide. Within the seat of the repair sole are the remains of a further repair piece. The edge/ flesh seam on one edge of this fragment indicates that it too was cut from a reused item.

<L161> Leather shoe (Fig 411) A<4441>, A[17820]; period 10, OA126
Incomplete; L 110mm, W at waist 45mm. Sole of small child's shoe. Pointed toe. Straight waist. Heel torn. Reused. A square shape had been roughly cut out of centre. Horizontal slash across heel and toe. Thong with looped end threaded through toe slash. Secondary function unknown.

<L162>–<L173> Leather soles: see CD-ROM

<L123>–<L158> Leather upper parts: see CD-ROM

8.16 Insect remains

Michelle Morris and David Smith

Introduction

Insect analysis was undertaken on 34 samples from periods 10 and 11. The samples were primarily selected according to archaeological criteria and apparent preservation. At the same time, samples were also selected so that they would be comparable to those used in the plant macrofossil analysis.

Methodology

The samples were processed using the standard method of paraffin flotation as outlined in Kenward et al (1980). The Coleoptera (beetles) were identified by direct comparison with the Gorham and Girling Collections of British Coleoptera. The insect faunas are presented in CD Table 54 and CD Table 55. The taxonomy of the Coleoptera follows Lucht (1987).

In order to aid interpretation, the faunas recovered were

divided into one or more ecological groups (CD Table 54; CD Table 55). The codes used and the nature of each group are explained in a key at the end of the table. These groupings are derived from the preliminary classifications outlined by Kenward (1978). The classification used here replicates that employed by Kenward and Hall (1995). Some of the Coleoptera have also been assigned codes based upon their degree of synanthropy. This includes the proportions of Kenward's 'house fauna' (species apparently particularly associated with human settlements: Hall and Kenward 1990; Kenward and Hall 1995) and those with known synanthropic preferences. These codes are derived from those used by Kenward (1997).

The dipterous (fly) puparia were identified using the drawings in K G V Smith (1973; 1989) and, where possible, by direct comparison with specimens identified by Skidmore (1999). The taxonomy follows that of K G V Smith (1989) for the Diptera.

Interpretation of the insect faunas

From the lists of insects (CD Table 54; CD Table 55) it is clear that across the site, and indeed across several deposit types, there is an almost ubiquitous fauna. Equally, these faunas do not appear to represent any single type of material. Recent work by Kenward (Carrot and Kenward 2001; Kenward and Hall 1995; 1997) has suggested that there are a range of 'indicator groups' of insects that may be specific to certain forms of craft activity, site use and deposits type. Unfortunately, though individual species from these 'indicator groups' are present, they do not dominate or appear significant in any individual fauna. The impression gained is that several types of material have been blended together during the formation of the deposits. In essence, the material sampled and studied had not remained in situ after its primary formation but had been redeposited. Both the insect faunas recovered and the ubiquitous nature of the distribution of species between samples are very similar to the findings from the early medieval site at Highgate, Beverley (Hall and Kenward 1980). At Highgate the origin of this material appears to have been the dumping of large quantities of organic waste, and this is also probably true of the majority of material from the Guildhall.

Regarding the individual species of beetle present, they are typical of dense urban settlement in the archaeological record (Hall and Kenward 1990; Kenward and Hall 1995). Many of the species recovered belong to the grouping of insects which Kenwood has labelled, perhaps misleadingly, as the 'house fauna' (Hall and Kenward 1990). This includes a range of synanthropic and quasi-synanthropic species typical of dry matter, often plant material, building up in housing. Examples of these species are *Lathridius minutus*, *Cryptophagus*, *Xylodromus concinnus* and probably the Colydidae *Aglenus brunneus*. Also included in this group of species are those that feed on the prepared timbers of buildings, such as *Anobium punctatum* (the 'woodworm') and *Lyctus brunneus* (the 'powder post' beetle). Recent statistical analysis by Carrot and Kenward (2001) has suggested that all these species are typical of house floors and other internal deposits in and around buildings.

Other species encountered belong to clear groupings of insects which are associated with foul and rotting organic wastes and rubbish. These species are characterised by ecological groupings 'rt' and 'rf' (CD Table 54; CD Table 55). They consist of a wide range of taxa such as the *Cercyon* species, the Histeridae ('pill beetles'), the majority of the Staphylinidae ('rove beetles'), the *Monotoma* and *Rhizophagus* species, and *Anthicus formicarius*. It seems that in both periods 10 and 11 this aspect of the fauna was dominant.

The soil micromorphology analysis at this site has raised the question of the presence of stabling deposits in several of the buildings. Stabling material seems to be one of the easier deposits to identify in the archaeological record using insect remains (Kenward and Hall 1997). Although members of the 'indicator groups' of species that are thought to be associated with stabling material are present, they fail to dominate in any single deposit. Unfortunately, the various species of lice and other ectoparasites that can be used as a clear indicator for stabling material were not encountered as they have been elsewhere (eg ibid; Kenward and Allison 1994; Smith et al 2000).

The condition of much of the material scattered across this site in both periods is also suggested by the species of fly puparia present. Many deposits contain *Musca domestica* (the common housefly), *Stomoyxs calcitrans* (the stable fly) and *Sepsis* flies. These are all species that are cosmopolitan and common around human housing, stabling and yards today. This is particularly true where rather liquid rubbish, excrement and carrion have been scattered (Smith 1973; 1989). A rather fluid and muddy nature of deposits is also suggested by the occurrence of *Platystethus cornutus*, *Oxytelus complanatus* and *Aphodius granarius*, quite often in large numbers. The recent work on the species associations found in the Anglo-Scandinavian deposits at 16–22 Coppergate, York, has found that these species are often associated with somewhat muddy external surfaces (Carrot and Kenward 2001). It is noticeable that these three species become much more dominant in the faunas at the Guildhall from period 11 and, although period 10 also had its deposits of foul material, this may suggest that the ground surfaces at the Guildhall became wetter during this phase.

Comparison with other sites

The insect faunas, in general, compare closely with those seen in both Roman and Anglo-Scandinavian York (Hall and Kenward 1990; Kenward and Hall 1995). These faunas are similar to ones from other medieval deposits that are accumulations of settlement rubbish. Two examples of such deposits are Highgate, Beverley, in Yorkshire (Hall and Kenward 1980) and Stone, Staffordshire (Moffet and Smith 1995). It is worth noting that a similar fauna indicative of mixed dumped deposits was also recovered from the Saxon site at Bull Wharf (BUF90: Smith 1998). Other archaeological sites in London have produced the same range of species, for example Roman and medieval 1 Poultry (ONE94: Smith 2000), medieval St Mary Spital (Smith 1997), medieval St John Clerkenwell (Smith and Chandler 2004), medieval Winchester Palace (Smith 2006) and Preacher's Court (Smith, D

N, 2002). Many of these medieval sites in London have yielded insect faunas, predominantly a range of flies, which seemed to be associated solely with deep and squalid cesspits (Smith 2000; Smith, D N, 2002; 2006). Another type of deposit identified using insect remains in London is stabling material (Smith and Chandler 2004). The major difference between the deposits at the Guildhall and some of the other sites is that here it is not possible to give a definite reconstruction of the use of any of the features concerned based on the insect remains.

8.17 Burial catalogue of the 11th- to 13th-century St Lawrence Jewry churchyard

William White (anthropological data), Damian Goodburn (timber grave furniture) and Ian Tyers (tree-ring dates)

Burials of the third quarter of the 11th century in the northern enclosure (OA101, period 10 phase 1)

All these burials (burials 1–6, Fig 412) were aligned west–east and laid out in a supine position with the head at the west end of the grave. All the wood used for the coffins was of local oak unless otherwise indicated.

BURIAL 1

Burial of a man aged 26–45 years old and 1.74m tall, who suffered from severe osteoarthritis. The body was buried in an unfastened coffin which must have been assembled in the grave at the time of the interment. The body was laid on a base board (tangentially-cleft and hewn) with a footboard wedged inside two side boards, and a lid was then laid on top of the two side boards. The foot board appears to have been fashioned with five sides. The bones inside the coffin were somewhat displaced. The base board produced a tree-ring date of after 1040.

BURIAL 2

Burial of a ?woman of indeterminate age. The body was buried in an unfastened coffin comprising a base board, side boards and a beech covering board, with no foot board (head end truncated) (Fig 360, e). The covering board produced a tree-ring date of ?1069. The feet were found with the toes pointing upwards, supported by two chalk blocks placed within the coffin on either side of the feet.

BURIAL 3

Burial of a woman aged 26–45 years old and 1.51m tall, with a bathrocranic skull (Fig 413), healed trepanation on the sagittal suture (Fig 426) and dental caries. The body did not appear to have been buried in any form of coffin, and was laid out with the hands at the sides, perhaps indicating that a shroud was not used.

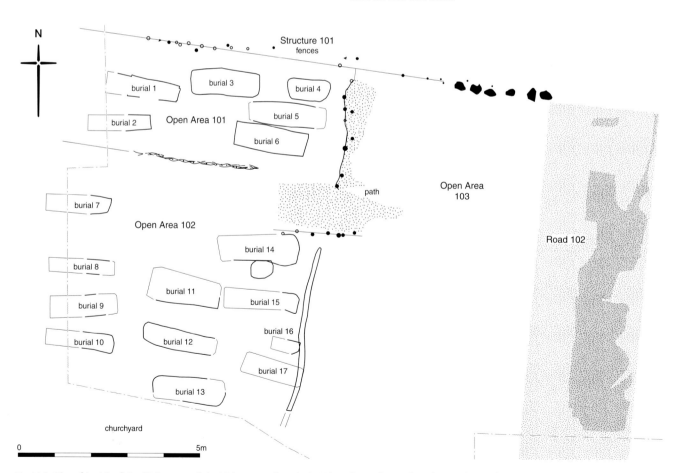

Fig 412 *Plan of burials of the third quarter of the 11th century (burials 1–17) in the northern and southern enclosures (OA101 and OA102) of the churchyard of St Lawrence Jewry (scale 1:100)*

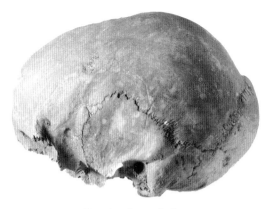

Fig 413 *Female skull of burial 3 showing bathrocrany*

BURIAL 4

Burial of a 2-year-old child. The body was placed in the grave with its hands on top of its pelvis and covered with two boards at c 45° to create a pitched roof effect (Fig 360, c). One of the boards produced a tree-ring date of 1040–76.

BURIAL 5

Burial of a man aged 17–25 years old and 1.68m tall, with a healed fracture of the left ankle. The body was laid out on a rectangular board with its hands by the sides and slightly under the pelvis (Fig 360, d; Fig 367). The head appeared to be supported in an upright fashion by stone and tile fragments placed on either side of it, and another rectangular board was used to cover the body. One of the boards produced a tree-ring date of 1061–90.

BURIAL 6

Burial of a woman aged 36–45 years old, with dental caries and osteoarthritis. The body was contained within an unfastened timber coffin with base board, side boards and a cover board (Fig 367). The base board and side boards were shorter than the body (c 1.46m long), stopping above the ankles, whereas the cover board covered the entire body (c 1.80m long). The head and feet were supported in an upright position by tile and stone fragments placed on one side of the head and either side of the feet. Adjacent to the left side of the body lay a willow/poplar (cf Salicaceae) rod extending from the pelvis to the knee. Three of the four boards (the base board and sides) were from the same tree. One of the boards produced a tree-ring date of ?1061, and another a date of ?1062.

Burials of the third quarter of the 11th century in the southern enclosure (OA102, period 10 phase 1)

All these burials (burials 7–17, Fig 412) were aligned west–east and laid out in a supine position with the head at the west end of the grave. All the wood used for the coffins was of local oak unless otherwise indicated.

BURIAL 7

Burial of a 6-month-old infant. The body was buried with the hands at the sides in a slightly tapered, pegged wooden coffin.

A few peg holes (for c 10mm diameter pegs of ?willow/poplar (cf Salicaceae)) were found along the edge of the lid and the ends of one of the side boards. A rod or stick was found under the base board.

BURIAL 8

Burial of an adolescent. The body was buried in a pegged and nailed wooden coffin. The side boards were nailed through into the end of the foot board and skew-pegged (cf burial 12) at an angle through to the base board. A rod or stick was found under the base board.

BURIAL 9

Burial of a man aged 17–25 years old and 1.64m tall. The body was buried in a nailed wooden coffin, with the sides nailed to the base and the foot board. The foot board produced a tree-ring date of 1041–77 and a side board a date of 1043–79.

BURIAL 10

Burial of an adolescent. The body was buried in a pegged wooden coffin with possible peg holes in the sides and base. The base board was extended by the addition of a short board (c 0.35m long) that was riveted or nailed to the longer board. The foot board produced a tree-ring date of after 1053 and the addition to the base board a date of 1051–?87. Three rods or sticks (one of ?willow/poplar (cf Salicaceae) and two of oak (*Quercus*) were found under the base board, one running along the length of the coffin and the two shorter ones at right angles.

BURIAL 11

Burial of a man aged 26–45 years old and 1.67m tall, with a healed skull wound (Fig 425). The body was buried in a pegged coffin made with thick, knotty, tangentially-cleft planks of oak. The coffin boards were retained for conservation and thus not sampled for tree-ring study, but the planks clearly derive from one or more slow-grown old parent trees (Fig 414). Judging from the large knots and curving grain in the side planks and lid, the parent log(s) used for those elements was probably cut from the upper parts of a large tree. That is quite different from the predominant use of high-quality butt logs for the fine radially-cleft boards used in nearly all the other graves.

The lid plank measured 1.74m long by 510mm wide and 60mm thick, and was somewhat distorted. The timber narrowed down to c 0.38m wide at the foot end, giving the coffin a markedly tapering form. The sapwood had decayed off at the edges, and the plank also had two large knots, which must have made it time-consuming and awkward to hew flat and true after cleaving. An incomplete axe-stop mark 110mm wide and slightly curved was found, and was broadly similar to the axe marks found on the faces of other planks used in the coffin, and on the end grain of several sections. It seems likely that one moderately heavy axe with a slightly curving thin blade over 120mm wide was used for all the smoothing and edge and end cutting. The two side planks were both a little distorted but can be seen to have been c 1.76m long by c 320mm wide and 45–50mm thick. It is quite clear from the shape of the bottom

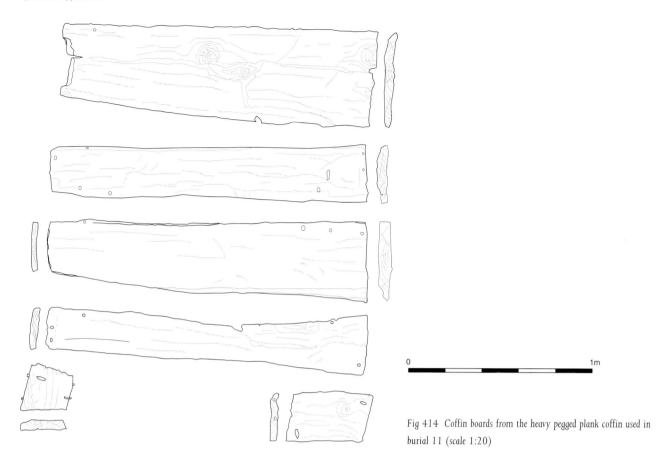

Fig 414 *Coffin boards from the heavy pegged plank coffin used in burial 11 (scale 1:20)*

and end planks that these two planks were markedly twisted and irregular (Fig 414). The base was made from the straightest-grained plank, but had a far from regular outline which had clearly been axe-cut to follow the twisted faces of the side planks. The knotty head board was set with the grain horizontally and was thinner than the other boards at c 35mm thick, while the narrower, 50mm thick foot board was set with the grain vertically. Both end boards had totally skewed quadrilateral shapes without any right angles.

The joining together of such irregular planks to form a coffin must have been challenging, although the thicker edges produced by this method of conversion must have made pegging easier. In fact, it would appear that the coffin was held together with at least three different types of fastenings, although the compression and distortion makes measuring peg hole diameters to a high degree of accuracy impossible. Pegs of c 9–10mm diameter were used in the base-to-sides and base-to-ends fastening, as well as several larger pegs c 18mm in diameter. Some of these pegs were of cleft oak while others were of some type of roundwood. Traces were also found of the use of at least one small iron nail in the lid plank. These additional fixings may have been necessary if the smaller pegs did not hold the heavy planks together sufficiently well.

The bones within the coffin were somewhat displaced.

BURIAL 12
Burial of a young man aged 17–25 years old with a large ossicle at bregma, dental caries and fractures of a rib and the right ulna. The body was buried in a pegged wooden coffin.

This coffin was the best-preserved of the more lightly-made coffins of a rectangular form, although its lid board was too broken and distorted to lift. All the surviving boards were of slow-grown, apparently new, oak (Fig 360, g; Fig 366; Fig 415). They were cleft from a log(s) c 1.0m in diameter from a parent wildwood tree 200–300 years old. Although the boards were clearly axe-trimmed on the faces, some abrasion and superficial decay had prevented clear toolmarks from surviving. The boards were all close to 1.9m long and 25–28mm thick, with the side boards being c 320mm wide and the base wider at 370mm. Both end boards were slightly damaged, and the eastern end seemed to have been split on site and to have lost part of its width. That board also appeared to have a small nail hole which may indicate that it was in second-hand use.

The edges of the boards had been fairly neatly axe-trimmed and the side boards were orientated with their thicker edges up and fastened to the base board by three pegs on each side. Where the side boards butted the thin edge of the base board with its typical wedge-shaped cross-section, the peg holes were deliberately bored to go through at an angle as they could not be accommodated in the thin edge of the base board. This rather surprising method of skew-pegging (cf burial 8) was also encountered in similar light boarded coffins of pre-Conquest date at St Peter's church, Barton-upon-Humber (Rodwell and Rodwell 1982, fig 11; Fig 415, c). The 15mm diameter facetted pegs were made of a pale-coloured wood, probably willow. The western end board was set with its thicker edge down and secured only to the sides with one skew-peg

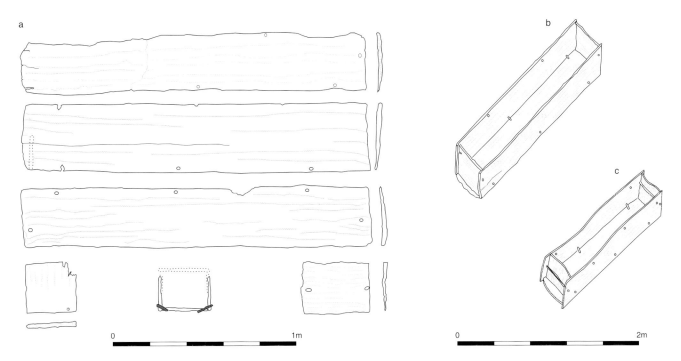

Fig 415 *An example of a light pegged coffin: a – coffin boards used in burial 12 (scale 1:20); b – reconstruction of burial 12 coffin; c – reconstruction of coffin from Barton-upon-Humber (after Rodwell and Rodwell 1982, fig 11) (scale 1:40)*

each side. The more fragmentary eastern end board was apparently set with its grain vertically. The southern side board bore traces of the fastening of the top, with a surviving peg hole, but no traces of other fastenings could be seen, and it is a little uncertain how the lid plank was fastened, if it was at all. It is hard to believe that such a lightly-built coffin could have been made to travel any distance.

The bones within the coffin where somewhat displaced, for example the head had rolled back. Within the coffin, fragments of stone and tile had been placed across the legs and on either side of the head; fragments of stone and tile were also placed on top of the coffin at the foot and head ends of the lid. The base board produced a tree-ring date of after 1052 and pottery from the grave fill dates to c 1050–c 1150.

BURIAL 13

Burial of a woman aged in her 40s with severe osteoarthritis. The body was laid out on a base board and covered with another board, with a further board at the head end of the grave. A redundant peg hole in the base board indicates that it was being reused. The board at the head end of the grave appeared to be too high and may be the remnants of a wooden grave marker; the top of the board had rotted off and its original height is lost. Two redundant peg holes in this board indicate that it too was reused. The body was laid out with its hands together over the pelvis and stones placed on either side of the head, knees and feet. The cover board produced a tree-ring date of 1030–?66.

BURIAL 14

Burial of a woman aged 26–45 years old and 1.54m tall, with severe osteoarthritis. The body was laid out with the hands at

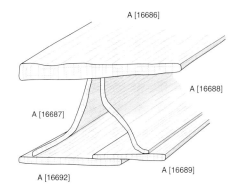

Fig 416 *Detail of collapsed unfastened coffin used in burial 14 (scale 1:20)*

the sides and was contained within an unfastened coffin. The structure consisted of a base made of two overlapping loose boards, two sides (one of beech) and a lid (Fig 364; Fig 416). Fragments of tile, stone and pottery were placed on either side of her head. The tree-ring dates from one of the base boards and a side board are intriguingly early (after AD 701 and AD 666), while the other base board produced a date of 1066–92.

BURIAL 15

Burial of an elderly woman aged over 45 years old, with severe osteoarthritis of the right shoulder joint and right elbow (Fig 417). The body was laid out with the hands at the sides in a pegged coffin. Peg holes and pegs indicated that the sides were pegged through to the end boards (two pegs) and base board (three pegs) and that the lid was fixed to the end boards. Some of these peg holes were skewed. The bones within the coffin where quite displaced. The base board produced a tree-ring date of after 1012.

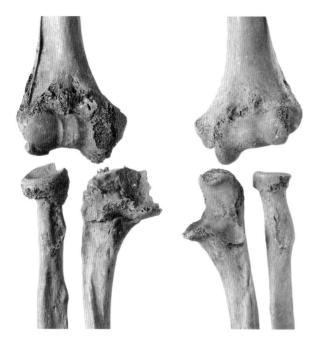

Fig 417 Burial 15, a woman with severe osteoarthritis showing eburnation (polished appearance) and incipient fusion of the right elbow joint

BURIAL 16

Burial of an infant aged about 6 months old. The body was contained within a poorly preserved coffin with a base, sides, ends and a lid; it was unclear whether this coffin had any fixings. The bones within the coffin were quite displaced.

BURIAL 17

Burial of a child aged 9–10 years old. The body was contained within a pegged coffin. The side boards were radially-cleft with the thick edge butted up to the base board. Each side of the coffin was fixed to the base board by three pegs through the base and into the edge of the side board (unlike the skewed pegs used in burial 13). The pegs that survived were of squared oak 8–10mm across. Two large fragments of tile and stone had been placed on the corners of the coffin lid at the head end. The bones within the coffin were quite displaced. One of the side boards produced a tree-ring date of 1036–68 and the base board a date of ?1046.

Early 12th-century burials (OA108, period 10 phase 4)

All these burials (burials 18–20, Fig 418) were aligned west–east and laid out in a supine position with the head at the west end of the grave. All the wood used for the coffins was of local oak unless otherwise indicated.

BURIAL 18

Burial of a man aged over 45 years and 1.71m tall, with a healed cranial wound and fractures to the ribs and fingers (Fig 425). Most of his teeth had been lost during his life and he also suffered from osteoarthritis. The body was laid out on a number

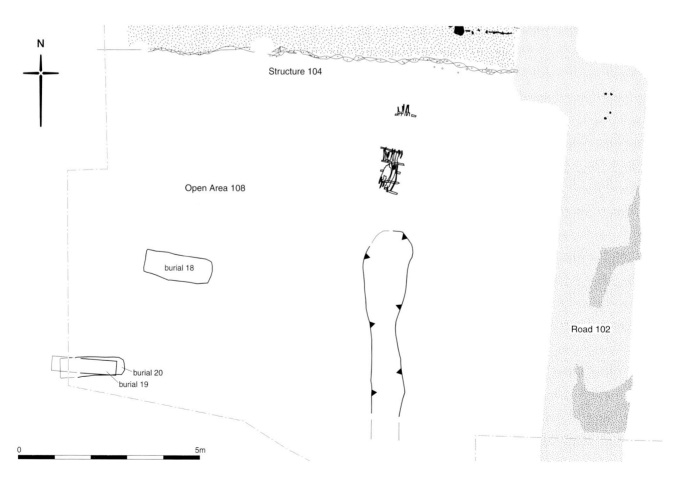

Fig 418 Plan of early 12th-century burials (burials 18–20) in the churchyard of St Lawrence Jewry (scale 1:100)

of thin planks which did not extend under the entire body. There were the decayed remnants of two side boards but no end boards. A single stone was placed against the left side of the head, perhaps to keep it in an upright position (Fig 365). After the body was placed in the grave, five or six regularly spaced sticks were placed across the body, presumably resting on the tops of the side boards (these sticks were originally thought to be wands: Bateman 2000, 48). This framework of sticks supported three thin beech boards which covered the body from the head to just above the ankles (Fig 360, f). One of the boards produced a tree-ring date of after 1080.

BURIAL 19

Burial of a man of indeterminate age with severe osteoarthritis in both knees. The body was buried in a pegged beech coffin; oblique peg holes show that the sides were skew-pegged to the base and foot end of the coffin. One of the pegs was c 8mm in diameter and made from ?willow/poplar (cf Salicaceae). The base board produced a tree-ring date of after 1096 and the foot board a date of after 1095.

BURIAL 20

Burial of an adult of indeterminate sex. The body was laid out with the hands in the centre of the pelvis and with a number of thin sticks lying parallel to and either side of it (Fig 369). The body was first placed in the grave and the 'coffin' assembled around it, consisting of two side boards and a cover

board made of radially-cleft beech that produced a tree-ring date of after 1096. These boards only covered the body to just below the knees.

Late 12th-century burials (OA115, period 11 phase 3)

All these burials (burials 21–45, Fig 419) were aligned east–west and laid out in a supine position with the head at the west end of the grave. All the wood used for the coffins was of local oak unless otherwise indicated.

BURIAL 21

Burial of a woman aged 26–45 years old. No surviving evidence for a coffin.

BURIAL 22

Burial of three people placed side by side and head to head in the same grave-cut: an adolescent in the middle, with a man (17–25 years old, 1.61m tall) to the north and another man (17–25 years old, with bathrocrany and dental caries) to the south. All three bodies were placed in the grave lying slightly on their left sides, and none had any surviving evidence for a coffin.

BURIAL 23

Burial of a child aged 10 years old, covered by an oak plank from the face down. The plank produced a tree-ring date of 1141–54.

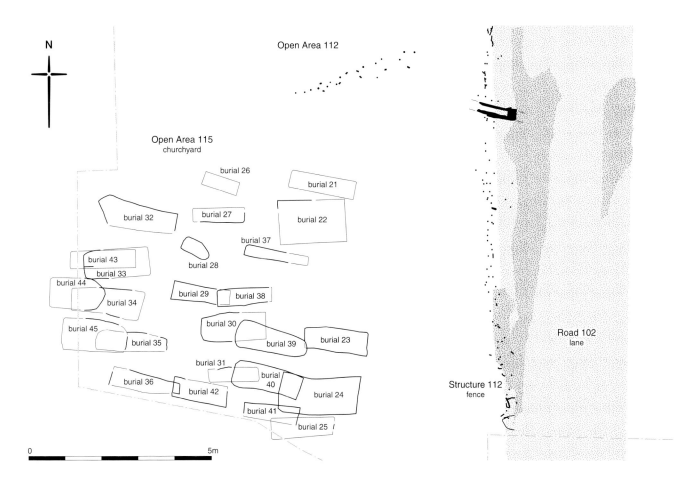

Fig 419 Plan of late 12th-century burials (burials 21–45) in the churchyard of St Lawrence Jewry (scale 1:100)

BURIAL 24

Double burial of a woman aged 17–25 years old and 1.56m tall, and a child aged 6–9 years old. The bodies were placed in the grave next to each other (head to head) and four branches or poles laid across them. Four radially-cleft oak boards were laid over the branches and entirely covered the bodies (Fig 360, b; Fig 361). The planks were of equal size and produced a combined tree-ring date of 1137–?71.

BURIAL 25

Burial of an adult, heavily truncated. No surviving evidence for a coffin.

BURIAL 26

Burial of a child aged 9 years old. No surviving evidence for a coffin.

BURIAL 27

Burial of an adolescent. No surviving evidence for a coffin.

BURIAL 28

Burial of a child aged about 18 months. No surviving evidence for a coffin.

BURIAL 29

Burial of a child aged 7 years old. The child was put in the grave and a single plank placed over the entire body. It is likely that this burial was in the same grave-cut as an adult buried in some form of coffin that was too decayed to record in any detail. The two bodies almost exactly overlay each other (head to head), with little or no gap between them, and thus are likely to have been buried at the same time. This burial is matched by a later burial to the west (burial 38).

BURIAL 30

Double burial of a 2–3-year-old child and a man aged 26–45 years old with Schmorl's nodes. The child was laid next to the man (head to head) and both the bodies were then covered with an oak plank, which produced a tree-ring date of 1124–?60. The plank did not cover their heads or the entire body of the child.

BURIAL 31

Burial of a child aged 9–12 years old, heavily truncated. No surviving evidence for a coffin.

BURIAL 32

Burial of a woman aged 17–25 years old and 1.52m tall, who suffered from osteoarthritis and had a healed ankle fracture. The body was entirely covered by a tangentially-faced oak plank. Residual pottery and early roofing tile from the grave fill dates to c 1135–c 1200.

BURIAL 33

Burial of a man aged 26–45 years old who suffered from osteoarthritis. No surviving evidence for a coffin.

BURIAL 34

Burial of a man aged 17–25 years old and 1.73m tall, who suffered from Osgood-Schlatter disease. No surviving evidence for a coffin.

BURIAL 35

Burial of a ?woman aged 26–45 years old and 1.59m tall, who suffered from severe osteoarthritis of the right knee joint (Fig 420). No surviving evidence for a coffin. An iron padlock A<236> was found in the torso region of the body. Residual pottery and early roofing tile from the grave fill dates to c 1135–c 1220.

BURIAL 36

Burial of an adolescent laid on a thin layer (c 20mm thick) of fine fragments of a white chalk-like material that covered the base of the grave-cut. The body was then entirely covered with a single oak plank.

BURIAL 37

Burial of an adult. No surviving evidence for a coffin.

BURIAL 38

Burial of an adolescent with cribra orbitalia. The body was buried in some form of wooden coffin of which only the lid survived well enough to be recorded in any detail. The foot end of the cover board, which produced a tree-ring date of 1127–?63, appeared to be axe-cut to a point. An adult in almost exactly the same location overlay the adolescent with little or no gap between the burials, and thus is likely to have been buried at the same time in the same grave-cut. The adult was buried in some form of coffin, of which only the base and sides survived in too decayed a condition to record in any detail. Unusually, the hands lay in the centre of the pelvis.

BURIAL 39

Burial of a man aged 26–45 years old and 1.81m tall, who had a rib fracture and suffered from osteoarthritis, dental caries and abscess. The body, wrapped in a shroud, was laid out on a boat-

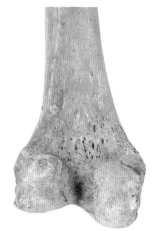

Fig 420 Burial 35, *probably a woman who had osteoarthritis, showing eburnation of the distal femur*

shaped bier and tied on with willow rope secured through small holes around the edge of the oak board. The bier and body could then be carried from the church to the churchyard and lowered into the grave, after which the body was covered with a rectangular oak plank. A small roundwood pole or staff c 60mm in diameter and 1.58m long, with axe-cut ends and the bark left on, was found laid along the right side of the body.

The bier timber used was a very wide, radially-split board of oak 2.03m long by 580mm wide and c 30mm thick, with a little sapwood left on (Fig 363; Fig 421). At the time of writing this is the widest recorded radially-split oak board excavated in London, and it must have been cleft from a very large straight-grained log a minimum of c 1.2m in diameter if the pith was off-centre, but with a more likely diameter of at least c 1.4m, allowing for the missing sapwood, bark and a little heart edge. The timber was of slow, regular growth. The surface of the board was in fairly good condition and faint, incomplete axe-stop marks survived up to 130mm wide, with slightly dished facets c 200mm wide, from the trimming of the 'as-cleft' torn surface. The axe used appears to have had a slightly curved, thin blade c 200mm wide or slightly more. An axe had also been used to trim the edges of the board to a lop-sided oval or boat-like shape; the reasons for using this unique shape are unclear, and no traces of it having been second-hand were found.

Around the perimeter of the board were 25 auger holes (c 10mm diameter) with a further four bored around the head end. Sections of pale-coloured roundwood (probably 1-year-old willow) were found in the holes, with the clear implication that damp, fine rods were used as a form of rope to bind the corpse on to the bier. Two perpendicularly aligned pairs of flattened fine rods (c 6mm diameter) could be seen impressed on to the underside of the cover board and may be the remnants of

binding. In one place, the concave 'dibit' of an unfinished spoon auger hole was found, indicating the form of bit used for drilling the holes.

The covering timber was a slightly decayed and truncated, tangentially-cleft and hewn oak plank. The timber survived 1.97m long by 500mm wide and 50mm thick. The damaged ends were sampled and found to have come from a slow-grown tree over 180 years old, but they could not be dated.

Traces of what appears to have been part of a coarse textile shroud or clothing were found impressed into the surface of the bier and underside of the covering plank in several places, and fragments of textile were also found on the body and legs.

The boat-shaped board was not sampled as it was selected for conservation, but a fragment of oak plank found underneath the bier produced a tree-ring date of after 1128.

BURIAL 40
Burial of a woman aged 26–45 years old (the pelvic bones of a child were collected with the adult bones). The body was laid in the grave and a bundle of four thin wooden rods or ?wands placed along its right side. The rods retained their bark and were 6–8mm in diameter and c 0.55m long; at the east end of the bundle was a copper-alloy bell (Fig 368). The bell is made of cast copper alloy and has an open-mouth form; the suspension tab at the top is broken off and the internal loop with clapper is also missing (the surviving dimensions are 26mm high and 28mm deep at the mouth). The interred body was entirely covered by an oak plank less distorted than most cover boards but otherwise typical of many examples from the churchyard (Fig 360, a). It was rectangular, 1.74m long by 425mm wide and c 30mm thick, with neatly axe-cut ends with some sapwood left on (Fig 422). It had been radially cleft and

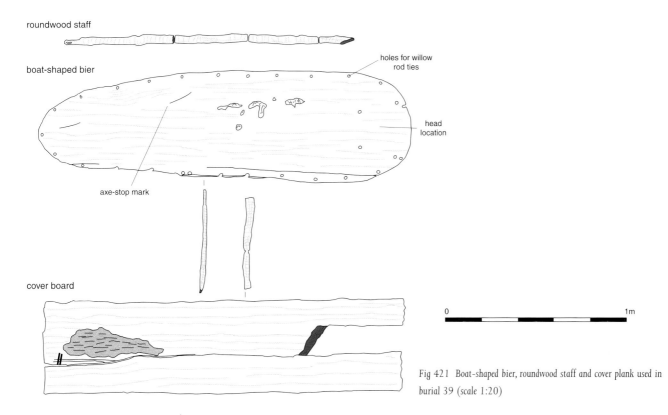

roundwood staff

boat-shaped bier

holes for willow rod ties

head location

axe-stop mark

cover board

0　　　　　　　　　　　　　　1m

Fig 421 *Boat-shaped bier, roundwood staff and cover plank used in burial 39 (scale 1:20)*

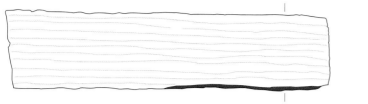

Fig 422 Cover board from burial 40 (scale 1:20)

hewn from a straight-grained oak log at least 1.1m in diameter which came from a slow-growing tree *c* 220–230 years old and of typical wildwood character. No clear toolmarks survived on the slightly eroded surfaces. Even in this simple construction, apparently new timber of good quality was used. The cover board produced a tree-ring date of 1150.

BURIAL 41

Burial of a child aged 7–8 years old with cribra orbitalia. The child was first laid in the grave and a single plank then placed over the entire body. Residual pottery and early roofing tile from the grave fill dates to *c* 1135–*c* 1220.

BURIAL 42

Burial of a 9-year-old child. No surviving evidence for a coffin.

BURIAL 43

Heavily truncated burial. No surviving evidence for a coffin.

BURIAL 44

Burial of an adolescent. The body was placed on a board in the grave and covered by another board. Both boards were too decayed to be recorded in detail.

BURIAL 45

Double burial of an adult, aged 17–25 years old, and an adolescent. The bodies were placed next to each other (head to head). No surviving evidence for a coffin or coffins. Residual pottery from the grave fill dates to *c* 1080–*c* 1200.

Early 13th-century burials (OA115, period 11 phase 4)

All these burials (burials 46–63, Fig 423) were aligned east–west and laid out in a supine position with the head at the west end of the grave. All the wood used for the coffins was of local oak unless otherwise indicated.

BURIAL 46

Burial of an elderly woman aged over 45 years old. The body was placed in a complete wooden coffin (whether pegged or unfastened is unclear). The base board of the coffin had clearly been reused and produced a tree-ring date of after 1205.

BURIAL 47

Burial of a man aged 17–25 years old and 1.71m tall, with Schmorl's nodes and spondylisis of the fifth lumbar vertebra. He was buried in a complete tapered wooden coffin (whether pegged or unfastened is unclear). The vertebrae and ribs were displaced but still lay between the arms. Residual pottery and early roofing tile from the grave fill dates to *c* 1140–*c* 1200.

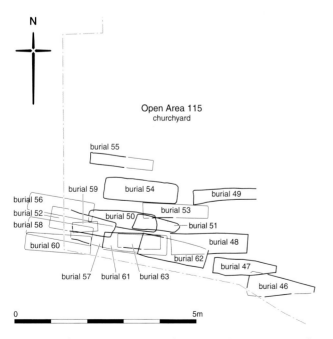

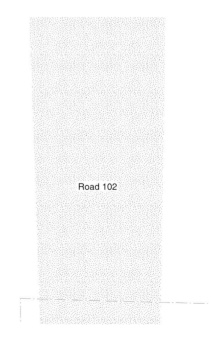

Fig 423 Plan of early 13th-century burials (burials 46–63) in the churchyard of St Lawrence Jewry (scale 1:100)

BURIAL 48

Burial of a man in his 30s and 1.61m tall, with osteoarthritis and Schmorl's nodes. He was buried in an almost complete tapered wooden coffin with base, sides, foot board and lid but no head board. There was no indication of how or whether the sides and base were joined. The base board produced a tree-ring date of 1146–52.

BURIAL 49

Burial of a woman aged 26–45 years old. The body was placed in a coffin, which employed two reused radially-cleft oak planks for the base, and had sides and ends but no lid. It was unclear how the different elements were joined together or whether the coffin was unfastened and assembled in the grave. One of the base boards produced a tree-ring date of after 1222.

BURIAL 50

Burial of a woman aged 26–45 years old and 1.51m tall. No surviving evidence for a coffin.

BURIAL 51

Burial of an adolescent. After the body had been placed in the grave, it was covered with a single oak plank. Residual pottery and early roofing tile from the grave fill dates to c 1135–c 1220.

BURIAL 52

Burial of a woman aged 17–25 years old and 1.54m tall, with spina bifida occulta. The body was laid out on a bier, which tapered towards the foot end, and tied on with rope secured through small holes around the edge of the oak board. The bier board used was a radially-cleft oak plank with faint, broad axe marks on the underside. Around the perimeter of the board were regularly spaced holes (c 15mm diameter), with a fragment of fibre or wood surviving in one of them. The bier and body could then be carried from the church to the churchyard and lowered into the grave, after which the body was covered with a rectangular plank (radially-cleft and hewn). The length of oak plank used was very knotty, and may have been an offcut rejected for other use. The bier board produced a tree-ring date of 1134–81 and residual pottery from the grave fill dates to c 1170–c 1240. The use of a base board with holes around the edge is also seen in burial 39.

BURIAL 53

Burial of an adult, heavily truncated. No surviving evidence for a coffin.

BURIAL 54

Burial of a man aged 26–30 years old and 1.73m tall. A number of stones were placed along or under the right side of the body, and the entire body was covered with a single board which tapered slightly towards the feet.

BURIAL 55

Burial of a woman aged 17–25 years old with a retained lower deciduous molar and spondylisis of the fifth lumbar vertebra. She was buried in some form of coffin which only survived as a stain.

BURIAL 56

Burial of an adult possibly interred in some form of coffin, as indicated by an organic deposit beneath the surviving body.

BURIAL 57

Burial of an adult in a nailed wooden coffin with lid, sides, ends and base. The coffin tapered towards the foot end, with the sides nailed through to the foot and head boards. The lid was also nailed through to the head and foot boards. The bones of the torso as well as the skull were somewhat displaced, which probably relates to the rare use of a full coffin well secured with nails. Residual pottery from the grave fill dates to c 1170–c 1240.

BURIAL 58

Burial of an adult, heavily truncated. No surviving evidence for a coffin.

BURIAL 59

Burial of a child. No surviving evidence for a coffin.

BURIAL 60

Burial of an adult. No surviving evidence for a coffin.

BURIAL 61

Burial of a woman aged 26–45 years old and 1.61m tall, with Schmorl's nodes. She was buried in a tapered wooden coffin, the sides and base of which only survived as stains while the lid had collapsed on to the body. Residual pottery from the grave fill dates to c 1170–c 1240.

BURIAL 62

Burial of woman aged 35–39 years old and 1.68m tall, with dental caries and osteoarthritis. She was buried in a complete wooden coffin.

BURIAL 63

Burial of an adult, heavily truncated. No surviving evidence for a coffin.

Mid 13th-century burials (OA140, period 12)

Both these burials (burials 64–65, Fig 424) were aligned east–west and laid out in a supine position with the head at the west end of the grave.

BURIAL 64

Burial of a man over 45 years old. No surviving evidence for a coffin. This burial was subjected to radiocarbon dating (below, 8.20), which produced a date of 1260–1410 cal AD at 95% confidence level.

BURIAL 65

Burial recorded in section only; no human remains recovered.

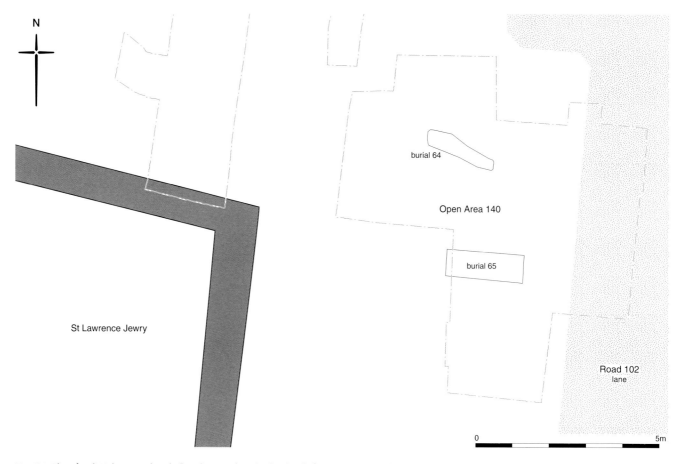

N

burial 64

Open Area 140

burial 65

Road 102
lane

St Lawrence Jewry

0   5m

Fig 424 Plan of mid 13th-century burials (burials 64–65) in the churchyard of St Lawrence Jewry (scale 1:100)

8.18 Human bones

William White

Introduction

The human bones from the medieval St Lawrence Jewry churchyard (OA101, OA102, OA108, OA115 and OA140, periods 10–12) were analysed in detail. Of the 72 people buried in 65 graves, 64 were available for full analysis along with three skulls from a contemporary pit.

Given the circumstances of excavation, the incomplete human bone assemblage from later medieval or post-medieval burials from the same churchyard (Chapter 4.3) did not warrant full analysis. In view of the small size of the surviving sample (five individuals) from the post-medieval burials in the Guildhall chapel (Chapter 4.5) they were only assessed for age and sex data and not subjected to full analysis. Full details of the analysis are available in the human bone research archive (White 2002). The 19th-century burials excavated in the St Lawrence Jewry 'Little Vault' have already been published (Bateman and Miles 1999, 130–9).

Preservation

The human bone tended to be well preserved in the earlier medieval burials but the post-medieval burials tended to be in a poorer state of preservation. Despite truncation of some of the burials, skeletal integrity generally was good, with 70% having more than half of the skeleton preserved. Indeed, 60% had more than 75% of the skeleton present at examination. This excellent recovery had an influence upon the extraction of information and on sex determination, in particular. The physical condition on each skeleton was scored on a scale of 1 to 3, and nearly all of the bone of medieval date fell into the best category, providing the bulk of the information that could be derived from a skeleton, including an estimate of the stature of the living individual in untruncated cases.

Methodology

The age of any immature individuals was estimated using dental development and state of epiphyseal fusion (Bass 1995, 13–15; Brothwell 1981, 64–7) and diaphyseal lengths (Sundick 1978; Hoffman 1979; Ferembach et al 1980; Ubelaker 1984, 46–53; Powers 1988), and of adults using tooth wear stages (Brothwell 1981, 71–2) and morphology of the pubic symphysis (Brooks and Suchey 1990). Sex was determined using skull and pelvic dimorphism (Phenice 1969; Ferembach et al 1980; Brothwell 1981, 59–63). Complementary data for sex determination was sought metrically (Bass 1995) but priority was given to the results of examination of the pelvis because this was regarded as the most reliable of the available techniques.

Conventional cranial and post-cranial measurements were

taken (Bass 1995, 68–81; Brothwell 1981, 79–87) and long-bone lengths were employed in the estimation of stature using the regression equations established by Trotter and Gleser (1952; 1958). Non-metric traits were recorded (Berry and Berry 1967; Finnegan 1978) and where appropriate tested in the elucidation of family relationship.

The jaws were examined for non-metric traits, dental hygiene and pathology (Berry 1978; Hillson 1986). Information on general pathology was recorded (Ortner and Putschar 1981), as was the evidence for infectious disease (Rogers and Waldron 1989), joint disease (Rogers and Waldron 1995) and epidemiology (Waldron 1994).

The subsamples of the population buried in the cemetery during periods 10–12 were too small for separate analysis, so data presented here are for the entire medieval sample. Osteological details of individual burials are integrated in the burial catalogue along with all other aspects of the burial (above, 8.17).

Human variation

Sex

Across periods 10 and 11 there were roughly equal numbers of men and women, with a slight preponderance of males in the earlier period and the reverse in the later one (Table 9; CD Table 56; CD Table 57). However, the numbers were too small to be of statistical significance.

Age

There was a relatively high proportion of immature persons buried in the cemetery (32.8%). There were no neonates but about half of the non-adults had survived into adolescence (Table 9; CD Table 56; CD Table 57). This is a rare finding in cemeteries of any date. The best-known example of burials with a high proportion of adolescents occurred in one of the cemetery areas at St Mary Spital, London (Conheeney 1997, 222).

Most of the adults (80%) could have an age assigned to them. However, only 10% of the adults, or 6% of the medieval sample, were demonstrably over the age of 45 when they died. This proportion is rather low for medieval London.

Table 9 Combined sex and age analysis of the burials from periods 10–12

Age group (yrs)	Male	?Male	Sex Unknown	?Female	Female	Total
1–5			5			5
6–12			8			8
13–16			9			9
17–25	8	1	1		5	15
26–45	7				10	17
45+	2				2	4
Unknown		1	7	1		9
Total	17	2	30	1	17	67

Metric variation

Stature

Stature estimates are usually more reliable based on the bones of the leg, rather than of the arm, in using the appropriate regression equations (Trotter and Gleser 1952; 1958). Choosing the left femur as the bone to be used in height calculations, stature could be estimated for 20 medieval adults from the site. Nine women ranged in height from 1.51m to 1.68m (mean 1.57m). The range for 11 men was from 1.61m to 1.81m (mean 1.71m). Stature therefore was comparable to other medieval sites (CD Table 58).

Physique

Several skulls were sufficiently intact for craniometry. The cranial index, based on 11 skulls, was 78.5. The population as a whole was therefore mesocranic (Brothwell 1981, 87). The same is true of other early medieval samples from London (eg St Nicholas Shambles) and has a bearing upon the 'transitional' nature of the Saxo-Norman population (Palliser 1980, 82; White 1988, 30–1).

The customary measurements were made upon the antero-posterior and medio-lateral diameters of the proximal shafts of both femora. The aim was to look for evidence of antero-posterior flattening of this part of the bone, possibly caused by adaptation to mechanical forces on the appropriate muscles as the result of manual work or other environmental effects (Wells 1964, 132). The Meric Index (the ratio of the antero-posterior to the medio-lateral diameter x100) is an expression of the degree of shaft flattening: a value of 84.9 or less showing platymeria, and a value of 85.0 or more showing a greater tendency to roundness of the shaft (eurymeria).

For females the mean Meric Index for the right and left femora was 73.2 and 73.1 respectively, while for males the means were 78.0 and 77.9. The differences between the sexes are not statistically significant, there merely being a tendency to a flattening of the femur shaft in both. With both sexes affected equally, it is difficult to see an occupational reason underlying such an observation. However, it is interesting that the men and women from the site were platymeric because most large series of post-medieval skeletons examined have been eurymeric. The Guildhall skeletons are comparable to those from other medieval sites in the London area, which are also borderline platymeric.

Non-metric variation

Where skulls were sufficiently undamaged they were examined superficially and their features assigned to subjective categories. Discontinuous or non-metric variation in the human skeleton has a heritable element and has been used in attempts to deduce the presence of family groups in a cemetery. The skeletons were examined for cranial and post-cranial traits, and evidence was found for certain epigenetic traits.

The traits were recorded and attempts made to find clusters of non-metric variation indicative of family burial plots. This approach was inconclusive, and in particular there was no osteological evidence that the two occupants of each double grave were close family members.

General pathology

Conditions of the spine and joints

OSTEOARTHRITIS

As is usual for an attrition cemetery, the most frequently encountered expression of pathology was osteoarthritis of the joints and the spine. During period 10 the degeneration of elements in the vertebral column appeared universal in everyone over the age of 25 years. In addition some individuals exhibited 'wear and tear' of a particular limb joint. Joints affected included the shoulder, elbow, wrist, knee and ankle.

DISH

Diffuse idiopathic skeletal hyperostosis (DISH) is a disease that affects predominantly males over the age of 50 who are obese and living on a calorie-rich diet, and may be linked to late-onset diabetes (Rogers and Waldron 2001, 260). None of the skeletons showed any evidence of DISH.

SCHMORL'S NODES

Schmorl's nodes are herniations in the vertebral body caused by prolapse of the intervertebral disc, and are thought to result from stress or strain during adolescence or early adult life. They are more common in males than in females. At this site Schmorl's nodes were equally present in both sexes in the later medieval period but were entirely lacking during period 10.

SPINA BIFIDA

Spina bifida occulta is a symptomless condition caused by the failure of one or more of the arches in the neural canal of the sacrum to fuse. It may be congenital in origin. None of the skeletons from the site had all five arches open. There was a single example of partial spina bifida occulta, with three neural arches open, but the overall prevalence of the complete condition obviously was much lower than today (5–10%).

Trauma

FRACTURES

Healed fractures were seen chiefly in the ribcage. There were isolated examples of a fracture of an ulna, one of the hand and two of the ankle.

INTER-PERSONAL VIOLENCE

An older man from Open Area 108 showed multiple wounds (burial 18, Fig 425). He had a healed cranial injury, possibly representing a depressed fracture caused by a blow. In addition, he had healed fractures of two ribs and of some of the metacarpals of the left hand. Another man showed a well-healed injury from an edged weapon on the right side of the coronal suture (burial 11, Fig 425).

Surgery

A mature woman from the early cemetery phase showed evidence of a well-healed trepanation (burial 3, Fig 426). Trepanation appears to be rare in medieval skeletons from London. This example is earlier in date than the two so far known from St Mary Spital (B Connell, pers comm). Many Anglo-Saxon examples are recorded from other parts of England (Lucy 2000, 72). It is believed that the operation performed in antiquity was done probably for the same reason as modern trephination, to relieve pressure on the brain (often caused by blood clotting).

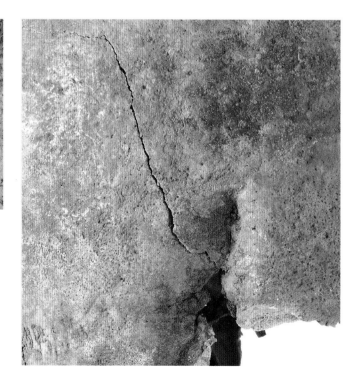

Fig 425 *Examples of inter-personal violence: a healed depressed fracture of the skull and healed metatarsal fracture in the same individual (burial 18) and a healed cranial injury (burial 11)*

Fig 426 *Calvarium with healed trepanation in a mature woman (burial 3)*

Other acquired disease

The bones of the left leg of an older woman (burial 16) were much more slender than the right. This limb appears to have wasted or become atrophied through disuse, perhaps because of paralysis.

Infections

Non-specific infections

Periostitis (inflammation of the bone surface) was present in the lower legs of several women, men and adults of unknown sex. The low prevalence (2% of possible cases) resembles that of a rural community rather than one in an urban environment (Manchester 1992; Mays 1997, 124).

Specific infections

Tuberculosis primarily affects the soft tissues but bone can be involved in 3–5% of cases. However, no instances of tuberculosis were observed in the spines or joints of any of the people from this site.

Dietary and developmental conditions

Mineral deficiency

Pitting seen in the upper part of the eye sockets may be caused by a diet that is deficient in iron, possibly made worse by internal parasites. This condition was observed in several children from the site.

Vitamin deficiency

There was no evidence of rickets (caused by a deficiency of vitamin D in the diet) or scurvy (caused by vitamin C deficiency).

Developmental conditions

A young man had suffered from Osgood-Schlatter disease (burial 34). This may have been caused by over-exercise of the knee joints during adolescence.

Neoplasms

There were no malignant bone tumours. One of the three skulls found in the same pit (OA102, period 10) had a large benign osteoma on the posterior arc of the sagittal suture.

Dental disease

Dental calculus accumulation on the teeth of the population was rather light, suggesting that there was some form of regular tooth-cleaning habit. Periodontal disease was rare. Loss of teeth during life was 3.6% but dental abscess formation was low (<1%). Dental caries infection was very low at 5.9% overall, which is consistent with the low prevalence in Anglo-Saxon and early medieval England, such as at Raunds, Northamptonshire (Powell 1996, 124) or St Nicholas Shambles, London (White 1988, 44).

8.19 Tree-ring analysis of medieval timbers

Ian Tyers

Introduction

Some 1200 timbers were sampled during and after the excavations by either the field team, the wood recording team or the author. Interim spot-dates on some of the medieval samples were produced between 1993 and 1995. In particular, the sampling and analysis of the coffin boards were undertaken during the excavation and recording of this delicate and fragile material. The rest of the material was catalogued, and stored until it was assessed and analysed in 2000–1. The remaining analytical work, the compilation of the final archive report incorporating the interpretative stratigraphic framework, and the publication text were completed in 2003 (Tyers 2003). The information in this monograph synthesises this work. Details of the results from individual samples from these excavations are not provided here but may be referred to in the research archive (ibid). The dating tables accompanying the chronological narrative include the tree-ring dating for the earlier medieval periods.

A near-complete sampling strategy was implemented to maximise the potential of dendrochronology for such a complex, multi-period and deeply stratified site. A number of timbers suitable for dendrochronological analysis were diverted to conservation and have not been sampled.

The number of samples analysed was significantly lower since many were unsuitable for dendrochronological analysis; some were of unsuitable species, others contained too few rings, and others again presented anatomical problems that prevented reliable measurement.

Dendrochronology or tree-ring dating

A general guide to dendrochronology has been published by English Heritage (1998), and the principles and limitations of the method as applied to complex archaeological sites in London are discussed in greater detail by Watson et al (2001, 3, 180–90). To summarise, tree-ring dating employs the patterns of tree-growth to determine the calendar dates for the period during which the sampled trees were alive. The amount of wood laid down in any one year by most trees is determined by the climate and other environmental factors. Trees can exhibit similar patterns of growth over relatively wide geographical areas, and this enables dendrochronologists to assign dates to some samples by matching the growth pattern with other ring sequences that have already been linked together to form reference chronologies.

The successful matching of a particular ring sequence with a specific reference chronology, while providing absolute calendar dates for the ring sequence, does not in itself always provide a precise date for the felling of that tree. This is because the full complement of rings to the bark-edge of the tree is required for the felling date to be established with annual precision, and these outermost rings are often missing. There are several reasons why many of the samples considered here had an incomplete sequence and, as a consequence, can not be used to provide a precise date for the construction of the structure with which they were associated. Firstly, the outermost sapwood rings of an oak tree are significantly less resistant to physical damage and to insect and fungal attack than the heartwood, and so do not often survive burial and excavation. Secondly, sapwood is often removed during the physical conversion of the whole, round log into a usable timber.

Interpretation of the dates

The interpretation of the dates depends upon the nature of the final rings in the sample. If the sample ends in the heartwood of the original tree, a *terminus post quem* for the felling of the tree is indicated by the date of the last ring plus the addition of the minimum expected number of sapwood rings that are likely to be missing. This is expressed in the dating tables and text thus: after 1060 (note that this date may be many decades prior to the true felling date). A different level of interpretation is possible where some of the outer sapwood or the heartwood/sapwood boundary survives on the sample; here a felling date range can be calculated using the maximum and minimum numbers of sapwood rings likely to have been present. This is expressed in the dating tables and text thus: 1060–80. The most precise level of interpretation occurs where the bark-edge survives, in which case a felling date can be directly derived from the date of the last surviving ring. This is expressed in the dating tables and text thus: 1066. Both the latter interpretations can be qualified by a question mark when there is only a tentative identification of either the heartwood/sapwood boundary (eg 1030–?60) or the bark-edge (eg ?1060) because the physical condition of the sample prevents the certain identification of these surfaces. Where more than one dated timber is present in a structure, the combined interpretation is obtained by calculating the narrowest date range common to each dated component within the group. The sapwood estimates used in this publication are a minimum of ten and maximum of 46 annual rings, where these figures indicate the 95% confidence limits of the range. These figures are applicable to oaks from England and Wales (Tyers 1998).

The dates obtained by tree-ring analysis do not by themselves necessarily indicate the date of the structure from which they are derived. It is necessary to incorporate other specialist evidence concerning the reuse of timbers and the repair of structures before the dates can be reliably interpreted as reflecting the construction date of individual phases.

Medieval timbers

In total the sequences from 120 post-Roman samples were successfully dated, all from site A. They provide mostly 11th-century dates for period 10 and later 11th- or early 12th-century dates for period 11; except for a single dated timber from period 13, none of the other post-Roman periods on the sites produced dendrochronologically suitable material (Fig 427). The results are given in summary form in the dating tables in the chronological narrative, and in discussion of some of the individual structures and artefacts. Of particular significance are the results from the coffins (Chapter 6.12; above, 8.17) and the identification of an early example of an imported barrel (Chapter 6.2, 'Cooperage finds').

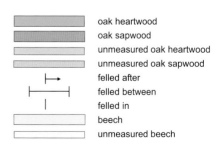

Fig 427 (*right and over*) *Bar diagram of dated medieval timbers from periods 10, 11 and 13 (for key see above)*

Period 10

Span of ring sequences

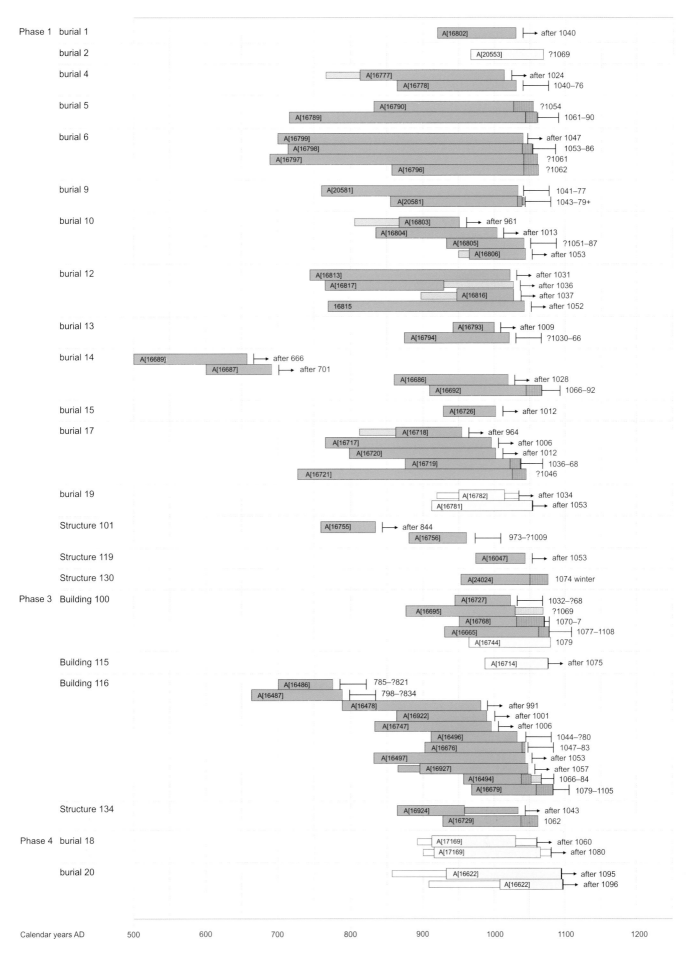

Phase 1 burial 1   A[16802]   → after 1040

burial 2   A[20553]   ?1069

burial 4   A[16777] → after 1024   A[16778] 1040–76

burial 5   A[16790] ?1054   A[16789] 1061–90

burial 6   A[16799] → after 1047   A[16798] 1053–86   A[16797] ?1061   A[16796] ?1062

burial 9   A[20581] 1041–77   A[20581] 1043–79+

burial 10   A[16803] → after 961   A[16804] → after 1013   A[16805] ?1051–87   A[16806] → after 1053

burial 12   A[16813] → after 1031   A[16817] → after 1036   A[16816] → after 1037   16815 → after 1052

burial 13   A[16793] → after 1009   A[16794] ?1030–66

burial 14   A[16689] → after 666   A[16687] → after 701   A[16686] → after 1028   A[16692] 1066–92

burial 15   A[16726] → after 1012

burial 17   A[16718] → after 964   A[16717] → after 1006   A[16720] → after 1012   A[16719] 1036–68   A[16721] ?1046

burial 19   A[16782] → after 1034   A[16781] → after 1053

Structure 101   A[16755] → after 844   A[16756] 973–?1009

Structure 119   A[16047] → after 1053

Structure 130   A[24024] 1074 winter

Phase 3 Building 100   A[16727] 1032–?68   A[16695] ?1069   A[16768] 1070–7   A[16665] 1077–1108   A[16744] 1079

Building 115   A[16714] → after 1075

Building 116   A[16486] 785–?821   A[16487] 798–?834   A[16478] → after 991   A[16922] after 1001   A[16747] → after 1006   A[16496] 1044–?80   A[16676] 1047–83   A[16497] → after 1053   A[16927] → after 1057   A[16494] 1066–84   A[16679] 1079–1105

Structure 134   A[16924] → after 1043   A[16729] 1062

Phase 4 burial 18   A[17169] → after 1060   A[17169] → after 1080

burial 20   A[16622] → after 1095   A[16622] → after 1096

Calendar years AD   500   600   700   800   900   1000   1100   1200

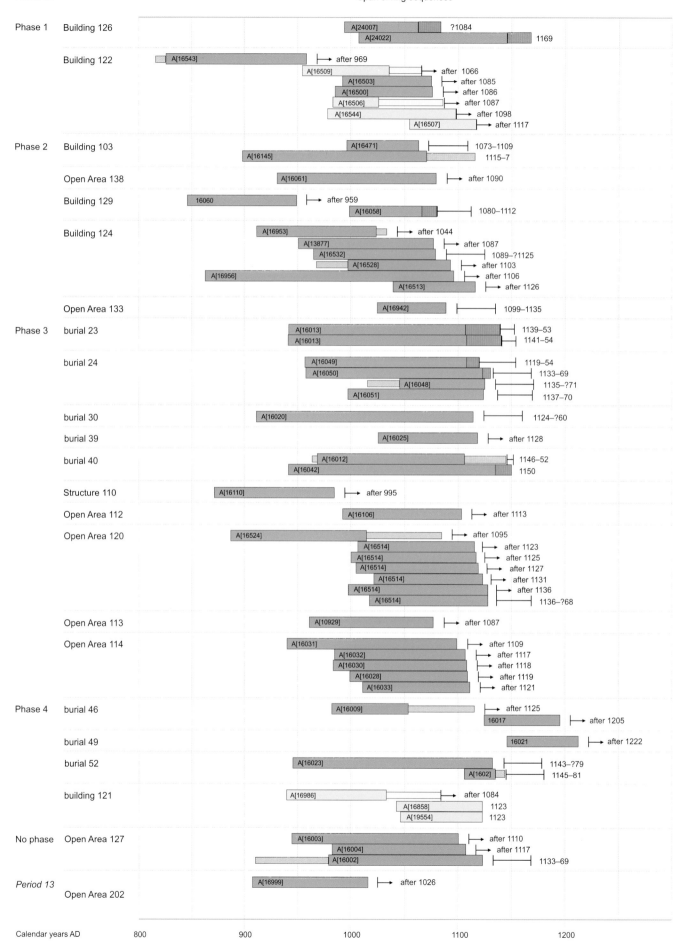

Period 11

Span of ring sequences

Phase 1 · Building 126 · A[24007] ?1084 · A[24022] 1169

Building 122 · A[16543] after 969 · A[16509] after 1066 · A[16503] after 1085 · A[16500] after 1086 · A[16506] after 1087 · A[16544] after 1098 · A[16507] after 1117

Phase 2 · Building 103 · A[16471] 1073–1109 · A[16145] 1115–7

Open Area 138 · A[16061] after 1090

Building 129 · 16060 after 959 · A[16058] 1080–1112

Building 124 · A[16953] after 1044 · A[13877] after 1087 · A[16532] 1089–?1125 · A[16528] after 1103 · A[16956] after 1106 · A[16513] after 1126

Open Area 133 · A[16942] 1099–1135

Phase 3 · burial 23 · A[16013] 1139–53 · A[16013] 1141–54

burial 24 · A[16049] 1119–54 · A[16050] 1133–69 · A[16048] 1135–?71 · A[16051] 1137–70

burial 30 · A[16020] 1124–?60

burial 39 · A[16025] after 1128

burial 40 · A[16012] 1146–52 · A[16042] 1150

Structure 110 · A[16110] after 995

Open Area 112 · A[16106] after 1113

Open Area 120 · A[16524] after 1095 · A[16514] after 1123 · A[16514] after 1125 · A[16514] after 1127 · A[16514] after 1131 · A[16514] after 1136 · A[16514] 1136–?68

Open Area 113 · A[10929] after 1087

Open Area 114 · A[16031] after 1109 · A[16032] after 1117 · A[16030] after 1118 · A[16028] after 1119 · A[16033] after 1121

Phase 4 · burial 46 · A[16009] after 1125 · 16017 after 1205

burial 49 · 16021 after 1222

burial 52 · A[16023] 1143–?79 · A[1602] 1145–81

building 121 · A[16986] after 1084 · A[16858] 1123 · A[19554] 1123

No phase · Open Area 127 · A[16003] after 1110 · A[16004] after 1117 · A[16002] 1133–69

Period 13 · Open Area 202 · A[16999] after 1026

Calendar years AD · 800 · 900 · 1000 · 1100 · 1200

8.20 Radiocarbon dating

Beta Analytic Inc, Florida, USA

Human bone from burial 64 was selected for radiocarbon dating. The radiocarbon date has been calibrated using the INTCAL98 calibration curve (Stuiver et al 1998) and the OxCal calibration programme (Bronk Ramsey 2003) version 3.9, using the probability method. Ranges encompass 95.4% of the possible ages and rounded out to the nearest 10 years.

Burial 64, D[138]; period 12, OA140

Beta	166062	
Measured radiocarbon age	660±60 BP	
Convention radiocarbon age	750±60 BP	
Calibrated age ranges (95.4%)	cal 1260–1410 AD	cal BP 760–640

FRENCH AND GERMAN SUMMARIES

Résumé

Les fouilles archéologiques du site de Guildhall eurent lieu entre 1985 et 1999 alors que l'ancienne Corporation de Londres (aujourd'hui connue comme la Corporation de la Cité de Londres) achevait un ambitieux programme de reconstruction nécessité par les destructions massives de la seconde guerre mondiale. De la fin des années 80 au milieu des années 90, l'essentiel du travail archéologique fut associé à la construction de la nouvelle galerie d'Art de la Cité de Londres, qui fut achevée en 1999. Cet ouvrage rend compte de ces fouilles et de travaux antérieurs, en ayant recours à des sources inédites comme à des études historiques et architecturales. L'objectif est de combiner les données stratigraphiques, mobilières, textuelles, environnementales et architecturales afin de restituer l'histoire du site de la manière la plus complète possible.

L'analyse de l'amphithéâtre romain, l'une des découvertes archéologiques majeures de Londres, fait l'objet d'un volume séparé (Bateman et al in prep). Cet ouvrage-ci commence par la présentation des traces d'activité postérieures à l'époque romaine qui prirent la forme d'une petite ferme du Xe apr. J.-C. siècle située au nord de la ville (chapitre 2).

L'une des découvertes médiévales les plus importantes de la fouille est celle d'un chemin des XIe-XIIe siècles et des terrains avoisinants qui incluent le cimetière paroissial de St Lawrence Jewry (chapitre 3). Le cimetière (et par déduction l'église) fut fondé dans le troisième quart du XIe siècle, un certain nombre de tombes étant datées de manière sûre des années 1050 par dendrochronologie. Dans les années 1070, plusieurs bâtiments en bois furent construits à l'extrémité nord d'un des chemins du cimetière qui devint au siècle suivant un axe plus structuré puisqu'il fut étendu pour atteindre le Guildhall nouvellement édifié et reçut des maisons de part et d'autre. Au XIIIe siècle, cette voie fut transformée en place devant le Guildhall et les maisons subsistantes furent démolies. L'ampleur de la fouille et la bonne conservation des matériaux organiques ont permis l'observation de nombreux éléments périssables, tels que des bois de construction ou encore une grande diversité de cercueils et de planches de coffrages dans le cimetière adjacent.

La nature de l'occupation commença à changer dans la seconde moitié du XIIe siècle quand de riches marchands juifs firent édifier de vastes maisons en pierre le long de Cat Street, dans la partie sud de la zone fouillée (chapitres 3 et 6.5). Un *mikveh* ou bain juif rituel subsistait dans une annexe à l'arrière de l'une des maisons. L'occupation juive s'est poursuivie au XIIIe siècle et les sources écrites révèlent le sort des habitants jusqu'à l'expulsion de toute la communauté juive d'Angleterre en 1290.

Autour de 1200, une grande salle seigneuriale, plus tard connue sous le nom de Blackwell Hall, fut construite le long de Basinghall Street, dans la partie orientale du site (chapitre 6.8 et 6.9). Les transformations du bâtiment dans le courant du XIIIe siècle ont pu être restituées par la fouille tandis que sa conversion en marché pour les draps de laine à la fin du XIVe siècle est attestée par les sources écrites. Ce marché perdura jusqu'en 1820 et les changements qu'il connut aux XVIe et XVIIe siècles sont également analysés et cartographiés.

D'autres aspects de l'histoire de Basinghall Street, Cat Street et Aldermanbury sont explorés à partir de nouvelles recherches documentaires et en intégrant les données archéologiques à l'évolution de la propriété médiévale et moderne (chapitre 4).

L'un des apports majeurs de l'ouvrage est l'analyse du Guildhall et de son enclos, le siège du gouvernement de la Cité de Londres depuis le XIIe siècle (chapitres 3, 4, 5 et 6.7). Le premier bâtiment fut construit, pense-t-on, dans les années 1120 et on en suit les principales transformations au début du XIVe siècle, au XVe siècle, à la fin du XVIIe siècle (à la suite du Grand Incendie de 1666) ainsi qu'à la fin du XVIIIe siècle, au XIXe siècle, enfin dans la seconde moitié du XXe siècle. Le statut et la richesse du gouvernement de la Cité permirent l'intervention de plusieurs architectes célèbres, tels que John Croxtone, au XVe siècle, Christopher Wren et Robert Hooke au XVIIe siècle, George Dance le Jeune à la fin du XVIIIe et au début du XIXe siècle, enfin Giles Gilbert Scott au XXe siècle. De nouvelles données concernant l'apparence de la construction elle-même, en particulier son porche, sont présentées et d'autres bâtiments de l'enclos sont étudiés et illustrés en détail, dont la chapelle et la bibliothèque médiévales ainsi que les bâtiments à usage administratif de l'époque médiévale et au-delà.

Un certain nombre d'essais thématiques (chapitre 6) discutent certains points de manière plus détaillée. Outre l'analyse des principales structures (la voie des XIe-XIIe siècles, l'occupation juive, Blackwell Hall et Guildhall), ces sections considèrent les données relatives à l'activité artisanale conduite sur le site (en particulier le travail d'alliages cuivreux), aux auberges médiévales et plus tardives (qui sont attestées pour la première fois dans Cat Street à la fin du XIVe siècle) et aux deux églises paroissiales situées dans la zone d'étude (St Lawrence Jewry et St Michael Bassishaw).

Le chapitre 7 synthétise les principales conclusions et propose des pistes de recherche pour l'avenir et un dernier chapitre (chapitre 8) complété par un CD-ROM fournit les données spécialisées, y compris plusieurs catalogues de mobilier.

Zusammenfassung

Die archäologischen Ausgrabungen an der Guildhall fanden zwischen 1985 und 1999 statt, als die ehemalige Corporation of London (heute die City of London Corporation genannt) ihr ehrgeiziges Wiederaufbauprogramm vollendete, das die großflächige Zerstörung der Guildhall und ihres Bezirks im Zweiten Weltkrieg beheben sollte. Der Hauptteil der archäologischen Arbeit zwischen den späten 80er und Mitte der 90er Jahren war eine Antwort auf die Planung und Konstruktion der neuen Kunstgalerie der City of London, die 1999 fertiggestellt wurde. Der vorliegende Band stellt diese und einige frühere Ausgrabungen vor und zieht Material aus publizierten sowie unpublizierten historischen und architektonischen Studien hinzu. Die Veröffentlichung zielt darauf ab, die verschiedenen Arten der Evidenz, nämlich

Stratigraphie, historische Dokumentation, archäologische Funde und Befunde, Umwelt-Archäologie und Architektur zusammenzuführen, um zu einem besseren Verständnis der Geschichte des Fundplatzes zu gelangen.

Die Geschichte des römischen Amphitheaters, einer der wichtigsten Entdeckungen, die jemals in London gemacht wurden, wird in einem separaten Band erzählt (Bateman et al in prep). Die vorliegende Publikation beginnt mit den wenigen Belegen für nachrömische Aktivitäten in und um das alte Amphitheater herum (Kapitel 2). Die Wiedernutzung dieses Teils von London begann im 10. Jh. n. Chr. mit einem kleinen Gehöft nördlich der spätangelsächsischen Stadt.

Einer der bedeutendsten Funde mittelalterlichen Zeitstellung während der Ausgrabung ist der Nachweis für eine Gasse des 11. und 12. Jhs und die daran angrenzenden Besitzungen, welche den Friedhof der Gemeindekirche St Lawrence Jewry einschließen (Kapitel 3). Der Friedhof (und davon ausgehend die Kirche auch) war im dritten Viertel des 11. Jhs eingerichtet worden: Eine Anzahl von Gräber wird durch Dendrodaten mit Sicherheit in die 1050er Jahre datiert. Einige Holzbauten wurden in den 1070er Jahren am nördlichen Ende eines Friedhofweges errichtet. Der Weg entwickelte sich im 12. Jh. zu einer Stadtgasse von offiziellerem Charakter: Er wurde verlängert, um die neu erbaute Guildhall zu erreichen, und von eng angeordneten Häusern flankiert. Im 13. Jh. kam es zu einer hofartigen Verbreiterung der Gasse vor der Guildhall und die noch bestehende Häuser entlang der Gasse wurden abgerissen. Die Größe der Ausgrabung und die Konservierungsbedingungen am Fundplatz erbrachten eine Menge archäologischen und organischen Materials; insbesondere überlebten viele Elemente der Holzbauten sowie eine große Bandbreite an Särgen und Totenbrettern im benachbarten Friedhof.

Die Besiedlung des untersuchten Gebietes fing an sich zu ändern, als in der zweiten Hälfte des 12. Jhs wohlhabende Juden große Steinhäuser entlang der Cat Street im Süden dieses Gebietes errichteten (Kapitel 3 und 6.5). Die *Mikweh*, das jüdische Bad für rituelle Zwecke, war in einem Nebengebäude hinter einem dieser Häuser gut erhalten. Juden lebten hier weiter im 13. Jh., und mit Hilfe der schriftlichen Überlieferung werden die Schicksale der Bewohner bis zu ihrer Ausweisung gezeigt, die zusammen mit der aller englischen Juden im Jahre 1290 stattfand.

Gegen 1200 wurde eine adlige Residenz, später als Blackwell Hall bekannt, in Basinghall Street, im östlichen Bereich des Ausgrabungsgebietes, erbaut (Kapitel 6.8 und 6.9). Die Umbauten des Gebäudes im 13. Jh. werden verfolgt; am Ende des 14. Jhs geschieht seine Umwandlung in einen städtischen Wolltextilmarkt. Der Blackwell Hall-Markt war bis 1820 in Betrieb, und seine verschiedenen Veränderungen im 16. und 17. Jh. werden ebenfalls untersucht und dokumentiert.

Andere Aspekte der Entwicklung von Basinghall Street, Cat Street und Aldermanbury werden beleuchtet, wobei neue Auswertungen der schriftlichen Quellen genutzt werden und der archäologische Befund in ein Rahmenwerk der mittelalterlichen und späteren Besitzverhältnisse integriert wird (Kapitel 4).

Eines der Hauptthemen der Veröffentlichung ist eine Analyse der Entwicklung der Guildhall und ihres Bezirks, dem Zentrum der Kommunalverwaltung der City of London seit dem 12. Jh. (Kapitel 3, 4, 5 und 6.7). Es wird argumentiert, daß die erste Guildhall in den 1120ern erbaut wurde. Größere Veränderungen an der Halle und ihrem Bezirk im frühen 14., 15., späten 17. (nach dem großen Stadtbrand von 1666), späten 18. und 19. Jh. sowie in der zweiten Hälfte des 20. Jhs werden beschrieben. Status und Wohlstand der City stellten sicher, daß einige bekannte Architekten an der Guildhall und ihrem Bezirk arbeiteten, unter ihnen John Croxtone im 15. Jh., Christopher Wren und Robert Hooke im 17. Jh., George Dance der Jüngere im späten 18. und frühen 19. Jh. sowie Giles Gilbert Scott im 20. Jh. Neue Informationen zum Aussehen der Guildhall, besonders ihrer Eingangshalle, werden vorgelegt, und andere Gebäude des Bezirks besprochen und im Detail illustriert, einschließlich der mittelalterlichen Kapelle und Bibliothek und der mittelalterlichen und späteren Verwaltungsbauten.

Einige Abhandlungen zu bestimmten Themen (Kapitel 6) befassen sich mit Forschungszielen und einer eingehenderen Diskussion verschiedener Aspekte der Evidenz. Außer einer Analyse der Stadtgasse im 11. und 12. Jh., der jüdischen Besiedlung, Blackwell Hall und der Guildhall geht es in diesen Aufsätzen um Belege für handwerkliche Tätigkeiten an der Fundstelle (insbesondere Verarbeitung von Kupferlegierung), für mittelalterliche und spätere Gastwirtschaften (deren erste in Cat Street im späten 14. Jh. nachgewiesen sind) und für die zwei im Untersuchungsgebiet gelegenen Gemeindekirchen (St Lawrence Jewry und St Michael Bassishaw).

In der Schlussdiskussion (Kapitel 7) wird eine Synthese aller Befunde versucht und Forschungsthemen für die Zukunft skizziert. Weitere Informationen der Spezialisten, inklusive der verschiedenen Fundkataloge, finden sich in Kapitel 8 und auf der begleitenden CD-ROM.

GLOSSARY OF SPECIALIST ARCHITECTURAL, WOODWORKING AND DOCUMENTARY TERMS

Blind
Used to describe tracery defining an unglazed part of a wall. A blind portico refers to the front features of a portico when applied to a wall

Board-and-muntin
A system of building timber walls whereby thicker **staves** with grooved edges alternate with thinner boards set into the grooves (see Fig 294)

Bulwark
Also *bulvaerk*, *bulhus* (Danish), *Bohlenwand* (German), *slepvegg* (Norwegian); a system of building timber walls with horizontal elements set into the sides of grooved posts (see Fig 294). Widespread in south Scandinavia, north Germany and Poland, in some areas until recent times

Cinquefoil
Consisting of five lobes or 'foils'; used to describe the 'cusp' or upper point of the window **light**

Clerestory
Upper part of the main elevation of a building, pierced by windows

Coppice
System of **woodmanship** at least 5000 years old in Britain, whereby trees are cut repeatedly near ground level for a crop of regrowth poles or rods

Engaged column
Column that is attached to a wall or arch

Hammerbeam roof
Open roof in which the principal rafters are supported by cantilevered brackets (hammerbeams) on the upper part of the wall, as opposed to being linked by a **tie-beam** to form a **truss**

Lierne
Subsidiary ribs in the crown of a vault that run between other ribs rather than springing from columns

Light
The compartment or panel of a window

Messuage
Usually a house or dwelling (Norman French *mese*; modern French *maison*) but synonymous with the tenement ('holding') on which the house was built. Title deeds commonly use the formula 'messuage or tenement' from the medieval period into the 18th century to describe or refer to a property

Mullion
The vertical bar dividing the **lights** in a window

Ogee
The very pointed arch form resulting from a 'double curve' using both convex and concave elements

Pollard

A tree repeatedly cut at chest height or above for a crop of regrowth poles or rods

Posthole

A small pit in which a post is inserted; the rest of the pit is then backfilled with soil or rubble

Post-pad

A small piece of timber or a stone placed on the ground surface and used to support a building post; the technique is often used for internal aisle posts

Purlin

Longitudinal roof timber

Quitclaim

The formal surrender of any rights held in a property, or of any rent (see **quitrent**) that derived from a property. The seller would therefore 'quitclaim' the purchaser as a normal part of the sale transaction

Quitrent

In addition to an active market in 'freehold' properties, there was an even more active one in 'quitrents', rents payable from properties, which the occupant would have to pay annually to the holder of the quitrent. They originated as a means of endowing religious houses without disposing of the whole property; the obligation to pay the quitrent would be passed on from owner to owner of the house on which they were charged. In time, they were also granted to ordinary citizens who, like religious houses, might sometimes have large portfolios of them. They could also be surrendered (usually in exchange for something else) and this would be done by means of a **quitclaim**

Raking post

A timber rising at an angle from the ground and with its other end set against the wall of a building to act as a buttress; represented by a **posthole** or **post-pad** beyond the wall-line of a building

Rear-arch

The arch on the inside of a wall that encloses a window or door

Respond

Half-column or pier attached to a wall and supporting an arch

Soke

A private lordship, administered by a regular court whose fines and profits would go to the owner. It compares with the rural manor, and so by analogy the soke must have had some definite geographical identity. Several early London **wards** (eg of Aldersgate, Cripplegate and Aldgate) first appear as sokes in the Late Saxon period, and had probably been entrusted to

persons responsible for guarding (warding) the gates they served

Spandrel

Approximately triangular space left between an arch (or window) and its rectangular frame

Stave

A vertically-set timber of plank-like section

Stave-and-muntin

See **board-and-muntin** (see Fig 294)

Tabernacle

Architectural niche or enclosure for a statue or tomb

Tie-beam

A horizontal timber tying together the opposed post-heads of timber-framed walls or the upper surfaces of solid walls

Timber

Wood used for constructional purposes; in early medieval south-east England usually oak, beech or ash with a diameter greater than 150mm

Transom

Horizontal bar across a window **light**

Treeland

Land on which trees are growing, from **wildwood** to managed woodlands, hedgerows and orchards

Truss

The rigid, triangular timber framework (composed of the horizontal **tie-beam** and two principal rafters) supporting each bay of a roof

Ward

By the 12th century the City was divided into 20 wards, generally centred on similarly-named streets, which were secular administrative units of the civic government (the smaller and more numerous parishes being the religious unit). The wards were responsible for maintaining order, sanitation and trading; as the City grew in size and population, the numbers of wards were increased

Wildwood

Ancient natural woodland little affected by humans. In south-east England during this period it was various forms of tall, dark, deciduous woodland with many large, straight, old trees. Includes 'wildwood-type woodland' which had grown on anciently cleared land for many hundreds of years

Woodmanship

Ancient sustainable systems of woodland management such as forms of **coppicing** and **pollarding**

BIBLIOGRAPHY

Manuscript sources

Balliol College Archives, Oxford (BCAO)

B.19.4, B.19.20, B.19.21, B.19.22 plans relating to St Lawrence Jewry

British Library, London (BL)

Add MS 5415 art 56 Leake, J, 'An Exact surveigh of the streets, lanes and churches, comprehended within the ruines of the City of London, first described in six platts in December Anno Domini 1666' (engraved by Vertue 1723; copy in BL, Crace Collection)

Harley MS 57 E37 charter of c 1395 granting land in the parish of St Michael Bassishaw

L.R. 301.bb.12 Paget, G, 1957 'An official, genealogical, and heraldic baronage of England: an account of the ancient nobility of this realm, from the time of the Norman Conquest till the close of the 15th century' (4 vols), typescript

MS 2879 Anon, c 1822 List of surviving funeral monuments in the Guildhall chapel in 1822

Clothworkers' Company, City of London (CC)

Benefactors (1480–1720) and conveyances, wills and current leases (1456–1723) (unfoliated)

Lute Charity, box 58

Rentals, bequests and leases (c 1605–12)

Corporation of London (from 2006, City of London Corporation) Department of Technical Services (CLDTS)

Jeffery archive: four files (containing notes, photos and photcopies) and seven typescripts compiled in the 1990s by Sally Jeffery, former architectural historian of the Corporation of London, detailing her research and architectural recording work:

Guildhall great hall information (file)

Guildhall great hall – general works 1994–5, window 1995–6, lighting 1995 (file)

Guildhall crypts (file)

Guildhall stucco and ironwork and east window (file)

Guildhall – chronological sequence (1994 typescript with 1996 and 1998 revisions)

Stucco work on the Guildhall 1805–7 by Francis Bernasconi (1995 typescript)

Folders and rolls of drawings for the Guildhall and its precincts held by Dick Gilbert Scott and seen by Sally Jeffery on 24 July 1995 (1995 typescript)

Guildhall summary (1998 typescript with 1999 information on porch)

The old library, Guildhall, Corporation of London (1998 typescript, revised 2000)

Guildhall crypts (1999 typescript)

The Guildhall (1999 typescript)

Corporation of London Record Office (from 2006, records administered by LMA and recatalogued) (CLRO)

CCA City Cash Accounts

CCL Comptroller's City Lands plans (with plan no.)

CD Comptroller's Deeds (with box letter)

CLC City Lands Contracts

CLCP City Lands Committee Papers

CLD Comptroller's City Lands Deeds (with box no.)

CLGB City Lands Grant Book

CR Committee for Repairs (Misc MS 117/3, below)

HR Husting Roll

JCCC Journals of the Court of Common Council of the City of London

JCLC Journals of the City Lands Committee

LB (A, B etc) Letter Books A–ZZ of the City of London

MD Miscellaneous Deeds (with box no.)

Misc MS 117/3 Committee for Repairing and Beautifying the Guildhall (1706–8)

Misc MSS 135/22, 159/16 warrants from the Committee for the Rebuilding of the Guildhall to the City chamberlain for the payment of contractors (1670–2)

Misc MS 210/7 proceedings of the Courts of Aldermen and Common Council (1709) concerning Guildhall building works

Misc MS 351/6 Guildhall chapel, memorial inscriptions: City officers and their families (1671–1763)

New 208A Sharpe, Reginald R, correspondence, Vol 1, letters 166, 168, 170, 171 (correspondence relating to the statues on the west front of the former Guildhall chapel)

PD Printed Documents

Plans, Guildhall Great Hall 1951–2 (engineers' drawings); Guildhall reconstruction ('phase IV', plans and elevations of Guildhall porch)

Prints

Repertory Repertories (minute books) of the Court of Aldermen of the City of London

RP Research Papers, 12.5 (Aldous, V E, 1985 'The Guildhall fire of 1786')

SCLB Surveyor's City Lands Building plans (with plan no.)

Guildhall Library, City of London (GL)

COLLAGE online image database containing works from the Guildhall Library Print Room and the Guildhall Art Gallery, http://collage.cityoflondon.gov.uk (COLLAGE reference nos have superceded old catalogue nos)

E.2.1 elevations, plans and sections of 50 churches designed and built under the direction of Sir Christopher Wren

Jones, P E, 1961 'The Guildhall crypt', lecture to the Guildhall Historical Association (typescript)

Map Case 172–4 and 368 series of 1950s architect's drawings of St Lawrence Jewry

MD 20518 Miscellaneous Deeds

MS 11616 Grocers' Company: register of grants and wills (1524)

MS 12849 Christ's Hospital: accounts for the rebuilding of Blackwell Hall after the Fire and subsequent repairs (1666–1708)

MS 12851 Christ's Hospital: Blackwell Hall Committee minute book (1697/8–1761)

MS 251[…] St Paul's Dean and Chapter: deeds

MS 25504 St Paul's Dean and Chapter: MSS, 'Liber L'

MS 25636 St Paul's Dean and Chapter: accounts

MS 2590/1 St Lawrence Jewry: vestry minutes (1556–1669)

MS 2590/2 St Lawrence Jewry: vestry minutes (1669–1720)

MS 2593/1 St Lawrence Jewry: churchwardens' accounts (1579–1640)

MS 2593/2 St Lawrence Jewry: churchwardens' accounts (1640–98)

MS 2596/1 St Mary Magdalen Milk Street: churchwardens' accounts (1518–1606)

MS 2597/1 St Mary Magdalen Milk Street: vestry minutes (1619–68)

MS 2598/1 St Michael Bassishaw: vestry minutes (1669–1715)

MS 2601/1 St Michael Bassishaw: churchwardens' accounts (1617–1716)

MS 31350 Christ's Hospital: deeds

MS 3556/2 St Mary Aldermanbury: churchwardens' accounts (1631–77) (unfoliated)

MS 7531/2 Coopers' Company: deeds

MS 7549 Coopers' Company: benefactors' book (1468–1844)

London Metropolitan Archives (formerly Greater London Record Office), City of London (LMA)

LCC/GLC 96[…] Survey drawings index: City of London National Monument Record fiches

Mercers' Company, City of London (MC)

First register of leases (1478–1572)

Card index of mercers (based principally on the Company's wardens' account books (1348, 1391–1464) and Acts of Court (1453 onwards)

National Monuments Record, Swindon (NMR)

Royal Commission on the Historical Monuments of England (RCHME) archive church of St Lawrence Jewry, London: inventory notes and photos (file BF094276) and measured surveys (drawings MD49/00419–20) created by RCHME while preparing the City volume (1929) of the *Inventory of London* series (includes plans and sections marked 'RIBA Studentships 1911')

Ministry of Public Building and Works (MPBW), Ancient Monuments Branch archive the Guildhall, London: series of plans and sections of architectural recording by the MPBW carried out 1967–70, prior to reconstruction works; album of annotated photographs during the works, 1970–2; series of 1960s plans and sections by architects, Sir Giles Scott Son and Partners, with site annotations (1970–?2) in pencil

The National Archives (TNA): Public Record Office, London (PRO)

C143 Ancient Deeds

C146 Ancient Deeds

C147 Ancient Deeds

E40 Ancient Deeds

E42 Ancient Deeds

E315 Ancient Deeds: Court of Augmentations, miscellaneous leases

E318 Ancient Deeds: particulars for grants

LR14 Ancient Deeds

University of Nottingham, online catalogue of deeds (UN)

NC catalogue of deeds in the Newcastle (Clumber) Collection (1st deposit), http://mss.library.nottingham.ac.uk/cats/ne_1_deeds_part_4.html

Printed and other secondary works

Ainsley, C, 2004 Animal by-products, in Howe and Lakin 2004, 105–6

Albarella, U, and Davis, S J M, 1996 Mammals and birds from Launceston Castle, Cornwall: decline in status and the rise of agriculture, *Circaea* 12(1), 1–156

Alexander, J, 1995 Building stone from the east Midlands quarries: sources, transportation and usage, *Medieval Archaeol* 39, 107–35

Alexander, J, and Binski, P (eds), 1987 *Age of Chivalry: art in Plantagenet England 1200–1400*, Roy Acad Arts exhibition catalogue, London

Allan, G A T, 1937 *Christ's Hospital*, London

Amorosi, T, 1989 *A postcranial guide to domestic neo-natal and juvenile mammals*, BAR Int Ser 533, Oxford

Anderberg, A-L, 1994 *Atlas of seeds and small fruits of north-west European plant species: Part 4, Resedaceae–Umbelliferae*, Stockholm

Anderson, M D, 1971 *History and images in British churches*, Edinburgh

Anon ('E.T.C.'), 1820 Description of Guildhall Chapel, London, *Gentleman's Mag* 90 (August), 116–18

Anon, 1822 [Discovery of coffin at Guildhall], *Gentleman's Mag* 92 (July), 3

Archer-Thomson, W, 1942 *Drapers' Company: history of the company's properties and trusts* (2 vols), London

Archibald, M M, 1991 Anglo-Saxon and Norman lead objects with official coin types, in Vince 1991a, 326–46

Armitage, K H, Pearce, J E, and Vince, A G, 1981 A late medieval bronze mould from Copthall Avenue, London, *Antiq J* 61, 362–4

Armitage, P L, 1994 Unwelcome companions: ancient rats reviewed, *Antiquity* 68, 231–40

Armitage, P L, Locker, A, and Straker, V, with West, B, 1987 Environmental archaeology in London: a review, in

Environmental archaeology: a regional review, Vol 2 (ed H C M Keeley), Engl Heritage Occas Pap 1, 252–331, London

Arwidsson, G, and Berg, G, 1983 *The Mästermyr find: a Viking Age tool chest from Gotland*, Stockholm

Askew, P, 1998 Broadgate phase 12/13, land to the west of Norton Folgate and due north of Primrose Street, London EC2: an archaeological assessment, unpub MoL rep

Assize of nuisance London assize of nuisance 1301–1431 (eds H M Chew and W Kellaway), London Rec Soc Pub 10, 1973, London

Astill, G, and Grant, A (eds), 1988 *The countryside of medieval England*, Oxford

Astill, G, Hirst, S, and Wright, S M, 2004 The Bordesley Abbey Project reviewed, *Archaeol J* 161, 106–58

Atkinson, D R, and Oswald, A, 1969 London clay tobacco pipes, *J Brit Archaeol Ass* 3 ser 32, 171–227

Avery, B W, and Bascomb, C L, 1974 *Soil survey laboratory techniques*, Soil Survey Tech Monogr 14, Harpenden

Ayre, J, and Wroe-Brown, R, with Malt, D, in prep *Queenhithe: excavations at Thames Court, City of London, 1989–97*, MoLAS epublication Ser

Babel, U, 1975 Micromorphology of soil organic matter, in *Soil components: organic components* (ed J E Giesking), 369–473, New York

Baddeley, J, 1927 *The Guildhall of the City of London*, 6 edn (rev), London

Baddeley, J, 1941 (1939) *The Guildhall of the City of London*, 7 edn (rev, with 'Epilogue' for 1941), London

Badham, S, and Norris, M, 1999 *Early incised slabs and brasses from the London marblers*, Res Rep Soc Antiq London 60, London

Bakels, C C, 1988 Pollen from plaggen soils in the province of North Brabant, the Netherlands, in *Man-made soils* (eds M Robinson and W Groenman-van Waateringe), BAR Int Ser 410, 55–66, Oxford

Baker, T, 1970 *Medieval London*, London

Bal, L, 1982 Zoological ripening of soils, Res Rep Centre for Agr Publishing Documentation, Wageningen

Ball, D F, 1964 Loss-on-ignition as an estimate of organic matter and organic carbon in non-calcareous soils, *J Soil Sci* 15, 84–92

Bangs, C, 1995 *The Lear Collection: a study of copper-alloy socket candlesticks, AD 200–1700*, Easton, Pa

Bannerman, W B (ed), 1914–15 *The registers of St Mary le Bowe, Cheapside, All Hallows, Honey Lane, and of St Pancras, Soper Lane, London*, Harleian Soc Pub 44–5, London

Bannerman, W B (ed), 1931–2 *The registers of St Mary the Virgin, Aldermanbury, London: Vols 1–2*, Harleian Soc Pub 61–2, London

Barber, B, and Bowsher, D, 2000 *The eastern cemetery of Roman London: excavations 1983–90*, MoLAS Monogr Ser 4, London

Barber, B, Chew, S, and White, B, 2004 *The Cistercian abbey of St Mary Stratford Langthorne: archaeological excavations for the London Underground Limited Jubilee Line Extension Project*, MoLAS Monogr Ser 18, London

Barker, T C, 1957 *The Girdlers' Company: a second history*, London

Barrère, M, 1990 [Catalogue entries], in *Archéologie et vie quotidienne aux XIIIe et XIVe siècles en Midi-Pyrénées* (eds M Barrère and M Rey-Delqué), Musée des Augustins exhibition catalogue, Toulouse

Barron, C M, 1969 Richard Whittington: the man behind the myth, in Hollaender and Kellaway 1969, 197–248

Barron, C M, 1974 The medieval Guildhall of London, London

Barron, C M, 1995 Centres of conspicuous consumption: the aristocratic town house in London 1200–1500, London J 20(1), 1–16

Barron, C M, 1996 The expansion of education in 15th-century London, in The cloister and the world: essays in honour of Barbara Harvey (eds J Blair and B Golding), 219–45, Oxford

Barron, C M, 2002 Church music in English towns 1450–1550: an interim report, Urban Hist 29(1), 83–91

Barron, C M, 2004a London in the later Middle Ages, Oxford

Barron, C M, 2004b The political culture of medieval London, in The 15th century: Vol 4, Political culture in late medieval Britain (eds L Clark and C Carpenter), 111–33, Woodbridge

Barron, C M, and Rousseau, M-H, 2004 Cathedral, city and state 1300–1540, in Keene et al 2004, 33–44

Bass, W M, 1995 Human osteology: a laboratory and field manual, 4 edn, Missouri Archaeol Soc Spec Pap 2, Columbia

Bassett, S (ed), 1992 Death in towns: urban responses to the dying and the dead, 100–1600, Leicester

Bateman, N, 1997 The early 11th- to mid 12th-century graveyard at Guildhall, City of London, in De Boe and Verhaeghe 1997b, 115–20

Bateman, N, 1999 The dedication of Guildhall chapel, in Medieval London: recent archaeological work and research: papers given at the CBA Mid-Anglia Group conference on 14 February 1998, Trans London Middlesex Archaeol Soc 50, 23–8

Bateman, N, 2000 Gladiators at the Guildhall: the story of London's Roman amphitheatre and medieval Guildhall, London

Bateman, N, 2003 John Carpenter's library: corporate charity and London's Guildhall, in Gaimster and Gilchrist 2003, 356–70

Bateman, N, 2004 From rags to riches: Blackwell Hall and the wool cloth trade, c 1450–1790, Post-Medieval Archaeol 38, 1–15

Bateman, N, and Miles, A, 1999 St Lawrence Jewry from the 11th to 19th centuries, Trans London Middlesex Archaeol Soc 50, 109–43

Bateman, N, and Porter, G, 1997 Guildhall Yard East, City of London, EC2: an archaeological assessment of excavations over the Roman amphitheatre 1985–97 and updated project design, unpub MoL rep

Bateman, N, Rowsome, P, and Malcolm, G, 1999 Guildhall Yard East, City of London, EC2 (GYE92): the proposed scope of the research design, analysis and publication of the excavations over the Roman amphitheatre 1985–97, unpub MoL rep

Bateman, N, Cowan, C, and Wroe-Brown, R, in prep London's Roman amphitheatre: excavations at the Guildhall, City of London, MoLAS Monogr Ser

Bayley, J, 1991 Alloy nomenclature, in Egan and Pritchard 1991, 13–17

Bayley, J, 1992 Metalworking ceramics, Medieval Ceram 16, 3–10

Bayley, J, Freestone, I, Jenner, A, and Vince, A, 1991 Metallurgy, in Vince 1991a, 389–405

Beckman, G G, and Smith, K J, 1974 Micromorphological changes in surface soils following wetting, drying and trampling, in Soil microscopy (ed G K Rutherford), 832–45, Kingston, Ont

Beckwith, J, 1972 Ivory carvings in early medieval England, London

Beijerinck, W, 1947 Zadenatlas der Nederlandsche flora: I–II, Veenman and Zonen, Wageningen

Bell, M, Fowler, M J, and Hillson, S W, 1996 The Experimental Earthwork Project, 1960–92, CBA Res Rep 100, York

Bell, M, Caseldine, A, and Neumann, H, 2000 Prehistoric intertidal archaeology in the Welsh Severn estuary, CBA Res Rep 120, York

Belshaw, R, 1989 A note on the recovery of Thoracochaeta zosterae (Halliday) (Diptera: Sphaeroceridae) from archaeological deposits, Circaea 6(1), 39–41

Bennett, K D, Whittington, G, and Edwards, K J, 1994 Recent plant nomenclature changes and pollen morphology in the British Isles, Quat Newsl 73, 1–6

Berggren, G, 1969 Atlas of seeds and small fruits of north-west European plant species: Part 2, Cyperaceae, Stockholm

Berggren, G, 1981 Atlas of seeds and small fruits of north-west European plant species: Part 3, Salicaceae–Cruciferae, Stockholm

Bergman, K, and Billberg, I, 1976 Metallhåntverk, in Uppgrävt förflutet för PK Banken i Lund (ed A W Mertensson), Archaeologica Lundensia 7, 119–212, Lund

Berry, A C, 1978 Anthropological and family studies in minor variants of the dental crown, in Development, function and evolution of the teeth (eds P M Butler and K A Joysey), 81–98, London

Berry, A C, and Berry, R J, 1967 Epigenetic variation in the human cranium, J Anatomy 101, 361–79

Betts, I M, 1990 Building materials, in Schofield et al 1990, 220–9

Betts, I M, 1991 Medieval and later building material: Billingsgate Fish Market car park, Lower Thames Street (BIG82), unpub MoL rep

Betts, I M, 1996 Glazed 11th-century wall tiles from London, Medieval Ceram 20, 19–24

Betts, I M, 2002a Medieval 'Westminster' floor tiles, MoLAS Monogr Ser 11, London

Betts, I M, 2002b Medieval and later building material: Northgate House (MRG95)/Kent House (KHS98), unpub MoL rep

Betts, I M, 2003 Ceramic building material research archive for the Guildhall project (medieval and post-medieval), unpub MoL rep

Betts, I M, 2007 Ceramic and stone building material, in Miller and Saxby 2007, 195–214

Betts, I M, in prep a The building material, in Steele, A, in prep Excavations at the monastery of St Saviour Bermondsey, Southwark, MoLAS Monogr Ser

Betts, I M, in prep b The ceramic and stone building material, in Blatherwick, S, and Bluer, R, in prep Great houses, moats and mills on the south bank of the Thames: medieval and Tudor Southwark and Rotherhithe, MoLAS Monogr Ser

Betts, I M, and Cromwell, T G, in prep Windsor Castle Governor's House tiled floor (Norman Gate, south tower, first floor), Engl Heritage Centre for Archaeol rep

Betts, I M, and Smith, T P, in prep Ceramic and stone building material, in Blair, I, in prep *Excavations at Monument House, 30–35 Botolph Lane, City of London*, 1998

Betts, I M, Bateman, N, and Porter, G, 1995 Two late Anglo-Saxon tiles and the early history of St Lawrence Jewry, London, *Medieval Archaeol* 39, 165–9

Biddle, M (ed), 1976 *Winchester in the early Middle Ages*, Winchester Stud 1, Oxford

Biddle, M, 1989 A city in transition: 400–800, in Lobel 1989, 20–9

Biddle, M (ed), 1990 *Object and economy in medieval Winchester: artefacts from medieval Winchester*, Winchester Stud 7(2) (2 vols), Oxford

Binney, M, 1972 Penshurst Palace, Kent – I. The seat of the Viscount de l'Isle, VC, KG, *Country Life* 151, 554–8

Binski, P, 2005 The cult of Edward the Confessor, *History Today* 55(11), 21–9

Birch, W de G, 1887 *The historical charters and constitutional documents of the City of London*, London

Birch, W de G, 1892 *Catalogue of seals in the Department of Manuscripts in the British Museum: Vol 2*, London

Black, M, 1985 *Food and cooking in medieval Britain: history and recipes*, London

Blackmore, L, and Pearce, J, in prep *A dated type-series of London medieval pottery: Part 5, Shelly-sandy ware and south Hertfordshire greyware*, MoLAS Monogr Ser

Blades, N W, 1995 Copper alloys from English archaeological sites 400–1600 AD: an analytical study using ICP-AES, unpub PhD thesis, Univ London

Blair, C, and Blair, J, 1991 Copper alloys, in *English medieval industries: craftsmen, techniques, products* (eds J Blair and N Ramsay), 81–106, London

Blair, I, 2000 15–17 King Street and 44–46 Gresham street, London EC2: an archaeological assessment report and updated project design (KIG95), unpub MoL rep

Blair, I, 2002 A moated manor at Low Hall, Walthamstow, *Essex Archaeol Hist* 33, 191–220

Blair, I, and Watson, B, 2004 Blossoms Inn, 30 Gresham Street, City of London, EC2: a post-excavation assessment and updated project design (GHT00), unpub MoL rep

Blair, I, Hillaby, J, Howell, I, Sermon, R, and Watson, B, 2001a The discovery of two medieval mikva'ot in London and a reinterpretation of the Bristol mikveh, *Trans Jewish Hist Soc* 37, 15–40

Blair, I, Hillaby, J, Howell, I, Sermon, R, and Watson, B, 2001b Two medieval Jewish ritual baths – mikva'ot – found at Gresham Street and Milk Street in London, *Trans London Middlesex Archaeol Soc* 52, 127–37

Blyth, D, 1990 *Flemish cities explored: Bruges, Ghent, Antwerp, Mechelen and Brussels*, London

Boddington, A, 1987 Chaos, disturbance and decay in an Anglo-Saxon cemetery, in Boddington et al 1987, 27–43

Boddington, A, Garland, A N, and Janaway, R C (eds), 1987 *Death, decay and reconstruction: approaches to archaeology and forensic science*, Manchester

Bosworth, J, 1882–98 *An Anglo-Saxon dictionary based on the manuscript collections of the late Joseph Bosworth* (ed T Northcote Toller), Oxford

Bradley, S, and Pevsner, N, 1997 *The buildings of England: London 1, The City of London*, London

Bramwell, D, 1975 Bird remains from medieval London, *London Naturalist* 54, 15–20

Brewer, T, 1865 *Memoir of the life and times of John Carpenter, Town Clerk of London*, London

Brigham, T, 1992 Reused timbers from the Billingsgate site, 1982–3, in Milne 1992, 86–105

Brigham, T, Goodburn, D, Milne, G, and Tyers, I, 1992 Terminology and dating, in Milne 1992, 14–22

Britton, F, 1987 *London delftware*, London

Bronk Ramsey, C, 2001 Development of the radiocarbon program OxCal, *Radiocarbon* 43, 355–63 (http://www.rlaha.ox.ac.uk/oxcal/oxcal.htm)

Brooke, C N L, assisted by Keir, G, 1975 *London 800–1216: the shaping of a city*, London

Brooks, S T, and Suchey, J M, 1990 Skeletal age determination based on the os pubis: comparison of the Acsádi-Nemeskéri and Suchey-Brooks methods, *J Human Evol* 5, 227–38

Brothwell, D, 1981 *Digging up bones: the excavation, treatment and study of human skeletal remains*, 3 edn, Oxford

Brothwell, D, 1987 Decay and disorder in the York Jewbury skeletons, in Boddington et al 1987, 22–7

Brunning, R, 1995 Joinery and structural carpentry, in Coles, J, and Minnitt, S, *Industrious and fairly civilised: the Glastonbury lake village*, 117–20, Taunton

Buckland, P C, and Perry, D W, 1989 Ectoparasites of sheep from Storaborg, Iceland, and their interpretation: piss, parasites and people, a palaeoecological perspective, *Hikuin* 15, 37–46

Bullock, P, Fedoroff, N, Jongerius, A, Stoops, G, and Tursina, T, 1985 *Handbook for soil thin section description*, Wolverhampton

Burch, M, and Treveil, P, with Keene, D, in prep *The development of early medieval and later Poultry and Cheapside: excavations at 1 Poultry and vicinity, City of London*, MoLAS Monogr Ser

Burford, E, J, 1990 *Wits, wenchers and wantons*, London

Butler, L A S, 1956 Medieval gravestones of Cambridgeshire, Huntingdonshire and the Soke of Peterborough, *Proc Cambridge Antiq Soc* 50, 89–100

Cal Chart R Calendar of the charter rolls, 1226–1516, Public Rec Office, 1903–27, London

Cal Close R Calendar of the close rolls, Public Rec Office, 1892–1975, London

Cal Fire Court The Fire Court: calendar to the judgments and decrees of the court of judicature appointed to determine differences between landlords and tenants as to rebuilding after the Great Fire (ed P E Jones) (2 vols), 1966–70, London

Cal Inq Misc Calendar of inquisitions miscellaneous, Public Rec Office, 1916–69, London

Cal Inq PM Calendar of inquisitions post mortem, Public Rec Office, 1904–74, London

Cal LB A–L Calendar of the letter books preserved among the archives of the Corporation of the City of London at the Guildhall, A to L (ed R R Sharpe) (11 vols), 1899–1912, London

Cal M Court R Calendar of early Mayor's Court rolls preserved among the archives of the Corporation of the City of London at the Guildhall, AD 1298–1307 (ed A H Thomas), 1924, Cambridge

Cal Pat R Calendar of the patent rolls, Public Rec Office, 1894–1974, London

Cal Plea & Mem R Calendar of plea and memoranda rolls preserved among the archives of the Corporation of the City of London at the Guildhall: Vols 1–4, 1323–1437 (ed A H Thomas, 1926–43); Vols 5–6, 1437–82 (ed P E Jones, 1953–61), Cambridge

Cal Poss Assizes London possessory assizes: a calendar (ed H M Chew), London Rec Soc Pub 1, 1965, London

Cal Wills Calendar of wills proved and enrolled in the Court of Husting, London, 1258–1688 (ed R R Sharpe), 1889–90, London

Cammas, C, 1994 Approche micromorphologique de la stratigraphie urbaine à Lattes: premiers résultats, Lattara ARALO, Lattes

Campbell, B M S, Galloway, J A, Keene, D, and Murphy, M, 1993 A medieval capital and its grain supply: agrarian production and distribution in the London region c 1300, Hist Geogr Res Ser 30, London

Campbell, J, 2004 University of Cambridge Department for Architecture website, section on Sir Christopher Wren (http://www.arct.cam.ac.uk/personal-page/james/phd/wren/architect.html)

Carlin, M, 1998 Fast food and urban living standards in medieval England, in Food and eating in medieval Europe (eds M Carlin and J T Rosenthal), 27–52, London

Carrott, J, and Kenward, H K, 2001 Species associations amongst insect remains from urban archaeological deposits and their significance in reconstructing the past human environment, J Archaeol Sci 28, 887–905

Cart Antiq R The cartae antiquae, rolls 11–20 (ed J C Davies), Pipe Roll Soc ns 33, 1960, London

Cart Holy Trinity The cartulary of Holy Trinity Priory, Aldgate (ed G A J Hodgett), London Rec Soc Pub 7, 1971, London

Cart Ramsey Cartularium monasterii de Rameseia (eds W H Hart and P A Lyons), Rolls Ser 79 (3 vols), 1884–93, London

Cart St Mary Clerkw The cartulary of St Mary Clerkenwell (ed W O Hassall), Camden Soc 3 ser 71, 1949, London

Casson, L, Drummond-Murray, J, and Francis, A, in prep Excavations at 10 Gresham Street, City of London, MoLAS Monogr Ser

Cat Anc Deeds A descriptive catalogue of ancient deeds, Public Rec Office, 1890–1915, London

Chron Ramsey Chronicon abbatiae Ramesiensis (ed W D Macray), Rolls Ser, 1886, London

Clapham, A R, Tutin, T G, and Moore, D M, 1987 Flora of the British Isles, 3 edn, Cambridge

Clark, J, 1991 [Various contributions], in Treasures and trinkets: jewellery in London from pre-Roman times to the 1930s (ed T Murdoch), Museum of London exhibition catalogue, London

Clark, J, 1995 The medieval horse and its equipment, HMSO Medieval Finds from Excavations in London Ser 5, London

Clarke, H, and Ambrosiani, B, 1994 (1991) Towns in the Viking Age, rev edn, London

Cobb, G, 1989 (1977) London City churches, 2 edn (rev N Redman), London

Cobb, H S (ed), 1990 The overseas trade of London: Exchequer customs accounts 1480–1, London Rec Soc Pub 27, London

Cocke, T, 1995 900 years: the restorations of Westminster Abbey, London

Cohen, N, 1994 Church investigation in the City of London 1878–1968, unpub MA thesis, Univ London

Cohen, N, 2001 St Alban's Wood Street, in Milne 2001, 86–100

CoL, 1950 The Corporation of London: its origin, constitution, powers and duties, London

CoL, 1992 The official guide to the Guildhall, London

Colardelle, R, and Colardelle, M, 1980 L'Habitat médiéval immergé de Colletière, à Charavines (Isère): premier bilan des fouilles, Archéologie Médiévale 10, 167–269

Coldstream, N, 1994 The Decorated style: architecture and ornament 1240–1360, London

Colvin, H, 1995 A biographical dictionary of British architects 1600–1840, 3 edn, New Haven and London

Conheeney, J, 1997 The human bone, in Thomas et al 1997, 218–31

Cook, G H, 1947 Mediaeval chantries and chantry chapels, London

Cook, G H, 1954 The English mediaeval parish church, London

Cooper, M, 2003 Hooke's career, in London's Leonardo: the life and work of Robert Hooke (eds J Bennett, M Cooper, M Hunter, and L Jardine), 1–61, Oxford

Courty, M A, 2001 Microfacies analysis assisting archaeological stratigraphy, in Earth sciences and archaeology (ed C R Ferring), 205–39, New York

Courty, M A, Goldberg, P, and Macphail, R I, 1989 Soils and micromorphology in archaeology, Cambridge

Courty, M A, Goldberg, P, and Macphail, R I, 1994 Ancient people – lifestyles and cultural patterns, in Transactions of the 15th World Congress of Soil Science, International Society of Soil Science, Mexico, 250–69, Acapulco

Cowie, R, and Blackmore, L, in prep Early and Middle Saxon rural settlement in the London region, MoLAS Monogr Ser

Crowfoot, E, Pritchard, F, and Staniland, K, 1992 Textiles and clothing c 1150–c 1450, HMSO Medieval Finds from Excavations in London Ser 4, London

Crowther, J, and Barker, P, 1995 Magnetic susceptibility: distinguishing anthropogenic effects from the natural, Archaeol Prospection 2, 207–15

Crowther, J, Macphail, R I, and Cruise, G M, 1996 Short-term burial change in a humic rendzina, Overton Down Experimental Earthwork, Wiltshire, England, Geoarchaeol 11(2), 95–117

Cruise, G M, and Macphail, R I, 2000 Microstratigraphical signatures of experimental rural occupation deposits and archaeological sites, in Interpreting stratigraphy (ed S Roskams), 183–91, York

Culpeper, N, 1653 The complete herbal, np

Curgy, J J, 1965 Apparition et soudres des points d'ossification des membres chez les mammifères, Mémoires du Musée National d'Histoire Naturelle, ser A (Zoologie), 32 fasc 3, Paris

Curl, J S, 2000 The Honourable The Irish Society and the plantation of Ulster 1608–2000, Chichester

Cushing, E J, 1967 Evidence for differential pollen preservation in late Quaternary sediments in Minnesota, Rev Palaeobotany & Palynology 4, 87–101

Dam, J D van, 1991 (1988) Nederlandse tegels, 2 edn, Amsterdam

Daniell, C, 1997 Death and burial in medieval England, London

Davis, A, 2002 The plant remains from 1 Poultry (ONE94), unpub MoL rep

Davis, A, 2003 The plant remains, in Malcolm and Bowsher 2003, 289–302

Davis, H W C, 1925 London lands and liberties of St Paul's, 1066–1135, in *Essays in medieval history presented to Thomas Frederick Tout* (eds A G Little and F M Powicke), 45–59, Manchester

Davis, R H C, 1990 (1967) *King Stephen, 1135–54*, 3 edn, London

Davis, S J M, 2002 British agriculture: texts for the zooarchaeologist, *J Human Palaeoecol* 7, 47–60

De Boe, G, and Verhaeghe, F (eds), 1997a *Papers of the 'Medieval Europe Brugge 1997' conference: Vol 1, Urbanism in medieval Europe*, IAP Rapporten 1, Zellik

De Boe, G, and Verhaeghe, F (eds), 1997b *Papers of the 'Medieval Europe Brugge 1997' conference: Vol 2, Death and burial in medieval Europe*, IAP Rapporten 2, Zellik

Delcourt, P A, and Delcourt, H R, 1980 Pollen preservation and Quaternary environmental history in the southeastern United States, *Palynology* 4, 215–31

Denison, S, 1999 No small fry in Saxon fishing industry, *Brit Archaeol* 41, 5

Dick, W A, and Tabatabai, M A, 1977 An alkaline oxidation method for the determination of total phosphorus in soils, *J Soil Sci Soc America* 41, 511–14

Dimbleby, G W, 1985 *The palynology of archaeological sites*, London

Dobney, K, and Harwood, J, 1998 Here to stay? Archaeological evidence for the introduction of commensal and economically important mammals to the north of England, in *The Holocene history of the European vertebrate fauna: modern aspects of research* (ed N Benecke), Archäologie in Eurasien 6, 373–87, Berlin

DoE, 1990 Department of the Environment, *Planning policy guidance: archaeology and planning (PPG16)*, London

Douglas, D C, and Greenaway, G W, 1981 *English historical documents: Vol 2, 1042–1189*, 2 edn, London

Driesch, A von den, 1976 *A guide to the measurement of animal bones from archaeological sites*, Peabody Mus Bull 1, Cambridge, Mass

Drift, J van der, 1964 Soil fauna and soil profile in some inland-dune habitats, in *Soil micromorphology* (ed A Jongerius), 69–81, Amsterdam

Driver, J C, 1982 Medullary bone as an indicator of sex in bird remains from archaeological sites, in Wilson et al 1982, 251–4

Drummond-Murray, J, and Liddle, J, 2003 Medieval industry in the Walbrook valley, *London Archaeol* 10(4), 87–94

Duffy, E A J, 1953 *Coleoptera: Scolytidae and Platypodidae*, Handbooks for the Identification of British Insects Vol 15, London

Dungworth, D, 2000a Analysis of the metal fragments, in Blaylock, S R, Excavation of an early post-medieval bronze foundry at Cowick Street, Exeter, 1999–2000, *Devon Archaeol Soc Proc* 58, 72–8

Dungworth, D, 2000b A note on the analysis of crucibles and moulds, *Hist Metall* 34, 83–6

Dungworth, D, 2001 Metalworking evidence from Housesteads Roman fort, Northumberland, unpub Engl Heritage Centre for Archaeol rep 109/2001

Dungworth, D, 2003 Chemical analysis of the founding assemblages from Guildhall (GYE92 and GAG87), unpub Engl Heritage Ancient Monuments Lab rep

Dyson, T, 1977 Historical survey, in Blurton, T R, with Rhodes, M, Excavations at Angel Court, Walbrook, 1974, *Trans London Middlesex Archaeol Soc* 28, 15–16

Dyson, T, 1990 King Alfred and the restoration of London, *London J* 15, 99–110

Dyson, T, 2003 Documentary research archive for the Guildhall project, unpub MoL rep

Dyson, T, and Schofield, J, 1984 Saxon London, in *Anglo-Saxon towns in southern England* (ed J Haslam), 285–313, Chichester

Eames, E S, 1980 *Catalogue of medieval lead-glazed earthenware tiles in the Department of Medieval and Later Antiquities, British Museum* (2 vols), London

Edlin, H, 1949 *Woodland crafts in Britain*, London

Eeles, F C, 1910 Discoveries during the demolition of the church of St Michael, Bassishaw, *Trans London Middlesex Archaeol Soc* 2(1), 164–78

Egan, G, 1991 Industry and economics on the medieval and later London waterfront, in *Waterfront archaeology: proceedings of the 3rd International Conference on Waterfront Archaeology held at Bristol, 23–26 September 1988* (eds G L Good, R H Jones, and M W Ponsford), CBA Res Rep 74, 9–18, London

Egan, G, 1995 *Lead cloth seals and related items in the British Museum*, Brit Mus Occas Pap 93, London

Egan, G, 1996a *Playthings from the past*, London

Egan, G, 1996b Some archaeological evidence for metalworking in London c 1050–c 1700 AD, *Hist Metall* 30, 83–94

Egan, G, 1997 *Dice*, Finds Res Grp 700–1700 Datasheet 23, Oxford

Egan, G, 1998 *The medieval household: daily living c 1150–c 1450*, HMSO Medieval Finds from Excavations in London Ser 6, London

Egan, G, 2000 Butcher, baker, spoon and candlestick maker? Some early highly decorated medieval leadwares in northern Europe, in *Lost and found: essays on medieval archaeology presented to H J E van Beuningen* (eds D Kicken, A M Koldeweij, and J R ter Molen), Rotterdam Pap 11, 102–15, Rotterdam

Egan, G, 2001 Cloth seals, in *Salisbury and South Wiltshire Museum medieval catalogue: Part 3* (ed P Saunders), 43–86, Salisbury

Egan, G, 2002 Copper alloy founding, in Howe, E, *Roman defences and medieval industry: excavations at Baltic House, City of London*, MoLAS Monogr Ser 7, 48–61, London

Egan, G, 2003 Two medieval copper alloy foundry excavations in London, in *Archaeometallugy in Europe: pre-printed papers of the Associazione Italiana di Metallurgia conference: Vol 2*, 243–52, Milan

Egan, G, 2005a *Material culture in London in an age of transition: Tudor and Stuart period finds c 1450–c 1700 from excavations at riverside sites in Southwark*, MoLAS Monogr Ser 19, London

Egan, G, 2005b [Foundry finds], in Sygrave, J, Development and industry in Whitechapel: excavations at 27–29 Whitechapel High Street and 2–4 Colchester Street, London E1, *Trans London Middlesex Archaeol Soc* 56, 77–96

Egan, G, in prep a Byzantium in London?, in *Wellbeing in Byzantium* (ed A Muthesius)

Egan, G, in prep b *Excavated textile manufacturing evidence from London, c 1150–c 1750*

Egan, G, in prep c [Various contributions], in Griffiths, D, Philpott, D, and Egan, G, in prep *Meols: the archaeology of the north Wirral coast: discoveries and observations in the 19th and 20th centuries, with a catalogue of collections*, Oxford Univ School Archaeol Monogr Ser

Egan, G, in prep d The earliest English lead tokens?, in *Festschrift for Marian Archibald*

Egan, G, and Pritchard, F, 1991 *Dress accessories c 1150–c 1450*, HMSO Medieval Finds from Excavations in London Ser 3, London

Egan, G, Blades, N, and Goodburn Brown, D, 1992 Evidence for the mass production of copper-alloy dress accessories and other items in the late medieval City of London, in *Pre-printed papers of the 'Medieval Europe York 1992' conference: Vol 3, Technology and innovation*, 111–16, York

Ekwall, E, 1954 *Street-names of the City of London*, Oxford

Ellenberg, H, 1988 *Vegetation ecology of central Europe*, 4 edn, Cambridge

Elsner, H, nd *Vikinger-Museum Haithabu: Schaufenster einer frühen Stadt*, Neumünster

Encyclop Jud *Encyclopaedia Judaica* (16 vols), 1971, Jerusalem

Endrei, W, and Egan, G, 1982 The sealing of cloth in Europe with special reference to the English evidence, *Textile Hist* 13(1), 47–75

Engelmark, R, 1992 A review of farming economy in south Scania based on botanical evidence, in *The archaeology of the cultural landscape: field work and research in a south Swedish rural region* (eds L Larsson, J Callmer, and B Stjernquist), 369–75, Stockholm

Engelmark, R, and Linderholm, J, 1996 Prehistoric land management and cultivation: a soil chemical study, *Arkaeologiske Rapporter fra Esbjerg Museum*, 315–22

Engelmark, R, and Viklund, K, 1986 Järnålders-jordbruk i Norrland – teori och praktik, *Populär Arkeologi* 4(2), 22–34

English Heritage, 1988 The Guildhall and Guildhall Yard, City of London: Appendix A of unpub Public Enquiry rep

English Heritage, 1998 *Dendrochronology: guidelines on producing and interpreting dendrochronological dates*, London

English Heritage, 2001 *Archaeometallurgy*, Engl Heritage Centre for Archaeol Guidelines 1, Swindon

Faithorne, W, and Newcourt, R, 1658 'An Exact Delineation of the Cities of London and Westminster and the suburbs thereof together with the Borough of Southwark', reproduced in Margary 1981

Farmer, D, 1997 *The Oxford dictionary of saints*, 4 edn, Oxford

Ferembach, D, Schwidetzky, I, and Stloukal, M, 1980 Recommendations for age and sex diagnosis of skeletons, *J Human Evol* 9, 517–49

Fernie, E C, 1993 *An architectural history of Norwich Cathedral*, Oxford

Finnegan, M, 1978 Non-metric variation in the infracranial skeleton, *J Anatomy* 125, 23–37

Fitch, M, 1969 *Index to testamentary records in the Commissary Court of London: Vol 1, 1374–1488*, Brit Rec Soc & HMC Joint Pub 12, London

Fitch, M, 1973 *Index to testamentary records in the Commissary Court of London: Vol 2, 1489–1570*, Brit Rec Soc & HMC Joint Pub 13, London

Fitter, R S R, 1990 (1945) *London's natural history*, The New Naturalist 3, repr, London

Fletcher, B F, 1943 *A history of architecture on the comparative method for students, craftsmen and amateurs*, 11 edn, London

Fleury, M, and France-Lanord, A, 1998 *Les Trésors mérovingiens de la basilique de Saint-Denis*, Luxemburg

Fossier, R (ed), 1997 *The Cambridge history of the Middle Ages: Vol 2, 950–1250*, Cambridge

Foster, W, 1961 *A short history of the worshipful Company of Coopers of London*, Cambridge

Foulsham, L, 2001 An analysis of dog breeds in the medieval and post-medieval periods, unpub BSc dissertation, Univ London

Friedman, T, 1984 *James Gibbs*, New Haven and London

Friel, I, 1995 *Ships, shipbuilding and technology in England, 1200–1520*, London

Fry, G S (ed), 1896 *Abstracts of inquisitions post mortem relating to the City of London returned into the Court of Chancery: Part 1, 1485–1561*, Brit Rec Soc Pub 15, London

Fry, G S (ed) 1906 *Abstracts of inquisitions post mortem relating to the City of London returned into the Court of Chancery: Part 3, 1577–1603*, Brit Rec Soc Pub 38, London

Fryde, E B (ed), 1986 *Handbook of British chronology*, 3 edn, London

Gadd, D, and Dyson, T, 1981 Bridewell Palace: excavations at 9–11 Bridewell Place and 1–3 Tudor Street, City of London, 1978, *Post-Medieval Archaeol* 15, 1–79

Gaimster, D, and Gilchrist, R (eds), 2003 *The archaeology of Reformation, 1480–1580*, Soc Post-Medieval Archaeol Monogr Ser 1, Leeds

Galinou, M (ed), 1990 *London's pride: the glorious history of the capital's gardens*, London

Ganiaris, H, and Bateman, N, 2004 From arena to art gallery: the preservation of London's Roman amphitheatre in situ, in *Preserving archaeological remains in situ?: proceedings of the 2nd conference, 12–14 September 2001* (ed T Nixon), 198–201, London

Garmonsway, G N (trans/ed), 1972 *The Anglo-Saxon Chronicle*, London

Gebhardt, A, and Langohr, R, 1999 Micromorphological study of construction materials and living floors in the medieval motte of Werken (West Flanders, Belgium), *Geoarchaeol* 14(7), 595–620

GeoQuest, 1993 Archaeomagnetic study of a tiln kiln at Niblett Hall, City of London, unpub MoL rep

Gesta abbatum Gesta abbatum monasterii Sancti Albani (ed H T Riley), Rolls Ser (3 vols), 1867, London

Giertz, W, 1996 Middle Meuse valley ceramics of Huy-type: a preliminary analysis, *Medieval Ceram* 20, 33–64

Gilchrist, R, and Sloane, B, 2005 *Requiem: the medieval monastic cemetery in Britain*, London

Giorgi, J, 1997 Guildhall: assessment of the plant remains, unpub MoL rep

Giorgi, J, 1999 The plant remains from Bull Wharf, unpub MoL rep

Giorgi, J, 2003 The plant remains from the Guildhall, unpub MoL rep

Giorgi, J, 2004 The botanical remains, in Howe and Lakin 2004, 128–9

Giorgi, J, 2006 Plant remains, in Thomas et al 2006, 188–202

Goldberg, P, Macphail, R I, and Arpin, T, in prep *Colour guide to geoarchaeological microstratigraphy*

Goodall, A R, 1984 Objects of non-ferrous metal, in *Medieval and post-medieval finds from Exeter 1971–80* (ed J P Allan), Exeter Archaeol Rep 3, 337–48, Exeter

Goodburn, D, 1992 Wood and woodlands: carpenters and carpentry, in Milne 1992, 106–30

Goodburn, D, 1993a Fragments of a 10th-century timber arcade from Vintners Place on the London waterfront, *Medieval Archaeol* 37, 78–92

Goodburn, D, 1993b Spontning i London under vikingatid och medeltid, *Forntida Teknik (Utblick)* 1993(2), 17–23

Goodburn, D, 1994 Trees underground: new insights into trees and woodmanship in south-east England c 800–1300, *Botanical J Scotl* 46(4), 658–62

Goodburn, D, 1995 Beyond the posthole: notes on stratigraphy and timber buildings from a London perspective, in *Interpreting stratigraphy 5: proceedings of a conference held at Norwich Castle Museum, 16 June 1994* (ed L Shepherd), 43–52, Norwich

Goodburn, D, 1997a London's early medieval timber buildings: little-known traditions of construction, in De Boe and Verhaeghe 1997a, 249–57

Goodburn, D, 1997b The production of timber for building in England before and after c 1180 AD, in De Boe and Verhaeghe 1997a, 155–61

Goodburn, D, 1998 The death of the wildwood and birth of woodmanship in south-east England, in *Hidden dimensions* (ed C Bernick), 130–8, Vancouver

Goodburn, D, 1999 A summary of the evidence for early medieval woodwork found at Cheapside, in Hill and Woodger 1999, 47–51

Goodburn, D, 2003a Coffin construction, in Watson, S, *An excavation in the western cemetery of Roman London: Atlantic House, City of London*, MoLAS Archaeol Stud Ser 7, 61–3, London

Goodburn, D, 2003b Prehistoric woodwork, in Masefield, R, Branch, N, et al, A later Bronze Age well complex at Swalecliffe, Kent, *Antiq J* 83, 98–105

Goodburn, D, in prep Ancient woodwork, in Hill, J, and Rowsome, P, in prep *Roman London and the Walbrook stream crossing: excavations at 1 Poultry and vicinity, City of London*, MoLAS Monogr Ser

Goodburn, D, and Redknap, M, 1988 Replicas and wrecks from the Thames area, *London Archaeol* 6(1), 7–10, 19–22

Goubitz, O, van Driel-Murray, C, and Groenman-van Waateringe, W, 2001 *Stepping through time: archaeological footwear from prehistoric times until 1800*, Zwolle

Graham, I D G, and Scollar, I, 1976 Limitations on magnetic prospection in archaeology imposed by soil properties, *Archaeo-Physika* 6, 1–124

Graham-Campbell, J (ed), 1994 *Cultural atlas of the Viking world*, Oxford

Grant, A, 1975 The animal bones, in Cunliffe, B, *Excavations at Portchester Castle: Vol 1, Roman*, Rep Res Comm Soc Antiq London 32, 378–408, London

Grant, A, 1982 The use of tooth wear as a guide to the age of domestic ungulates, in Wilson et al 1982, 91–108

Grant, A, 1988 Animal resources, in Astill and Grant 1988, 149–87

Great Chron The Great chronicle of London (eds A H Thomas and I D Thornley), 1938, London

Greig, J, 1984 The palaeoecology of some British hay meadow types, in *Plants and ancient man: studies in palaeoethnobotany* (eds W van Zeist and W A Casparie), 213–26, Rotterdam

Greig, J, 1988 Plant resources, in Astill and Grant 1988, 108–27

Greig, J, 1991 The British Isles, in *Progress in Old World palaeoethnobotany: a retrospective view on the occasion of 20 years of the International Work Group for Palaeoethnobotany* (eds W van Zeist, K Wasylikowa, and K Behre), 299–334, Rotterdam

Grenville, J, 2003 Statue of Discipline or Temperance, in Marks and Williamson 2003, 260, cat no. 122

Grew, F, and de Neergaard, M, 1988 *Shoes and pattens*, HMSO Medieval Finds from Excavations in London Ser 2, London

Grigson, C, 1982 Sex and age determination of some bones and teeth of domestic cattle: a review of the literature, in Wilson et al 1982, 7–24

Grigson, J, 1987 *The Englishman's flora*, London

Grimes, W F, 1968 *The excavation of Roman and mediaeval London*, London

Guélat, M, and Federici-Schenardi, M, 1999 Develier-Courtételle (Jura): l'histoire d'une cabane en fosse reconstituée grâce à la micromorphologie, *Helvetia Archaeologica* 118/119, 58–63

Guildhall Art Gallery, 1999 *The history of Guildhall Art Gallery*, London

Guildhall Museum, 1908 *Catalogue of the collection of London antiquities in the Guildhall Museum*, 2 edn, London

Hagen, A, 1992 *A handbook of Anglo-Saxon food: processing and consumption*, Pinner

Hagen, A, 1995 *A second handbook of Anglo-Saxon food and drink: production and distribution*, Hockwold cum Wilton

Hall, A, 2003 Recognition and characterisation of turves in archaeological occupation deposits by means of macrofossil plant remains, unpub Engl Heritage Centre for Archaeol rep 16/2003

Hall, A R, and Kenward, H K, 1980 An interpretation of biological remains from Highgate, Beverley, *J Archaeol Sci* 7, 33–51

Hall, A R, and Kenward, H K, 1990 *Environmental evidence from the colonia*, Archaeol York 14/6, London

Hall, J, 1979 *Hall's dictionary of subject and symbols in art*, rev edn, London

Hall, R, 1984 *The Viking dig*, London

Hall, R, 1994 *English Heritage book of Viking Age York*, London

Hall, S J G, and Clutton-Brock, J, 1995 *200 years of British farm livestock*, London

Hammond, P W, 1993 *Food and feast in medieval England*, Stroud

Hansen, M, 1987 *The Hydrophiloidea (Coleoptera) of Fennoscandia and Denmark*, Fauna Entomologica Scandinavica Vol 18, Leiden

Harben, H, 1918 *A dictionary of the City of London*, London

Harding, C, 1986 Post-Roman gazetteer, unpub MoL (LAARC) rep

Harding, V, 1990 The population of London, 1550–1700: a

review of the published evidence, *London J* 15, 111–28

Harding, V, 1992 Burial choice and burial location, in Bassett 1992, 119–35

Harding, V, 2002 *The dead and the living in Paris and London, 1500–1670*, Cambridge

Hare, J N, 1985 *Battle Abbey: the eastern range and the excavations of 1978–80*, HBMCE Archaeol Rep 2, London

Harvey, J H, 1954 *English mediaeval architects: a biographical dictionary down to 1550*, London

Harvey, J H, 1978 *The Perpendicular style, 1330–1485*, London

Harvey, J H, 1984 *English mediaeval architects: a biographical dictionary down to 1550*, rev edn, Gloucester

Hatton, E, 1708 *A new view of London* (2 vols), London

Havinga, A J, 1984 A 20-year experimental investigation into the corrosion susceptibility of pollen and spores in various soil types, *Pollen et Spores* 26, 541–58

Hay, M, 1995 *Westminster Hall and the medieval kings*, London

Hayden, A, 2000 West side story: archaeological excavations at Cornmarket and Bridge Street Upper, Dublin – a summary account, in *Medieval Dublin I: proceedings of the Friends of Medieval Dublin symposium 1999* (ed S Duffy), 84–116, Dublin

Hessen, O von, 1984 *Il bacile bronzeo romanico da Empoli*, Quaderni del Dipartimento di archeologia e storia delle arti, Università di Siena, Sezione archeologia 4, Florence

Heyworth, M, 1991 Metallurgical analysis of the dress accessories, in Egan and Pritchard 1991, 387–95

Higgins, D A, and Davey, P, 1988 Draft guidelines for using the clay tobacco pipe record sheets, unpub MoL rep

Hill, J, and Woodger, A, 1999 *Excavations at 72–75 Cheapside/83–93 Queen Street, City of London*, MoLAS Archaeol Stud Ser 2, London

Hillaby, J, 1992 London: the 13th-century Jewry revisited, *Trans Jewish Hist Soc* 32, 89–158

Hillaby, J, 1994 The London Jewry: William I to John, *Trans Jewish Hist Soc* 33, 1–44

Hillson, S, 1986 *Teeth*, Cambridge

Hinton, D, 1990 Relief-decorated strap ends, in Biddle 1990, 497–500

Hinton, D, 2000 *A smith in Lindsey: the Anglo-Saxon grave at Tattershall Thorpe, Lincolnshire*, Soc Medieval Archaeol Monogr Ser 16, London

Hinton, P, 1996 Charred plant remains, in Andrews, P, and Crockett, A, *Three excavations along the Thames and its tributaries, 1994: Neolithic to Saxon settlement and burial in the Thames, Colne and Kennet valleys*, 43–7, Salisbury

HMC, 1874 Historical Manuscripts Commission, *Fourth report* (Balliol College, Oxford), London

HMC, 1883 Historical Manuscripts Commission, *Ninth report* (Dean and Chapter of St Paul's), London

HMC, 1899 Historical Manuscripts Commission, *Calendar of MSS of the Marquis of Salisbury preserved at Hatfield House, Salisbury*, London

Hodder, M A, 1991 *Excavations at Sandwell Priory and Hall, 1982–8: a Mesolithic settlement, medieval monastery and post-medieval country house in West Bromwich*, South Staffordshire Archaeol Hist Soc Trans 31, Stafford

Hodgson, J M, 1997 *Soil survey field handbook*, Soil Survey Land Res Centre Tech Monogr 5, Silsoe

Hoffman, J, 1979 Age estimation from diaphyseal length: 2 months to 12 years, *J Forensic Sci* 24, 461–9

Hoffman, K, 1970 *The year 1200: the exhibition*, Cloisters Stud Medieval Art 1, New York

Holden, E W, 1989 Slate roofing in medieval Sussex – a reappraisal, *Sussex Archaeol Collect* 127, 73–88

Holder, N, 1998 Inscriptions, writing and literacy in Saxon London, *Trans London Middlesex Archaeol Soc* 49, 81–97

Holder, N, 2003 The Guildhall basement, London EC2: archaeological assessment of the exposed medieval masonry recorded by the Museum of London in the excavations of the 1990s, unpub MoL rep

Hollaender, A E J, and Kellaway, W (eds), 1969 *Studies in London history presented to Philip Edmund Jones*, London

Hollar, Wenceslaus, c 1647 *Long View of London*, reproduced in London Topogr Soc Pub 19 for 1906–7, Pub 112 for 1970

Holloway, S, 1992 *Courage high! A history of firefighting in London*, London

Horsman, V, Milne, C, and Milne, G, 1988 *Aspects of Saxo-Norman London: Vol 1, Building and street development near Billingsgate and Cheapside*, London Middlesex Archaeol Soc Spec Pap 11, London

Howard, F E, 1936 *Mediaeval styles of the English parish church*, London

Howe, E, and Lakin, D, 2004 *Roman and medieval Cripplegate, City of London: archaeological excavations 1992–8*, MoLAS Monogr Ser 21, London

Howgego, J, 1978 *Printed maps of London c 1553–1850*, 2 edn, Folkestone

Huff, C, 1997 Falconers, fowlers and nobles: the sport of falconry in Anglo-Saxon England, *Medieval Life* 7, 7–9

Hughes, R, 2004 Wattle and daub: a technical and experimental study based on materials from the National Portrait Gallery, in Leary, J, *Tatberht's Lundenwic: archaeological excavations in Middle Saxon London*, Pre-Construct Archaeol Monogr Ser 2, 115–40, London

Hughes Clarke, A W (ed), 1940 *The registers of St Lawrence Jewry, London, 1538–1676*, Harleian Soc Pub 70, London

Hughes Clarke, A W (ed), 1941 *The registers of St Lawrence Jewry and St Mary Magdalen Milk Street, London, 1677–1812*, Harleian Soc Pub 71, London

Hughes Clarke, A W (ed), 1942 *The registers of St Mary Magdalen Milk Street, 1558–1666, and St Michael Bassishaw, London, 1528–1625*, Harleian Soc Pub 72, London

Hughes Clarke, A W (ed), 1943 *The registers of St Michael Bassishaw, London, 1626–1735*, Harleian Soc Pub 73, London

Hughes Clarke, A W (ed), 1944 *The registers of St Michael Bassishaw, London, 1736–1892*, Harleian Soc Pub 74, London

Hurst, J G, Neal, D S, and van Beuningen, H J E, 1986 *Pottery produced and traded in north-west Europe 1350–1650*, Rotterdam Pap 6, Rotterdam

Hyde, H M, 1940 *Judge Jeffreys*, London

Isserlin, R, 1996 Building Jerusalem in the 'Islands of the Sea': the archaeology of medieval Anglo-Jewry, in *Building Jerusalem: Jewish architecture in Britain* (ed S Kadish), 34–53, London

Jardine, L, 2002 *On a grander scale: the outstanding career of Sir Christopher Wren*, London

Jardine, L, 2003 *The curious life of Robert Hooke: the man who measured London*, London

Jeffery, P, 1996 *The City churches of Sir Christopher Wren*, London

Jeffery, S, 2003 Mansion House, in Lever 2003, 422–49

Jenner, A, and Vince, A G, 1983 A dated type-series of London medieval pottery: Part 3, A late medieval Hertfordshire glazed ware, *Trans London Middlesex Archaeol Soc* 34, 151–70

Johns, H, 1989 Introduction to the maps, in Lobel 1989, 57–62

Johnson, M, and Allen, S, 2004 Coffins at Beverley Minster, *Archaeologist* 52, 36–7

Jones, G, Straker, V, and Davis, A, 1991 Early medieval plant use and ecology, in Vince 1991a, 347–79

Jones, M, and Dimbleby, G (eds), 1981 *The environment of man: the Iron Age to the Anglo-Saxon period*, BAR Brit Ser 87, Oxford

Jordan, W K, 1960 *The charities of London 1480–1660*, London

Kaldi, J, 1986 Diagenesis of nearshore carbonate rocks in the Sprotborough Member of the Cadeby (Magnesian Limestone) Formation (Upper Permian) of eastern England, in *The English Zechstein and related topics* (eds G M Harwood and D S Smith), 90–7, Oxford

Keen, L, 1993 Pre-Conquest glazed relief tiles from All Saints church, Pavement, York, *J Brit Archaeol Ass* 3 ser 146, 67–86

Keen, L, 2002 Windsor Castle and the Penn tile industry, in *Windsor: medieval archaeology, art and architecture of the Thames valley* (eds L Keen and E Scarff), Brit Archaol Ass Conf Trans 25, 219–37, Leeds

Keene, D, 1990 Wooden vessels, in Biddle 1990, 959–66

Keene, D, 1996 Metalworking in medieval London: an historical survey, *Hist Metall* 30, 95–102

Keene, D, 2003a Alfred in London, in *Alfred the Great: papers from the 11th-centenary conferences* (ed T Reuter), 235–49, Aldershot

Keene, D, 2003b Civic institutions, in Marks and Williamson 2003, 262–4

Keene, D, 2004 From Conquest to capital: St Paul's *c* 1100–1300, in Keene et al 2004, 17–32

Keene, D, Burns, A, and Saint, A (eds), 2004 *St Paul's: the cathedral church of London, 604–2004*, New Haven and London

Keller, C, 1995 Pingsdorf-type ware: an introduction, *Medieval Ceram* 19, 19–28

Kemble, J M, 1839–48 *Codex diplomaticus Aevi Saxonum*, London

Kenward, H K, 1978 *The analysis of archaeological insect assemblages: a new approach*, Archaeol York 19/1, London

Kenward, H K, 1997 Synanthropic insects and the size, remoteness and longevity of archaeological occupation sites: applying concepts from biogeography to past 'islands' of human occupation, *Quat Proc* 5, 135–52

Kenward, H K, and Allison, E P, 1994 A preliminary view of the insect assemblages from the early Christian rath site at Deer Park Farms, Northern Ireland, in *Environment and economy in Anglo-Saxon England* (ed J Rackham), CBA Res Rep 89, 88–103, London

Kenward, H K, and Hall, A R, 1995 *Biological evidence from Anglo-Scandinavian deposits at 16–22 Coppergate*, Archaeol York 14/7, London

Kenward, H K, and Hall, A R, 1997 Enhancing bio-archaeological interpretation using indicator groups: stable manure as a paradigm, *J Archaeol Sci* 24, 663–73

Kenward, H K, Hall, A R, and Jones, A K G, 1980 A tested set of techniques for the extraction of plant and animal macro-fossils from waterlogged archaeological deposits, *Sci & Archaeol* 22, 3–15

Ker, N R (ed), 1964 *Medieval libraries of Great Britain: a list of surviving books*, Roy Hist Soc Guides & Handbooks 3, 2 edn, London

Keys, L, 2003 Report on the iron slag from the Guildhall Yard excavations (GYE92), unpub MoL rep

Kilmurry, K, 1980 *The pottery industry of Stamford, Lincolnshire, c AD 850–1250*, BAR Brit Ser 84, Oxford

Kingsford, C L (ed), 1905 *Chronicles of London*, Oxford

Kingsford, C L, 1916 Historical notes on medieval London houses, *London Topogr Rec* 10, 44–144

Kinmonth, C, 1993 *Irish country furniture 1700–1950*, New Haven and London

Kjølbye-Biddle, B, 1990 Early medieval spoons, in Biddle 1990, 828–31

Klemperer, W D, 1992 The study of burials at Hulton Abbey, in *Pre-printed papers of the 'Medieval Europe York 1992' conference: Vol 4, Death and burial*, 85–91, York

Koldeweij, E, 2001 *The English candlestick 1425–1925*, London

Kurath, H, Kuhn, S, and Lewis, R (eds), 1956–99 *Middle English dictionary*, Ann Arbor, Mi

La Neve, J, with Greenway, D E, 1968 *Fasti ecclesiae anglicanae 1066–1300: Vol 1, St Paul's, London*, London

L&P Hen VIII Letters and papers, foreign and domestic, of the reign of Henry VIII (eds J S Brewer, J Gairdner, and R H Brodie) (22 vols in 35), Public Rec Office, 1864–1932, London

Latham, R, and Matthews, W (eds), 1970–83 *The diary of Samuel Pepys: a new and complete transcription* (11 vols), London

Lawson, A J, 2000 *Potterne 1982–5: animal husbandry in later prehistoric Wiltshire*, Wessex Archaeol Rep 17, Salisbury

Lawson, G, 1980 Stringed musical instruments: artefacts in the archaeology of Western Europe, 500 BC to AD 1200, unpub PhD thesis, Univ Cambridge

Lawson, G, 1985 Musical instrument pegs, in Hare 1985, 151–4

Lawson, G, 1990 Musical instruments, in Biddle 1990, 710–18

Lawson, G, 1993 An important cache of musical instrument components, in Knight, J K, Excavations at Montgomery Castle: Part 3, The finds other than metalwork, *Archaeol Cambrensis* 148, 196–203

Lea, R, 1987 Guildhall Yard East: chapel, unpub MoL rep

Leake, J, 1667 A map of the City of London showing the extent of the damage caused by the Great Fire of 1666, reproduced in Margary 1981

Letts, J, 2001 Medieval thatch, *Brit Archaeol* 58, 11–13

Lever, J, 2003 *Catalogue of the drawings of George Dance the younger (1741–1825) and of George Dance the elder (1695–1768) from the collection of Sir John Soane's Museum*, London

Liber Cust Liber custumarum in munimenta Gildhallae Londoniensis (ed H T Riley), Rolls Ser 12 (3 vols in 4), 1859–62, London

Liddle, J, 2007 Animal bone from the phase 2 backfilling of the city ditch (OA17), in Lyon, J, *Within these walls: Roman and medieval defences north of Newgate at the Merrill Lynch Financial Centre, City of London*, MoLAS Monogr Ser 33, 109–11, London

Lillywhite, B, 1963 *London coffee houses: a reference book of the coffee houses of the 17th, 18th and 19th centuries*, London

Lillywhite, B, 1972 *London signs: a reference book of London signs from earliest times to about the mid-19th century*, London

Lindroth, C H, 1974 *Coleoptera: Carabidae*, Handbooks for the Identification of British Insects Vol 4 (part 2), London

Litten, J, 1991 *The English way of death: the common funeral since 1450*, London

Lloyd, B, 1978 Monumental inscriptions found in the chapel of St Mary Magdalen by Guildhall usually known as Guildhall chapel on its demolition in 1822, unpub typescript in Guildhall Library

Lobel, M D (ed), 1989 *British atlas of historic towns: Vol 3, The City of London, from prehistoric times to c 1520*, Oxford

Locker, A, 2001 The role of stored fish in England 900–1750 AD: the evidence from historical and archaeological data, unpub PhD thesis, Univ Southampton

Locker, A, 2006 Vertebrate remains: contribution on fish bone, in Seeley et al 2006, 140–1

Loengard, J S (ed), 1989 *London viewers and their certificates 1508–58*, London Rec Soc Pub 26, London

London, H S (ed), 1967 *Glover's roll, c 1253–8, and Walford's roll, c 1273*, in *Rolls of arms: Henry III* (ed A Wagner), Aspilogia 2, 87–204, London

Lubin, H, 1990 *The Worcester pilgrim*, Worcester Cathedral Pub 1, Worcester

Lucht, W H, 1987 *Die Käfer Mitteleuropas: Katalog*, Krefeld

Lucy, S, 2000 *The Anglo-Saxon way of death*, Stroud

Lyon, J, 2004 New work on Cripplegate fort: excavations at 25 Gresham Street, 2000–01, *Trans London Middlesex Archaeol Soc* 55, 153–82

Mabey, R, 1972 *Food for free: a guide to the edible wild plants of Britain*, London

McClean, T, 1981 *English medieval gardens*, London

MacGregor, A, Mainman, A J, and Rogers, N S H, 1999 *Craft, industry and everyday life: bone, antler, ivory and horn from Anglo-Scandinavian and medieval York*, Archaeol York 17/12, York

McKellar, E, 1999 *The birth of modern London: the development and design of the city 1660–1720*, Manchester

McNeilage, T, 1995 Polychrome stone in the Guildhall, London, *Conserv News* 56 (March), 28

Macphail, R I, 1981 Soil and botanical studies of the 'dark earth', in Jones and Dimbleby 1981, 309–31

Macphail, R I, 1988 Soil report on the Middle Saxon floor and 'dark earth' at Jubilee Hall, in Cowie, R, and Whytehead, R L, with Blackmore, L, Two Middle Saxon occupation sites: excavations at Jubilee Hall and 21–22 Maiden Lane, *Trans London Middlesex Archaeol Soc* 39, 156–9

Macphail, R I, 2001 Dragon Hall, King Street, Norwich: soil micromorphology and chemistry, unpub Norfolk Archaeol Unit rep

Macphail, R I, 2002 *Pevensey Castle: soil micromorphology and chemistry of the Roman deposits and 'dark earth'*, Reading

Macphail, R I, 2003 Industrial activities – some suggested microstratigraphic signatures: ochre, building materials and iron working, in *The environmental archaeology of industry* (eds P

Murphy and P E J Wiltshire), Symposia Ass Envir Archaeol 20, 94–106, Oxford

Macphail, R I, and Courty, M A, 1985 Interpretation and significance of urban deposits, in *Proceedings of the 3rd Nordic Conference on the Application of Scientific Methods in Archaeology: Mariehamn, Åland, Finland, 8–11 October 1984* (eds T Edgren and H Jungner), 71–83, Helsinki

Macphail, R I, and Cruise, G M, 1993 King Edward Buildings (KEB92): assessment of soils and pollen, unpub MoL rep

Macphail, R I, and Cruise, G M, 1995 Guildhall Yard East (GYE92): brief assessment of microstratigraphy (soil micromorphology and pollen), unpub MoL rep

Macphail, R I, and Cruise, G M, 2001 The soil micromorphologist as team player: a multianalytical approach to the study of European microstratigraphy, in *Earth science and archaeology* (ed R Ferring), 241–67, New York

Macphail, R I, and Goldberg, P, 1995 Recent advances in micromorphological interpretations of soils and sediments from archaeological sites, in *Archaeological sediments and soils: analysis, interpretation and management* (ed R I Macphail), 1–24, London

Macphail, R I, and Linderholm, J, in prep Soil micromorphology, in Burch and Treveil in prep

Macphail, R I, Courty, M A, Hather, J, and Wattez, J, 1997 The soil micromorphological evidence of domestic occupation and stabling activities, in *Arene Candide: a functional and environmental assessment of the Holocene sequence (excavations Bernabò Brea-Cardini, 1949–50)* (ed R Maggi), Memorie dell'Instituto Italiano di Paleontologia Umana, 53–88, Rome

Macphail, R I, Cruise, G M, Mellalieu, S J, and Niblett, R, 1998 Micromorphological interpretation of a 'turf-filled' funerary shaft at St Albans, United Kingdom, *Geoarchaeol* 13(6), 617–44

Macphail, R I, Crowther, J, Acott, T G, Bell, M G, and Cruise, G M, 2003a The Experimental Earthwork at Wareham, Dorset, after 33 years: changes to the buried LFH and Ah horizon, *J Archaeol Sci* 30, 77–93

Macphail, R I, Crowther, J, and Cruise, G M, 2003b Microstratigraphy: soil micromorphology, chemistry and pollen: the Roman amphitheatre of London and its surroundings, unpub MoL rep

Macphail, R I, Crowther, J, and Cruise, G M, 2003c Microstratigraphy: soil micromorphology, chemistry and pollen: the Guildhall of London, from an 11th-century settlement to a civic and commercial capital, unpub MoL rep

Madge, S J (ed), 1901 *Abstracts of inquisitions post mortem relating to the City of London returned into the Court of Chancery: Part 2, 1561–77*, Brit Rec Soc Pub 26, London

Maitland, W, 1756 *The history and survey of London* (2 vols), London

Malcolm, G, and Bowsher, D, with Cowie, R, 2003 *Middle Saxon London: excavations at the Royal Opera House 1989–99*, MoLAS Monogr Ser 15, London

Maloney, C, 1980 A witch bottle from Duke's Place, Aldgate, *Trans London Middlesex Archaeol Soc* 31, 157–8

Maltby, M, 1981 Iron Age, Romano-British and Anglo-Saxon animal husbandry: a review of the faunal evidence, in Jones and Dimbleby 1981, 155–203

Maltby, M, 1979 Faunal studies from urban sites: the animal bones from Exeter 1971–5, Exeter Archaeol Rep 2, Sheffield

Manchester, K, 1992 The palaeopathology of urban infections, in Bassett 1992, 8–15

Manzione, C K, 1997 Christ's Hospital of London, 1552–98: 'a passing deed of pity', Selinsgrove, Pa

Margary, H, 1981 A collection of early maps of London 1553–1667, Margary in assoc Guildhall Library, Kent

Markham, G, 1633 Country contentments: or, the husbandmans recreations, London

Marks, R, and Williamson, P (eds), 2003 Gothic: art for England 1400–1547, Victoria and Albert Museum exhibition catalogue, London

Marsden, P, 1968 Archaeological finds in the City of London, 1965–6, Trans London Middlesex Archaeol Soc 22(1), 1–17

Mardsen, P, 1981 The pre-1411 Guildhall of London, London Archaeol 4(5), 115–20

Marsh, B, 1914 Records of the worshipful Company of Carpenters: Vol 2, Warden's account book 1438–1516, Oxford

Marstein, O, 1989 Sko og andre gjenstander i laer, Fortiden i Trondheim Bygrunn: Folkebibliotekstomten, Meddelelser 23, Trondheim

Marzinzik, S, 2003 Early Anglo-Saxon buckles (late 5th to early 8th centuries AD): their classification and context, BAR Brit Ser 357, Oxford

Masters, B, 1969 The mayor's household before 1600, in Hollaender and Kellaway 1969, 95–114

Masters, B, 1973 The City Surveyor, the City Engineer and the City Architect and Planning Officer, Guildhall Misc 4, 237–55

Masters, B, 1988 The chamberlain of the City of London 1237–1987, London

Matthews, W, French, C A I, Lawrence, T, Cutler, D F, and Jones, M K, 1997 Microstratigraphic traces of site formation processes and human activity, World Archaeol 29, 281–308

Mays, S, 1997 Life and death in a medieval village, in De Boe and Verhaeghe 1997b, 121–5

Merrifield, R, 1954 The use of bellarmines as witch-bottles, Guildhall Misc 3, 3–15

Merrifield, R, 1965 The Roman City of London, London

Milbourn, T, 1881 The church of St Stephen Walbrook, Trans London Middlesex Archaeol Soc os 5, 327–402

Miles, A W, 2003 The crypt of St Andrew Holborn: an archaeological watching brief, unpub MoL rep

Miller, P, and Saxby, D, 2007 The Augustinian priory of St Mary Merton, Surrey: excavations 1976–90, MoLAS Monogr Ser 34, London

Miller, P, and Stephenson, R, 1999 A 14th-century pottery site in Kingston upon Thames, Surrey: excavations at 70–76 Eden Street, MoLAS Archaeol Stud Ser 1, London

Mills, P, and Oliver, J, 1666–7 The survey of building sites in the City of London after the great fire of 1666 by Peter Mills and John Oliver (eds P E Jones and T F Reddaway), London Topogr Soc Pub 97–9, 101, 103 (5 vols), 1962–7, London

Milne, G, 1986 The Great Fire of London, London

Milne, G, 1992 Timber building techniques in London, c 900–1400: an archaeological study of waterfront installations and related material, London Middlesex Archaeol Soc Spec Pap 15, London

Milne, G, 1997 St Bride's church, London: archaeological research 1952–60 and 1992–5, Engl Heritage Archaeol Rep 11, London

Milne, G, with Cohen, N, 2001 Excavations at medieval Cripplegate, London: archaeology after the Blitz, 1946–68, Engl Heritage Archaeol Rep, Swindon

Mitchiner, M, 1988 Jettons, medalets and tokens: Vol 1, The medieval period and Nuremberg, London

Mitchiner, M, and Skinner, A, 1983 English tokens c 1200–1425, Brit Numis J 53, 29–77

Moe, D, 1983 Palynology of sheep's faeces: relationship between pollen content, diet and local pollen rain, Grana 22, 105–13

Moffett, L C, and Smith, D N, 1995 Insects and plants from a late medieval and early post-medieval tenement in Stone, Staffordshire, UK, Circaea 12(2), 157–75

Moore, P D, Webb, J A, and Collinson, M E, 1991 Pollen analysis, Oxford

Moorhouse, S, 1972 Medieval distilling apparatus of glass and pottery, Medieval Archaeol 16, 79–121

Moorhouse, S, 1988 Documentary evidence for medieval ceramic roofing materials and its archaeological implications: some thoughts, Medieval Ceram 12, 33–55

Morris, C, 2000 Wood and woodworking in Anglo-Scandinavian and medieval York, Archaeol York 17/13, York

Morris, R K, 1992 An English glossary of medieval mouldings: with an introduction to mouldings c 1040–1240, Architect Hist 35, 1–17

Mortimer, C, 2002 Bedern and the foundry: analysis of material from high-temperature processes, including a re-examination of material from the foundry, in Ottaway, P, and Rogers, N, Craft, industry and everyday life: finds from medieval York, Archaeol York 17/15, 2708–12, York

Mortimer, J, 1712 The whole art of husbandry; or, the way of managing and improving of land, 3 edn, London

Mould, Q, Carlisle, I, and Cameron, E, 2003 Craft, industry and everyday life: leather and leatherworking in Anglo-Scandinavian and medieval York, Archaeol York 17/16, York

Moulins, D de, 1989 Plant remains: National Gallery extension, in Whytehead, R L, and Cowie, R, with Blackmore, L, Excavations at the Peabody site, Chandos Place, and the National Gallery, Trans London Middlesex Archaeol Soc 40, 141–8

Moulins, D de, in prep The weeds from the thatch roofs of medieval cottages from the south of England, in Vegetation history and archaeobotany

MPRG, 1998 A guide to the classification of medieval ceramic forms, Medieval Pottery Res Grp Occas Pap 1, London

Mücher, H J, Slotboom, R T, and ter Veen, W J, 1990 Palynology and micromorphology of a man-made soil: a reconstruction of the agricultural history since late-medieval times of the Posteles in the Netherlands, Catena 17, 55–67

Murray, H, 1983 Viking and early medieval buildings in Dublin: a study of the buildings excavated under the direction of A B Ó Ríordáin in High Street, Winetavern Street and Christchurch Place, Dublin, 1962–3, 1967–76, BAR Brit Ser 119, Oxford

Museum of London, 1994 (1980) Archaeological site manual, 3 edn, London

Nailer, A, and Reid, P, in prep Post-Roman footwear, in Burch and Treveil in prep

Nenk, B, and Pearce, J E, 1994 Two Stamford-type ware

modelled birds from London, *Medieval Ceram* 18, 77–80

Newcourt, R, 1708–10 *Repertorium ecclesiasticum parochiale Londinense* (2 vols), London

Nichols, J B, 1819 *A brief account of the Guildhall of the City of London*, London

Nightingale, P, 1987 The origin of the Court of Husting and the Danish influence on London's development into a capital city, *Engl Hist Rev* 404 (July), 559–78

Nightingale, P, 1995 *A medieval mercantile community: the Grocers' Company and the politics and trade of London 1000–1485*, New Haven and London

Norman, P, 1905 The church of St Lawrence Jewry, *Trans St Paul's Ecclesiol Soc* 5, 263–4

North, J J, 1975 *English hammered coinage: Vol 2, Edward I to Charles II, 1272–1662*, London

O'Connor, S J, 1993 *A calendar of the cartularies of John Pyel and Adam Fraunceys*, Camden Soc 5 ser 2, London

O'Connor, T P, 1989 *Bones from Anglo-Scandinavian levels at 16–22 Coppergate*, Archaeol York 15/3, London

O'Connor, T P, 1991 *Bones from 46–54 Fishergate*, Archaeol York 15/4, London

ODNB *Oxford dictionary of national biography* (eds H C G Matthew and B Harrison), 2004, Oxford

Ogilby, J, and Morgan, W, 1676 'Large and Accurate Map of the City of London', reproduced in Margary, H, 1976, *'Large and Accurate Map of the City of London' by John Ogilby and William Morgan, 1676*, Margary in assoc Guildhall Library, Kent

Oldroyd, H, 1964 *The natural history of the flies*, London

Ortner, D J, and Putschar, W G J, 1981 *Identification of pathological conditions in human skeletal remains*, Washington, DC

Oswald, A, 1975 *Clay pipes for the archaeologist*, BAR Brit Ser 14, Oxford

Palliser, D M, 1978 The medieval street-names of York, *York Historian* 2, 2–16

Palliser, D M, 1980 Historical assessment, in Dawes, J D, and Magilton, J R, *The cemetery of St Helen-on-the-Walls, Aldwark*, Archaeol York 12/1, 82–3, London

Pantin, W A, 1961 Medieval inns, in *Studies in building history: essays in recognition of the work of B H St J O'Neil* (ed E M Jope), 166–91, London

Papworth, J W, 1874 *Papworth's ordinary of British armorials*, London

Parsons, D (ed), 1990 *Stone quarrying and building in England AD 43–1525*, London

Payne, A, 2003 Aldermen of London, in Marks and Williamson 2003, 268, cat no. 130

Pearce, J, 1992 *Post-medieval pottery in London 1500–1700: Part 1, Border wares*, London

Pearce, J, 1997 Evidence for the early 16th-century Surrey-Hampshire border ware industry from the City of London, *Medieval Ceram* 21, 43–60

Pearce, J, 1998a Ceramic curfews, in Egan 1998, 122–5

Pearce, J, 1998b Hanging lamps: ceramic, in Egan 1998, 127–9

Pearce, J, 2004 Metalworking, in Howe and Lakin 2004, 102–5

Pearce, J, and Vince, A G, 1988 *A dated type-series of London medieval pottery: Part 4, Surrey whitewares*, London Middlesex Archaeol Soc Spec Pap 10, London

Pearce, J, Vince, A G, and White, R, 1982 A dated type-series of London medieval pottery: Part 1, Mill Green ware, *Trans London Middlesex Archaeol Soc* 33, 266–98

Pearce, J, Vince, A G, and Jenner, M A, 1985 *A dated type-series of London medieval pottery: Part 2, London-type ware*, London Middlesex Archaeol Soc Spec Pap 6, London

Pearson, E, in prep Plant remains from Billingsgate

Pelling, R, and Robinson, M, 2000 Saxon emmer wheat from the upper and middle Thames valley, England, *Envir Archaeol* 5, 117–19

Pepper, G, 1992 An archaeology of the Jewry in medieval London, *London Archaeol* 7(1), 3–6

Perks, S, 1910 *The restoration and recent discoveries at the Guildhall, London: a paper read at the Royal Society of Arts, on Wednesday, June 1st, 1910*, London

Peterken, G, 1996 *Natural woodland*, Cambridge

Pevsner, N, 1957 *The buildings of England: London 1, The Cities of London and Westminster*, Harmondsworth

Phenice, T W, 1969 A newly developed visual method of sexing the os pubis, *American J Phys Anthropol* 30, 297–302

Platt, C, and Coleman-Smith, R, 1975 *Excavations in medieval Southampton 1953–69: Vol 2, The finds*, Leicester

Pluis, J, 1997 *The Dutch tile: designs and names*, Leiden

PMSA Public Monuments and Sculpture Association, national recording project (http://pmsa.courtauld.ac.uk/pmsa/CL/CLCOL41x.htm)

Porter, G, 1997 An early medieval settlement at Guildhall, City of London, in De Boe and Verhaeghe 1997a, 147–52

Porter, S, 1996 *The Great Fire of London*, Stroud

Powell, F, 1996 The human bone, in Boddington, A, *Raunds Furnells: the Anglo-Saxon church and churchyard*, Engl Heritage Archaeol Rep 7, 113–24, London

Powers, R, 1988 A tool for coping with juvenile human bones from archaeological excavations, in White 1988, 74–8

Price, J E, 1886 *A descriptive account of the Guildhall of the City of London, its history and associations*, London

Pritchard, F, 1982 Building material: Swan Lane car park, Upper Thames Street (SWA81), unpub MoL rep

Pritchard, F, 1988 Embroidery, in Grew and de Neergaard 1988, 75–9

Pritchard, F, 1991 Small finds, in Vince 1991a, 120–278

Prummel, W, and Frisch, H J, 1986 A guide for the distinction of species, sex and body side in bones of sheep and goat, *J Archaeol Sci* 13, 567–77

Rackham, O, 1976 *Trees and woodland in the British landscape*, London

RCHME, 1929 Roy Comm Hist Monuments Engl, *An inventory of the historical monuments in London: Vol 4, The City of London*, London

Reddaway, T F, 1940 *The rebuilding of London*, London

Remnant, M, 1986 *English bowed instruments from Anglo-Saxon to Tudor times*, Oxford

Reynolds, P, 1979 *Iron Age farm: the Butser experiment*, London

Reynolds, P, 1987 *Ancient farming*, Aylesbury

RIBA, 1865 [Report on the discussion following the paper on the restoration of the Guildhall presented by the architect of the new roof, Horace Jones], *Roy Inst Brit Architects, Pap* (1864–5)

Rielly, K, 1997 Assessment of the animal bones from the Guildhall excavations, unpub MoL rep

Rielly, K, in prep The animal bones, in Burch and Treveil in prep

Rigg, J M (ed), 1902 Select pleas, starrs, and other records from the rolls of the Exchequer of the Jews, AD 1220–84, Selden Soc 15 (Jewish Hist Soc Spec Vol), London

Riley, H T (ed), 1868 Memorials of London and London life in the 13th, 14th and 15th centuries: being a series of extracts, local, social and political, from the early archives of the City of London, AD 1276–1419, London

Roberts, C, and Cox, M, 2003 Health and disease in Britain from prehistory to the present day, Stroud

Rodwell, J S (ed), 2000 British plant communities: Vol 5, Maritime communities and vegetation of open habitats, Cambridge

Rodwell, W, and Rodwell, K, 1982 St Peter's church, Barton-upon-Humber: excavation and structural study 1978–81, Antiq J 62(2), 283–315

Rocsdahl, E, and Wilson, D M (eds), 1992 From Viking to Crusader: the Scandinavians and Europe 800–1200, 22nd Council of Europe exhibition catalogue, New York

Rogers, J, and Waldron, T, 1989 Infections in palaeopathology: the basis of classification according to most probable cause, J Archaeol Sci 16, 611–25

Rogers, J, and Waldron, T, 1995 A field guide to joint disease in archaeology, Chichester

Rogers, J, and Waldron, T, 2001 DISH and the monastic way of life, Int J Osteol 11, 357–65

Roth, C, 1949 (1941) A history of the Jews in England, 2 edn, Oxford

Ryan, P, 1996 Brick in Essex from the Roman Conquest to the Reformation, Chelmsford

Salter, H E, 1931 Particulars of properties in the City of London belonging to St John's College, Oxford, London Topogr Rec 15, London

Samuel, M W, 1989 The 15th-century garner at Leadenhall, London, Antiq J 69(1), 119–53

Samuel, M W, 1999 St Paul's Cathedral: excavations in the crypt 1994–6: archaeological post-excavation assessment of the architectural fragments, unpub MoL rep

Samuel, M W, 2003 Guildhall east window, Guildhall, Aldermanbury, EC2, City of London: the medieval stone and iron elements removed in the 1995 intervention, unpub MoL rep

Samuel, M W, 2005 The Guildhall: architectural reconstruction, worked stone and petrological analysis, unpub MoL rep

Samuel, M, and Milne, G, 1992 The 'Ledene hall' and medieval market, in Milne, G, From Roman basilica to medieval market: archaeology in action in the City of London, 39–50, London

Saunders, A, and Schofield, J (eds), 2001 Tudor London: a map and a view, London Topogr Soc Pub 159, London

Savage, A (trans/coll), 1982 The Anglo-Saxon chronicles, London

Sawyer, P H, 1968 Anglo-Saxon charters: an annotated list and bibliography, Roy Hist Soc Guides & Handbooks 8, London

Schmid, E, 1972 Atlas of animal bones for prehistorians, archaeologists and Quaternary geologists, London

Schofield, J (ed), 1987 The London surveys of Ralph Treswell, London Topogr Soc Pub 135, London

Schofield, J, 1988 The cemetery of St Nicholas Shambles, in White 1988, 7–27

Schofield, J, 1994 Saxon and medieval parish churches in the City of London: a review, Trans London Middlesex Archaeol Soc 45, 23–145

Schofield, J (ed), with Maloney, C, 1998 Archaeology in the City of London 1907–91: a guide to records of excavations by the Museum of London and its predecessors, MoL Archaeol Gazetteer Ser 1, London

Schofield, J, 1999 (1984) The building of London from the Conquest to the Great Fire, 3 edn, Stroud

Schofield, J, 2001 The view of the City of London from the north, in Saunders and Schofield 2001, 33–57

Schofield, J, 2003a (1995) Medieval London houses, rev edn, New Haven and London

Schofield, J, 2003b Some aspects of the reformation of religious space in London, 1540–1660, in Gaimster and Gilchrist 2003, 310–24

Schofield, J, and Lea, R, 2005 Holy Trinity Priory, Aldgate, City of London: an archaeological reconstruction and history, MoLAS Monogr Ser 24, London

Schofield, J, Allen, P, and Taylor, C, 1990 Medieval buildings and property development in the area of Cheapside, Trans London Middlesex Archaeol Soc 41, 39–237

Schweingruber, F H, 1990 Anatomy of European woods: an atlas for the identification of European trees, shrubs and dwarf shrubs, Bern

Scott, D A, 2001 The application of scanning X-ray fluorescence microanalysis in the examination of cultural materials, Archaeometry 43, 472–78

Scull, C, in prep The composite belt suite, in Cowie, R, and Blackmore, L, in prep Lundenwic: excavations in Middle Saxon London 1987–2000, MoLAS Monogr Ser

Seeley, D, Phillpotts, C, and Samuel, M, 2006 Winchester Palace: excavations at the Southwark residence of the bishops of Winchester, MoLAS Monogr Ser 31, London

Serjeantson, D, 1989 Animal remains and the tanning trade, in Diet and craft in towns (eds D Serjeantson and T Waldron), BAR Brit Ser 199, 129–46, Oxford

Seymour, R, 1734 A survey of London, London

Shelley, H C, 1909 Inns and taverns of old London, London

Sheppard, F, 1998 London: a history, Oxford

Silverside, A J, 1977 A phytosociological survey of British arable weed and related communities, unpub PhD thesis, Univ Durham

Simpson, I A, Milek, K B, and Gudmundsson, G, 1999 A reinterpretation of the great pit at Hofstadir, Iceland, using sediment thin-section micromorphology, Geoarchaeol 14, 511–30

Skidmore, P, 1999 The mineralised flies, in Connor, A, and Buckley, R, Roman and medieval occupation in Causeway Lane, Leicester, Leicester Archaeol Monogr Ser 5, 341–3, Leicester

Smirnova, L, 2001 Utilization of rare bone materials in medieval Novgorod, in Crafting bone: skeletal technologies through time and space: proceedings of the 2nd meeting of the (ICAZ) Worked Bone Research Group, Budapest, 31 August–5 September 1999 (eds A M Choyke and L Bartosiewicz), BAR Int Ser 937, 9–17, Oxford

Smith, D N, 1997 The insect fauna, in Thomas et al 1997, 245–7

Smith, D N, 1998 The insect remains from Saxon and medieval deposits at Bull Wharf, London, unpub MoL rep

Smith, D N, 2000 The insect remains from 1 Poultry, London, unpub Univ Birmingham Envir Archaeol Services rep 13

Smith, D N, 2002 Insect remains, in Barber, B, and Thomas, C, The London Charterhouse, MoLAS Monogr Ser 10, 113–15, London

Smith, D N, 2006 Insect remains, in Seeley et al 2006, 142–4

Smith, D N, and Chandler, G, 2004 The insect remains, in Sloane, B, and Malcolm, G, Excavations at the priory of the Order of the Hospital of St John of Jerusalem, Clerkenwell, London, MoLAS Monogr Ser 20, 389–94, London

Smith, D N, Osborne, P, and Barratt, J, 2000 Beetles and evidence of past environments at Goldcliff, in Bell et al 2000, 245–60

Smith, K G V, 1973 Insects and other arthropods of medical importance, London

Smith, K G V, 1989 An introduction to the immature stages of British flies, Handbooks for the Identification of British Insects Vol 10 (part 14), London

Smith, R, 1952 The library at Guildhall in the 15th and 16th centuries, Guildhall Misc 1, 3–9

Smith, R, 1956 The library at Guildhall in the 15th and 16th centuries, Guildhall Misc 6, 3–6

Smith, R N, 1969 Fusion of ossification centres in the cat, J Small Anim Pract 10, 523–30

Smith, T, 2002 London wool warehouses, GLIAS Newsl (April)

Smith, T P, 1999a London's earliest medieval roofing tiles: a comparative study, Medieval Ceram 22/23, 66–71

Smith, T P, 1999b London pantiles: use and status – a cautionary tale, London Middlesex Archaeol Soc Newsl 96, 7–9

Smith, T P, with Betts, I M, 2004 Ceramic building materials, in Barber et al 2004, 138–46

Spencer, B, 1998 Pilgrim souvenirs and secular badges, HMSO Medieval Finds from Excavations in London Ser 7, London

Stace, C, 1991 New flora of the British Isles, Cambridge

Steane, J M, 2001 The archaeology of power, Stroud

Steer, C, in prep Funeral monuments in medieval London, PhD thesis, Royal Holloway, Univ London

Stenton, F M, 1970 Preparatory to Anglo-Saxon England, Oxford

Stockmarr, J, 1971 Tablets with spores used in absolute pollen analysis, Pollen et Spores 13, 615–21

Stoops, G, 1996 Complementary techniques for the study of thin sections of archaeological materials, in Proceedings of the 13th International Congress of Prehistoric and Protohistoric Sciences, Forlì-Italia, 8–14 September 1996, 175–82, Forlì

Stott, P, 1990 The medieval garden, in Galinou 1990, 30–41

Stow, J, 1603 A survey of London (ed C L Kingsford) (2 vols), 1908 repr 1971, Oxford

Streeton, A D F, 1985 Ceramic building material, in Hare 1985, 79–100

Stroud, D, 1971 George Dance, architect, 1741–1825, London

Stroud, G, 1994 The population, in Lilley, J M, Stroud, G, Brothwell, D R, and Williamson, M H, The Jewish burial ground at Jewbury, Archaeol York 12/3, 424–94, London

Stroud, G, and Kemp, R L, 1993 Cemeteries of the church and priory of St Andrew, Fishergate, Archaeol York 12/2, London

Strype, J (ed), 1720 A survey of the Cities of London and Westminster from 1633 to the present (2 vols in 6), London

Stuiver, M, Reimer, P J, Bard, E, Beck, J W, Burr, G S, Hughen, K A, Kromer, B, McCormac, F G, van der Plicht, J, and Spurk, M, 1998 INTCAL98 radiocarbon age calibration, 24,000–0 cal BP, Radiocarbon 40, 1041–83

Sundick, R L, 1978 Human skeletal growth and age determination, Homo 39, 297–33

Sutton, A, 1992 Merchants, music and social harmony: the London Puy and its French and London contexts c 1300, London J 17(1), 1–17

Sutton, A, 2005 The mercery of London: trade, goods and people, 1130–1578, Aldershot

Swann, J, 2001 History of footwear in Norway, Sweden and Finland, Stockholm

Taylor, G, 1996 Medieval founding at Deansway, Worcester, Hist Metall 30, 111–15

Telfer, A, 2004 Fast food in the medieval city: excavations at 29–30 Queen Street and 1–7 Great St Thomas Apostle, London EC4, Trans London Middlesex Archaeol Soc 55, 211–27

Thomas, C, 2002 The archaeology of medieval London, Stroud

Thomas, C, 2004 Life and death in London's East End: 2000 years at Spitalfields, London

Thomas, C, Sloane, B, and Phillpotts, C, 1997 Excavations at the priory and hospital of St Mary Spital, London, MoLAS Monogr Ser 1, London

Thomas, C, Cowie, R, and Sidell, J, 2006 The royal palace, abbey and town of Westminster on Thorney Island: archaeological excavations (1991–8) for the London Underground Limited Jubilee Line Extension Project, MoLAS Monogr Ser 22, London

Thomas, S, 1980 Medieval footwear from Coventry: a catalogue of the collection of Coventry Museums, Coventry

Thorpe, B, 1840 Ancient laws and institutes of England: Vol 1, Secular laws, London

Thurley, S, 1999 Whitehall Palace: an architectural history of the royal apartments, 1240–1698, New Haven and London

Tite, M S, and Mullins, C E, 1971 Enhancement of magnetic susceptibility of soils on archaeological sites, Archaeometry 13, 209–19

Trotter, M, and Gleser, G C, 1952 Estimation of stature from long bones of American whites and negroes, American J Physical Anthropol 10, 463–514

Trotter, M, and Gleser, G C, 1958 A re-evaluation of estimation of stature based on measurements of stature taken during life and long bones after death, American J Physical Anthropol 16, 79–123

Trow-Smith, R, 1957 A history of British livestock husbandry to 1700, London

Twigg, G, 1993 Plague in London: spatial and temporal aspects of mortality, in Epidemic disease in London (ed J A I Champion), Centre for Metropolitan Hist Working Pap Ser 1, 1–17, London

Tyers, I, 1998 Tree-ring analysis and wood identification of timbers excavated on the Magistrates Court site, Kingston upon Hull, East Yorkshire, unpub ARCUS rep 410

Tyers, I, 2003 Wattle analysis for the Guildhall sites, unpub MoL rep

Tyers, I, and Hibberd, H, 1993 Dendrochronology, wood identification and wattle analysis for the Fleet valley developer's report, unpub MoL rep

Tyler, K, Stephenson, R, and Betts, I M, in prep *London's delftware industry: the tin-glazed pottery industries of Southwark and Lambeth*, MoLAS Monogr Ser

Ubelaker, D H, 1984 *Human skeletal remains: excavation, analysis, interpretation*, Washington, DC

Underhill, R, 1986 *The woodwright's workbook*, Chapel Hill, NC

Urry, W, 1967 *Canterbury under the Angevin kings*, London

Viklund, K, Engelmark, R, and Linderholm, J (eds), 1998 *Fåhus från bronsålder till idag*, Skrifter om Skogs- och Lantbrukshistoria 12, Lund

Vince, A, 1990 *Saxon London: an archaeological investigation*, London

Vince, A G (ed), 1991a *Aspects of Saxo-Norman London: Vol 2, Finds and environmental evidence*, London Middlesex Archaeol Soc Spec Pap 12, London

Vince, A G, 1991b Early medieval London: refining the chronology, *London Archaeol* 6(10), 263–71

Vince, A G, and Jenner, A, 1991 The Saxon and early medieval pottery of London, in Vince 1991a, 19–119

Wagner, L, 1924 *London inns and taverns*, London

Waldron, T, 1994 *Counting the dead: the epidemiology of skeletal populations*, Chichester

Wallace, P, 1992 *The Viking Age buildings of Dublin*, Medieval Dublin Excavations 1962–81 Ser A 1, Dublin

Ward-Perkins, J B, 1940 *London Museum medieval catalogue*, London

Wardle, A, 1998 Musical instruments, in Egan 1998, 283–90

Watson, B, 1998 'Dark earth' and urban decline in late Roman London, in *Roman London: recent archaeological work* (ed B Watson), J Roman Archaeol Suppl Ser 24, 100–6, Portsmouth, RI

Webb, G, 1956 *Architecture in Britain: the Middle Ages*, London

Weever, J, 1631 *Ancient funerall monuments within the united monarchie of Great Britaine*, London

Weinstein, R, 1990 London's market gardens in the early modern period, in Galinou 1990, 80–99

Weitzmann-Fiedler, J, 1981 *Romanische gravierte Bronzeschalen*, Berlin

Welch, C, 1910 Recent discoveries in City churches, with historical notes on the church and parish of St Michael, Bassishaw, *Trans London Middlesex Archaeol Soc* 2(1), 149–63

Wells, C, 1964 *Bones, bodies and disease: evidence of disease and abnormality in early man*, London

West, B, 1985 Chicken legs revisited, *Circaea* 3(1), 11–14

Wheeler, A H, 1978 *Key to the fishes of northern Europe*, London

Wheeler, A H, 1979 *The tidal Thames: the history of a river and its fishes*, London

Wheeler, R E M, 1927 *London and the Vikings*, London Museum Catalogues 6, London

White, W J, 1988 *Skeletal remains from the cemetery of St Nicholas Shambles, City of London*, London Middlesex Archaeol Soc Spec Pap 9, London

White, W J, 2002 Human bone from the Guildhall site (GYE92), unpub MoL rep

Whiteley, M, 2005 The Hôtel Saint-Pol, Paris, main residence of the Valois kings, 1364–1422, unpub Brit Archaeol Ass lecture (2 March)

Whitelock, D (ed), 1955 *English historical documents: Vol 1, c 500–1042*, London

Whitelock, D (ed), 1979 *English historical documents: Vol 1, c 500–1042*, 2 edn, London

Wightman, E A, 1970 *Roman Trier and the Treveri*, London

Williams, D, 1996 Some recent finds from east Surrey, *Surrey Archaeol Collect* 83, 165–86

Williams, D, 1997 *Late Saxon stirrup mounts: a classification and catalogue*, CBA Res Rep 111, York

Williams, G, 1963 *Medieval London: from commune to capital*, London

Williams, J H, 1979 *St Peter's Street, Northampton: excavations 1973–6*, Northampton Devel Corp Archaeol Monogr 2, Northampton

Wilson, B, Grigson, C, and Payne, S (eds), 1982 *Ageing and sexing animal bones from archaeological sites*, BAR Brit Ser 109, Oxford

Wilson, C, 1976 The original design of the City of London Guildhall, *J Brit Archaeol Ass* 3 ser 129, 1–14

Wilson, C, 1990 *The Gothic cathedral: the architecture of the great church 1130–1530*, London

Wilson, C, 2003 'Excellent, new and uniforme': Perpendicular architecture c 1400–1547, in Marks and Williamson 2003, 98–119

Wilson, C A, 1973 *Food and drink in Britain: from the Stone Age to recent times*, London

Wilson, C A, 1991 *Food and drink in Britain: from the Stone Age to recent times*, rev edn, London

Wilson, R, and Edwards, P, 1993 Butchery of horse and dog at Witney Palace, Oxfordshire, and the knackering and feeding of meat to hounds during the post-medieval period, *Post-Medieval Archaeol* 27, 43–56

Wood, M, 1965 *The English mediaeval house*, London

Wright, S M, 1987 Much Park Street, Coventry: the development of a medieval street: excavations 1970–4, *Trans Birmingham Warwicks Archaeol Soc* 92, 1–132, 2 microfiches

YAT, 1978 York Archaeological Trust, 2000 years of York: the archaeological story, York

Yeoman, P, 1999 *Pilgrimage in medieval Scotland*, London

Youngs, S M, and Clark, J, 1982 Medieval Britain in 1981, *Medieval Archaeol* 26, 164–227

INDEX: PARTS I and II

Compiled by Ann Hudson